MERGERS AND ACQUISITIONS: LAW AND FINANCE

EDITORIAL ADVISORS

Vicki Been
Boxer Family Professor of Law
New York University School of Law

Erwin Chemerinsky
Dean and Distinguished Professor of Law
University of California, Irvine, School of Law

Richard A. Epstein
Laurence A. Tisch Professor of Law
New York University School of Law
Peter and Kirsten Bedford Senior Fellow
The Hoover Institution
Senior Lecturer in Law
The University of Chicago

Ronald J. Gilson
Charles J. Meyers Professor of Law and Business
Stanford University
Marc and Eva Stern Professor of Law and Business
Columbia Law School

James E. Krier
Earl Warren DeLano Professor of Law
The University of Michigan Law School

Richard K. Neumann, Jr.
Professor of Law
Maurice A. Deane School of Law at Hofstra University

Robert H. Sitkoff
John L. Gray Professor of Law
Harvard Law School

David Alan Sklansky
Yosef Osheawich Professor of Law
University of California at Berkeley School of Law

ASPEN CASEBOOK SERIES

MERGERS AND ACQUISITIONS: LAW AND FINANCE

ROBERT B. THOMPSON
Peter P. Weidenbruch Jr. Professor of Business Law
Georgetown University Law Center

Second Edition

Copyright © 2014 CCH Incorporated.

Published by Wolters Kluwer Law & Business in New York.

Wolters Kluwer Law & Business serves customers worldwide with CCH, Aspen Publishers, and Kluwer Law International products. (www.wolterskluwerlb.com)

No part of this publication may be reproduced or transmitted in any form or by any means, electronic or mechanical, including photocopy, recording, or utilized by any information storage or retrieval system, without written permission from the publisher. For information about permissions or to request permissions online, visit us at www.wolterskluwerlb.com, or a written request may be faxed to our permissions department at 212-771-0803.

To contact Customer Service, e-mail customer.service@wolterskluwer.com, call 1-800-234-1660, fax 1-800-901-9075, or mail correspondence to:

> Wolters Kluwer Law & Business
> Attn: Order Department
> PO Box 990
> Frederick, MD 21705

Printed in the United States of America.

1 2 3 4 5 6 7 8 9 0

ISBN 978-1-4548-3765-7 (Casebound)

ISBN 978-1-4548-4838-7 (Loose-leaf)

Library of Congress Cataloging-in-Publication Data

Thompson, Robert B., 1949- author.
  Mergers and acquisitions : law and finance / Robert B. Thompson, Peter P. Weidenbruch, Jr. Professor of Business Law, Georgetown University Law Center. — Second edition.
    p. cm.
  Includes bibliographical references and index.
  ISBN 978-1-4548-3765-7 (alk. paper)
1. Consolidation and merger of corporations — Law and legislation — United States. I. Title.
  KF1477.T478 2014
  346.73'06626 — dc23

2014004642

Certified Chain of Custody
Promoting Sustainable Forestry
www.sfiprogram.org
SFI-01347

About Wolters Kluwer Law & Business

Wolters Kluwer Law & Business is a leading global provider of intelligent information and digital solutions for legal and business professionals in key specialty areas, and respected educational resources for professors and law students. Wolters Kluwer Law & Business connects legal and business professionals as well as those in the education market with timely, specialized authoritative content and information-enabled solutions to support success through productivity, accuracy and mobility.

Serving customers worldwide, Wolters Kluwer Law & Business products include those under the Aspen Publishers, CCH, Kluwer Law International, Loislaw, ftwilliam.com and MediRegs family of products.

CCH products have been a trusted resource since 1913, and are highly regarded resources for legal, securities, antitrust and trade regulation, government contracting, banking, pension, payroll, employment and labor, and healthcare reimbursement and compliance professionals.

Aspen Publishers products provide essential information to attorneys, business professionals and law students. Written by preeminent authorities, the product line offers analytical and practical information in a range of specialty practice areas from securities law and intellectual property to mergers and acquisitions and pension/benefits. Aspen's trusted legal education resources provide professors and students with high-quality, up-to-date and effective resources for successful instruction and study in all areas of the law.

Kluwer Law International products provide the global business community with reliable international legal information in English. Legal practitioners, corporate counsel and business executives around the world rely on Kluwer Law journals, looseleafs, books, and electronic products for comprehensive information in many areas of international legal practice.

Loislaw is a comprehensive online legal research product providing legal content to law firm practitioners of various specializations. Loislaw provides attorneys with the ability to quickly and efficiently find the necessary legal information they need, when and where they need it, by facilitating access to primary law as well as state-specific law, records, forms and treatises.

ftwilliam.com offers employee benefits professionals the highest quality plan documents (retirement, welfare and non-qualified) and government forms (5500/PBGC, 1099 and IRS) software at highly competitive prices.

MediRegs products provide integrated health care compliance content and software solutions for professionals in healthcare, higher education and life sciences, including professionals in accounting, law and consulting.

Wolters Kluwer Law & Business, a division of Wolters Kluwer, is headquartered in New York. Wolters Kluwer is a market-leading global information services company focused on professionals.

To my family—Dottie, Blake, Beth, Mira, Hunter, Adrianne, Lucy, Isaiah, and Micah, who have made this journey enjoyable

SUMMARY OF CONTENTS

Contents		xi
Preface		xix
Chapter 1.	WHY MERGERS HAPPEN: MACROECONOMIC TRENDS	1
Chapter 2.	FINANCIAL AND ECONOMIC INCENTIVES THAT SHAPE MERGERS	11
Chapter 3.	LEGAL SHAPING OF DEALS	23
Chapter 4.	DEAL STRATEGY: THE BIDDER'S APPROACH	65
Chapter 5.	THE TARGET'S APPROACH: REMAINING INDEPENDENT OR GETTING THE BEST DEAL FROM THE FIRST OR ANOTHER BIDDER	95
Chapter 6.	JUDICIAL REVIEW OF DEFENSIVE TACTICS	141
Chapter 7.	POISON PILLS: A CASE STUDY OF DEFENSIVE TACTICS AND JUDICIAL REVIEW	225
Chapter 8.	IS A DEFENSE AFFECTING VOTING DIFFERENT?	281
Chapter 9.	FINANCE FOUNDATION FOR VALUATION	319
Chapter 10.	CASH-OUT MERGERS	331
Chapter 11.	SALE OF CONTROL FOR A PREMIUM	423
Chapter 12.	DISCLOSURE AND LIMITS ON THE USE OF INFORMATION	455
Chapter 13.	FINANCIAL REORGANIZATIONS: HIGHLY LEVERAGED TRANSACTIONS, GOING PRIVATE, ASSET RESTRUCTURING	491
Chapter 14.	ACTIVIST SHAREHOLDERS	535
Chapter 15.	INTERNATIONAL TRANSACTIONS	563
Appendix A: Delaware General Corporation Law		*573*
Appendix B: Federal Statutes & Regulations		*605*
Table of Cases		*633*
Index		*637*

CONTENTS

Preface ... xix

1. WHY MERGERS HAPPEN: MACROECONOMIC TRENDS ... 1

A. Merger Waves ... 1
B. Macroeconomic Factors That Contributed to Merger Waves ... 3
C. Who Captures the Benefits of Acquisitions? ... 5
    1. Target Shareholders and Acquirer Managers ... 5
    2. Impact on Other Stakeholders ... 8

2. FINANCIAL AND ECONOMIC INCENTIVES THAT SHAPE MERGERS ... 11

A. Synergies ... 11
B. Change of Control Benefits and Changes in Financial Aspects of the Business ... 12
C. Summary of Gains from Acquisitions ... 13
D. Costs of Acquisitions; Why Acquisitions Fail ... 14
    1. Costs Incurred in Acquisitions ... 15
    2. How Acquisitions Destroy Wealth ... 15
E. Acquisition Financing Decisions ... 16
    1. How Much of the Target Does the Bidder Wish to Acquire? ... 17
    2. Currency Choices ... 17
        a. Stock or Cash ... 17
        b. Economic Effects of Financing Choices ... 18
        c. Impact on the Acquirer's Capital Structure and Costs of Capital ... 18
        d. Ownership Structure ... 19
        e. Tax Liability ... 19
        f. Risks Bearing Under Alternative Currencies ... 20
            Problems ... 21

3. LEGAL SHAPING OF DEALS 23

- A. The Law's Distinctive Roles — 23
- B. Mergers and Other Acquisitions as a Decision Governed by Law — 24
  1. Corporate Law Reduced to Three (Overly Simplified) Rules — 24
  2. The Merger Form as a Template for Understanding Legal Regulation of Acquisition Transactions — 26
  3. Alternative Legal Structures for Acquisition That Permit Planners to Avoid One or More of the Requirements of the Merger Template — 28
- C. Judicial Limits on Private Planning to Avoid Particular Merger Effects: De Facto Merger — 34
  - *Hariton v. Arco Electronics, Inc.* — 34
  - *Farris v. Glen Alden Corp.* — 36
  - *Terry v. Penn Central Corp.* — 42
  - Notes and Questions — 47
- D. Federal Law Affecting Deals — 51
  1. Securities Law — 51
     - a. "Disclosure, Again Disclosure, and Still More Disclosure" — 51
       - *Prudent Real Estate Trust v. Johncamp Realty, Inc.* — 54
       - Notes and Questions — 58
     - b. Substantive Regulations from Securities Law, Particularly Tender Offers — 60
     - c. Avoiding Securities Regulation — 60
  2. Tax — 61
  3. Antitrust — 62
  4. National Security — 64

4. DEAL STRATEGY: THE BIDDER'S APPROACH 65

- A. Beginning the Deal Dance: Who to Approach? — 65
- B. Getting to a Definitive Agreement — 67
  1. Deal Terms: Financial, Legal, and Social — 67
  2. Due Diligence — 68
  3. Negotiating the Acquisition Agreement — 69
     - *In re IBP, Inc. Shareholders Litigation* — 70
     - Notes and Questions — 79
     - *Martin Marietta Materials, Inc. v. Vulcan Materials Co.* — 80
     - Notes and Questions — 92

Contents

5. THE TARGET'S APPROACH: REMAINING INDEPENDENT OR GETTING THE BEST DEAL FROM THE FIRST OR ANOTHER BIDDER — 95

- A. The Legal and Economic Framework — 95
  1. Financial Defenses — 96
  2. Legal Defenses — 97
- B. Fiduciary Duties and Legal Challenges to Board Action — 98
  - *Smith v. Van Gorkom* — 98
  - Notes and Questions — 117
  - *Gantler v. Stephens* — 119
  - Notes and Questions — 128
  - *Lyondell Chemical Co. v. Ryan* — 131
  - Notes and Questions — 139

6. JUDICIAL REVIEW OF DEFENSIVE TACTICS — 141

- A. The Corporate Law Template for Considering Takeover Defenses — 141
  - *Unocal Corp. v. Mesa Petroleum Co.* — 143
  - Notes and Questions — 150
  - *Revlon, Inc. v. MacAndrews & Forbes Holdings, Inc.* — 152
  - Notes and Questions — 159
- B. Applying *Unocal* and *Revlon*—The Two Paramounts — 160
  - *Paramount Communications, Inc. v. Time Inc.* — 160
  - Notes and Questions — 170
  - *Paramount Communications, Inc. v. QVC Network Inc.* — 172
  - Notes and Questions — 188
- C. The Evolution of *Unocal*; Deal Protection Devices — 189
  - *Louisiana Municipal Police Employees' Retirement System v. Crawford* — 189
  - *Omnicare, Inc. v. NCS Healthcare, Inc.* — 191
  - Notes and Questions — 206
- D. State Anti-Takeover Statutes as Defensive Mechanisms — 210
  - *Amanda Acquisition Corp. v. Universal Foods Corp.* — 213
  - Notes and Questions — 222

7. POISON PILLS: A CASE STUDY OF DEFENSIVE TACTICS AND JUDICIAL REVIEW — 225

- A. The Challenge Facing the Drafters of the Poison Pill — 225
  - Wachtell, Lipton, Rosen & Katz, The Share Purchase Rights Plan — 226
  - Notes and Questions — 232

B. Judicial Review of Director Action to Implement or Continue a Poison Pill ... 234
        Moran v. Household International, Inc. ... 234
        Notes and Questions ... 242
        City Capital Associates Ltd. Partnership v. Interco Inc. ... 243
        Notes and Questions ... 257
        Air Products and Chemicals, Inc. v. Airgas, Inc. ... 259
        Notes and Questions ... 263
C. Evolution in the Poison Pill and Judicial Responses ... 264
        Carmody v. Toll Brothers, Inc. ... 265
        Quickturn Design Systems, Inc. v. Shapiro ... 271
        Notes and Questions ... 275

8. IS A DEFENSE AFFECTING VOTING DIFFERENT?   281

        Schnell v. Chris-Craft Industries, Inc. ... 282
        Blasius Industries, Inc. v. Atlas Corp. ... 286
        Notes and Questions ... 295
        Unitrin, Inc. v. American General Corp. ... 295
        Notes and Questions ... 306
        MM Companies, Inc. v. Liquid Audio, Inc. ... 308
        Notes and Questions ... 317

9. FINANCE FOUNDATION FOR VALUATION   319

A. Introduction ... 319
B. A Primer on Financial Theory Underlying the Discounted Cash Flow Method of Valuation ... 320
        Problem ... 323
C. The Mechanics of a Discounted Cash Flow Analysis ... 323
   1. Forecasting Free Cash Flow ... 324
      a. The Explicit Forecast Period (i.e., The First Five Years) ... 324
      b. Terminal Value ... 326
   2. Picking an Appropriate Discount Rate ... 326
   3. Adjustments ... 327
   4. Forecasting Change in Free Cash Flow from the Merger ... 327
D. Deal Comparables, Company Comparables, and Other Measures ... 327

10. CASH-OUT MERGERS   331

A. Majority Power, Minority Rights to Exit Via Appraisal or Gain Judicial Review for Breach of Fiduciary Duty ... 331
        Weinberger v. UOP, Inc. ... 331

		Notes and Questions	345
		Cede & Co. v. Technicolor, Inc.	*349*
		Notes and Questions	360
B.	Valuation Techniques		362
		In re Emerging Communications, Inc. Shareholders Litigation	*362*
		Notes and Questions	385
C.	Short-Form Mergers		386
		Glassman v. Unocal Exploration Corp.	*386*
		Notes and Questions	391
		Berger v. Pubco Corp.	*392*
D.	Planning to Minimize Judicial Review		400
		In re Cox Communications, Inc. Shareholders Litigation	*400*
		Notes and Questions	416

11. SALE OF CONTROL FOR A PREMIUM — 423

		Perlman v. Feldmann	*424*
		Notes and Questions	429
		Mendel v. Carroll	*431*
		Notes and Questions	443
		In re Synthes, Inc. Shareholder Litigation	*443*
		Notes and Questions	453

12. DISCLOSURE AND LIMITS ON THE USE OF INFORMATION — 455

A.	Risk Arbitrage, Mandatory Disclosure, and the Search for Information		455
B.	Law's Effect on Information		459
	1.	Mandatory Disclosure from Federal Law	459
	2.	Mandatory Disclosure's Impact on Information About Merger Transactions and the Additional Effect of Antifraud Prohibitions	461
		a. When Will Merger Information Have to Be Disclosed?	461
		b. Remedies for Failure to Comply with Mandatory Disclosure or Antifraud Provisions Relating to Mergers	464
	3.	Disclosure Duties Arising from State Law Fiduciary Duty	464
C.	Law's Limits on the Use of Inside Information		466
	1.	Classic Insiders	466
		Chiarella v. United States	*466*
	2.	Tippee Liability and Constructive Insiders	470
		Dirks v. Securities and Exchange Commission	*470*
		Note	478

	3. Misappropriation and Rule 14e-3 Liability	479
	United States v. O'Hagan	479
	Notes and Questions	487
	4. Assembling the Bases for Insider Trading Liability	488

13. FINANCIAL REORGANIZATIONS: HIGHLY LEVERAGED TRANSACTIONS, GOING PRIVATE, ASSET RESTRUCTURING   491

A.	Leveraged Buyouts, Going Private, and Other Transactions Making Use of Leverage	491
	1. Economic Factors Used to Create Wealth in LBOs	492
	2. It's Not for Everyone: The Ideal Candidate for an LBO; Empirical Evidence on Post-Transaction Performance	494
	3. Exit	495
	4. Law Shaping the LBO Deal	496
	Metropolitan Life Insurance Co. v. RJR Nabisco, Inc.	498
	5. HCA's LBO as a Case Study	511
	6. *Topps* as a Case Study of the Overlap of Federal Disclosure and State Intermediate Scrutiny	517
	In re The Topps Co. Shareholders Litigation	517
	Notes and Questions	526
B.	Leveraged Recapitalizations	528
C.	Asset Restructuring	531
	1. Divestitures	531
	2. Carve-Outs	532
	3. Spinoff	533

14. ACTIVIST SHAREHOLDERS   535

A.	Who Are Activist Shareholders?	535
B.	Patterns of Engagement	536
	CSX Corp. v. Children's Inv. Fund Management (UK) LLP	540
	Notes and Questions	561

15. INTERNATIONAL TRANSACTIONS   563

A.	Determining Which Law	564
B.	More Expansive Roles for Shareholders in Friendly Deals	565
C.	Roles for Groups Other than Shareholders	566
D.	Different Approaches to Ability of Management to Oppose Deals Favored by Shareholders	567
E.	Different Rules in Deals by a Controlling Shareholder	567

| F. | Different Methods of Conflict Resolution | 568 |
| G. | Cadbury/Kraft as a Case Study | 568 |

Appendix A: Delaware General Corporation Law   *573*
Appendix B: Federal Statutes & Regulations   *605*
Table of Cases   *633*
Index   *637*

PREFACE

This book focuses on mergers and more particularly on how lawyers create value in a transactional setting. As befitting a course that typically comes late in one's law school education, this material moves the focus from case analysis to understanding the deal. We study not only the legal rules but also the economic and financial principles that shape the strategy of lawyers in this area and the clients they advise. Experience has shown that lawyers with knowledge of these adjacent fields create greater value in transactions.

Examples of this broadened focus include these:

- The first item that follows each case is most often a note entitled "The Deal." This structure asks you to understand who the parties were, but also what they were trying to accomplish, where the value would come from in the deal, and the choices available to planners because of those sources of value. In the *Revlon* case, for example, it makes a difference that what had been a grocery store company (albeit one with a raider at its helm) was making a hostile run at the sophisticated cosmetic giant Revlon.
- There is a separate chapter on the "poison pill" that both illustrates this entrepreneurial lawyerly innovation and provides a template for understanding defensive tactics that are a key part of the mergers and acquisitions landscape. The legal case is placed within the context of the specific problem that the lawyers needed to solve—to create a barrier against one of the few things that shareholders are permitted to do under corporate law that could undercut directors' control of the corporation—and shows how the poison pill did that in a creative and unusual way. Later parts of the chapter trace how the provision continued to evolve and how the strategies and techniques morphed with each new deal, an evolutionary pattern that prospective lawyers will want to understand throughout the study of mergers and acquisitions.
- The book begins by asking what planners are trying to accomplish in an acquisition, in financial terms of how new value is created, and in legal terms of the law's contribution to value added through use of legal forms and entities.

- Valuation is crucial to understanding deals and this book contains a rich but accessible introduction of the core principles that underlie how courts and finance experts value companies. Specific merger cases in the appraisal setting are then used to provide a way to work through the principles just introduced.
- Insider trading and the wonderful cases that populate the area that arise most often in a takeover setting are put within a broader discussion of the economic value of information.

Students come to a mergers course with a variety of prior experiences in corporate law. The pedagogical challenge is to get everyone to the same foundational level as quickly as possible. Thus, in Chapter 5, core principles of corporate governance are presented in a way that both jogs the memory of those who have dealt with these legal issues in other courses and sets the stage for a richer exploration of these principles in the context of mergers and acquisitions. My approach is informed by a decade of co-teaching mergers to a class made up of both law and business students that provided an ongoing laboratory in working through the most effective way to teach finance to law students and law to business students without simultaneously having the other half of the class tune out the discussion. I am grateful to my law and management students at Vanderbilt who regularly improved the presentation of ideas covered in this book and later classes of students at Georgetown. I am particularly grateful to my co-teacher in those classes, Ron Masulis, an energetic and distinguished finance professor, whose curiosity is broad, whose questions are precise and right-on, and whose willingness to make things better is tireless. In those classes and elsewhere, I have also benefited from distinguished practitioners in both finance and law who have been willing to share their insights, including particularly, Delaware jurist Leo Strine, New York practitioner David Katz, and Nashville's Jim Cheek, who regularly co-taught a follow-on course for students interested in mergers.

I gratefully acknowledge Wachtell, Lipton, Rosen & Katz for granting permission to reprint The Wachtell Lipton Share Purchase Rights Plan.

I welcome comments, questions, and suggestions at thompson@law.georgetown.edu.

Robert B. Thompson

March 2014
Washington, D.C.

Mergers and Acquisitions: Law and Finance

1. WHY MERGERS HAPPEN: MACROECONOMIC TRENDS

Mergers and other acquisitions occur because planners see benefits that could come from combining two or more businesses. In Chapter 2 we study in more detail the specific incentives that motivate such individual deals. But first, we begin our study with a look at a few global trends to set the stage for future learning. This chapter presents a brief survey of the historical trends reflected in mergers, a somewhat more detailed look at the macroeconomic factors that cause the number of acquisitions to be larger in some eras and smaller in others, and a brief examination of who gains or loses when mergers occur.

A. MERGER WAVES

Mergers and related acquisitions have occurred in the United States in a series of waves over the last century or more, as can be seen on the chart below. In one sense, the peaks in the chart coincide with certain of the macroeconomic trends discussed in the next section: good economic conditions, expansive credit, etc. But equally compelling for our study is the change in regulation that flowed from each of the peaks. Over time, mergers have been increasing; and in recent times, the growth has been steeper outside of the United States.

The 1890s. The first notable wave of mergers roughly coincides with the roaring 90s, the 1890s that is, when large growth spurred in part by the Industrial Revolution led to increases in the size and scope of business and legal rules made mergers easier to accomplish than before. Prior to the

Chart 1-1

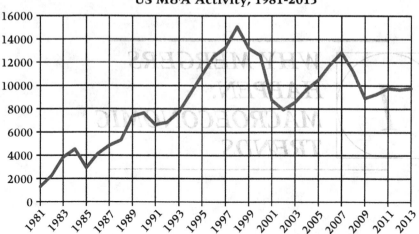

1890s, mergers required the unanimous approval of shareholders of each company, a daunting task as the number of shareholders grew and their interests became more disparate. If done outside of the merger form, acquisition by purchase of assets or similar contractual deals triggered large transactional costs. With the introduction into state corporations codes of a supermajority requirement (often a two-thirds vote), the way was open for mergers. The most notable regulatory change associated with this era was the trust-busting of Theodore Roosevelt and others who introduced the first dramatic government antitrust controls on firms and their deals.

The 1920s. A second peak in acquisitions is visible in the roaring 20s, when the economic expansion that followed World War I produced a period of economic growth and an increase in the number of deals. The growth of managerial capitalism and innovative management patterns in firms like General Motors provided new justifications for acquisitions that could create efficiencies in business forms. The market crash of 1929 and the Great Depression which followed ended this merger wave and also brought us a greatly expanded governmental presence in business and markets, including the Securities Act of 1933 and the Securities Exchange Act of 1934, with their focus on government intervention through disclosure and an effort to invigorate shareholders as a check on managerialist control of corporations.

The 1960s. This decade presents a third peak in the number of acquisitions at a time when the economy experienced a sustained period of economic growth. Notably, this takeover era was marked by a visible increase in the presence of hostile acquisitions, through proxy fights and then the developing tactic of a public tender offer offering cash for the shares of a publicly held company. This unwelcome and often surprising challenge to the status quo of managerialists' control of corporations left its calling card on the regulatory side in the form of the Williams Act, a 1968 amendment to the Securities Exchange Act of 1934, which imposed disclosure obligations on one making a tender offer for control of a company similar to those previously imposed on proxy fights and also led to regulation of the substance of tender offers, such as mandating equal treatment for all shareholders.

The 1980s. The growing number of takeovers in the 1980s reflected not just the economic growth the United States experienced after a severe bout with inflation and unemployment, but also the deregulatory approach that grew during the Reagan administration. Changes in the shareholder make-up also influenced the market. The increase of institutional investors facilitated a more active takeover market. Changes in financial markets, such as growth in leveraged buyouts and an increase in private equity, heightened the role of entrepreneurs as a motivator of takeovers. The primary legal legacy of this takeover era was in giving form to the law's approach to defensive tactics that still shapes our study of takeovers. The focus here was state corporate law, principally that of the small state of Delaware, which is the key player in corporate law. This era gave rise to the poison pills and other private ordering innovations by which takeover advisers sought to insulate a company from attack. This era gave us the *Unocal* and *Revlon* cases, which were the responses of the Delaware courts to such lawyer innovations that essentially gave boards of directors additional space to resist raiders who sought to go over their heads to shareholders in order to achieve a hostile takeover.

Late 1990s-2001. The technological growth of the 1990s spurred yet another peak in acquisitions, particularly driven by financial innovations in Silicon Valley and elsewhere. The abrupt bursting of this bubble set back the wave of takeovers and provided new regulation in the form of the Sarbanes-Oxley Act and its new rules for corporate governance.

Mid 2000s. The most recent peak in deals in 2007 reflected the easy money of the period between Enron and the credit crunch and the financial crisis, which saw a rise in private equity and other financial bidders to a degree not seen since the 1980s. The severe corrections in 2008 and thereafter brought fewer deals and additional regulations that will shape the next peak for which your study in this course is directed.

B. MACROECONOMIC FACTORS THAT CONTRIBUTED TO MERGER WAVES

If you examine which factors are associated with the peaks and troughs of the merger waves discussed in the prior section, you will likely see a number of factors that are not randomly distributed, but rather can shape your understanding of why mergers happen. Our focus here is on the macroeconomic factors that contribute to a merger wave.

1. ***Economic Conditions.*** The health of the economy is a key factor associated with mergers. More mergers occur when the economy is growing and at the top of the business cycle. A rising stock market provides currency to finance mergers and may present situations in which insiders' view of information about the value of the company is different than the market's. This asymmetry may itself encourage mergers to happen. Just as the economic factors shaping the economy move in cycles, the level of mergers and acquisitions is also affected by the cognitive state of investors and other market participants. Bubbles and similar cognitive impulses may also appear in waves, similar to changes in core economic conditions.

2. ***Credit Availability.*** Available money to borrow is a key for financing mergers, and this factor is not constant across a business cycle or even the same at the top parts of various business cycles. When there are low interest rates and cheap money, it is not surprising that there are more deals.

3. ***Industry Shocks, Changes in Government Policy, and Innovation.*** Mergers are not evenly spread across all sectors of the economy. They tend to be clustered in particular industries and respond to specific changes in the economy or in those industries. For example, deregulation of airlines in the 1970s or banks in the 1990s generated a spike in mergers in those industries. It was said to be cheaper to drill for oil on Wall Street in the 1980s than in oil fields themselves. Sometimes these shocks are related to changes in government policy, as when many countries denationalized major segments of their economies after the fall of the Berlin Wall or changed their antitrust policies, leading to an increase in mergers. At other times, it has been technological change that has generated merger possibilities. The development of computers has expanded the capacity to use information and lowered costs in many industries which, in turn, created opportunity for mergers. Such technology has birthed entire new industries and spurred acquisitions in telecom and related industries, as during the dotcom bubble around the turn of the century. More generally, the spread of cheaper communication and information devices has facilitated the growth of institutional investors and, more specifically, activist investors.

4. ***Globalization.*** Growth of computer power and reduction in costs to communicate across borders and to transport goods around the

world has been a major contributor to economic activity in mergers and acquisitions (M&A). These changes have opened up markets that previously were separate and permitted new entrants whose competition puts pressure on existing market participants, resulting in takeover activity. These larger markets, in turn, create the possibility of economies of scale that previously may not have been possible, which itself becomes an inducement to merger activity. Government policies interact with these trends; for example, a spread in trade liberalization can also be a basis for M&A activity. Chapter 15 discusses this topic in more detail.

C. WHO CAPTURES THE BENEFITS OF ACQUISITIONS?

1. *Target Shareholders and Acquirer Managers*

Acquisitions both produce and transfer wealth, spread unevenly among various participants. Shareholders of target companies have received the largest gains. Studies over the last several decades show shareholder gains averaging 30 percent or more, as measured by the change in the market value of their stock against the price before the announcement of the takeover. *See, e.g.,* Robert G. Bruner, APPLIED MERGERS AND ACQUISITIONS (University Ed. 2004) at 37, Exhibit 3.3 (summarizing the findings of 25 studies which reveal returns are material and significant; "significant" in such studies refers to statistical significance, that the results are not due to chance) [hereinafter Bruner]. Chart 1-2 presents a distribution of premiums across deals.

In contrast, shareholders of an acquiring company do not see similar increases in the value of their shares and frequently sustain a small loss, as measured by the change in the market price of their shares prior to the announcement of the acquisition. *See* Bruner at 36-44 (summarizing 22 studies that report negative returns and 32 that report positive returns, about two-thirds of which are statistically significant). Professor Bruner observes, "A reasonable conclusion from these studies is that in the aggregate, abnormal (or market-adjusted) returns to buyer shareholders from M&A activity are essentially zero." Buyers basically break even in the sense that they earn their required return on investment. Bruner at 44.

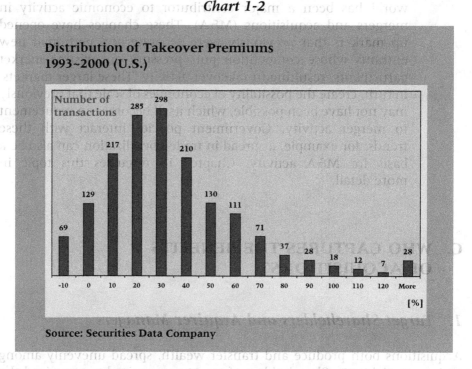

Chart 1-2

Distribution of Takeover Premiums 1993~2000 (U.S.)

Source: Securities Data Company

What might explain such differences between targets and bidders? Acquirers are usually larger than their targets, so the takeover is likely to have a greater relative impact on the target. Economic factors such as supply and demand can explain some differences. Legal rules requiring shareholder approval, which we discuss later, permit those shareholders to extract more of the gain. The different incentives of managers in the two companies also may contribute to this pattern.

Managers are a second group who usually do well in a takeover. On the acquirer side, whose managers are likely to control the combined entity, the benefits may be in the form of empire building, producing a higher ongoing compensation for managers to direct larger pools of assets, and perhaps lowering the risks of bankruptcy for the larger firm. Managers of the target firm, if they don't continue in the merged enterprise, often receive golden parachutes or other benefits from compensation agreements that may serve to counter their economic incentive for the status quo.

Such management agency costs, and the bid process itself, can lead to bidder overpayment in an acquisition setting. Beyond direct management incentives, hubris might push managers toward takeovers that don't provide an immediate return to their shareholders. *See, e.g.,* John C. Coffee, *Regulating the Market for Corporate Control: A Critical Assessment of the Tender Offer's Role in Corporate Governance*, 84 COLUM. L. REV. 1145, 1162-1173

C. Who Captures the Benefits of Acquisitions?

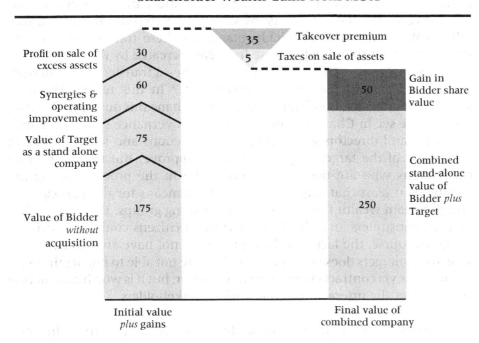

Chart 1-3

Shareholder Wealth Gains from M&A

(1984) (discussing disciplinary hypothesis for takeovers, synergy hypothesis, empire-building hypothesis and exploitation hypothesis). The bidding process itself can lead to a winner's curse that can result in acquiring companies overpaying. *See, e.g.,* Bernard S. Black, *Bidder Overpayment in Takeovers: Manager Ignorance and the Winner's Curse*, 41 STAN. L. REV. 597 (1989).

What if we combine returns to the targets and bidders, adjusting for their difference in size in an effort to measure net economic gain? Studies have sought to examine such data by constructing a portfolio of target and bidders weighting their inclusion by size or by examining absolute dollar values in the takeover. Bruner reports findings of 24 studies, almost all reporting positive combined returns and a majority being positive in a statistically significant sense. Bruner at 47. Those measures derive from immediate changes in market value of stock. Financial economists and others have sought to measure if acquisitions produce gains over longer periods of time. The majority of these show a loss. *See* Bruner at 44. Other studies evaluate how acquiring companies, measured by operational measures such as return on assets, tend to be more equivocal. Dennis Mueller, after editing a collection of studies of M&A profitability across seven nations, concluded "Any economic efficiency gains from the mergers would appear to be small, judging from these statistics." THE DETERMINANTS AND EFFECTS OF MERGERS: AN INTERNATIONAL COMPARISON (Dennis C. Mueller ed., 1980).

2. Impact on Other Stakeholders

An analysis of the size of the overall gains produced by takeovers and our relative certainty about those gains should also consider the extent that other stakeholders may be disadvantaged by these transactions. Do the returns to target shareholders arise from gains created by the acquisitions, discussed in the next chapter, or instead are they a transfer of wealth from some other constituency of the corporations? In this regard, the legal structure that is a focus of later materials may shape this outcome. Acquisitions, as we see in Chapter 3, occur within a governance system in which managers and directors get to propose transactions and shareholders, at least those of the target corporation, must approve. But there are other constituents who are not given a direct role in the process, raising the possibility at least that acquisitions may be a means for the participating groups to gain wealth from the non-participating groups. Employees, debt holders, consumers, and the larger society of citizens could be disadvantaged. Of course, the fact that these groups do not have an explicit role in approving mergers does not mean that they are not able to impact the deals or the terms via contract claims or market power, but it is worth considering at the outset the interaction of the various stakeholders.

Employees. Employees can be hurt to the extent that the gain produced in the acquisition comes from a reduction in the number of jobs as business combinations create economies of scale, which permit the same work to be done with fewer employees. Wages could be reduced in a similar setting. If, on the other hand, new efficiencies generated by the acquisition permit expansion in products or market, the impact on employees could be positive.

Debt holders. Acquisitions can directly impact the value of existing debt. The price charged by the creditors to extend credit reflects the risk of the prior company, its balance sheet, etc. To the extent that an acquirer completes an acquisition that increases its size dramatically, increases risks of bankruptcy, or otherwise impacts the price at which it can borrow funds, the preexisting creditors may find themselves with an interest rate that reflects the pre-acquisition borrower and a risk level that has increased dramatically. Studies of the change in the value of debt holder interest in companies that have been acquired show no overall loss. Creditors often protect themselves against such change of risk by contract, e.g., by including covenants in their debt documents that trigger a resetting of their interest rate, but there may be gaps in their contract. Metropolitan Life, which saw the value of its debt from R.J. Reynolds decline after the leveraged buyout of that firm, was unsuccessful in seeking legal redress for such an adverse change. *See* Metropolitan Life Ins. Co. v. RJR Nabisco, Inc., 716 F. Supp. 1504 (1989).

Government. Acquisitions often bring large changes to what the government receives in taxes. To the extent that acquisitions are financed by borrowed money, as they often are, businesses can deduct the interest they pay from their taxable income and reduce the tax owed. This means that the government, in effect, is paying for a portion of the cost of the takeover. For example, if a corporation is in the 35 percent corporate income tax bracket and borrows to finance the deal, every $100 that the company pays in interest will reduce the tax on its income by $35, effectively reducing the cost of borrowing by more than one-third. This is sometimes called a "tax shield."

Consumers, competitors, suppliers, host communities. If acquisitions create monopoly power and otherwise increase the participants' influence over prices, there may be a transfer of wealth from such customers to the acquisition participant. To a lesser extent, suppliers and host communities who lose company headquarters and the community support that often comes with such headquarters may also see a loss after a takeover. Takeover policy is sometimes influenced by such concerns. *See* Roberta Romano, *The Political Economy of Takeover Statutes*, 73 VA. L. REV. 111 (1987).

2 FINANCIAL AND ECONOMIC INCENTIVES THAT SHAPE MERGERS

A. SYNERGIES

Mergers occur when two companies decide that their combination will create greater value than if they continued to operate as freestanding entities (taking into account the costs to be incurred in any such combination). When the economic gains result from changes in the combined use of assets of the previously separate firms, they are often called synergistic gains (2+2 = 5), which can derive from several sources.

- *Economies of scale.* If a combination of companies in the same industry, or perhaps the same geographic market, permits one or both of the entities to more efficiently use particular assets that are being used at less than optimal capacity, an acquisition can produce synergies. Often this means that the newly combined entity can service the same customer base with fewer assets than the sum of both companies in their uncombined state. For example, two banks in the same market may realize costs savings from combining branches on the same block, or airlines may be able to reduce excess capacity by combining overlapping routes.
- *Vertical integration.* In other settings, efficiencies may come not from a horizontal combination as above, but from the combined firm's better ability to link the vertical parts of a production process, upstream or downstream from the portion of the production process performed by the original firm. When firms pass on products to the next stage of the production process, there may be large transaction costs, e.g., transportation costs. Where the production requires firm-specific assets in which the value to the highest value

user is more than to the second best user, the company may be unwilling to make the needed investment if the counterparty could renege after making the agreement and seek to opportunistically renegotiate the price. Vertical integration may be an economically advantageous solution to such risks.

- *Economies of scope*. If potential merger partners engage in complementary products or processes, it may be that the expertise (perhaps not being fully utilized in the original firm) can be transferred to the complementary line of business and produce gains. An example would be an advertising firm with excess capacity extending its expertise to an underperforming beer brand or a firm with strong research and development or distribution capacity transferring those skills to a firm in a complementary industry that lacks such expertise.
- *Market power*. Sometimes, a combination of two firms can create market power that enables the combined firms to raise prices in a monopoly or monopsony context. Such combinations, of course, may attract the attention of antitrust regulators.

B. CHANGE OF CONTROL BENEFITS AND CHANGES IN FINANCIAL ASPECTS OF THE BUSINESS

Increase in value can also occur without the need to involve the assets of another firm. Here, the gain can be attributed to rearranging the control or operations of an individual firm. Examples include:

- *Replacing weak managers or reversing bad management decisions*. Markets reflect the value of the company's assets in current use and controlled by current management. If that use is not the most efficient or managers leave something to be desired, it will be possible to create value by replacing those managers and/or those policies. A particular example that we discuss later is the takeover of Technicolor, a firm that was long dominant in the colorization process of movies but eventually found itself with new competition and the need to move into new businesses. The company's choice to open a series of One Hour Photo (OHP) businesses proved disastrous from a financial standpoint. The ability of a bidder to acquire control of the company led to the immediate closing of the OHP business and a large increase in the firm's share price.
- *Improving management incentives*. Sometimes it is not necessary to change the management at all in order to increase value. A new

owner may increase monitoring of managers or change the managers' incentives. For example, by offering managers an increased ownership position that aligns their interests with those of the shareholders and providing them a greater return if share value goes up, a more efficient operation can result.
- *Financial and asset restructuring.* In a firm with little or no borrowing, financial change to increase the leverage of the company can sometimes produce financial gain. Because the government permits companies to deduct interest payments before figuring their income tax, the government in effect takes on part of the cost of borrowing. If management can use the borrowed funds to produce a return that exceeds the costs of the debt, they will be able to increase return. Financial economists talk about this factor in terms of measuring the firm's distance from its optimal borrowing level. This computation also includes the increased risk of bankruptcy (and the costs which will be incurred if that were to occur) because the increased leverage can add to financial pressure on the firm, particularly in times of economic stress. As an alternative to borrowing to provide cash for what appear to be positive net present value investments, new owners can cause the entity to sell assets that do not fit with the firm's business plan.
- *Purchasing undervalued assets.* Gain can also occur in an acquisition if a bidder has been able to identify undervalued assets that can be purchased for what appears to be a bargain price. This may be more likely to occur in purchasing privately held firms where there is no publicly available information about the target.

C. SUMMARY OF GAINS FROM ACQUISITIONS

As the prior sections highlight, value in an acquisition derives from multiple sources which do not always fall into neat categories suggested in the prior discussion or can easily expand beyond such a list. For a deal professional, however, there is benefit in understanding the sources of value motivating a particular deal and identifying what that tells you about the motives of the players and how the deal is likely to unfold. Consider the chart that follows placing the various motivations for acquisitions just discussed.

The boxes on the left side of the graph reflect the synergy motivations discussed in section A. Those on the right side of the graph reflect the financial reasons in section B. All of the sources of possible gains will not be available in all transactions. For example, the synergistic boxes require the combination of two operating companies to create economies of scale or

Chart 2-1
Economic Gains from Acquisitions

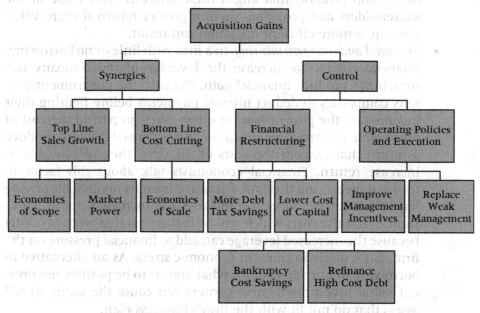

Source: Ronald Masulis

vertical integration, while those on the right side do not. Those gains are available to any bidder, even one without any operating assets. The two sides of the graph thus reflect a division between strategic bidders and financial bidders. Sometimes a deal may be attractive to both kinds of bidders, but often, economic circumstances or the specifics of a particular deal may favor one over the other. For example, in times of easily available credit and high savings, financial bidders such as hedge funds or private equity may have higher visibility in deals. In a credit crunch, as seen in 2008 and 2009, strategic buyers take center stage. Takeover defenses, too, may reflect such difference so that you should try to identify economic sources that are motivating the deal.

D. COSTS OF ACQUISITIONS; WHY ACQUISITIONS FAIL

Of course, gains are only part of the equation in considering acquisitions; costs incurred to acquire those gains should also be put into the

D. Costs of Acquisitions; Why Acquisitions Fail

computations. More generally, those planning acquisitions should be aware why acquisitions fail: factors that lead gains to be overestimated or costs to be underestimated or weak implementation that means anticipated gains are not realized.

1. Costs Incurred in Acquisitions

Any acquisition plan needs to include a realistic estimate of costs that will be incurred in the deal. These include:

- *Merger integration costs.* Combining assets, production processes, and personnel is a complex task that can ruin many acquisition estimates. Successful integration begins as soon as the first meeting between the parties, even as the deal is being worked out. Companies often work out a system to establish the goals of the merger, pick the teams who will be charged with implementing it (usually with members from both companies), and follow a system shown by past deals to have facilitated integration.
- *Taxes.* Anything paid to the government in taxes reduces any gains otherwise created in an acquisition. As a result, planners will often seek a form of acquisition that will defer or reduce the amount of taxes paid. Income tax often is the focus of the tax planner, and a key question is whether the transaction will cause income to be realized. Stock-for-stock acquisitions often do not trigger a realization event, while cash payments usually do. The result may be that when shareholders of the target know they will immediately incur a payment to the government, they will require a higher premium for the taxable transaction.
- *M&A advisory fees.* While merger transactions often create large gains, there are often significant fees incurred. Investment banking fees are often the largest, but attorneys' fees can also take a noticeable chunk, and accountants' and other fees are a cost that reduce any gains created by the acquisition.

2. How Acquisitions Destroy Wealth

Just as there are predictable patterns by which gains are created in mergers, there are recurring factors visible when deals go bad. The focus here is often on the acquiring firm and the economic factors that contribute to weak management incentives in choosing the deal or in the implementations of the deal.

- *Empire building and weak performance incentives.* Managers recognize that personal compensation, such as salary, often correlates with the size of the enterprise that they manage so that the desire to implement an acquisition in order to create a larger enterprise may be pursued by managers even if the likelihood of gain is not as great as investors might prefer. Management with weak pay for performance incentives has less reason to resist the siren call of empire building.
- *Acquisitions to hide poor performance.* A firm with below-average returns for its sector, but with sufficient cash or other resources, or in an industry or economic period where acquisitions are plentiful, may be able to hide otherwise poor relative performance by one or more acquisitions of companies with strong current earnings.
- *Hubris; overconfidence.* Failed acquisitions can sometimes be explained by factors that are more psychological than economic. Managers may be more likely than the average person to fall prey to hubris or to have an overconfidence bias that the acquisition will work or that the combination will produce gains at the high end of a range.
- *Entrenchment.* The factors cited thus far apply more often to managers in the corporate hierarchy. But, in the corporate legal structure, decisions such as mergers are made by the board of directors who can countermand management weaknesses or monitor their selfish decisions. In this regard, if a board lacks the necessary experience in the industry to monitor management or is otherwise captured, acquisitions that fail to produce expected gains may result. (Board entrenchment on the target side can be a reason why acquisitions do not take place, as discussed in more detail in Chapter 5).
- *Weak implementation* can prevent those gains from being achieved. This can be because of poor "due diligence" in the acquirer's examination of the target's business. Poor integration is a common challenge, as discussed in the prior section. Poor post-deal management of the target can also dissipate gains anticipated in a merger.

E. ACQUISITION FINANCING DECISIONS

Key questions in any acquisition include what the bidder is acquiring and what currency choices are available to pay for the target and its assets.

E. Acquisition Financing Decisions

1. How Much of the Target Does the Bidder Wish to Acquire?

Once planners of an acquisition have identified a target where synergies or other gains could result from an acquisition, they must also ask whether they want to acquire all of the assets of the target or just some of them. More important may be the question of whether the acquirer wants to assume all of the liabilities of the target, some of them, or none of them. These decisions will be guided by the economic factors discussed above and will affect the size of the deal and the acquisition price. The actual means by which this choice is implemented reflects the legal choices that are discussed in more detail in Chapter 3.

2. Currency Choices

a. Stock or Cash

A key financial choice when putting together a deal is which type of currency should be used to pay for the acquisition: (1) the acquirer's stock;

Chart 2-2

US M&A Financing Breakdown

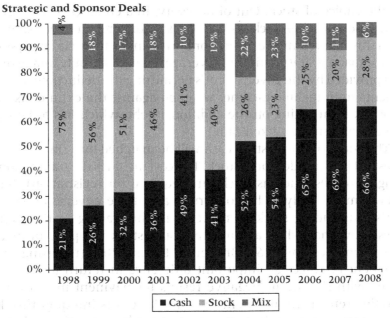

Source: Dealogic as of September 26, 2008.
(1) Excludes transactions less than $1 billion.
(2) Excludes financial sponsor transactions.

(2) cash; or (3) some combination of the two, including hybrid instruments that include elements of each. Further, to the extent that cash is the currency, there are multiple sources of cash in an acquisition. The most accessible will be an acquiring firm's retained earnings; alternatively, cash can be provided by a bank or other lender. It is common in acquisitions for cash to be obtained by selling assets, either the acquirer's existing assets or some of the target's assets that won't produce synergies with the acquirer.

b. Economic Effects of Financing Choices

A planner must be attuned to the different economic effects of the financing choice. These include (1) impact on the acquirer's capital structure, debt capacity, and cost of capital; (2) the effect on the acquirer's ownership structure; (3) who will bear the risks of the enterprise going forward; and (4) tax liabilities (what you have to pay the government and when).

c. Impact on the Acquirer's Capital Structure and Costs of Capital

The choice of cash or currency will reflect the practical reality of how much it costs to borrow. An acquirer in a weak financial position may only have the choice of stock. Out of necessity, in a credit crunch most buyers find themselves using stock instead of cash. For companies who have access to cash through retained earnings or borrowing, a financial analyst will ask if the company is at its optimum leverage level to take advantage of the tax shield provided by the government's permitting the deductibility of interest payments from taxable income, weighed against the extra costs of bankruptcy risk from taking on the additional debt, which has to be repaid in specified amounts at a fixed time.

This focus on the costs of cash will be matched by a similar analysis of the costs of issuing additional stock. The cost includes the transaction cost of issuing securities (such as disclosure required for registration), but managers are more likely to be concerned about the adverse impact on the issuer's outstanding stock as reflected in the trading market. Empirical studies show that when a company issues stock the price of its existing shares often goes down. *See* Bruner, at Exhibit 20-2 (reporting that form of payment produces an important difference in return to bidder shareholders, with significant negative results for payment in stock and zero to positive returns for payment in cash). Investors interpret this decision to issue stock as a signal from management, who made the decision to use cash instead of stock, that the stock may be overvalued and react accordingly. A stock issuance also requires compliance with SEC disclosure rules

E. Acquisition Financing Decisions

regarding issuance of stock (in this case to the shareholders of the target company who are purchasing stock by receiving bidder shares in the deal shares). This regulatory process can take months longer than a similar deal in which the currency is cash. Planners may worry that this additional time increases the risk of the deal not closing by giving more time to potential competing bidders, but a stock offer may raise the liquidity of the trading shares of the company's stock with more shares now being in circulation.

d. Ownership Structure

The two alternatives, cash or stock, have different results as to who are the shareholders of the acquirer. More precisely, a cash offer produces no change in the shareholder roster of the acquiring company — whatever was the ownership structure before, and the particular ownership percentage of individual block holders, family members, or managers, will be the same after the deal is completed. But if stock were used as the currency, the additional shares issued to the target shareholder will dilute the percentage of any existing shareholder of the acquiring company, who may not welcome that change. And if the target corporation had a controlling shareholder or large bloc holder, existing acquiring company shareholders may worry that the change will introduce an agency cost concern for them in terms of possible selfish acts by a new group of managers for which the shareholders want additional consideration. Further, the result may be to introduce a new personality into the ownership dynamic of the resulting company. When Time Inc. acquired Turner Broadcasting, and its CNN and other brands, it also acquired the outspoken Ted Turner as a large shareholder. *See* Sallie Hofmeister, *Turner to Leave Time Warner*, L.A. TIMES, Feb. 25, 2006 (reporting "Maverick entrepreneur Ted Turner said Friday that he would step down as a Time Warner Inc. director in May, ending his colorful and volatile 10-year affiliation with the world's largest entertainment company.").

e. Tax Liability

The Internal Revenue Code provides several methods to complete an acquisition without triggering immediate tax liability for the corporation or the shareholders. The applicable law is found in Section 368 of the Internal Revenue Code and provides three core types of reorganization that can qualify for the favorable tax deferred treatment. These are usually termed A, B, and C reorganizations, tracking the provisions of that section. A stock transaction can often qualify for these reorganizations; a transaction in which cash is the currency likely will not and thus trigger possible income tax liability for the shareholders of the target. See the additional discussion at the end of Chapter 4.

f. Risk Bearing Under Alternative Currencies

Parties contemplating a merger will be concerned about what the transaction will do to risks carried by the shareholders going forward. These risks include the risk of the combined business after the merger in terms of changes affecting the economy and the combined company, and the risk of the transaction not closing or being delayed. If cash is the chosen consideration, the buying shareholders will bear all of the risks of the extent to which synergies and operating improvements promised for the merger actually occur. In contrast, if stock is the chosen consideration, this risk will now be shared by the two sets of shareholders in proportion to their ownership of the combined entity. There may be reasons why the parties prefer one allocation of another. In a merger pitched as a merger of equals, for example, takeover premiums are small or non-existent. Thus, it is seen as important that both sets of shareholders share in the risks and benefits going forward and that both sets of managers share in control of the combined entity going forward.

As for the more short-term risk during the time until the transaction closes, cash fixes the consideration, and any change in the acquirer's stock or the economy in general will be carried by the acquiring shareholders. In contrast, if stock consideration is used, this risk, too, is shared by the two sets of shareholders. In a stock-for-stock setting, planners often shape

Chart 2-3
M&A FINANCING EFFECTS

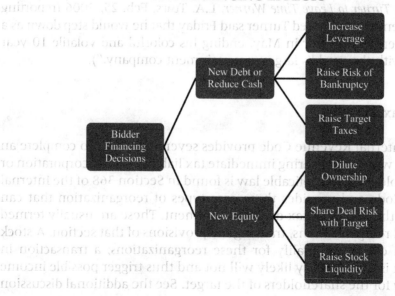

E. Acquisition Financing Decisions

this allocation of risk by providing a "collar," i.e., stating a floor or ceiling for how much the selling shareholders are to receive and thereby bounding the risks being taken on by those shareholders.

Planners can similarly address the long-term risk by contract, such as providing that the equity consideration is linked to contingent payments — e.g., if certain earnings or other benchmarks are met, the amount of stock to be received by the target shareholders increases. Can you see why selling shareholders might not be entirely satisfied with this resolution of the uncertainties of future performance?

Finally, another way of addressing risk and possible differences is to give selling shareholders a choice of currency, assuming that meets the capital and ownership needs of the business and doesn't adversely affect the preferred tax treatment planners desire for the transaction.

PROBLEM 2-1:

Bank of America (B of A) acquires Fleet by an exchange rate of .553 shares of B of A for every share of Fleet. How is the risk of that transaction different than if the offer was for a fixed cash amount for each Fleet share?

PROBLEM 2-2:

The board of a target company and a potential acquirer are discussing an acquisition in the shadow of a possible second bidder from a company whom the target board would definitely prefer not to see in control of their company. What form of consideration would you suggest?

PROBLEM 2-3:

How will choice of currency differ for strategic and financial bidders?

3 LEGAL SHAPING OF DEALS

A. THE LAW'S DISTINCTIVE ROLES

Apart from the economic and financial factors discussed in the last chapter that provide incentives for acquisition activity, law frames the choices for those planning deals. The distinctive role of law can be seen in several visible effects on transactions:

- *Providing an efficient form for transactions to realize synergy and other gains from acquisition, as compared to the methods that the parties would have to implement if relegated to contract.* Consider the empowering effects of Delaware §259 entitled "Status, Rights, Liabilities, of Constituent and Surviving or Resulting Corporations Following Merger." Once a merger has occurred, the statute decrees that: "the separate existence of all the constituent corporations . . . shall cease," the new or surviving corporation shall possess "all of the rights, privileges, powers and franchises" of each of the merged corporations, and "all property . . . and all debts" of each of the merged corporations "shall be vested in the corporation surviving." This instantaneous and global transformation of control and legal title, without any additional paperwork other than the filing of the merger documents with a state official, seems almost magical in contrast to the multitudinous bills of sales and various contract documents that would be required to effectively transfer control in the absence of such a statute.
- *Permitting private planners to create separate corporate entities wholly owned by their creator but recognized as separate from their parent.* These separate entities can be used in acquisitions (and elsewhere)

to limit the parent's obligation for liabilities included in or incurred by the subsidiary without the need to separately contract for such protection or draft the terms of such an agreement. This leads, for example, to triangular mergers discussed below or other alternative structuring of acquisition transactions.

- *Protecting various constituencies or the government as a whole by regulatory requirements that an acquisition must satisfy.* For example, state corporations law puts all corporate powers in the hands of the board of directors (*see* Del. §141) but then empowers shareholders to elect those directors and requires their consent for a merger to take place. Federal securities law seeks to protect the exercise of the shareholder franchise by requiring substantial disclosure to shareholders who are asked to make such decisions. Federal antitrust law provides a means to block transactions that could harm consumers by leading to monopoly or similar market constraints. Government likewise retains the power to specify when transactions require tax payments or otherwise dictates the tax treatment resulting from an acquisition.

Acquisitions can trigger a host of legal and regulatory issues that go well beyond the capacity of this or any single law school course. Our focus here is on four principal sources of law: corporate law; securities regulation; antitrust; and tax, where significant issues are likely to arise in most acquisitions, and even here the greatest focus is on corporate law. Each of those topics often occupies a separate course (or more) in law school, and the discussion here, at least for the last three in this book, is admittedly cursory, flagging issues for later pursuit by one entering the transactional world.

B. MERGERS AND OTHER ACQUISITIONS AS A DECISION GOVERNED BY LAW

1. Corporate Law Reduced to Three (Overly Simplified) Rules

Corporate law is the source of the "creation" function described above. More centrally for our discussion, it names the corporate players; indeed, only three types of participants are provided for in corporate statutes: shareholders, directors, and officers. For mergers, corporate law specifies who is the "decider" for decisions like mergers and as we will see, sometimes provides exit rights for shareholders from the corporation itself. While it is dangerous, if not foolhardy, to telescope your learning from a prior corporations or business associations course into such a capsulated form, let's begin the discussion with three broad, overly simplified points that you might remember from your prior study and which provide a jumping-off point for a more detailed discussion of corporate law in the merger context in the chapters that follow.

- *Rule #1. Directors rule (most of the time).* This principle derives from a bedrock point of corporate law found in all American corporate statutes. *See* Del. §141, MBCA §8.01(b).[1] The power given to the board includes product decisions, hiring and firing employees and making compensation contracts with them, buying and selling assets in the ordinary course of business, and issuing shares and other securities (provided they have been authorized in the corporation's articles of incorporation). In other words, directors (and the officers they are authorized to appoint) get to do most everything. The business judgment rule, a presumption of judicial deference to director decisions discussed in more detail in Chapter 5, reflects this same principle. Empowering a centralized group to speak for the entity provides efficiency benefits in an economy where shareholding is widely dispersed. As a centralized decision-maker, directors can negotiate on behalf of shareholders and other constituencies. At the same time, directors with this broad power to direct other people's money might not pay the attention to this effort that the shareholders would like them to pay or may use their power to benefit themselves or the managers who they fail to monitor sufficiently. This leads to Rules 2 and 3 below. Mergers, sale of substantially all of the entity's assets, and charter amendments are partial exceptions to this rule in that they may require a shareholder vote after board approval, as discussed below.
- *Rule #2. Shareholders check directors, but only in three limited ways — vote, sell, and sue.* Shareholders are not given plenary powers to decide corporate policy. Rather, they are conceived as simple creatures who, like babies, exercise three basic functions. First, they are permitted to elect directors once a year (with additional limitations that we consider in more detail in later chapters) and vote on mergers and other fundamental changes, once the directors have decided they want to put such a matter to the shareholders. Shareholder power to amend the corporation's bylaws in some situations without the board playing a gate-keeping role has taken on broader importance in takeovers in recent years. Second, shareholders can sell their shares, either in the market or in response to a tender offer made to them by a bidder seeking to acquire control. Third, they

---

1. In this book most statutory references are to the Delaware General Corporation Law, under whose laws the majority of American public corporations are incorporated, and to the Model Business Corporation Act ("MBCA"), the template for corporations statutes in 30 states. Key statutory provisions appear in the Appendix.

can bring suit as part of the judicial function described below. This power given to shareholders reflects the concern that directors, while providing the advantages of centralized control, may, if unconstrained, act in ways that benefit themselves or otherwise harm shareholders. Shareholders, so the argument goes, are best positioned as the residual claimant of the enterprise to perform this monitoring function.

- *Rule #3. Judicial review to check agency power via fiduciary duties.* American corporate law relies on courts to constrain director decisions (and possible abuse of their centralized power) by enforcing fiduciary duties of care and loyalty. Much of our specific focus in later chapters focuses on how intrusive judicial review is in the takeover setting, ranging from a deferential business judgment standard to the much more intrusive "entire fairness" review, with the intermediate standards of *Unocal* and *Revlon* occupying space between the other two.

2. The Merger Form as a Template for Understanding Legal Regulation of Acquisition Transactions

If a possible bidder decides it makes economic sense to acquire another company, there are a variety of legal forms for the transaction that can each result in transferring control of the assets to the bidder and the deal consideration to the target and its shareholders. The statutory merger form is presented here as the touchstone for understanding the various alternatives available to the deal planner. Among the legal forms, it is the one with the most extensive set of requirements so that it also provides an accessible template for understanding the differences in the other forms.

The statutory requirements for a merger are straightforward and can be found by examining the first three subsections of §251 of the Delaware General Corporations Law:

(a) Any 2 ... corporations ... may merge ... pursuant to an agreement of (a) merger ... ;
(b) The board of directors of each corporation ... shall adopt a resolution (b) approving an agreement of merger ... ;
(c) The agreement ... shall be submitted to the stockholders of each constituent (c) corporation. ...

Later language in (c) specifies that if the agreement is adopted by a majority vote of the shareholders and filed with the secretary of state, the merger will become effective. An additional key merger requirement for our analysis is found in §262(a), which specifies any stockholder of the constituent corporations who meets various conditions discussed below is entitled to appraisal, basically the right to insist that the corporation

B. Mergers and Other Acquisitions as a Decision Governed by Law

pay the shareholder fair value for the shares, in contrast to the usual corporate rule that shareholders are not entitled to force the corporation to return the capital or value of the shares.

Thus we see a statutory form with the following core requirements:

- *An agreement or plan of merger.* This will often be negotiated by the management team covering many of the financial items covered in Chapter 2. §251 requires that the agreement specify items such as which corporation will merge into the other and the consideration and conversion of shares.
- *Approval of the plan by the board of directors* of each constituent corporation and recommending it to shareholders. Since a merger necessarily involves two (or more) corporations, this requires action by the boards on each side of the transaction.
- *Adoption of the plan by the shareholders* of each constituent corporation, again opening up the need to address actions by shareholders on both sides of the transaction. At this point it is necessary to read deeper into §251, particularly subsection (f), which begins "Notwithstanding the requirements of subsection (c) . . . no vote of stockholders of a constituent corporation surviving a merger shall be necessary . . . if: . . ." This distinction between the acquiring and target corporation (the acquiring corporation is usually the surviving corporation) is one you will need to remember and continue to analyze. The triggers for removal of the vote of shareholders of the acquiring corporation turns on the presence of three factors with the key one being if the exchange terms of the merger require no more than 20 percent of new shares of the acquirer to be issued.
- *Exit rights for shareholders* of constituent corporations as specified in §262. However, there are exceptions to who gets exit rights that make understanding the voting exception just discussed look like a walk in the park. Begin with §262(b), which states that appraisal rights are available for specified transactions such as a §251 merger and grants appraisal rights to stockholders who have "perfected" those rights. §262(b)(1) begins with a "Provided, however," which reverses the rule you have just learned and denies appraisal where the company is publicly traded. But before you get too settled on that rule, you must take into account §262(b)(2), which begins "Notwithstanding paragraph (1)," thus returning appraisal rights to shareholders of a subset of public companies. However, understanding those shareholders entitled to appraisal becomes difficult because of the double negative construction of the sentence (in a section that has already turned you around twice!). The exception restores appraisal for those shareholders who receive anything *except* four named types of consideration.

Stock is on the list, so the usual public company stock-for-stock merger will not provide appraisal for shareholders of the target corporation. Cash makes the exception list, but only if in lieu of fractional shares. A straight-up cash-out, as in *Weinberger v. UOP* thus becomes the type of merger that provides target shareholders with appraisal rights. The statute should be a lesson to statutory drafters everywhere. The comparable sections of the Model Business Corporation Act's Chapter 13 are more direct, although still difficult to follow for one confronting them for the first time.

With this background, it is possible to define the legal requirements that are in play for a deal planner in comparing a merger to the various alternative transactions using the following template, with "A Corp." referring to the acquiring corporation and "T Corp." referring to the target corporation.

Legal Effects

1. A Corp. Board Vote	2. T Corp. Board Vote
3. A Shareholders Vote	4. T Shareholders Vote
5. A Shareholders Exit	6. T Shareholders Exit
	7. T Liabilities Assumed by A?
	8. Taxes Currently Due?

3. Alternative Legal Structures for Acquisition That Permit Planners to Avoid One or More of the Requirements of the Merger Template

A merger planner would want to be able to distinguish the following variations:

- *Merger, sometimes referred to as a Statutory Merger,* usually in which one corporation (the "Target" or disappearing corporation) merges into another corporation (the "Acquiring" or surviving corporation).
- *Sale of assets*, an alternative transaction in which the Target sells its assets to the Acquiring corporation in exchange for consideration such as cash or stock. Frequently, the Target corporation will then dissolve and distribute its remaining assets (the consideration received in the transaction) to its shareholders.
- *Triangular Merger*, a statutory merger in which the Target merges into a subsidiary of the Acquiring corporation in exchange for consideration which may be shares of the Acquiring parent corporation received by the subsidiary in exchange for issuing all of the subsidiary's shares to the parent at the time of the subsidiary's formation.

- *Reverse Triangular Merger*, again a statutory merger between the Target and a subsidiary of the parent. This time, however, the subsidiary merges into the Target, which will be the surviving corporation, but the terms of the merger are still that the Target shareholders will receive shares of the Acquiring corporation.
- *Tender Offer*, a transaction in which the Acquiring corporation purchases shares of the Target corporation directly from the shareholders of the Target corporation. Such an offer is usually conditioned on tender by at least 50 percent of the Target's shareholders, so once the transaction has been completed, the Acquiring corporation will control a majority of the shares of the Target.

The discussion of each variation below assumes that the business deal is the same in each. That means that the consideration is the same. The examples assume that the Acquiring corporation will offer its own stock in exchange for the Target stock previously held by the Target shareholders at an exchange rate reflective of the relative values of the two companies. But the consideration could just as easily be cash in each of the variations without changing the core legal structure. As you work through each transaction, try to answer the same basic questions:

1. Who ends up with control of the business and assets of the Target?
2. What are the roles for the directors of A corp. and T corp.?
3. What are the roles for the shareholders of A? For T? More specifically, what are their rights to participate in the decision and their rights to exit?
4. What are the roles for the court and the government?

1. Merger

Acquirer ←—Target

In a merger, each corporation (in this case A and T) will need to satisfy the applicable requirements of Section 251 of the Delaware code, if they are Delaware corporations, or a comparable provision of the corporations code of their state of incorporation.

(a) *Plan of Merger.* Under §251(a) there must be a plan of merger, which must include items such as who is to be the surviving corporation and what T shareholders are to receive in exchange for their T shares. The two CEOs and their advisers will determine the contents of this plan, with the assistance of lawyers in drafting the document.

(b) *Board Approval.* Under §251(b) the board of each constituent corporation (here A and T) must approve the merger agreement and declare its advisability.

(c) *Shareholder Approval.* Under §251(c) the shareholders of each constituent corporation approve the merger, with the vote specified to be a majority of all outstanding stock of the corporation, a requirement for an absolute majority which effectively counts any non-voters as no.

(d) *Shareholder Exit.* From a separate statute, §262, shareholders of a constituent corporation to the merger must be given exit rights, i.e., the right to require the corporation to purchase their shares for "fair value" as an alternative to receiving the merger consideration or whatever may be available if the shareholder would sell the shares in the market.

From this template, with these four positive requirements, it is essential to consider how the last two of these requirements are sometimes modified even within the statutory merger setting. For example, §251(f) begins: "Notwithstanding the requirements of subsections (c) . . . no vote of stockholders . . . shall be necessary . . . if": the first two specified requirements under (f) result in the subsection only applying to a surviving corporation since only its certificate of incorporation will not be changed and the shares of its shareholders will remain outstanding. The third requirement removes the vote for such acquiring shareholders for any merger plan in which the surviving corporation doesn't issue more than an additional 20 percent of its stock.

The modification as to exit rights is much more complex and one of the greatest failings of the Delaware corporations law in terms of plain English writing. Section 262(b) begins with the straightforward rule that appraisal rights are available to stockholders of any constituent corporation (again, A and T in our example) for a statutory §251 merger and various other similar transactions. Subsection (b)(1), beginning "provided however," then takes away such appraisal rights for a set of corporations defined with some complexity, but reducible for our discussion to companies with publicly traded shares. This is the "market out" exception—if a shareholder has access to the market as a source of liquidity, law does not provide an alternative that can be expensive and time consuming. But we haven't completed our journey through the statute. Subsection (b)(2) then reverses subsection (1) and makes appraisal available for a subset of public companies. This subset, however, is defined in a complex way that is likely to confuse. A stockholder is within the exception to the exception (and therefore entitled to appraisal) when receiving by the terms of the merger, anything other than specified types of consideration including: (a) stock of the surviving corporation; (b) shares of any other public corporation (for example, a parent corporation) so that stock for stock mergers would continue to be covered by the market out exception and the shareholders left with no appraisal rights; and (c) cash, which would seem to take out the other significant type of currency consideration, as discussed in Chapter 2. But the reference to cash is not unmodified. It only refers to "cash in lieu of fractional shares," an anachronism from the days before computers when there was a desire to keep ownership in whole shares, and to permit merger plans that permitted cash payment for any fractional shares created by the conversion rate agreed between the parties.

Thus the dominant illustrations of mergers that will fit within this exception to the exception are those where stockholders receive cash for their whole shares. Even if you have followed the explanation until now, you will not yet understand that the practical effect of this provision is to preserve appraisal for cash-out mergers (i.e., the target shareholders are forced to take cash and not just for fractional shares), such as *Weinberger v. UOP Inc.*, where the parent corporation already owns greater than the 51 percent of the target that would be necessary to approve a merger. The Model Business Corporation Act, in changes since 1999, has been better about writing its appraisal statute to more clearly identify its focus for mergers in which the majority shareholder has a conflict of interest.

2. Sale of Assets

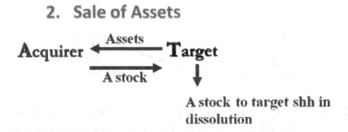

A sale of assets is a contractual purchase and sale agreement in which the Target conveys assets (and perhaps liabilities) to the Acquiring company, and in return, the Acquirer provides the consideration (which, for our discussion, you should assume is the same as what was specified in the merger agreement in the prior example). The purchase and sale is between the two corporations, so that the consideration remains within the Target corporation. But often in the acquisition world, the sale of assets is followed by the dissolution of the Target, in which the Target distributes its remaining assets proportionately to its shareholders. The result after both these steps, therefore, is the financial equivalent of a merger. The Target's assets and liabilities have moved to the Acquirer and the T shareholders have become shareholders of A, if the consideration was stock for stock. Of course, the sale of assets form is often useful when the buyer desires to acquire the Target's assets but not its liabilities, or only some of its assets or liabilities. Our focus is on the availability of the sale of assets form in the same economic setting as the merger but with fewer legal requirements than the template with which we began. Delaware's §271 specifies approval requirements for the seller corporation similar to, but not identical to, what we have already seen: a sale itself, with less formality specified than the "plan" identified in §251(a), entered into by the board of the selling company and approved by the majority of the outstanding shares. But there are two significant differences.

First, there is no mention of the purchasing corporation in these requirements, so the requirements for action by that corporation will fall back on the default rules in corporate law outside of the acquisition context, i.e., director decision-making under §141. Second, the right to exit is more constrained than in mergers. If you return to the appraisal section and examine the list of statutes for which appraisal is provided in Delaware, the sale of assets form is missing. So, selling company shareholders have a vote but no statutory exit. In this regard, Delaware differs from most other states. The Model Business Corporation Act, which provides the basis for the corporations statute of a majority of states, specifically gives appraisal rights to selling company shareholders for sale of assets, but as to acquiring shareholders, it is like Delaware in providing no rights for shareholders to vote or exit.

3. Forward Triangular Merger

A triangular merger is a variation of the §251 statutory merger in that one company merges into another. The Acquiring company forms a wholly owned subsidiary to be the party to the merger and this subsidiary corporation ("S") enters into the merger agreement with the target. In setting up the Subsidiary, the parent subscribes for the shares of the Subsidiary, paid for by providing the Subsidiary the Acquiring company shares or cash that the Subsidiary will then use for the merger with Target. The merger then proceeds just as before. The plan specifies that T will merge into S and S will be the surviving company. It also provides that every shareholder of T will receive the agreed-upon consideration (usually A shares or cash at the agreed-upon exchange rate). When completed, A will control the assets of T, but through a wholly owned subsidiary, which can provide some liability protection if A would prefer not to expose its set of assets to risk accruing from the T assets.

The requirements of §§251(b) and (c) and 262 will apply as before with the vote of each board of directors and each set of shareholders and the exit rights for shareholders. But note the uncertainty as to those approvals that have been removed. S's board is likely to be as amenable as the A board to approving the mergers; on the acquirer side, the vote of the shareholders could go much smoother than in a statutory merger since the vote of S shareholders means there is one voter, A, Inc., and A's board is entitled to act for it. Likewise, this one S shareholder will not seek appraisal, should it be available, so the risk of the corporate treasury being diluted by shareholders seeking their money will not occur.

4. Reverse Triangular Merger

A reverse triangular merger follows on the preceding form as a merger between the target and a subsidiary of the acquiring firm. But now the plan of merger specifies that the Subsidiary will merge into the Target with the Target as the surviving company. The plan will still specify that every shareholder of T will receive the consideration of A stock or cash as previously discussed. Once the deal is completed, A will control the use of T's assets and liabilities through a wholly owned subsidiary, which can provide the liability protection discussed above. The difference is that T is the surviving entity, which could be important if T has a valuable brand name or contract rights that cannot be easily transferred.

5. Tender Offer

Acquirer ← T shares **Target**

A shares → Target shareholders

A tender offer differs from the other transactions already described in that it is between A, Inc. and the shareholders of T. A, Inc. offers to buy the T shares from the T shareholders for the same stock or cash consideration as previously used. Once the transaction is completed, A, Inc. will control the use and direction of T assets (assuming it has conditioned its offer upon tender of at least 51 percent of the shares which will enable it to elect T's board). As with the triangular transactions, this means that A will now control T's assets and liabilities through a separate corporation which can provide the same kind of liability insulation previously discussed. If A, Inc. desires to own all of the T shares, as opposed to just a majority, it can follow up the tender offer with a cash-out merger in which the consideration is the same as in the first step. Under this §251 transaction it can easily satisfy the requirements of director and shareholder approval, and as seen below, the litigation risk of having to pay a higher amount in appraisal will not be great.

Tender offers are essentially a series of contractual exchanges without the need for collective action that is governed by corporate law. Beyond contract law, legal regulation is more likely to come from federal securities law. The Williams Act, 1968 amendments to the Securities Exchange Act of 1934, imposed disclosure requirements on a bidder making a tender offer that essentially mirrors the then existing disclosure obligations of an acquirer using a proxy fight to seek control of a company. See §14(d) of the Act and compare it to §14(a). Disclosure is discussed in more detail in Chapter 12. In addition to this §14(d) disclosure triggered by the tender offer itself, the Williams Act also added an "early warning" type of disclosure for any shareholder who acquires more than 5 percent of the equity of a public company and a requirement to report subsequent changes in that holding. See §13(d) of the Act. Additional disclosure triggered by §13, requiring institutional shareholders to report their holdings, can also shape a takeover battle. See §13(g).

While disclosure is the principal regulatory tool visible in the Williams Act, and in the 1934 Act more generally, there is also some substantive regulation of tender offers from the statute and implementing rules that you should note. Congressional worry about mistreatment of tendering shareholders in tender offers led to requirements of withdrawal rights for shareholders who tender (§14(d)(5)), a requirement that if more shares are tendered than the bidder seeks, shares must be purchased pro rata (§14(d)(6)), and requiring any increase in the tender price during the offer be paid to all who tender (§14(d)(7). SEC rules require equal treatment of all shareholders (*see* Rule 14d-10) and require that tender offers stay open a minimum of 20 business days (*see* Rule 14e-1).

C. JUDICIAL LIMITS ON PRIVATE PLANNING TO AVOID PARTICULAR MERGER EFFECTS: DE FACTO MERGER

Hariton v. Arco Electronics, Inc.
188 A.2d 123 (Del. Sup. Ct. 1963)

SOUTHERLAND, Chief Justice.

This case involves a sale of assets under §271 of the corporation law, 8 Del. C. It presents for decision the question presented, but not decided, in Heilbrunn v. Sun Chemical Corporation, Del., 150 A.2d 755. It may be stated as follows:

A sale of assets is effected under §271 in consideration of shares of stock of the purchasing corporation. The agreement of sale embodies also a

C. Judicial Limits on Private Planning

plan to dissolve the selling corporation and distribute the shares so received to the stockholders of the seller, so as to accomplish the same result as would be accomplished by a merger of the seller into the purchaser. Is the sale legal?

The facts are these:

The defendant Arco and Loral Electronics Corporation, a New York corporation, are both engaged, in somewhat different forms, in the electronic equipment business. In the summer of 1961 they negotiated for an amalgamation of the companies. As of October 27, 1961, they entered into a "Reorganization Agreement and Plan." The provisions of this Plan pertinent here are in substance as follows:

1. Arco agrees to sell all its assets to Loral in consideration (inter alia) of the issuance to it of 283,000 shares of Loral.
2. Arco agrees to call a stockholders meeting for the purpose of approving the Plan and the voluntary dissolution.
3. Arco agrees to distribute to its stockholders all the Loral shares received by it as a part of the complete liquidation of Arco.

At the Arco meeting all the stockholders voting (about 80%) approved the Plan. It was thereafter consummated.

Plaintiff, a stockholder who did not vote at the meeting, sued to enjoin the consummation of the Plan on the grounds (1) that it was illegal, and (2) that it was unfair. The second ground was abandoned. Affidavits and documentary evidence were filed, and defendant moved for summary judgment and dismissal of the complaint. The Vice Chancellor granted the motion and plaintiff appeals.

The question before us we have stated above. Plaintiff's argument that the sale is illegal runs as follows:

The several steps taken here accomplish the same result as a merger of Arco into Loral. In a "true" sale of assets, the stockholder of the seller retains the right to elect whether the selling company shall continue as a holding company. Moreover, the stockholder of the selling company is forced to accept an investment in a new enterprise without the right of appraisal granted under the merger statute. §271 cannot therefore be legally combined with a dissolution proceeding under §275 and a consequent distribution of the purchaser's stock. Such a proceeding is a misuse of the power granted under §271, and a *de facto* merger results.

The foregoing is a brief summary of plaintiff's contention.

Plaintiff's contention that this sale has achieved the same result as a merger is plainly correct. The same contention was made to us in Heilbrunn v. Sun Chemical Corporation, Del., 150 A.2d 755. Accepting it as correct, we noted that this result is made possible by the overlapping scope of the merger statute and section 271, mentioned in Sterling v. Mayflower Hotel Corporation, 33 Del. Ch. 293, 93 A.2d 107, 38 A.L.R.2d 425. We also adverted to the increased use, in connection with corporate reorganization plans, of §271 instead of the merger statute. Further, we observed that no Delaware case has held such procedure to be improper, and that two cases appear to assume its legality. Finch v. Warrior Cement Corporation, 16 Del. Ch. 44, 141 A. 54, and Argenbright v. Phoenix Finance Co., 21 Del. Ch. 288, 187 A. 124. But we were not required in the *Heilbrunn* case to decide the point.

We now hold that the reorganization here accomplished through §271 and a mandatory plan of dissolution and distribution is legal. This is so because the sale-of-assets statute and the merger statute are independent of each other. They are, so to speak, of equal dignity, and the framers of a reorganization plan may resort to either type of corporate mechanics to achieve the desired end. This is not an anomalous result in our corporation law. As the Vice Chancellor pointed out, the elimination of accrued dividends, though forbidden under a charter amendment (Keller v. Wilson & Co., 21 Del. Ch. 391, 190 A. 115) may be accomplished by a merger. Federal United Corporation v. Havender, 24 Del. Ch. 318, 11 A.2d 331.

In Langfelder v. Universal Laboratories, D.C., 68 F. Supp. 209, Judge Leahy commented upon "the general theory of the Delaware Corporation Law that action taken pursuant to the authority of the various sections of that law constitute acts of independent legal significance and their validity is not dependent on other sections of the Act." 68 F. Supp. 211, footnote....

Plaintiff concedes, as we read his brief, that if the several steps taken in this case had been taken separately they would have been legal. That is, he concedes that a sale of assets, followed by a separate proceeding to dissolve and distribute, would be legal, even though the same result would follow. This concession exposes the weakness of his contention. To attempt to make any such distinction between sales under §271 would be to create uncertainty in the law and invite litigation.

We are in accord with the Vice Chancellor's ruling, and the judgment below is affirmed.

Farris v. Glen Alden Corp.
143 A.2d 25 (Pa. Sup. Ct. 1958)

COHEN, Justice.

We are required to determine on this appeal whether, as a result of a "Reorganization Agreement" executed by the officers of Glen Alden Corporation and List Industries Corporation, and approved by the shareholders of the former company, the rights and remedies of a dissenting shareholder accrue to the plaintiff.

C. Judicial Limits on Private Planning

Glen Alden is a Pennsylvania corporation engaged principally in the mining of anthracite coal and lately in the manufacture of air conditioning units and fire-fighting equipment. In recent years the company's operating revenue has declined substantially, and in fact, its coal operations have resulted in tax loss carryovers of approximately $14,000,000. In October 1957, List, a Delaware holding company owning interests in motion picture theaters, textile companies and real estate, and to a lesser extent, in oil and gas operations, warehouses and aluminum piston manufacturing, purchased through a wholly owned subsidiary 38.5% of Glen Alden's outstanding stock.[2] This acquisition enabled List to place three of its directors on the Glen Alden board.

On March 20, 1958, the two corporations entered into a "reorganization agreement," subject to stockholder approval, which contemplated the following actions:

1. Glen Alden is to acquire all of the assets of List, excepting a small amount of cash reserved for the payment of List's expenses in connection with the transaction. These assets include over $8,000,000 in cash held chiefly in the treasuries of List's wholly owned subsidiaries.
2. In consideration of the transfer, Glen Alden is to issue 3,621,703 shares of stock to List. List in turn is to distribute the stock to its shareholders at a ratio of five shares of Glen Alden stock for each six shares of List stock. In order to accomplish the necessary distribution, Glen Alden is to increase the authorized number of its shares of capital stock from 2,500,000 shares to 7,500,000 shares without according pre-emptive rights to the present shareholders upon the issuance of any such shares.
3. Further, Glen Alden is to assume all of List's liabilities including a $5,000,000 note incurred by List in order to purchase Glen Alden stock in 1957, outstanding stock options, incentive stock options plans, and pension obligations.
4. Glen Alden is to change its corporate name from Glen Alden Corporation to List Alden Corporation.
5. The present directors of both corporations are to become directors of List Alden.
6. List is to be dissolved and List Alden is to then carry on the operations of both former corporations.

Two days after the agreement was executed notice of the annual meeting of Glen Alden to be held on April 11, 1958, was mailed to the shareholders together with a proxy statement analyzing the reorganization agreement and recommending its approval as well as approval of certain

---

2. Of the purchase price of $8,719,109, $5,000,000 was borrowed.

amendments to Glen Alden's articles of incorporation and bylaws necessary to implement the agreement. At this meeting the holders of a majority of the outstanding shares, (not including those owned by List), voted in favor of a resolution approving the reorganization agreement.

On the day of the shareholders' meeting, plaintiff, a shareholder of Glen Alden, filed a complaint in equity against the corporation and its officers seeking to enjoin them temporarily until final hearing, and perpetually thereafter, from executing and carrying out the agreement.

The gravamen of the complaint was that the notice of the annual shareholders' meeting did not conform to the requirements of the Business Corporation Law, 15 P.S. §2852-1 et seq., in three respects: (1) It did not give notice to the shareholders that the true intent and purpose of the meeting was to effect a merger or consolidation of Glen Alden and List; (2) It failed to give notice to the shareholders of their right to dissent to the plan of merger or consolidation and claim fair value for their shares; and (3) It did not contain copies of the text of certain sections of the Business Corporation Law as required.[3]

By reason of these omissions, plaintiff contended that the approval of the reorganization agreement by the shareholders at the annual meeting was invalid and unless the carrying out of the plan were enjoined, he would suffer irreparable loss by being deprived of substantial property rights.

The defendants answered admitting the material allegations of fact in the complaint but denying that they gave rise to a cause of action because the transaction complained of was a purchase of corporate assets as to which shareholders had no rights of dissent or appraisal. For these reasons the defendants then moved for judgment on the pleadings.[5]

The court below concluded that the reorganization agreement entered into between the two corporations was a plan for a *de facto* merger, and that therefore the failure of the notice of the annual meeting to conform to the pertinent requirements of the merger provisions of the Business Corporation Law rendered the notice defective and all proceedings in furtherance of the agreement void. . . . This appeal followed.

When use of the corporate form of business organization first became widespread, it was relatively easy for courts to define a "merger" or a "sale of assets" and to label a particular transaction as one or the other.

---

3. The proxy statement included the following declaration:

Appraisal Rights.
    In the opinion of counsel, the shareholders of neither Glen Alden nor List Industries will have any rights of appraisal or similar rights of dissenters with respect to any matter to be acted upon at their respective meetings.

5. Counsel for the defendants concedes that if the corporation is required to pay the dissenting shareholders the appraised fair value of their shares, the resultant drain of cash would prevent Glen Alden from carrying out the agreement. On the other hand, plaintiff contends that if the shareholders had been told of their rights as dissenters, rather than specifically advised that they had no such rights, the resolution approving the reorganization agreement would have been defeated.

C. Judicial Limits on Private Planning

See, e.g., 15 Fletcher, CORPORATIONS §§7040-7045 (rev. vol. 1938); *In re Buist's Estate*, 1929, 297 Pa. 537, 541, 147 A. 606; *Koehler v. St. Mary's Brewing Co.*, 1910, 228 Pa. 648, 653-654, 77 A. 1016. But prompted by the desire to avoid the impact of adverse, and to obtain the benefits of favorable, government regulations, particularly federal tax laws, new accounting and legal techniques were developed by lawyers and accountants which interwove the elements characteristic of each, thereby creating hybrid forms of corporate amalgamation. Thus, it is no longer helpful to consider an individual transaction in the abstract and solely by reference to the various elements therein determine whether it is a "merger" or a "sale." Instead, to determine properly the nature of a corporate transaction, we must refer not only to all the provisions of the agreement, but also to the consequences of the transaction and to the purposes of the provisions of the corporation law said to be applicable. We shall apply this principle to the instant case.

Section 908, subd. A of the Pennsylvania Business Corporation Law provides: "If any shareholder of a domestic corporation which becomes a party to a plan of merger or consolidation shall object to such plan of merger or consolidation . . . such shareholder shall be entitled to . . . [the fair value of his shares upon surrender of the share certificate or certificates representing his shares]." Act of May 5, 1933, P.L. 364, as amended, 15 P.S. §2852-908, subd. A.

This provision had its origin in the early decision of this Court in *Lauman v. Lebanon Valley R. R. Co.*, 1858, 30 Pa. 42. There a shareholder who objected to the consolidation of his company with another was held to have a right in the absence of statute to treat the consolidation as a dissolution of his company and to receive the value of his shares upon their surrender.

The rationale of the *Lauman* case, and of the present section of the Business Corporation Law based thereon, is that when a corporation combines with another so as to lose its essential nature and alter the original fundamental relationships of the shareholders among themselves and to the corporation, a shareholder who does not wish to continue his membership therein may treat his membership in the original corporation as terminated and have the value of his shares paid to him. See *Lauman v. Lebanon Valley R.R. Co.*, supra, 30 Pa. at pages 46-47. See also *Bloch v. Baldwin Locomotive Works*, C.P. Del. 1950, 75 Pa. Dist. & Co. R. 24, 36-38.

Does the combination outlined in the present 'reorganization agreement so fundamentally change the corporate character of Glen Alden and the interest of the plaintiff as a shareholder therein, that to refuse him the rights and remedies of a dissenting shareholder would in reality force him to give up his stock in one corporation and against his will accept shares in another? If so, the combination is a merger within the meaning of section 908, subd. A of the corporation law. See *Bloch v. Baldwin Locomotive Works*, supra. Cf. *Marks v. Autocar Co.*, D.C.E.D. Pa. 1954, 153 F. Supp. 768. See also *Troupiansky v. Henry Disston & Sons*, D.C.E.D. Pa. 1957, 151 F. Supp. 609.

If the reorganization agreement were consummated plaintiff would find that the "List Alden" resulting from the amalgamation would be quite a different corporation than the "Glen Alden" in which he is now a shareholder. Instead of continuing primarily as a coal mining company, Glen Alden would be transformed, after amendment of its articles of incorporation, into a diversified holding company whose interests would range from motion picture theaters to textile companies. Plaintiff would find himself a member of a company with assets of $169,000,000 and a long-term debt of $38,000,000 in lieu of a company one-half that size and with but one-seventh the long-term debt.

While the administration of the operations and properties of Glen Alden as well as List would be in the hands of management common to both companies, since all executives of List would be retained in List Alden, the control of Glen Alden would pass to the directors of List; for List would hold eleven of the seventeen directorships on the new board of directors.

As an aftermath of the transaction plaintiff's proportionate interest in Glen Alden would have been reduced to only two-fifths of what it presently is because of the issuance of an additional 3,621,703 shares to List which would not be subject to pre-emptive rights. In fact, ownership of Glen Alden would pass to the stockholders of List who would hold 76.5% of the outstanding shares as compared with but 23.5% retained by the present Glen Alden shareholders.

Perhaps the most important consequence to the plaintiff, if he were denied the right to have his shares redeemed at their fair value, would be the serious financial loss suffered upon consummation of the agreement. While the present book value of his stock is $38 a share after combination it would be worth only $21 a share. In contrast, the shareholders of List who presently hold stock with a total book value of $33,000,000 or $7.50 a share, would receive stock with a book value of $76,000,000 or $21 a share.

Under these circumstances it may well be said that if the proposed combination is allowed to take place without right of dissent, plaintiff would have his stock in Glen Alden taken away from him and the stock of a new company thrust upon him in its place. He would be projected against his will into a new enterprise under terms not of his own choosing. It was to protect dissident shareholders against just such a result that this Court one hundred years ago in the *Lauman* case, and the legislature thereafter in section 908, subd. A, granted the right of dissent. And it is to accord that protection to the plaintiff that we conclude that the combination proposed in the case at hand is a merger within the intendment of section 908, subd. A.

Nevertheless, defendants contend that the 1957 amendments to sections 311 and 908 of the corporation law preclude us from reaching this result and require the entry of judgment in their favor. Subsection F of section 311 dealing with the voluntary transfer of corporate assets provides: "The shareholders of a business corporation which acquires by

C. Judicial Limits on Private Planning

sale, lease or exchange all or substantially all of the property of another corporation by the issuance of stock, securities or otherwise shall not be entitled to the rights and remedies of dissenting shareholders. . . ." Act of July 11, 1957, P.L. 711, §1, 15 P.S. §2852-311, subd. F.

And the amendment to section 908 reads as follows: "The right of dissenting shareholders . . . shall not apply to the purchase by a corporation of assets whether or not the consideration therefor be money or property, real or personal, including shares or bonds or other evidences of indebtedness of such corporation. The shareholders of such corporation shall have no right to dissent from any such purchase." Act of July 11, 1957, P.L. 711, §1, 15 P.S. §2852-908, subd. C.

Defendants view these amendments as abridging the right of shareholders to dissent to a transaction between two corporations which involves a transfer of assets for a consideration even though the transfer has all the legal incidents of a merger. They claim that only if the merger is accomplished in accordance with the prescribed statutory procedure does the right of dissent accrue. In support of this position they cite to us the comment on the amendments by the Committee on Corporation Law of the Pennsylvania Bar Association, the committee which originally drafted these provisions. The comment states that the provisions were intended to overrule cases which granted shareholders the right to dissent to a sale of assets when accompanied by the legal incidents of a merger. See 61 Ann. Rep. Pa. Bar Ass'n 277, 284 (1957).[7]

Whatever may have been the intent of the *committee*, there is no evidence to indicate that the *legislature* intended the 1957 amendments to have the effect contended for. But furthermore, the language of these two provisions does not support the opinion of the committee and is inapt to achieve any such purpose. The amendments of 1957 do not provide that a transaction between two corporations which has the effect of a merger but which includes a transfer of assets for consideration is to be exempt from the protective provisions of sections 908, subd. A and 515. They provide only that the shareholders of a corporation which acquires the property or purchases the assets of another corporation, *without more*, are not

---

7. "The amendment to Section 311 expressly provides that a sale, lease or exchange of substantially all corporate assets in connection with its liquidation or dissolution is subject to the provisions of Article XI of the Act, and that no consent or authorization of shareholders other than what is required by Article XI is necessary. The recent decision in *Marks v. Autocar Co.*, D.C.E.D. Pa., Civil Action No. 16075 [153 F. Supp. 768] is to the contrary. This amendment, together with the proposed amendment to Section 1104 expressly permitting the directors in liquidating the corporation to sell only such assets as may be required to pay its debts and distribute any assets remaining among shareholders (Section 1108, [subd.] B now so provides in the case of receivers) have the effect of overruling *Marks v. Autocar Co.*, . . . which permits a shareholder dissenting from such a sale to obtain the fair value of his shares. The *Marks* case relies substantially on *Bloch v. Baldwin Locomotive Works*, 75 [Pa.] Dist. & Co. R. 24, also believed to be an undesirable decision. That case permitted a holder of stock in a corporation which *purchased* for stock all the assets of another corporation to obtain the fair value of his shares. That case is also in effect overruled by the new Sections 311 [subd.] F and 908 [subd.] C." 61 Ann. Rep. Pa. Bar Ass'n, 277, 284 (1957).

entitled to the right to dissent from the transaction. So, as in the present case, when as part of a transaction between two corporations, one corporation dissolves, its liabilities are assumed by the survivor, its executives and directors take over the management and control of the survivor, and, as consideration for the transfer, its stockholders acquire a majority of the shares of stock of the survivor, then the transaction is no longer simply a purchase of assets or acquisition of property to which sections 311, subd. F and 908, subd. C apply, but a merger governed by section 908, subd. A of the corporation law. To divest shareholders of their right of dissent under such circumstances would require express language which is absent from the 1957 amendments.

Even were we to assume that the combination provided for in the reorganiation agreement is a "sale of assets" to which section 908, subd. A does not apply, it would avail the defendants nothing; we will not blind our eyes to the realities of the transaction. Despite the designation of the parties and the form employed, Glen Alden does not in fact acquire List, rather, List acquires Glen Alden, cf. Metropolitan Edison Co. v. Commissioner, 3 Cir., 1938, 98 F.2d 807, affirmed sub nom., Helvering v. Metropolitan Edison Co., 1939, 306 U.S. 522, 59 S. Ct. 634, 83 L. Ed. 957, and under section 311, subd. D[8] the right of dissent would remain with the shareholders of Glen Alden.

We hold that the combination contemplated by the reorganization agreement, although consummated by contract rather than in accordance with the statutory procedure, is a merger within the protective purview of sections 908, subd. A and 515 of the corporation law. The shareholders of Glen Alden should have been notified accordingly and advised of their statutory rights of dissent and appraisal. The failure of the corporate officers to take these steps renders the stockholder approval of the agreement at the 1958 shareholders' meeting invalid. The lower court did not err in enjoining the officers and directors of Glen Alden from carrying out this agreement.

Decree affirmed at appellants' cost.

Terry v. Penn Central Corp.
668 F.2d 188 (3d Cir. 1981)

ADAMS, Circuit Judge.

The Penn Central Corporation ("Penn Central"), an appellee in this case, has sought to acquire Colt Industries Inc. ("Colt"), also an appellee, by merging Colt with PCC Holdings, Inc. ("Holdings"), a wholly-owned

---

8. "If any shareholder of a business corporation which sells, leases or exchanges all or substantially all of its property and assets otherwise than (1) in the usual and regular course of its business, (2) for the purpose of relocating its business, or (3) in connection with its dissolution and liquidation, shall object to such sale, lease or exchange and comply with the provisions of section 515 of this act, such shareholder shall be entitled to the rights and remedies of dissenting shareholders as therein provided." Act of July 11, 1957, P.L. 711, 15 P.S. §2852-311, subd. D.

C. Judicial Limits on Private Planning 43

subsidiary of Penn Central. Howard L. Terry and W.H. Hunt, the appellants, are shareholders of Penn Central who objected to the transaction. In a diversity action before the United States District Court for the Eastern District of Pennsylvania, appellants sought injunctive and declaratory relief to enforce voting and dissenters' rights to which appellants asserted they were entitled. Appellants further sought to enjoin Holdings from proceeding with the proposed merger, and in particular moved to enjoin a vote on the transaction, scheduled for October 29, 1981, by the shareholders of Penn Central. In an opinion issued on October 22, 1981, Judge Pollak denied appellants' requests. Appellants thereupon filed an appeal in this Court. . . . The shareholders of Penn Central voted, as scheduled, on October 29. . . .

After argument on appeal, the shareholders disapproved of the merger, and the corporations thereafter publicly announced their abandonment of this particular merger. Penn Central, however, has not abandoned its proposed series of acquisitions, of which the Colt acquisition was merely one instance.

I.

Penn Central is the successor to the Penn Central Transportation Corporation, which underwent a reorganization under the bankruptcy laws that was completed in 1978. No longer involved in the railroading business, Penn Central, since 1978, has had the advantage, for tax purposes, of a large loss carry-forward. In order to put that loss carry-forward to its best use, Penn Central has embarked on a program of acquiring corporations whose profits could be sheltered. To this end Penn Central created Holdings, a wholly-owned subsidiary which was to acquire the businesses that Penn Central desired. The first acquisition under the plan was Marathon Manufacturing Company ("Marathon"), in 1979. In the Marathon acquisition, a class of preferred Penn Central stock was created, and 30 million shares of "First Series Preference Stock" was issued to the owners of Marathon stock. Appellants were shareholders of Marathon who thereby obtained shares of this First Series Preference Stock. Terry was promptly elected to the Penn Central board of directors.

In 1981, Penn Central decided upon another acquisition: Colt. The management and directors of Colt and Penn Central agreed upon a merger of Colt into Holdings, compensated for by issuance of a second series of Penn Central preference stock to Colt shareholders. Terry opposed the merger at the directors' meeting, and sought to preclude the consummation of the transaction. . . .

Because Colt and Penn Central have now announced their abandonment of the proposed merger, the request for injunctive relief considered by the district court is now conceded by all parties to be moot. However, the appellants' request for declaratory relief, which the appellants now contend is moot as well, involves legal questions that go to Penn Central's plan of acquisitions, rather than to the Colt transaction alone, and these questions appear likely to recur in future disputes between the parties here. It is clear from the record that the Colt merger was one in a series of similar acquisitions by Penn Central. The appellants, one of whom has now objected to each of the last two proposed acquisitions by Penn Central, will continue to have a lively interest in challenging any future amalgamations structured in roughly the same manner as the transaction before us now. The declaratory relief requested here thus arises from a genuine and continuing controversy, and involves adverse parties who have diligently presented their cases to this Court. The continuing threat of legal action creates some present injury, and not merely a speculative future injury, to Penn Central: without a judgment on the merits of this appeal, Penn Central's present ability to negotiate other acquisitions will be severely impaired by the desire of potential merger partners to avoid the legal complications faced by Penn Central and Colt. In a case such as this, a voluntary termination by the parties of the specific activity challenged in the lawsuit—here, the proposed treatment of the dissenting preferred shareholders in the Colt-Holdings plan—does not render the action moot because there is "a reasonable likelihood that the parties or those in privity with them will be involved in a suit on the same issues in the future." *American Bible Society v. Blount*, 446 F.2d 588, 595 (3d Cir. 1971); *Marshall v. Whittaker Corp.*, 610 F.2d 1141, 1147 (3d Cir. 1979).

III.

Terry and Hunt contend that under Pennsylvania law they are entitled to dissent and appraisal rights if a merger is approved by the Penn Central shareholders. . . . Briefly, appellants' argument is that the proposed merger between Holdings and Colt constitutes a de facto merger between Colt and Penn Central, and that the Penn Central shareholders are therefore entitled to the protections for dissenting shareholders that Pennsylvania corporate law provides for shareholders of parties to a merger. Although this reasoning, with its emphasis on the substance of the transaction rather than its formal trappings, may be attractive as a matter of policy, see, e.g., Note, Three-Party Mergers: The Fourth Form of Corporate Acquisition, 57 VA. L. REV. 1242 (1971), it contravenes the language employed by the Pennsylvania legislature in setting out the rights of shareholders.

Section 908 of the Pennsylvania Business Corporation Law (PBCL), 15 P.S. §1908, provides that shareholders of corporations that are parties to a plan of merger are entitled to dissent and appraisal rights, but adds that for an acquisition other than such a merger, the only rights are those provided for in Section 311 of the PBCL, 15 P.S. §1311 (Purdon 1967 & Supp. 1981-82). Section 311, in turn, provides for dissent and appraisal rights only when an acquisition has been accomplished by "the issuance

C. Judicial Limits on Private Planning

of voting shares of such corporation to be outstanding immediately after the acquisition sufficient to elect a majority of the directors of the corporation." In this case the shares of Penn Central stock to be issued in the Colt transaction do not exceed the number of shares already existing, and thus the transaction is not covered by Section 311. Any statutory dissent and appraisal rights for Penn Central shareholders are therefore contingent upon Penn Central's status as a party to the merger within the meaning of Section 908. And as the district court points out, the PBCL describes the parties to a merger as those entities that are actually combined into a single corporation. Section 907, 15 P.S. §1907 (Purdon Supp. 1981-82), states that:

> Upon the merger or consolidation becoming effective, the several corporations parties to the plan of merger or consolidation shall be a single corporation which, in the case of a merger, shall be that corporation designated in the plan of merger as the surviving corporation. . . .

At the consummation of the proposed merger plan here, both Holdings and Penn Central would survive as separate entities, and it would therefore appear that Penn Central is not a party within the meaning of the Section 907. We can discern no reason to infer that the legislature intended the word "party" to have different meanings in Sections 907 and 908, and accordingly conclude that Penn Central is not a party to the merger.

Appellants argue that Penn Central is nevertheless brought into the amalgamation by the de facto merger doctrine as set out in Pennsylvania law in *Farris v. Glen Alden Corp.*, 393 Pa. 427, 143 A.2d 25 (1958). *Farris* was the penultimate step in a pas de deux involving the Pennsylvania courts and the Pennsylvania legislature regarding the proper treatment for transactions that reached the same practical result as a merger but avoided the legal form of merger and the concomitant legal obligations. In the 1950s the Pennsylvania courts advanced the doctrine that a transaction having the effect of an amalgamation would be treated as a de facto merger. See, e.g., *Bloch v. The Baldwin Locomotive Works*, 75 Pa. D.&C. 24 (1950). The legislature responded with efforts to constrict the de facto merger doctrine. *Farris*, addressing those efforts, held that the doctrine still covered a reorganization agreement that had the effect of merging a large corporation into a smaller corporation. In a 1959 response to *Farris*, the legislature made explicit its objection to earlier cases that found certain transactions to be de facto mergers. The legislature enacted a law, modifying inter alia Sections 311 and 908, entitled in part:

> An Act . . . changing the law as to . . . the acquisition or transfer of corporate assets, the rights of dissenting shareholders, . . . abolishing the doctrine of de facto mergers or consolidation and reversing the rules laid down in *Bloch v. Baldwin Locomotive Works*, 75 D & C 24, and *Marks v. The Autocar Co.*, 153 F. Supp. 768. . . .

Act of November 10, 1959 (P.L. 1406, No. 502).

Following this explicit statement, the de facto merger doctrine has rarely been invoked by the Pennsylvania courts. Only once has the Pennsylvania Supreme Court made reference to it, in *In re Jones & Laughlin Steel Corp.*, 488 Pa. 524, 412 A.2d 1099 (1980). Even there, the Court's reference was oblique. It merely cited *Farris* for the proposition that shareholders have the right to enjoin "proposed unfair or fraudulent corporate actions." 488 Pa. at 533, 412 A.2d at 1104. This Court, sitting in diversity in *Knapp v. North American Rockwell Corp.*, 506 F.2d 361 (3d Cir. 1974), cert. denied, 421 U.S. 965, 95 S. Ct. 1955, 44 L. Ed. 2d 452 (1975), made reference to the de facto merger doctrine to hold that a transaction structured as a sale of assets could nevertheless be deemed a merger for purposes of requiring the merging corporation to assume the acquired corporation's liability for damages to a worker who was injured by a faulty piece of equipment manufactured by the acquired company. Perhaps the broadest application of the doctrine was made in *In re Penn Central Securities Litigation*, 367 F. Supp. 1158 (E.D. Pa. 1973), in which the district court held that the doctrine provided the plaintiffs in that case with standing for a 10b-5 lawsuit alleging fraud and also gave rise to dissent and appraisal rights in a triangular merger situation.

None of these cases persuades us that a Pennsylvania court would apply the de facto merger doctrine to the situation before us. Although *Jones & Laughlin Steel* suggests that dissent and appraisal rights might be available if fraud or fundamental unfairness were shown, we are not faced with such a situation. No allegation of fraud has been advanced, and the only allegation of fundamental unfairness is that the appellants will, if the merger is consummated, be forced into what they consider a poor investment on the part of Penn Central without the opportunity to receive an appraised value for their stock. Even if appellants' evaluation of the merits of the proposed merger is accurate, poor business judgment on the part of management would not be enough to constitute unfairness cognizable by a court. And the denial of appraisal rights to dissenters cannot constitute fundamental unfairness, or the de facto merger doctrine would apply in every instance in which dissenters' rights were sought and the 1959 amendments by the legislature would be rendered nugatory.[7]

The two federal cases invoking the doctrine, *Knapp* and *Penn Central Securities*, are not persuasive as to the applicability of the de facto merger to the present situation. *Knapp* was not concerned with the rights of shareholders as the Pennsylvania legislature was in 1959. Although *Penn Central Securities* did hold, in part, that the triangular merger there constituted a de facto merger, it is clear from the briefs submitted to the district court in that case that the court was not made aware of the post-*Farris* 1959

---

7. A different result might be reached if here, as in *Farris*, the acquiring corporation were significantly smaller than the acquired corporation such that the acquisition greatly transformed the nature of the successor corporation. But in this situation we do not have such a case; after the merger Penn Central would remain a major, diversified corporation, and would continue on the course of acquiring other corporations.

amendments or the legislative statement of intent to limit the de facto merger doctrine.

In the absence of any explicit guidance to the contrary by the Pennsylvania courts, we conclude that the language of the legislature in 1959 precludes a decision that the transaction in this case constitutes a de facto merger sufficient to entitle Penn Central shareholders to dissent and appraisal rights. We therefore hold that appellants do not possess such rights if a transaction such as the one involved here is consummated.

NOTES AND QUESTIONS

1. **The economics of the deals.** In each case, assets that previously were separately managed in a corporation have become part of a larger enterprise with control passing to the larger enterprise and the former shareholders being paid with the currency of shares. What are the likely economic explanations for such a combination? Make sure you follow the core economic changes, particularly in the *Farris* case where the legal form actually suggests a form of transaction that is upside down from the actual economics of the deal. This, in turn, leads to a discussion of the legal form, as does the use of a triangular merger form in *Terry*, but your understanding of the legal strategy will be enhanced if you start with a clear picture of what the deal was designed to accomplish in an economic sense.

2. **The legal choices available for the planners.** The planners in the first two cases seem to anticipate some benefit from doing the deal as a sale of assets as opposed to a merger. What would be the law's default position for who makes the decision for the corporation as to selling assets? *Hint*: Recall Rule #1 from the opening section of this chapter. Second, what have you learned about how and when that default rule is changed by statutes like Delaware §251 as to statutory mergers? Third, how are the rules specified by §271 for sale of substantially all the assets of a corporation different, and more specifically, which of the statutory merger requirements do the planners of the Hariton transaction seek to avoid by structuring the deal as a sale of assets? *Farris* and *Terry* likewise illustrate planners of an acquisition seeking to avoid one or more of the usual requirements of a statutory merger by doing the transaction in a different legal form. Can you identify which one?

3. **Why are exit rights so costly to firms?** Planners would like to avoid exits rights available in the standard merger template because of the drain of the corporation's treasury and the anticipated costs associated with having to replace that existing *internal* capital with capital from an external market. If shareholders exercise their statutory appraisal right to require the corporation to purchase their stock, the payment will both reduce the firm's equity capital and likely move it further away from its optimal debt ratio. For example, a firm with $10 million in capital, of which $6 million is

equity and $4 million is debt, has a 40 percent debt ratio. If shareholders holding $1 million of shares were to exercise their appraisal right, the corporation's capital would be $9 million, with $5 million in equity and $4 million in debt, the leverage having now risen to 44 percent. This, in turn, can increase the firm's bankruptcy risk and reduce the firm's debt capacity, which can reduce the firm's ability to invest in profitable new investments. To avoid these negative effects, the firm would need to make a new equity offering to offset the loss of equity capital from the shareholder exit. Empirical studies on firms making such offerings, called seasoned equity offerings (SEO), show that these offering are often priced at a 2 percent discount from the firm's prior market price, and underwriting costs absorb about 5 percent of the offerings proceeds. In addition, the SEO announcement typically reduces a firm's stock price on the market (and thus its entire equity capitalization) by an average of 3 percent. This "hit" affects not just the new stock being sold (which, for example, may be 10 percent of the firm's equity outstanding) but also the other 90 percent. Thus, not 3 percent, but 30 percent of the new equity raised will be absorbed by the changes due to the SEO, contributing to a significant dilution of the equity interests of the existing shareholders.

4. Differences between the law of Delaware and other states as to sale of assets and differences in all states as to protection offered shareholders of a target corporation versus shareholders of an acquiring corporation. Consider how the facts of *Farris v. Glen Alden* differ from *Hariton*. It is again a sale of assets for shares, but somewhat surprisingly, the buyer is much smaller than the seller. This can be seen by comparing the total number of shares Glen Alden is to issue to List in exchange for the List assets as compared to the number of Glen Alden shares previously outstanding. When the additional facts of the makeup of the board are considered, it is clear that this is really List acquiring Glen Alden and not the other way around. Pennsylvania law (and the law of most other states) differs from Delaware in that it requires that shareholders of the seller of substantially all assets receive appraisal rights, but the deal can be done on the purchaser side by the directors alone with no exit rights for shareholders. In contrast to *Hariton*'s holding that courts will respect the planner's choice between a merger and sale of assets, *Farris* suggests a refusal to respect the choice to let planners redefine a transaction where the result is to deprive shareholders of the selling corporation of their appraisal rights. The Third Circuit's decision in *Terry*, which otherwise supports the planner's decision to pick a transaction that removes exit rights, notes in footnote 7 that "a different result might be reached" in a case, where like *Farris*, the recharacterization permits a "minnow to swallow a whale." This possible distinction between protection for the target company from the acquiring company is *not* limited to these cases but is reflected in the pattern of alternative transactions studied above as to the statutory merger requirements that can be avoided by planners. In the use

C. Judicial Limits on Private Planning

of triangular mergers and sale of assets, the law permits planners to avoid votes by the shareholders of the acquiring corporation, but not the target corporation. Does such a distinction reflect economic realities? Professor Ronald Gilson has argued that law does not replicate other protections that exist for shareholders, and that this additional statutory protection for target shareholders reflects that the impending disappearance of their corporation means that target management is in a "final period" and will no longer be constrained by the market and other constraints that usually affect managers, such that their shareholders are more vulnerable to their directors agreeing to a deal that disadvantages these shareholders. Such reasoning would support use of a de facto doctrine in a *Farris*-type transaction but not a *Hariton*-type transaction. *See* Ronald Gilson, *A Structural Approach to Corporations: The Case Against Defensive Tactics in Tender Offers*, 33 STAN. L. REV. 819, 839 (1981).

5. **Voting.** Why are the Penn Central shareholders voting? The planners have chosen a triangular merger pattern in which the target, Colt, is merging into a Penn Central subsidiary via a statutory merger, such as that provided by §251 of the Delaware law discussed above. (Note that this merger is governed by Pennsylvania law, which is similar on the core requirements for a statutory merger with an important difference discussed below.) In such a setting, the boards and shareholders of the two constituent corporations vote, but that means the subsidiary's shareholders will vote and not the parent's shareholders, which, of course, would be one reason why planners would want to do a triangular or some other alternative to a statutory merger. The appellate decision does not explain the reason why the parent corporation's shareholders vote in this case, but the reason can be found in the district court opinion, 527 F. Supp. 118, 120 (E.D. Pa. 1981). The listing standards of the New York Stock Exchange require a vote of shareholders beyond the vote required by state law. Standard 21.003(c) specified that shareholder approval is required prior to the issuance of common stock in any transaction or series of related transactions where the number of shares issued is in excess of 20 percent of the number of common stock outstanding before the issuance. The first step of a triangular merger is the creation of the subsidiary, and often the issuance of parent shares to the subsidiary in exchange for the new shares being issued by the subsidiary, and this triggers the parent shareholders' right to vote.

6. **Tender offers as an alternative structure.** The Time/Warner deal presented later in this book illustrates how tender offers can play a role parallel to the triangular merger and sale of asset forms just discussed. The boards of directors of Time, Inc. and Warner Communications signed an agreement for a stock-for-stock merger on March 3, 1989, culminating three years of discussion between the two media companies. Time's traditional business of magazine and book publishing had expanded to include both cable television franchises and subsidiaries, such as Home Box Office

and Cinemax that provided content for this growing entertainment pipeline. Warner, a long-recognized name in the movie-business, possessed an international distribution system, a large presence in the music and recording business, and cable television systems. Warner was to merge with a wholly owned Time subsidiary (TW Sub, Inc.), with Warner as the surviving corporation. The common stock of Warner would be converted into the common stock of Time, Inc. at an agreed upon ratio by which former Warner stockholders would own about 62 percent of the stock of the combined company. Time's board had recognized the potential need to pay a premium for the stock in exchange for achieving a favorable governance arrangement that would protect the "Time culture" (i.e., the board was evenly split between the two companies, co-CEOs were specified with an eventual succession to a Time person, and special committees of the board, controlled by members from each of the former companies, would control the publication and the music business of the companies).

Time's shareholders were scheduled to meet on June 23 to approve the merger. On June 7, Paramount, another entertainment company, announced an all-cash tender offer for all Time shares (but not Warner) for $175, a substantial premium over the $126 price where Time had traded after announcement of the Warner merger. The Time board, believing that the Warner transaction offered long-time value to the stockholders, took several actions discussed in a later chapter of this book. What is relevant for our purposes here is that these actions included abandoning the merger form and replacing it with a tender offer by Time, Inc. for 51 percent of the outstanding shares of Warner Communications. How did the change in the form of the transaction alter the legal requirements and the economic realities of the deal? What did the planners gain by using a tender offer instead of the merger to accomplish the transaction?

7. Planning to avoid even the requirements of the alternative transactional structures. It is possible to go even farther in planning than has been suggested so far. Instead of the alternative triangular transactions or statutory sale of assets, consider how a contractual agreement could accomplish a similar economic result and not have to deal with pesky problems like having to pay out cash via appraisal right proceedings. *Compare* Pratt v. Ballman-Cummings Furniture Co., 495 S.W.2d 509 (Ark. 1973) (where two corporations with the same majority shareholder entered into a partnership that effectively combined their identity, management, and marketing, a prima facie case for establishing application of de facto merger was established), and Good v. Lackawanna Leather Co., 233 A.2d 201 (N.J. Super. Ct. 1967) (two companies, one the principal supplier of the other, each with the same majority shareholders, pursued a merger that was abandoned after 20 percent of the shareholders of one of the companies voted against the merger that would have entitled them to appraisal rights; in the following years, the business of one shifted to the other by contract and loans and other means; the court declined to provide appraisal:

"Although many of the economic objectives sought to be accomplished under the proposed and rejected statutory merger in fact have been achieved, this without more does not constitute a de facto merger.").

D. FEDERAL LAW AFFECTING DEALS

The transactional questions considered so far in this chapter derive mostly from state corporations law, but an acquisition will also trigger various requirements of federal law. We address four here — securities, tax, antitrust, and national security — but we only scratch the surface as each of the first three is the subject of its own separate course in most law schools.

1. Securities Law

Securities law is designed to protect investors in buying and selling securities (and sometimes in other functions, such as voting). Unlike corporate law, discussed earlier in this chapter, securities law comes from the federal government and not the 50 states, so that there is one common source of regulation in the United States. Two principal laws are relevant to our study, the Securities Act of 1933 and the Securities Exchange Act of 1934, both of which were enacted in the early days of the New Deal in response to the economic crisis that followed the Great Depression.

a. "Disclosure, Again Disclosure, and Still More Disclosure"[3]

Securities laws, in contrast to the corporate laws previously discussed, focus mostly on disclosure as opposed to the substance of various governance relationships. Securities laws require disclosure to enable investors to make decisions, although there are a few exceptions that we see discussed in the next subsection, such as a tender offer law that ensures all shareholders who tender will get the best price.

The disclosure requirements can best be described as episodic as opposed to plenary or continuous. Although the spread of regulation has expanded to sometimes produce a result that appears to require continuous disclosure, you will gain a greater understanding of the laws if you focus on

---

3. Louis Loss, in discussing the purpose of the federal securities regulation in Securities Regulation (2d ed. 1961) at 21.

the different specific triggers of disclosure obligations and how each impacts the universe of acquisition transactions. These include:

- *Issuance of securities.* This was the earliest of the contexts for which disclosure was required and was the subject of the Securities Act of 1933, passed during the first hundred days of Franklin Roosevelt's administration. Under the terms of the Act, a person cannot sell securities (Section 5) without full disclosure, usually provided in a registration statement (i.e., S-1 or S-3) that is filed with the SEC and contained in a prospectus (Section 10) that is delivered to buyers. The issuer is strictly liable for any misstatements that appear in the registration statement (Section 11), and various gatekeepers (e.g., underwriters, accountants, and directors) are liable if they don't satisfy their due diligence obligations relating to the truthfulness of the disclosures. When does a merger involve an issuance? If the consideration for the deal (as discussed in Chapter 2) is a security (e.g., stock) as opposed to cash.
- *Proxy solicitation.* Section 14(a) of the Securities Exchange Act, passed in 1934, requires disclosure whenever a person solicits a proxy, i.e., the right to vote a shareholder's stock. The disclosure required for this activity is governed by rules promulgated by the Securities and Exchange Commission under the 1934 Act and found in Schedule 14A. The actual disclosure substantially overlaps with that found in S-1 and other registration statements; each refers you to a set of integrated disclosure provisions called Regulation S-K. S-K is a daunting read with over 60 items covering more than 100 pages of the federal rule book. The application of proxy disclosure to acquisitions takes more than one step. The actual trigger for disclosure is when someone "solicits" a proxy. Who does that? The most likely actor is management, who seeks to implement a merger or other transactions (such as a sale of assets) for which state law requires a vote of the shareholders. In almost any widely dispersed corporation, management could not obtain the majority vote required by state law without soliciting proxies, so that disclosure is going to be required for most transactions because of the interaction of state and federal law. But if the deal is done outside of a form that requires a shareholder vote, this particular trigger of disclosure will not occur. The regulation also applies to persons other than the issuer who solicit proxies from more than ten persons.
- *Tender offer.* Shareholders whose corporation is taken over via a cash tender offer will not receive disclosure under the proxy rules, a gap that led to the Williams Act in 1968, which amended the 1934 Act to require disclosure when public shareholders receive a tender offer. The Supreme Court described the purpose of the Williams Act as to "insure that public shareholders who are

confronted by a cash tender offer for their stock will not be required to respond without adequate information regarding the qualifications and intentions of the offering party." Rondeau v. Mosinee Paper Corp., 422 U.S. 49, 58-59 (1975), quoting S. Rep. No. 550, 90th Cong., 1st Sess. 3 (1967); H.R. Rep. No. 1711, 90th Cong., 2d Sess. 4 (1968). The required disclosure schedule (this time in Schedule TO and Regulation M-A) requires some information similar to what will be in a proxy and some that is unique to the tender offer context, for example, the terms of the tender offer. What subset of acquisitions needs to meet this disclosure requirement? Only those acquisitions that the acquirer's management has chosen to structure as a tender offer (with stock or cash as the consideration to be paid). Section 13(d), also added by the Williams Act, requires disclosure when a shareholder acquires at least 5 percent of an issuer's shares, providing something of an early warning device of possible takeover interest. Additional rules apply to formation of groups and require institutional investors to make disclosure of certain block holdings.

- *Going private transactions.* Specific disclosure is required for a transaction causing a publicly held stock to be delisted or deregistered. This will often occur in a deal involving management. *See* Chapter 13. A firm initiating such a transaction is required to file disclosure on Schedule 13e-3, which requires information about the source of funds to be used in the transaction, management's equity participation in the deal, certain employment arrangements, potential conflicts of interest, and any offers from unaffiliated parties over the past 18 months. The most noticeable difference in the disclosure required here as compared to that previously discussed is that the disclosure must include a statement as to whether the board believes the transaction is fair, a requirement that ventures more into the realm of substance than most securities disclosures.
- *Periodic disclosure.* In addition to the various transactions described above that trigger disclosure obligations, there is a separate set of obligations triggered by the calendar. Public companies over a certain size[4] must make annual disclosure on Form 10-K and quarterly disclosures on Form 10-Q. These forms also use Regulation S-K as a base, so the disclosure should be familiar for one who has already absorbed the previous requirements. The periodic disclosure requirements include Item 303 from

---

4. As of 2012, companies with 2000 shareholders of record and more than $10 million dollars in assets were subject to these requirements with the coverage also extending to companies with 500 or more "non-accredited" shareholders of record, with accredited being based on wealth or sophistication categories that would permit investors to fend for themselves.

Regulation S-K, Management's Discussion and Analysis (MD&A), which is designed to expand what management tells investors. In addition to Forms 10-K and 10-Q, there is also disclosure required by Form 8-K, which gets closer to real time or continuous disclosure. Traditionally, this involved a limited number of items (such as bankruptcy or a change of control), but after Enron, Congress expanded the number of items that must be disclosed to more than 20. Most track specific allegations of the Enron/WorldCom crisis, but the specific disclosure can occur in some mergers.

- *Antifraud Liability.* Additional disclosure may be required to avoid running afoul of the antifraud provisions of the 1934 act, if necessary to avoid half-truths or if remaining silent when there is a duty to speak (discussed in more detail in Chapter 12).

The case below illustrates the effect of disclosure, here in the specific context of a tender offer.

Prudent Real Estate Trust v. Johncamp Realty, Inc.
599 F.2d 1140 (2d Cir. 1979)

FRIENDLY, Circuit Judge:

[Prudent Real Estate Trust (Prudent), the target of a tender offer by the defendant Johncamp Realty, Inc. (Johncamp), sought a temporary injunction against the continuation of a tender offer on the ground that the material filed with the Securities and Exchange Commission (SEC) pursuant to Schedule 14D implementing §14(d) of the Securities and Exchange Act was insufficient and that, because of certain statements and omissions, the offer violated §14(e) of the Act.]

... Defendant Johncamp is a Delaware close corporation which was founded by Johncamp Netherlands Antilles, N.V. (Johncamp N.V.) and The Pacific Company, a California corporation (Pacific). Johncamp N.V. owns 60% and Pacific 40% of the common shares of Johncamp. All of the stock of Johncamp N.V. is owned by Campeau Corporation (Campeau), a publicly held Ontario corporation; Robert Campeau, a resident of Canada, is chairman of its board and chief executive officer. John E. Wertin, a resident of California, is president, secretary and a director of Johncamp, president and a director and sole stockholder of Pacific, and president and director of John Wertin Development Corporation (JWDC), a California corporation, 95% of the stock of which is owned by Pacific. ...

On March 12, 1979, Johncamp filed with the SEC a Schedule 14D-1 as required for a tender offer by 17 C.F.R. §240.14d-100. The schedule contained the form of offer, which was advertised the following day in the New York Times. The offer, which was to expire on March 23 unless extended, was to purchase any and all of Prudent's outstanding shares at $7

D. Federal Law Affecting Deals

net per share, as against the last available market price of 4, and was not conditioned upon any minimum number of shares being tendered. . . .

The offer went on to state that 80% of the required funds would be furnished by Johncamp N.V. which would obtain them from Campeau, out of the latter's own funds or from a $50,000,000 (Canadian) line of bank credit described in some detail, and that 20% would be supplied by Pacific which would obtain the funds from JWDC and Wertin. The purpose of the offer was to acquire all the shares of Prudent but if this did not occur pursuant to the offer, Johncamp, Campeau, Johncamp N.V. and Pacific desired to acquire enough shares to exercise control. The purchaser intended to reconstitute the board of trustees of Prudent as soon and as much as possible. Although no specific plans for Prudent's future had been formulated, Johncamp N.V. and Pacific had established a procedure to increase the likelihood that Campeau's investment in Johncamp would be fully recovered; pursuant to such procedure Johncamp N.V. could cause a liquidation of Prudent if Johncamp acquired at least two-thirds of the outstanding shares. . . .

The only other portion of the Schedule 14D here relevant is *Item 9. Financial Statements of Certain Bidders.* This was answered: "Not applicable, but see Exhibit 1." Exhibit 1 consisted of the printed annual reports of Campeau for 1976 and 1977 and audited consolidated financial statements for 1978.

On March 16, 1979, Prudent initiated this action to enjoin the defendants from proceeding with the tender offer, and moved for a temporary restraining order and a preliminary injunction on various grounds. . . . [The ground discussed here is] the failure to disclose in the Offer or the Schedule any financial information about the Wertin interests, to wit, Pacific, JWDC, and Wertin himself, as 17 C.F.R. §240. 14d-100, Item 9, allegedly requires. . . .

The relevant sections of the Securities Exchange Act, §14(d)(1) and (e), added by the Williams Act of 1968, are too familiar to require extended exposition. . . . The House Interstate and Foreign Commerce Committee explained the need for the new legislation as follows:

> Where one company seeks control of another by means of a stock-for-stock exchange, the offer must be registered under the Securities Act of 1933. The shareholder gets a prospectus setting forth all material facts about the offer. He knows who the purchaser is, and what plans have been made for the company. He is thus placed in a position to make an informed decision whether to hold his stock or to exchange it for the stock of the other company. . . .
>
> In contrast when a cash tender offer is made, no information need be filed or disclosed to shareholders. Such an offer can be made on the most minimal disclosure; yet the investment decision — whether to retain the security or sell it — is in substance little different from the decision made on an original purchase of a security, or on an offer to exchange one security for another. . . .

> The persons seeking control . . . have information about themselves and about their plans which, if known to investors, might substantially change the assumptions on which the market price is based. This bill is designed to make the relevant facts known so that shareholders have a fair opportunity to make their decision. (H. Rep. No. 1711, 90th Cong., 2d Sess., reprinted in 2 U.S. Code Cong. & Ad. News 2811, 2812-13 (1968).)

This discussion reflected views earlier expressed by the late Manuel F. Cohen, Chairman of the SEC, in A Note on Takeover Bids and Corporate Purchases of Stock, 22 Bus. Law. 149, 149-50 (1966). See also Sen. Rep. No. 539, 90th Cong., 1st Sess., at 2 and 3. . . .

[I]n a release appearing on July 28, 1977, 42 F.R. 38341-50 new regulations were issued, which for the first time adopted a Schedule 14D, specifically tailored to §14(d) of the Act. The schedule included as Item 9:

> *Item 9. Financial Statements of Certain Bidders.* Where the bidder is other than a natural person and the bidder's financial condition is material to a decision by a security holder of the subject company whether to sell, tender or hold securities being sought in the tender offer, furnish current, adequate financial information concerning the bidder. . . .

Emphasizing that Item 9 retained the concept of materiality and that this was dependent on the facts and circumstances, the Commission said, 42 F.R. at 38346:

> These may include, but are not limited to: (1) the terms of the tender offer, particularly those terms concerning the amount of securities being sought, such as any or all, a fixed minimum with the right to accept additional shares tendered, all or none, and a fixed percentage of the outstanding; (2) whether the purpose of the tender offer is for control of the subject company; (3) the plans or proposals of the bidder described in Item 5 of the Schedule; and (4) the ability of the bidder to pay for the securities sought in the tender offer and/or to repay any loans made by the bidder or its affiliates in connection with the tender offer or otherwise. It should be noted that the factors described above are not exclusive nor is it necessary that any or all such factors be present in order to trigger the materiality test. . . .

The parties accept that the test of materiality is that stated in TSC Industries, Inc. v. Northway, Inc., 426 U.S. 438, 449 (1976), although that case arose under Rule 14a-9 concerning proxy contests. . . . The Court's formulation was, 426 U.S. at 449:

> An omitted fact is material if there is a substantial likelihood that a reasonable shareholder would consider it important in deciding how to vote. . . .

In applying this test to a cash tender offer, it is necessary to appreciate the problem faced by a stockholder of the target company in deciding whether to tender, to sell or to hold part or all of his securities. It is true that, in the case of an "any and all" offer such as that here at

D. Federal Law Affecting Deals

issue, a stockholder who has firmly decided to tender has no interest in the financial position of the offeror other than its ability to pay — a point not here at issue — since he will have severed all financial connections with the target. It is also true that in the case of such an offer, there is less reason for him to seek to eliminate the risk of being partly in and partly out by selling to arbitrageurs, usually at a price somewhere between the previous market and the offered price, than where the offer is for a stated number or percentage of the shares (with or without the right to accept additional shares) or is conditioned on a minimum number being obtained. Still, the shareholder of the target company faces a hard problem in determining the most advantageous course of action, a problem whose difficulty is enhanced by his usual ignorance of the course other shareholders are adopting. If the bidder is in a flourishing financial condition, the stockholder might decide to hold his shares in the hope that, if the offer was only partially successful, the bidder might raise its bid after termination of the offer or infuse new capital into the enterprise. *Per contra*, a poor financial condition of the bidder might cause the shareholder to accept for fear that control of the company would pass into irresponsible hands. The force of these considerations is diminished but not altogether removed in this case by the fact that the Wertin interests were supplying only 20% of the financing and that Campeau's annual reports for 1976 and 1977 and its financial statements for 1978, which were incorporated in the Schedule 14D, showed it to be a company of substance. As against this, the stockholders' agreement gave Wertin the right to vote all acquired Prudent shares and the district court found that Wertin was to manage the properties. The case came within item (2) and possibly item (3) of the SEC's release, 42 F.R. 38346.

Johncamp relies on statements by SEC Chairman Cohen before the House Committee at the hearings that led to the Williams Act wherein he analogized the information required by the bill to be provided to stockholders with that required in proxy contests, where Regulation 14A does not require a challenger to file its financial statements unless it proposes a merger or consolidation or the issuance "of securities of another issuer," even if its objective is to gain control. Prudent counters with the language from the House Committee report quoted above, echoing Chairman Cohen's article, that in the case of a cash tender offer "the investment decision — whether to retain the security or sell it — is in substance little different from the decision made on an original purchase of a security, or on an offer to exchange one security for another." See to the same effect Sen. Rep. No. 550, 90th Cong., 1st Sess. at 3. In truth the situation is not precisely like any of these models. It differs from the proxy contest *simpliciter* in that an investment decision is being made; it differs from an original purchase of a security or an offer to exchange one security for another in that the stockholder does not have to appraise what he is buying. It differs also from an ordinary sale in that the investment decision is influenced not solely by general factors affecting the prospects of the economy, the market, or the company, but importantly by the particular proposal being made. In any event we must look to some extent to what the Congressional committees said rather than to what the facts are.

From the beginning of litigation under the Williams Act, this court has been conscious of its responsibility not to allow management to "resort to the courts on trumped-up or trivial grounds as a means for delaying and thereby defeating tender offers." Electronic Specialty Co. v. International Controls Corp., 409 F.2d 937, 947 (1969).... An important factor here is the impracticability of obtaining information about the Wertin interests from other sources. At the very least there is "fair ground for litigating" the issue of materiality and the balance of hardships tips heavily in Prudent's favor. Hamilton Watch Co. v. Benrus Watch Co., 206 F.2d 738, 740 (2 Cir. 1953). We are further influenced by the fact that our decision imposes no serious impediment to cash tender offers. Even in this case the omission can be readily corrected; in future cases presumably it will not be made....

We therefore reverse the order under appeal and direct the district court to issue a temporary injunction. It will be sufficient if this extends only until Johncamp makes the necessary corrections and allows a reasonable period for withdrawal of stock already tendered; we see no need for the further cooling-off period that Prudent requests.... Since Prudent conceded that its only reason for declining to make its stockholder list available to Johncamp was the alleged defects in the offer and Schedule 14D, the order should direct that this be done once the corrections are made if litigation in the New York courts has not yet produced that result....

NOTES AND QUESTIONS

1. **Ability to pay**. The ability to pay, which Judge Friendly says would be the sole financial concern of a shareholder who had firmly decided to tender, was not an issue in *Prudent Real Estate Trust v. Johncamp Realty*. It was an issue in MAI Basic Four, Inc. v. Prime Computer, Inc., 871 F.2d 212 (1st Cir. 1989), however, where a trial and appeals court enjoined a tender offer pending disclosure of further information about the investment banking firm that was helping finance the bidders' acquisition. The court quoted with approval the dissent of an earlier decision: "In the event of doubt on a particular disclosure question, courts should exercise liberality in order to carry out the remedial purposes of the [Williams Act]. Excess information may well be harmless, but inadequate disclosure could be disastrous to the shareholder." 871 F.2d at 219, quoting City Capital Assoc. Ltd. Partnership v. Interco, Inc., 860 F.2d 60, 68 (3d Cir. 1988) (Weis, J., dissenting). The court

D. Federal Law Affecting Deals

held that Drexel the investment banking firm a bidder, pointing to "Drexel's early and pervasive role in the planning and execution of the present offer, its erstwhile board representation in the corporation controlling the sole equity participant in the bidder group, and record evidence sufficient to reasonably suggest an expectation though not a contractual obligation that Drexel would itself provide additional financing if it could not place the $875 (million) in junk bonds elsewhere." 871 F.2d at 219.

2. Groups. The issue as to who must make disclosure under the Williams Act has arisen more frequently as to the definition of groups, disussed in the *CSX* case contained in chapter 14. The statutory definition in §13(d)(3) of a group as an aggregation of persons or entities who "act as a . . . group for the purpose of acquiring, holding or disposing of securities" has been given fairly broad interpretation by the courts. In Wellman v. Dickinson, 682 F.2d 355 (2d Cir. 1982), cert. denied, 460 U.S. 1069 (1983), Fairleigh S. Dickinson, Jr., the son of a founder of Becton, Dickinson & Co. and holder of more than 4 percent of the company's stock, lost an internal power struggle and was removed as chairman. Dickinson hired the investment banking firm of Salomon Brothers to assist him in locating a company that would be interested in purchasing his substantial holdings in Becton and those of his friends for a complete or partial takeover of the company. Dickinson and his friends could deliver 13 percent of the outstanding stock. The court of appeals supported the district court's findings that Dickinson and his friends "were all part of a group formed to dispose of their shares to aid a third party acquisition of a controlling interest in [Becton]," 682 F.2d at 363.

Rule 13d-5(b) adopts the holding of GAF Corp. v. Milstein, 453 F.2d 709 (2d Cir. 1971), cert. denied, 406 U.S. 910 (1972), that a group cannot wait until it makes its first concerted acquisition or disposition of shares but must file immediately upon formation of the group.

3. Remedy — Private actions. The Williams Act provides no express private cause of action. In Piper v. Chris-Craft Industries, Inc., 430 U.S. 1 (1977), the Supreme Court ruled that a losing bidder did not have standing to sue under §14(e) to recover $27 million in damages allegedly caused when the competing bidder used misleading statements to acquire a majority of shares in a target company. The Court found that "the sole purpose of the Williams Act was the protection of investors who are confronted with a tender offer. . . . [There is] no hint in the legislative history . . . that Congress contemplated a private cause of action for damages by one of several contending offerors against a successful bidder or by a losing bidder against a target corporation." 430 U.S. at 35. Subsequent lower courts found that target companies can seek equitable relief such as corrective disclosure (*see* Florida Commercial Banks v. Culverhouse, 772 F.2d 1513 (11th Cir. 1985)), and that target shareholders can sue for an injunction or damages (*see* Plaine v. McCabe, 797 F.2d 713 (9th Cir. 1986)). *Cf.* In re Phillips Petroleum Securities Litigation, 881 F.2d 1236 (3d Cir. 1989) (false filing that bidder would not accept purchase of shares on terms different from those of other shareholders could justify an action under Rule 10b-5).

4. What purpose for disclosure? If courts are reluctant to enforce a remedy other than corrective disclosure, what effect does §14(d) have and, even more, what purpose is served by the early warning requirement of §13(d)? In one sense, disclosure gives the target a litigation opportunity to stall an unwanted tender offer while seeking out a white knight or implementing another defensive strategy. *See* Jarrell, *The Wealth Effects of Litigation by Targets: Do Interests Diverge in a Merger?*, 28 J.L. & Econ. 151 (1985). In a broader sense, the disclosure serves to encourage an auction, with the possible impact that tender offers that are undertaken will produce higher returns for target shareholders, but that fewer tender offers will occur as potential bidders find fewer incentives to seek out potential targets. *See* Macey and Netter, *Regulation 13D and the Regulatory Process*, 65 Wash. U. L.Q. 131 (1987).

b. Substantive Regulations from Securities Law, Particularly Tender Offers

While many court opinions emphasize the disclosure orientation of the Williams Act, significant substantive regulation is also included. The clearest purpose of many of these rules is to limit the pressure on shareholders to tender quickly.

Under SEC Rule 14e-1 an offer must remain open for 20 business days. If a bidder seeks to buy less than all of a target's shares, Section 14(d)(6) requires that the purchases be pro rata from all those who tendered during the offering period. Thus a bidder cannot use a first-come, first-served limited time offer to force an immediate shareholder response. Section 14(d)(5), as supplemented by Rule 14d-7, permits a shareholder to withdraw tendered securities during the entire offer, thus freeing a shareholder from one peril of an immediate decision. The "best-price rule" of §14(d)(7) and Rule 14d-10 requiring that the tender offer be open to all shareholders may reflect a concern for equal treatment of shareholders in a way that broadens federal law beyond its traditional disclosure focus.

c. Avoiding Securities Regulation

A tender offer may be an alternative way to achieve control without triggering some of the merger requirements discussed in the previous part, but there will be times when planners do not wish their conduct to trigger the federal tender offer regulations discussed in this part. Whether a transaction is a tender offer or not has been addressed by courts under a multi-factor test: (1) active and widespread solicitation

D. Federal Law Affecting Deals

of public shareholders; (2) for a substantial percentage of the issuer's stock; (3) at a premium over the prevailing market price; (4) on terms that are firm rather than negotiable; (5) contingent on a fixed number of shared to be tendered or purchased; (6) via an offer open only for a limited period of time; (7) with recipients subject to pressure to sell stock; and (8) perhaps public announcement of a purchasing program preceding or accompanying the rapid accumulation of large amount of the target's stock. *See* Wellman v. Dickinson, 475 F. Supp. 783, 823-24 (S.D.N.Y. 1982), *aff'd on other grounds*, 682 F.2d 355 (2d Cir. 1982), and S.E.C. v. Carter Hawley Hale Stores, Inc., 760 F.2d 945 (9th Cir. 1985). In Hanson Trust PLC v. SCM Corp., 774 F.2d 47 (2d Cir. 1985), a hostile bidder's tender offer had been met by the target's agreeing to an alternative proposal from a white knight. The frustrated bidder then terminated its tender offer and acquired 25 percent of the target's stock via five privately negotiated cash transactions and one open market purchase. These acquisitions provided the disappointed bidder sufficient votes to defeat the transaction contemplated by the white knight. The Second Circuit held the bidder's purchases were not a tender offer triggering the additional regulations.

2. Tax

There will be tax aspects to any acquisition that will require the advice of a specialist. Two questions that you will want to address in terms of general planning for the deal are: (1) Does the form of transaction trigger tax recognition for the shareholders?, and (2) Can the deal be structured so that the deductibility of interest paid on debt reduces the cost of capital of the combined company?

Transaction triggering recognition of gain for shareholders of the target company. If the shares of the target are being sold for more than the purchase price paid by the various shareholders, they will care if the transaction triggers an immediate recognition of gain, and the corresponding tax liability, or instead permits them to defer the gain until a time in the future, perhaps at a time of their choice. Sellers required to share part of their consideration with the government are likely to ask a higher price for their shares, raising the costs of the transaction.

Such immediate recognition can be avoided if the transaction comes within Section 368 of the Internal Revenue Code, which defines those transactions that get tax-deferred status. That section protects three types of transactions that are well-enough known that participants refer to each transaction by the subsection of Section 368. You should be able to place these tax-free sections within the frame of the transaction choices discussed above. Subsection A grants tax deferred-status to Statutory Mergers, the idea being that a continuation of each business has occurred by becoming part of the combined business, rather than a sale that would trigger income recognition. Subsection (B), written in terms of a Stock Acquisition, covers sales of stock in exchange for stock, as would occur in a tender offer (for stock, not cash consideration) or if a block purchaser would offer stock in exchange for the target stock. Subsection (C) is written in terms of an Asset Acquisition in which the target has sold substantially all of its assets in exchange for stock of the acquirer followed by the target dissolving and distributing the acquired stock to the target shareholders. For each method, there are limits on the amount of consideration other than stock (i.e., cash) that can be received without triggering the recognition of income.

Transactions that increase the tax shield of debt. If an acquiring company plans to finance the acquisition with borrowed money (as would be the dominant source, for example, in a leveraged buyout (LBO) and would regularly be used in many other acquisitions), the deal may shield a greater portion of the acquirer's profits from income tax because interest payments are a deduction before taxable income is determined. Such a deduction means the government in effect pays a share of the cost of raising the capital needed for the acquisition; this could contribute to a more favorable cost of capital for the firm. Financial analysts sometimes think of a firm's capital structure in terms of how far the entity is from its ideal cost of capital. If a firm is below such a number, an acquisition funded by debt can contribute to a more favorable response in the financial community. There are countervailing costs, such as increased bankruptcy risk, which also needs to be included in such analysis. There are also other tax benefits that in effect create government subsidies for the acquisition, which, if available, may impact the reasons for the acquisition.

3. *Antitrust*

Antitrust is another branch of law that can have large effects on planning for an acquisition. Like taxes and securities, the source of this law is primarily federal. The traditional concern arises from laws aimed at monopoly and restraint of trade contained in the Sherman Act and Clayton Act that date to the period before the First World War. More recent legislation, the Hart-Scott-Rodino Act of 1976, adds to the antitrust regulation by requiring that advance notice be given for every acquisition over a fairly low threshold of deal size. With the increasing globalization of deals, planners regularly also have to deal with possible antitrust regulation by the European Union, China, or other countries, who may hold up a deal even if the United States regulators do not.

D. Federal Law Affecting Deals

Section 2 of the Sherman Act prohibits monopoly, attempts to monopolize, or conspiracy that can cover many acquisitions by competitors in the same industry. Section 1 of the Sherman Act similarly prohibits contracts or combinations in restraint of trade. Section 7 of the Clayton Act applies to stock or asset purchases where the effect "*may* be substantially to lessen competition or to tend to create a monopoly." Companies can face government suits seeking injunctive relief or treble damages from private litigants.

The pre-merger notification requirements of the Hart-Scott-Rodino Act shapes the timetable for any acquisition beyond its size threshold (e.g., if one party's sales or assets exceed $100 million and the other's sales or assets exceed $10 million, both as adjusted for inflation, but still not a large threshold in today's economy). The Act also covers "creeping acquisitions" if an acquirer passes 15 percent of the target's shares. Once covered by the Act, the deal planner will need to pay attention to a three-part timetable. First, certain information is required to be given to the government. Second, there is a waiting period (usually 30 days, but 15 for a cash tender offer). Third, there is the possibility of a second request by the government for more information. If the additional information does not satisfy the government, enforcement action may follow.

Satisfaction of this requirement can be a massive undertaking. In one merger in the chemical industry, one of the companies put 2.5 million documents in a database and hired scores of contract attorneys to respond to a "second request" from the government. That request included items like "list each relevant product manufactured or sold and for each relevant product state sales for each relevant area in units and dollars including portions in U.S. and outside the U.S." Not only does data compilation take months, but government review will likewise take longer, so that in some circumstances, this part of the case can be what is holding up the closing date.

Enforcement of the antitrust laws is split between two federal agencies, the Antitrust Division of the Department of Justice (DOJ) and the Federal Trade Commission (FTC). The division of work between the two agencies is such that either may be involved in your transaction. In terms of risk of litigation, numbers for the year 2000 showed that the Antitrust Division opened 178 files, made second requests in 55 of those, obtained consent decrees in 18 of those, 13 deals were abandoned, and two went to trial. The numbers for FTC prosecutions were similar. In addition to this general federal effort, there may be specialized rules for particular industries such as banks or railroads. State attorneys general are also able to bring antitrust proceedings.

The basis for government interests in an acquisition vary over time. Definition of the applicable market has been a point of debate as technology has rearranged traditional boundaries between industries and introduced new competitors to existing businesses. There was a substantial change in the direction of less government litigation and greater trusting of the markets in the period after 1980. The Department of Justice and the Federal Trade Commission have published joint merger guidelines at different points over the last thirty years. The 2010 revision sets out multiple methods to evaluate competitive effects sometimes looking at changes in market concentration, as measured, for example, by the Herfindahl-Hirschmann index (HHI) and in other contexts looking at unilateral effects. *See http://ftc.gov/os/2010/08/100819hmg.pdf.*

4. National Security

The state law merger statutes discussed earlier in this chapter do not condition mergers on prior government approval. However federal law gives the President the authority to block, or order the divestiture of, any acquisition of control of a U.S. business by a foreign party on a finding that the acquisition might pose a significant threat to U.S. national security. That finding is not subject to judicial review. This executive review has been delegated to the Committee on Foreign Investment in the United States (CFIUS). *See* 50 U.S.C. §2170; 31 C.F.R. §§600.101 et seq. This review provides an entry for political concern about some foreign takeovers which has been enough, for example, to derail proposed acquisitions by foreign owners of U.S. ports or oil companies (although a Chinese purchaser of the leading American pork producers went through.)

4 DEAL STRATEGY: THE BIDDER'S APPROACH

A. BEGINNING THE DEAL DANCE: WHO TO APPROACH?

Assuming that a potential acquiring firm has identified a transaction that would produce value for one of the reasons set out in Chapter 2, what is the best way to approach the prospective target? This strategy is shaped both by legal and financial factors, illustrating the need of being conversant in both disciplines.

Often, the first overture to the target company is made to the managers of the target, or more specifically, one manager: the chief executive officer. In the vernacular of the deal dance, this is sometimes called a "casual pass." The acquiring company CEO calls his or her counterpart at the target, and over dinner or coffee or something less formal, suggests the acquiring company is interested in a combination and perhaps a discussion of why such a combination makes sense. If the target CEO is interested, additional conversations may ensue, other parties at each company may become involved, and the discussion may proceed to completion of a friendly merger agreement or other form of acquisition.

If, as is often the case, the target CEO responds with less enthusiasm, the bidder may redirect the offer to another governance level of the target, its board of directors. In what is sometimes called a "bear hug," the acquiring firm writes or otherwise communicates with the target board identifying its interest and setting the outlines of possible terms. If the target CEO did not inform the target board of the initial conversations in the casual pass, such a communication may open a wedge between the target CEO and board that will be relevant to the later discussions. This bear hug is often a private communication to the target board, but in particular situations, the acquiring company can suggest that if the target's board is unresponsive, it will make the bear hug public. As before, if the target board is interested in this overture, discussions could proceed to an agreement for a friendly merger or other acquisition.

If, as is often the case, the target board responds with less enthusiasm than the acquirer might prefer, the bidder may redirect its offer to yet another governance level of the target, this time the shareholders, in the form of a hostile tender offer or perhaps a proxy fight to gain control of the board of directors (discussed in more detail in the chapters that follow). Although defensive tactics discussed in subsequent chapters may in some sense seem to permit the target board to fend off unwanted tender offers (see, for example, the discussion of "just say no" in Chapter 7), defensive tactics often, instead, lead to a deal with the initial bidder (perhaps on improved terms) or with a white knight. So, even where the bidder goes over the head of the directors to the shareholders, the result may still be a friendly agreement between the boards of the two corporations.

The decision tree that follows outlines the choices just discussed. For deals that either start or end up on a friendly plane, the parties' discussions will move through a predictable pattern. Parties' discussions will be confidential (see the discussion of risk arbitrage and insider trading in Chapter 12). Often, parties will move to a letter of intent and then to a definitive merger agreement.

Chart 4-1
The Deal Dance: Acquisition Decision Tree

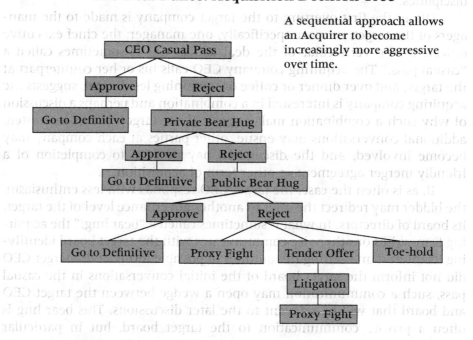

Source: Ronald Masulis

B. GETTING TO A DEFINITIVE AGREEMENT

1. Deal Terms: Financial, Legal, and Social

At the top of the bidder's concerns during this period (and the target, too, for that matter) will be the core of the terms, already addressed in prior chapters, that will be included in a definitive merger agreement. These include: (1) the form the acquisition will take; (2) who will be the surviving corporation; (3) the amount to be paid for the target and any adjustments based on post-agreement changes in the market or earn-outs based on post-closing performance of the target; and (4) the currency to be used.

Beyond the economic terms and the timetable for the deal, the merger agreement will also cover a series of social issues. Failure to find a resolution on these issues can sometimes block the deal as effectively as not being able to come to a price. Key issues include:

(1) *Who will be the chief executive officer of the combined company?* It should not surprise you that many deals arise when the target company CEO is at or near retirement age. Outside that context, compensation for the CEO who is not picked to lead the new company will likely need to be addressed; heads of key divisions may be selected during this time, as well as compensation for key employees who are going or staying.

(2) *The makeup of the board of directors and its split between the acquiring and target directors.* The acquiring company will usually get a majority of the board seats, with a few seats parceled out to key target board members or managers. In a "Merger of Equals," the board may be split equally between members of the two previous boards. Merger of Equals (MOE) is not a legal category but a designation placed on the deal by the parties themselves to communicate how they want the deal to be viewed. They are typically stock-for-stock deals in which no or little premium is offered to either set of shareholders who will share in the risks and rewards of the venture going forward. Frequently, there is a parallel effort to involve employees from both companies in the venture going forward. Such MOEs may provide for co-CEOs and a shared succession order, although more than one CEO-in-waiting has been disappointed in deals termed a Merger of Equals.

(3) *The name of the new company going forward.* The name of the acquiring company often survives in the same way its corporate form does, but there are alternatives, such as a blended name (ExxonMobil, for example) or a completely new name where the planners want to emphasize a new direction.

(4) *The headquarters of the new company.* Even for acquisitions labeled as a Merger of Equals, the place named as the headquarters can be a giveaway as to where real power is likely to lie going forward. The name of the company and who will be CEO similarly help define the extent to which a Merger of Equals may include one side that is more equal.

(5) *The place of incorporation of the new company.* This can be particularly important in a cross-border deal where different business cultures may shape the choice planners make for their acquisition.

(6) *Role of block holders or founding families.* It may be important in negotiating an acquisition to address the role of important block holders or the founding family. If the deal is for stock, it may dilute the holdings of a large shareholder of the acquiring company in a way that would lead them to oppose the deal. On the other side of the transaction, a large block holder of the target may care about the impact of the deal on that holder's taxes or investment profile.

2. Due Diligence

Bidders don't start (or even end) the acquisition process with complete information. Incompleteness or inaccuracies can create risk which, in turn, calls for some kind of response or strategy in addressing such risk. This subsection and the one that follows address in a general way how parties approach due diligence, the role of representations and warranties, and other parts of an acquisition agreement. It concludes with a case in which a court had to interpret one clause of an acquisition agreement, a Material Adverse Change (MAC) clause.

Due diligence is an important part of what the prospective bidder and its financial and legal advisers do, both before an agreement is reached and post-agreement but prior to the closing. Due diligence is about information and using that to reduce uncertainty in the deal process.

Timing. Some due diligence will occur before the initial approach to a potential target. Public documents, e.g., SEC filings, analysts' reports, and news stories provide data points that help determine price and flag possible risk points. One disadvantage of a hostile bid is that a bidder will not be able to go beyond these sources, which means the valuation is likely to have a greater range of uncertainty. During negotiations, but before a definitive agreement has been signed, the target will make more information available, tempered by its desire not to disrupt its business. More detailed information may be linked to a prospective bidder signing a confidentiality agreement or entering into a standstill agreement. After the acquisition has been signed, due diligence may continue to test the information provided in the representations and warranties and to prepare necessary disclosure documents needed for closing.

Topics. The subject of due diligence spans a range of finance and legal issue and will involve investment bankers, accountants, lawyers, and others in analyzing the information produced. Representative topics include:

- Finance documents including various accounting reports and reports as to market presence and sales issues, cash flow, and costs;
- Operations issues involving IT, assets, intellectual property, organization, and human resources;
- Legal issues such as assuring proper corporate organization, verifying ownership of assets, identifying pending or anticipated litigation, and regulatory issues; and
- Liability and risk assessment, including insurance, exposure to environmental or other claims, and exposure to taxes.

3. Negotiating the Acquisition Agreement

The acquisition agreement will be negotiated once there has been a meeting of the minds of the principals. It will be completed prior to the vote by the boards of directors of the two companies. Agreements typically includes provisions from these categories:

Price and structure. These sections will reflect the results of the items discussed in Chapter 2.

Representations and warranties. These are legal statements of facts on which the other party seeks to rely and can cover a variety of areas.

Covenants. Covenants are promises of what the parties will do after the signing of the agreement and, in part, will track the representations and warranties to insure they will continue to be true until closing. There may be specific covenants covering certain prohibited conduct concerning assets and business. In a stock-for-stock merger, the buyer may be asked to make covenants for things that could affect the value of its stock.

Conditions. These clauses are more specific in effect in stating conditions for the parties' obligation to close. The continuing veracity of the representations and warranties will be a condition and satisfaction of the promise in the covenants. There could be a financing contingency, depending on market conditions and which side is more anxious for a deal. Government approval for things like antitrust and tax are likely to show up here. The Material Adverse Change clause, discussed in the case below, is written as an escape to the parties' obligation to close but has seldom worked in litigated cases.

Other. This could include indemnification, if any, or any guarantees of parents. Termination fees and their exclusivity are commonly a topic in agreements. For sample clauses, see *Appendices*, 10 U. MIAMI BUS. L. REV. 219 (2002).

In re IBP, Inc. Shareholders Litigation
789 A.2d 14 (Del. Ch. 2001)

STRINE, Vice Chancellor.

This post-trial opinion addresses a demand for specific performance of a "Merger Agreement" by IBP, Inc., the nation's number one beef and number two pork distributor. By this action, IBP seeks to compel the "Merger" between itself and Tyson Foods, Inc., the nation's leading chicken distributor, in a transaction in which IBP stockholders will receive their choice of $30 a share in cash or Tyson stock, or a combination of the two.

The IBP-Tyson Merger Agreement resulted from a vigorous auction process that pitted Tyson against the nation's number one pork producer, Smithfield Foods. To say that Tyson was eager to win the auction is to slight its ardent desire to possess IBP. During the bidding process, Tyson was anxious to ensure that it would acquire IBP, and to make sure Smithfield did not. By succeeding, Tyson hoped to create the world's preeminent meat products company — a company that would dominate the meat cases of supermarkets in the United States and eventually throughout the globe.

During the auction process, Tyson was given a great deal of information that suggested that IBP was heading into a trough in the beef business. Even more, Tyson was alerted to serious problems at an IBP subsidiary, DFG, which had been victimized by accounting fraud to the tune of over $30 million in charges to earnings and which was the active subject of an asset impairment study. Not only that, Tyson knew that IBP was projected to fall seriously short of the fiscal year 2000 earnings predicted in projections prepared by IBP's Chief Financial Officer in August, 2000.

By the end of the auction process, Tyson had come to have great doubts about IBP's ability to project its future earnings, the credibility of IBP's management, and thought that the important business unit in which DFG was located — Foodbrands — was broken.

Yet, Tyson's ardor for IBP was such that Tyson raised its bid by a total of $4.00 a share after learning of these problems. Tyson also signed the Merger Agreement, which permitted IBP to recognize unlimited additional liabilities on account of the accounting improprieties at DFG. It did so without demanding any representation that IBP meet its projections for future earnings, or any escrow tied to those projections.

After the Merger Agreement was signed on January 1, 2001, Tyson trumpeted the value of the merger to its stockholders and the financial community, and indicated that it was fully aware of the risks that attended the cyclical nature of IBP's business. In early January, Tyson's stockholders ratified the merger agreement and authorized its management to take whatever action was needed to effectuate it.

During the winter and spring of 2001, Tyson's own business performance was dismal. Meanwhile, IBP was struggling through a poor first quarter. Both companies' problems were due in large measure to a severe winter, which adversely affected livestock supplies and vitality. As these struggles deepened, Tyson's desire to buy IBP weakened.

This cooling of affections first resulted in a slow-down by Tyson in the process of consummating a transaction, a slow-down that was attributed to IBP's on-going efforts to resolve issues that had been raised about its financial statements by the Securities and Exchange Commission ("SEC"). The most important of these issues was how to report the problems at DFG, which Tyson had been aware of at the time it signed the Merger Agreement. Indeed, all the key issues that the SEC raised with IBP were known by Tyson at the time it signed the Merger Agreement. The SEC first raised these issues in a faxed letter on December 29, 2000, to IBP's outside counsel. Neither IBP management nor Tyson learned of the letter until the second week of January, 2001. After learning of the letter, Tyson management put the Merger Agreement to a successful board and stockholder vote.

But the most important reason that Tyson slowed down the Merger process was different: it was having buyer's regret. Tyson wished it had paid less especially in view of its own compromised 2001 performance and IBP's slow 2001 results.

By March, Tyson's founder and controlling stockholder, Don Tyson, no longer wanted to go through with the Merger Agreement. He made the decision to abandon the Merger. His son, John Tyson, Tyson's Chief Executive Officer, and the other Tyson managers followed his instructions. Don Tyson abandoned the Merger because of IBP's and Tyson's poor results in 2001, and not because of DFG or the SEC issues IBP was dealing with. Indeed, Don Tyson told IBP management that he would blow DFG up if he were them.

After the business decision was made to terminate, Tyson's legal team swung into action. They fired off a letter terminating the Agreement at the same time as they filed suit accusing IBP of fraudulently inducing the Merger that Tyson had once so desperately desired. . . .

In this opinion, I address IBP's claim that Tyson had no legal basis to avoid its obligation to consummate the Merger Agreement, as well as

Tyson's contrary arguments. The parties' extensive claims are too numerous to summarize adequately, as are the court's rulings.

At bottom, however, I conclude as follows:

- The Merger Agreement and related contracts were valid and enforceable contracts that were not induced by any material misrepresentation or omission;
- The Merger Agreement specifically allocated certain risks to Tyson, including the risk of any losses or financial effects from the accounting improprieties at DFG, and these risks cannot serve as a basis for Tyson to terminate the Agreement;
- None of the non-DFG related issues that the SEC raised constitute a contractually permissible basis for Tyson to walk away from the Merger;
- IBP has not suffered a Material Adverse Effect within the meaning of the Agreement that excused Tyson's failure to close the Merger; and
- Specific performance is the decisively preferable remedy for Tyson's breach, as it is the only method by which to adequately redress the harm threatened to IBP and its stockholders. . . .

D. Was Tyson's Termination Justified Because IBP Has Suffered a Material Adverse Effect?

Tyson argues that it was also permitted to terminate because IBP had breached §5.10 of the Agreement, which is a representation and warranty that IBP had not suffered a material adverse effect since the "Balance Sheet Date" of December 25, 1999, except as set forth in the Warranted Financials or Schedule 5.10 of the Agreement. Under the contract, a material adverse effect (or "MAE") is defined as "any event, occurrence or development of a state of circumstances or facts which has had or reasonably could be expected to have a Material Adverse Effect" . . . "on the condition (financial or otherwise), business, assets, liabilities or results of operations of [IBP] and [its] Subsidiaries taken as whole. . . ."

Tyson asserts that the decline in IBP's performance in the last quarter of 2000 and the first quarter of 2001 evidences the existence of a Material Adverse Effect. It also contends that the DFG Impairment Charge constitutes a Material Adverse Effect. And taken together, Tyson claims that it is virtually indisputable that the combination of these factors amounts to a Material Adverse Effect.

In addressing these arguments, it is useful to be mindful that Tyson's publicly expressed reasons for terminating the Merger did not include an assertion that IBP had suffered a Material Adverse Effect. The post-hoc nature of Tyson's arguments bear on what it felt the contract meant when contracting, and suggests that a short-term drop in IBP's performance

B. Getting to a Definitive Agreement

would not be sufficient to cause a MAE. To the extent the facts matter, it is also relevant that Tyson gave no weight to DFG in contracting.

The resolution of Tyson's Material Adverse Effect argument requires the court to engage in an exercise that is quite imprecise. The simplicity of §5.10's words is deceptive, because the application of those words is dauntingly complex. On its face, §5.10 is a capacious clause that puts IBP at risk for a variety of uncontrollable factors that might materially affect its overall business or results of operation as a whole. Although many merger contracts contain specific exclusions from MAE clauses that cover declines in the overall economy or the relevant industry sector, or adverse weather or market conditions, §5.10 is unqualified by such express exclusions.

IBP argues, however, that statements in the Warranted Financials that emphasize the risks IBP faces from swings in livestock supply act as an implicit carve-out, because a Material Adverse Effect under that section cannot include an Effect that is set forth in the Warranted Financials. I agree with Tyson, however, that these disclaimers were far too general to preclude industry-wide or general factors from constituting a Material Adverse Effect. Had IBP wished such an exclusion from the broad language of §5.10, IBP should have bargained for it. At the same time, the notion that §5.10 gave Tyson a right to walk away simply because of a downturn in cattle supply is equally untenable. Instead, Tyson would have to show that the event had the required materiality of effect.[148]

The difficulty of addressing that question is considerable, however, because §5.10 is fraught with temporal ambiguity. By its own terms, it refers to any Material Adverse Effect that has occurred to IBP since December 25, 1999, unless that Effect is covered by the Warranted Financials or Schedule 5.10. Moreover, Tyson's right to refuse to close because a Material Adverse Effect has occurred is also qualified by the other express disclosures in the Schedule, by virtue of (i) the language of the Annexes that permits Tyson to refuse to close for breach of a warranty unless that breach results from "actions specifically permitted" by the Agreement; and (ii) the language of the Agreement that makes all disclosure schedules apply to Schedule 5.10 where that is the reasonably apparent intent of the drafters. Taken together, these provisions can be read to require the court to examine whether a MAE has occurred against the December 25, 1999, condition of IBP as adjusted by the specific disclosures of the Warranted Financials and the Agreement itself. This approach makes commercial sense because it establishes a baseline that roughly reflects the status of IBP as Tyson indisputably knew it at the time of signing the Merger Agreement.

---

148. *But see Pittsburgh Coke & Chem. Co. v. Bollo*, 421 F. Supp. 908, 930 (E.D.N.Y. 1976) (where Material Adverse Condition ("MAC") clause applied to a company's "financial condition," "business," or "operations," court read that clause narrowly to exclude "technological and economic changes in the aviation industry which undoubtedly affected the business of all who had dealings with that industry").

But describing this basic contractual approach is somewhat easier than applying it. For example, the original IBP 10-K for FY 1999 revealed the following five-year earnings from operations and earnings per share before extraordinary items:

	1999	1998	1997	1996	1995
Earnings from Operations (in thousands)	$528,473	$373,735	$226,716	$322,908	$480,096
Net Earnings Per Share	$3.39	$2.21	$1.26	$2.10	$2.96

The picture that is revealed from this data is of a company that is consistently profitable, but subject to strong swings in annual EBIT and net earnings. The averages that emerge from this data are of EBIT of approximately $386 million per year and net earnings of $2.38 per share. If this average is seen as weighting the past too much, a three-year average generates EBIT of $376 million and net earnings of $2.29 per share.

The original Warranted Financials in FY 2000 also emphasize that swings in IBP's performance were a part of its business reality. For example, the trailing last twelve month's earnings from operations as of the end of third quarter of FY 2000 were $462 million, as compared to $528 million for full year 1999, as originally reported. In addition, the third quarter 10-Q showed that IBP's earnings from operations for the first 39 weeks of 2000 were lagging earnings from operations for the comparable period in 1999 by $40 million, after adjusting for the CFBA Charges.

The financial statements also indicate that Foodbrands [the processed food portion of the business] was hardly a stable source of earnings, and was still much smaller in importance than IBP's fresh meat operations. Not only that, FY 2000 Foodbrands performance was lagging 1999, even accounting for the unusual, disclosed items.

The Rawhide Projections [developed by management at the request of a special board committee when a leveraged buyout was being considered] add another dimension to the meaning of §5.10. These Projections indicated that IBP would not reach the same level of profitability as originally reported *until FY 2004*. In FY 2001, IBP was expected to have earnings from operations of $446 and net profits of $1.93 a share, down from what was expected in FY 2000. This diminishment in expectations resulted from concern over an anticipated trough in the cattle cycle that would occur during years 2001 to 2003. Moreover, the performance projected for FY 2001 was a drop even from the reduced FY 2000 earnings that Tyson expected as of the time it signed the Merger Agreement.

These negotiating realities bear on the interpretation of §5.10 and suggest that the contractual language must be read in the larger context

B. Getting to a Definitive Agreement

in which the parties were transacting. To a short-term speculator, the failure of a company to meet analysts' projected earnings for a quarter could be highly material. Such a failure is less important to an acquiror who seeks to purchase the company as part of a long-term strategy.[151] To such an acquiror, the important thing is whether the company has suffered a Material Adverse Effect in its business or results of operations that is consequential to the company's earnings power over a commercially reasonable period, which one would think would be measured in years rather than months. It is odd to think that a strategic buyer would view a short-term blip in earnings as material, so long as the target's earnings-generating potential is not materially affected by that blip or the blip's cause.[152]

In large measure, the resolution of the parties' arguments turns on a difficult policy question. In what direction does the burden of this sort of uncertainty fall: on an acquiror or on the seller? What little New York authority exists is not particularly helpful, and cuts in both directions. One New York case held a buyer to its bargain even when the seller suffered a very severe shock from an extraordinary event, reasoning that the seller realized that it was buying the stock of a sound company that was, however, susceptible to market swings.[153] Another case held that a Material Adverse Effect was evidenced by a short-term drop in sales, but in a commercial context where such a drop was arguably quite critical.[154] Non-New York authorities cited by the parties provide no firmer guidance.

In another New York case, *Katz v. NVF Co.*, 100 A.D.2d 470, 473 N.Y.S.2d 786 (1984), two merger partners agreed that one partner has suffered a material adverse change when its full year results showed a *net loss* of over $6.3 million, compared to a $2.1 million profit a year before, and steep operating losses due to plant closure. *Id.* at 788. The *Katz* case thus presents a negative change of much greater magnitude and duration than exists in this case.

---

151. James C. Freund, *Anatomy of a Merger: Strategies and Techniques for Negotiating Corporate Acquisitions* 246 (LAW JOURNALS SEMINARS-PRESS 1975) ("[W]hatever the concept of materiality may mean, at the very least it is always relative to the situation.").

152. *Pine State Creamery Co. v. Land-O-Sun Dairies, Inc.*, 201 F.3d 437 (4th Cir. 1999) (*per curiam*) (whether severe losses during a two-month period evidenced a MAC was a jury question where there was evidence that the business was seasonal and that such downturns were expected as part of the earnings cycle of the business).

153. *Bear Stearns Co. v. Jardine Strategic Holdings*, No. 31371187, slip. op. (N.Y. Supr. June 17, 1988), *aff'd mem.*, 143 A.D.2d 1073, 533 N.Y.S.2d 167 (1988) (Tender offeror who was to purchase 20% of Bear Stearns could not rely on the MAC clause to avoid contract despite $100 million loss suffered by Bear Stearns on Black Monday, October 19, 1997, and the fact that Bear Stearns suffered a $48 million quarterly loss, its first in history. The buyer knew that Bear Stearns was in a volatile cyclical business.).

154. In *Pan Am Corp. v. Delta Air Lines*, 175 B.R. 438, 492-493 (S.D.N.Y. 1994), Pan Am airlines suffered sharp decline in bookings over a three-month period that was shocking to its management. The court held that a MAC had occurred. It did so, however, in a context where the party relying on the MAC clause was providing funding in a work-out situation, making any further deterioration of Pan Am's already compromised condition quite important.

Practical reasons lead me to conclude that a New York court would incline toward the view that a buyer ought to have to make a strong showing to invoke a Material Adverse Effect exception to its obligation to close. Merger contracts are heavily negotiated and cover a large number of specific risks explicitly. As a result, even where a Material Adverse Effect condition is as broadly written as the one in the Merger Agreement, that provision is best read as a backstop protecting the acquiror from the occurrence of unknown events that substantially threaten the overall earnings potential of the target in a durationally-significant manner.[155] A short-term hiccup in earnings should not suffice; rather the Material Adverse Effect should be material when viewed from the longer-term perspective of a reasonable acquiror. In this regard, it is worth noting that IBP never provided Tyson with *quarterly* projections.

When examined from this seller-friendly perspective, the question of whether IBP has suffered a Material Adverse Effect remains a close one. IBP had a very sub-par first quarter. The earnings per share of $.19 it reported exaggerate IBP's success, because part of those earnings were generated from a windfall generated by accounting for its stock option plan, a type of gain that is not likely to recur. On a normalized basis, IBP's first quarter of 2001 earnings from operations ran 64% behind the comparable period in 2000. If IBP had continued to perform on a straight-line basis using its first quarter 2001 performance, it would generate earnings from operations of around $200 million. This sort of annual performance would be consequential to a reasonable acquiror and would deviate materially from the range in which IBP had performed during the recent past.[156]

Tyson says that this impact must also be coupled with the DFG Impairment Charge of $60.4 million. That Charge represents an indication that DFG is likely to generate far less cash flow than IBP had previously anticipated.[157] At the very least, the Charge is worth between $.50 and $.60 cents per IBP share, which is not trivial. It is worth even more, says Tyson, if one realizes that the Rawhide Projections portrayed Foodbrands as the driver of increased profitability in an era of flat fresh meats profits. This deficiency must be considered in view of the overall poor performance of Foodbrands so far in FY 2001. The Rawhide Projections had targeted Foodbrands to earn $137 million in 2001. In a January 30, 2001, presentation to Tyson, Bond had presented an operating plan that hoped to achieve $145 million from Foodbrands. As of the end of the first quarter,

---

155. A contrary rule will encourage the negotiation of extremely detailed "MAC" clauses with numerous carve-outs or qualifiers. An approach that reads broad clauses as addressing fundamental events that would materially affect the value of a target to a reasonable acquiror eliminates the need for drafting of that sort.

156. *See Raskin v. Birmingham Steel Corp.*, Del. Ch., 1990 WL 193326, at *5, Allen, C. (Dec. 4, 1990) (while "a reported 50% decline in earnings over two consecutive quarters might not be held to be a material adverse development, it is, I believe unlikely to think that might happen").

157. The Impairment Charge was, of course, signaled by Shipley's reduced estimate for DFG in FY 2001, and his indication that an impairment study was underway.

B. Getting to a Definitive Agreement

Foodbrands had earned only $2 million, and thus needed another $135 million in the succeeding three quarters to reach its Rawhide Projection. IBP's overall trailing last twelve month's earnings had declined from $488 million as of the end of the third quarter of 2000 to $330 million.

As a result of these problems, analysts following IBP issued sharply reduced earnings estimates for FY 2001. Originally, analysts were predicting that IBP would exceed the Rawhide Projections in 2001 by a wide margin. After IBP's poor first quarter, some analysts had reduced their estimate from $2.38 per share to $1.44 a share. *Even accounting for Tyson's attempts to manipulate the analyst community's perception of IBP*, this was a sharp drop.

Tyson contends that the logical inference to be drawn from the record evidence that is available is that IBP will likely have its worst year since 1997, a year which will be well below the company's average performance for all relevant periods. As important, the company's principal driver of growth is performing at markedly diminished levels, thus compromising the company's future results as it enters what is expected to be a tough few years in the fresh meats business.

IBP has several responses to Tyson's evidence. IBP initially notes that Tyson's arguments are unaccompanied by expert evidence that identifies the diminution in IBP's value or earnings potential as a result of its first quarter performance.[160] The absence of such proof is significant. Even after Hankins [Tyson's CFO] generated extremely pessimistic projections for IBP in order to justify a lower deal price, Merrill Lynch [Tyson's investment banker] still concluded that a purchase of IBP at $30 per share was still within the range of fairness and a great long-term value for Tyson. The Merrill Lynch analysis casts great doubt on Tyson's assertion that IBP has suffered a Material Adverse Effect.[161]

IBP also emphasizes the cyclical nature of its businesses. It attributes its poor first quarter to an unexpectedly severe winter. This led ranchers to hold livestock back from market, causing a sharp increase in prices that hurt both the fresh meats business and Foodbrands. Once April was concluded, IBP began to perform more in line with its recent year results, because supplies were increasing and Foodbrands was able to begin to make up its winter margins. Bond testified at trial that he expects IBP to meet or exceed the Rawhide Projection of $1.93 a share in 2001, and the company has publicly indicated that it expects earnings of $1.80 to $2.20 a share. Peterson expressed the same view.

---

160. It has admittedly taken its own payment multiples based on the Rawhide Projections and simply "valued" the effect that way. But IBP never warranted that it would meet those Projections.

161. Tyson's only expert on this subject testified that a MAE would have occurred in his view even if IBP met the Rawhide Projections, because those Projections were more bearish than the analysts. This academic theory is of somewhat dubious practical utility, as it leaves the enforceability of contracts dependent on whether predictions by third-parties come true.

IBP also notes that any cyclical fall is subject to cure by the Agreement's termination date, which was May 15, 2001. By May 15, IBP had two weeks of strong earnings that signaled a strong quarter ahead. Moreover, by that time, cattle that had been held back from market were being sold, leading to plentiful supplies that were expected to last for most of the year.

Not only that, IBP notes that not all analyst reporting services had been as pessimistic as Tyson portrays. In March, Morningstar was reporting a mean analyst prediction of $1.70 per share for IBP in 2001. By May, this had grown to a mean of $1.74 a share. Throughout the same period, Morningstar's consensus prediction was an FY 2002 performance of $2.33 range in March, and $2.38 in May. Therefore, according to Morningstar, the analyst community was predicting that IBP would return to historically healthy earnings next year, and that earnings for this year would fall short of the Rawhide Projections by less than $.20 per share.

IBP also argues that the Impairment Charge does not approach materiality as a big picture item. That Charge is a one-time, non-cash charge, and IBP has taken large charges of that kind as recently as 1999. While IBP does not deny that its decision to buy DFG turned out disastrously, it reminds me that DFG is but a tiny fraction of IBP's overall business and that a total shutdown of DFG would likely have little effect on the future results of a combined Tyson/IBP. And as a narrow asset issue, the charge is insignificant to IBP as a whole.

I am confessedly torn about the correct outcome. As Tyson points out, IBP has only pointed to two weeks of truly healthy results in 2001 before the contract termination date of May 15. Even these results are suspect, Tyson contends, due to the fact that IBP expected markedly better results for the second week just days before the actual results come out. In view of IBP's demonstrated incapacity to accurately predict near-term results, Tyson says with some justification that I should be hesitant to give much weight to IBP's assurances that it will perform well for the rest of the year.

In the end, however, Tyson has not persuaded me that IBP has suffered a Material Adverse Effect. By its own arguments, Tyson has evinced more confidence in stock market analysts than I personally harbor. But its embrace of the analysts is illustrative of why I conclude that Tyson has not met its burden.

As of May 2001, analysts were predicting that IBP would earn between $1.50 to around $1.74 per share in 2001. The analysts were also predicting that IBP would earn between $2.33 and $2.42 per share in 2002. These members are based on reported "mean" or "consensus" analyst numbers. Even at the low end of this *consensus* range, IBP's earnings for the next two years would not be out of line with its historical performance during troughs in the beef cycle. As recently as years 1996-1998, IBP went through a period with a three year average earnings of $1.85 per share. At the high end of the analysts' consensus range, IBP's results would exceed this figure by $.21 per year.

This predicted range of performance from the source that Tyson vouches for suggests that no Material Adverse Effect has occurred.[170] Rather, the analyst views support the conclusion that IBP remains what the baseline evidence suggests it was—a consistently but erratically profitable company struggling to implement a strategy that will reduce the cyclicality of its earnings. Although IBP may not be performing as well as it and Tyson had hoped, IBP's business appears to be in sound enough shape to deliver results of operations in line with the company's recent historical performance. Tyson's own investment banker still believes IBP is fairly priced at $30 per share. The fact that Foodbrands is not yet delivering on the promise of even better performance for IBP during beef troughs is unavailing to Tyson, since §5.10 focuses on IBP as a whole and IBP's performance as an entire company is in keeping with its baseline condition.

Therefore, I conclude that Tyson has not demonstrated a breach of §5.10. I admit to reaching this conclusion with less than the optimal amount of confidence. The record evidence is not of the type that permits certainty.[172]

NOTES AND QUESTIONS

1. The deal. What do the three parties have in common—the nation's leading beef distributor (IBP), leading chicken distributor (Tyson) and leading pork producer (Smithfield)? Each is competing for shelf space in supermarkets and seeking to survive and prosper in a changing food industry. Can you see the evidence of buyer's remorse? Tyson's has triumphed in what the court calls a vigorous auction process that it "ardently" desired to win, but now is having second thoughts. How is it that the merger agreement was signed on January 1 and had already been approved by Tyson shareholders within days? What would have happened if, as is common in most American public corporations, voting control was not held within the founding family, but dispersed among many shareholders? The vote required by state law and more importantly, the proxy solicitation process and disclosure required by federal law to obtain the

---

170. Again, I emphasize that my conclusion is heavily influenced by my temporal perspective, which recognizes that even good businesses do not invariably perform at consistent levels of profitability. If a different policy decision is the correct one, a contrary conclusion could be reached. That different, more short-term approach will, I fear, make merger agreements more difficult to negotiate and lead to Material Adverse Effect clauses of great prolixity.

172. If I am incorrect and IBP bore the burden to prove the absence of a Material Adverse Effect by clear and convincing evidence in order to obtain an order of specific performance, it would not have met that burden. It would prevail under a preponderance standard, regardless of whether it bore the burden of persuasion.

necessary approval would normally take 3-4 months. What would you have expected Tyson's shareholders to do at that point if events had continued along the same timeline as set out in the case?

2. Gap-filling and contract interpretation. Is the contract ambiguous? What approach does the vice-chancellor take to merger agreements? Is it different than other contract that you have studied?

Martin Marietta Materials, Inc. v. Vulcan Materials Co.
68 A.3d 1208 (Del. 2012)

JACOBS, Justice:

[After a trial in this action initially brought by Martin Marietta Materials, Inc. ("Martin") against Vulcan Materials Company ("Vulcan"), the Court of Chancery enjoined Martin, for a four-month period, from continuing to prosecute its pending Exchange Offer and Proxy Contest to acquire control of Vulcan. That injunctive relief was granted to remedy Martin's adjudicated violations of two contracts between Martin and Vulcan: a Non-Disclosure Letter Agreement (the "NDA") and a Common Interest, Joint Defense and Confidentiality Agreement (the "JDA")[1] (referred to collectively in this Opinion as the "Confidentiality Agreements.") The Supreme Court affirmed.

THE FACTS
A. Background Leading to the Confidentiality Agreements

Vulcan and Martin are the two largest participants in the United States construction aggregates industry. That industry engages in mining certain commodities and processing them into materials used to build and repair roads, buildings and other infrastructure. Vulcan, a New Jersey corporation headquartered in Birmingham, Alabama, is the country's largest aggregates business; and Martin, a North Carolina corporation headquartered in Raleigh, North Carolina, is the country's second-largest.

Since the early 2000s, Vulcan and Martin episodically discussed the possibility of a business combination, but the discussions were unproductive and no significant progress was made. [Discussions resumed in 2010 after Ward Nye, who had served as Martin's Chief Operating Officer since 2006, was appointed Martin's Chief Executive Officer ("CEO").] . . .

---

1. Both agreements expressly provided that they would be construed under Delaware law. [Vulcan first alleged its breach of contract claims in a lawsuit it brought in an Alabama federal court. Eventually, the parties agreed that the Chancery action would proceed first, ahead of both the Alabama action and related litigation pending in New Jersey.]

B. Getting to a Definitive Agreement

At the outset Nye was receptive to a combination with Vulcan, in part because he believed the timing was to Martin's advantage. Vulcan's relative strength in markets that had been hard hit by the financial crisis, such as Florida and California, had now become a short-term weakness. As a result, Vulcan's financial and stock price performance were unfavorable compared to Martin's, whose business was less concentrated in those beleaguered geographic regions. To Nye, therefore, a timely merger — before a full economic recovery and before Vulcan's financial results and stock price improved — was in Martin's interest. Moreover, Nye had only recently been installed as Martin's CEO, whereas [Don] James, Vulcan's CEO, was nearing retirement age with no clear successor. To Nye, that suggested that a timely merger would also create an opportunity for him to end up as CEO of the combined companies.

Relatedly, although Nye was willing to discuss a possible merger with his Vulcan counterpart, he was not willing to risk being supplanted as CEO. The risk of Nye being displaced would arise if Martin were put "in play" by a leak of its confidential discussions with Vulcan, followed by a hostile takeover bid by Vulcan or a third party. Nye's concern about a hostile deal was not fanciful: recently Martin had engaged in friendly talks with a European company that had turned hostile. The European company's hostile attempt to acquire Martin failed only because the financial crisis "cratered" the bidder's financing.

Understandably, therefore, when Nye first spoke to Vulcan's banker, Goldman Sachs, in April 2010, he stressed that Martin was not for sale, and that Martin was interested in discussing the prospect of a friendly merger, but not a hostile acquisition of Martin by Vulcan. As the Chancellor found, Nye's notes prepared for a conversion with Vulcan's banker made it clear that "(i) Martin ... would talk and share information about a *consensual* deal only, and not for purposes of facilitating an *unwanted* acquisition of Martin ... by Vulcan; and even then only if (ii) absolute confidentiality, even as to the fact of their discussions, was maintained." When James and Nye first met in April 2010, they agreed that their talks must remain completely confidential, and they operated from the "shared premise" that any information exchanged by the companies would be used only to facilitate a friendly deal.

To secure their understanding, Nye and James agreed that their respective companies would enter into confidentiality agreements. That led to the drafting and execution of the two Confidentiality Agreements at issue in this case: the NDA and the JDA.

B. The NDA

Nye [instructed] Roselyn Bar, Esquire, Martin's General Counsel ... to prepare the NDA. In drafting the NDA,. Consistent with Nye's desire for strict confidentiality, Bar proposed changes [from an] earlier template agreement that were "unidirectional," *i.e.*, that enlarged the scope of the information subject to its restrictions and limited the permissible uses and disclosures of that covered information.

In its final form, the NDA prohibited both the "use" and the "disclosure" of "Evaluation Material," except where expressly allowed. Paragraph 2 permitted either party to *use* the other party's Evaluation Material, but *"solely for the purpose of evaluating a Transaction."* Paragraph 2 also categorically prohibited either party from *disclosing* Evaluation Material to anyone except the receiving party's representatives. The NDA defined "Evaluation Material" as "any nonpublic information furnished or communicated by the disclosing party" as well as "all analyses, compilations, forecasts, studies, reports, interpretations, financial statements, summaries, notes, data, records or other documents and materials prepared by the receiving party . . . that contain, reflect, are based upon or are generated from any such nonpublic information. . . ." The NDA defined "Transaction" as "a possible business combination transaction . . . between [Martin] and [Vulcan] or one of their respective subsidiaries."

Paragraph 3 of the NDA also prohibited the disclosure of the merger negotiations between Martin and Vulcan, and certain other related information, except for disclosures that were "legally required." . . . Paragraph 4 defined specific conditions under which "legally required" disclosure of Evaluation Material (and certain other information covered by Paragraph 3) would be permitted. . . . As the Chancellor found, "Paragraph (4) establishes the Notice and Vetting Process for disclosing Evaluation Material and Transaction Information that would otherwise be confidential under the NDA in circumstances [where] a party is 'required' to do so in the sense that the party had received an External Demand." The Chancellor further concluded that Ms. Bar's addition of the words "Subject to paragraph (4)" at the beginning of NDA paragraph (3), is "most obviously read as being designed to prevent any reading of ¶ 3 that would permit escape from ¶ 4's narrow definition of legally required and ¶ 4's rigorous Notice and Vetting Process."

Vulcan shared Martin's confidentiality concerns. It therefore agreed to include in the NDA the changes that Ms. Bar proposed to the predecessor template agreement.

C. The JDA

Because the parties were exploring a combination of the two largest companies in their industry, antitrust scrutiny appeared unavoidable. After the NDA was signed, the two companies' inside and outside counsel met to discuss that issue. The discussions implicated nonpublic, privileged information and attorney work-product, leading Martin and Vulcan also to

B. Getting to a Definitive Agreement

execute the JDA (which was drafted by outside counsel) to govern those exchanges.

The JDA, like the NDA, prohibits and limits the use and the disclosure of information that the JDA describes as "Confidential Materials." The critical prohibitions and limitations are found in JDA Paragraphs 2 and 4. Paragraph 2 prohibits the disclosure of Confidential Materials without "the consent of all Parties who may be entitled to claim any privilege or confidential status with respect to such materials. . . ." JDA Paragraph 4 relevantly provides that "Confidential Materials will be used, consistent with the maintenance of the privileged and confidential status of those materials, solely for purposes of pursuing and completing *the Transaction.*" The JDA defines "Transaction" as "a *potential transaction being discussed* by Vulcan and Martin[ ] . . . involving the combination or acquisition of all or certain of their assets or stock. . . ."

D. Martin's Use and Disclosure of Vulcan's Information Covered by the NDA and JDA

After the JDA and the NDA were executed, Vulcan provided to Martin nonpublic information that gave Martin a window into Vulcan's organization, including detailed confidential information about Vulcan's business, revenues, and personnel. Those disclosures enabled Martin to project more reliably the value of synergistic cost-cutting measures that could be achieved from a combination of the two companies. Therefore, Martin needed Vulcan's nonpublic information to evaluate the two "gating issues" critical to any business combination transaction: possible antitrust-related divestitures and merger synergies.

The Court of Chancery found, and Martin does not dispute, that Martin used and disclosed Vulcan's nonpublic information in preparing its Exchange Offer and its Proxy Contest to oust some of Vulcan's board members (collectively, the "hostile takeover bid"). Martin's position is that its use and disclosure of that nonpublic information was not legally prohibited by the Confidentiality Agreements. [Antitrust counsel on both sides met and prepared a joint antitrust analysis in 2010; a meeting between Martin's and Vulcan's CFOs and controllers took place in Match 2011.] The information exchanged at that meeting and the nonpublic information Martin had previously received, caused Martin to revise its estimated merger synergies upwards by as much as $100 million annually, from the $150–$200 million it previously estimated. That synergy jump, plus the fact that Martin's stock price had increased in relation to Vulcan's, led Martin to conclude that it "could offer Vulcan's shareholders a premium in a stock-for-stock exchange, yet still justify the deal to Martin's stockholders" on economic grounds. Martin knew, however, that if it wanted to use all of its projected synergistic gains to justify the transaction, time was of the essence. Not only did current market conditions favor Martin, but also Vulcan already had plans to obtain certain cost savings on its own, independent of any deal with Martin.

... [A]s the talks floundered soon after the March 8 meeting, Martin and its bankers began using Vulcan's confidential, nonpublic information to consider alternatives to a friendly deal. By April 2011, Martin's bankers were evaluating the constraints imposed by the NDA upon a non-consensual transaction. At a mid-August 2011 meeting, Martin's board formally authorized management to pursue alternatives to a friendly deal. Four months later, Martin launched its unsolicited Exchange Offer.

As a regulatory matter, an exchange offer carries a line-item requirement under federal securities law to disclose past negotiations. Martin announced its Exchange Offer on December 12, 2011, by sending Vulcan a public "bear hug" letter and filing a Form S-4 with the United States Securities and Exchange Commission ("SEC"). On January 24, 2012, Martin announced its Proxy Contest and filed a proxy statement in connection therewith.

Both before and after Martin commenced its hostile takeover bid, Martin disclosed Vulcan's nonpublic information, first to third party advisors (investment bankers, lawyers and public relations advisors), and later publicly. Martin did that without Vulcan's prior consent and without adhering to the Notice and Vetting Process mandated by the NDA. Regarding Martin's public relations advisors, the Chancellor found:

> Despite the Confidentiality Agreements, no effort was made to shield these advisors from receiving Evaluation Material or information relating to James' and Nye's negotiations. To the contrary, it is plain that the public relations advisors were given a blow-by-blow of Nye's and [Martin's CFO's] view of the negotiations with Vulcan and access to other Evaluation Material, and they advised Martin ... management how the process and substance of information sharing and negotiation could be translated into a public communications strategy that would exert pressure on Vulcan to accept an unsolicited bid from Martin....

As for its public disclosures, Martin's Form S–4 disclosed not only the history of the negotiations, but also other detailed information that constituted "Evaluation Material" and "Confidential Materials" under the respective Confidentiality Agreements. Those details, as the Court of Chancery found, included:

- Martin's anticipated annual cost synergies of $200 million to $250 million resulting from a merger with Vulcan;
- James' estimates of "achievable synergies" from a merger at different stages of the discussions, "including his belief as of June 2010 that 'a combination of the companies would result in approximately $100 million in synergies,' and not 'synergies at the $175 million to $200 million levels that Mr. Nye believed were

B. Getting to a Definitive Agreement

achievable'; and James' supposed belief at the time the merger discussions ended, that 'the cost synergies to be achieved in a combination would [not] be greater than $50 million;'"
- "James' view of alternative deal structures designed to minimize tax leakage;"
- "James' conclusion, based on the merger discussions, that the 'potential tax leakage (*i.e.*, taxes arising from the sale or other disposition of certain assets that may be required to obtain regulatory approvals) and the ability to divest overlap[ping] business were significant impediments to a transaction;'" and
- "The fact that 'the legal teams did not identify any significant impediments to a business combination transaction' at their antitrust meeting on May 19, 2010."

The disclosures by Martin to the SEC, the Chancellor found, "were ... a tactical decision influenced by [Martin's] flacks," and "the influence of these public relations advisors is evident in the detailed, argumentative S-4 filed by Martin[ ]." Those disclosures, the trial court found, "exceeded the scope of what was legally required," and involved "selectively using that [Evaluation] Material and portraying it in a way designed to cast Vulcan's management and board in a bad light, to make Martin['s] own offer look attractive, and to put pressure on Vulcan's board to accept a deal on Martin['s] terms."

Lastly, the Chancellor found that after it launched its hostile takeover bid, Martin disclosed Evaluation Material and other confidential information "in push pieces to investors, off the record and on the record communications to the media, and investor conference calls." Those disclosures "include[d] a detailed history of the discussions [and] negotiations that [had taken] place concerning 'the Transaction,' [and] references revealing the 'opinions,' 'analyses' and 'non-public information' of Vulcan" regarding issues such as required antitrust divestitures and synergies.

E. The Court of Chancery's Post-Trial Determinations

On December 12, 2011, the same day it launched its hostile takeover bid, Martin commenced this Court of Chancery action for a declaration that nothing in the NDA barred Martin from conducting its Exchange Offer and Proxy Contest. Vulcan counterclaimed for a mirror-image determination that Martin breached the NDA, and later amended its counterclaim to add claims that Martin had violated the JDA. [After trial, the Chancellor enjoined] Martin from (among other things) proceeding with its Exchange Offer and Proxy Contest for a four month period. Martin then terminated its Exchange Offer and Proxy Contest, and appealed to this Court from the trial court's final order and judgment.

In its Opinion, the Court of Chancery ultimately determined that Martin had breached the NDA and the JDA by impermissibly using and disclosing Evaluation Material under the NDA and Confidential Materials under the JDA. . . . [T]he Court of Chancery found that, although the Confidentiality Agreements did not contain a "standstill" provision, they did bar Martin (and Vulcan) from:

- "Using the broad class of 'evaluation material' defined by the confidentiality agreements except for the consideration of a contractually negotiated business combination transaction between the parties, and not for a combination that was to be effected by hostile, unsolicited activity of one of the parties;"
- "Disclosing either the fact that the parties had merger discussions or any evaluation material shared under the confidentiality agreements unless the party was legally required to disclose because: (i) it had received 'oral questions, interrogatories, requests for information or documents in legal proceedings, subpoena, civil investigative demand or other similar process;' and (ii) its legal counsel had, after giving the other party notice and the chance for it to comment on the extent of disclosure required, limited disclosure to the minimum necessary to satisfy the requirements of law;" and
- "Disclosing information protected from disclosure by the confidentiality agreements through press releases, investor conference calls, and communications with journalists that were in no way required by law."

ANALYSIS . . .

B. Martin's Violations of the JDA

The Chancellor determined that Martin, in making its hostile bid, both "used" and "disclosed" Vulcan Confidential Materials in violation of the JDA. That agreement (the trial court found) unambiguously prohibits the use of "Confidential Materials" without Vulcan's consent, except "for purposes of pursuing and completing the Transaction," which the JDA defines as "a potential transaction being discussed by Vulcan and Martin. . . ." The Court of Chancery found as fact that "the only transaction that was 'being discussed' at the time the parties entered into the JDA was a negotiated merger," and that "neither [the] Exchange Offer nor [the] Proxy Contest . . . was 'the' transaction that was 'being discussed' at the time that the JDA was negotiated."

. . . The trial court properly found that the relevant operative language of the JDA—"a potential transaction being discussed"—is unambiguous, and Martin does not seriously contend otherwise. The only remaining dispute, accordingly, is factual: what transaction was "being discussed?" The *only* transaction being discussed, the trial court found, was a negotiated merger. To say that that finding is not "clearly wrong" would be an understatement: the finding is amply supported by the evidence. Nye told Vulcan that Martin was not for sale. Nye told Vulcan that Martin was interested in discussing the prospect of a merger, *not* an acquisition, whether by Vulcan or otherwise. And, Nye described the transaction under discussion as a "modified merger of equals."

Equally unpersuasive is Martin's alternative contention that even if "Transaction" means a negotiated merger, Martin did not violate the JDA's use restriction, because the JDA expressly allowed Martin to use Confidential Materials "for purposes of pursuing and completing the Transaction," and Martin's hostile bid "ultimately will facilitate . . . a negotiated transaction." That claim fails because the Chancellor found as fact that the only transaction being discussed would be "friendly" or "negotiated." That finding expressly and categorically excluded Martin's "hostile bid or a business combination . . . effected by a pressure strategy."

C. Martin's Violations of the NDA

We next consider Martin's challenges to the Chancellor's determination that Martin violated the disclosure restrictions of the NDA. The Chancellor found as fact that Martin disclosed Vulcan confidential information, including Evaluation Material, in the course of pursuing its hostile bid, and Martin does not contest that finding. Rather, Martin's claim before us is that its disclosure of Vulcan confidential information was permitted by Paragraph 3 of the NDA, and that the Court of Chancery erred in holding otherwise. This claim rests upon a somewhat intricate (and fragile) structure of subsidiary arguments, which run as follows: (i) Martin was entitled to disclose Vulcan confidential information, including Evaluation Material, that was otherwise protected under the NDA without Vulcan's prior consent, if disclosure was "legally required;" (ii) the disclosure of Vulcan's confidential information in publicly filed documents was "legally required" by SEC Rules applicable to exchange offers; (iii) the Vulcan confidential information that Martin disclosed to investors was legally permitted because that disclosure was already "legally required" by SEC Rules; and (iv) Martin was not contractually obligated to give Vulcan prior notice of any intended disclosures, or to engage in a pre-disclosure vetting process, because those procedural requirements applied only to disclosures made in response to an "External Demand" arising in the course of a legal proceeding, and no such External Demand was ever made. . . .

[W]e conclude, as a matter of law based upon the NDA's unambiguous terms, that: (i) Paragraph 3, of itself, does not authorize the disclosure of "Evaluation Material," even if such disclosure is otherwise "legally required;" (ii) Paragraph 4 is the only NDA provision that authorizes the disclosure of Evaluation Material; (iii) any disclosure under Paragraph 4 is permitted only in response to an External Demand and after complying with the pre-disclosure Notice and Vetting Process mandated by that paragraph; and (iv) because no External Demand was made and Martin never engaged in the Notice and Vetting Process, its disclosure of Vulcan's Evaluation Material violated the disclosure restrictions of the NDA.

The contract provisions that relate to this issue are Paragraphs 2, 3 and 4 of the NDA. Paragraph 2, entitled *"Use of Evaluation Material,"* categorically prohibits the disclosure of a party's Evaluation Material to anyone other than the receiving party's representatives. Paragraph 3, which is entitled *"Non-Disclosure of Discussions; Communications,"* also prohibits the disclosure of certain information relating to merger "discussions or negotiations" between Martin and Vulcan. But, Paragraph 3 also carves out an exception that permits disclosure of that information where disclosure is "legally required":

> Subject to paragraph (4), each party agrees that, without the prior written consent of the other party, it and its Representatives will not disclose to any other person, other than as legally required, the fact that any Evaluation Material has been made available hereunder, that discussions or negotiations have or are taking place concerning a Transaction or any of the terms, conditions or other facts with respect thereto (including the status thereof or that this letter agreement exists).

At this point it is helpful to pause and identify which "legally required" disclosures Paragraph 3 does—and does not—permit. By its terms, Paragraph 3 covers only three categories of information: (a) the fact that any Evaluation Material has been made available; (b) the fact that discussions or negotiations concerning a Transaction have been taken or are taking place; and (c) any of the terms, conditions or other facts with respect thereto [*i.e.,* to the negotiations] including the status thereof [*i.e.,* the negotiations] or that the NDA exists. *Not included within those categories is the substance of a party's Evaluation Material*—as distinguished from "the fact that . . . Evaluation Material has been made available."

The omission of Evaluation Material from the coverage of Paragraph 3 is both intentional and logical. Although Paragraph 3 does not expressly prohibit the disclosure of Evaluation Material, it does not need to. Paragraph 2 accomplishes that. Evaluation Material does not fall with Paragraph 3's "legally required" carve-out exception, because that exception can *only* apply to the confidential information specifically identified in Paragraph 3. Moreover—and of critical importance—the permitted disclosure of Evaluation Material is explicitly and separately made the subject of Paragraph 4, which is entitled *"Required Disclosure."* Paragraph 4, by its terms, addresses the disclosure of "any of the other party's Evaluation Material *or* any of the facts, the disclosure of which is prohibited under paragraph (3) of [the NDA]."

B. Getting to a Definitive Agreement 89

Paragraph 4 also mandates a procedural framework within which legally required disclosure of Evaluation Material is permissible. That framework has two elements. The first is that Evaluation Material must be the subject of an External Demand. The second is that a party contemplating disclosure of that information must give pre-disclosure notice of any intended disclosure and (where applicable) engages in a vetting process.

To illustrate how these two elements operate structurally, we divide Paragraph 4 into two parts. The first creates a right to prior notice to enable the adversely affected party to seek appropriate judicial relief:

> In the event that a party or any of its Representatives are requested or required (by oral questions, interrogatories, requests for information or documents in legal proceedings, subpoena, civil investigative demand or other similar process) to disclose any of the other party's Evaluation Material or any of the facts, the disclosure of which is prohibited under paragraph (3) of this letter agreement, the party requested or required to make the disclosure shall provide the other party with prompt notice of any such request or requirement so that the other party may seek a protective order or other appropriate remedy and/or waive compliance with the provisions of this letter agreement.

The second part comes into play if a contracting party, for whatever reason, does not seek or obtain court protection. In those circumstances, Paragraph 4 mandates an extrajudicial "vetting" process:

> If, in the absence of a protective order or other remedy or the receipt of a waiver by such other party, the party requested or required to make the disclosure or any of its Representatives should nonetheless, in the opinion of such party's [or its Representative's] counsel, be legally required to make the disclosure, such party or its Representative may, without liability hereunder, disclose only that portion of the other party's Evaluation Material which such counsel advises is legally required to be disclosed; provided that the party requested or required to make the disclosure exercises its reasonable efforts to preserve the confidentiality of the other party's Evaluation Material, including, without limitation, by cooperating with the other party to obtain an appropriate protective order or other reliable assurance that confidential treatment will be accorded the other party's Evaluation Material.

To recapitulate, Paragraphs 2, 3, and 4, both internally and when read together, unambiguously permit a party to the NDA to disclose "legally required" Evaluation Material. But, that may be done *only* if an External Demand for such information has first been made, and *only* if the non-disclosing party is then given prior notice of any intended disclosure and (where applicable) an opportunity to vet the information sought to be disclosed. The Court of Chancery properly so concluded. In our view, that interpretation is compelled by the text of these NDA provisions, their relationship to each other, and by the canon of construction that requires all contract provisions to be harmonized and given effect where possible. That also is the only interpretation that is consistent with the found facts relating to the NDA's overall purpose and import, and the parties' reasons for negotiating the specific language of the disputed NDA provisions.

Martin's contrary argument rests on the premise that Evaluation Material is textually included within the purview of Paragraph 3. Martin claims that the following italicized phrase in Paragraph 3 captures Evaluation Material: "[E]ach party agrees [not to disclose, other than as legally required,] . . . that discussions or negotiations have or are taking place concerning a Transaction or any of the terms, conditions, or *other facts with respect thereto* (including the status thereof or that this letter agreement exists).

Martin's argued-for interpretation—that "other facts with respect thereto" must be read to cover Evaluation Material—finds no support in the specific language and structure of the NDA. It is also unreasonable. Any doubt about the scope of the phrase "other facts with respect thereto" is put to rest by considering the broader language of which that phrase is but one moving part. The context clarifies that the phrase, "other facts with respect *thereto*," means specific facts indicating that there were "discussions or negotiations . . . concerning a Transaction," including the fact that the NDA even exists. That peripheral species of information differs markedly from the substantive, company-specific internal information that the parties exchanged in order to facilitate their discussions or negotiations (*i.e.*, Evaluation Material).

Evaluation Material is a term that is central to, and defined in, the NDA. That term is specifically referred to by name throughout the agreement. Martin's interpretation of the NDA attempts to shoehorn "Evaluation Material" into language in Paragraph 3 that does not, and is not intended to, include "Evaluation Material." If the drafters of the NDA intended to include Evaluation Material within the category of information disclosable under Paragraph 3, they easily could have done that by referring directly to "Evaluation Material," as they did repeatedly elsewhere in the NDA.

The NDA also clearly distinguishes Evaluation Material from the disclosable information covered by Paragraph 3. Paragraph 4 addresses the disclosure of "any of the other party's Evaluation Material *or* any of the facts, the disclosure of which is prohibited under paragraph (3) of this letter agreement." The disjunctive "or" plainly contradicts Martin's claim that Evaluation Material falls within the purview of Paragraph 3. And, the basic logic and structure of the NDA makes the trial court's reading the only reasonable one, because Paragraph 2 (which precedes Paragraph 3) flatly prohibits the disclosure of Evaluation Material, and Paragraph 4 expressly mandates the conditions and procedures that must be complied with before Evaluation Material may be disclosed (assuming disclosure is otherwise "legally required").

We conclude, for these reasons, that the only reasonable construction of the NDA is that Paragraph 4 alone permitted the disclosure of Evaluation Material, and even then only if triggered by an External Demand and preceded by compliance with Paragraph 4's Notice and Vetting Process. The

Court of Chancery found as fact that Martin disclosed Evaluation Material in the course of conducting its hostile bid, without having received an External Demand and without having engaged in the Notice and Vetting Process. Martin has not challenged that finding. We therefore uphold the Court of Chancery's determination that Martin breached the NDA's disclosure restrictions.

D. The Remedy

... Paragraph 9 of the NDA both parties stipulated that "money damages would not be [a] sufficient remedy for *any* breach ... by either party," and that "the non-breaching party *shall be entitled to equitable relief,* including injunction and specific performance, as a remedy for any such breach." The JDA has a similar provision that obligates the parties to pursue "equitable or injunctive relief"—and *not* monetary damages—in the event of a breach of that agreement.

Our courts have long held that "contractual stipulations as to irreparable harm alone suffice to establish that element for the purpose of issuing ... injunctive relief." Martin offers no persuasive reason why the parties' stipulation in the NDA that "money damages would not be [a] sufficient remedy for any breach" should not be regarded as a stipulation to irreparable injury, nor why the stipulation that "any breach ... shall entitle[ ]" the non-breaching party "to equitable relief" should not be given effect in this case. Nor does Martin persuade us that, although the JDA expressly disclaims any right to a money damages remedy, the harm imposed by a breach of that contract is not "irreparable" for injunctive purposes.

Martin's assertions also fail factually, because the Chancellor did make a finding of "actual"—and irreparable—injury. The trial court found, as fact, that "Vulcan is now suffering from exactly the same kind of harm Nye demanded the Confidentiality Agreements shield Martin [ ] from[;]" that Vulcan was injured by Martin's "contractually improper selective revelation of nonpublic Vulcan information[;]" and that Vulcan suffered a loss of "negotiating leverage."

Unable to deny that the trial court so found, Martin shifts ground and asserts that any finding of harm was "speculative" and made "without any support." To the contrary, the adjudicated harm was not speculative and is supported by ample record evidence. For example, Vulcan's CEO James testified that when Martin revealed publicly the fact of the negotiations, "[i]t put us in play at a time that we would not have wanted to be put into play," because "this industry is in a recession." James also testified that "our employees were very concerned," and that "[o]ur executive team obviously is completely distracted from pursuing our internal strategic plan." That and other non-speculative record evidence solidly supports the Court of Chancery's finding of "actual" irreparable injury.

Martin also attacks the scope of the remedy itself, claiming that the injunction was unreasonable because it would delay Martin's Proxy Contest by one year, rather than four months. In different circumstances that kind of harm might be a legally cognizable factor that a court will take into account in balancing the equities for and against granting an injunction. Here, however, the "delay" is attributable to the NDA's May 3, 2012 expiration date, which — when combined with Vulcan's advance notice bylaw — precluded Martin from disclosing Vulcan confidential information to support its Proxy Contest in time for Vulcan's 2012 annual meeting. Because New Jersey law requires director elections to be held annually, the practical reality was that Martin's first opportunity to disclose that information lawfully to promote a Proxy Contest would not occur until 2013.

Given those facts, the Court of Chancery did not abuse its discretion by holding that the equities favored Vulcan, because "Martin's breaches prevented Vulcan from seeking injunctive relief before the confidential information was made public" and Vulcan "[had] been measured in its request for injunctive relief." The court properly balanced the need to "vindicat[e] Vulcan's reasonable [contractual] expectations" against the "delay" imposed on Martin as a "result of its own conduct." The Chancellor stated that although "an argument can be made that a longer injunction would be justified by the pervasiveness of Martin['s] breaches," an injunction lasting four months was "a responsible period" reflecting the time interval between when Martin launched its Exchange Offer on December 12, 2011, and the NDA's May 3, 2012 expiration date. That this measured form of relief also resulted in delaying Martin for a longer period from seeking to replace the Vulcan board, does not detract from the propriety of the relief the court granted.

NOTES AND QUESTIONS

1. The deal. This was a strategic merger between the two biggest players in their industry. What social factors, such as those discussed in section B1 of this chapter shape this deal coming together (and then falling apart) when it did? Consider why this deal moved from a friendly discussion to a hostile offer. What is Martin Marietta seeking to accomplish by its use of information in this new environment? How effective is its use of SEC disclosure requirements, illustrating the federal rules discussed in Chapter 3?

2. Separating the different kinds of provisions in acquisitions agreements. The court distinguished "standstill agreement" and "confidentiality agreement" as qualitatively different and not necessarily, or even customarily, embodied in separate instruments. Contracts denominated as standstill agreements may also contain confidentiality provisions, and instruments denominated as confidentiality agreements may contain standstill provisions." The court made this distinction:

A standstill agreement expressly prohibits specific conduct by a contracting party to acquire control of the other contracting party. Typically, a standstill agreement will prohibit a hostile bid in any form, including a hostile tender offer to acquire stock control of the other contracting party and/or a proxy contest to replace all or some of its directors. Standstill prohibitions do not require, or in any way depend upon, a contracting party's use or disclosure of the other party's confidential, nonpublic information. Rather, a standstill agreement is intended to protect a contracting party against hostile takeover behavior, as distinguished from the unauthorized use or disclosure of the other party's confidential nonpublic information.

A confidentiality agreement, in contrast, is intended and structured to prevent a contracting party from using and disclosing the other party's confidential, nonpublic information except as permitted by the agreement. In that respect it is qualitatively distinguishable from a prohibition that precludes a party categorically from engaging in specified hostile takeover activity. Thus, a confidentiality agreement will not typically preclude a contracting party from making a hostile bid to acquire control of the other party, so long as the bid does not involve the use or disclosure of the other party's confidential, nonpublic information. A confidentiality agreement is intended to protect a contracting party's non-public information, not its corporate ownership and control.

It is undisputed that the Confidentiality Agreements in this case were true confidentiality agreements, not standstill agreements. They did not categorically preclude Martin from making a hostile takeover bid for Vulcan. What they did was preclude Martin from using and disclosing Vulcan's confidential, nonpublic information except insofar as the agreements themselves permitted.

68 A.3d at 1218, note 43.

3. How is the remedy tailored to the timetable of a deal under federal and state law? The injunction blocks Martin's offer for four months, but the practical effect is three times that long because of the impact of state corporate law rules about shareholder meetings and federal law governing proxy solicitation. What can be expected to change during that period? What might Martin do to speed up that timeline?

4. Damages for a winning bidder. Terms negotiated as part of the Acquisition Agreement can have liability creating consequences. In Ventas, Inc. v. HCP, Inc., 647 F.3d 291 (6th Cir. 2011) a federal appellate court affirmed a jury verdict of $100 million in favor of the winning bidder in an auction who had been injured by the subsequent actions of the losing bidder found to have violated a standstill agreement. The standstill, signed at the time that parties entered into confidential negotiations, prohibited the participants from making or announcing any bid outside of the auction process for 18 months. When the losing bidder in fact pursued a bid, the winning bidder had to increase its price by 10 percent to complete the deal. The court found:

> Although courts should be circumspect in adjudicating claims between competitors, wrongful and anti-competitive conduct should not be insulated from liability. Indeed, the public interest in full and fair competition is furthered by imposing liability on a market player, such as HCP, for fraudulently leveraging a public market to

sabotage a competitor, as liability for such conduct will deter similar future conduct and promote economic certainty in the marketplace.

For the reasons set forth above, we AFFIRM the judgment of the district court in the amount of $101,672,807.00 in favor of Ventas.

647 F.3d 291, at 311, 318 (6th Cir. 2011).

5. Damages for a losing bidder. Similar liability can arise for the benefit of the losing bidder when the acquired corporation breaches a no-shop and similar provisions. In a Delaware case where two bidders were pursuing a target, the initial bidder had signed a merger agreement but ultimately lost out to a higher bidder. The losing bidder was a strategic bidder and the complaint alleged that the target's senior management feared they would lose their job following a strategic deal such that they favored the other bidder, a financial buyer that needed a management team. The court permitted a suit to go forward based on violations of the no-shop provision and a related provision requiring the bidder to take commercially reasonable efforts to keep the initial bidder informed of the offer and status of any Superior Proposals as defined under the agreement. The litigation was also allowed to proceed against the successful bidder for tortious interference. The court saw the possibility of damages even beyond the $4 million termination fee bargained for by the losing bidder and $2 million in expense reimbursement. The court said:

> Bidders in particular secure rights under acquisition agreements to protect themselves against being used as a stalking horse and as consideration for making target-specific investment of time and resources in particular acquisitions, Target entities secure important rights as well. It is critical to our law that these bargained for rights be enforced. Both through equitable remedies such an injunctive relief and specific performance, and in appropriate cases through monetary remedies including awards of damages.

NACCO Indus., Inc. v. Applica, Inc., 997 A.2d 1, 19 (Del Ch. 2009).

5. THE TARGET'S APPROACH: REMAINING INDEPENDENT OR GETTING THE BEST DEAL FROM THE FIRST OR ANOTHER BIDDER

A. THE LEGAL AND ECONOMIC FRAMEWORK

While the bidder might see great possibilities for creating value from synergies or change of control, its views of the target are not the only relevant ones. Most prominently, the current managers and directors of the target may have a different view. This chapter focuses on their perspective and the judicial response to actions they may take. They may want to make a deal and have that deal be able to resist shareholder claims challenging their action. Alternatively, they may believe the company will do better if it continues independently of the bidder or that the current bid is too low or that another bidder will be a better fit. They want to be able to take action to fend off a low bidder and be able to resist shareholder claims challenging their action. Consider the range of responses available to them and how much room they will have to enact them.

A target facing an acquisition bid (and the board and managers who usually speak for that target) might have a variety of reasons why they don't want to accept the bidder's offer, at least immediately. The range of possible actions they might take in response might be financial in nature or legal. There are a host of economic and market factors that necessarily shape a target's response, so that law is only part of what you must know to be an effective deal participant. Indeed, the financial factors that determine value, as discussed in Chapter 2, may be the key determinants in how a target responds. Directors and managers themselves respond to various financial incentives and monitoring constraints that are part of the context in which deals are considered and need to be part of the knowledge base with which you approach takeovers.

1. Financial Defenses

Target managers and directors have available to them a range of actions that will make the takeover more expensive for the bidder, make the target less attractive to the bidder (which can lower the bidder's return even if not directly raising its costs), or pursue an alternative deal on terms that are more attractive to the target's shareholders or managers. You will see many more defenses than those listed here, but instead of getting lost in a seemingly inexhaustible list, you ought to try to analyze each new tactic as implementing the core strategies just identified to make the offer financially more expensive to the bidder. Specific examples include:

- *Getting rid of excess cash*. As discussed in Chapter 2, bidders often seek value creation by a more efficient use of the target's assets, and excess cash is particularly valued in such a strategy. Such cash can be a way of paying for the costs of an acquisition or lowering the costs of the acquirer's borrowing to fund the acquisition, so that a target which depletes its cash, by a dividend for example, may seem less attractive.
- *Purchasing another company* or other assets can deplete cash (if that is the form of consideration the target uses to make the acquisition). A possible side benefit is that the purchase could create antitrust problems for the bidder or otherwise make the combination less attractive.
- *Share repurchases* work to deplete the target's cash while providing shareholders an immediate cash return on their investment (in a way that can provide capital gains income tax treatment).
- *Selling the crown jewel* of the target's assets from which the bidder may have anticipated synergies can make the target less attractive, although it may be necessary to combine this with a dividend distribution of the cash received in return.
- *Golden parachutes* are contracts with senior officers providing them substantial payouts triggered by a takeover that, in turn, will deplete the target's treasury.
- *White knight* refers to a second bidder recruited by management in response to an initial hostile bid who management thinks will provide a better fit for the target or at least a more accommodating host for management's continued employment and control of the target's assets within the white knight's structure.
- *White squire* describes a friendly bidder who is willing to buy into the target and provide beneficial funding, but without necessarily taking control of the target.

2. Legal Defenses

Any of the actions described in the list above likely come within Rule #1 in Chapter 3, that directors get to make decisions for the corporation, including acquiring or disposing of assets, determining dividends and salary, and the like. The core part of a legal defense is to focus on those few things that directors cannot do, as described in Rule #2 in Chapter 3. Put simply, protection is needed *only* against the few things that someone other than directors are permitted to do. The two most obvious illustrations are the shareholders' right to vote and their power to sell their shares. The core of a legal defense strategy for any target will be to narrow or close off those channels for such shareholder action. This can best be described by focusing on what have been the most prevalent tactic against shareholder selling—the poison pill—and against shareholder voting—the staggered board.

Over the last two decades, those defenses have been very effective in shutting off those two avenues for shareholder action, such that other legal defenses, including various state takeover statutes, have receded in importance. As with the financial defenses, though, if you understand the core problem to which legal defenses are directed—closing off the few avenues for decision-making by anyone other than directors—you will be able to include any new evolutions of defenses within your understanding. A poison pill, discussed in more detail in Chapter 7, essentially imposes a severe financial penalty on a bidder who acquires shares through a tender offer to which the target board has not consented. A staggered board essentially requires two annual meetings for a hostile bidder to gain control of a board via the vote, thereby increasing the costs for a control fight to include two proxy fights and requiring the board to take the risk that any return on investment cannot come for some time with the attendant risk that the economy may be different and the ability to increase value may no longer exist in the same way.

As you think about those legal defenses, you should also consider the antidotes that are available against those defenses, since neither set is impregnable but vulnerable particularly to eventual use of the shareholder vote. In such a setting, particularly with the large number of institutional investors and activist investors included in the shareholder census, bidders can continue to press the financial and market incentives of an attractive bid. Since 2000, for example, regulatory changes to enhance shareholder voting and market changes that have made it more worthwhile for institutional shareholders to exercise their voting rights have led to a dramatic reduction in the presence of staggered boards, at least in the largest American corporations, and more muted use of poison pills. In addition, directors have to consider their fiduciary duties and possible challenges to the takeover defenses described below.

B. FIDUCIARY DUTIES AND LEGAL CHALLENGES TO BOARD ACTION

Delaware's corporate law gives directors very broad power to act for the corporation. (Recall Rule #1 from Chapter 3.) This authority is broad enough that it would cover any number of defensive tactics which might be taken, as set out in the previous section. Statutes in states other than Delaware likewise provide directors with a very broad swath of authority. In exercising this broad control over other people's money, directors are constrained by fiduciary duties as determined by the Delaware courts in suits brought by shareholders on behalf of the corporation or as class actions. Indeed, the Delaware Supreme Court has declared that the defining tension in corporate governance is between director decision-making and judicial review based on fiduciary duty. Omnicare, Inc. v. NCS Healthcare, Inc., 818 A.2d 914, 927 (Del. 2003).

Apart from self-help via selling in the market or voting, a judicial challenge based on fiduciary duty is sometimes a way to constrain what directors do. Such duties, which have been a part of corporate law for almost two centuries, focus on a director's duty of care and loyalty in undertaking the powers given to them by corporation statutes such as Delaware §141.

Loyalty is the most common challenge to director action and regularly is based on conflict of interest, usually in a transaction in which the directors are on one side and the corporation, or its shareholders, on the other. *Weinberger v. UOP*, contained in Chapter 10, defines the broad duty that leads to intense judicial review: "where one stands on both sides of a transaction, he has the burden of establishing the entire fairness sufficient to pass the test of careful scrutiny by the courts." Weinberger v. UOP, Inc., 457 A.2d 701, 710 (Del. 1983).

The duty of care for directors generally is set out in a key acquisition case, *Smith v. Van Gorkom*. You should focus on the substantive standard for director behavior that the court sets out and the procedural approach that a court will take in addressing a challenge made to director action based on fiduciary duty.

Smith v. Van Gorkom
488 A.2d 858 (Del. Sup. Ct. 1985)

HORSEY, Justice (for the majority):

This appeal from the Court of Chancery involves a class action brought by shareholders of the defendant Trans Union Corporation ("Trans Union" or "the Company"), originally seeking rescission of a cash-out merger of

B. Fiduciary Duties and Legal Challenges to Board Action

Trans Union into the defendant New T Company ("New T"), a wholly-owned subsidiary of the defendant, Marmon Group, Inc. ("Marmon"). Alternate relief in the form of damages is sought against the defendant members of the Board of Directors of Trans Union, New T, and Jay A. Pritzker and Robert A. Pritzker, owners of Marmon.

Following trial, the former Chancellor granted judgment for the defendant directors by unreported letter opinion dated July 6, 1982. . . .

I.

A.

Trans Union was a publicly-traded, diversified holding company, the principal earnings of which were generated by its railcar leasing business. During the period here involved, the Company had a cash flow of hundreds of millions of dollars annually. However, the Company had difficulty in generating sufficient taxable income to offset increasingly large investment tax credits (ITCs). Accelerated depreciation deductions had decreased available taxable income against which to offset accumulating ITCs. The Company took these deductions, despite their effect on usable ITCs, because the rental price in the railcar leasing market had already impounded the purported tax savings.

In the late 1970's, together with other capital-intensive firms, Trans Union lobbied in Congress to have ITCs refundable in cash to firms which could not fully utilize the credit. During the summer of 1980, defendant Jerome W. Van Gorkom, Trans Union's Chairman and Chief Executive Officer, testified and lobbied in Congress for refundability of ITCs and against further accelerated depreciation. By the end of August, Van Gorkom was convinced that Congress would neither accept the refundability concept nor curtail further accelerated depreciation.

Beginning in the late 1960's, and continuing through the 1970's, Trans Union pursued a program of acquiring small companies in order to increase available taxable income. In July 1980, Trans Union Management prepared the annual revision of the Company's Five-Year Forecast. This report was presented to the Board of Directors at its July, 1980 meeting. The report projected an annual income growth of about 20%. The report also concluded that Trans Union would have about $195 million in spare cash between 1980 and 1985, "with the surplus growing rapidly from 1982 onward." . . .

B.

On August 27, 1980, Van Gorkom met with Senior Management of Trans Union. Van Gorkom reported on his lobbying efforts in Washington and his desire to find a solution to the tax credit problem more permanent than a continued program of acquisitions. Various alternatives were suggested and discussed preliminarily, including the sale of Trans Union to a company with a large amount of taxable income.

Donald Romans, Chief Financial Officer of Trans Union, stated that his department had done a "very brief bit of work on the possibility of a leveraged buy-out." This work had been prompted by a media article which Romans had seen regarding a leveraged buy-out by management. The work consisted of a "preliminary study" of the cash which could be generated by the Company if it participated in a leveraged buy-out. As Romans stated, this analysis "was very first and rough cut at seeing whether a cash flow would support what might be considered a high price for this type of transaction."

On September 5, at another Senior Management meeting which Van Gorkom attended, Romans again brought up the idea of a leveraged buy-out as a "possible strategic alternative" to the Company's acquisition program. Romans and Bruce S. Chelberg, President and Chief Operating Officer of Trans Union, had been working on the matter in preparation for the meeting. According to Romans: They did not "come up" with a price for the Company. They merely "ran the numbers" at $50 a share and at $60 a share with the "rough form" of their cash figures at the time. Their "figures indicated that $50 would be very easy to do but $60 would be very difficult to do under those figures." This work did not purport to establish a fair price for either the Company or 100% of the stock. It was intended to determine the cash flow needed to service the debt that would "probably" be incurred in a leveraged buy-out, based on "rough calculations" without "any benefit of experts to identify what the limits were to that, and so forth." These computations were not considered extensive and no conclusion was reached.

At this meeting, Van Gorkom stated that he would be willing to take $55 per share for his own 75,000 shares. He vetoed the suggestion of a leveraged buy-out by Management, however, as involving a potential conflict of interest for Management. Van Gorkom, a certified public accountant and lawyer, had been an officer of Trans Union for 24 years, its Chief Executive Officer for more than 17 years, and Chairman of its Board for 2 years. It is noteworthy in this connection that he was then approaching 65 years of age and mandatory retirement.

For several days following the September 5 meeting, Van Gorkom pondered the idea of a sale. He had participated in many acquisitions as a manager and director of Trans Union and as a director of other companies. He was familiar with acquisition procedures, valuation methods, and negotiations; and he privately considered the pros and cons of whether Trans Union should seek a privately or publicly-held purchaser.

Van Gorkom decided to meet with Jay A. Pritzker, a well-known corporate takeover specialist and a social acquaintance. However, rather than approaching Pritzker simply to determine his interest in acquiring Trans

Union, Van Gorkom assembled a proposed per share price for sale of the Company and a financing structure by which to accomplish the sale. Van Gorkom did so without consulting either his Board or any members of Senior Management except one: Carl Peterson, Trans Union's Controller. Telling Peterson that he wanted no other person on his staff to know what he was doing, but without telling him why, Van Gorkom directed Peterson to calculate the feasibility of a leveraged buy-out at an assumed price per share of $55. Apart from the Company's historic stock market price,[1] and Van Gorkom's long association with Trans Union, the record is devoid of any competent evidence that $55 represented the per share intrinsic value of the Company.

Having thus chosen the $55 figure, based solely on the availability of a leveraged buy-out, Van Gorkom multiplied the price per share by the number of shares outstanding to reach a total value of the Company of $690 million. Van Gorkom told Peterson to use this $690 million figure and to assume a $200 million equity contribution by the buyer. Based on these assumptions, Van Gorkom directed Peterson to determine whether the debt portion of the purchase price could be paid off in five years or less if financed by Trans Union's cash flow as projected in the Five Year Forecast, and by the sale of certain weaker divisions identified in a study done for Trans Union by the Boston Consulting Group ("BCG study"). Peterson reported that, of the purchase price, approximately $50-80 million would remain outstanding after five years. Van Gorkom was disappointed, but decided to meet with Pritzker nevertheless.

Van Gorkom arranged a meeting with Pritzker at the latter's home on Saturday, September 13, 1980. Van Gorkom prefaced his presentation by stating to Pritzker: "Now as far as you are concerned, I can, I think, show how you can pay a substantial premium over the present stock price and pay off most of the loan in the first five years." . . . If you could pay $55 for this Company, here is a way in which I think it can be financed."

Van Gorkom then reviewed with Pritzker his calculations based upon his proposed price of $55 per share. Although Pritzker mentioned $50 as a more attractive figure, no other price was mentioned. However, Van Gorkom stated that to be sure that $55 was the best price obtainable, Trans Union should be free to accept any better offer. Pritzker demurred, stating that his organization would serve as a "stalking horse" for an "auction contest" only if Trans Union would permit Pritzker to buy 1,750,000 shares of Trans Union stock at market price which Pritzker could then sell to any higher bidder. After further discussion on this point, Pritzker told Van Gorkom that he would give him a more definite reaction soon.

---

1. The common stock of Trans Union was traded on the New York Stock Exchange. Over the five-year period from 1975 through 1979, Trans Union's stock had traded within a range of a high of $39 1/2 and a low of $24 1/4. Its high and low range for 1980 through September 19 (the last trading day before announcement of the merger) was $38 1/4 - $29 1/2.

On Monday, September 15, Pritzker advised Van Gorkom that he was interested in the $55 cash-out merger proposal and requested more information on Trans Union. Van Gorkom agreed to meet privately with Pritzker, accompanied by Peterson, Chelberg, and Michael Carpenter, Trans Union's consultant from the Boston Consulting Group. The meetings took place on September 16 and 17. Van Gorkom was "astounded that events were moving with such amazing rapidity."

On Thursday, September 18, Van Gorkom met again with Pritzker. At that time, Van Gorkom knew that Pritzker intended to make a cash-out merger offer at Van Gorkom's proposed $55 per share. Pritzker instructed his attorney, a merger and acquisition specialist, to begin drafting merger documents. There was no further discussion of the $55 price. However, the number of shares of Trans Union's treasury stock to be offered to Pritzker was negotiated down to one million shares; the price was set at $38 — 75 cents above the per share price at the close of the market on September 19. At this point, Pritzker insisted that the Trans Union Board act on his merger proposal within the next three days, stating to Van Gorkom: "We have to have a decision by no later than Sunday [evening, September 21,] before the opening of the English stock exchange on Monday morning." Pritzker's lawyer was then instructed to draft the merger documents, to be reviewed by Van Gorkom's lawyer, "sometimes with discussion and sometimes not, in the haste to get it finished."

On Friday, September 19, Van Gorkom, Chelberg, and Pritzker consulted with Trans Union's lead bank regarding the financing of Pritzker's purchase of Trans Union. The bank indicated that it could form a syndicate of banks that would finance the transaction. On the same day, Van Gorkom retained James Brennan, Esquire, to advise Trans Union on the legal aspects of the merger. Van Gorkom did not consult with William Browder, a Vice-President and director of Trans Union and former head of its legal department, or with William Moore, then the head of Trans Union's legal staff.

On Friday, September 19, Van Gorkom called a special meeting of the Trans Union Board for noon the following day. He also called a meeting of the Company's Senior Management to convene at 11:00 A.M., prior to the meeting of the Board. No one, except Chelberg and Peterson, was told the purpose of the meetings. Van Gorkom did not invite Trans Union's investment banker, Salomon Brothers, or its Chicago-based partner, to attend.

Of those present at the Senior Management meeting on September 20, only Chelberg and Peterson had prior knowledge of Pritzker's offer. Van Gorkom disclosed the offer and described its terms, but he furnished no copies of the proposed Merger Agreement. Romans announced that his department had done a second study which showed that, for a leveraged buy-out, the price range for Trans Union stock was between $55 and

$65 per share. Van Gorkom neither saw the study nor asked Romans to make it available for the Board meeting.

Senior Management's reaction to the Pritzker proposal was completely negative. No member of Management, except Chelberg and Peterson, supported the proposal. Romans objected to the price as being too low;[2] he was critical of the timing and suggested that consideration should be given to the adverse tax consequences of an all-cash deal for low-basis shareholders; and he took the position that the agreement to sell Pritzker one million newly-issued shares at market price would inhibit other offers, as would the prohibitions against soliciting bids and furnishing inside information to other bidders. Romans argued that the Pritzker proposal was a "lock up" and amounted to "an agreed merger as opposed to an offer." Nevertheless, Van Gorkom proceeded to the Board meeting as scheduled without further delay.

Ten directors served on the Trans Union Board, five inside (defendants Bonser, O'Boyle, Browder, Chelberg, and Van Gorkom) and five outside (defendants Wallis, Johnson, Lanterman, Morgan and Reneker). All directors were present at the meeting, except O'Boyle who was ill. Of the outside directors, four were corporate chief executive officers and one was the former Dean of the University of Chicago Business School. None was an investment banker or trained financial analyst. All members of the Board were well informed about the Company and its operations as a going concern. They were familiar with the current financial condition of the Company, as well as operating and earnings projections reported in the recent Five Year Forecast. The Board generally received regular and detailed reports and was kept abreast of the accumulated investment tax credit and accelerated depreciation problem.

Van Gorkom began the Special Meeting of the Board with a twenty-minute oral presentation. Copies of the proposed Merger Agreement were delivered too late for study before or during the meeting.[3] He reviewed the Company's ITC and depreciation problems and the efforts theretofore made to solve them. He discussed his initial meeting with Pritzker and his motivation in arranging that meeting. Van Gorkom did not disclose to the Board, however, the methodology by which he alone had arrived at the $55 figure, or the fact that he first proposed the $55 price in his negotiations with Pritzker.

---

2. Van Gorkom asked Romans to express his opinion as to the $55 price. Romans stated that he "thought the price was too low in relation to what he could derive for the company in a cash sale, particularly one which enabled us to realize the values of certain subsidiaries and independent entities."

3. The record is not clear as to the terms of the Merger Agreement. The Agreement, as originally presented to the Board on September 20, was never produced by defendants despite demands by the plaintiffs. Nor is it clear that the directors were given an opportunity to study the Merger Agreement before voting on it. All that can be said is that Brennan had the Agreement before him during the meeting.

Van Gorkom outlined the terms of the Pritzker offer as follows: Pritzker would pay $55 in cash for all outstanding shares of Trans Union stock upon completion of which Trans Union would be merged into New T Company, a subsidiary wholly-owned by Pritzker and formed to implement the merger; for a period of 90 days, Trans Union could receive, but could not actively solicit, competing offers; the offer had to be acted on by the next evening, Sunday, September 21; Trans Union could only furnish to competing bidders published information, and not proprietary information; the offer was subject to Pritzker obtaining the necessary financing by October 10, 1980; if the financing contingency were met or waived by Pritzker, Trans Union was required to sell to Pritzker one million newly-issued shares of Trans Union at $38 per share.

Van Gorkom took the position that putting Trans Union "up for auction" through a 90-day market test would validate a decision by the Board that $55 was a fair price. He told the Board that the "free market will have an opportunity to judge whether $55 is a fair price." Van Gorkom framed the decision before the Board not as whether $55 per share was the highest price that could be obtained, but as whether the $55 price was a fair price that the stockholders should be given the opportunity to accept or reject.[4]

Attorney Brennan advised the members of the Board that they might be sued if they failed to accept the offer and that a fairness opinion was not required as a matter of law.

Romans attended the meeting as chief financial officer of the Company. He told the Board that he had not been involved in the negotiations with Pritzker and knew nothing about the merger proposal until the morning of the meeting; that his studies did not indicate either a fair price for the stock or a valuation of the Company; that he did not see his role as directly addressing the fairness issue; and that he and his people "were trying to search for ways to justify a price in connection with such a [leveraged buy-out] transaction, rather than to say what the shares are worth." Romans testified:

> "I told the Board that the study ran the numbers at 50 and 60, and then the subsequent study at 55 and 65, and that was not the same thing as saying that I have a valuation of the company at X dollars. But it was a way—a first step towards reaching that conclusion."

Romans told the Board that, in his opinion, $55 was "in the range of a fair price," but "at the beginning of the range."

Chelberg, Trans Union's President, supported Van Gorkom's presentation and representations. He testified that he "participated to make sure that the Board members collectively were clear on the details of the

---

4. In Van Gorkom's words: The "real decision" is whether to "let the stockholders decide it" which is "all you are being asked to decide today."

agreement or offer from Pritzker"; that he "participated in the discussion with Mr. Brennan, inquiring of him about the necessity for valuation opinions in spite of the way in which this particular offer was couched"; and that he was otherwise actively involved in supporting the positions being taken by Van Gorkom before the Board about "the necessity to act immediately on this offer," and about "the adequacy of the $55 and the question of how that would be tested."

The Board meeting of September 20 lasted about two hours. Based solely upon Van Gorkom's oral presentation, Chelberg's supporting representations, Romans' oral statement, Brennan's legal advice, and their knowledge of the market history of the Company's stock,[5] the directors approved the proposed Merger Agreement. However, the Board later claimed to have attached two conditions to its acceptance: (1) that Trans Union reserved the right to accept any better offer that was made during the market test period; and (2) that Trans Union could share its proprietary information with any other potential bidders. While the Board now claims to have reserved the right to accept any better offer received after the announcement of the Pritzker agreement (even though the minutes of the meeting do not reflect this), it is undisputed that the Board did not reserve the right to actively solicit alternate offers.

The Merger Agreement was executed by Van Gorkom during the evening of September 20 at a formal social event that he hosted for the opening of the Chicago Lyric Opera. Neither he nor any other director read the agreement prior to its signing and delivery to Pritzker. . . .

On February 10, the stockholders of Trans Union approved the Pritzker merger proposal. Of the outstanding shares, 69.9% were voted in favor of the merger; 7.25% were voted against the merger; and 22.85% were not voted.

II.

We turn to the issue of the application of the business judgment rule to the September 20 meeting of the Board.

The Court of Chancery concluded from the evidence that the Board of Directors' approval of the Pritzker merger proposal fell within the protection of the business judgment rule. . . .

The defendants deny that the Trial Court committed legal error in relying upon post-September 20, 1980 events and the directors' later acquired knowledge. The defendants further submit that their decision to accept $55 per share was informed because: (1) they were "highly

---

5. The Trial Court stated the premium relationship of the $55 price to the market history of the Company's stock as follows: . . . the merger price offered to the stockholders of Trans Union represented a premium of 62% over the average of the high and low prices at which Trans Union stock had traded in 1980, a premium of 48% over the last closing price, and a premium of 39% over the highest price at which the stock of Trans Union had traded any time during the prior six years.

qualified"; (2) they were "well-informed"; and (3) they deliberated over the "proposal" not once but three times. On essentially this evidence and under our standard of review, the defendants assert that affirmance is required. We must disagree.

Under Delaware law, the business judgment rule is the offspring of the fundamental principle, codified in 8 Del. C. §141(a), that the business and affairs of a Delaware corporation are managed by or under its board of directors. In carrying out their managerial roles, directors are charged with an unyielding fiduciary duty to the corporation and its shareholders. The business judgment rule exists to protect and promote the full and free exercise of the managerial power granted to Delaware directors. The rule itself "is a presumption that in making a business decision, the directors of a corporation acted on an informed basis, in good faith and in the honest belief that the action taken was in the best interests of the company." [Aronson v. Lewis, Del. Supr., 473 A.2d 805, 812 (1984).] Thus, the party attacking a board decision as uninformed must rebut the presumption that its business judgment was an informed one.

The determination of whether a business judgment is an informed one turns on whether the directors have informed themselves "prior to making a business decision, of all material information reasonably available to them." Id.

Under the business judgment rule there is no protection for directors who have made "an unintelligent or unadvised judgment." [Mitchell v. Highland-Western Glass, Del. Ch., 167 A. 831, 833 (1933).] A director's duty to inform himself in preparation for a decision derives from the fiduciary capacity in which he serves the corporation and its stockholders. Since a director is vested with the responsibility for the management of the affairs of the corporation, he must execute that duty with the recognition that he acts on behalf of others. Such obligation does not tolerate faithlessness or self-dealing. But fulfillment of the fiduciary function requires more than the mere absence of bad faith or fraud. Representation of the financial interests of others imposes on a director an affirmative duty to protect those interests and to proceed with a critical eye in assessing information of the type and under the circumstances present here.

Thus, a director's duty to exercise an informed business judgment is in the nature of a duty of care, as distinguished from a duty of loyalty. Here, there were no allegations of fraud, bad faith, or self-dealing, or proof thereof. Hence, it is presumed that the directors reached their business judgment in good faith, and considerations of motive are irrelevant to the issue before us.

The standard of care applicable to a director's duty of care has also been recently restated by this Court. In *Aronson*, supra, we stated: "While the Delaware cases use a variety of terms to describe the applicable standard of care, our analysis satisfies us that under the business judgment rule director liability is predicated upon concepts of gross negligence." 473 A.2d at 812.

We again confirm that view. We think the concept of gross negligence is also the proper standard for determining whether a business judgment reached by a board of directors was an informed one.

In the specific context of a proposed merger of domestic corporations, a director has a duty under 8 Del. C. §251(b), along with his fellow directors, to act in an informed and deliberate manner in determining whether to approve an agreement of merger before submitting the proposal to the stockholders. Certainly in the merger context, a director may not abdicate that duty by leaving to the shareholders alone the decision to approve or disapprove the agreement.

It is against those standards that the conduct of the directors of Trans Union must be tested, as a matter of law and as a matter of fact, regarding their exercise of an informed business judgment in voting to approve the Pritzker merger proposal.

III.

... The issue of whether the directors reached an informed decision to "sell" the Company on September 20, 1980, must be determined only upon the basis of the information then reasonably available to the directors and relevant to their decision to accept the Pritzker merger proposal. This is not to say that the directors were precluded from altering their original plan of action, had they done so in an informed manner. What we do say is that the question of whether the directors reached an informed business judgment in agreeing to sell the Company, pursuant to the terms of the September 20 Agreement presents, in reality, two questions: (A) whether the directors reached an informed business judgment on September 20, 1980; and (B) if they did not, whether the directors' actions taken subsequent to September 20 were adequate to cure any infirmity in their action taken on September 20. We first consider the directors' September 20 action in terms of their reaching an informed business judgment.

A.

On the record before us, we must conclude that the Board of Directors did not reach an informed business judgment on September 20, 1980, in voting to "sell" the Company for $55 per share pursuant to the Pritzker cash-out merger proposal. Our reasons, in summary, are as follows:

The directors (1) did not adequately inform themselves as to Van Gorkom's role in forcing the "sale" of the Company and in establishing the per share purchase price; (2) were uninformed as to the intrinsic value of the Company; and (3) given these circumstances, at a minimum, were grossly negligent in approving the "sale" of the Company upon two hours' consideration, without prior notice, and without the exigency of a crisis or emergency.

As has been noted, the Board based its September 20 decision to approve the cash-out merger primarily on Van Gorkom's representations. None of the directors, other than Van Gorkom and Chelberg, had any prior knowledge that the purpose of the meeting was to propose a cash-out merger of Trans Union. No members of Senior Management were present, other than Chelberg, Romans and Peterson; and the latter two had only learned of the proposed sale an hour earlier. Both general counsel Moore and former general counsel Browder attended the meeting, but were equally uninformed as to the purpose of the meeting and the documents to be acted upon.

Without any documents before them concerning the proposed transaction, the members of the Board were required to rely entirely upon Van Gorkom's 20-minute oral presentation of the proposal. No written summary of the terms of the merger was presented; the directors were given no documentation to support the adequacy of $55 price per share for sale of the Company; and the Board had before it nothing more than Van Gorkom's statement of his understanding of the substance of an agreement which he admittedly had never read, nor which any member of the Board had ever seen.

Under 8 Del. C. §141(e), "directors are fully protected in relying in good faith on reports made by officers." The term "report" has been liberally construed to include reports of informal personal investigations by corporate officers. However, there is no evidence that any "report," as defined under §141(e), concerning the Pritzker proposal was presented to the Board on September 20. Van Gorkom's oral presentation of his understanding of the terms of the proposed Merger Agreement, which he had not seen, and Romans' brief oral statement of his preliminary study regarding the feasibility of a leveraged buy-out of Trans Union do not qualify as §141(e) "reports" for these reasons: The former lacked substance because Van Gorkom was basically uninformed as to the essential provisions of the very document about which he was talking. Romans' statement was irrelevant to the issues before the Board since it did not purport to be a valuation study. At a minimum for a report to enjoy the status conferred by §141(e), it must be pertinent to the subject matter upon which a board is called to act, and otherwise be entitled to good faith, not blind, reliance. Considering all of the surrounding circumstances—hastily calling the meeting without prior notice of its subject matter, the proposed sale of the Company without any prior consideration of the issue or necessity therefor, the urgent time constraints imposed by Pritzker, and the total absence of any documentation whatsoever—the directors were duty bound to make reasonable inquiry of Van Gorkom and Romans, and if they had done so, the inadequacy of that upon which they now claim to have relied would have been apparent.

B. Fiduciary Duties and Legal Challenges to Board Action

The defendants rely on the following factors to sustain the Trial Court's finding that the Board's decision was an informed one: (1) the magnitude of the premium or spread between the $55 Pritzker offering price and Trans Union's current market price of $38 per share; (2) the amendment of the Agreement as submitted on September 20 to permit the Board to accept any better offer during the "market test" period; (3) the collective experience and expertise of the Board's "inside" and "outside" directors; and (4) their reliance on Brennan's legal advice that the directors might be sued if they rejected the Pritzker proposal. We discuss each of these grounds seriatim:

(1)

A substantial premium may provide one reason to recommend a merger, but in the absence of other sound valuation information, the fact of a premium alone does not provide an adequate basis upon which to assess the fairness of an offering price. Here, the judgment reached as to the adequacy of the premium was based on a comparison between the historically depressed Trans Union market price and the amount of the Pritzker offer. Using market price as a basis for concluding that the premium adequately reflected the true value of the Company was a clearly faulty, indeed fallacious, premise, as the defendants' own evidence demonstrates.

The record is clear that before September 20, Van Gorkom and other members of Trans Union's Board knew that the market had consistently undervalued the worth of Trans Union's stock, despite steady increases in the Company's operating income in the seven years preceding the merger. The Board related this occurrence in large part to Trans Union's inability to use its ITCs as previously noted. Van Gorkom testified that he did not believe the market price accurately reflected Trans Union's true worth; and several of the directors testified that, as a general rule, most chief executives think that the market undervalues their companies' stock. Yet, on September 20, Trans Union's Board apparently believed that the market stock price accurately reflected the value of the Company for the purpose of determining the adequacy of the premium for its sale....

The parties do not dispute that a publicly-traded stock price is solely a measure of the value of a minority position and, thus, market price represents only the value of a single share. Nevertheless, on September 20, the Board assessed the adequacy of the premium over market, offered by Pritzker, solely by comparing it with Trans Union's current and historical stock price.

Indeed, as of September 20, the Board had no other information on which to base a determination of the intrinsic value of Trans Union as a going concern. As of September 20, the Board had made no evaluation of the Company designed to value the entire enterprise, nor had the Board ever previously considered selling the Company or consenting to a buy-out merger. Thus, the adequacy of a premium is indeterminate unless it is assessed in terms of other competent and sound valuation information that reflects the value of the particular business.

Despite the foregoing facts and circumstances, there was no call by the Board, either on September 20 or thereafter, for any valuation study or documentation of the $55 price per share as a measure of the fair value of the Company in a cash-out context. It is undisputed that the major asset of Trans Union was its cash flow. Yet, at no time did the Board call for a valuation study taking into account that highly significant element of the Company's assets.

We do not imply that an outside valuation study is essential to support an informed business judgment; nor do we state that fairness opinions by independent investment bankers are required as a matter of law. Often insiders familiar with the business of a going concern are in a better position than are outsiders to gather relevant information; and under appropriate circumstances, such directors may be fully protected in relying in good faith upon the valuation reports of their management. See 8 Del. C. §141(e).

Here, the record establishes that the Board did not request its Chief Financial Officer, Romans, to make any valuation study or review of the proposal to determine the adequacy of $55 per share for sale of the Company. On the record before us: The Board rested on Romans' elicited response that the $55 figure was within a "fair price range" within the context of a leveraged buy-out. No director sought any further information from Romans. No director asked him why he put $55 at the bottom of his range. No director asked Romans for any details as to his study, the reason why it had been undertaken or its depth. No director asked to see the study; and no director asked Romans whether Trans Union's finance department could do a fairness study within the remaining 36-hour period available under the Pritzker offer.

Had the Board, or any member, made an inquiry of Romans, he presumably would have responded as he testified: that his calculations were rough and preliminary; and, that the study was not designed to determine the fair value of the Company, but rather to assess the feasibility of a leveraged buy-out financed by the Company's projected cash flow, making certain assumptions as to the purchaser's borrowing needs. Romans would have presumably also informed the Board of his view, and the widespread view of Senior Management, that the timing of the offer was wrong and the offer inadequate.

The record also establishes that the Board accepted without scrutiny Van Gorkom's representation as to the fairness of the $55 price per share for sale of the Company—a subject that the Board had never previously considered. The Board thereby failed to discover that Van Gorkom had suggested the $55 price to Pritzker and, most crucially, that Van Gorkom had arrived at the $55 figure based on calculations designed solely to determine the feasibility of a leveraged buy-out.[19] No questions were raised either as to the tax implications of a cash-out merger or how the price for the one million share option granted Pritzker was calculated.

We do not say that the Board of Directors was not entitled to give some credence to Van Gorkom's representation that $55 was an adequate or fair price. Under §141(e), the directors were entitled to rely upon their chairman's opinion of value and adequacy, provided that such opinion was reached on a sound basis. Here, the issue is whether the directors informed themselves as to all information that was reasonably available to them. Had they done so, they would have learned of the source and derivation of the $55 price and could not reasonably have relied thereupon in good faith.

None of the directors, Management or outside, were investment bankers or financial analysts. Yet the Board did not consider recessing the meeting until a later hour that day (or requesting an extension of Pritzker's Sunday evening deadline) to give it time to elicit more information as to the sufficiency of the offer, either from inside Management (in particular Romans) or from Trans Union's own investment banker, Salomon Brothers, whose Chicago specialist in merger and acquisitions was known to the Board and familiar with Trans Union's affairs.

Thus, the record compels the conclusion that on September 20 the Board lacked valuation information adequate to reach an informed business judgment as to the fairness of $55 per share for sale of the Company.

(2)

This brings us to the post-September 20 "market test" upon which the defendants ultimately rely to confirm the reasonableness of their September 20 decision to accept the Pritzker proposal. In this connection, the directors present a two-part argument: (a) that by making a "market test" of Pritzker's $55 per share offer a condition of their September 20 decision to accept his offer, they cannot be found to have acted impulsively or in an uninformed manner on September 20; and (b) that the adequacy of the $17 premium for sale of the Company was conclusively established over the following 90 to 120 days by the most reliable evidence available — the marketplace. Thus, the defendants impliedly contend that the "market test" eliminated the need for the Board to perform any other form of fairness test either on September 20, or thereafter.

---

19. As of September 20 the directors did not know: that Van Gorkom had arrived at the $55 figure alone, and subjectively, as the figure to be used by Controller Peterson in creating a feasible structure for a leveraged buy-out by a prospective purchaser; that Van Gorkom had not sought advice, information or assistance from either inside or outside Trans Union directors as to the value of the Company as an entity or the fair price per share for 100% of its stock; that Van Gorkom had not consulted with the Company's investment bankers or other financial analysts; that Van Gorkom had not consulted with or confided in any officer or director of the Company except Chelberg; and that Van Gorkom had deliberately chosen to ignore the advice and opinion of the members of his Senior Management group regarding the adequacy of the $55 price.

Again, the facts of record do not support the defendants' argument. There is no evidence: (a) that the Merger Agreement was effectively amended to give the Board freedom to put Trans Union up for auction sale to the highest bidder; or (b) that a public auction was in fact permitted to occur....

The directors' unfounded reliance on both the premium and the market test as the basis for accepting the Pritzker proposal undermines the defendants' remaining contention that the Board's collective experience and sophistication was a sufficient basis for finding that it reached its September 20 decision with informed, reasonable deliberation. Compare Gimbel v. Signal Companies, Inc., Del. Ch., 316 A.2d 599 (1974), aff'd per curiam, Del. Supr., 316 A.2d 619 (1974). There, the Court of Chancery preliminary enjoined a board's sale of stock of its wholly-owned subsidiary for an alleged grossly inadequate price. It did so based on a finding that the business judgment rule had been pierced for failure of management to give its board "the opportunity to make a reasonable and reasoned decision." 316 A.2d at 615. The Court there reached this result notwithstanding the board's sophistication and experience; the company's need of immediate cash; and the board's need to act promptly due to the impact of an energy crisis on the value of the underlying assets being sold — all of its subsidiary's oil and gas interests. The Court found those factors denoting competence to be outweighed by evidence of gross negligence; that management in effect sprang the deal on the board by negotiating the asset sale without informing the board; that the buyer intended to "force a quick decision" by the board; that the board meeting was called on only one-and-a-half days' notice; that its outside directors were not notified of the meeting's purpose; that during a meeting spanning "a couple of hours" a sale of assets worth $480 million was approved; and that the Board failed to obtain a *current* appraisal of its oil and gas interests. The analogy of *Signal* to the case at bar is significant. ...

(4)

... We conclude that Trans Union's Board was grossly negligent in that it failed to act with informed reasonable deliberation in agreeing to the Pritzker merger proposal on September 20; and we further conclude that the Trial Court erred as a matter of law in failing to address that question before determining whether the directors' later conduct was sufficient to cure its initial error. ...

[The court further concluded that the board's later conduct did not cure its initial error.] ...

V.

The defendants ultimately rely on the stockholder vote of February 10 for exoneration. The defendants contend that the stockholders' "overwhelming" vote approving the Pritzker Merger Agreement had the legal effect of curing any failure of the Board to reach an informed business judgment in its approval of the merger.

The parties tacitly agree that a discovered failure of the Board to reach an informed business judgment in approving the merger constitutes a voidable, rather than a void, act. Hence, the merger can be sustained, notwithstanding the infirmity of the Board's action, if its approval by majority vote of the shareholders is found to have been based on an informed electorate. . . .

The settled rule in Delaware is that "where a majority of fully informed stockholders ratify action of even interested directors, an attack on the ratified transaction normally must fail." Gerlach v. Gillam, Del. Ch., 139 A.2d 591, 593 (1958). The question of whether shareholders have been fully informed such that their vote can be said to ratify director action, "turns on the fairness and completeness of the proxy materials submitted by the management to the . . . shareholders." *Michelson v. Duncan*, supra at 220. As this Court stated in Gottlieb v. Heyden Chemical Corp., Del. Supr., 91 A.2d 57, 59 (1952):

> [T]he entire atmosphere is freshened and a new set of rules invoked where a formal approval has been given by a majority of independent, fully informed stockholders. . . .

In *Lynch v. Vickers Energy Corp.*, supra, this Court held that corporate directors owe to their stockholders a fiduciary duty to disclose all facts germane to the transaction at issue in an atmosphere of complete candor. We defined "germane" in the tender offer context as all "information such as a reasonable stockholder would consider important in deciding whether to sell or retain stock." Id. at 281. *Accord Weinberger v. UOP, Inc.*, supra; *Michelson v. Duncan*, supra; Schreiber v. Pennzoil Corp., Del. Ch., 419 A.2d 952 (1980). In reality, "germane" means material facts.

Applying this standard to the record before us, we find that Trans Union's stockholders were not fully informed of all facts material to their vote on the Pritzker Merger and that the Trial Court's ruling to the contrary is clearly erroneous. We list the material deficiencies in the proxy materials:

(1) The fact that the Board had no reasonably adequate information indicative of the intrinsic value of the Company, other than a concededly depressed market price, was without question material to the shareholders voting on the merger. See *Weinberger*, supra at 709 (insiders' report that cash-out merger price up to $24 was good investment held material); *Michelson*, supra at 224 (alleged terms and intent of stock option plan held not germane); *Schreiber*, supra at 959 (management fee of $650,000 held germane).

Accordingly, the Board's lack of valuation information should have been disclosed. Instead, the directors cloaked the absence of such information in both the Proxy Statement and the Supplemental Proxy Statement. Through artful drafting, noticeably absent at the September 20 meeting, both documents create the impression that the Board knew the intrinsic worth of the Company. In particular, the Original Proxy Statement contained the following:

> [a]lthough the Board of Directors regards the intrinsic value of the Company's assets to be significantly greater than their book value . . . , systematic liquidation of such a large and complex entity as Trans Union is simply not regarded as a feasible method of realizing its inherent value. Therefore, a business combination such as the merger would seem to be the only practicable way in which the stockholders could realize the value of the Company.

The Proxy stated further that "[i]n the view of the Board of Directors . . . , the prices at which the Company's common stock has traded in recent years have not reflected the inherent value of the Company." What the Board failed to disclose to its stockholders was that the Board had not made any study of the intrinsic or inherent worth of the Company; nor had the Board even discussed the inherent value of the Company prior to approving the merger on September 20, or at either of the subsequent meetings on October 8 or January 26. Neither in its Original Proxy Statement nor in its Supplemental Proxy did the Board disclose that it had no information before it, beyond the premium-over-market and the price/earnings ratio, on which to determine the fair value of the Company as a whole.

(2) We find false and misleading the Board's characterization of the Romans report in the Supplemental Proxy Statement. The Supplemental Proxy stated:

> At the September 20, 1980 meeting of the Board of Directors of Trans Union, Mr. Romans indicated that while he could not say that $55,00 per share was an unfair price, he had prepared a preliminary report which reflected that the value of the Company was in the range of $55.00 to $65.00 per share.

Nowhere does the Board disclose that Romans stated to the Board that his calculations were made in a "search for ways to justify a price in connection with" a leveraged buy-out transaction, "rather than to say what the shares are worth," and that he stated to the Board that his conclusion thus arrived at "was not the same thing as saying that I have a valuation of the Company at X dollars." Such information would have been material to a reasonable shareholder because it tended to invalidate the fairness of the merger price of $55. Furthermore, defendants again failed to disclose the absence of valuation information, but still made repeated reference to the "substantial premium."

(3) We find misleading the Board's references to the "substantial" premium offered. The Board gave as their primary reason in support of

the merger the "substantial premium" shareholders would receive. But the Board did not disclose its failure to assess the premium offered in terms of other relevant valuation techniques, thereby rendering questionable its determination as to the substantiality of the premium over an admittedly depressed stock market price. . . .

The burden must fall on defendants who claim ratification based on shareholder vote to establish that the shareholder approval resulted from a fully informed electorate. On the record before us, it is clear that the Board failed to meet that burden. *Weinberger v. UOP, Inc.*, supra at 703; *Michelson v. Duncan*, supra. . . .

For the foregoing reasons, we conclude that the director defendants breached their fiduciary duty of candor by their failure to make true and correct disclosures of all information they had, or should have had, material to the transaction submitted for stockholder approval.

VI.

To summarize: we hold that the directors of Trans Union breached their fiduciary duty to their stockholders (1) by their failure to inform themselves of all information reasonably available to them and relevant to their decision to recommend the Pritzker merger; and (2) by their failure to disclose all material information such as a reasonable stockholder would consider important in deciding whether to approve the Pritzker offer.

We hold, therefore, that the Trial Court committed reversible error in applying the business judgment rule in favor of the director defendants in this case.

On remand, the Court of Chancery shall conduct an evidentiary hearing to determine the fair value of the shares represented by the plaintiffs' class, based on the intrinsic value of Trans Union on September 20, 1980. Such valuation shall be made in accordance with *Weinberger v. UOP, Inc.*, supra at 712-715. Thereafter, an award of damages may be entered to the extent that the fair value of Trans Union exceeds $55 per share.

Reversed and Remanded for proceedings consistent herewith.

McNeilly, Justice, dissenting (joined by Christie, C.J.)

The majority opinion reads like an advocate's closing address to a hostile jury.

And I say that not lightly. Throughout the opinion great emphasis is directed only to the negative, with nothing more than lip service granted the positive aspects of this case. In my opinion Chancellor Marvel (retired) should have been affirmed. The Chancellor's opinion was the product of well reasoned conclusions, based upon a sound deductive process, clearly supported by the evidence and entitled to deference in this appeal. Because of my diametrical opposition to all evidentiary conclusions of the majority, I respectfully dissent.

It would serve no useful purpose, particularly at this late date, for me to dissent at great length. I restrain myself from doing so, but feel compelled to at least point out what I consider to be the most glaring deficiencies in the majority opinion. The majority has spoken and has effectively said that Trans Union's Directors have been the victims of a "fast shuffle" by Van Gorkom and Pritzker. That is the beginning of the majority's comedy of errors. The first and most important error made is the majority's assessment of the directors' knowledge of the affairs of Trans Union and their combined ability to act in this situation under the protection of the business judgment rule.

Trans Union's Board of Directors consisted of ten men, five of whom were "inside" directors and five of whom were "outside" directors. The "inside" directors were Van Gorkom, Chelberg, Bonser, William B. Browder, Senior Vice-President-Law, and Thomas P. O'Boyle, Senior Vice-President-Administration. At the time the merger was proposed the inside five directors had collectively been employed by the Company for 116 years and had 68 years of combined experience as directors. The "outside" directors were A.W. Wallis, William B. Johnson, Joseph B. Lanterman, Graham J. Morgan and Robert W. Reneker. With the exception of Wallis, these were all chief executive officers of Chicago based corporations that were at least as large as Trans Union. The five "outside" directors had 78 years of combined experience as chief executive officers, and 53 years cumulative service as Trans Union directors.

The inside directors wear their badge of expertise in the corporate affairs of Trans Union on their sleeves. But what about the outsiders? Dr. Wallis is or was an economist and math statistician, a professor of economics at Yale University, dean of the graduate school of business at the University of Chicago, and Chancellor of the University of Rochester. Dr. Wallis had been on the Board of Trans Union since 1962. He also was on the Board of Bausch & Lomb, Kodak, Metropolitan Life Insurance Company, Standard Oil and others.

William B. Johnson is a University of Pennsylvania law graduate, President of Railway Express until 1966, Chairman and Chief Executive of I.C. Industries Holding Company, and member of Trans Union's Board since 1968.

Joseph Lanterman, a Certified Public Accountant, is or was President and Chief Executive of American Steel, on the Board of International Harvester, Peoples Energy, Illinois Bell Telephone, Harris Bank and Trust Company, Kemper Insurance Company and a director of Trans Union for four years.

Graham Morgan is a chemist, was Chairman and Chief Executive Officer of U.S. Gypsum, and in the 17 and 18 years prior to the Trans Union transaction had been involved in 31 or 32 corporate takeovers.

Robert Reneker attended University of Chicago and Harvard Business Schools. He was President and Chief Executive of Swift and Company, director of Trans Union since 1971, and member of the Boards of seven other corporations including U.S. Gypsum and the Chicago Tribune.

Directors of this caliber are not ordinarily taken in by a "fast shuffle." I submit they were not taken into this multi-million dollar corporate transaction without being fully informed and aware of the state of the art as it pertained to the entire corporate panorama of Trans Union. True, even directors such as these, with their business acumen, interest and expertise, can go astray. I do not believe that to be the case here. These men knew Trans Union like the back of their hands and were more than well qualified to make on the spot informed business judgments concerning the affairs of Trans Union including a 100% sale of the corporation. Lest we forget, the corporate world of then and now operates on what is so aptly referred to as "the fast track." These men were at the time an integral part of that world, all professional business men, not intellectual figureheads. . . .

NOTES AND QUESTIONS

1. **The deal.** Trans Union had a stable business, including leasing rail cars, but the company had been unable to take full advantage of investment tax credits available for that business. The company's efforts to change the tax law or to make acquisitions to produce additional income to make use of the credits had been tried without complete success. A buyer who had sufficient income that would be offset by those unused credits might well value the business above its current market value and pay a higher price. Returning to the typology introduced in Chapter 2, this deal seems to illustrate financial gains as opposed to synergistic or operational gain opportunity. Within that context, a leveraged buyout is a recurring acquisition form (discussed in more detail in Chapter 13) in which the tax deductibility of debt incurred by the bidder means that the government is in effect subsidizing part of the costs of the takeover. Many leveraged buyouts involve existing management in key roles, usually then termed a management buyout or MBO. This one did not. The current CEO, Mr. Van Gorkom, was approaching retirement age and vetoed an MBO. Instead, he approached Jay Pritzker, a well-known Chicago financier, best known for his family's ownership of the Hyatt Hotels. Van Gorkom, clearly a mover and shaker, was able to put together a deal quickly; the company's existing bank was quick to say it could provide the financing for the deal.

2. **How good was the price?** The price paid in the takeover was 48 percent higher than the recent trading price, which itself was at the very high end of the trading range of the stock for the previous six years. Was the deal bad for shareholders? If so, was it because the directors did not take sufficient care? How good were the incentives of directors to seek the best price? Were Van Gorkom's interests the same as the shareholders?

3. **Personal liability for directors.** The result of the *Van Gorkom* case was to hold the directors personally liable for their breach of fiduciary duty. Procedurally, the breach of fiduciary duty rebutted the deference of the business judgment rule and meant that the directors now had the burden of proving the entire fairness of the transaction with any shortcoming coming out of their own pocket. This raised an immediate concern in the director and business community. The following year, the Delaware legislature passed a new section 102(b)(7) permitting corporations to add a provision to its articles of incorporation eliminating damages liability for its directors (but not officers) for violations of duty of care (but not duty of loyalty or good faith). Every large Delaware corporation added such a provision, and similar statutes appear in other states so that this is a dominant feature of American corporate governance. The duty of care can be the basis for an injunction but not damages. Not surprisingly, it led to efforts to re-characterize particular facts as being either care or loyalty depending on which side you were on. This development is taken up after the next case.

4. **The procedural setting as a key to understanding fiduciary duty cases.** Your consideration of the substance of the legal rules will benefit if you keep in mind the clear and identifiable procedural context and pattern for these cases that can be seen as a predictable starting point for a judge in any fiduciary duty case. It is as if there is a big X marked on the floor that the judge will move to when the issue is fiduciary duty. This starting point is one of deference to the actions of the directors. It is reflected in the business judgment rule, which the courts describe as a presumption that "in making a business decision the directors of a corporation acted on an informed basis, in good faith, and in the honest belief that the action taken was in the best interest of the corporation." Aronson v. Lewis, 473 A.2d 805, 812 (Del. 1984). The practical result is that unless the plaintiff comes up with a reason to move the court off of this starting point, the board's action will stand. *Id.* What will suffice to rebut this presumption? The clearest example is where a fiduciary enters into a self-dealing contract with the corporation. As the Delaware Supreme Court said in *Weinberger*, "where one stands on both sides of a transaction, he has the burden of establishing the entire fairness sufficient to pass the test of careful scrutiny by the courts." Weinberger v. UOP, Inc., 457 A.2d 701, 710 (Del. 1983). That quote captures not just the trigger for the move from deference, but also the procedural frame that results—a more intrusive form of judicial review in which the defendant has the burden of proof as to fairness. While conflict, as set out in *Weinberger*, is the most common reason for moving away from the deference starting point, it is not the only one. Delaware courts have made clear that breaches of other fiduciary duties, such as care, will trigger a similar shift, as in *Smith v. Van Gorkom*.

B. *Fiduciary Duties and Legal Challenges to Board Action* 119

Gantler v. Stephens
965 A.2d 695 (Del. Sup. Ct. 2009) (en banc)

JACOBS, Justice.

The plaintiffs in this breach of fiduciary duty action, who are certain shareholders of First Niles Financial, Inc. ("First Niles" or the "Company"), appeal from the dismissal of their complaint by the Court of Chancery. The complaint alleges that the defendants, who are officers and directors of First Niles, violated their fiduciary duties by rejecting a valuable opportunity to sell the Company, deciding instead to reclassify the Company's shares in order to benefit themselves, and by disseminating a materially misleading proxy statement to induce shareholder approval. We conclude that the complaint pleads sufficient facts to overcome the business judgment presumption, and to state substantive fiduciary duty and disclosure claims....

[First Niles was a one bank/savings association holding company operating Home Federal Savings & Loan Association ("Home Federal" or "Bank") in the small town of Niles, Ohio. These events unfolded between 2003 and 2006 at a time when the bank] was operating in a depressed local economy, with little to no growth in the Bank's assets and anticipated low growth for the future. At that time Stephens, who was Chairman, President, CEO and founder of First Niles and the Bank, was beyond retirement age and there was no heir apparent among the Company's officers. The acquisition market for banks like Home Federal was brisk, however, and First Niles was thought to be an excellent acquisition for another financial institution. Accordingly, the First Niles Board sought advice on strategic opportunities available to the Company, and in August 2004, decided that First Niles should put itself up for sale (the "Sales Process")

[At the time, the board included:

- Stephens, owning 109,652 shares or 7.9 percent;
- Leonard Gantler, an accountant, who became a plaintiff in this case (owning 3.6 percent);
- P. James Kramer, a local HVAC contractor for whom the bank was a major customer (with less than 5000 shares);
- William S. Eddy, a local osteopath (with 1149 shares);
- Ralph Zuzolo, a principal in the law firm of Zuzolo, Zuzolo & Zuzolo that frequently provided legal services to the Bank and sole owner of a local real estate title company that provided title services for nearly all of the Bank's real estate closings.]

[In August 2004, the board authorized the sale of the Company and retained an investment bank, Keefe, Bruyette & Woods (the "Financial Advisor"), and a law firm, Silver, Freedman & Taft ("Legal Counsel"). But the following month, Management (Stephens and others)] advocated abandoning the Sales Process in favor of a proposal to "privatize" the

Company. Under Management's proposal, First Niles would delist its shares from the NASDAQ SmallCap Market, convert the Bank from a federally chartered to a state chartered bank, and reincorporate in Maryland. The Board did not act on that proposal, and the Sales Process continued.

In December 2004, three potential purchasers—Farmers National Banc Corp. ("Farmers"), Cortland Bancorp ("Cortland"), and First Place Financial Corp. ("First Place")—sent bid letters to Stephens. Farmers stated in its bid letter that it had no plans to retain the First Niles Board, and the Board did not further pursue the Farmers' offer. In its bid letter, Cortland offered $18 per First Niles share, 49% in cash and 51% in stock, representing a 3.4% premium over the current First Niles share price. Cortland also indicated that it would terminate all the incumbent Board members, but would consider them for future service on Cortland's board. First Place's bid letter, which made no representation regarding the continued retention of the First Niles Board, proposed a stock-for-stock transaction valued at $18 to $18.50 per First Niles Share, representing a 3.4% to 6.3% premium.

The Board considered these bids at its next regularly scheduled meeting in December 2004. At that meeting the Financial Advisor opined that all three bids were within the range suggested by its financial models, and that accepting the stock-based offers would be superior to retaining First Niles shares. The Board took no action at that time. Thereafter, at that same meeting, Stephens also discussed in further detail Management's proposed privatization.

On January 18, 2005, the Board directed the Financial Advisor and Management to conduct due diligence in connection with a possible transaction with First Place or Cortland. The Financial Advisor met with Stephens and Safarek, and all three reviewed Cortland's due diligence request. Stephens and Safarek [first vice-president and treasurer] agreed to provide the materials Cortland requested and scheduled a due diligence session for February 6. Cortland failed to receive the materials it requested, canceled the February 6 meeting, and demanded the submission of those materials by February 8. The due diligence materials were never furnished, and Cortland withdrew its bid for First Niles on February 10. Management did not inform the Board of these due diligence events until after Cortland had withdrawn its bid.

First Place made its due diligence request on February 7, 2005, and asked for a due diligence review session the following week. Initially, Stephens did not provide the requested materials to First Place and resisted setting a date for a due diligence session. After Cortland withdrew its bid, however, Stephens agreed to schedule a due diligence session.

First Place began its due diligence review on February 13, 2005, and submitted a revised offer to First Niles on March 4. As compared to its original offer, First Place's revised offer had an improved exchange ratio. Because of a decline in First Place's stock value, the revised offer represented a lower implied price per share ($17.25 per First Niles share), but since First Niles' stock price had also declined, the revised offer still represented an 11% premium over market price. The Financial Advisor opined that First Place's revised offer was within an acceptable range, and that it exceeded the mean and median comparable multiples for previous acquisitions involving similar banks.

On March 7, 2005, at the next regularly scheduled Board meeting, Stephens informed the directors of First Place's revised offer. Although the Financial Advisor suggested that First Place might again increase the exchange ratio, the Board did not discuss the offer. Stephens proposed that the Board delay considering the offer until the next regularly scheduled Board meeting. After the Financial Advisor told him that First Place would likely not wait two weeks for a response, Stephens scheduled a special Board meeting for March 9 to discuss the First Place offer.

On March 8, First Place increased the exchange ratio of its offer to provide an implied value of $17.37 per First Niles share. At the March 9 special Board meeting, Stephens distributed a memorandum from the Financial Advisor describing First Place's revised offer in positive terms. Without any discussion or deliberation, however, the Board voted 4 to 1 to reject that offer, with only Gantler voting to accept it. After the vote, Stephens discussed Management's privatization plan and instructed Legal Counsel to further investigate that plan.

C. The Reclassification Proposal

Five weeks later, on April 18, 2005, Stephens circulated to the Board members a document describing a proposed privatization of First Niles ("Privatization Proposal"). That Proposal recommended reclassifying the shares of holders of 300 or fewer shares of First Niles common stock into a new issue of Series A Preferred Stock on a one-to-one basis (the "Reclassification"). The Series A Preferred Stock would pay higher dividends and have the same liquidation rights as the common stock, but the Preferred holders would lose all voting rights except in the event of a proposed sale of the Company. The Privatization Proposal claimed that the Reclassification was the best method to privatize the Company because it allowed maximum flexibility for future capital management activities, such as open market purchases and negotiated buy-backs. Moreover, First Niles could achieve the Reclassification without having to buy back shares in a fair market appraisal.

On April 20, 2005, the Board appointed Zuzolo to chair a special committee to investigate issues relating to the Reclassification, specifically: (1) reincorporating in a state other than Delaware, (2) changing the Bank's charter from a federal to a state charter, (3) deregistering from NASDAQ, and (4) delisting. However, Zuzolo passed away before any other directors were appointed to the special committee.

On December 5, 2005, Powell Goldstein, First Niles' outside counsel specially retained for the Privatization ("Outside Counsel"), orally presented the Reclassification proposal to the Board. The Board was not furnished any written materials. After the presentation, the Board voted 3 to 1 to direct Outside Counsel to proceed with the Reclassification program. Gantler cast the only dissenting vote.

Thereafter, the makeup of the Board changed. Shaker [a local attorney] replaced Zuzolo [who had died] in January of 2006, and Csontos [a full-time employee serving as compliance officer and corporate secretary] replaced Gantler in April of 2006. From that point on, the Board consisted of Stephens, Kramer, Eddy, Shaker and Csontos.

On June 5, 2006, the Board determined, based on the advice of Management and First Niles' general counsel, that the Reclassification was fair both to the First Niles shareholders who would receive newly issued Series A Preferred Stock, and to those shareholders who would continue to hold First Niles common stock. On June 19, the Board voted unanimously to amend the Company's certificate of incorporation to reclassify the shares held by owners of 300 or fewer shares of common stock into shares of Series A Preferred Stock that would have the features and terms described in the Privatization Proposal.

D. The Reclassification Proxy and the Shareholder Vote

On June 29, 2006, the Board submitted a preliminary proxy to the United States Securities and Exchange Commission ("SEC"). An amended version of the preliminary proxy was filed on August 10. Plaintiffs initiated this lawsuit after the amended filing, claiming that the preliminary proxy was materially false and misleading in various respects. On November 16, 2006, the Board, after correcting some of the alleged deficiencies, disseminated a definitive proxy statement ("Reclassification Proxy" or "Proxy") to the First Niles shareholders. On November 20, the plaintiffs filed an amended complaint, alleging (inter alia) that the Reclassification Proxy contained material misstatements and omissions.

In the Reclassification Proxy, the Board represented that the proposed Reclassification would allow First Niles to "save significant legal, accounting and administrative expenses" relating to public disclosure and reporting requirements under the Exchange Act. The Proxy also disclosed the benefits of deregistration as including annual savings of $142,500 by reducing the number of common shareholders, $81,000 by avoiding Sarbanes-Oxley related compliance costs, and $174,000 by avoiding a one-time consulting fee to design a system to improve the Company's internal control structure. The negative features and estimated costs of the transaction included $75,000 in Reclassification-related expenses, reduced liquidity for both the to-be-reclassified preferred and common shares, and the loss of certain investor protections under the federal securities laws.

The Reclassification Proxy also disclosed alternative transactions that the Board had considered, including a cash-out merger, a reverse stock-split, an issue tender offer, expense reduction and a business combination. The Proxy stated that each of the directors and officers of First Niles had "a conflict of interest with respect to [the Reclassification] because he or she is in a position to structure it in such a way that benefits his or her interests differently from the interests of unaffiliated shareholders." The Proxy further disclosed that the Company had received one firm merger offer, and that "[a]fter careful deliberations, the board determined in its business judgment the proposal was not in the best interests of the Company or our shareholders and rejected the proposal."

The Company's shareholders approved the Reclassification on December 14, 2006. Taking judicial notice of the Company's Rule 13e-3 Transaction Statement, the trial court concluded that of the 1,384,533 shares outstanding and eligible to vote, 793,092 shares (or 57.3%) were voted in favor and 11,060 shares abstained. Of the unaffiliated shares, however, the proposal passed by a bare 50.28% majority vote.

E. Procedural History

The amended complaint asserts three separate claims. Count I alleges that the defendants breached their fiduciary duties to the First Niles shareholders by rejecting the First Place merger offer and abandoning the Sales Process. Count II alleges that the defendants breached their fiduciary duty of disclosure by disseminating a materially false and misleading Reclassification Proxy. Count III alleges that the defendants breached their fiduciary duties by effecting the Reclassification.

ANALYSIS

I. THE COURT OF CHANCERY ERRONEOUSLY DISMISSED COUNT I OF THE COMPLAINT

Count I of the complaint alleges that the defendants breached their duties of loyalty and care as directors and officers of First Niles by abandoning the Sales Process. Specifically, plaintiffs claim that the defendants improperly: (1) sabotaged the due diligence aspect of the Sales Process, (2) rejected the First Place offer, and (3) terminated the Sales Process, all for the purpose of retaining the benefits of continued incumbency.

[The court affirmed the chancellor's decision not to apply the intermediate scrutiny standard of *Unocal*, since the complaint did not allege any "defensive" action by the Board, noting that rejecting an acquisition offer, without more, is not "defensive action" under *Unocal*. It then moved to address the Chancery Court's ruling that the plaintiff had failed to rebut the business judgment rule.]

... Because the Board had "initiated the Sales Process on its own accord, seemingly as a market check as part of an exploration of strategic alternatives[,]" that supported the Board's stated business purpose—to reduce corporate expense associated with federal securities law compliance. The Vice Chancellor also concluded that the complaint failed to plead facts sufficient to infer disloyalty, and that given the Board's extensive discussions with, and receipt of reports from, the Financial Advisor, and given the involvement of specially retained Outside Counsel, the alleged facts were insufficient to establish a violation of the duty of care. The court therefore concluded that the challenged conduct was entitled to business judgment protection, which required the dismissal of Count I. ...

B. The Court of Chancery Misapplied the Business Judgment Standard

The plaintiffs next claim that the legal sufficiency of Count I should have been reviewed under the entire fairness standard. That claim is assessed within the framework of the business judgment standard, which is "a presumption that in making a business decision the directors of a corporation acted on an informed basis, in good faith and in the honest belief that the action taken was in the best interests of the company."

Procedurally, the plaintiffs have the burden to plead facts sufficient to rebut that presumption. On a motion to dismiss, the pled facts must support a reasonable inference that in making the challenged decision, the board of directors breached either its duty of loyalty or its duty of care. If the plaintiff fails to satisfy that burden, "a court will not substitute its judgment for that of the board if the ... decision can be 'attributed to any rational business purpose.'"

We first consider the sufficiency of Count I as against the Director Defendants. That Count alleges that those defendants (together with non-party director Zuzolo) improperly rejected a value-maximizing bid from First Place and terminated the Sales Process. Plaintiffs allege that the defendants rejected the First Place bid to preserve personal benefits, including retaining their positions and pay as directors, as well as valuable outside business opportunities. The complaint further alleges that the Board failed to deliberate before deciding to reject the First Place bid and to terminate the Sales Process. Indeed, plaintiffs emphasize, the Board retained the Financial Advisor to advise it on the Sales Process, yet repeatedly disregarded the Financial Advisor's advice.

A board's decision not to pursue a merger opportunity is normally reviewed within the traditional business judgment framework. In that context the board is entitled to a strong presumption in its favor, because

B. Fiduciary Duties and Legal Challenges to Board Action

implicit in the board's statutory authority to propose a merger, is also the power to decline to do so.[29]

Our analysis of whether the Board's termination of the Sales Process merits the business judgment presumption is two pronged. First, did the Board reach its decision in the good faith pursuit of a legitimate corporate interest? Second, did the Board do so advisedly? For the Board's decision here to be entitled to the business judgment presumption, both questions must be answered affirmatively.

We consider first whether Count I alleges a cognizable claim that the Board breached its duty of loyalty. In *TW Services v. SWT Acquisition Corporation*, the Court of Chancery recognized that a board's decision to decline a merger is often rooted in distinctively corporate concerns, such as enhancing the corporation's long term share value, or "a plausible concern that the level of debt likely to be borne by [the target company] following any merger would be detrimental to the long term function of th[at][c]ompany." A good faith pursuit of legitimate concerns of this kind will satisfy the first prong of the analysis.

Here, the plaintiffs allege that the Director Defendants had a disqualifying self-interest because they were financially motivated to maintain the status quo. A claim of this kind must be viewed with caution, because to argue that directors have an entrenchment motive solely because they could lose their positions following an acquisition is, to an extent, tautological. By its very nature, a board decision to reject a merger proposal could always enable a plaintiff to assert that a majority of the directors had an entrenchment motive. For that reason, the plaintiffs must plead, in addition to a motive to retain corporate control, other facts sufficient to state a cognizable claim that the Director Defendants acted disloyally.[32]

The plaintiffs have done that here. At the time the Sales Process was terminated, the Board members were Stephens, Kramer, Eddy, Zuzolo and Gantler. Only Gantler voted to accept the First Place merger bid. The pled facts are sufficient to establish disloyalty of at least three (i.e., a majority) of the remaining directors, which suffices to rebut the business judgment presumption. First, the Reclassification Proxy itself admits that the Company's directors and officers had "a conflict of interest with respect to [the Reclassification] because he or she is in a position to structure it in a way

---

29. *See* 8 Del. C. §251 for the grant of authority to enter into a merger; *see also TW Servs.*, 1989 WL 20290, at *10-11; *see generally Kahn v. MSB Bancorp, Inc.*, 1998 WL 409355 (Del. Ch. July 16, 1998), *aff'd*, 734 A.2d 158 (Table) (Del. 1999) (describing a board's power under Section 251 and reviewing a decision not to negotiate a merger under the business judgment standard).

32. *See Pogostin v. Rice*, 480 A.2d 619, 627 (Del. 1984), *overruled on other grounds by Brehm v. Eisner*, 746 A.2d 244 (Del. 2000) ("plaintiffs have failed to plead any facts supporting their claim[s] that the . . . board rejected the . . . offer solely to retain control. Rather, plaintiffs seek to establish a motive or primary purpose to retain control only by showing that the . . . board opposed a tender offer. Acceptance of such an argument would condemn any board, which successfully avoided a takeover, regardless of whether that board properly determined that it was acting in the best interests of the shareholders.").

that benefits his or her interests differently from the interest of the unaffiliated stockholders." Second, a director-specific analysis establishes (for Rule 12(b)(6) purposes) that a majority of the Board was conflicted.

Stephens: Aside from Stephens losing his long held positions as President, Chairman and CEO of First Niles and the Bank, the plaintiffs have alleged specific conduct from which a duty of loyalty violation can reasonably be inferred. Stephens never responded to Cortland's due diligence request. The Financial Advisor noted that Stephens' failure to respond had caused Cortland to withdraw its bid. Even after Cortland had offered First Niles an extension, Stephens did not furnish the necessary due diligence materials, nor did he inform the Board of these due diligence problems until after Cortland withdrew. Cortland had also explicitly stated in its bid letter that the incumbent Board would be terminated if Cortland acquired First Niles. From these alleged facts it may reasonably be inferred that what motivated Stephens' unexplained failure to respond promptly to Cortland's due diligence request was his personal financial interest, as opposed to the interests of the shareholders. That same inference can be drawn from Stephens' response to the First Place bid: Count I alleges that Stephens attempted to "sabotage" the First Place due diligence request in a manner similar to what occurred with Cortland.

Thus, the pled facts provide a sufficient basis to conclude, for purposes of a Rule 12(b)(6) motion to dismiss, that Stephens acted disloyally.

Kramer: Director Kramer's alleged circumstances establish a similar disqualifying conflict. Kramer was the President of William Kramer & Son, a heating and air conditioning company in Niles that provided heating and air conditioning services to the Bank. It is reasonable to infer that Kramer feared that if the Company were sold his firm would lose the Bank as a client. The loss of such a major client would be economically significant, because the complaint alleges that Kramer was a man of comparatively modest means, and that his company had few major assets and was completely leveraged. Because Kramer would suffer significant injury to his personal business interest if the Sales Process went forward, those pled facts are sufficient to support a reasonable inference that Kramer disloyally voted to terminate the Sales Process and support the Privatization Proposal.

Zuzolo: As earlier noted, Director Zuzolo was a principal in a small law firm in Niles that frequently provided legal services to First Niles and the Bank. Zuzolo was also the sole owner of a real estate title company that provided title services in nearly all of Home Federal's real estate transactions. Because Zuzolo, like Kramer, had a strong personal interest in having the Sales Process not go forward, the same reasonable inferences that flow from Kramer's personal business interest can be drawn in Zuzolo's case.

In summary, the plaintiffs have alleged facts sufficient to establish, for purposes of a motion to dismiss, that a majority of the First Niles Board

B. Fiduciary Duties and Legal Challenges to Board Action

acted disloyally. Because a cognizable claim of disloyalty rebuts the business judgment presumption, we need not reach the separate question of whether, in deciding to terminate the Sales Process, the Director Defendants acted advisedly (i.e., with due care). Because the claim of disloyalty was subject to entire fairness review, the Court of Chancery erred in dismissing Count I as to the Director Defendants on the basis of the business judgment presumption.

In dismissing Count I as to the Officer Defendants, the Court of Chancery similarly erred. The Court of Chancery has held, and the parties do not dispute, that corporate officers owe fiduciary duties that are identical to those owed by corporate directors. That issue — whether or not officers owe fiduciary duties identical to those of directors — has been characterized as a matter of first impression for this Court. In the past, we have implied that officers of Delaware corporations, like directors, owe fiduciary duties of care and loyalty, and that the fiduciary duties of officers are the same as those of directors. We now explicitly so hold. The only question presented here is whether the complaint alleges sufficiently detailed acts of wrongdoing by Stephens and Safarek to state a claim that they breached their fiduciary duties as officers. We conclude that it does.

Stephens and Safarek were responsible for preparing the due diligence materials for the three firms that expressed an interest in acquiring First Niles. The alleged facts that make it reasonable to infer that Stephens violated his duty of loyalty as a director, also establish his violation of that same duty as an officer. It also is reasonably inferable that Safarek aided and abetted Stephens' separate loyalty breach. Safarek, as First Niles' Vice President and Treasurer, depended upon Stephen's continued good will to retain his job and the benefits that it generated. Because Safarek was in no position to act independently of Stephens, it may be inferred that by assisting Stephens to "sabotage" the due diligence process, Safarek also breached his duty of loyalty.

The Court of Chancery found otherwise. Having characterized Safarek's actions as causing "a delay of a matter of days, or at most a couple of weeks," the Vice Chancellor observed that he could not see how that "conceivably could be a breach of Safarek's fiduciary duties." This analysis is inappropriate on a motion to dismiss. The complaint alleges that Safarek never responded to Cortland's due diligence requests and that as a result, Cortland withdrew a competitive bid for First Niles. Those facts support a reasonable inference that Safarek and Stephens attempted to sabotage the Cortland and First Place due diligence process. On a motion to dismiss, the Court of Chancery was not free to disregard that reasonable inference, or to discount it by weighing it against other, perhaps contrary, inferences that might also be drawn. By dismissing Count I as applied to Stephens and Safarek as officers of First Niles, the trial court erred.

NOTES AND QUESTIONS

1. **The deal.** Compare where value would likely arise from the various potential bidders. Three other banking companies indicated interest in buying in a stock-for-stock transaction at a small premium. The privatization transaction offered the possibility as described in the company's proxy to "save significant legal, accounting and administrative expenses" including costs attributed to compliance with the requirements added by the Sarbanes-Oxley Act in 2002 (e.g., requirements for more intense internal controls). Those receiving the new preferred shares would get a higher dividend, but both preferred shareholders and common shareholders would have reduced liquidity as the stock would no longer be traded on Nasdaq.

2. **Alternative legal forms.** The firm's proxy statement disclosed the board had considered various alternatives including a cash-out merger, a reverse stock split, and an issuer tender offer. What was the advantage of the recapitalization that the board ultimately undertook? The discussion in Chapter 3 should be a tip off here.

3. **Federal going private regulation.** This case illustrates the federal disclosure imposed under §13e of the Securities Exchange Act of 1934 and Rule 13e-3 triggered by a transaction in which shareholders will lose their publicly registered status and the disclosure to shareholders and other investor protections that come with such status.

4. **Shareholder ratification of possible director breach of fiduciary duty.** Both *Van Gorkom* and *Gantler* allege director and officer actions said to violate a fiduciary duty followed by a subsequent shareholder vote on the transaction which the defendants would like to rely on for exoneration. *Van Gorkom* cited the settled rule in Delaware that "where a majority of fully informed stockholders ratify action of even interested directors, an attack on the ratified transaction normally must fail." But the court found the Trans Union shareholders were not fully informed because of multiple material deficiencies in the proxy statement. In *Gantler*, the court found two deficiencies that blocked ratification:

> First, because a shareholder vote was required to amend the certificate of incorporation, that approving vote could not also operate to "ratify" the challenged conduct of the interested directors. Second, the adjudicated cognizable claim that the Reclassification Proxy contained a material misrepresentation, eliminates an essential predicate for applying the doctrine, namely, that the shareholder vote was fully informed.

The second reason parallels *Van Gorkom*, but the first is in some conflict with the import of the earlier case so that the court holds "to the extent that *Van Gorkom* holds otherwise, it is overruled." The court explained its understanding of ratification this way:

> Under current Delaware case law, the scope and effect of the common law doctrine of shareholder ratification is unclear, making it difficult to apply that doctrine in a

B. Fiduciary Duties and Legal Challenges to Board Action

coherent manner. As the Court of Chancery has noted in *In re Wheelabrator Technologies, Inc., Shareholders Litigation* [663 A.2d 1194, 1202 and n.4 (Del. Ch. 1995)]:

> [The doctrine of ratification] might be thought to lack coherence because the decisions addressing the effect of shareholder "ratification" have fragmented that subject into three distinct compartments.... In its "classic" ... form, shareholder ratification describes the situation where shareholders approve board action that, legally speaking, could be accomplished without any shareholder approval.... "[C]lassic" ratification involves the voluntary addition of an independent layer of shareholder approval in circumstances where shareholder approval is not legally required. But "shareholder ratification" has also been used to describe the effect of an informed shareholder vote that was statutorily required for the transaction to have legal existence.... That [the Delaware courts] have used the same term is such highly diverse sets of factual circumstances, without regard to their possible functional differences, suggests that "shareholder ratification" has now acquired an expanded meaning intended to describe any approval of challenged board action by a fully informed vote of shareholders, irrespective of whether that shareholder vote is legally required for the transaction to attain legal existence.

To restore coherence and clarity to this area of our law, we hold that the scope of the shareholder ratification doctrine must be limited to its so-called "classic" form; that is, to circumstances where a fully informed shareholder vote approves director action that does *not* legally require shareholder approval in order to become legally effective. Moreover, the only director action or conduct that can be ratified is that which the shareholders are specifically asked to approve. With one exception, the "cleansing" effect of such a ratifying shareholder vote is to subject the challenged director action to business judgment review, as opposed to "extinguishing" the claim altogether (*i.e.*, obviating all judicial review of the challenged action).[54]

To avoid confusion about the doctrinal clarifications set forth in Part III A of this Opinion, we note that they apply only to the common law doctrine of shareholder ratification. They are not intended to affect or alter our jurisprudence governing the effect of an approving vote of disinterested shareholders under 8 Del. C. §144....

The Court of Chancery held that although Count III of the complaint pled facts establishing that the Reclassification Proposal was an interested transaction not entitled to business judgment protection, the shareholders' fully informed vote "ratifying" that Proposal reinstated the business judgment presumption. That ruling was legally erroneous, for several reasons. First, the ratification doctrine does not apply to transactions where shareholder approval is statutorily required. Here, the Reclassification could not become legally effective without a statutorily mandated shareholder vote approving the amendment to First Niles' certificate of incorporation. Second, because

---

54. To the extent that *Smith v. Van Gorkom* holds otherwise, it is overruled. 488 A.2d 858, 889-90 (Del. 1985). The only species of claim that shareholder ratification can validly extinguish is a claim that the directors lacked the authority to take action that was later ratified. Nothing herein should be read as altering the well-established principle that void acts such as fraud, gift, waste and ultra vires acts cannot be ratified by a less than unanimous shareholder vote. *See Michelson v. Duncan*, 407 A.2d 211, 219 (Del. 1979) ("[W]here a claim of gift or waste of assets, fraud or [u]ltra vires is asserted that a less than unanimous shareholder ratification is not a full defense."); *see also Harbor Fin. Partners v. Huizenga*, 751 A.2d 879, 896 (Del. Ch. 1999) (explaining that ultra vires, fraud, and gift or waste of corporate assets are "void" acts that cannot be ratified by less than unanimous shareholder consent); *accord Solomon v. Armstrong*, 747 A.2d at 1115. "Voidable" acts are those beyond management's powers, but where they are performed in the best interests of the corporation they may be ratified by a majority vote of disinterested shareholders. *See Michelson*, 407 A.2d at 219.

we have determined that the complaint states a cognizable claim that the Reclassification Proxy was materially misleading (*see* Part II, *supra*, of this Opinion), that precludes ruling at this procedural juncture, as a matter of law, that the Reclassification was fully informed. Therefore, the approving shareholder vote did not operate as a "ratification" of the challenged conduct in any legally meaningful sense.

In limiting traditional ratification, the court is not saying the director action cannot stand, just that it will be tested in other ways. *See, e.g.*, In re Wayport, Inc. Litigation, 76 A.3d 296, 314-15 (Del. Ch. 2013) and the discussion of disclosure duties in Chapter 12 of this book.

5. Conflicts when a board considers a deal. Facts that give rise to a possible breach of duty of loyalty to rebut the business judgment rule, as occurred in *Gantler*, can arise in variety of situations. In a Delaware case, the court found plaintiff could survive a motion to dismiss based on well-pleaded facts showing that a 37-percent shareholder who needed liquidity dominated the board through "a pattern of threats aimed at intimidating them, thus rendering them non-independent for purposes of voting on the Merger." New Jersey Carpenters Pension Fund v. Infogroup, Inc., 2011 WL 4825888 (Del. Ch. Oct. 6, 2011). But see, In re Synthes, Inc. Shareholder Litigation, 50 A.3d 1022 (Del. Ch. 2012) (no breach based on asserted need for liquidity on facts where all shareholders got same premium). Another Delaware case illustrates how conflict plays out given the exculpation discussed in this chapter. The primary conflict in that case, involving a going private transaction of the Del Monte Foods Company, related to the investment banker, Barclays Capital (Barclays). Barclays began as a financial adviser to Del Monte but did not disclose its explicit goal of later providing buy-side financing to the acquirer (which apparently would bring a larger fee). It steered one of Del Monte's owners into a "club bid" with the potential bidder with whom Barclays had the strongest relationship. Later Barclays asked that bidder for a third of the buy-side financing. That is a conflict as to the banker, but what impact does it have on the actions of the directors? The court found (on the basis of the preliminary record presented) a claim of a violation of the directors' fiduciary duty by "failing to provide the serious oversight that would have checked Barclays' misconduct." What kind of duty is that given what you have seen in *Van Gorkom* and *Gantler*? It is closer to *Van Gorkom*. But what about §102(b)(7)? The court noted "unless further discovery reveals different facts, the one-two punch of exculpation under §102(b)(7) and full protection under §141(e) makes the chances of a judgment for money damages vanishingly small." In re Del Monte Foods Company Shareholders Litigation, 25 A.3d 813, 818 (Del Ch. 2012). What then? The exculpation does not affect injunctive relief, which the court gave in the form of postponing the vote for 20 days and noted that aiders and abettors were not protected by §102(b)(7) in the same way as directors against the possibility of money damages. *Id.* at 818-819. After the shareholders approved the deal, the case settled for $89.4 million payment, funded by the new owners of the company and the banker.

6. Good faith. The availability of this "care" channel to move courts off deference was dramatically affected by Delaware's exculpation statute §102(b)(7), which blocks director liability for damages that might arise for alleged breaches of duty of care. The omission of loyalty and good faith from this exculpation not surprisingly provided incentives for litigants to categorize director failings as within those categories. *See, e.g.,* Stone v. Ritter, 911 A.2d 362 (Del. 2006).

It also led to an effort to develop good faith, previously a term not well-defined, to do more work as a possible way to avoid exculpation, eventually resulting in a narrowing interpretation of the Delaware Supreme Court in the case which follows.

Lyondell Chemical Co. v. Ryan
970 A.2d 235 (Del. Sup. Ct. 2009) (en banc)

BERGER, Justice.

We accepted this interlocutory appeal to consider a claim that directors failed to act in good faith in conducting the sale of their company. The Court of Chancery decided that "unexplained inaction" permits a reasonable inference that the directors may have consciously disregarded their fiduciary duties. The trial court expressed concern about the speed with which the transaction was consummated; the directors' failure to negotiate better terms; and their failure to seek potentially superior deals. But the record establishes that the directors were disinterested and independent; that they were generally aware of the company's value and its prospects; and that they considered the offer, under the time constraints imposed by the buyer, with the assistance of financial and legal advisors. At most, this record creates a triable issue of fact on the question of whether the directors exercised due care. There is no evidence, however, from which to infer that the directors knowingly ignored their responsibilities, thereby breaching their duty of loyalty. Accordingly, the directors are entitled to the entry of summary judgment.

FACTUAL AND PROCEDURAL BACKGROUND

Before the merger at issue, Lyondell Chemical Company ("Lyondell") was the third largest independent, publicly traded chemical company in North America. Dan Smith ("Smith") was Lyondell's Chairman and CEO. Lyondell's other ten directors were independent and many were, or had been, CEOs of other large, publicly traded companies. Basell AF ("Basell") is a privately held Luxembourg company owned by Leonard Blavatnik ("Blavatnik") through his ownership of Access Industries. Basell is in the business of polyolefin technology, production and marketing.

In April 2006, Blavatnik told Smith that Basell was interested in acquiring Lyondell. A few months later, Basell sent a letter to Lyondell's board offering $26.50-$28.50 per share. Lyondell determined that the price was inadequate and that it was not interested in selling. During the next year, Lyondell prospered and no potential acquirors expressed interest in the company. In May 2007, an Access affiliate filed a Schedule 13D with the Securities and Exchange Commission disclosing its right to acquire an 8.3% block of Lyondell stock owned by Occidental Petroleum Corporation. The Schedule 13D also disclosed Blavatnik's interest in possible transactions with Lyondell.

In response to the Schedule 13D, the Lyondell board immediately convened a special meeting. The board recognized that the 13D signaled to the market that the company was "in play,"[1] but the directors decided to take a "wait and see" approach. A few days later, Apollo Management, L.P. contacted Smith to suggest a management-led LBO, but Smith rejected that proposal. In late June 2007, Basell announced that it had entered into a $9.6 billion merger agreement with Huntsman Corporation ("Huntsman"), a specialty chemical company. Basell apparently reconsidered, however, after Hexion Specialty Chemicals, Inc. made a topping bid for Huntsman. Faced with competition for Huntsman, Blavatnik returned his attention to Lyondell.

On July 9, 2007, Blavatnik met with Smith to discuss an all-cash deal at $40 per share. Smith responded that $40 was too low, and Blavatnik raised his offer to $44-$45 per share. Smith told Blavatnik that he would present the proposal to the board, but that he thought the board would reject it. Smith advised Blavatnik to give Lyondell his best offer, since Lyondell really was not on the market. The meeting ended at that point, but Blavatnik asked Smith to call him later in the day. When Smith called, Blavatnik offered to pay $48 per share. Under Blavatnik's proposal, Basell would require no financing contingency, but Lyondell would have to agree to a $400 million break-up fee and sign a merger agreement by July 16, 2007.

Smith called a special meeting of the Lyondell board on July 10, 2007 to review and consider Basell's offer. The meeting lasted slightly less than one hour, during which time the board reviewed valuation material that had been prepared by Lyondell management for presentation at the regular board meeting, which was scheduled for the following day. The board also discussed the Basell offer, the status of the Huntsman merger, and the likelihood that another party might be interested in Lyondell. The board instructed Smith to obtain a written offer from Basell and more details about Basell's financing.

Blavatnik agreed to the board's request, but also made an additional demand. Basell had until July 11 to make a higher bid for Huntsman, so

---

1. On the day that the 13D was made public, Lyondell's stock went from $33 to $37 per share.

B. Fiduciary Duties and Legal Challenges to Board Action 133

Blavatnik asked Smith to find out whether the Lyondell board would provide a firm indication of interest in his proposal by the end of that day. The Lyondell board met on July 11, again for less than one hour, to consider the Basell proposal and how it compared to the benefits of remaining independent. The board decided that it was interested, authorized the retention of Deutsche Bank Securities, Inc. ("Deutsche Bank") as its financial advisor, and instructed Smith to negotiate with Blavatnik.

Basell then announced that it would not raise its offer for Huntsman, and Huntsman terminated the Basell merger agreement. From July 12-July 15 the parties negotiated the terms of a Lyondell merger agreement; Basell conducted due diligence; Deutsche Bank prepared a "fairness" opinion; and Lyondell conducted its regularly scheduled board meeting. The Lyondell board discussed the Basell proposal again on July 12, and later instructed Smith to try to negotiate better terms. Specifically, the board wanted a higher price, a go-shop provision,[2] and a reduced break-up fee. As the trial court noted, Blavatnik was "incredulous." He had offered his best price, which was a substantial premium, and the deal had to be concluded on his schedule. As a sign of good faith, however, Blavatnik agreed to reduce the break-up fee from $400 million to $385 million.

On July 16, 2007, the board met to consider the Basell merger agreement. Lyondell's management, as well as its financial and legal advisers, presented reports analyzing the merits of the deal. The advisors explained that, notwithstanding the no-shop provision in the merger agreement, Lyondell would be able to consider any superior proposals that might be made because of the "fiduciary out" provision. In addition, Deutsche Bank reviewed valuation models derived from "bullish" and more conservative financial projections. Several of those valuations yielded a range that did not even reach $48 per share, and Deutsche Bank opined that the proposed merger price was fair. Indeed, the bank's managing director described the merger price as "an absolute home run." Deutsche Bank also identified other possible acquirors and explained why it believed no other entity would top Basell's offer. After considering the presentations, the Lyondell board voted to approve the merger and recommend it to the stockholders. At a special stockholders' meeting held on November 20, 2007, the merger was approved by more than 99% of the voted shares. . . .

DISCUSSION

The class action complaint challenging this $13 billion cash merger alleges that the Lyondell directors breached their "fiduciary duties of care, loyalty and candor . . . and . . . put their personal interests ahead of the interests of the Lyondell shareholders." Specifically, the complaint alleges

---

2. A "go-shop" provision allows the seller to seek other buyers for a specified period after the agreement is signed.

that: 1) the merger price was grossly insufficient; 2) the directors were motivated to approve the merger for their own self-interest;[5] 3) the process by which the merger was negotiated was flawed; 4) the directors agreed to unreasonable deal protection provisions; and 5) the preliminary proxy statement omitted numerous material facts. The trial court rejected all claims except those directed at the process by which the directors sold the company and the deal protection provisions in the merger agreement.

The remaining claims are but two aspects of a single claim, under *Revlon v. MacAndrews & Forbes Holdings, Inc.*, that the directors failed to obtain the best available price in selling the company. As the trial court correctly noted, *Revlon* did not create any new fiduciary duties. It simply held that the "board must perform its fiduciary duties in the service of a specific objective: maximizing the sale price of the enterprise." The trial court reviewed the record, and found that Ryan might be able to prevail at trial on a claim that the Lyondell directors breached their duty of care. But Lyondell's charter includes an exculpatory provision, pursuant to 8 Del. C. §102(b)(7), protecting the directors from personal liability for breaches of the duty of care. Thus, this case turns on whether any arguable shortcomings on the part of the Lyondell directors also implicate their duty of loyalty, a breach of which is not exculpated. Because the trial court determined that the board was independent and was not motivated by self-interest or ill will, the sole issue is whether the directors are entitled to summary judgment on the claim that they breached their duty of loyalty by failing to act in good faith.

This Court examined "good faith" in two recent decisions. In *In re Walt Disney Co. Deriv. Litig.*,[9] the Court discussed the range of conduct that might be characterized as bad faith, and concluded that bad faith encompasses not only an intent to harm but also intentional dereliction of duty:

> [A]t least three different categories of fiduciary behavior are candidates for the "bad faith" pejorative label. The first category involves so-called "subjective bad faith," that is, fiduciary conduct motivated by an actual intent to do harm. . . . [S]uch conduct constitutes classic, quintessential bad faith. . . .
>
> The second category of conduct, which is at the opposite end of the spectrum, involves lack of due care — that is, fiduciary action taken solely by reason of gross negligence and without any malevolent intent. . . . [W]e address the issue of whether gross negligence (including failure to inform one's self of available material facts), without more, can also constitute bad faith. The answer is clearly no. . . .
>
> That leaves the third category of fiduciary conduct, which falls in between the first two categories. . . . This third category is what the Chancellor's definition of bad faith — intentional dereliction of duty, a conscious disregard for one's responsibilities — is intended to capture. The question is whether such misconduct

---

5. The directors' alleged financial interest is the fact that they would receive cash for their stock options.

9. 906 A.2d 27 (Del. 2006).

B. Fiduciary Duties and Legal Challenges to Board Action 135

is properly treated as a non-exculpable, nonindemnifiable violation of the fiduciary duty to act in good faith. In our view, it must be. . . .

The *Disney* decision expressly disavowed any attempt to provide a comprehensive or exclusive definition of "bad faith."

A few months later, in *Stone v. Ritter*,[11] this Court addressed the concept of bad faith in the context of an "oversight" claim. We adopted the standard articulated ten years earlier, in *In re Caremark Int'l Deriv. Litig.*:[12]

> [W]here a claim of directorial liability for corporate loss is predicated upon ignorance of liability creating activities within the corporation . . . only a sustained or systematic failure of the board to exercise oversight — such as an utter failure to attempt to assure a reasonable information and reporting system exists — will establish the lack of good faith that is a necessary condition to liability.

The *Stone* Court explained that the *Caremark* standard is fully consistent with the *Disney* definition of bad faith. *Stone* also clarified any possible ambiguity about the directors' mental state, holding that "imposition of liability requires a showing that the directors knew that they were not discharging their fiduciary obligations."

The Court of Chancery recognized these legal principles, but it denied summary judgment in order to obtain a more complete record before deciding whether the directors had acted in bad faith. Under other circumstances, deferring a decision to expand the record would be appropriate. Here, however, the trial court reviewed the existing record under a mistaken view of the applicable law. Three factors contributed to that mistake. First, the trial court imposed *Revlon* duties on the Lyondell directors before they either had decided to sell, or before the sale had become inevitable. Second, the court read *Revlon* and its progeny as creating a set of requirements that must be satisfied during the sale process. Third, the trial court equated an arguably imperfect attempt to carry out *Revlon* duties with a knowing disregard of one's duties that constitutes bad faith.

Summary judgment may be granted if there are no material issues of fact in dispute and the moving party is entitled to judgment as a matter of law. The facts, and all reasonable inferences, must be considered in the light most favorable to the non-moving party. The Court of Chancery identified several undisputed facts that would support the entry of judgment in favor of the Lyondell directors: the directors were "active, sophisticated, and generally aware of the value of the Company and the conditions of the markets in which the Company operated." They had reason to believe that no other bidders would emerge, given the price Basell had offered and the limited universe of companies that might be interested in acquiring Lyondell's unique assets. Smith negotiated the price up from $40 to $48 per

---

11. 911 A.2d 362 (Del. 2006).
12. 698 A.2d 959, 971 (Del. Ch. 1996).

share—a price that Deutsche Bank opined was fair. Finally, no other acquiror expressed interest during the four months between the merger announcement and the stockholder vote.

Other facts, however, led the trial court to "question the adequacy of the Board's knowledge and efforts. . . . After the Schedule 13D was filed in May, the directors apparently took no action to prepare for a possible acquisition proposal. The merger was negotiated and finalized in less than one week, during which time the directors met for a total of only seven hours to consider the matter. The directors did not seriously press Blavatnik for a better price, nor did they conduct even a limited market check. Moreover, although the deal protections were not unusual or preclusive, the trial court was troubled by "the Board's decision to grant considerable protection to a deal that may not have been adequately vetted under *Revlon*."

The trial court found the directors' failure to act during the two months after the filing of the Basell Schedule 13D critical to its analysis of their good faith. The court pointedly referred to the directors' "two months of slothful indifference despite *knowing* that the Company was in play," and the fact that they "languidly awaited overtures from potential suitors. . . ." In the end, the trial court found that it was this "failing" that warranted denial of their motion for summary judgment:

> [T]he Opinion clearly questions whether the Defendants "engaged" in the sale process. . . . This is where the 13D filing in May 2007 and the subsequent two months of (apparent) Board inactivity become critical. . . . [T]he Directors made *no apparent effort* to arm themselves with *specific knowledge* about the present value of the Company in the May through July 2007 time period, despite *admittedly knowing* that the 13D filing . . . effectively put the Company "in play," and, therefore, presumably, also knowing that an offer for the sale of the Company could occur at any time. It is these facts that raise the specter of "bad faith" in the present summary judgment record. . . .

The problem with the trial court's analysis is that *Revlon* duties do not arise simply because a company is "in play."[23] The duty to seek the best available price applies only when a company embarks on a transaction—on its own initiative or in response to an unsolicited offer—that will result in a change of control.[24] Basell's Schedule 13D did put the Lyondell directors, and the market in general, on notice that Basell was interested in acquiring Lyondell. The directors responded by promptly holding a special meeting to consider whether Lyondell should take any action. The directors decided that they would neither put the company up for sale nor institute defensive measures to fend off a possible hostile offer. Instead, they decided to take a "wait and see" approach. That decision was an entirely appropriate exercise of the directors' business judgment. The time for action under

---

23. *Paramount Communications, Inc. v. Time, Inc.*, 571 A.2d 1140, 1151 (Del. 1989).
24. *In re Santa Fe Pac. Corp. S'holder Litig.*, 669 A.2d 59, 71 (1995).

Revlon did not begin until July 10, 2007, when the directors began negotiating the sale of Lyondell.

The Court of Chancery focused on the directors' two months of inaction, when it should have focused on the one week during which they considered Basell's offer. During that one week, the directors met several times; their CEO tried to negotiate better terms; they evaluated Lyondell's value, the price offered and the likelihood of obtaining a better price; and then the directors approved the merger. The trial court acknowledged that the directors' conduct during those seven days might not demonstrate anything more than lack of due care. But the court remained skeptical about the directors' good faith—at least on the present record. That lingering concern was based on the trial court's synthesis of the *Revlon* line of cases, which led it to the erroneous conclusion that directors must follow one of several courses of action to satisfy their *Revlon* duties.

There is only one *Revlon* duty—to "[get] the best price for the stockholders at a sale of the company." No court can tell directors exactly how to accomplish that goal, because they will be facing a unique combination of circumstances, many of which will be outside their control. As we noted in *Barkan v. Amsted Industries, Inc.*," there is no single blueprint that a board must follow to fulfill its duties." That said, our courts have highlighted both the positive and negative aspects of various boards' conduct under *Revlon*. The trial court drew several principles from those cases: directors must "engage actively in the sale process,"[28] and they must confirm that they have obtained the best available price either by conducting an auction, by conducting a market check, or by demonstrating "an impeccable knowledge of the market."

The Lyondell directors did not conduct an auction or a market check, and they did not satisfy the trial court that they had the "impeccable" market knowledge that the court believed was necessary to excuse their failure to pursue one of the first two alternatives. As a result, the Court of Chancery was unable to conclude that the directors had met their burden under *Revlon*. In evaluating the totality of the circumstances, even on this limited record, we would be inclined to hold otherwise. But we would not question the trial court's decision to seek additional evidence if the issue were whether the directors had exercised due care. Where, as here, the issue is whether the directors failed to act in good faith, the analysis is very different, and the existing record mandates the entry of judgment in favor of the directors.

---

28. *See, e.g., Barkan v. Amsted Industries, Inc.*, 567 A.2d at 1287 [(Del. 1989)] (Directors need not conduct a market check if they have reliable basis for belief that price offered is best possible); *Paramount Communications, Inc. v. QVC Network, Inc.*, 637 A.2d 34, 49 (Del. 1994) (No-shop provision impermissibly interfered with directors' ability to negotiate with another known bidder); *In re Netsmart Technologies, Inc., Shareholders Litig.*, 924 A.2d 171, 199 (Del. Ch. 2007) (Plaintiff likely to succeed on claim based on board's failure to consider strategic buyers).

As discussed above, bad faith will be found if a "fiduciary intentionally fails to act in the face of a known duty to act, demonstrating a conscious disregard for his duties." The trial court decided that the *Revlon* sale process must follow one of three courses, and that the Lyondell directors did not discharge that "known set of [*Revlon*] 'duties.'" But, as noted, there are no legally prescribed steps that directors must follow to satisfy their *Revlon* duties. Thus, the directors' failure to take any specific steps during the sale process could not have demonstrated a conscious disregard of their duties. More importantly, there is a vast difference between an inadequate or flawed effort to carry out fiduciary duties and a conscious disregard for those duties.

Directors' decisions must be reasonable, not perfect.[33] "In the transactional context, [an] extreme set of facts [is] required to sustain a disloyalty claim premised on the notion that disinterested directors were intentionally disregarding their duties."[34] The trial court denied summary judgment because the Lyondell directors' "unexplained inaction" prevented the court from determining that they had acted in good faith. But, if the directors failed to do all that they should have under the circumstances, they breached their duty of care. Only if they knowingly and completely failed to undertake their responsibilities would they breach their duty of loyalty. The trial court approached the record from the wrong perspective. Instead of questioning whether disinterested, independent directors did everything that they (arguably) should have done to obtain the best sale price, the inquiry should have been whether those directors utterly failed to attempt to obtain the best sale price.

Viewing the record in this manner leads to only one possible conclusion. The Lyondell directors met several times to consider Basell's premium offer. They were generally aware of the value of their company and they knew the chemical company market. The directors solicited and followed the advice of their financial and legal advisors. They attempted to negotiate a higher offer even though all the evidence indicates that Basell had offered a "blowout" price.[37] Finally, they approved the merger agreement, because "it was simply too good not to pass along [to the stockholders] for their consideration." We assume, as we must on summary judgment, that the Lyondell directors did absolutely nothing to prepare for Basell's offer, and that they did not even consider conducting a market check before agreeing to the merger. Even so, this record clearly establishes that the Lyondell directors did not breach their duty of loyalty by failing to act in good faith. In concluding otherwise, the Court of Chancery reversibly erred.

---

33. *Paramount Communications, Inc. v. QVC Network, Inc.*, 637 A.2d at 45.
34. *In re Lear Corp. S'holder Litig.*, 2008 WL 4053221 at *11 (Del. Ch.).
37. . . . The trial court disparages the Lyondell directors' characterization of $48 per share as a "blowout" premium. But the record evidence—including testimony from Basell directors who voted against the merger because they believed the price was too high—supports such a description.

CONCLUSION

Based on the foregoing, the decision of the Court of Chancery is reversed and this matter is remanded for entry of judgment in favor of the Lyondell directors. Jurisdiction is not retained.

NOTES AND QUESTIONS

1. **The deal.** The target, Lyondell, a chemical company, was not necessarily looking to sell when Len Blavatnik, a Russian-born entrepreneur who had acquired a variety of businesses, first contacted Lyondell's CEO about a possible deal. Lyondell's rebuff of that offer did not end Blavatnik's pursuit, and a year later his company contracted for the right to acquire an 8 percent block in Lyondell. This last action led to a public Schedule 13D filing under the Williams Act. In the ensuing weeks, Blavatnik entered a merger agreement to purchase another chemical company, Huntsman, and was in the middle of a bidding competition with a private equity fund-backed bidder for that company. The two CEOs in this deal finally met in early July when Blavatnik first offered $40 cash per share and later that same day raised the price to $48. The court doesn't tell you, but Lyondell had been trading in the low $30s prior to the Schedule 13D, and its five-year high had been about $39. Lyondell's board then became involved, and over the next week, Blavatnik let go of his pursuit of Huntsman and the two sides came to a deal with no financing contingency. How different is the board's behavior here than in *Van Gorkom*?

2. **Postscript.** The deal was signed in July 2007, which in retrospect turned out to be the high tide of easy financing. The purchaser was able to close in November 2007, but only with interim bank financing and not longer-term takeout financing. It proved to be difficult to obtain the necessary longer-term financing as the financial system meltdown played out during the following year and LyondellBasell filed for bankruptcy reorganization in January 2009, followed by its parent in March 2009, with several large international banks taking a loss. Blavatnik himself later sued JP Moran Chase for his own investment losses. Meanwhile, the other chemical company deal that Blavatnik lost, the Huntsman purchase by Hexion, led to high litigation in Delaware in which the purchaser sought to use a Material Adverse Change clause to avoid closing. The Delaware court ruled the purchaser could not get out of the deal. Hexion Specialty Chemicals, Inc. v. Huntsman Corp., 965 A.2d 715 (Del. Ch. 2008). William Bratton traces this history of the deal in William W. Bratton, Lyondell: A Note of Approbation, 55 N.Y.L. Sch. L. Rev. 561 (2010/2011).

3. **Good faith in a transactional context.** *Lyondell* seemingly closed the book on a two decades long flirtation of Delaware law with

using good faith as a means to judicially monitor director conduct outside of loyalty. The *Van Gorkom* court's imposition of liability on directors for their action or inaction in approving a merger generated quick legislative response in the insertion of §102(b)(7) into the Delaware General Corporation Law. That section permitted corporations to insert provisions into their charter that eliminated director liability for damages based on duty of care, and Delaware public corporations were quick to use that authority. That exculpation provision, however, continued to permit claims based on self-dealing or good faith. For a time, it seemed like good faith would be the hook to police management, a trend that evolved in a series of cases occurring outside of a deal setting that focused on directors' oversight, not their direct decision-making, and their duty to monitor the activities of others in the corporation. *See, e.g.*, In re Caremark Int'l Inc. Derivative Litigation, 698 A.2d 959 (1966), and the *Disney* litigation challenging its payment of $140 million or so to its President, Michael Ovitz, who CEO Michael Eisner pushed out after a year in the business. Brehm v. Eisner, 746 A.2d 244 (2000) (ultimately leading to a trial and Chancery decision finding no good-faith violation); In re The Walt Disney Company Derivative Litigation, 907 A.2d 693 (Del. Ch. 2005), *aff'd*, 906 A.2d 27 (Del 2006). The Delaware Supreme Court's decision in *Stone v. Ritter* narrowed the use of good faith in a monitoring setting and the decision in *Lyondell* extends such narrowing to a transactional setting. Is there less need for judicial monitoring outside of a self-dealing conflict allegation in a deal setting where the market is actively monitoring director response to a takeover and shareholders have an opportunity to vote on the deal?

6 JUDICIAL REVIEW OF DEFENSIVE TACTICS

A. THE CORPORATE LAW TEMPLATE FOR CONSIDERING TAKEOVER DEFENSES

Prior to the takeover wave of the early 1980s, Delaware and other courts generally applied the two-part template of business judgment deference or entire fairness to fiduciary duty challenges that arose in a takeover context. In situations where, for example, the directors used corporate funds to purchase shares from a greenmailer or otherwise responded to a threat from an unwanted suitor, the Delaware court observed a conflict of interest, but not "the same 'self-dealing interest' as is present, for example, when a director sells property to the corporation." Cheff v. Mathes, 199 A.2d 548, 555 (Del. 1964). The court in that 1964 case upheld the board's actions to protect the founding family's control of the corporation based on their good faith and reasonable investigation of a danger to corporate policy. When the takeover wave of the early 1980s provided a plethora of new defense tactics challenged as breaches of fiduciary duty, courts applied this two-part deference/fairness system in ways that often provided substantial room for defensive action. In *Johnson v. Trueblood*, for example, a federal decision interpreting Delaware law, Judge Seitz, himself a former chancellor of Delaware, found Delaware law to be that "at a minimum, the plaintiff must make a showing that the sole or primary purpose of the defendant was to retain control."

> It is . . . obvious that if directors were held to the same standard as ordinary fiduciaries the corporation could not conduct business. For example, an ordinary fiduciary may not have the slightest conflict of interest in any transaction he undertakes on behalf of

the trust. Yet by the very nature of corporate life a director has a certain amount of self-interest in everything he does. The very fact that the director wants to enhance corporate profits is in part attributable to his desire to keep shareholders satisfied so that they will not oust him.

... The business judgment rule seeks to alleviate this problem by validating certain situations that otherwise would involve a conflict of interest for the ordinary fiduciary. The rule achieves this purpose by postulating that if actions are arguably taken for the benefit of the corporation, then the directors are presumed to have been exercising their sound business judgment rather than responding to any personal motivations.

Because the rule presumes that business judgment was exercised, the plaintiff must make a showing from which a factfinder might infer that impermissible motives predominated in the making of the decision in question.

The plaintiffs' theory that "a" motive to control is sufficient to rebut the rule is inconsistent with this purpose. Because the rule is designed to validate certain transactions despite conflicts of interest, the plaintiffs' rule would negate that purpose, at least in many cases. As already noted, control is always arguably "a" motive in any action taken by a director. Hence plaintiffs could always make this showing and thereby undercut the purpose of the rule.

In short, we believe that under Delaware law, at a minimum the plaintiff must make a showing that the sole or primary motive of the defendant was to retain control. If he makes a showing sufficient to survive a directed verdict, the burden then shifts to the defendant to show that the transaction in question had a valid corporate business purpose.

Johnson v. Trueblood, 629 F.2d 287, 292-93 (3d Cir. 1980) (declining to shift burden where the 53 percent shareholder pursued a series of financial steps in response to the corporation's financial distress, preferring these steps over the minority shareholder's offer to provide the financing that would have shifted control of the corporation).

Another federal court declined to move from the business judgment deference absent bad faith "so long as it can be attributed to any rational business purpose."

> As the *Trueblood* court concluded, "at a minimum, the Delaware cases require that the plaintiff must show some sort of bad faith on the part of the defendant. We do not think that a showing of 'a' motive to retain control, without more, constitutes bad faith in this context unless we are to ignore the realities of corporate life." 629 F.2d at 293. Because our examination of the board's conduct does not reveal such bad faith, we do not believe an evaluation of the fairness or wisdom of the board's conduct is called for as long as it can be attributed to any rational business purpose.

Panter v. Marshall Field, 646 F.2d 271 (7th Cir. 1981) (upholding target's strategy designed to create antitrust problems for a bidder in the same business who sought to take over Marshall Field's, the department store).

In the aftermath of such judicial holdings, the Delaware Supreme Court offered an expanded choice for judicial review as set out in the cases that follow.

Unocal Corp. v. Mesa Petroleum Co.
493 A.2d 946 (Del. Sup. Ct. 1985)

MOORE, Justice.

We confront an issue of first impression in Delaware — the validity of a corporation's self-tender for its own shares which excludes from participation a stockholder making a hostile tender offer for the company's stock.

The Court of Chancery granted a preliminary injunction to the plaintiffs, Mesa Petroleum Co., Mesa Asset Co., Mesa Partners II, and Mesa Eastern, Inc. (collectively "Mesa"),[1] enjoining an exchange offer of the defendant, Unocal Corporation (Unocal) for its own stock. The trial court concluded that a selective exchange offer, excluding Mesa, was legally impermissible. We cannot agree with such a blanket rule. . . .

I.

. . . On April 8, 1985, Mesa, the owner of approximately 13% of Unocal's stock, commenced a two-tier "front loaded" cash tender offer for 64 million shares, or approximately 37%, of Unocal's outstanding stock at a price of $54 per share. The "back-end" was designed to eliminate the remaining publicly held shares by an exchange of securities purportedly worth $54 per share. However, pursuant to an order entered by the United States District Court for the Central District of California on April 26, 1985, Mesa issued a supplemental proxy statement to Unocal's stockholders disclosing that the securities offered in the second-step merger would be highly subordinated, and that Unocal's capitalization would differ significantly from its present structure. Unocal has rather aptly termed such securities "junk bonds."

Unocal's board consists of eight independent outside directors and six insiders. It met on April 13, 1985, to consider the Mesa tender offer. Thirteen directors were present, and the meeting lasted nine and one-half hours. The directors were given no agenda or written materials prior to the session. However, detailed presentations were made by legal counsel regarding the board's obligations under both Delaware corporate law and the federal securities laws. The board then received a presentation from Peter Sachs on behalf of Goldman Sachs & Co. (Goldman Sachs) and Dillon, Read & Co. (Dillon Read) discussing the bases for their opinions that the Mesa proposal was wholly inadequate. Mr. Sachs opined that the minimum cash value that could be expected from a sale or orderly liquidation for 100% of Unocal's stock was in excess of $60 per share. In making his presentation, Mr. Sachs showed slides outlining the valuation techniques used by the financial advisors, and others, depicting recent business

---
1. T. Boone Pickens, Jr., is President and Chairman of the Board of Mesa Petroleum and President of Mesa Asset and controls the related Mesa entities.

combinations in the oil and gas industry. The Court of Chancery found that the Sachs presentation was designed to apprise the directors of the scope of the analyses performed rather than the facts and numbers used in reaching the conclusion that Mesa's tender offer price was inadequate.

Mr. Sachs also presented various defensive strategies available to the board if it concluded that Mesa's two-step tender offer was inadequate and should be opposed. One of the devices outlined was a self-tender by Unocal for its own stock with a reasonable price range of $70 to $75 per share. The cost of such a proposal would cause the company to incur $6.1-6.5 billion of additional debt, and a presentation was made informing the board of Unocal's ability to handle it. The directors were told that the primary effect of this obligation would be to reduce exploratory drilling, but that the company would nonetheless remain a viable entity.

The eight outside directors, comprising a clear majority of the thirteen members present, then met separately with Unocal's financial advisors and attorneys. Thereafter, they unanimously agreed to advise the board that it should reject Mesa's tender offer as inadequate, and that Unocal should pursue a self-tender to provide the stockholders with a fairly priced alternative to the Mesa proposal. The board then reconvened and unanimously adopted a resolution rejecting as grossly inadequate Mesa's tender offer. Despite the nine and one-half hour length of the meeting, no formal decision was made on the proposed defensive self-tender.

On April 15, the board met again with four of the directors present by telephone and one member still absent. This session lasted two hours. Unocal's Vice President of Finance and its Assistant General Counsel made a detailed presentation of the proposed terms of the exchange offer. A price range between $70 and $80 per share was considered, and ultimately the directors agreed upon $72. The board was also advised about the debt securities that would be issued, and the necessity of placing restrictive covenants upon certain corporate activities until the obligations were paid. The board's decisions were made in reliance on the advice of its investment bankers, including the terms and conditions upon which the securities were to be issued. Based upon this advice, and the board's own deliberations, the directors unanimously approved the exchange offer. Their resolution provided that if Mesa acquired 64 million shares of Unocal stock through its own offer (the Mesa Purchase Condition), Unocal would buy the remaining 49% outstanding for an exchange of debt securities having an aggregate par value of $72 per share. The board resolution also stated that the offer would be subject to other conditions that had been described to the board at the meeting, or which were deemed necessary by Unocal's officers, including the exclusion of Mesa from the proposal (the Mesa exclusion).

Unocal's exchange offer was commenced on April 17, 1985, and Mesa promptly challenged it by filing this suit in the Court of Chancery. On April 22, the Unocal board met again and was advised by Goldman Sachs and

Dillon Read to waive the Mesa Purchase Condition as to 50 million shares. This recommendation was in response to a perceived concern of the shareholders that, if shares were tendered to Unocal, no shares would be purchased by either offeror. The directors were also advised that they should tender their own Unocal stock into the exchange offer as a mark of their confidence in it.

Another focus of the board was the Mesa exclusion. Legal counsel advised that under Delaware law Mesa could only be excluded for what the directors reasonably believed to be a valid corporate purpose. The directors' discussion centered on the objective of adequately compensating shareholders at the "back-end" of Mesa's proposal, which the latter would finance with "junk bonds." To include Mesa would defeat that goal, because under the proration aspect of the exchange offer (49%) every Mesa share accepted by Unocal would displace one held by another stockholder. Further, if Mesa were permitted to tender to Unocal, the latter would in effect be financing Mesa's own inadequate proposal. . . .

III.

We begin with the basic issue of the power of a board of directors of a Delaware corporation to adopt a defensive measure of this type. Absent such authority, all other questions are moot. Neither issues of fairness nor business judgment are pertinent without the basic underpinning of a board's legal power to act.

The board has a large reservoir of authority upon which to draw. Its duties and responsibilities proceed from the inherent powers conferred by 8 Del. C. §141(a), respecting management of the corporation's "business and affairs." Additionally, the powers here being exercised derive from 8 Del. C. §160(a), conferring broad authority upon a corporation to deal in its own stock. From this it is now well established that in the acquisition of its shares a Delaware corporation may deal selectively with its stockholders, provided the directors have not acted out of a sole or primary purpose to entrench themselves in office. *Cheff v. Mathes*, Del. Supr., 199 A.2d 548, 554 (1964); *Bennett v. Propp*, Del. Supr., 187 A.2d 405, 408 (1962); *Martin v. American Potash & Chemical Corporation*, Del. Supr., 92 A.2d 295, 302 (1952); *Kaplan v. Goldsamt*, Del. Ch., 380 A.2d 556, 568-569 (1977); *Kors v. Carey*, Del. Ch., 158 A.2d 136, 140-141 (1960). . . .

When a board addresses a pending takeover bid it has an obligation to determine whether the offer is in the best interests of the corporation and its shareholders. In that respect a board's duty is no different from any other responsibility it shoulders, and its decisions should be no less entitled to the respect they otherwise would be accorded in the realm of business judgment. *See also Johnson v. Trueblood*, 629 F.2d 287, 292-293 (3d Cir. 1980). There are, however, certain caveats to a proper exercise of this function. Because of the omnipresent specter that a board may be acting primarily in its own interests, rather than those of the corporation and its shareholders, there is an enhanced duty which calls for judicial examination at the threshold before the protections of the business judgment rule may be conferred.

This Court has long recognized that:

> We must bear in mind the inherent danger in the purchase of shares with corporate funds to remove a threat to corporate policy when a threat to control is involved. The directors are of necessity confronted with a conflict of interest, and an objective decision is difficult.

Bennett v. Propp, Del. Supr., 187 A.2d 405, 409 (1962). In the face of this inherent conflict directors must show that they had reasonable grounds for believing that a danger to corporate policy and effectiveness existed because of another person's stock ownership. *Cheff v. Mathes*, 199 A.2d at 554-555. However, they satisfy that burden "by showing good faith and reasonable investigation. . . ." *Id.* at 555. Furthermore, such proof is materially enhanced, as here, by the approval of a board comprised of a majority of outside independent directors who have acted in accordance with the foregoing standards. *See Aronson v. Lewis*, 473 A.2d at 812, 815; *Puma v. Marriott*, Del. Ch., 283 A.2d 693, 695 (1971); *Panter v. Marshall Field & Co.*, 646 F.2d 271, 295 (7th Cir. 1981).

IV.

A.

In the board's exercise of corporate power to forestall a takeover bid our analysis begins with the basic principle that corporate directors have a fiduciary duty to act in the best interests of the corporation's stockholders. *Guth v. Loft, Inc.*, Del. Supr., 5 A.2d 503, 510 (1939). As we have noted, their duty of care extends to protecting the corporation and its owners from perceived harm whether a threat originates from third parties or other shareholders.[10] But such powers are not absolute. A corporation does not have unbridled discretion to defeat any perceived threat by any Draconian means available.

The restriction placed upon a selective stock repurchase is that the directors may not have acted solely or primarily out of a desire to perpetuate themselves in office. *See Cheff v. Mathes*, 199 A.2d at 556; *Kors v. Carey*, 158 A.2d at 140. Of course, to this is added the further caveat that inequitable action may not be taken under the guise of law. *Schnell v. Chris-Craft Industries, Inc.*, Del. Supr., 285 A.2d 437, 439 (1971). The standard of proof established in

---

10. It has been suggested that a board's response to a takeover threat should be a passive one. Easterbrook & Fischel, *supra*, 36 Bus. Law. at 1750. However, that clearly is not the law of Delaware, and as the proponents of this rule of passivity readily concede, it has not been adopted either by courts or state legislatures. Easterbrook & Fischel, *supra*, 94 Harv. L. Rev. at 1194.

A. The Corporate Law Template for Considering Takeover Defenses   147

Cheff v. Mathes and discussed *supra* at page 16, is designed to ensure that a defensive measure to thwart or impede a takeover is indeed motivated by a good faith concern for the welfare of the corporation and its stockholders, which in all circumstances must be free of any fraud or other misconduct. *Cheff v. Mathes*, 199 A.2d at 554-555. However, this does not end the inquiry.

B.

A further aspect is the element of balance. If a defensive measure is to come within the ambit of the business judgment rule, it must be reasonable in relation to the threat posed. This entails an analysis by the directors of the nature of the takeover bid and its effect on the corporate enterprise. Examples of such concerns may include: inadequacy of the price offered, nature and timing of the offer, questions of illegality, the impact on "constituencies" other than shareholders (i.e., creditors, customers, employees, and perhaps even the community generally), the risk of no consummation, and the quality of securities being offered in the exchange. *See* Lipton and Brownstein, *Takeover Responses and Directors' Responsibilities: An Update*, p. 7, ABA National Institute on the Dynamics of Corporate Control (December 8, 1983). While not a controlling factor, it also seems to us that a board may reasonably consider the basic stockholder interests at stake, including those of short term speculators, whose actions may have fueled the coercive aspect of the offer at the expense of the long term investor. Here, the threat posed was viewed by the Unocal board as a grossly inadequate two-tier coercive tender offer coupled with the threat of greenmail.

Specifically, the Unocal directors had concluded that the value of Unocal was substantially above the $54 per share offered in cash at the front end. Furthermore, they determined that the subordinated securities to be exchanged in Mesa's announced squeeze out of the remaining shareholders in the "back-end" merger were "junk bonds" worth far less than $54. It is now well recognized that such offers are a classic coercive measure designed to stampede shareholders into tendering at the first tier, even if the price is inadequate, out of fear of what they will receive at the back end of the transaction. Wholly beyond the coercive aspect of an inadequate two-tier tender offer, the threat was posed by a corporate raider with a national reputation as a "greenmailer."

In adopting the selective exchange offer, the board stated that its objective was either to defeat the inadequate Mesa offer or, should the offer still succeed, provide the 49% of its stockholders, who would otherwise be forced to accept "junk bonds," with $72 worth of senior debt. We find that both purposes are valid.

However, such efforts would have been thwarted by Mesa's participation in the exchange offer. First, if Mesa could tender its shares, Unocal would effectively be subsidizing the former's continuing effort to buy

Unocal stock at $54 per share. Second, Mesa could not, by definition, fit within the class of shareholders being protected from its own coercive and inadequate tender offer.

Thus, we are satisfied that the selective exchange offer is reasonably related to the threats posed. It is consistent with the principle that "the minority stockholder shall receive the substantial equivalent in value of what he had before." *Sterling v. Mayflower Hotel Corp.*, Del. Supr., 93 A.2d 107, 114 (1952). *See also Rosenblatt v. Getty Oil Co.*, Del. Supr., 493 A.2d 929, 940 (1985). This concept of fairness, while stated in the merger context, is also relevant in the area of tender offer law. Thus, the board's decision to offer what it determined to be the fair value of the corporation to the 49% of its shareholders, who would otherwise be forced to accept highly subordinated "junk bonds," is reasonable and consistent with the directors' duty to ensure that the minority stockholders receive equal value for their shares.

V.

Mesa contends that it is unlawful, and the trial court agreed, for a corporation to discriminate in this fashion against one shareholder. It argues correctly that no case has ever sanctioned a device that precludes a raider from sharing in a benefit available to all other stockholders. However, as we have noted earlier, the principle of selective stock repurchases by a Delaware corporation is neither unknown nor unauthorized. *Cheff v. Mathes*, 199 A.2d at 554; *Bennett v. Propp*, 187 A.2d at 408; *Martin v. American Potash & Chemical Corporation*, 92 A.2d at 302; *Kaplan v. Goldsamt*, 380 A.2d at 568-569; *Kors v. Carey*, 158 A.2d at 140-141; 8 *Del. C.* §160. The only difference is that heretofore the approved transaction was the payment of "greenmail" to a raider or dissident posing a threat to the corporate enterprise. All other stockholders were denied such favored treatment, and given Mesa's past history of greenmail, its claims here are rather ironic.

However, our corporate law is not static. It must grow and develop in response to, indeed in anticipation of, evolving concepts and needs. Merely because the General Corporation Law is silent as to a specific matter does not mean that it is prohibited. *See Providence and Worcester Co. v. Baker*, Del. Supr., 378 A.2d 121, 123-124 (1977). In the days when *Cheff, Bennett, Martin,* and *Kors* were decided, the tender offer, while not an unknown device, was virtually unused, and little was known of such methods as two-tier "front-end" loaded offers with their coercive effects. Then, the favored attack of a raider was stock acquisition followed by a proxy contest. Various defensive tactics, which provided no benefit whatever to the raider, evolved. Thus, the use of corporate funds by management to counter a proxy battle was approved. *Hall v. Trans-Lux Daylight Picture Screen Corp.*, Del. Supr., 171 A. 226 (1934); *Hibbert v. Hollywood Park, Inc.*, Del. Supr., 457 A.2d 339 (1983). Litigation, supported by corporate funds, aimed at the raider has long been a popular device.

More recently, as the sophistication of both raiders and targets has developed, a host of other defensive measures to counter such ever mounting threats has evolved and received judicial sanction. These include defensive charter amendments and other devices bearing some rather exotic, but apt, names: Crown Jewel, White Knight, Pac Man, and Golden Parachute. Each has highly selective features, the object of which is to deter or defeat the raider.

Thus, while the exchange offer is a form of selective treatment, given the nature of the threat posed here the response is neither unlawful nor unreasonable. If the board of directors is disinterested, has acted in good faith and with due care, its decision in the absence of an abuse of discretion will be upheld as a proper exercise of business judgment.

Mesa contends that the basis of this action is punitive, and solely in response to the exercise of its rights of corporate democracy. Nothing precludes Mesa, as a stockholder, from acting in its own self-interest. *See e.g., DuPont v. DuPont*, 251 Fed. 937 (D. Del. 1918), *aff'd*, 256 Fed. 129 (3d Cir. 1918); *Ringling Bros.-Barnum & Bailey Combined Shows, Inc. v. Ringling*, Del. Supr., 53 A.2d 441, 447 (1947); *Heil v. Standard Gas & Electric Co.*, Del. Ch., 151 A. 303, 304 (1930). *But see, Allied Chemical & Dye Corp. v. Steel & Tube Co. of America*, Del. Ch., 120 A. 486, 491 (1923) (majority shareholder owes a fiduciary duty to the minority shareholders). However, Mesa, while pursuing its own interests, has acted in a manner which a board consisting of a majority of independent directors has reasonably determined to be contrary to the best interests of Unocal and its other shareholders. In this situation, there is no support in Delaware law for the proposition that, when responding to a perceived harm, a corporation must guarantee a benefit to a stockholder who is deliberately provoking the danger being addressed. There is no obligation of self-sacrifice by the corporation and its shareholders in the face of such a challenge.

VI.

In conclusion, there was directorial power to oppose the Mesa tender offer, and to undertake a selective stock exchange made in good faith and upon a reasonable investigation pursuant to a clear duty to protect the corporate enterprise. Further, the selective stock repurchase plan chosen by Unocal is reasonable in relation to the threat that the board rationally and reasonably believed was posed by Mesa's inadequate and coercive two-tier tender offer. Under those circumstances the board's action is entitled to be measured by the standards of the business judgment rule. Thus, unless it is shown by a preponderance of the evidence that the directors' decisions were primarily based on perpetuating themselves in office, or some other breach of fiduciary duty such as fraud, overreaching, lack of good faith, or being uninformed, a Court will not substitute its judgment for that of the board.

In this case that protection is not lost merely because Unocal's directors have tendered their shares in the exchange offer. Given the validity of the Mesa exclusion, they are receiving a benefit shared generally by all other stockholders except Mesa. In this circumstance the test of *Aronson v. Lewis*, 473 A.2d at 812, is satisfied. *See also Cheff v. Mathes*, 199 A.2d at 554. If the stockholders are displeased with the action of their elected representatives, the powers of corporate democracy are at their disposal to turn the board out. *Aronson v. Lewis*, Del. Supr., 473 A.2d 805, 811 (1984). *See also* 8 Del. C. §§141(k) and 211(b).

With the Court of Chancery's findings that the exchange offer was based on the board's good faith belief that the Mesa offer was inadequate, that the board's action was informed and taken with due care, that Mesa's prior activities justify a reasonable inference that its principle objective was greenmail, and implicitly, that the substance of the offer itself was reasonable and fair to the corporation and its stockholders if Mesa were included, we cannot say that the Unocal directors have acted in such a manner as to have passed an "unintelligent and unadvised judgment." *Mitchell v. Highland-Western Glass Co.*, Del. Ch., 167 A. 831, 833 (1933). The decision of the Court of Chancery is therefore REVERSED, and the preliminary injunction is VACATED.

NOTES AND QUESTIONS

1. **The deal.** Consider how value might be created by this transaction. On the acquirer side was T. Boone Pickens from a small, independent (meaning not vertically integrated) oil producer in Amarillo, Texas (population about 175,000) on the windswept plains of the Texas panhandle. His target was Unocal Corporation, then number 27 on the Fortune 500 list of America's largest companies, an integrated oil company headquartered in a gleaming tower overlooking Los Angeles. Pickens had acquired 13 percent of Unocal shares in anonymous market transactions (where the price had been in the low $40s). He now offered $54 cash for an additional 37 percent of the shares, which would take him over the 50 percent threshold needed for majority status. Thereafter, he planned to cash out the remaining shares in a cash-out merger providing those shareholders with subordinated securities with a face value of $54 per share. The high risk of non-payment of these subordinated promises led the court to describe them as "junk bonds."

2. **Valuation.** How would a Unocal shareholder value such an offer? At first glance, a shareholder who, for simplicity's sake, owned a block of 100 Unocal shares would expect cash for a portion of the 100 shares and subordinated securities for the remaining portion and would calculate the weighted average of the two payments to determine the value of the offer. The 37 percent Pickens needed to acquire would have to come from the 87 percent he did not already own, so that if all shareholders tendered in response to the offer (a rational choice given the premium over prior market

price) our shareholder, like all others, could expect to get the cash for 37/87 or 42.5 of her 100 shares. (Federal tender offer rules require that the bidder buy the asked for amount pro rata from all shareholders who tender in the prescribed 20-business day window that a tender offer must remain open.) For the remaining 57.5 shares, our shareholder would expect to receive the subordinated securities. If the junk bonds are in fact worth their face value of $54, the weighted average calculation is straightforward and produces $54 in value for each of the 100 shares. If, however, the risky nature of the junk bonds drives their true value to a lower number, the weighted average sum will decrease. If the value of the junk bonds go low enough, the result would be less than the current market value of the shares.

    3. Prisoner's dilemma. What would you expect shareholders to do if analysts and others in the market valued the junk bonds at $24, so that the weighted average was $36.75. A prospective seller who owned the entire block would do what any other seller does when offered an inadequate price and tell the buyer to take a hike. But the two-tiered, front-end loaded nature of the deal creates the possibility of a prisoner's dilemma for the shareholders. Like two prisoners kept isolated from each other who cannot coordinate their strategy, each has to worry that the other will defect. If one defects and the other does not, the defector will be able to get the higher $54 cash value for that shareholder's entire block of 100 shares, leaving the non-defector with the lower junk bonds for her entire block of 100 shares. Given this risk, each shareholder will tender and get the weighted average. The Court clearly viewed this possibility as a threat to the shareholders, given its discussion in Part IV.B of the opinion.

    4. Directors as the shareholders' champion. How might the shareholders be protected? Given the core approach of Delaware corporate law, it should not surprise you to see that the Court sees the directors as a centralized actor who can fill this role. The Court's explicit and emphatic rejection of Easterbrook & Fischel's then-current argument in footnote 10 calling for director passivity tells you something as to how the Court views the role of directors and implicitly the extent to which it views the market as an alternative source of such protection.

    5. Omnipresent specter. Having accepted the central role for directors, the Court is unwilling to continue with the existing deference/entire fairness set of choices for judicial review and defines a specific intermediate review role for courts, which it inserts as a threshold that must be crossed before business judgment deference is available.

    a. What is a sufficient threat and how would a board go about showing the existence of such danger? Compare the threat to Unocal from threats found permissible in the cases which follow.

    b. What is the board's response and is it proportional? To answer this last question you will need to focus on how the board's response changed as the deal unfolded. How attractive is the $72 it offered for the Unocal stock not taken in the first tier of Mesa's offer? What is Pickens's response likely to be? Is this the company and a set of assets and liabilities that Pickens was willing to put up so much of a premium to buy? If Pickens were to walk, what result for the Unocal shareholders then? Removing the condition on the company's $72 offer for 50 million of the outstanding shares was a response to what was likely a strong investor push back to the company. Now consider if the Unocal shareholder's response in deciding whether to tender into the company's $72 offer is similar to their dilemma if they were forced to respond to the original Pickens offer. Should that influence the Court's discussion of proportionality?

6. **Federal regulation of two-tier offers.** After this case, the SEC passed a new tender offer rule, Rule 14d-10, usually referred to as the Best Price rule, requiring an offeror to give any shareholder the best price. The result was to practically remove the threat of a two-tiered coercive bust-up offer. But the structure constructed by the Delaware court in response to this now mothballed tactic has survived to govern all defensive tactics.

Revlon, Inc. v. MacAndrews & Forbes Holdings, Inc.
506 A.2d 173 (Del. Sup. Ct. 1986)

MOORE, Justice:

In this battle for corporate control of Revlon, Inc. (Revlon), the Court of Chancery enjoined certain transactions designed to thwart the efforts of Pantry Pride, Inc. (Pantry Pride) to acquire Revlon. The defendants are Revlon, its board of directors, and Forstmann Little & Co. and the latter's affiliated limited partnership (collectively, Forstmann). The injunction barred consummation of an option granted Forstmann to purchase certain Revlon assets (the lock-up option), a promise by Revlon to deal exclusively with Forstmann in the face of a takeover (the no-shop provision), and the payment of a $25 million cancellation fee to Forstmann if the transaction was aborted. The Court of Chancery found that the Revlon directors had breached their duty of care by entering into the foregoing transaction and effectively ending an active auction for the company. The trial court ruled that such arrangements are not illegal *per se* under Delaware law, but that their use under the circumstances here was impermissible. We agree. *See MacAndrews & Forbes Holdings, Inc. v. Revlon, Inc.*, Del. Ch., 501 A.2d 1239 (1985). Thus, we granted this expedited interlocutory appeal to consider for the first time the validity of such defensive measures in the face of an active bidding contest for corporate control. Additionally, we address for the first time the extent to which a corporation may consider the impact of a takeover threat on constituencies other than shareholders. *See Unocal Corp. v. Mesa Petroleum Co.*, Del. Supr., 493 A.2d 946, 955 (1985).

In our view, lock-ups and related agreements are permitted under Delaware law where their adoption is untainted by director interest or other breaches of fiduciary duty. The actions taken by the Revlon directors, however, did not meet this standard. Moreover, while concern for various corporate constituencies is proper when addressing a takeover threat, that principle is limited by the requirement that there be some rationally related benefit accruing to the stockholders. We find no such benefit here.

Thus, under all the circumstances we must agree with the Court of Chancery that the enjoined Revlon defensive measures were inconsistent with the directors' duties to the stockholders. Accordingly, we affirm.

I.

[In the summer of 1985, Revlon's chief executive officer, Michel C. Bergerac, rejected overtures from his counterpart at Pantry Pride, Ronald O. Perelman, concerning the possible acquisition of Revlon by Pantry Pride in the $40-42 per share range if friendly or $45 if the acquisition were hostile. This and all subsequent overtures were rebuffed, perhaps in part, the court noted, because of Mr. Bergerac's strong personal antipathy to Mr. Perelman.

Revlon's board met in August to consider the impending hostile bid. Of the 14 directors, six were part of the company's senior management, two held significant blocks of stock, and four of the remaining six had had some relationship with companies doing business with Revlon. The court noted that on this record "we cannot conclude that this board is entitled to certain presumptions that generally attach to the decisions of a board whose majority consists of truly outside independent directors."

After hearing from Felix Rohatyn and William Loomis of Lazard Freres, the company's investment banker, and from its special counsel, Martin Lipton, the board adopted two defensive tactics: a poison pill plan and the company's repurchase of 5 million of its 30 million shares.

After Pantry Pride launched a hostile tender offer at $47.50, Revlon commenced its own tender offer, now increased to 10 million shares. Eighty-seven percent of Revlon's shareholders tendered in response to this offer, and the company purchased the shares pro rata from those who tendered. The consideration for the 10 million shares was not cash but senior subordinated notes (and a fractional share of cumulative convertible preferred stock). Lazard Freres opined that the notes would trade at their face value on a fully distributable basis. The notes contained covenants that limited Revlon's ability to incur additional debt, sell assets, or pay dividends unless otherwise approved by the "independent" (non-management) members of the board.

During the next six weeks, Pantry Pride made four additional cash bids at successively higher prices. Revlon pursued negotiations with other bidders and agreed on October 3 to a leveraged buyout by Forstmann. Under the terms of the buyout, a new company formed by Forstmann would purchase each Revlon share for $56 cash, Revlon management would purchase stock in the new company by exercising their Revlon golden parachutes, Forstmann would assume Revlon's $475 million debt incurred in the issuance of the notes, and Revlon would redeem the poison pill and waive the restrictive covenants of the notes for Forstmann or in connection with any offer superior to Forstmann's. The agreement contemplated either Revlon or an acquirer selling off various divisions of Revlon, including its cosmetics and fragrance division, to provide cash for the transaction.

The announcement of this agreement, including the waiver of the note covenants, led to a decline in the price of the notes. One director later reported a deluge of telephone calls from irate noteholders, and the Wall Street Journal reported threats of litigation by the noteholders.

Pantry Pride again raised its offer, this time to $56.25. Efforts to reach agreement failed. Pantry Pride announced that it would engage in fractional bidding and top any Forstmann offer by a slightly higher one. The court found that Forstmann, but not Pantry Pride, had been made privy to certain Revlon financial data. With this data Forstmann made a $57.25 offer subject to these conditions:

- Forstmann would receive a lock-up option to purchase two Revlon divisions for $525 million, some $100-$175 million below the value ascribed to them by Lazard Freres;
- Revlon would agree to a no-shop provision, blocking its discussion with other suitors;
- Revlon would pay a $25 million cancellation fee to Forstmann if the deal fell through;
- Revlon's current management would not participate in the merger;
- The poison pill would be redeemed and the note covenants would be waived. Forstmann agreed to support the par value of the notes by an exchange of new notes.

Forstmann said it would withdraw its offer if it were not immediately accepted. The Revlon board unanimously approved Forstmann's proposal because (1) it was for a higher price than the Pantry Pride bid (although the court noted that the Forstmann proposal must be discounted for the time value of money because of the delay in approving the merger and consummating the transaction, so that the exact difference between the two bids remained unsettled); (2) it protected the noteholders; and (3) Forstmann's financing was firmly in place.

Pantry Pride filed suit and raised its offer to $58 conditioned upon nullification of the poison pill, waiver of the covenants, and an injunction of the Forstmann lock-up. The trial court concluded that the Revlon directors had breached their duty of loyalty by making concessions to Forstmann out of concern for directors' liability to the noteholders rather than maximizing the sales price of the company for the stockholders' benefit.]

II.

[To determine the propriety of a preliminary injunction, the court looked to Pantry Pride's probability of success on the merits, addressing first the directors' responsibility for managing the business and affairs of the corporation subject to their fiduciary duties and describing the court's role as governed by the business judgment rule as set out in *Unocal*. Under these standards the court found the adoption of the poison pill to be valid and found any further challenge to the poison pill as moot since the board had agreed to redeem the pill for any cash proposal of $57.25 or more per share.]

C.

The second defensive measure adopted by Revlon to thwart a Pantry Pride takeover was the company's own exchange offer for 10 million of its shares. The directors' general broad powers to manage the business and affairs of the corporation are augmented by the specific authority conferred under 8 Del. C. §160(a), permitting the company to deal in its own stock. *Unocal*, 493 A.2d at 953-54; *Cheff v. Mathes*, 41 Del. Supr. 494, 199 A.2d 548, 554 (1964); *Kors v. Carey*, 39 Del. Ch. 47, 158 A.2d 136, 140 (1960). However, when exercising that power in an effort to forestall a hostile takeover, the board's actions are strictly held to the fiduciary standards outlined in *Unocal*. These standards require the directors to determine the best interests of the corporation and its stockholders, and impose an enhanced duty to abjure any action that is motivated by considerations other than a good faith concern for such interests. *Unocal*, 493 A.2d at 954-55; *see Bennett v. Propp*, 41 Del. Supr. 14, 187 A.2d 405, 409 (1962).

The Revlon directors concluded that Pantry Pride's $47.50 offer was grossly inadequate. In that regard the board acted in good faith, and on an informed basis, with reasonable grounds to believe that there existed a harmful threat to the corporate enterprise. The adoption of a defensive measure, reasonable in relation to the threat posed, was proper and fully accorded with the powers, duties, and responsibilities conferred upon directors under our law. *Unocal*, 493 A.2d at 954; *Pogostin v. Rice*, 480 A.2d at 627.

D.

However, when Pantry Pride increased its offer to $50 per share, and then to $53, it became apparent to all that the break-up of the company was inevitable. The Revlon board's authorization permitting management to negotiate a merger or buyout with a third party was a recognition that the company was for sale. The duty of the board had thus changed from the preservation of Revlon as a corporate entity to the maximization of the company's value at a sale for the stockholders' benefit. This significantly altered the board's responsibilities under the *Unocal* standards. It no longer faced threats to corporate policy and effectiveness, or to the stockholders' interests, from a grossly inadequate bid. The whole question of defensive measures became moot. The directors' role changed from defenders of the corporate bastion to auctioneers charged with getting the best price for the stockholders at a sale of the company.

III.

This brings us to the lock-up with Forstmann and its emphasis on shoring up the sagging market value of the Notes in the face of threatened litigation by their holders. Such a focus was inconsistent with the changed concept of the directors' responsibilities at this stage of the developments. The impending waiver of the Notes covenants had caused the value of the Notes to fall, and the board was aware of the noteholders' ire as well as their subsequent threats of suit. The directors thus made support of the Notes an integral part of the company's dealings with Forstmann, even though their primary responsibility at this stage was to the equity owners.

The original threat posed by Pantry Pride—the break-up of the company—had become a reality which even the directors embraced. Selective dealing to fend off a hostile but determined bidder was no longer a proper objective. Instead, obtaining the highest price for the benefit of the stockholders should have been the central theme guiding director action. Thus, the Revlon board could not make the requisite showing of good faith by preferring the noteholders and ignoring its duty of loyalty to the shareholders. The rights of the former already were fixed by contract. *Wolfensohn v. Madison Fund, Inc.*, Del. Supr., 253 A.2d 72, 75 (1969); *Harff v. Kerkorian*, Del. Ch., 324 A.2d 215 (1974). The noteholders required no further protection, and when the Revlon board entered into an auction-ending lock-up agreement with Forstmann on the basis of impermissible considerations at the expense of the shareholders, the directors breached their primary duty of loyalty.

The Revlon board argued that it acted in good faith in protecting the noteholders because *Unocal* permits consideration of other corporate constituencies. Although such considerations may be permissible, there are fundamental limitations upon that prerogative. A board may have regard for various constituencies in discharging its responsibilities, provided there are rationally related benefits accruing to the stockholders. *Unocal*, 493 A.2d at 955. However, such concern for non-stockholder interests is inappropriate when an auction among active bidders is in progress, and the object no longer is to protect or maintain the corporate enterprise but to sell it to the highest bidder.

Revlon also contended that by *Gilbert v. El Paso Co.*, Del. Ch., 490 A.2d 1050, 1054-55 (1984), it had contractual and good faith obligations to consider the noteholders. However, any such duties are limited to the principle that one may not interfere with contractual relationships by improper actions. Here, the rights of the noteholders were fixed by agreement, and there is nothing of substance to suggest that any of those terms were violated. The Notes covenants specifically contemplated a waiver to permit sale of the company at a fair price. The Notes were accepted by the holders on that basis, including the risk of an adverse market effect stemming from a waiver. Thus, nothing remained for Revlon to legitimately protect, and no rationally related benefit thereby accrued to the stockholders. Under such circumstances we must conclude that the merger agreement with Forstmann was unreasonable in relation to the threat posed.

A lock-up is not *per se* illegal under Delaware law. Its use has been approved in an earlier case. *Thompson v. Enstar Corp.*, Del. Ch. [509 A.2d 578] (1984). Such options can entice other bidders to enter a contest for control of the corporation, creating an auction for the company and maximizing shareholder profit. Current economic conditions in the takeover market are such that a "white knight" like Forstmann might only enter the bidding for the target company if it receives some form of compensation to cover the risks and costs involved. Note, *Corporations-Mergers-"Lock-up" Enjoined Under Section 14(e) of Securities Exchange Act — Mobil Corp. v. Marathon Oil Co., 669 F.2d 366 (6th Cir. 1981)*, 12 SETON HALL L. REV. 881, 892 (1982). However, while those lock-ups which draw bidders into the battle benefit shareholders, similar measures which end an active auction and foreclose further bidding operate to the shareholders' detriment. Note, *Lock-up Options: Toward a State Law Standard*, 96 HARV. L. REV. 1068, 1081 (1983).

The Forstmann option had a ... destructive effect on the auction process. Forstmann had already been drawn into the contest on a preferred basis, so the result of the lock-up was not to foster bidding, but to destroy it. The board's stated reasons for approving the transactions were: (1) better financing, (2) noteholder protection, and (3) higher price. As the Court of Chancery found, and we agree, any distinctions between the rival bidders' methods of financing the proposal were nominal at best, and such a consideration has little or no significance in a cash offer for any and all shares. The principal object, contrary to the board's duty of care, appears to have been protection of the noteholders over the shareholders' interests.

While Forstmann's $57.25 offer was objectively higher than Pantry Pride's $56.25 bid, the margin of superiority is less when the Forstmann price is adjusted for the time value of money. In reality, the Revlon board ended the auction in return for very little actual improvement in the final bid. The principal benefit went to the directors, who avoided personal liability to a class of creditors to whom the board owed no further duty under the circumstances. Thus, when a board ends an intense bidding contest on an insubstantial basis, and where a significant by-product of that action is to protect the directors against a perceived threat of personal liability for consequences stemming from the adoption of previous defensive measures, the action cannot withstand the enhanced scrutiny which *Unocal* requires of director conduct. *See Unocal,* 493 A.2d at 954-55.

In addition to the lock-up option, the Court of Chancery enjoined the no-shop provision as part of the attempt to foreclose further bidding by Pantry Pride. *MacAndrews & Forbes Holdings, Inc. v. Revlon, Inc.,* 501 A.2d at 1251. The no-shop provision, like the lock-up option, while not *per se* illegal, is impermissible under the *Unocal* standards when a board's primary duty becomes that of an auctioneer responsible for selling the company to the highest bidder. The agreement to negotiate only with Forstmann ended rather than intensified the board's involvement in the bidding contest.

It is ironic that the parties even considered a no-shop agreement when Revlon had dealt preferentially, and almost exclusively, with Forstmann throughout the contest. After the directors authorized management to negotiate with other parties, Forstmann was given every negotiating advantage that Pantry Pride had been denied: cooperation from management, access to financial data, and the exclusive opportunity to present merger proposals directly to the board of directors. Favoritism for a white knight to the total exclusion of a hostile bidder might be justifiable when the latter's offer adversely affects shareholder interests, but when bidders make relatively similar offers, or dissolution of the company becomes inevitable, the directors cannot fulfill their enhanced *Unocal* duties by playing favorites with the contending factions. Market forces must be allowed to operate freely to bring the target's shareholders the best price available for their equity.[16] Thus, as the trial court ruled, the shareholders' interests necessitated that the board remain free to negotiate in the fulfillment of that duty.

The court below similarly enjoined the payment of the cancellation fee, pending a resolution of the merits, because the fee was part of the overall plan to thwart Pantry Pride's efforts. We find no abuse of discretion in that ruling....

V.

In conclusion, the Revlon board was confronted with a situation not uncommon in the current wave of corporate takeovers. A hostile and determined bidder sought the company at a price the board was convinced was inadequate. The initial defensive tactics worked to the benefit of the

---

16. By this we do not embrace the "passivity" thesis rejected in *Unocal. See* 493 A.2d at 954-55, nn.8-10. The directors' role remains an active one, changed only in the respect that they are charged with the duty of selling the company at the highest price attainable for the stockholders' benefit.

shareholders, and thus the board was able to sustain its *Unocal* burdens in justifying those measures. However, in granting an asset option lock-up to Forstmann, we must conclude that under all the circumstances the directors allowed considerations other than the maximization of shareholder profit to affect their judgment, and followed a course that ended the auction for Revlon, absent court intervention, to the ultimate detriment of its shareholders. No such defensive measure can be sustained when it represents a breach of the directors' fundamental duty of care. *See Smith v. Van Gorkom*, Del. Supr., 488 A.2d 858, 874 (1985). In that context the board's action is not entitled to the deference accorded it by the business judgment rule. The measures were properly enjoined. The decision of the Court of Chancery, therefore, is AFFIRMED.

NOTES AND QUESTIONS

1. **The deal.** Where was the value coming from in this deal? The acquirer was Pantry Pride, headquartered in Fort Lauderdale, Florida. The firm, recently renamed from Food Fair after coming out of bankruptcy, had its origins in the high-volume, minimum-overhead grocery business. As such, it seemed an unlikely suitor for Revlon, known for its glamour advertising and higher-margin cosmetics. But Pantry Pride had come under the wing of Ronald Perelman, who with this deal and others was going to build a fortune. How are these characteristics likely to impact the interest of Mr. Bergerac and the Revlon managers in doing a deal?

2. **The initial response of the Revlon board.** Do the math resulting from the share repurchase plan that was an initial focus of the directors. How much of a defensive tactic would that be to a subsequent offer? How would it be reviewed by a Delaware judge?

3. **The post-August 19 board action.** Why didn't the board stand pat after August 19? Likely for reasons similar to why the Unocal board decided to remove its conditions limiting their counteroffer to just 50 million shares. These takeovers are taking place in a dynamic market in which directors are hearing from investors and the market and feel a need to respond apart from the legal aspects. But the additional responses trigger a different legal review and one that is potentially much more burdensome to deal planners and their clients. How has the maneuvering room for the Revlon directors changed?

4. **"Revlonland."** This case generated the *Revlon* rule and the enhanced duty that flows from that. Most managers and directors would prefer to avoid being in Revlonland. How would you define the breakpoint at which this broader duty is created? If your clients wanted to avoid this status, what advice would you give?

B. APPLYING *UNOCAL* AND *REVLON*—THE TWO PARAMOUNTS

Paramount Communications, Inc. v. Time Inc.
571 A.2d 1140 (Del. Sup. Ct. 1989)

Horsey, Justice:

[This suit seeks to enjoin Time Incorporated's tender offer for 51 percent of the outstanding shares of Warner Communications, Inc. The tender offer replaced a planned merger agreement between Time and Warner that had been abandoned in the face of Paramount's all-cash offer to purchase all of the outstanding shares of Time for $175 per share. Paramount and shareholders of Time filed suits alleging that the merger agreement resulted in a change of control that effectively put Time up for sale, thereby triggering *Revlon* duties, and that Time's response to the Paramount tender offer breached its duties under *Unocal*.

The boards of directors of Time and Warner agreed to a stock-for-stock merger on March 3, 1989, culminating three years of discussions between the two media companies. Time's traditional business of magazine and book publication had been expanded to include pay television programming through its Home Box Office, Inc. and Cinemax subsidiaries and cable television franchises. Warner, a long-recognized name in the movie business, possessed an international distribution system, large interests in the music and recording business, and cable television systems.

In 1987, a special committee of executives proposed that Time should expand in the areas of ownership and creation of video programming. In the spring of 1987, Time and Warner discussed the possibility of a joint venture between the two companies through the creation of a jointly owned cable company that would produce and distribute movies. Tax considerations and other issues caused this plan to be abandoned, but Time's interest in Warner continued over the next year. In July 1988, the Time board considered several companies in the entertainment industry and concluded that Warner was a superior candidate for consolidation.

Discussions between the two companies reached an impasse over certain corporate governance issues. Warner insisted on a stock swap in order to preserve the Warner shareholders' equity in the resulting corporation. Time preferred to pay cash and/or securities to acquire Warner. Time wanted to dominate the discussion of who would be CEO at the merged company in order to preserve the "Time culture." The court noted that the primary concern of Time's outside directors—the preservation of the "Time culture"—sprang from Time's recognition as a respected journalistic institution. Several of Time's outside directors feared that a merger with an entertainment company would divert Time's focus from news journalism and threaten the Time culture.

B. Applying Unocal and Revlon — The Two Paramounts

During the fall of 1988, Time held informal discussions with several companies including Paramount. Time steadfastly maintained it was not placing itself up for sale and terminated talks with Capital Cities/ABC when that company wanted to control the resulting board.

Warner and Time resumed negotiations in January 1989, leading to the merger agreement in March. The agreement called for Warner to be merged with a wholly-owned Time subsidiary, with Warner becoming the surviving company. The resulting company would have a 24-member board with 12 members representing each corporation. The company would have co-CEOs for the first few years, with Time's president to be designated as sole CEO upon the retirement of Warner CEO, Steve Ross. The board would create an editorial committee with a majority of members representing Time and an entertainment committee controlled by Warner board members. The parties agreed on an exchange rate favoring Warner by which former Warner stockholders would own about 62 percent of the common stock of Time-Warner, Inc. Time's board had recognized the potential need to pay a premium in the stock ratio in exchange for dictating the governing arrangement of the new Time-Warner and to preserve the Time culture.

At its March 3 meeting, the Time board adopted several defensive tactics, including an automatic stock exchange where each company would acquire about 10 percent of the shares of the other, a no-shop clause preventing Time from considering any other consolidation proposals regardless of their merits, and agreements with various banks that the Chancellor found to be futile efforts to "dry up" money for a hostile takeover.

On June 7, 1989, after Time had sent out extensive proxy statements to its shareholders seeking approval of the merger, but before the shareholder's meeting scheduled for June 23, Paramount announced its all-cash offer. Paramount's offer was subject to several conditions, including requiring Time to terminate its merger and stock exchange agreement with Warner, and Time removing certain defensive tactics including its poison pill. In response to the Paramount offer of $175 per share, the trading price of Time stock rose from $126 to $170. Over the following eight days, Time's board met three times to discuss Paramount's offer. After hearing from Time's financial advisers, who said that Time's per share value was materially higher than $175 on an auction basis, the board concluded that Paramount's $175 bid was inadequate.

The court said that the board's prevailing belief was that Paramount's bid presented a threat to Time's control of its own destiny and retention of the Time culture. The board feared that Paramount's cash premium would be a tempting prospect to institutional investors who held large quantities of Time stock. Certain Time directors expressed their concern that their stockholders would not comprehend the long-term benefits of the Warner merger. Thus, the Time-Warner merger was recast as an outright cash and securities acquisition of Warner by Time, 51 percent to be acquired in a $70 per share cash tender offer with the remaining 49 percent to be acquired later for cash and securities. To provide the funds required for the acquisition, Time would take on $7-$10 billion of debt, thus eliminating the company's low-debt status, which had been one of the principal transaction-related benefits of the original merger. The Chancellor found the initial Time-Warner transaction to have been negotiated at arm's length and the restructured Time-Warner transaction to have resulted from Paramount's offer and its expected effect on a Time shareholder vote.

On June 23, Paramount raised its all-cash offer to $200 per share. The Time board reiterated its belief that the offer was still inadequate and that the Warner transaction offered a greater long-term value to the stockholders and, unlike Paramount, was not a threat to Time's survival and its "culture".]

II.

The Shareholder Plaintiffs first assert a *Revlon* claim. They contend that the March 4 Time-Warner agreement effectively put Time up for sale, triggering *Revlon* duties, requiring Time's board to enhance short-term shareholder value and to treat all other interested acquirors on an equal basis. The Shareholder Plaintiffs base this argument on two facts: (i) the ultimate Time-Warner exchange ratio of .465 favoring Warner, resulting in Warner shareholders' receipt of 62% of the combined company; and (ii) the subjective intent of Time's directors as evidenced in their statements that the market might perceive the Time-Warner merger as putting Time up "for sale" and their adoption of various defensive measures.

The Shareholder Plaintiffs further contend that Time's directors, in structuring the original merger transaction to be "takeover-proof," triggered *Revlon* duties by foreclosing their shareholders from any prospect of obtaining a control premium. In short, plaintiffs argue that Time's board's decision to merge with Warner imposed a fiduciary duty to maximize immediate share value and not erect unreasonable barriers to further bids. Therefore, they argue, the Chancellor erred in finding: that Paramount's bid for Time did not place Time "for sale"; that Time's transaction with Warner did not result in any transfer of control; and that the combined Time-Warner was not so large as to preclude the possibility of the stockholders of Time-Warner receiving a future control premium.

Paramount asserts only a *Unocal* claim in which the shareholder plaintiffs join. Paramount contends that the Chancellor, in applying the first part of the *Unocal* test, erred in finding that Time's board had reasonable grounds to believe that Paramount posed both a legally cognizable threat to Time shareholders and a danger to Time's corporate policy and effectiveness. Paramount also contests the court's finding that Time's board made a reasonable and objective investigation of Paramount's offer so as to be informed before rejecting it. Paramount further claims that the court erred in applying *Unocal*'s second part in finding Time's response to be "reasonable." Paramount points primarily to the preclusive effect of the revised agreement which denied Time shareholders the opportunity both to vote on the agreement and to respond to Paramount's tender offer. Paramount argues that the underlying motivation of Time's board in adopting these defensive measures was management's desire to perpetuate itself in office.

The Court of Chancery posed the pivotal question presented by this case to be: Under what circumstances must a board of directors abandon an in-place plan of corporate development in order to provide its shareholders with the option to elect and realize an immediate control premium? As applied to this case, the question becomes: Did Time's board, having developed a strategic plan of global expansion to be launched through a business combination with Warner, come under a fiduciary duty to jettison its plan and put the corporation's future in the hands of its shareholders?

While we affirm the result reached by the Chancellor, we think it unwise to place undue emphasis upon long-term versus short-term corporate strategy. Two key predicates underpin our analysis. First, Delaware law imposes on a board of directors the duty to manage the business and affairs of the corporation. 8 Del. C. §141(a). This broad mandate includes a conferred authority to set a corporate course of action, including time frame, designed to enhance corporate profitability. Thus, the question of "long-term" versus "short-term" values is largely irrelevant because directors, generally, are obliged to chart a course for a corporation which is in its best interests without regard to a fixed investment horizon. Second, absent a limited set of circumstances as defined under *Revlon*, a board of directors, while always required to act in an informed manner, is not under any *per se* duty to maximize shareholder value in the short term, even in the context of a takeover.[12] In our view, the pivotal question presented by this case is: "Did Time, by entering into the proposed merger with Warner, put itself up for sale?" A resolution of that issue through application of *Revlon* has a significant bearing upon the resolution of the derivative *Unocal* issue.

A.

We first take up plaintiffs' principal *Revlon* argument, summarized above. In rejecting this argument, the Chancellor found the original Time-Warner merger agreement not to constitute a "change of control" and concluded that the transaction did not trigger *Revlon* duties. The Chancellor's conclusion is premised on a finding that "[b]efore the merger

---

12. Thus, we endorse the Chancellor's conclusion that it is not a breach of faith for directors to determine that the present stock market price of shares is not representative of true value or that there may indeed be several market values for any corporation's stock. We have so held in another context. *See Van Gorkom*, 488 A.2d at 876.

agreement was signed, control of the corporation existed in a fluid aggregation of unaffiliated shareholders representing a voting majority — in other words, in the market." The Chancellor's findings of fact are supported by the record and his conclusion is correct as a matter of law. However, we premise our rejection of plaintiffs' *Revlon* claim on different grounds, namely, the absence of any substantial evidence to conclude that Time's board, in negotiating with Warner, made the dissolution or break-up of the corporate entity inevitable, as was the case in *Revlon*.

Under Delaware law there are, generally speaking and without excluding other possibilities, two circumstances which may implicate *Revlon* duties. The first, and clearer one, is when a corporation initiates an active bidding process seeking to sell itself or to effect a business reorganization involving a clear break-up of the company. *See, e.g., Mills Acquisition Co. v. Macmillan, Inc*, Del. Supr., 559 A.2d 1261 (1988). However, *Revlon* duties may also be triggered where, in response to a bidder's offer, a target abandons its long-term strategy and seeks an alternative transaction involving the breakup of the company. Thus, in *Revlon*, when the board responded to Pantry Pride's offer by contemplating a "bust-up" sale of assets in a leveraged acquisition, we imposed upon the board a duty to maximize immediate shareholder value and an obligation to auction the company fairly. If, however, the board's reaction to a hostile tender offer is found to constitute only a defensive response and not an abandonment of the corporation's continued existence, *Revlon* duties are not triggered, though *Unocal* duties attach.[14] *See, e.g., Ivanhoe Partners v. Newmont Mining Corp*., Del. Supr., 535 A.2d 1334, 1345 (1987).

The plaintiffs insist that even though the original Time-Warner agreement may not have worked "an objective change of control," the transaction made a "sale" of Time inevitable. Plaintiffs rely on the subjective intent of Time's board of directors and principally upon certain board members' expressions of concern that the Warner transaction *might* be viewed as effectively putting Time up for sale. Plaintiffs argue that the use of a lock-up agreement, a no-shop clause, and so-called "dry-up" agreements prevented shareholders from obtaining a control premium in the immediate future and thus violated *Revlon*.

We agree with the Chancellor that such evidence is entirely insufficient to invoke *Revlon* duties; and we decline to extend *Revlon*'s application to corporate transactions simply because they might be construed as putting a corporation either "in play" or "up for sale." *See Citron v. Fairchild*

---

14. Within the auction process, any action taken by the board must be reasonably related to the threat posed or reasonable in relation to the advantage sought, *see Mills Acquisition Co. v. Macmillan, Inc.*, Del. Supr., 559 A.2d 1261, 1288 (1988). Thus, a *Unocal* analysis may be appropriate when a corporation is in a *Revlon* situation and *Revlon* duties may be triggered by a defensive action taken in response to a hostile offer. Since *Revlon*, we have stated that differing treatment of various bidders is not actionable when such action reasonably relates to achieving the best price available for the stockholders. *Macmillan*, 559 A.2d at 1286-87.

B. Applying Unocal and Revlon — The Two Paramounts

Camera, Del. Supr., 569 A.2d 53 (1989); *Macmillan*, 559 A.2d at 1285 n.35. The adoption of structural safety devices alone does not trigger *Revlon*. Rather, as the Chancellor stated, such devices are properly subject to a *Unocal* analysis.

Finally, we do not find in Time's recasting of its merger agreement with Warner from a share exchange to a share purchase a basis to conclude that Time had either abandoned its strategic plan or made a sale of Time inevitable. The Chancellor found that although the merged Time-Warner company would be large (with a value approaching approximately $30 billion), recent takeover cases have proven that acquisition of the combined company might nonetheless be possible. *In re Time Incorporated Shareholder Litigation*, Del. Ch., C.A. No. 10670, Allen, C. (July 14, 1989), slip op. at 56. The legal consequence is that *Unocal* alone applies to determine whether the business judgment rule attaches to the revised agreement. Plaintiffs' analogy to *Macmillan* thus collapses and plaintiffs' reliance on *Macmillan* is misplaced.

B.

We turn now to plaintiffs' *Unocal* claim. We begin by noting, as did the Chancellor, that our decision does not require us to pass on the wisdom of the board's decision to enter into the original Time-Warner agreement. That is not a court's task. Our task is simply to review the record to determine whether there is sufficient evidence to support the Chancellor's conclusion that the initial Time-Warner agreement was the product of a proper exercise of business judgment. *Macmillan*, 559 A.2d at 1288.

We have purposely detailed the evidence of the Time board's deliberative approach, beginning in 1983-84, to expand itself. Time's decision in 1988 to combine with Warner was made only after what could be fairly characterized as an exhaustive appraisal of Time's future as a corporation. After concluding in 1983-84 that the corporation must expand to survive, and beyond journalism into entertainment, the board combed the field of available entertainment companies. By 1987 Time had focused upon Warner; by late July 1988 Time's board was convinced that Warner would provide the best "fit" for Time to achieve its strategic objectives. The record attests to the zealousness of Time's executives, fully supported by their directors, in seeing to the preservation of Time's "culture," i.e., its perceived editorial integrity in journalism. We find ample evidence in the record to support the Chancellor's conclusion that the Time board's decision to expand the business of the company through its March 3 merger with Warner was entitled to the protection of the business judgment rule. *See Aronson v. Lewis*, Del. Supr., 473 A.2d 805, 812 (1984).

. . . The court ruled that *Unocal* applied to all director actions taken, following receipt of Paramount's hostile tender offer, that were reasonably determined to be defensive. Clearly that was a correct ruling and no party disputes that ruling.

In *Unocal*, we held that before the business judgment rule is applied to a board's adoption of a defensive measure, the burden will lie with the board to prove (a) reasonable grounds for believing that a danger to corporate policy and effectiveness existed; and (b) that the defensive measure adopted was reasonable in relation to the threat posed. *Unocal*, 493 A.2d at 946. Directors satisfy the first part of the *Unocal* test by demonstrating good faith and reasonable investigation. We have repeatedly stated that the refusal to entertain an offer may comport with a valid exercise of a board's business judgment. *See, e.g., Macmillan*, 559 A.2d at 1285 n.35; *Van Gorkom*, 488 A.2d at 881; *Pogostin v. Rice*, Del. Supr., 480 A.2d 619, 627 (1984).

Unocal involved a two-tier, highly coercive tender offer. In such a case, the threat is obvious: shareholders may be compelled to tender to avoid being treated adversely in the second stage of the transaction. *Accord Ivanhoe*, 535 A.2d at 1344. In subsequent cases, the Court of Chancery has suggested that an all-cash, all-shares offer, falling within a range of values that a shareholder might reasonably prefer, cannot constitute a legally recognized "threat" to shareholder interests sufficient to withstand a *Unocal* analysis. *AC Acquisitions Corp. v. Anderson, Clayton & Co.*, Del. Ch., 519 A.2d 103 (1986); *see Grand Metropolitan, PLC v. Pillsbury Co.*, Del. Ch., 558 A.2d 1049 (1988); *City Capital Associates v. Interco, Inc.*, Del. Ch., 551 A.2d 787 (1988). In those cases, the Court of Chancery determined that whatever threat existed related only to the shareholders and only to price and not to the corporation.

From those decisions by our Court of Chancery, Paramount and the individual plaintiffs extrapolate a rule of law that an all-cash, all-shares offer with values reasonably in the range of acceptable price cannot pose any objective threat to a corporation or its shareholders. Thus, Paramount would have us hold that only if the value of Paramount's offer were determined to be clearly inferior to the value created by management's plan to merge with Warner could the offer be viewed — objectively — as a threat.

Implicit in the plaintiffs' argument is the view that a hostile tender offer can pose only two types of threats: the threat of coercion that results from a two-tier offer promising unequal treatment for nontendering shareholders; and the threat of inadequate value from an all-shares, all-cash offer at a price below what a target board in good faith deems to be the present value of its shares. *See, e.g., Interco*, 551 A.2d at 797; *see also BNS, Inc. v. Koppers*, D. Del., 683 F. Supp. 458 (1988). Since Paramount's offer was all-cash, the only conceivable "threat," plaintiffs argue, was inadequate value.[17]

---

17. Some commentators have suggested that the threats posed by hostile offers be categorized into not two but three types: "(i) *opportunity loss* . . . [where] a hostile offer might deprive target shareholders of the opportunity to select a superior alternative offered by target management [or, we would add, offered by another bidder]; (ii) *structural coercion*, . . . the risk that disparate treatment of non-

We disapprove of such a narrow and rigid construction of *Unocal*, for the reasons which follow.

Plaintiffs' position represents a fundamental misconception of our standard of review under *Unocal* principally because it would involve the court in substituting its judgment as to what is a "better" deal for that of a corporation's board of directors. To the extent that the Court of Chancery has recently done so in certain of its opinions, we hereby reject such approach as not in keeping with a proper *Unocal* analysis. *See, e.g., Interco*, 551 A.2d 787, and its progeny; *but see TW Services, Inc. v. SWT Acquisition Corp.*, Del. Ch., C.A. No. 1047, Allen, C. 1989 WL 20290 (March 2, 1989).

The usefulness of *Unocal* as an analytical tool is precisely its flexibility in the face of a variety of fact scenarios. *Unocal* is not intended as an abstract standard; neither is it a structured and mechanistic procedure of appraisal. Thus, we have said that directors may consider, when evaluating the threat posed by a takeover bid, the "inadequacy of the price offered, nature and timing of the offer, questions of illegality, the impact on 'constituencies' other than shareholders . . . the risk of nonconsummation, and the quality of securities being offered in the exchange." 493 A.2d at 955. The open-ended analysis mandated by *Unocal* is not intended to lead to a simple mathematical exercise: that is, of comparing the discounted value of Time-Warner's expected trading price at some future date with Paramount's offer and determining which is the higher. Indeed, in our view, precepts underlying the business judgment rule militate against a court's engaging in the process of attempting to appraise and evaluate the relative merits of a long-term versus a short-term investment goal for shareholders. To engage in such an exercise is a distortion of the *Unocal* process and, in particular, the application of the second part of *Unocal*'s test, discussed below.

In this case, the Time board reasonably determined that inadequate value was not the only legally cognizable threat that Paramount's all-cash, all-shares offer could present. Time's board concluded that Paramount's eleventh hour offer posed other threats. One concern was that Time shareholders might elect to tender into Paramount's cash offer in ignorance or a mistaken belief of the strategic benefit which a business combination with Warner might produce. Moreover, Time viewed the conditions attached to Paramount's offer as introducing a degree of uncertainty that skewed a comparative analysis. Further, the timing of Paramount's offer to follow issuance of Time's proxy notice was viewed as arguably designed to upset, if not confuse, the Time stockholders' vote. Given this record evidence, we

---

tendering shareholders might distort shareholders' tender decisions; and . . . (iii) *substantive coercion*, . . . the risk that shareholders will mistakenly accept an underpriced offer because they disbelieve management's representations of intrinsic value." The recognition of substantive coercion, the authors suggest, would help guarantee that the *Unocal* standard becomes an effective intermediate standard of review. Gilson & Kraakman, *Delaware's Intermediate Standard for Defensive Tactics: Is There Substance to Proportionality Review?*, 44 THE BUSINESS LAWYER 247, 267 (1989).

cannot conclude that the Time board's decision of June 6 that Paramount's offer posed a threat to corporate policy and effectiveness was lacking in good faith or dominated by motives of either entrenchment or self-interest.

Paramount also contends that the Time board had not duly investigated Paramount's offer. Therefore, Paramount argues, Time was unable to make an informed decision that the offer posed a threat to Time's corporate policy. Although the Chancellor did not address this issue directly, his findings of fact do detail Time's exploration of the available entertainment companies, including Paramount, before determining that Warner provided the best strategic "fit." In addition, the court found that Time's board rejected Paramount's offer because Paramount did not serve Time's objectives or meet Time's needs. Thus, the record does, in our judgment, demonstrate that Time's board was adequately informed of the potential benefits of a transaction with Paramount. We agree with the Chancellor that the Time board's lengthy pre-June investigation of potential merger candidates, including Paramount, mooted any obligation on Time's part to halt its merger process with Warner to reconsider Paramount. Time's board was under no obligation to negotiate with Paramount. *Unocal*, 493 A.2d at 954-55; *see also Macmillan*, 559 A.2d at 1285 n.35. Time's failure to negotiate cannot be fairly found to have been uninformed. The evidence supporting this finding is materially enhanced by the fact that twelve of Time's sixteen board members were outside independent directors. *Unocal*, 493 A.2d at 955; *Moran v. Household Intern., Inc.*, Del. Supr., 500 A.2d 1346, 1356 (1985).

We turn to the second part of the *Unocal* analysis. The obvious requisite to determining the reasonableness of a defensive action is a clear identification of the nature of the threat. As the Chancellor correctly noted, this "requires an evaluation of the importance of the corporate objective threatened; alternative methods of protecting that objective; impacts of the 'defensive' action, and other relevant factors." *In Re: Time Incorporated Shareholder Litigation*, Del. Ch., 1989 WL 79880 (July 14, 1989). It is not until both parts of the *Unocal* inquiry have been satisfied that the business judgment rule attaches to defensive actions of a board of directors. *Unocal*, 493 A.2d at 954. As applied to the facts of this case, the question is whether the record evidence supports the Court of Chancery's conclusion that the restructuring of the Time-Warner transaction, including the adoption of several preclusive defensive measures, was a *reasonable response* in relation to a perceived threat.

Paramount argues that, assuming its tender offer posed a threat, Time's response was unreasonable in precluding Time's shareholders from accepting the tender offer or receiving a control premium in the immediately foreseeable future. Once again, the contention stems, we believe, from a fundamental misunderstanding of where the power of corporate governance lies. Delaware law confers the management of the corporate enterprise to the stockholders' duly elected board representatives. 8 Del. C. §141(a). The fiduciary duty to manage a corporate enterprise includes the selection of a time frame for achievement of corporate goals. That

B. Applying Unocal *and* Revlon — *The Two Paramounts*

duty may not be delegated to the stockholders. *Van Gorkom*, 488 A.2d at 873. Directors are not obliged to abandon a deliberately conceived corporate plan for a short-term shareholder profit unless there is clearly no basis to sustain the corporate strategy. *See, e.g., Revlon,* 506 A.2d at 173.

Although the Chancellor blurred somewhat the discrete analyses required under *Unocal*, he did conclude that Time's board reasonably perceived Paramount's offer to be a significant threat to the planned Time-Warner merger and that Time's response was not "overly broad." We have found that even in light of a valid threat, management actions that are coercive in nature or force upon shareholders a management-sponsored alternative to a hostile offer may be struck down as unreasonable and nonproportionate responses. *Macmillan*, 559 A.2d at 1261; *AC Acquisitions Corp.*, 519 A.2d at 103.

Here, on the record facts, the Chancellor found that Time's responsive action to Paramount's tender offer was not aimed at "cramming down" on its shareholders a management-sponsored alternative, but rather had as its goal the carrying forward of a pre-existing transaction in an altered form.[19] Thus, the response was reasonably related to the threat. The Chancellor noted that the revised agreement and its accompanying safety devices did not preclude Paramount from making an offer for the combined Time-Warner company or from changing the conditions of its offer so as not to make the offer dependent upon the nullification of the Time-Warner agreement. Thus, the response was proportionate. We affirm the Chancellor's rulings as clearly supported by the record. Finally, we note that although Time was required, as a result of Paramount's hostile offer, to incur a heavy debt to finance its acquisition of Warner, that fact alone does not render the board's decision unreasonable so long as the directors could reasonably perceive the debt load not to be so injurious to the corporation as to jeopardize its well being.

C.

Conclusion

Applying the test for grant or denial of preliminary injunctive relief, we find plaintiffs failed to establish a reasonable likelihood of ultimate success on the merits. Therefore, we affirm.

---

19. The Chancellor cited *Shamrock Holdings, Inc. v. Polaroid Corp.*, Del. Ch., 559 A.2d 257 (1989), as a closely analogous case. In that case, the Court of Chancery upheld, in the face of a takeover bid, the establishment of an employee stock ownership plan that had a significant antitakeover effect. The Court of Chancery upheld the board's action largely because the ESOP had been adopted *prior* to any contest for control and was reasonably determined to increase productivity and enhance profits. The ESOP did not appear to be primarily a device to affect or secure corporate control.

NOTES AND QUESTIONS

1. **Reasons for the deal.** Evaluate how the Time-Warner combination might create value based on the various possibilities set out in Chapter 2. Time directors and management had been addressing how to create new value for several years. Several challenges and opportunities to the company given the then current business context seemed likely given the facts in the opinion:

- Time's traditional business of magazines (*Time, Sports Illustrated, People*) likely would have slower growth. Time had expanded into alternative entertainment ventures including both "content" (e.g., HBO and Cinemax) and the "pipe" for carrying content, but may not yet have developed sufficient economies of scale and scope for those industries;
- It may become more difficult to compete in the entertainment venues without expansion and new resources. Movies/content were becoming more expensive to make, likely requiring a greater ability to bear and spread risk;
- Globalization was another industry shock in terms of expanding the commitment required to be a player in the entertainment business as well as traditional businesses.

2. **Structure of the deal.** While the Time management and directors were aware of the benefits from such a combination, the terms of the deal reflected both these synergies and more particular concerns to the Time directors and managers:

- *Type of consideration.* What is the significance of the type of consideration given the economics of the deal discussed above?
- *Amount of consideration.* The facts tell you that Warner shareholders received a premium in terms of the portion of the combined business that will be owned by that set of shareholders once the combination occurs. Retain that fact when you evaluate the options the planners have once Paramount shows up. Although Time shareholders were to receive a smaller portion relative to Warner shareholders, the value of their shares nevertheless went up (to about $120 per share), suggesting the market believed that there was some real synergy in this deal.
- *Governance provisions.* Splitting the new board equally between the two old boards is common in mergers termed a "merger of equals," as this one was. Having co-CEOs is sometimes tried in these deals, but the results are not always as predicted. Having separate board committees for the journalist and entertainment parts of the

B. Applying Unocal and Revlon—The Two Paramounts

business is more unusual. Together, the provisions show a real effort of the Time managers to pick the terms for the combined business and likely suggests some mistrust of those movie guys from Hollywood in running what had become a pillar of the American media establishment.

3. Paramount's motivation to enter the fray. Paramount, like Warner, was one of the traditionally dominant American movie houses, although it had adapted to industry changes less than Warner and at the same time had a fair amount of cash from having recently sold a large unrelated business. What would you expect Paramount's strategic goals to be, given the environment in the entertainment business discussed in Note 1? Would you expect that Paramount would realize similar synergies in combining with Time? What do you make of Paramount offering $175 and then $200 for Time shares?

4. Decision time for the Time board and managers. Time's decision to merge with Warner reflected study by its managers and directors of what Time needed in the current environment. They had picked Warner from among other possible partners (including Paramount) and had negotiated governance provisions that insured the future of the top Time executives and protected the Time culture. All that remained was approval by the Time shareholders. (*Query:* Why was a vote by the surviving corporation shareholders required given the legal form chosen for this deal?) After the proxy statements had been mailed for the shareholder vote, Paramount made public its offer to acquire Time shares for $175. Consider your options as a Time director. How do you evaluate the likelihood of acquiring the necessary shareholder approval? How would you view the career prospects of the top Time executives if Paramount were to triumph? In this context, Time and their advisors chose to restructure the acquisition. The new form is very directly related to the legal requirements for acquisitions that we have already studied. What advantage was gained by moving to the new form? How did the new form change the financial aspects of the deal discussed in Note 1 above?

5. The *Unocal* test. This case is an important application of the *Unocal* test. Consider how this opinion alters the two parts of the enhanced scrutiny test as first set out in *Unocal*:

a. *Threat.* The Supreme Court quotes approvingly the expanded definition of threat by the Chancery Court in *Interco*, found in Chapter 7. What is the result of this phrasing on the range of space for director defensive action?

b. *Proportionality.* What does this opinion say about the relative roles of directors and shareholders in making decisions about takeovers? If you were to read the Chancery Court opinion in this case, you will find that Chancellor Allen took the side of directors on the facts of this case, and this opinion suggests additional space for managers to maneuver after this case.

6. **The *Revlon* test.** This opinion is more cited today for what it tells us about the trigger for the *Revlon* test. Look carefully at the two core circumstances that the court says trigger *Revlon*. Had Time done either one? So, having been found outside of "Revlonland," what result? We return to the default rule of corporate law that directors get to decide, and the Time-Warner transaction was completed. So what kinds of transactions will trigger *Revlon*? It is worthwhile to develop a test that fits the cases you have seen to this point, but you will want to be open to modification after reading the next case.

7. **After the marriage.** As for the two sets of shareholders, Warner shareholders got cash for a majority of their shares, at a premium. Time shareholders saw the value of their shares fall, not just away from the $200 that reflected the possibility of the Paramount bid, but also below the $120 benchmark prior to the change. What would account for the difference? Recall the change in the type of consideration and the debt Time had to take on for the alternative deal. Time later tried various things to pay down this debt, but its presence continued to weigh down its stock price. Time shareholders never saw a return to the $120 level, and its subsequent merger with AOL prolonged the period in which the stock failed to reach its earlier high. As for the co-CEOs, Warner's Steven Ross proved more adept at boardroom politics. Within a short period, he persuaded two Time directors to leave the board and not too long after, persuaded the board to end the shared CEO position. The result was that Warner shareholders got a premium for their shares, Warner's CEO ended up running the combined company, and Time shareholders experienced a prolonged period of a low share price relative to what would have been available in the Paramount offer. By 2014 Time Warner was spinning off its magazines and seeking a buyer for its cable business.

Paramount Communications, Inc. v. QVC Network Inc.
637 A.2d 34 (Del. Sup. Ct. 1994)

VEASEY, Chief Justice.

In this appeal we review an order of the Court of Chancery dated November 24, 1993 (the "November 24 Order"), preliminarily enjoining certain defensive measures designed to facilitate a so-called strategic alliance between Viacom Inc. ("Viacom") and Paramount Communications Inc. ("Paramount") approved by the board of directors of Paramount (the "Paramount Board" or the "Paramount directors") and to thwart an unsolicited, more valuable, tender offer by QVC Network Inc. ("QVC"). In affirming, we hold that the sale of control in this case, which is at the heart of the proposed strategic alliance, implicates enhanced judicial scrutiny of the conduct of the Paramount Board under *Unocal Corp. v. Mesa Petroleum Co.*, Del. Supr., 493 A.2d 946 (1985), and *Revlon, Inc. v. MacAndrews & Forbes Holdings, Inc.*, Del. Supr., 506 A.2d 173 (1986). We further hold that the conduct of the Paramount Board was not reasonable as to process or result.

QVC and certain stockholders of Paramount commenced separate actions (later consolidated) in the Court of Chancery seeking preliminary and permanent injunctive relief against Paramount, certain members of the Paramount Board, and Viacom. This action arises out of a proposed acquisition of Paramount by Viacom through a tender offer followed by a second-step merger (the "Paramount-Viacom transaction"), and a competing unsolicited tender offer by QVC. The Court of Chancery granted a preliminary injunction. *QVC Network, Inc. v. Paramount Communications Inc.*, Del. Ch., 635 A.2d 1245, Jacobs, V.C. (1993) (the "Court of Chancery Opinion"). We affirmed by order dated December 9, 1993. *Paramount Communications Inc. v. QVC Network Inc.*, Del. Supr., Nos. 427 and 428, 1993, 637 A.2d 828, Veasey, C.J. (Dec. 9, 1993) (the "December 9 Order").

I. Facts

... Paramount is a Delaware corporation with its principal offices in New York City. Approximately 118 million shares of Paramount's common stock are outstanding and traded on the New York Stock Exchange. The majority of Paramount's stock is publicly held by numerous unaffiliated investors. Paramount owns and operates a diverse group of entertainment businesses, including motion picture and television studios, book publishers, professional sports teams, and amusement parks.

There are 15 persons serving on the Paramount Board. Four directors are officer-employees of Paramount: Martin S. Davis ("Davis"), Paramount's Chairman and Chief Executive Officer since 1983; Donald Oresman ("Oresman"), Executive Vice-President, Chief Administrative Officer, and General Counsel; Stanley R. Jaffe, President and Chief Operating Officer; and Ronald L. Nelson, Executive Vice President and Chief Financial Officer. Paramount's 11 outside directors are distinguished and experienced business persons who are present or former senior executives of public corporations or financial institutions.

Viacom is a Delaware corporation with its headquarters in Massachusetts. Viacom is controlled by Sumner M. Redstone ("Redstone"), its Chairman and Chief Executive Officer, who owns indirectly approximately 85.2 percent of Viacom's voting Class A stock and approximately 69.2 percent of Viacom's nonvoting Class B stock through National Amusements, Inc. ("NAI"), an entity 91.7 percent owned by Redstone. Viacom has a wide range of entertainment operations, including a number of well-known cable television channels such as MTV, Nickelodeon, Showtime, and The Movie Channel. Viacom's equity co-investors in the Paramount-Viacom transaction include NYNEX Corporation and Blockbuster Entertainment Corporation.

QVC is a Delaware corporation with its headquarters in West Chester, Pennsylvania. QVC has several large stockholders, including Liberty Media Corporation, Comcast Corporation, Advance Publications, Inc., and Cox Enterprises Inc. Barry Diller ("Diller"), the Chairman and Chief Executive Officer of QVC, is also a substantial stockholder. QVC sells a variety of merchandise through a televised shopping channel. QVC has several equity co-investors in its proposed combination with Paramount including Bell-South Corporation and Comcast Corporation.

Beginning in the late 1980s, Paramount investigated the possibility of acquiring or merging with other companies in the entertainment, media, or communications industry. Paramount considered such transactions to be desirable, and perhaps necessary, in order to keep pace with competitors in the rapidly evolving field of entertainment and communications. Consistent with its goal of strategic expansion, Paramount made a tender offer for Time Inc. in 1989, but was ultimately unsuccessful. *See Paramount Communications, Inc. v. Time Inc.*, Del. Supr., 571 A.2d 1140 (1990) (*"Time-Warner"*).

Although Paramount had considered a possible combination of Paramount and Viacom as early as 1990, recent efforts to explore such a transaction began at a dinner meeting between Redstone and Davis on April 20, 1993. Robert Greenhill ("Greenhill"), Chairman of Smith Barney Shearson Inc. ("Smith Barney"), attended and helped facilitate this meeting. After several more meetings between Redstone and Davis, serious negotiations began taking place in early July.

It was tentatively agreed that Davis would be the chief executive officer and Redstone would be the controlling stockholder of the combined company, but the parties could not reach agreement on the merger price and the terms of a stock option to be granted to Viacom. [Negotiations broke down, but reopened when Davis learned of QVC's potential interest in Paramount.]

On September 12, 1993, the Paramount Board met again and unanimously approved the Original Merger Agreement whereby Paramount would merge with and into Viacom. The terms of the merger provided that each share of Paramount common stock would be converted into 0.10 shares of Viacom Class A voting stock, 0.90 shares of Viacom Class B nonvoting stock, and $9.10 in cash. In addition, the Paramount Board agreed to amend its "poison pill" Rights Agreement to exempt the proposed merger with Viacom. The Original Merger Agreement also contained several provisions designed to make it more difficult for a potential competing bid to succeed. We focus, as did the Court of Chancery, on three of these defensive provisions: a "no-shop" provision (the "No-Shop Provision"), the Termination Fee, and the Stock Option Agreement.

First, under the No-Shop Provision, the Paramount Board agreed that Paramount would not solicit, encourage, discuss, negotiate, or endorse any

B. Applying Unocal *and* Revlon — *The Two Paramounts*

competing transaction unless: (a) a third party "makes an unsolicited written, bona fide proposal, which is not subject to any material contingencies relating to financing"; and (b) the Paramount Board determines that discussions or negotiations with the third party are necessary for the Paramount Board to comply with its fiduciary duties.

Second, under the Termination Fee provision, Viacom would receive a $100 million termination fee if: (a) Paramount terminated the Original Merger Agreement because of a competing transaction; (b) Paramount's stockholders did not approve the merger; or (c) the Paramount Board recommended a competing transaction.

The third and most significant deterrent device was the Stock Option Agreement, which granted to Viacom an option to purchase approximately 19.9 percent (23,699,000 shares) of Paramount's outstanding common stock at $69.14 per share if any of the triggering events for the Termination Fee occurred. In addition to the customary terms that are normally associated with a stock option, the Stock Option Agreement contained two provisions that were both unusual and highly beneficial to Viacom: (a) Viacom was permitted to pay for the shares with a senior subordinated note of questionable marketability instead of cash, thereby avoiding the need to raise the $1.6 billion purchase price (the "Note Feature"); and (b) Viacom could elect to require Paramount to pay Viacom in cash a sum equal to the difference between the purchase price and the market price of Paramount's stock (the "Put Feature"). Because the Stock Option Agreement was not "capped" to limit its maximum dollar value, it had the potential to reach (and in this case did reach) unreasonable levels.

After the execution of the Original Merger Agreement and the Stock Option Agreement on September 12, 1993, Paramount and Viacom announced their proposed merger. In a number of public statements, the parties indicated that the pending transaction was a virtual certainty. Redstone described it as a "marriage" that would "never be torn asunder" and stated that only a "nuclear attack" could break the deal. Redstone also called Diller and John Malone of Tele-Communications Inc., a major stockholder of QVC, to dissuade them from making a competing bid.

Despite these attempts to discourage a competing bid, Diller sent a letter to Davis on September 20, 1993, proposing a merger in which QVC would acquire Paramount for approximately $80 per share[, thereafter QVC attempted to engage Paramount in Meaningful Merger negotiations].

On October 21, 1993, QVC filed this action and publicly announced an $80 cash tender offer for 51 percent of Paramount's outstanding shares (the "QVC tender offer"). Each remaining share of Paramount common stock would be converted into 1.42857 shares of QVC common stock in a second-step merger. The tender offer was conditioned on, among other things, the invalidation of the Stock Option Agreement, which was worth over $200 million by that point.[5] QVC contends that it had to commence a tender offer because of the slow pace of the merger discussions and the need to begin seeking clearance under federal antitrust laws.

Confronted by QVC's hostile bid, which on its face offered over $10 per share more than the consideration provided by the Original Merger Agreement, Viacom realized that it would need to raise its bid in order to remain competitive. . . .

At a special meeting on October 24, 1993, the Paramount Board approved the Amended Merger Agreement and an amendment to the Stock Option Agreement. . . .

Although the Amended Merger Agreement offered more consideration to the Paramount stockholders and somewhat more flexibility to the Paramount Board than did the Original Merger Agreement, the defensive measures designed to make a competing bid more difficult were not removed or modified. In particular, there is no evidence in the record that Paramount sought to use its newly-acquired leverage to eliminate or modify the No-Shop Provision, the Termination Fee, or the Stock Option Agreement when the subject of amending the Original Merger Agreement was on the table.

Viacom's tender offer commenced on October 25, 1993, and QVC's tender offer was formally launched on October 27, 1993. Diller sent a letter to the Paramount Board on October 28 requesting an opportunity to negotiate with Paramount, and Oresman responded the following day by agreeing to meet. The meeting, held on November 1, was not very fruitful, however, after QVC's proposed guidelines for a "fair bidding process" were rejected by Paramount on the ground that "auction procedures" were inappropriate and contrary to Paramount's contractual obligations to Viacom.

On November 6, 1993, Viacom unilaterally raised its tender offer price to $85 per share in cash and offered a comparable increase in the value of the securities being proposed in the second-step merger. At a telephonic meeting held later that day, the Paramount Board agreed to recommend Viacom's higher bid to Paramount's stockholders.

QVC responded to Viacom's higher bid on November 12 by increasing its tender offer to $90 per share and by increasing the securities for its second-step merger by a similar amount. In response to QVC's latest offer, the Paramount Board scheduled a meeting for November 15, 1993. Prior to the meeting, Oresman sent the members of the Paramount Board a document summarizing the "conditions and uncertainties" of QVC's offer. One director testified that this document gave him a very negative impression of the QVC bid.

At its meeting on November 15, 1993, the Paramount Board determined that the new QVC offer was not in the best interests of the

---

5. By November 15, 1993, the value of the Stock Option Agreement had increased to nearly $500 million based on the $90 QVC bid. *See* Court of Chancery Opinion, 635 A.2d 1245, 1271.

stockholders. The purported basis for this conclusion was that QVC's bid was excessively conditional. The Paramount Board did not communicate with QVC regarding the status of the conditions because it believed that the No-Shop Provision prevented such communication in the absence of firm financing. Several Paramount directors also testified that they believed the Viacom transaction would be more advantageous to Paramount's future business prospects than a QVC transaction. Although a number of materials were distributed to the Paramount Board describing the Viacom and QVC transactions, the only quantitative analysis of the consideration to be received by the stockholders under each proposal was based on then-current market prices of the securities involved, not on the anticipated value of such securities at the time when the stockholders would receive them. . . .

II. APPLICABLE PRINCIPLES OF ESTABLISHED DELAWARE LAW . . .

A. *The Significance of a Sale or Change of Control* . . .

When a majority of a corporation's voting shares are acquired by a single person or entity, or by a cohesive group acting together, there is a significant diminution in the voting power of those who thereby become minority stockholders. Under the statutory framework of the General Corporation Law, many of the most fundamental corporate changes can be implemented only if they are approved by a majority vote of the stockholders. Such actions include elections of directors, amendments to the certificate of incorporation, mergers, consolidations, sales of all or substantially all of the assets of the corporation, and dissolution. 8 Del. C. §§211, 242, 251-258, 263, 271, 275. Because of the overriding importance of voting rights, this Court and the Court of Chancery have consistently acted to protect stockholders from unwarranted interference with such rights.[11]

In the absence of devices protecting the minority stockholders, stockholder votes are likely to become mere formalities where there is a majority stockholder. For example, minority stockholders can be deprived of a continuing equity interest in their corporation by means of a cash-out merger. *Weinberger*, 457 A.2d at 703. Absent effective protective provisions,

---

11. *See Schnell v. Chris-Craft Indus., Inc.*, Del. Supr., 285 A.2d 437, 439 (1971) (holding that actions taken by management to manipulate corporate machinery "for the purpose of obstructing the legitimate efforts of dissident stockholders in the exercise of their rights to undertake a proxy contest against management" were "contrary to established principles of corporate democracy" and therefore invalid); *Giuricich v. Emtrol Corp.*, Del. Supr., 449 A.2d 232, 239 (1982) (holding that "careful judicial scrutiny will be given a situation in which the right to vote for the election of successor directors has been effectively frustrated"); *Centaur Partners, IV v. Nat'l Intergroup*, Del. Supr., 582 A.2d 923 (1990) (holding that supermajority voting provisions must be clear and unambiguous because they have the effect of disenfranchising the majority); *Stroud v. Grace*, Del. Supr., 606 A.2d 75, 84 (1992) (directors' duty of disclosure is premised on the importance of stockholders being fully informed when voting on a specific matter); *Blasius Indus., Inc. v. Atlas Corp.*, Del. Ch., 564 A.2d 651, 659 n.2 (1988) ("Delaware courts have long exercised a most sensitive and protective regard for the free and effective exercise of voting rights.").

minority stockholders must rely for protection solely on the fiduciary duties owed to them by the directors and the majority stockholder, since the minority stockholders have lost the power to influence corporate direction through the ballot. The acquisition of majority status and the consequent privilege of exerting the powers of majority ownership come at a price. That price is usually a control premium which recognizes not only the value of a control block of shares, but also compensates the minority stockholders for their resulting loss of voting power.

In the case before us, the public stockholders (in the aggregate) currently own a majority of Paramount's voting stock. Control of the corporation is not vested in a single person, entity, or group, but vested in the fluid aggregation of unaffiliated stockholders. In the event the Paramount-Viacom transaction is consummated, the public stockholders will receive cash and a minority equity voting position in the surviving corporation. Following such consummation, there will be a controlling stockholder who will have the voting power to: (a) elect directors; (b) cause a break-up of the corporation; (c) merge it with another company; (d) cash-out the public stockholders; (e) amend the certificate of incorporation; (f) sell all or substantially all of the corporate assets; or (g) otherwise alter materially the nature of the corporation and the public stockholders' interests. Irrespective of the present Paramount Board's vision of a long-term strategic alliance with Viacom, the proposed sale of control would provide the new controlling stockholder with the power to alter that vision.

Because of the intended sale of control, the Paramount-Viacom transaction has economic consequences of considerable significance to the Paramount stockholders. Once control has shifted, the current Paramount stockholders will have no leverage in the future to demand another control premium. As a result, the Paramount stockholders are entitled to receive, and should receive, a control premium and/or protective devices of significant value. There being no such protective provisions in the Viacom-Paramount transaction, the Paramount directors had an obligation to take the maximum advantage of the current opportunity to realize for the stockholders the best value reasonably available.

B. The Obligations of Directors in a Sale or Change of Control Transaction

In the sale of control context, the directors must focus on one primary objective—to secure the transaction offering the best value reasonably available for the stockholders—and they must exercise their fiduciary duties to further that end. The decisions of this Court have consistently emphasized this goal. *Revlon*, 506 A.2d at 182 ("The duty of the board . . . [is] the maximization of the company's value at a sale for the stockholders' benefit."); *Macmillan*, 559 A.2d at 1288 ("[I]n a sale of corporate control the responsibility of the directors is to get the highest value

B. Applying Unocal and Revlon — The Two Paramounts

reasonably attainable for the shareholders."); *Barkan*, 567 A.2d at 1286 ("[T]he board must act in a neutral manner to encourage the highest possible price for shareholders."). *See also Wilmington Trust Co. v. Coulter*, Del. Supr., 200 A.2d 441, 448 (1964) (in the context of the duty of a trustee, "[w]hen all is equal . . . it is plain that the Trustee is bound to obtain the best price obtainable").

In pursuing this objective, the directors must be especially diligent. *See Citron v. Fairchild Camera and Instrument Corp.*, Del. Supr., 569 A.2d 53, 66 (1989) (discussing "a board's active and direct role in the sale process"). In particular, this Court has stressed the importance of the board being adequately informed in negotiating a sale of control: "The need for adequate information is central to the enlightened evaluation of a transaction that a board must make." *Barkan*, 567 A.2d at 1287. . . .

In determining which alternative provides the best value for the stockholders, a board of directors is not limited to considering only the amount of cash involved, and is not required to ignore totally its view of the future value of a strategic alliance. *See Macmillan*, 559 A.2d at 1282 n.29. Instead, the directors should analyze the entire situation and evaluate in a disciplined manner the consideration being offered. Where stock or other non-cash consideration is involved, the board should try to quantify its value, if feasible, to achieve an objective comparison of the alternatives. In addition, the board may assess a variety of practical considerations relating to each alternative, including:

> [an offer's] fairness and feasibility; the proposed or actual financing for the offer, and the consequences of that financing; questions of illegality; . . . the risk of non-consum[m]ation; . . . the bidder's identity, prior background and other business venture experiences; and the bidder's business plans for the corporation and their effects on stockholder interests.

Macmillan, 559 A.2d at 1282 n.29. These considerations are important because the selection of one alternative may permanently foreclose other opportunities. While the assessment of these factors may be complex, the board's goal is straightforward: Having informed themselves of all material information reasonably available, the directors must decide which alternative is most likely to offer the best value reasonably available to the stockholders.

C. Enhanced Judicial Scrutiny of a Sale or Change of Control Transaction

Board action in the circumstances presented here is subject to enhanced scrutiny. Such scrutiny is mandated by: (a) the threatened diminution of the current stockholders' voting power; (b) the fact that an asset belonging to public stockholders (a control premium) is being sold and may never be available again; and (c) the traditional concern of Delaware courts for actions which impair or impede stockholder voting rights (see *supra* note 11). In *Macmillan*, this Court held:

> When *Revlon* duties devolve upon directors, this Court will continue to exact an enhanced judicial scrutiny at the threshold, as in *Unocal*, before the normal presumptions of the business judgment rule will apply.[15]

559 A.2d at 1288. The *Macmillan* decision articulates a specific two-part test for analyzing board action where competing bidders are not treated equally:[16]

> In the face of disparate treatment, the trial court must first examine whether the directors properly perceived that shareholder interests were enhanced. In any event the board's action must be reasonable in relation to the advantage sought to be achieved, or conversely, to the threat which a particular bid allegedly poses to stockholder interests.

Id. See also Roberts v. General Instrument Corp., Del. Ch., C.A. No. 11639, 1990 WL 118356, Allen, C. (Aug. 13, 1990), reprinted at 16 Del. J. Corp. L. 1540, 1554 ("This enhanced test requires a judicial judgment of reasonableness in the circumstances.").

The key features of an enhanced scrutiny test are: (a) a judicial determination regarding the adequacy of the decisionmaking process employed by the directors, including the information on which the directors based their decision; and (b) a judicial examination of the reasonableness of the directors' action in light of the circumstances then existing. The directors have the burden of proving that they were adequately informed and acted reasonably.

Although an enhanced scrutiny test involves a review of the reasonableness of the substantive merits of a board's actions, a court should not ignore the complexity of the directors' task in a sale of control. There are many business and financial considerations implicated in investigating and selecting the best value reasonably available. The board of directors is the corporate decisionmaking body best equipped to make these judgments. Accordingly, a court applying enhanced judicial scrutiny should be deciding whether the directors made a reasonable decision, not a perfect decision. If a board selected one of several reasonable alternatives, a court should not second-guess that choice even though it might have decided otherwise or subsequent events may have cast doubt on the board's determination. Thus, courts will not substitute their business judgment for that of the directors, but will determine if the directors' decision was, on balance, within a range of reasonableness. *See Unocal*, 493 A.2d at 955-56; *Macmillan*, 559 A.2d at 1288; *Nixon*, 626 A.2d at 1378.

---

15. Because the Paramount Board acted unreasonably as to process and result in this sale of control situation, the business judgment rule did not become operative.

16. Before this test is invoked, "the plaintiff must show, and the trial court must find, that the directors of the target company treated one or more of the respective bidders on unequal terms." *Macmillan*, 559 A.2d at 1288.

D. Revlon and Time-Warner Distinguished

The Paramount defendants and Viacom assert that the fiduciary obligations and the enhanced judicial scrutiny discussed above are not implicated in this case in the absence of a "break-up" of the corporation, and that the order granting the preliminary injunction should be reversed. This argument is based on their erroneous interpretation of our decisions in *Revlon* and *Time-Warner*.

In *Revlon*, we reviewed the actions of the board of directors of Revlon, Inc. ("Revlon"), which had rebuffed the overtures of Pantry Pride, Inc. and had instead entered into an agreement with Forstmann Little & Co. ("Forstmann") providing for the acquisition of 100 percent of Revlon's outstanding stock by Forstmann and the subsequent break-up of Revlon. Based on the facts and circumstances present in *Revlon*, we held that "[t]he directors' role changed from defenders of the corporate bastion to auctioneers charged with getting the best price for the stockholders at a sale of the company." 506 A.2d at 182. We further held that "when a board ends an intense bidding contest on an insubstantial basis, . . . [that] action cannot withstand the enhanced scrutiny which *Unocal* requires of director conduct." *Id.* at 184.

It is true that one of the circumstances bearing on these holdings was the fact that "the break-up of the company . . . had become a reality which even the directors embraced." *Id.* at 182. It does not follow, however, that a "break-up" must be present and "inevitable" before directors are subject to enhanced judicial scrutiny and are required to pursue a transaction that is calculated to produce the best value reasonably available to the stockholders. In fact, we stated in *Revlon* that "when bidders make relatively similar offers, or dissolution of the company becomes inevitable, the directors cannot fulfill their enhanced *Unocal* duties by playing favorites with the contending factions." *Id.* at 184. . . . *Revlon* thus does not hold that an inevitable dissolution or "break-up" is necessary.

The decisions of this Court following *Revlon* reinforced the applicability of enhanced scrutiny and the directors' obligation to seek the best value reasonably available for the stockholders where there is a pending sale of control, regardless of whether or not there is to be a break-up of the corporation. In *Macmillan*, this Court held:

> We stated in *Revlon*, and again here, that *in a sale of corporate control* the responsibility of the directors is to get the highest value reasonably attainable for the shareholders.

559 A.2d at 1288 (emphasis added). In *Barkan*, we observed further:

> We believe that the general principles announced in *Revlon*, in *Unocal Corp. v. Mesa Petroleum Co.*, Del. Supr., 493 A.2d 946 (1985), and in *Moran v. Household International, Inc.*, Del. Supr., 500 A.2d 1346 (1985), govern this case and every case in which a *fundamental change of corporate control* occurs or is contemplated.

567 A.2d at 1286 (emphasis added).

Although *Macmillan* and *Barkan* are clear in holding that a change of control imposes on directors the obligation to obtain the best value reasonably available to the stockholders, the Paramount defendants have interpreted our decision in *Time-Warner* as requiring a corporate break-up in order for that obligation to apply. The facts in *Time-Warner*, however, were quite different from the facts of this case, and refute Paramount's position here. In *Time-Warner*, the Chancellor held that there was no change of control in the original stock-for-stock merger between Time and Warner because Time would be owned by a fluid aggregation of unaffiliated stockholders both before and after the merger:

> If the appropriate inquiry is whether a change in control is contemplated, the answer must be sought in the specific circumstances surrounding the transaction. Surely under some circumstances a stock for stock merger could reflect a transfer of corporate control. That would, for example, plainly be the case here if Warner were a private company. But where, as here, the shares of both constituent corporations are widely held, corporate control can be expected to remain unaffected by a stock for stock merger. This in my judgment was the situation with respect to the original merger agreement. When the specifics of that situation are reviewed, it is seen that, aside from legal technicalities and aside from arrangements thought to enhance the prospect for the ultimate succession of [Nicholas J. Nicholas, Jr., president of Time], neither corporation could be said to be acquiring the other. *Control of both remained in a large, fluid, changeable and changing market.*
>
> The existence of a control block of stock in the hands of a single shareholder or a group with loyalty to each other does have real consequences to the financial value of "minority" stock. The law offers some protection to such shares through the imposition of a fiduciary duty upon controlling shareholders. *But here, effectuation of the merger would not have subjected Time shareholders to the risks and consequences of holders of minority shares.* This is a reflection of the fact that no control passed to anyone in the transaction contemplated. The shareholders of Time would have "suffered" dilution, of course, but they would suffer the same type of dilution upon the public distribution of new stock.

Paramount Communications Inc. v. Time Inc., Del. Ch., No. 10866, 1989 WL 79880, Allen, C. (July 17, 1989), reprinted at 15 Del. J. Corp. L. 700, 739 (emphasis added). Moreover, the transaction actually consummated in *Time-Warner* was not a merger, as originally planned, but a sale of Warner's stock to Time.

In our affirmance of the Court of Chancery's well-reasoned decision, this Court held that "The Chancellor's findings of fact are supported by the record and *his conclusion is correct as a matter of law."* 571 A.2d at 1150 (emphasis added). Nevertheless, the Paramount defendants here have argued that a break-up is a requirement and have focused on the following language in our *Time-Warner* decision:

> However, we premise our rejection of plaintiffs' *Revlon* claim on different grounds, namely, the absence of any substantial evidence to conclude that Time's board, in negotiating with Warner, made the dissolution or break-up of the corporate entity inevitable, as was the case in *Revlon*.

B. Applying Unocal and Revlon—The Two Paramounts

> Under Delaware law there are, generally speaking and *without excluding other possibilities,* two circumstances which may implicate *Revlon* duties. The first, and clearer one, is when a corporation *initiates an active bidding process seeking to sell itself* or to effect a business reorganization involving a clear break-up of the company. However, *Revlon* duties may also be triggered where, in response to a bidder's offer, a target abandons its long-term strategy and seeks an alternative transaction involving the breakup of the company.

Id. at 1150 (emphasis added) (citation and footnote omitted).

The Paramount defendants have misread the holding of *Time-Warner.* Contrary to their argument, our decision in *Time-Warner* expressly states that the two general scenarios discussed in the above-quoted paragraph are not the *only* instances where "*Revlon* duties" may be implicated. The Paramount defendants' argument totally ignores the phrase "without excluding other possibilities." Moreover, the instant case is clearly within the first general scenario set forth in *Time-Warner.* The Paramount Board, albeit unintentionally, had "initiate[d] an active bidding process seeking to sell itself" by agreeing to sell control of the corporation to Viacom in circumstances where another potential acquiror (QVC) was equally interested in being a bidder.

The Paramount defendants' position that *both* a change of control *and* a break-up are *required* must be rejected. Such a holding would unduly restrict the application of *Revlon,* is inconsistent with this Court's decisions in *Barkan* and *Macmillan,* and has no basis in policy. There are few events that have a more significant impact on the stockholders than a sale of control or a corporate break-up. Each event represents a fundamental (and perhaps irrevocable) change in the nature of the corporate enterprise from a practical standpoint. It is the significance of *each* of these events that justifies: (a) focusing on the directors' obligation to seek the best value reasonably available to the stockholders; and (b) requiring a close scrutiny of board action which could be contrary to the stockholders' interests.

Accordingly, when a corporation undertakes a transaction which will cause: (a) a change in corporate control; or (b) a break-up of the corporate entity, the directors' obligation is to seek the best value reasonably available to the stockholders. This obligation arises because the effect of the Viacom-Paramount transaction, if consummated, is to shift control of Paramount from the public stockholders to a controlling stockholder, Viacom. Neither *Time-Warner* nor any other decision of this Court holds that a "break-up" of the company is essential to give rise to this obligation where there is a sale of control.

III. BREACH OF FIDUCIARY DUTIES BY PARAMOUNT BOARD

We now turn to duties of the Paramount Board under the facts of this case and our conclusions as to the breaches of those duties which warrant injunctive relief.

A. The Specific Obligations of the Paramount Board

Under the facts of this case, the Paramount directors had the obligation: (a) to be diligent and vigilant in examining critically the Paramount-Viacom transaction and the QVC tender offers; (b) to act in good faith; (c) to obtain, and act with due care on, all material information reasonably available, including information necessary to compare the two offers to determine which of these transactions, or an alternative course of action, would provide the best value reasonably available to the stockholders; and (d) to negotiate actively and in good faith with both Viacom and QVC to that end.

Having decided to sell control of the corporation, the Paramount directors were required to evaluate critically whether or not all material aspects of the Paramount-Viacom transaction (separately and in the aggregate) were reasonable and in the best interests of the Paramount stockholders in light of current circumstances, including: the change of control premium, the Stock Option Agreement, the Termination Fee, the coercive nature of both the Viacom and QVC tender offers,[18] the No-Shop Provision, and the proposed disparate use of the Rights Agreement as to the Viacom and QVC tender offers, respectively.

These obligations necessarily implicated various issues, including the questions of whether or not those provisions and other aspects of the Paramount-Viacom transaction (separately and in the aggregate): (a) adversely affected the value provided to the Paramount stockholders; (b) inhibited or encouraged alternative bids; (c) were enforceable contractual obligations in light of the directors' fiduciary duties; and (d) in the end would advance or retard the Paramount directors' obligation to secure for the Paramount stockholders the best value reasonably available under the circumstances.

The Paramount defendants contend that they were precluded by certain contractual provisions, including the No-Shop Provision, from negotiating with QVC or seeking alternatives. Such provisions, whether or not they are presumptively valid in the abstract, may not validly define or limit the directors' fiduciary duties under Delaware law or prevent the Paramount directors from carrying out their fiduciary duties under Delaware law. To the extent such provisions are inconsistent with those duties, they are invalid and unenforceable. *See Revlon*, 506 A.2d at 184-85.

Since the Paramount directors had already decided to sell control, they had an obligation to continue their search for the best value reasonably available to the stockholders. This continuing obligation included the responsibility, at the October 24 board meeting and thereafter, to evaluate critically both the QVC tender offers and the Paramount-Viacom

---

18. Both the Viacom and the QVC tender offers were for 51 percent cash and a "back-end" of various securities, the value of each of which depended on the fluctuating value of Viacom and QVC stock at any given time. Thus, both tender offers were two-tiered, front-end loaded, and coercive. Such coercive offers are inherently problematic and should be expected to receive particularly careful analysis by a target board. *See Unocal*, 493 A.2d at 956.

transaction to determine if: (a) the QVC tender offer was, or would continue to be, conditional; (b) the QVC tender offer could be improved; (c) the Viacom tender offer or other aspects of the Paramount-Viacom transaction could be improved; (d) each of the respective offers would be reasonably likely to come to closure, and under what circumstances; (e) other material information was reasonably available for consideration by the Paramount directors; (f) there were viable and realistic alternative courses of action; and (g) the timing constraints could be managed so the directors could consider these matters carefully and deliberately.

B. The Breaches of Fiduciary Duty by the Paramount Board

The Paramount directors made the decision on September 12, 1993, that, in their judgment, a strategic merger with Viacom on the economic terms of the Original Merger Agreement was in the best interests of Paramount and its stockholders. Those terms provided a modest change of control premium to the stockholders. The directors also decided at that time that it was appropriate to agree to certain defensive measures (the Stock Option Agreement, the Termination Fee, and the No-Shop Provision) insisted upon by Viacom as part of that economic transaction. Those defensive measures, coupled with the sale of control and subsequent disparate treatment of competing bidders, implicated the judicial scrutiny of *Unocal, Revlon, Macmillan*, and their progeny. We conclude that the Paramount directors' process was not reasonable, and the result achieved for the stockholders was not reasonable under the circumstances.

When entering into the Original Merger Agreement, and thereafter, the Paramount Board clearly gave insufficient attention to the potential consequences of the defensive measures demanded by Viacom. The Stock Option Agreement had a number of unusual and potentially "draconian" provisions, including the Note Feature and the Put Feature. Furthermore, the Termination Fee, whether or not unreasonable by itself, clearly made Paramount less attractive to other bidders, when coupled with the Stock Option Agreement. Finally, the No-Shop Provision inhibited the Paramount Board's ability to negotiate with other potential bidders, particularly QVC which had already expressed an interest in Paramount.[20]

---

20. We express no opinion whether certain aspects of the No-Shop Provision here could be valid in another context. Whether or not it could validly have operated here at an early stage solely to prevent Paramount from actively "shopping" the company, it could not prevent the Paramount directors from carrying out their fiduciary duties in considering unsolicited bids or in negotiating for the best value reasonably available to the stockholders. *Macmillan*, 559 A.2d at 1287. As we said in *Barkan*: "Where a board has no reasonable basis upon which to judge the adequacy of a contemplated transaction, a no-shop restriction gives rise to the inference that the board seeks to forestall competing bids." 567 A.2d at 1288. *See also Revlon*, 506 A.2d at 184 (holding that "[t]he no-shop provision, like the lock-up option, while not *per se* illegal, is impermissible under the *Unocal* standards when a board's primary duty becomes that of an auctioneer responsible for selling the company to the highest bidder").

Throughout the applicable time period, and especially from the first QVC merger proposal on September 20 through the Paramount Board meeting on November 15, QVC's interest in Paramount provided the opportunity for the Paramount Board to seek significantly higher value for the Paramount stockholders than that being offered by Viacom. QVC persistently demonstrated its intention to meet and exceed the Viacom offers, and frequently expressed its willingness to negotiate possible further increases.

The Paramount directors had the opportunity in the October 23-24 time frame, when the Original Merger Agreement was renegotiated, to take appropriate action to modify the improper defensive measures as well as to improve the economic terms of the Paramount-Viacom transaction. Under the circumstances existing at that time, it should have been clear to the Paramount Board that the Stock Option Agreement, coupled with the Termination Fee and the No-Shop Clause, were impeding the realization of the best value reasonably available to the Paramount stockholders. Nevertheless, the Paramount Board made no effort to eliminate or modify these counterproductive devices, and instead continued to cling to its vision of a strategic alliance with Viacom. Moreover, based on advice from the Paramount management, the Paramount directors considered the QVC offer to be "conditional" and asserted that they were precluded by the No-Shop Provision from seeking more information from, or negotiating with, QVC.

By November 12, 1993, the value of the revised QVC offer on its face exceeded that of the Viacom offer by over $1 billion at then current values. This significant disparity of value cannot be justified on the basis of the directors' vision of future strategy, primarily because the change of control would supplant the authority of the current Paramount Board to continue to hold and implement their strategic vision in any meaningful way. Moreover, their uninformed process had deprived their strategic vision of much of its credibility. *See Van Gorkom*, 488 A.2d at 872; *Cede v. Technicolor*, 634 A.2d at 367; *Hanson Trust PLC v. ML SCM Acquisition Inc.*, 2d Cir., 781 F.2d 264, 274 (1986).

When the Paramount directors met on November 15 to consider QVC's increased tender offer, they remained prisoners of their own misconceptions and missed opportunities to eliminate the restrictions they had imposed on themselves. Yet, it was not "too late" to reconsider negotiating with QVC. The circumstances existing on November 15 made it clear that the defensive measures, taken as a whole, were problematic: (a) the No-Shop Provision could not define or limit their fiduciary duties; (b) the Stock Option Agreement had become "draconian"; and (c) the Termination Fee, in context with all the circumstances, was similarly deterring the realization of possibly higher bids. Nevertheless, the Paramount directors remained paralyzed by their uninformed belief that the QVC offer was "illusory." This final opportunity to negotiate on the stockholders' behalf and to fulfill their obligation to seek the best value reasonably available was thereby squandered.

IV. VIACOM'S CLAIM OF VESTED CONTRACT RIGHTS

Viacom argues that it had certain "vested" contract rights with respect to the No-Shop Provision and the Stock Option Agreement. In effect, Viacom's argument is that the Paramount directors could enter into an agreement in violation of their fiduciary duties and then render Paramount, and ultimately its stockholders, liable for failing to carry out an agreement in violation of those duties. Viacom's protestations about vested rights are without merit. This Court has found that those defensive measures were improperly designed to deter potential bidders, and that such measures do not meet the reasonableness test to which they must be subjected. They are consequently invalid and unenforceable under the facts of this case.

The No-Shop Provision could not validly define or limit the fiduciary duties of the Paramount directors. To the extent that a contract, or a provision thereof, purports to require a board to act or not act in such a fashion as to limit the exercise of fiduciary duties, it is invalid and unenforceable. *Cf. Wilmington Trust v. Coulter*, 200 A.2d at 452-54. Despite the arguments of Paramount and Viacom to the contrary, the Paramount directors could not contract away their fiduciary obligations. Since the No-Shop Provision was invalid, Viacom never had any vested contract rights in the provision.

As discussed previously, the Stock Option Agreement contained several "draconian" aspects, including the Note Feature and the Put Feature. While we have held that lock-up options are not *per se* illegal, *see Revlon*, 506 A.2d at 183, no options with similar features have ever been upheld by this Court. Under the circumstances of this case, the Stock Option Agreement clearly is invalid. Accordingly, Viacom never had any vested contract rights in that Agreement.

Viacom, a sophisticated party with experienced legal and financial advisors, knew of (and in fact demanded) the unreasonable features of the Stock Option Agreement. It cannot be now heard to argue that it obtained vested contract rights by negotiating and obtaining contractual provisions from a board acting in violation of its fiduciary duties. As the Nebraska Supreme Court said in rejecting a similar argument in *ConAgra, Inc. v. Cargill, Inc.*, 222 Neb. 136, 382 N.W.2d 576, 587-88 (1986), "To so hold, it would seem, would be to get the shareholders coming and going." Likewise, we reject Viacom's arguments and hold that its fate must rise or fall, and in this instance fall, with the determination that the actions of the Paramount Board were invalid.

V. Conclusion

The realization of the best value reasonably available to the stockholders became the Paramount directors' primary obligation under these facts in light of the change of control. That obligation was not satisfied, and the Paramount Board's process was deficient. The directors' initial hope and expectation for a strategic alliance with Viacom was allowed to dominate their decisionmaking process to the point where the arsenal of defensive measures established at the outset was perpetuated (not modified or eliminated) when the situation was dramatically altered. QVC's unsolicited bid presented the opportunity for significantly greater value for the stockholders and enhanced negotiating leverage for the directors. Rather than seizing those opportunities, the Paramount directors chose to wall themselves off from material information which was reasonably available and to hide behind the defensive measures as a rationalization for refusing to negotiate with QVC or seeking other alternatives. Their view of the strategic alliance likewise became an empty rationalization as the opportunities for higher value for the stockholders continued to develop.

It is the nature of the judicial process that we decide only the case before us—a case which, on its facts, is clearly controlled by established Delaware law. Here, the proposed change of control and the implications thereof were crystal clear. In other cases they may be less clear. The holding of this case on its facts, coupled with the holdings of the principal cases discussed herein where the issue of sale of control is implicated, should provide a workable precedent against which to measure future cases.

For the reasons set forth herein, the November 24, 1993, Order of the Court of Chancery has been AFFIRMED, and this matter has been REMANDED for proceedings consistent herewith, as set forth in the December 9, 1993, Order of this Court.

NOTES AND QUESTIONS

1. The deal: The sequel. What were the economic drivers of the Paramount and Viacom deal? The analysis from the prior case should help you here, for a couple of years have gone by, but Paramount is looking at the same landscape that faced Warner and Time. Martin Davis, CEO of Paramount, and Sumner Redstone, his counterpart at Viacom, have worked out a fit so that both of them would remain active in the combined business. Mr. Redstone, the older of the two, would become chairman, and Mr. Davis would be chief executive. But as in our last case, there are other parties eying the same assets. This time the spoiler is QVC, run by Barry Diller and including John Malone, two well-known dealmakers of the industry. They, too, are looking for synergies in the entertainment business, although Martin Davis may not have viewed QVC, with its Home Shopping Network, as the ideal partner.

2. **The choices for the Paramount planners.** Put yourself in the shoes of Martin Davis and his advisers at Paramount. They had negotiated a deal with Viacom that they believed best met the needs of the company going forward. A less attractive suitor now sought to crash the party. Davis might well say to himself: "I have seen this movie before, and I know that Delaware courts will protect director decision-making in such a setting. We will now do to QVC what Time did to us." So you can imagine how he might have greeted his lawyer coming to tell him the news that he and the company had now been on opposite sides of the same issue in two cases and lost both cases.

3. *Revlon* **after** *QVC*. This opinion requires us to recalibrate the trigger for Revlonland from where it stood after Paramount/Time. A stock-for-stock merger does not provide the breadth of insulation that might have appeared. But the exception set out in *QVC* seems clear enough — a stock-for-stock merger in which there is a controlling shareholder in the acquiring company means that control has passed out of the market to that controlling shareholder. That does not seem to fit very neatly within the two examples given in *Time-Warner*. And it seems to represent something of a shift in the policy that justifies this more intrusive level of judicial review. The focus now is on control premium, which usually doesn't exist in publicly held companies with shares dispersed in the market, but can show up in going private or a cash sale of the entire business. This seems to point *Revlon* to a more narrow set of transactions. Another setting for the law's approach to sale of control for a premium appears in Chapter 11.

C. THE EVOLUTION OF *UNOCAL*; DEAL PROTECTION DEVICES

Louisiana Municipal Police Employees' Retirement System v. Crawford
918 A.2d 1172, 1180-81 (Del. Ch. 2007)

CHANDLER, Chancellor: . . .

Whether the boards of Caremark and CVS were attempting to secure a merger of equals that offers considerable strategic benefit or protecting personal benefits that would flow from the merger, they made certain that the transaction contained a full complement of deal-protection devices. First, both boards are contractually bound to submit the merger to their shareholders under a "force the vote" provision. Second, both boards are subject to a "no shop" provision, under which neither board may speak with a competing bidder unless the board concludes, after examining a competing offer, that the offer either is a "Superior Proposal" or is likely to lead to one. A "last look" provision obligates the target board to disclose the terms of a competing Superior Proposal, and allows the other party a five-day window in which to match the bid.

The foundation of this intricate barricade, however, is undoubtedly the $675 million reciprocal termination fee, a provision inseparably linked with the other deal protection devices. The termination fee is triggered if, for almost any reason, either board withdraws or changes its recommendation of the merger. The fee must also be paid if either company's shareholders reject the merger agreement and then accept any *other* merger proposal within twelve months.

The "no shop" provision contains what defendants characterize as a road map by which a competing bidder may tiptoe around termination fee landmines in order to make a hostile offer. The map looks like this: a target board must receive an offer and determine that it constitutes, or may lead to, a Superior Proposal. The hostile bidder must also enter into a confidentiality agreement no less demanding than the one between CVS and Caremark. If, after providing its initial partner with a "last look" at the offer, the target board still wishes to change its recommendation, then the target board and the new party may enter into a conditional merger agreement. This new agreement is "conditional" because it may only become effective after: (a) the CVS/Caremark merger is terminated, *e.g.*, by shareholder vote; and (b) the third party pays the jilted suitor a $675 million consolation prize.[10]

Defendants attempt to build a bright line rule upon treacherous foundations, relying upon carefully-selected comments to contradict a clear principle of Delaware law. Our courts do not "presume that all business

---

10. The parties make passionate arguments with respect to the appropriateness of the deal protections. Defendants maintain that these are no more than a customary set of devices employed regularly by market participants and their lawyers. Particularly with respect to the termination fee, this argument by custom fails to convince.

It is true, as defendants note, that this Court has upheld termination fees of greater than three percent of total deal value. *See, e.g., McMillan v. Intercargo Corp.*, 768 A.2d 492, 505-06 (Del. Ch. 2000) (describing 3.5% lockup as an "insubstantial obstacle"); *Lewis v. Leaseway Transp. Corp.*, 1990 WL 67383, at *8 (Del. Ch. May 16, 1990) (dismissing challenge to a transaction that included a breakup fee and related expenses of approximately 3% of transaction value); *Kysor Indus. Corp. v. Margaux, Inc.*, 674 A.2d 889, 897 (Del. Super. 1996) (finding termination fee of 2.8% of Kysor's offer reasonable); *Goodwin v. Live Entm't*, 1999 WL 64265, at *20 (Del. Ch. Jan. 25, 1999) (approving termination fee of 3.125% *plus* $1 million in expenses for a total percentage of 4.167%). Defendants also pluck particular language from opinions in order to suggest that a three percent fee is somehow *presumptively* reasonable. *See, e.g., In re Pennaco Energy, Inc.*, 787 A.2d 691, 702 (Del. Ch. 2001) ("settled on a termination fee at the more traditional level of 3%"); *id.* at 707 ("only the modest and reasonable advantages of a 3% termination fee and matching rights"); *McMillan*, 768 A.2d at 505-06 ("Although in purely percentage terms, the termination fee was at the high end of what our courts have approved, it was still within the range that is generally considered reasonable. . . . From a preclusion perspective, it is difficult to see how a 3.5% fee would have deterred a rival bidder. . . .").

circumstances are identical or that there is any naturally occurring rate of deal protection, the deficit or excess of which will be less than economically optimal." *In re Toys "R" Us, Inc., S'holder Litig.,* 877 A.2d 975, 1016 (2005). Rather, a court focuses upon "the real world risks and prospects confronting [directors] when they agreed to the deal protections." *Id.* That analysis will, by necessity, require the Court to consider a number of factors, including without limitation: the overall size of the termination fee, as well as its percentage value; the benefit to shareholders, including a premium (if any) that directors seek to protect; the absolute size of the transaction, as well as the relative size of the partners to the merger; the degree to which a counterparty found such protections to be crucial to the deal, bearing in mind differences in bargaining power; and the preclusive or coercive power of *all* deal protections included in a transaction, taken as a whole. The inquiry, by its very nature fact intensive, cannot be reduced to a mathematical equation. Though a "3% rule" for termination fees might be convenient for transaction planners, it is simply too blunt an instrument, too subject to abuse, for this Court to bless as a blanket rule.

Nor may plaintiffs rely upon some naturally-occurring rate or combination of deal protection measures, the existence of which will invoke the judicial blue pencil. Rather, plaintiffs must specifically demonstrate how a given set of deal protections operate in an unreasonable, preclusive, or coercive manner, under the standards of this Court's *Unocal* jurisprudence, to inequitably harm shareholders.

Nevertheless, because I conclude that plaintiffs are not subject to any irreparable harm so long as shareholders are given the opportunity to exercise a fully-informed vote, I need not address the specific deal protections at this stage in litigation.

Omnicare, Inc. v. NCS Healthcare, Inc.
818 A.2d 914 (Del. Sup. Ct. 2003) (en banc)

HOLLAND, Justice, for the majority:

NCS Healthcare, Inc. ("NCS"), a Delaware corporation, [a leading independent provider of pharmacy services to long-term care institutions including skilled nursing facilities, assisted living facilities and other institutional healthcare facilities] was the object of competing acquisition bids, one by Genesis Health Ventures, Inc. ("Genesis"), a Pennsylvania corporation, [a leading provider of healthcare and support services to the elderly] and the other by Omnicare, Inc. ("Omnicare"), a Delaware corporation [in the institutional pharmacy business, with annual sales in excess of $2.1 billion during its last fiscal year]. . . . [After a period of seeking various financial solutions in what had been a difficult time in its industry, including discussion with Omnicare, the NCS board and the two shareholders who controlled a majority of its voting stock, agreed to a merger with

Genesis.] The merger agreement between Genesis and NCS contained a provision authorized by Section 251(c) of Delaware's corporation law [now found in Section 146]. It required that the Genesis agreement be placed before the corporation's stockholders for a vote, even if the NCS board of directors no longer recommended it. At the insistence of Genesis, the NCS board also agreed to omit any effective fiduciary [out] clause from the merger agreement. In connection with the Genesis merger agreement, two stockholders of NCS, who held a majority of the voting power, agreed unconditionally to vote all of their shares in favor of the Genesis merger. Thus, the combined terms of the voting agreements and merger agreement guaranteed, *ab initio*, that the transaction proposed by Genesis would obtain NCS stockholder's approval.

[Several months after approving the merger agreement, but before the stockholder vote was scheduled, the NCS board of directors withdrew its prior recommendation in favor of the Genesis merger in the face of an Omnicare deal described as offering "the NCS stockholders an amount of cash equal to more than twice the then current market value of the shares to be received in the Genesis merger."] The Court of Chancery ruled that the voting agreements, when coupled with the provision in the Genesis merger agreement requiring that it be presented to the stockholders for a vote pursuant to 8 Del. C. §251(c), constituted defensive measures within the meaning of *Unocal Corp. v. Mesa Petroleum Co*. After applying the *Unocal* standard of enhanced judicial scrutiny, the Court of Chancery held that those defensive measures were reasonable. We have concluded that, in the absence of an effective fiduciary out clause, those defensive measures are both preclusive and coercive. Therefore, we hold that those defensive measures are invalid and unenforceable. . . .

FACTUAL BACKGROUND[6]

NCS common stock consists of Class A shares and Class B shares. The Class A shares are entitled to one vote per share and the Class B shares are entitled to ten votes per share. The shares are virtually identical in every other respect. As of July 28, 2002, NCS had 18,461,599 Class A shares and 5,255,210 Class B shares outstanding. Two of the four directors own 65 percent of the voting stock. Jon H. Outcalt, Chairman of the board of directors, owns 202,063 shares of NCS Class A common stock and 3,476,086 shares of Class B common stock. Kevin B. Shaw, President, CEO, and a director of NCS, owned at the time the merger agreement was executed with Genesis, owned 28,905 shares of NCS Class A common stock and 1,141,134 shares of Class B common stock.

---

6. [This is a condensed and edited version of the court's presentation of the facts, sometimes reordered to present the story.—ED.]

The NCS board has two other members, defendants Boake A. Sells and Richard L. Osborne. Sells is a graduate of the Harvard Business School. He was Chairman and CEO at Revco Drugstores in Cleveland, Ohio from 1987 to 1992, when he was replaced by new owners. Sells currently sits on the boards of both public and private companies. Osborne is a full-time professor at the Weatherhead School of Management at Case Western Reserve University. He has been at the university for over thirty years. Osborne currently sits on at least seven corporate boards other than NCSBeginning in late 1999, changes in the timing and level of reimbursements by government and third-party providers adversely affected market conditions in the health care industry. As a result, NCS began to experience greater difficulty in collecting accounts receivables, which led to a precipitous decline in the market value of its stock. NCS common shares that traded above $20 in January 1999 were worth as little as $5 at the end of that year. By early 2001, NCS was in default on approximately $350 million in debt. . . . After these defaults, NCS common stock traded in a range of $0.09 to $0.50 per share until days before the announcement of the transaction at issue in this case.

As NCS's financial condition continued to deteriorate, it sought investment banking assistance, first from UBS Warburg, L.L.C. to identify potential acquirers and possible equity investors, resulting in only one nonbinding indication of interest valued at $190 million, substantially less than the face value of NCS's senior debt; thereafter it hired Brown, Gibbons, Lang & Company. Noteholders, whose notes were in default, formed a committee to represent their financial interests (the "Ad Hoc Committee"). At that time, full recovery for NCS's creditors was a remote prospect, and any recovery for NCS stockholders seemed impossible.

In response to an NCS invitation, Omnicare proposed to acquire NCS in a bankruptcy sale, first for $225 million, subject to satisfactory completion of due diligence, later increased to $270 million, and then, in secret discussions between Omnicare and Judy Mencher, a representative of the Ad Hoc Committee, to $313 million. Discovery had revealed that, at the same time, Omnicare was attempting to lure away NCS's customers through what it characterized as the "NCS Blitz." The "NCS Blitz" was an effort by Omnicare to target NCS's customers. Omnicare has engaged in an "NCS Blitz" a number of times, most recently while NCS and Omnicare were in discussions in July and August 2001.

By early 2002, NCS's operating performance was improving, and the NCS directors began to believe that it might be possible for NCS to enter into a transaction that would provide some recovery for NCS stockholders' equity. In March 2002, NCS decided to form an independent committee of board members who were neither NCS employees nor major NCS stockholders (the "Independent Committee"). The NCS board thought this was necessary because, due to NCS's precarious financial condition, it felt that fiduciary duties were owed to the enterprise as a whole rather than solely to

NCS stockholders. Sells and Osborne were selected as the members of the committee and given authority to consider and negotiate possible transactions for NCS. The entire four member NCS board, however, retained authority to approve any transaction. The Independent Committee retained the same legal and financial counsel as the NCS board. The Independent Committee met for the first time on May 14, 2002. At that meeting Glenn Pollack (from Brown Gibbons) suggested that NCS seek a "stalking-horse merger partner" to obtain the highest possible value in any transaction. The Independent Committee agreed with the suggestion.

Genesis, which itself had recently emerged from bankruptcy after suffering, like NCS, from dwindling government reimbursement, had been contacted by members of the Ad Hoc Committee in January 2002 concerning a possible transaction with NCS and in response executed NCS's standard confidentiality agreement and began a due diligence review. In May 2002, the two members of the Independent Committee and Scott Berlin of Brown Gibbons, Glen Pollack and Boake Sells met with George Hager, CFO of Genesis, and Michael Walker, who was Genesis's CEO. At that meeting, Genesis made it clear that if it were going to engage in any negotiations with NCS, it would not do so as a "stalking horse." As one of its advisors testified, "We didn't want to be someone who set forth a valuation for NCS which would only result in that valuation . . . being publicly disclosed, and thereby creating an environment where Omnicare felt to maintain its competitive monopolistic positions, that they had to match and exceed that level." Thus, Genesis "wanted a degree of certainty that to the extent [it] w[as] willing to pursue a negotiated merger agreement . . . , [it] would be able to consummate the transaction [it] negotiated and executed."

In June 2002, Genesis proposed a transaction that would take place outside the bankruptcy context and provided the possibility that NCS stockholders would be able to recover something for their investment. As discussions continued, the terms proposed by Genesis continued to improve. On June 25, the economic terms of the Genesis proposal included repayment of the NCS senior debt in full, full assumption of trade credit obligations, an exchange offer or direct purchase of the NCS Notes . . . , and $20 million in value for the NCS common stock. Structurally, the Genesis proposal continued to include consents from a significant majority of the Note holders as well as support agreements from stockholders owning a majority of the NCS voting power. After further conversations, Genesis agreed to offer a total of $24 million in consideration for the NCS common stock, or an additional $4 million, in the form of Genesis common stock. Prior to the second offer, Genesis's representatives demanded that before any further negotiations take place NCS agree to enter into an exclusivity agreement with it. As Hager from Genesis explained it: "[I]f they wished us to continue to try to move this process to a definitive agreement, that they would need to do it on an exclusive basis with us. We were going to, and already had incurred significant expense, but we would incur additional expenses . . . , both internal and external, to bring this transaction to a definitive signing. We wanted them to work with us on an exclusive basis for a short period of time to see if we could reach agreement."

NCS director Sells testified, Pollack told the Independent Committee at a July 3, 2002, meeting that:

> "Genesis felt that they had suffered at the hands of Omnicare and others. I guess maybe just Omnicare. I don't know much about Genesis [sic] acquisition history. But they had suffered before at the 11:59:59 and that they wanted to have a pretty much bulletproof deal or they were not going to go forward. . . . Genesis had tried to acquire, I suppose, an institutional pharmacy, I don't remember the name of it. Thought they had a deal and then at the last minute, Omnicare outbid them for the company in a like 11:59 kind of thing, and that they were unhappy about that. And once burned, twice shy."

After NCS executed the exclusivity agreement, Genesis provided NCS with a draft merger agreement, a draft Note holders' support agreement, and draft voting agreements for Outcalt and Shaw, who together held a majority of the voting power of the NCS common stock. Genesis and NCS negotiated the terms of the merger agreement over the next three weeks. During those negotiations, the Independent Committee and the Ad Hoc Committee persuaded Genesis to improve the terms of its merger. As negotiations continued the exclusivity agreement was extended to July 26 and then July 31.

By this time, Omnicare came to believe that NCS was negotiating a transaction, possibly with Genesis or another of Omnicare's competitors, that would potentially present a competitive threat to Omnicare. Omnicare also came to believe, in light of a run-up in the price of NCS common stock, that whatever transaction NCS was negotiating probably included a payment for its stock. Thus, the Omnicare board of directors met on the morning of July 26 and on the recommendation of its management, authorized a proposal to acquire NCS that did not involve a sale of assets in bankruptcy. On the afternoon of July 26, 2002, Omnicare faxed to NCS a letter outlining a proposed acquisition. The letter suggested a transaction in which Omnicare would retire NCS's senior and subordinated debt at par plus accrued interest and pay the NCS stockholders $3 cash for their shares. Omnicare's proposal, however, was expressly conditioned on negotiating a merger agreement, obtaining certain third party consents, and completing its due diligence.

Mencher saw the July 26 Omnicare letter and realized that, while its economic terms were attractive, the "due diligence" condition substantially undercut its strength. In an effort to get a better proposal from Omnicare, Mencher telephoned Gemunder (of Omnicare) and told him that Omnicare was unlikely to succeed in its bid unless it dropped the "due diligence outs." She explained this was the only way a bid at the last minute would be able to succeed. Gemunder considered Mencher's warning "very real" and followed up with his advisors. They, however, insisted that he retain the due diligence condition "to protect [him] from doing something foolish." Taking this advice to heart, Gemunder decided not to drop the due diligence condition.

Late in the afternoon of July 26, 2002, NCS representatives received voicemail messages from Omnicare asking to discuss the letter. The exclusivity agreement prevented NCS from returning those calls. In relevant part, that agreement precluded NCS from "engag[ing] or particpat[ing] in any discussions or negotiations with respect to a Competing Transaction or a proposal for one." The July 26 letter from Omnicare met the definition of a "Competing Transaction." [The Independent Committee concluded that discussions with Omnicare about its July 26 letter presented an unacceptable risk that Genesis would abandon merger discussions. It believed that, given Omnicare's past bankruptcy proposals and unwillingness to consider a merger, as well as its decision to negotiate exclusively with the Ad Hoc Committee, the risk of losing the Genesis proposal was too substantial. Nevertheless, the Independent Committee instructed Pollack to use Omnicare's letter to negotiate for improved terms with Genesis.

Genesis responded to the NCS request to improve its offer with substantially improved terms. First, it proposed to retire the Notes in accordance with the terms of the indenture, thus eliminating the need for Noteholders to consent to the transaction.] Second, Genesis increased the exchange ratio for NCS common stock to one-tenth of a Genesis common share for each NCS common share, an 80 percent increase. Third, it agreed to lower the proposed termination fee in the merger agreement from $10 million to $6 million. In return for these concessions, Genesis stipulated that the transaction had to be approved by midnight the next day, July 28, or else Genesis would terminate discussions and withdraw its offer.

The Independent Committee and the NCS board both scheduled meetings for July 28. The committee met first. Although that meeting lasted less than an hour, the Court of Chancery determined the minutes reflect that the directors were fully informed of all material facts relating to the proposed transaction. After concluding that Genesis was sincere in establishing the midnight deadline, the committee voted unanimously to recommend the transaction to the full board.

The full board met thereafter. After receiving similar reports and advice from its legal and financial advisors, the board concluded that "balancing the potential loss of the Genesis deal against the uncertainty of Omnicare's letter, results in the conclusion that the only reasonable alternative for the Board of Directors is to approve the Genesis transaction." The board first voted to authorize the voting agreements with Outcalt and Shaw, for purposes of Section 203 of the Delaware General Corporation Law ("DGCL"). The board was advised by its legal counsel that "under the terms of the merger agreement and because NCS shareholders representing in excess of 50% of the outstanding voting power would be *required* by Genesis to enter into stockholder voting agreements contemporaneously with the signing of the merger agreement, and would agree to vote their shares in favor of the merger agreement, shareholder approval of the merger would be assured even if the NCS Board were to withdraw or change its recommendation. *These facts would prevent NCS from engaging in any alternative or superior transaction in the future."* (emphasis added).

A definitive merger agreement between NCS and Genesis and the stockholder voting agreements were executed later that day. [Outcalt and Shaw, in their capacity as NCS stockholders, entered into voting agreements with Genesis. NCS was also required to be a party to the voting agreements by Genesis, agreeing to vote all of their shares in favor of the merger agreement.]

Hours after the NCS/Genesis transaction was executed, Omnicare faxed a letter to NCS restating its conditional proposal and attaching a draft merger agreement. Later that morning, Omnicare issued a press release publicly disclosing the proposal. On August 1, 2002, Omnicare filed a lawsuit attempting to enjoin the NCS/Genesis merger, and announced that it intended to launch a tender offer for NCS's shares at a price of $3.50 per share. Omnicare continued to condition its proposal on satisfactory completion of a due diligence investigation of NCS. Twice in August, the NCS Independent Committee and full board of directors met separately to consider the Omnicare tender offer in light of the Genesis merger agreement. NCS's outside legal counsel and NCS's financial advisor attended both meetings. The board was unable to determine that Omnicare's expressions of interest were likely to lead to a "Superior Proposal," as the term was defined in the NCS/Genesis merger agreement.

On September 10, 2002, NCS requested and received a waiver from Genesis allowing NCS to enter into discussions with Omnicare without first having to determine that Omnicare's proposal was a "Superior Proposal." On October 6, 2002, Omnicare irrevocably committed itself to a transaction with NCS. Pursuant to the terms of its proposal, Omnicare agreed to acquire all the outstanding NCS Class A and Class B shares at a price of $3.50 per share in cash. As a result of this irrevocable offer, on October 21, 2002, the NCS board withdrew its recommendation that the stockholders vote in favor of the NCS/Genesis merger agreement. NCS's financial advisor withdrew its fairness opinion of the NCS/Genesis merger agreement as well. However, pursuant to the terms of the merger agreement, Even if the NCS board "changes, withdraws or modifies" its recommendation, as it did, it must still submit the merger to a stockholder vote. As explained in a subsequent filing with the Securities and Exchange Commission ("SEC") states: "Notwithstanding the foregoing, the NCS independent committee and the NCS board of directors recognize that (1) the existing contractual obligations to Genesis currently prevent NCS from accepting the Omnicare irrevocable merger proposal; and (2) the existence of the voting agreements entered into by Messrs. Outcalt and Shaw, whereby Messrs. Outcalt and Shaw agreed to vote their shares of NCS Class A common stock and NCS Class B common stock in favor of the Genesis merger, ensure NCS stockholder approval of the Genesis merger." This litigation was commenced to prevent the consummation of the inferior Genesis transaction.

LEGAL ANALYSIS

Business Judgment or Enhanced Scrutiny

The "defining tension" in corporate governance today has been characterized as "the tension between deference to directors' decisions and the scope of judicial review."[E. Norman Veasey, *The Defining Tension in Corporate Governance in America*, 52 Bus. Law. 393, 403 (1997).] The appropriate standard of judicial review is dispositive of which party has the burden of proof as any litigation proceeds from stage to stage until there is a substantive determination on the merits. Accordingly, identification of the correct analytical framework is essential to a proper judicial review of challenges to the decision-making process of a corporation's board of directors. . . .

. . . Deal Protection Devices Require Enhanced Scrutiny

The dispositive issues in this appeal involve the defensive devices that protected the Genesis merger agreement. The Delaware corporation statute provides that the board's management decision to enter into and recommend a merger transaction can become final only when ownership action is taken by a vote of the stockholders. Thus, the Delaware corporation law expressly provides for a balance of power between boards and stockholders which makes merger transactions a shared enterprise and ownership decision. Consequently, a board of directors' decision to adopt defensive devices to protect a merger agreement may implicate the stockholders' right to effectively vote contrary to the initial recommendation of the board in favor of the transaction. . . .

There are inherent conflicts between a board's interest in protecting a merger transaction it has approved, the stockholders' statutory right to make the final decision to either approve or not approve a merger, and the board's continuing responsibility to effectively exercise its fiduciary duties at all times after the merger agreement is executed. These competing considerations require a threshold determination that board-approved defensive devices protecting a merger transaction are within the limitations of its statutory authority and consistent with the directors' fiduciary duties. Accordingly, in *Paramount v. Time*, we held that the business judgment rule applied to the Time board's original decision to merge with Warner. We further held, however, that defensive devices adopted by the board to protect the original merger transaction must withstand enhanced judicial scrutiny under the *Unocal* standard of review, even when that merger transaction does not result in a change of control.

Enhanced Scrutiny Generally

. . . A board's decision to protect its decision to enter a merger agreement with defensive devices against uninvited competing transactions that may emerge is analogous to a board's decision to protect against dangers to corporate policy and effectiveness when it adopts defensive measures in a hostile takeover contest. . . .

[I]n applying enhanced judicial scrutiny to defensive devices designed to protect a merger agreement, a court must first determine that those measures are not preclusive or coercive *before* its focus shifts to the "range of reasonableness" in making a proportionality determination.

. . . Defensive devices taken to protect a merger agreement executed by a board of directors are intended to give that agreement an advantage over any subsequent transactions that materialize before the merger is approved by the stockholders and consummated. This is analogous to the favored treatment that a board of directors may properly give to encourage an initial bidder when it discharges its fiduciary duties under *Revlon*.

Therefore, in the context of a merger that does not involve a change of control, when defensive devices in the executed merger agreement are challenged *vis-à-vis* their effect on a subsequent competing alternative merger transaction, this Court's analysis in *Macmillan* is didactic. In the context of a case of defensive measures taken against an existing bidder, we stated in *Macmillan*:

> In the face of disparate treatment, the trial court must first examine whether the directors properly perceived that shareholder interests were enhanced. In any event the board's action must be reasonable in relation to the advantage sought to be achieved [by the merger it approved], or conversely, to the threat which a [competing transaction] poses to stockholder interests. If on the basis of this enhanced *Unocal* scrutiny the trial court is satisfied that the test has been met, then the directors' actions necessarily are entitled to the protections of the business judgment rule.

The latitude a board will have in either maintaining or using the defensive devices it has adopted to protect the merger it approved will vary according to the degree of benefit or detriment to the stockholders' interests that is presented by the value or terms of the subsequent competing transaction. . . .

Deal Protection Devices

Defensive devices, as that term is used in this opinion, is a synonym for what are frequently referred to as "deal protection devices." Both terms are used interchangeably to describe any measure or combination of measures that are intended to protect the consummation of a merger transaction. Defensive devices can be economic, structural, or both.

Deal protection devices need not all be in the merger agreement itself. In this case, for example, the Section 251(c) provision in the merger agreement was combined with the separate voting agreements to provide a structural defense for the Genesis merger agreement against any subsequent superior transaction. Genesis made the NCS board's defense of its transaction absolute by insisting on the omission of any effective fiduciary out clause in the NCS merger agreement.

Genesis argues that stockholder voting agreements cannot be construed as deal protection devices taken by a board of directors because stockholders are entitled to vote in their own interest. . . . In this case, the stockholder voting agreements were inextricably intertwined with the defensive aspects of the Genesis merger agreement. In fact, the voting agreements with Shaw and Outcalt were the linchpin of Genesis' proposed tripartite defense. Therefore, Genesis made the execution of those voting agreements a non-negotiable condition precedent to its execution of the merger agreement. In the case before us, the Court of Chancery held that the acts which locked-up the Genesis transaction were the Section 251(c) provision and "the execution of the *voting agreement* by Outcalt and Shaw."

With the assurance that Outcalt and Shaw would irrevocably agree to exercise their majority voting power in favor of its transaction, Genesis insisted that the merger agreement reflect the other two aspects of its concerted defense, i.e., the inclusion of a Section 251(c) provision and the omission of any effective fiduciary out clause. Those dual aspects of the merger agreement would not have provided Genesis with a complete defense in the absence of the voting agreements with Shaw and Outcalt.

These Deal Protection Devices Unenforceable

In this case, the Court of Chancery correctly held that the NCS directors' decision to adopt defensive devices to *completely* "lock up" the Genesis merger mandated "special scrutiny" under the two-part test set forth in *Unocal*. That conclusion is consistent with our holding in *Paramount v. Time* that "safety devices" adopted to protect a transaction that did not result in a change of control are subject to enhanced judicial scrutiny under a *Unocal* analysis. The record does not, however, support the Court of Chancery's conclusion that the defensive devices adopted by the NCS board to protect the Genesis merger were reasonable and proportionate to the threat that NCS perceived from the potential loss of the Genesis transaction.

Pursuant to the judicial scrutiny required under *Unocal*'s two-stage analysis, the NCS directors must first demonstrate "that they had reasonable grounds for believing that a danger to corporate policy and effectiveness existed. . . ." To satisfy that burden, the NCS directors are required to show they acted in good faith after conducting a reasonable investigation. The threat identified by the NCS board was the possibility of losing the Genesis offer and being left with no comparable alternative transaction.

The second stage of the *Unocal* test requires the NCS directors to demonstrate that their defensive response was "reasonable in relation to the threat posed." This inquiry involves a two-step analysis. The NCS directors must first establish that the merger deal protection devices adopted in response to the threat were not "coercive" or "preclusive," and then

C. The Evolution of Unocal; Deal Protection Devices

demonstrate that their response was within a "range of reasonable responses" to the threat perceived. In *Unitrin*, [651 A.2d 1361, 1387-88] we stated:

- A response is "coercive" if it is aimed at forcing upon stockholders a management-sponsored alternative to a hostile offer.
- A response is "preclusive" if it deprives stockholders of the right to receive all tender offers or precludes a bidder from seeking control by fundamentally restricting proxy contests or otherwise.

This aspect of the *Unocal* standard provides for a disjunctive analysis. If defensive measures are either preclusive or coercive they are draconian and impermissible. In this case, the deal protection devices of the NCS board were *both* preclusive and coercive.

This Court enunciated the standard for determining stockholder coercion in the case of *Williams v. Geier*. A stockholder vote may be nullified by wrongful coercion "where the board or some other party takes actions which have the effect of causing the stockholders to vote in favor of the proposed transaction for some reason other than the merits of that transaction." In *Brazen v. Bell Atlantic Corporation*, we applied that test for stockholder coercion and held "that although the termination fee provision may have influenced the stockholder vote, there were 'no structurally or situationally coercive factors' that made an otherwise valid fee provision impermissibly coercive" under the facts presented.

... In this case, the Court of Chancery did not expressly address the issue of "coercion" in its *Unocal* analysis. It did find as a fact, however, that NCS's public stockholders (who owned 80% of NCS and overwhelmingly supported Omnicare's offer) will be forced to accept the Genesis merger because of the structural defenses approved by the NCS board. Consequently, the record reflects that any stockholder vote would have been robbed of its effectiveness by the impermissible coercion that predetermined the outcome of the merger without regard to the merits of the Genesis transaction at the time the vote was scheduled to be taken. Deal protection devices that result in such coercion cannot withstand *Unocal's* enhanced judicial scrutiny standard of review because they are not within the range of reasonableness.

Although the minority stockholders were not forced to vote for the Genesis merger, they were required to accept it because it was a *fait accompli*. The record reflects that the defensive devices employed by the NCS board are preclusive and coercive in the sense that they accomplished a *fait accompli*. In this case, despite the fact that the NCS board has withdrawn its recommendation for the Genesis transaction and recommended its rejection by the stockholders, the deal protection devices approved by the NCS board operated in concert to have a preclusive and coercive effect. Those tripartite defensive measures—the Section 251(c) provision, the voting agreements, and the absence of an effective fiduciary out clause — made it "mathematically impossible" and "realistically unattainable" for the Omnicare transaction or any other proposal to succeed, no matter how superior the proposal.

The deal protection devices adopted by the NCS board were designed to coerce the consummation of the Genesis merger and preclude the consideration of any superior transaction. The NCS directors' defensive devices are not within a reasonable range of responses to the perceived threat of losing the Genesis offer because they are preclusive and coercive. Accordingly, we hold that those deal protection devices are unenforceable.

Effective Fiduciary Out Required

The defensive measures that protected the merger transaction are unenforceable not only because they are preclusive and coercive but, alternatively, they are unenforceable because they are invalid as they operate in this case. Given the specifically enforceable irrevocable voting agreements, the provision in the merger agreement requiring the board to submit the transaction for a stockholder vote and the omission of a fiduciary out clause in the merger agreement completely prevented the board from discharging its fiduciary responsibilities to the minority stockholders when Omnicare presented its superior transaction. "To the extent that a [merger] contract, or a provision thereof, purports to require a board to act or not act in such a fashion as to limit the exercise of fiduciary duties, it is invalid and unenforceable."[74]

In *QVC*, this Court recognized that "[w]hen a majority of a corporation's voting shares are acquired by a single person or entity, or by *a cohesive group acting together* [as in this case], there is a significant diminution in the voting power of those who thereby become minority stockholders." Therefore, we acknowledged that "[i]n the absence of devices protecting the minority stockholders, stockholder votes are likely to become mere formalities," where a cohesive group acting together to exercise majority voting powers have already decided the outcome. Consequently, we concluded that since the minority stockholders lost the power to influence corporate direction through the ballot, "minority stockholders must rely for protection solely on the fiduciary duties owed to them by the directors."

Under the circumstances presented in this case, where a cohesive group of stockholders with majority voting power was irrevocably committed to the merger transaction, "[e]ffective representation of the financial interests of the minority shareholders imposed upon the [NCS board] an affirmative responsibility to protect those minority shareholders' interests."

---

74. Paramount Communications, Inc. v. QVC Network, Inc. 637 A.2d 34, 51 (Del. 1993). . . . Restatement (Second) of Contracts §193. . . .

C. The Evolution of Unocal; Deal Protection Devices

The NCS board could not abdicate its fiduciary duties to the minority by leaving it to the stockholders alone to approve or disapprove the merger agreement because two stockholders had already combined to establish a majority of the voting power that made the outcome of the stockholder vote a foregone conclusion.

The Court of Chancery noted that Section 251(c) of the Delaware General Corporation Law now permits boards to agree to submit a merger agreement for a stockholder vote, even if the Board later withdraws its support for that agreement and recommends that the stockholders reject it.... Taking action that is otherwise legally possible, however, does not *ipso facto* comport with the fiduciary responsibilities of directors in all circumstances.... The directors of a Delaware corporation have a continuing obligation to discharge their fiduciary responsibilities, as future circumstances develop, after a merger agreement is announced. Genesis anticipated the likelihood of a superior offer after its merger agreement was announced and demanded defensive measures from the NCS board that *completely* protected its transaction. Instead of agreeing to the absolute defense of the Genesis merger from a superior offer, however, the NCS board was required to negotiate a fiduciary out clause to protect the NCS stockholders if the Genesis transaction became an inferior offer. By acceding to Genesis' ultimatum for complete protection *in futuro*, the NCS board disabled itself from exercising its own fiduciary obligations at a time when the board's own judgment is most important, i.e. receipt of a subsequent superior offer.

Any board has authority to give the proponent of a recommended merger agreement reasonable structural and economic defenses, incentives, and fair compensation if the transaction is not completed. To the extent that defensive measures are economic and reasonable, they may become an increased cost to the proponent of any subsequent transaction. Just as defensive measures cannot be draconian, however, they cannot limit or circumscribe the directors' fiduciary duties. Notwithstanding the corporation's insolvent condition, the NCS board had no authority to execute a merger agreement that subsequently prevented it from effectively discharging its ongoing fiduciary responsibilities.

The stockholders of a Delaware corporation are entitled to rely upon the board to discharge its fiduciary duties at all times. The fiduciary duties of a director are unremitting and must be effectively discharged in the specific context of the actions that are required with regard to the corporation or its stockholders as circumstances change. The stockholders with majority voting power, Shaw and Outcalt, had an absolute right to sell or exchange their shares with a third party at any price. This right was not only known to the other directors of NCS, it became an integral part of the Genesis agreement. In its answering brief, Genesis candidly states that its offer "came with a condition—Genesis would not be a stalking horse and would not agree to a transaction to which NCS's controlling shareholders were not committed."

The NCS board was required to contract for an effective fiduciary out clause to exercise its continuing fiduciary responsibilities to the minority stockholders.[88] The issues in this appeal do not involve the general validity of either stockholder voting agreements or the authority of directors to insert a Section 251(c) provision in a merger agreement. In this case, the NCS board combined those two otherwise valid actions and caused them to operate in concert as an absolute lock up, in the absence of an effective fiduciary out clause in the Genesis merger agreement.

In the context of this preclusive and coercive lock up case, the protection of Genesis' contractual expectations must yield to the supervening responsibility of the directors to discharge their fiduciary duties on a continuing basis. The merger agreement and voting agreements, as they were combined to operate in concert in this case, are inconsistent with the NCS directors' fiduciary duties. To that extent, we hold that they are invalid and unenforceable.

VEASEY, Chief Justice, with whom STEELE, Justice, joins dissenting. . . .

An Analysis of the Process Leading to the Lock-Up Reflects a Quintessential, Disinterested and Informed Board Decision Reached in Good Faith

. . . Going into negotiations with Genesis, the NCS directors knew that, up until that time, NCS had found only one potential bidder, Omnicare. Omnicare had refused to buy NCS except at a fire sale price through an asset sale in bankruptcy. Omnicare's best proposal at that stage would not have paid off all creditors and would have provided nothing for stockholders. The Noteholders, represented by the Ad Hoc Committee, were willing to oblige Omnicare and force NCS into bankruptcy if Omnicare would pay in full the NCS debt. Through the NCS board's efforts, Genesis expressed interest that became increasingly attractive. Negotiations with Genesis led to an offer paying creditors off and conferring on NCS stockholders $24 million — an amount infinitely superior to the prior Omnicare proposals.

But there was, understandably, a sine qua non. In exchange for offering the NCS stockholders a return on their equity and creditor payment, Genesis demanded certainty that the merger would close. If the NCS board would not have acceded to the Section 251(c) provision, if Outcalt and Shaw had not agreed to the voting agreements and if NCS

---

88. *See Paramount Communications Inc. v. QVC Network Inc.*, 637 A.2d at 42-43. Merger agreements involve an ownership decision and, therefore, cannot become final without stockholder approval. Other contracts do not require a fiduciary out clause because they involve business judgments that are within the *exclusive* province of the board of directors' power to manage the affairs of the corporation. *See Grimes v. Donald*, 673 A.2d 1207, 1214-15 (Del. 1996).

had insisted on a fiduciary out, there would have been no Genesis deal! Thus, the only value-enhancing transaction available would have disappeared. NCS knew that Omnicare had spoiled a Genesis acquisition in the past, and it is not disputed by the Majority that the NCS directors made a reasoned decision to accept as real the Genesis threat to walk away.

When Omnicare submitted its conditional eleventh-hour bid, the NCS board had to weigh the economic terms of the proposal against the uncertainty of completing a deal with Omnicare. Importantly, because Omnicare's bid was conditioned on its satisfactorily completing its due diligence review of NCS, the NCS board saw this as a crippling condition, as did the Ad Hoc Committee. As a matter of business judgment, the risk of negotiating with Omnicare and losing Genesis at that point outweighed the possible benefits. The lock-up was indisputably a sine qua non to any deal with Genesis.

A lock-up permits a target board and a bidder to "exchange certainties." Certainty itself has value. The acquirer may pay a higher price for the target if the acquirer is assured consummation of the transaction. The target company also benefits from the certainty of completing a transaction with a bidder because losing an acquirer creates the perception that a target is damaged goods, thus reducing its value....

Situations will arise where business realities demand a lock-up so that wealth-enhancing transactions may go forward. Accordingly, any brightline rule prohibiting lock-ups could, in circumstances such as these, chill otherwise permissible conduct.

Our Jurisprudence Does Not Compel This Court to Invalidate the Joint Action of the Board and the Controlling Stockholders

... Outcalt and Shaw were fully informed stockholders. As the NCS controlling stockholders, they made an informed choice to commit their voting power to the merger. The minority stockholders were deemed to know that when controlling stockholders have 65% of the vote they can approve a merger without the need for the minority votes. Moreover, to the extent a minority stockholder may have felt "coerced" to vote for the merger, which was already a *fait accompli*, it was a meaningless coercion — or no coercion at all — because the controlling votes, those of Outcalt and Shaw, were already "cast." Although the fact that the controlling votes were committed to the merger "precluded" an overriding vote against the merger by the Class A stockholders, the pejorative "preclusive" label applicable in a *Unitrin* fact situation has no application here. Therefore, there was no meaningful minority stockholder voting decision to coerce.

In applying *Unocal* scrutiny, we believe the Majority incorrectly preempted the proportionality inquiry. In our view, the proportionality inquiry must account for the reality that the contractual measures protecting this merger agreement were necessary to obtain the Genesis deal. The

Majority has not demonstrated that the director action was a disproportionate response to the threat posed. Indeed, it is clear to us that the board action to negotiate the best deal reasonably available with the only viable merger partner (Genesis) who could satisfy the creditors and benefit the stockholders, was reasonable in relation to the threat, by any practical yardstick.

An Absolute Lock-Up Is Not a Per Se Violation of Fiduciary Duty

... In this case, Genesis made it abundantly clear early on that it was willing to negotiate a deal with NCS but only on the condition that it would not be a "stalking horse." Thus, it wanted to be certain that a third party could not use its deal with NCS as a floor against which to begin a bidding war. As a result of this negotiating position, a "fiduciary out" was not acceptable to Genesis. The Majority Opinion holds that such a negotiating position, if implemented in the agreement, is invalid per se where there is an absolute lock-up. We know of no authority in our jurisprudence supporting this new rule, and we believe it is unwise and unwarranted.

The Majority relies on our decision in *QVC* to assert that the board's fiduciary duties prevent the directors from negotiating a merger agreement without providing an escape provision. Reliance on *QVC* for this proposition, however, confuses our statement of a board's responsibilities when the directors confront a superior transaction and turn away from it to lock up a less valuable deal with the very different situation here, where the board committed itself to the *only* value-enhancing transaction available. . . .

The Majority also mistakenly relies on our decision in *QVC* to support the notion that the NCS board should have retained a fiduciary out to save the minority stockholder from Shaw's and Outcalt's voting agreements. Our reasoning in *QVC*, which recognizes that minority stockholders must rely for protection on the fiduciary duties owed to them by directors, does not create a *special* duty to protect the minority stockholders from the consequences of a controlling stockholder's ultimate decision unless the controlling stockholder stands on both sides of the transaction, which is certainly not the case here. . . . Unlike the stockholders who are confronted with a transaction that will relegate them to a minority status in the corporation, the Class A stockholders of NCS purchased stock knowing that the Charter provided Class B stockholders voting control.

NOTES AND QUESTIONS

1. **The deal.**

    a. **The economics of certainty.** A merger negotiation is like many other economic transactions in which the seller has to decide

C. The Evolution of Unocal; Deal Protection Devices

whether to make an immediate deal with the buyer, forgoing the possibility of a higher price that might show up later from another bidder, against the possibility that not making an immediate deal will drive the first bidder away, thereby lowering the price for the company or the asset and likely forgoing the possible premium found in the initial bid. For a first bidder such as Genesis, the concern is investing money to develop the initial bid and putting a price on the table, only to be used by the seller as a "stalking horse" to get a higher price from another bidder. The first bidder not only faces the possibility of being out the "sunk costs" it has invested, but may also be at an economic disadvantage in competing with the second bidder to the extent that the work of the first bidder saves the second bidder search costs that permit the second bidder to free ride on the valuable information the first bidder has paid to develop about the target. The usual give and take over the value of certainty is seen in the negotiations between Genesis and the NCS board in July.

b. **How shareholder voting in a typical merger creates additional uncertainty.** Merger statutes add an additional degree of uncertainty to the core negotiations just described to buy and sell the company, one that arises from the governance requirement that shareholders must approve fundamental changes. Federal disclosure rules, triggered whenever proxies are sought from shareholders in a public company, not only publicize the terms of the deal but also add three months or more to the time line during which another bidder might show up. Recall the appearance of Paramount late in the Time-Warner negotiations. The requirement of shareholder approval, ostensibly designed to provide a means of checking agency costs of directors with control of other people's money within the target corporation, also acts as an option to the target to walk away if another bidder emerges (or the economy changes) over the period waiting for the vote. Buyers would like to minimize the risk of this additional uncertainty and the board and managers of the Seller, to the extent they believe (doing the core economic calculation described in the previous paragraph) that the first bidder's deal is the best for the corporations, often seek to provide such assurances.

c. **Providing more certainty in the Genesis/NCS deal.** The merger agreement between Genesis and NCS incorporates a variety of deal protection devices that are common to mergers:
- *Termination Fee.* Here $6 million that NCS must pay if it does not complete the deal.
- *Force the vote provision.* The NCS's board agreement that even if the board were to change its mind about the merger during the period before the shareholder vote (perhaps because of the

appearance of the second bid or changes in the economy), they will not pull the vote off the shareholder's agenda; such a provision was explicitly permitted by an addition to the Delaware statute §251(c) made in 1999 (since moved to §146 of the Delaware code).

- *No shop/no talk.* The target board's agreement not to affirmatively seek out other bidders or to talk to other bidders who might seek information as part of due diligence or otherwise.

In addition this deal included a deal protection clause not usually found in most deals:

- *Shareholders' agreement.* A contract in which the two controlling shareholders agreed to vote for the merger.

Finally there is a Negative Deal Protection that the parties chose not to put into the merger agreement that is important to the Court's analysis:

- *Fiduciary out clause* that would permit the directors of the target to rescind the merger agreement if necessary to satisfy their fiduciary duty to their shareholders.

Each of these provisions (and their cumulative effect) leads to a court having to weigh a possible tradeoff between protecting the power of shareholders to overturn merger decisions made by managers and directors versus the impact on the certainty of transactions that will necessarily arise because of the delay and the possibility that the target will use the extra time to take a better deal that would not have been available at the time the merger agreement was sealed by the boards.

2. Revising "old learning": Deal protection and intermediate scrutiny. As with many mergers, at the time of the initial Genesis discussions, the second bidder's offer had not yet surfaced. By what standard should such initial director actions be judged in such a setting? The court seems clear that the intermediate test of *Unocal* will be applied.

    a. Do you see any difference in how the court here phrases the standard here as compared to the standard to be met in *Revlon*? This opinion discusses both the triggers for enhanced scrutiny and how directors meet enhanced scrutiny if this review is triggered. How is the court's examination of reasonableness different than the deference of the business judgment rule?

    b. As to the *Unocal* test, this opinion discusses *Unitrin*, where the Court discussed application of the second "proportionality" prong of *Unocal* as itself a two-step analysis, looking first at whether the defensive tactics were "coercive or "preclusive" (as illustrations of "draconian") and then at whether the response was within a range of reasonableness. Further illustration of this test is visible in Chapter 7 and in the *Unitrin* case itself that appears in Chapter 8. For the moment, consider how often coercive or preclusive will be found in takeovers. Separately, what is it about the facts of this case that suggest the combination of defensive tactics here is not likely to reappear frequently??

3. Accounting for the non-typical aspects of this case. The Court concludes that "the public shareholders will be forced to accept the Genesis merger." What is the source of the coercion? The suggestion is that directors have misused their authority in the same way alleged in Time/Paramount and Paramount/QVC and the Court is using *Unocal* to preserve the rightful sphere of shareholder decision-making and shareholder value. But the shareholder/director relationship in NCS does not track the typical dispersed shareholder template of American public corporations. Instead there are two shareholders who hold a majority of the votes. In *Mendel v. Carroll*, included in Chapter 11 below, Chancellor Allen discusses the duties of directors when there is a controlling shareholder and concludes that directors cannot use their authority to intrude on the control decisions of a controlling shareholder. As the dissent in this case points out, the two shareholders (who are also two of the four directors) agreed to the Genesis deal, making the economic trade-off described above. The majority's focus on the directors' duty to public shareholders skates past this crucial difference (a result that undoubtedly pleased the controlling shareholders who now were able to share in the largess of what had turned out to be a better deal from Omnicare).

4. Omnicare's application in the more typical deal protection case. Must deal planners include a fiduciary out clause in every merger agreement that they draft? The common law methodology of this case means the actual holding only applied to the four corners of this case, or more specifically, to a situation where there was: (a) a §251(c)/§146 clause; (b) a shareholder voting agreement; and (c) the absence of a fiduciary out. The atypical nature of this control shareholder case means that there remains uncertainty about the legal rule in the more typical merger agreement.

5. A California alternative and other Delaware applications. A California court in Monty v. Leis, 193 Cal. App. 4th 1367, 123 Cal. Rptr. 3d 641 (2 Dist. 2011), declined to follow Omnicare, noting it had been criticized in Delaware (*See* In re Toys "R" Us, Inc., Shareholder Litigation (Del. Ch. 2005) 877 A.2d 975, 1016, n.68, Omnicare "represents... an aberrational departure from [the] long accepted principle" that what matters is whether the board acted reasonably in light of all the circumstances), and following instead Jewel Companies, Inc. v. Pay Less Drug Stores Northwest, Inc. (9th Cir.1984) 741 F.2d 1555, a case decided under California law. In *Jewel*, the court held that a board of directors may lawfully bind itself in a merger agreement to forbear from negotiating or accepting competing offers. (*Id.* at p. 1564.) The court reasoned:

> "An exclusive board-negotiated merger agreement may confer considerable benefits upon the shareholders of a firm. A potential merger partner may be reluctant to agree to a merger unless it is confident that its offer will not be used by the board simply to trigger an auction for the firm's assets. Therefore, an exclusive merger agreement may be necessary to secure the best offer for the shareholders of a firm. ... It is true that in certain situations the shareholders may suffer a lost opportunity as a result of the board's entering into an exclusive merger agreement. As the district court took great pains to point out, subsequent to a contractual commitment unanticipated business opportunities and exigencies of the marketplace may render a proposed merger less desirable than when originally bargained for. But all contracts are formed at a single point in time and are based on the information available at that moment. The pursuit of competitive advantage has never been recognized at law as a sufficient reason to render void, or voidable, an otherwise valid contract, and in our view, it was not the intention of the drafters of California's Corporate Code to make this any less true of negotiated merger agreements."

Jewel Companies, Inc. v. Pay Less Drug Stores Northwest, Inc., supra, 741 F.2d at pp. 1563-1564.

In a subsequent Delaware case, the Chancery Court declined to enjoin a deal where there was no shareholder agreement as in *Omnicare*, but written consent was secured from a majority of the shareholders within one day of the board's approval (and the board members held 59% of the outstanding stock). Although the deal lacked "an auction, a fairness opinion, a broad pre-signing-solicitation, a fiduciary-out, or a post-agreement market check," the Court declined to interfere with the decision of the non-conflicted board of a small public corporation. *See* In re OPENLANE, Inc. Shareholder Litigation, 2011 WL 4599662 (Del. Ch. Sept. 30, 2011).

D. STATE ANTI-TAKEOVER STATUTES AS DEFENSIVE MECHANISMS

The defensive tactics discussed in this chapter involve director action challenged as a breach of the directors' fiduciary duty under common law developments of those doctrines. But prior to full flowering of that common law and the room it provided directors to oppose unwanted offers, state legislatures provided a host of statutes that functionally aimed at the same purpose of blocking an unwanted offer. This statutory development arrived in three waves. After 1968, when hostile takeovers first took off, three-fourths of the states passed statutes. These first-generation statutes tilted the playing field in favor of targets by requiring even more disclosure by bidders than did the federal Williams Act and also required review by a state official or

D. State Anti-Takeover Statutes as Defensive Mechanisms

imposed other procedural requirements that could substantially delay a tender offer. The Supreme Court struck down such a statute in 1982 in Edgar v. MITE Corp., 457 U.S. 624 (1982), as impermissible interference with interstate commerce.

After *MITE*, state legislators desirous of slowing the rate of takeovers, developed a second-generation group of anti-takeover statutes that focused not on regulating bidder conduct but rather empowering shareholders to approve changes in control or allowing directors to act as centralized agents for the corporation, matters that traditionally had been a state concern within corporations law. One of these statutes was upheld by the U.S. Supreme Court in CTS Corp. v. Dynamics Corp. of America, 481 U.S. 69 (1987), against claims that it was preempted by the Williams Act and that it was impermissible state interference with interstate commerce.

The states' success in CTS led to even more statutes, sometimes called third-generation statutes as described in the case below. The statutes follow multiple patterns with courts often passing two, three, or even six or more. These include:

1. ***Moratorium statutes.*** Delaware G.C.L. §203, described in the case below, is a moratorium or business combination statute, first passed in New York and subsequently widely adopted. These statutes prohibit business combinations between certain acquiring shareholders and the target corporation for a period of time (three years in Delaware, five years in New York) unless the acquirer gains the approval of Target's pre-acquisition board of directors or acquires a supermajority of the voting stock (85 percent in Delaware). A business combination is usually defined to include not just mergers and similar transactions, but any transaction that confers a financial benefit on the interested shareholder so that, absent compliance with the statute, the acquirer would have to operate the newly acquired corporation at arm's length for the moratorium period specified by the statute.

2. ***Control share acquisition statutes.*** The Indiana statute upheld in *CTS* is an example of this type of statute. These statutes provide that when an acquiring shareholder crosses certain thresholds, such as 20 percent, 33-1/3 percent, or 50 percent, the acquired shares will lack voting rights unless voting power is reinstated by a majority vote of the disinterested shareholders. Encouraged by the Supreme Court's approval of the Indiana statute, many states enacted a similar statute. Proponents of control share acquisition statutes analogize the shareholder approval of tender offers to shareholder approval of mergers long required by state law. However, the effect of these statutes often is to require an acquirer to launch two efforts — the acquisition of the shares and a proxy fight to persuade the remaining shareholders to give a vote to the acquired shares.

3. ***Supermajority/fair price statutes.*** These statutes operate similarly to the moratorium statutes in that they condition completion of a second-step merger following a tender offer on the merger receiving a supermajority vote or the remaining shareholders receiving a statutorily defined fair price, often defined in a way that would provide the remaining shareholders more than what had been initially offered in the tender offer.

4. ***Appraisal statutes.*** A few states provide that a tender offer triggers the right of any remaining shareholders to seek appraisal of their shares, but the definition of fair price is more like the fair price statutes than the merger appraisal statutes. Such statutes, in effect, prevent partial bids, a result that is also mandated by takeover rules in the United Kingdom.

5. ***Other constituencies.*** Statutes in most states specifically authorize boards of directors to consider constituencies beyond shareholders in responding to tender offers. These other constituencies include bondholders, employees, neighbors, and the community. Such statutes seem designed to give directors substantial room to maneuver in response to an unwanted suitor, consistent with the approach of the Delaware court in *Paramount Communications v. Time, Inc.* A 1990 Pennsylvania statute extends these statutes by stating that "directors shall not be required . . . to regard any corporate interest or the interest of any particular group affected by such action as a dominant or controlling interest or factor." Pennsylvania Stat. Ann. Tit. 15, §1715(b) (Purdon). This direct affront to the primacy of director duty to shareholders has provoked substantial criticism of the Pennsylvania law. Critics argue that this break in accountability to shareholders leaves managers without sufficient constraint, absent the threat of being replaced at the next election. Proponents see the law as a way to change director focus on short-term share price maximization, a perception often linked with perceived social and economic injury to nonshareholder constituencies from takeovers.

6. ***Disgorgement.*** A 1990 Pennsylvania statute permits a target company to recover the profits made by an unwanted suitor on target stock acquired within 24 months before or 18 months after the unwanted suitor becomes a controlling person or group. Pennsylvania Stat. Ann. Tit. 15, §2575 (Purdon). The definition of controlling person or group is broadly defined to include (1) those acquiring, offering to acquire, or publicly disclosing or causing to be disclosed, directly or indirectly, an intent to acquire voting power over at least 20 percent of the votes that all shareholders would be entitled to cast in an election of directors; and (2) those who directly or indirectly publicly disclose or cause to be disclosed

D. State Anti-Takeover Statutes as Defensive Mechanisms

that they may seek to acquire control through any means. Pennsylvania Stat. Ann. Tit. 15 §2573 (Purdon).

7. **Severance compensation.** Pennsylvania legislation provides for one-time lump sum severance payments to employees terminated within 24 months of a control share approval. The statute also protects labor contracts made with acquired companies. Pennsylvania Stat. Ann. Tit. 15, §§2582, 2587 (Purdon). The severance payment statutes extend to a larger group of employees the benefit of "golden parachute" agreements that boards frequently give key management employees to protect them against loss of compensation after a takeover.

The success of internal corporate defensive tactics discussed in this and the next chapters—e.g., poison pills to block shareholder selling and staggered boards to block shareholder voting—muted the impact of state anti-takeover provisions even after their constitutionality was established. Put simply, planners on the defense side obtained such sufficient protection from poison pills and staggered boards that they didn't need to aggressively pursue use of these state statutes. As poison pills and staggered boards have receded in recent years, the potential usefulness of these statutes may provide the means for a return of these statutes to a more central place in takeovers, requiring understanding as to how they might be used and how a court would approach a challenge to their use.

These statutes operate similarly to the other defensive tactics already studied. They raise the costs to the bidder (for example, in the fair price, disgorgement, or severance pay statutes) or they narrow the space for shareholders to overcome a director decision not to pursue a takeover (by requiring such a high vote of shareholders that a minority can exercise a veto of the majority shareholder action).

Amanda Acquisition Corp. v. Universal Foods Corp.
877 F.2d 496 (7th Cir. 1989), cert. denied, 493 U.S. 955 (1989)

EASTERBROOK, Circuit Judge.

States have enacted three generations of takeover statutes in the last 20 years. . . .

Wisconsin has a third-generation takeover statute. Enacted after *CTS*, it postpones the kinds of transactions that often follow tender offers (and often are the reason for making the offers in the first place). Unless the target's board agrees to the transaction in advance, the bidder must wait three years after buying the shares to merge with the target or acquire more than 5% of its assets. We must decide whether this is consistent with the Williams Act and Commerce Clause.

I.

Amanda Acquisition Corporation is a shell with a single purpose: to acquire Universal Foods Corporation, a diversified firm incorporated in Wisconsin and traded on the New York Stock Exchange. Universal is covered by Wisconsin's antitakeover law. Amanda is a subsidiary of High Voltage Engineering Corp., a small electronics firm in Massachusetts. Most of High Voltage's equity capital comes from Berisford Capital PLC, a British venture capital firm, and Hyde Park Partners L.P., a partnership affiliated with the principals of Berisford. Chase Manhattan Bank has promised to lend Amanda 50% of the cost of the acquisition, secured by the stock of Universal.

In mid-November 1988 Universal's stock was trading for about $25 per share. On December 1 Amanda commenced a tender offer at $30.50, to be effective if at least 75% of the stock should be tendered. This all-cash, all-shares offer has been increased by stages to $38.00. Amanda's financing is contingent on a prompt merger with Universal if the offer succeeds, so the offer is conditional on a judicial declaration that the law is invalid. . . .

No firm incorporated in Wisconsin and having its headquarters, substantial operations, or 10% of its shares or shareholders there may "engage in a business combination with an interested stockholder . . . for 3 years after the interested stockholder's stock acquisition date unless the board of directors of the [Wisconsin] corporation has approved, before the interested stockholder's stock acquisition date, that business combination or the purchase of stock," Wis. Stat. §180.726(2). An "interested stockholder" is one owning 10% of the voting stock, directly or through associates (anyone acting in concert with it), §180.726(1)(e). A "business combination" is a merger with the bidder or any of its affiliates, sale of more than 5% of the assets to bidder or affiliate, liquidation of the target, or a transaction by which the target guarantees the bidder's or affiliates debts or passes tax benefits to the bidder or affiliate, §180.726(1)(e). The law, in other words, provides for almost hermetic separation of bidder and target for three years after the bidder obtains 10% of the stock — unless the target's board consented before then. No matter how popular the offer, the ban applies: obtaining 85% (even 100%) of the stock held by non-management shareholders won't allow the bidder to engage in a business combination, as it would under Delaware law. Wisconsin firms cannot opt out of the law, as many corporations subject to almost all other state takeover statutes. In Wisconsin it is management's approval in advance, or wait three years. Even when the time is up, the bidder needs the approval of a majority of the remaining investors, without any provision disqualifying shares still held by the managers who resisted the transaction, §180.726(3)(b). The district court found that this statute "effectively eliminates hostile leveraged buyouts." As a practical matter, Wisconsin prohibits any offer contingent on a merger between bidder and target, a condition attached to about 90% of contemporary tender offers. . . .

II.

A.

If our views of the wisdom of state law mattered, Wisconsin's takeover statute would not survive. Like our colleagues who decided *MITE* and *CTS*, we believe that antitakeover legislation injures shareholders. Managers frequently realize gains for investors via voluntary combinations (mergers). If gains are to be had, but managers balk, tender offers are investors' way to go over managers' heads. If managers are not maximizing the firm's value—perhaps because they have missed the possibility of a synergistic combination, perhaps because they are clinging to divisions that could be better run in other hands, perhaps because they are just not the best persons for the job—a bidder that believes it can realize more of the firm's value will make investors a higher offer....

Although a takeover-proof firm leaves investors at the mercy of incumbent managers (who may be mistaken about the wisdom of their business plan even when they act in the best of faith), a takeover-resistant firm may be able to assist its investors. An auction may run up the price, and delay may be essential to an auction. Auctions transfer money from bidders to targets, and diversified investors would not gain from them (their left pocket loses what the right pocket gains); diversified investors would lose from auctions if the lower returns to bidders discourage future bids. But from targets' perspectives, once a bid is on the table an auction may be the best strategy. The full effects of auctions are hard to unravel, sparking scholarly debate. Devices giving managers some ability to orchestrate investors' responses, in order to avoid panic tenders in response to front-end-loaded offers, also could be beneficial, as the Supreme Court emphasized in *CTS*, 481 U.S. at 92-93. ("Could be" is an important qualifier; even from a perspective limited to targets' shareholders given a bid on the table, it is important to know whether managers use this power to augment bids or to stifle them, and whether courts can tell the two apart.)

State anti-takeover laws do not serve these ends well, however. Investors who prefer to give managers the discretion to orchestrate responses to bids may do so through "fair-price" clauses in the articles of incorporation and other consensual devices. Other firms may choose different strategies. A law such as Wisconsin's does not add options to firms that would like to give more discretion to their managers; instead it destroys the possibility of divergent choices. Wisconsin's law applies even when the investors prefer to leave their managers under the gun, to allow the market full sway. Karpoff and Malatesta found that state antitakeover laws have little or no effect on the price of shares if the firm already has poison pills (or related devices) in place, but strongly negative effects on price when firms have no such contractual devices. To put this differently, state laws have bite only when investors, given the choice, would deny managers the power to interfere with tender offers (maybe already *have* denied managers that power). See also Roberta Romano, *The Political Economy of Takeover Statutes*, 73 VA. L. REV. 111, 128-131 (1987)....

B.

Skepticism about the wisdom of a state's law does not lead to the conclusion that the law is beyond the state's power, however. We have not been elected custodians of investors' wealth. States need not treat investors' welfare as their summum bonum. Perhaps they choose to protect managers' welfare instead, or believe that the current economic literature reaches an incorrect conclusion and that despite appearances takeovers injure investors in the long run. Unless a federal statute or the Constitution bars the way, Wisconsin's choice must be respected.

Amanda relies on the Williams Act of 1968, incorporated into §§13(d), (e) and 14(d)-(f) of the Securities Exchange Act of 1934, 15 U.S.C. §§78m(d), (e), 78n(d)-(f). The Williams Act regulates the conduct of tender offers. Amanda believes that Congress created an entitlement for investors to receive the benefit of tender offers, and that because Wisconsin's law makes tender offers unattractive to many potential bidders, it is preempted. See *MITE*, 633 F.2d at 490-99, and Justice White's views, 457 U.S. at 630-640. . . .

There is a big difference between what Congress *enacts* and what it *supposes* will ensue. Expectations about the consequences of a law are not themselves law. To say that Congress wanted to be neutral between bidder and target—a conclusion reached in many of the Court's opinions, e.g., Piper v. Chris-Craft Industries, Inc., 430 U.S. 1 (1977)—is not to say that it also forbade the states to favor one of these sides. Every law has a stopping point, likely one selected because of a belief that it would be unwise (for now, maybe forever) to do more. Nothing in the Williams Act says that the federal compromise among bidders, targets' managers, and investors is the only permissible one. See Daniel R. Fischel, *From* MITE *to* CTS: *State Anti-Takeover Statutes, the Williams Act, the Commerce Clause, and Insider Trading*, 1987 Sup. Ct. Rev. 47, 71-74. Like the majority of the Court in *CTS*, however, we stop short of the precipice.

The Williams Act regulates the *process* of tender offers: timing, disclosure, proration if tenders exceed what the bidder is willing to buy, best-price rules. It slows things down, allowing investors to evaluate the offer and management's response. Best-price, proration, and short-tender rules ensure that investors who decide at the end of the offer get the same treatment as those who decide immediately, reducing pressure to leap before looking. After complying with the disclosure and delay requirements, the bidder is free to take the shares. *MITE* held invalid a state law that increased the delay and, by authorizing a regulator to nix the offer, created a distinct possibility that the bidder would be unable to buy the stock (and the holders to sell it) despite compliance with federal law. Illinois tried to regulate the process of tender offers, contradicting in some respects the federal rules. Indiana, by contrast, allowed the tender offer to take its course as the Williams Act specified but "sterilized" the acquired shares until the

D. State Anti-Takeover Statutes as Defensive Mechanisms 217

remaining investors restored their voting rights. Congress said nothing about the voting power of shares acquired in tender offers. Indiana's law reduced the benefits the bidder anticipated from the acquisition but left the process alone. So the Court, although accepting Justice White's views for the purpose of argument, held that Indiana's rules do not conflict with the federal norms.

CTS observed that laws affecting the voting power of acquired shares do not differ in principle from many other rules governing the internal affairs of corporations. Laws requiring staggered or classified boards of directors delay the transfer of control to the bidder; laws requiring super-majority vote for a merger may make a transaction less attractive or impossible. Yet these are not preempted by the Williams Act, any more than state laws concerning the *effect* of investors' votes are preempted by the portions of the Exchange Act, 15 U.S.C. §78n(a)-(c), regulating the process of soliciting proxies. Federal securities laws frequently regulate process while state corporate law regulates substance. Federal proxy rules demand that firms disclose many things, in order to promote informed voting. Yet states may permit or compel a supermajority rule (even a unanimity rule) rendering it all but impossible for a particular side to prevail in the voting. See Robert Charles Clark, CORPORATE LAW §9.1.3 (1986). Are the state laws therefore preempted? How about state laws that allow many firms to organize without traded shares? Universities, hospitals, and other charities have self-perpetuating boards and cannot be acquired by tender offer. Insurance companies may be organized as mutuals, without traded shares; retailers often organize as co-operatives, without traded stock; some decently large companies (large enough to be "reporting companies" under the '34 Act) issue stock subject to buy-sell agreements under which the investors cannot sell to strangers without offering stock to the firm at a formula price; Ford Motor Co. issued non-voting stock to outside investors while reserving voting stock for the family, thus preventing outsiders from gaining control (dual- class stock is becoming more common); firms issue and state law enforces poison pills. All of these devices make tender offers unattractive (even impossible) and greatly diminish the power of proxy fights, success in which often depends on buying votes by acquiring the equity to which the vote is attached. See Douglas H. Blair, Devra L. Golbe & James M. Gerard, *Unbundling the Voting Rights and Profit Claims of Common Shares*, 97 J. POL. ECON. 420 (1989). None of these devices could be thought preempted by the Williams Act or the proxy rules. If they are not preempted, neither is Wis. Stat. §180.726.

Any bidder complying with federal law is free to acquire shares of Wisconsin firms on schedule. Delay in completing a second-stage merger may make the target less attractive, and thus depress the price offered or even lead to an absence of bids; it does not, however, alter any of the procedures governed by federal regulation. Indeed Wisconsin's law does not depend in any way on how the acquiring firm came by its stock:

open-market purchases, private acquisitions of blocs, and acquisitions via tender offers are treated identically. Wisconsin's law is no different in effect from one saying that for the three years after a person acquires 10% of a firm's stock, a unanimous vote is required to merge. Corporate law once had a generally-applicable unanimity rule in major transactions, a rule discarded because giving every investor the power to block every reorganization stopped many desirable changes. (Many investors could use their "hold-up" power to try to engross a larger portion of the gains, creating a complex bargaining problem that often could not be solved.) Wisconsin's more restrained version of unanimity also may block beneficial transactions, but not by tinkering with any of the procedures established in federal law.

Only if the Williams Act gives investors a right to be the beneficiary of offers could Wisconsin's law run afoul of the federal rule. No such entitlement can be mined out of the Williams Act, however. Schreiber v. Burlington Northern, Inc., 472 U.S. 1 (1985), holds that the cancellation of a pending offer because of machinations between bidder and target does not deprive investors of their due under the Williams Act. The Court treated §14(e) as a disclosure law, so that investors could make informed decisions; it follows that events leading bidders to cease their quest do not conflict with the Williams Act any more than a state law leading a firm not to issue new securities could conflict with the Securities Act of 1933. See also Panter v. Marshall Field & Co., 646 F.2d 271, 283-85 (7th Cir. 1981); Lewis v. McGraw, 619 F.2d 192 (2d Cir. 1980), both holding that the evaporation of an opportunity to tender one's shares when a defensive tactic leads the bidder to withdraw the invitation does not violate the Williams Act. Investors have no right to receive tender offers. More to the point — since Amanda sues as bidder rather than as investor seeking to sell — the Williams Act does not create a right to profit from the business of making tender offers. It is not attractive to put bids on the table for Wisconsin corporations, but because Wisconsin leaves the process alone once a bidder appears, its law may co-exist with the Williams Act.

C.

The Commerce Clause, Art. I, §8, cl. 3 of the Constitution, grants Congress the power "[to] regulate Commerce . . . among the several States." . . .

Illinois's law, held invalid in *MITE*, regulated sales of stock elsewhere. Illinois tried to tell a Texas owner of stock in a Delaware corporation that he could not sell to a buyer in California. By contrast, Wisconsin's law, like the Indiana statute sustained by *CTS*, regulates the internal affairs of firms incorporated there. Investors may buy or sell stock as they please. Wisconsin's law differs in this respect not only from that of Illinois but also from that of Massachusetts, which forbade any transfer of shares for one year after the failure

D. State Anti-Takeover Statutes as Defensive Mechanisms

to disclose any material fact, a flaw that led the First Circuit to condemn it. Hyde Park Partners, L.P. v. Connolly, 839 F.2d 837, 847-48 (1st Cir. 1988).

Buyers of stock in Wisconsin firms may exercise full rights as investors, taking immediate control. No interstate transaction is regulated or forbidden. True, Wisconsin's law makes a potential buyer less willing to buy (or depresses the bid), but this is equally true of Indiana's rule. Many other rules of corporate law—supermajority voting requirements, staggered and classified boards, and so on—have similar or greater effects on some person's willingness to purchase stock. *CTS*, 481 U.S. at 89-90. States could ban mergers outright, with even more powerful consequences. Louisville & Nashville R.R. v. Kentucky, 161 U.S. 677, 701-04 (1896); see also Kansas City, Memphis & Birmingham R.R. v. Stiles, 242 U.S. 111, 117 (1916); Ashley v. Ryan, 153 U.S. 436, 443 (1894). Wisconsin did not allow mergers among firms chartered there until 1947. We doubt that it was violating the Commerce Clause all those years. Cf. Edmund W. Kitch, *Regulation and the American Common Market*, in REGULATION, FEDERALISM, AND INTERSTATE COMMERCE 7 (A. Dan Tarlock ed., 1981). Every rule of corporate law affects investors who live outside the state of incorporation, yet this has never been thought sufficient to authorize a form of cost-benefit inquiry through the medium of the Commerce Clause.

Wisconsin, like Indiana, is indifferent to the domicile of the bidder. . . . "Because nothing in the [Wisconsin] Act imposes a greater burden on out-of-state offerors than it does on similarly situated [Wisconsin] offerors, we reject the contention that the Act discriminates against interstate commerce." *CTS*, 481 U.S. at 88. For the same reason, the Court long ago held that state blue sky laws comport with the Commerce Clause. Hall v. Geiger-Jones Co., 242 U.S. 539 (1917); Caldwell v. Sioux Falls Stock Yards Co., 242 U.S. 559 (1917); Merrick v. N.W. Halsey & Co., 242 U.S. 568 (1917). Blue sky laws may bar Texans from selling stock in Wisconsin, but they apply equally to local residents' attempts to sell. That their application blocks a form of commerce altogether does not strip the states of power.

Wisconsin could exceed its powers by subjecting firms to inconsistent regulation. Because §180.726 applies only to a subset of firms incorporated in Wisconsin, however, there is no possibility of inconsistent regulation. Here, too, the Wisconsin law is materially identical to Indiana's. This leaves only the argument that Wisconsin's law hinders the flow of interstate trade "too much." *CTS* dispatched this concern by declaring it inapplicable to laws that apply only to the internal affairs of firms incorporated in the regulating state. States may regulate corporate transactions as they choose without having to demonstrate under an unfocused balancing test that the benefits are "enough" to justify the consequences.

To say that states have the power to enact laws whose costs exceed their benefits is not to say that investors should kiss their wallets goodbye. States compete to offer corporate codes attractive to firms. Managers who want to raise money incorporate their firms in the states that offer the combination of rules investors prefer. Ralph K. Winter, Jr., *State Law, Shareholder Protection, and the Theory of the Corporation*, 6 J. LEGAL STUDIES 251 (1977); Fischel, supra, 1987 SUP. CT. REV. at 74-84. Laws that in the short run injure investors and protect managers will in the longer run make the state less attractive to firms that need to raise new capital. If the law is "protectionist," the protected class is the existing body of managers (and other workers), suppliers, and so on, which bears no necessary relation to state boundaries. States regulating the affairs of domestic corporations cannot in the long run injure anyone but themselves. Professor Fischel makes the point, 1987 SUP. CT. REV. at 84:

> In the short run, states can enact welfare-decreasing legislation that imposes costs on residents of other states. State anti-takeover statutes . . . may be paradigm examples of cost-exporting legislation that is enacted in response to lobbying pressure by in-state constituents. [The managers who gain from the law live in-state; the investors who lose may live elsewhere.] In the long run, however, states have no ability to export costs to non-resident investors. When entrepreneurs want to raise capital for a corporate venture, they must decide where to incorporate. The choice of where to incorporate in turn affects the price investors are willing to pay for shares. And because shares of stock have many perfect substitutes which offer the same risk-return combinations, it is impossible for the entrepreneur to pass on the effects of the law to investors. . . . Nor can a state export costs to the founding entrepreneur since corporations can be incorporated anywhere, regardless of the firm's physical location. States that enact laws that are harmful to investors will cause entrepreneurs to incorporate elsewhere.

The long run takes time to arrive, and it is tempting to suppose that courts could contribute to investors' welfare by eliminating laws that impose costs in the short run. See Gregg A. Jarrell, *State Anti-Takeover Laws and the Efficient Allocation of Corporate Control: An Economic Analysis of* Edgar v. MITE Corp., 2 SUP. CT. ECON. REV. 111 (1983). The price of such warfare, however, is a reduction in the power of competition among states. Courts seeking to impose "good" rules on the states diminish the differences among corporate codes and dampen competitive forces. Too, courts may fail in their quest. How do judges know which rules are best? Often only the slow forces of competition reveal that information. Early economic studies may mislead, or judges (not trained as social scientists) may misinterpret the available data or act precipitously. Our Constitution allows the states to act as laboratories; slow migration (or national law on the authority of the Commerce Clause) grinds the failures under. No such process weeds out judicial errors, or decisions that, although astute when rendered, have become anachronistic in light of changes in the economy. Judges must hesitate for these practical reasons — and not only because of limits on their constitutional competence — before trying to "perfect" corporate codes.

D. State Anti-Takeover Statutes as Defensive Mechanisms

The three district judges who have considered and sustained Delaware's law delaying mergers did so in large measure because they believed that the law left hostile offers "a meaningful opportunity for success." BNS, Inc. v. Koppers Co., [683 F. Supp. 458, 469 (D. Del. 1988)]. See also [RP Acquisition Corp. v. Staley Continental Inc., 686 F. Supp. 476, 482-484, 488 (D. Del. 1988); City Capital Associates L.P. v. Interco, Inc., 696 F. Supp. 1551, 1555 (D. Del. 1988)]. Delaware allows a merger to occur forthwith if the bidder obtains 85% of the shares other than those held by management and employee stock plans. If the bid is attractive to the bulk of the unaffiliated investors, it succeeds. Wisconsin offers no such opportunity, which Amanda believes is fatal.

Even in Wisconsin, though, options remain. Defenses impenetrable to the naked eye may have cracks. Poison pills are less fatal in practice than in name (some have been swallowed willingly), and corporate law contains self-defense mechanisms. Investors concerned about stock-watering often arranged for firms to issue pre-emptive rights, entitlements for existing investors to buy stock at the same price offered to newcomers (often before the newcomers had a chance to buy in). Poison pills are dilution devices, and so pre-emptive rights ought to be handy countermeasures.[11] So too there are countermeasures to statutes deferring mergers. The cheapest is to lower the bid to reflect the costs of delay. Because every potential bidder labors under the same drawback, the firm placing the highest value on the target still should win. Or a bidder might take down the stock and pledge it (or its dividends) as security for any loans. That is, the bidder could operate the target as a subsidiary for three years. The corporate world is full of partially owned subsidiaries. If there is gain to be had from changing the debt-equity ratio of the target, that can be done consistent with Wisconsin law. The prospect of being locked into place as holders of illiquid minority positions would cause many persons to sell out, and the threat of being locked in would cause many managers to give assent in advance, as Wisconsin allows. (Or bidders might demand that directors waive the protections of state law, just as Amanda believes that the directors' fiduciary duties compel them to redeem the poison pill rights.) Many bidders would find lock-in unattractive because of the potential for litigation by minority investors, and the need to operate the firm as a subsidiary might foreclose savings or synergies from merger. So none of these options is a perfect substitute for immediate merger, but each is a crack in the defensive wall allowing some value-increasing bids to proceed.

---

11. Imagine a series of Antidote rights, issued by would-be bidding firms, that detach if anyone exercises flip-over rights to purchase the bidder's stock at a discount. Antidote rights would entitle the bidder's investors, other than those who exercise flip-over rights, to purchase the bidder's stock at the same discount available to investors exercising flip-over rights. Antidotes for flip-in rights also could be issued. In general, whenever one firm can issue rights allowing the purchase of cheap stock, another firm can issue the equivalent series of contingent preemptive rights that offsets the dilution.

At the end of the day, however, it does not matter whether these countermeasures are "enough." The Commerce Clause does not demand that states leave bidders a "meaningful opportunity for success." Maryland enacted a law that absolutely banned vertical integration in the oil business. No opportunities, "meaningful" or otherwise, remained to firms wanting to own retail outlets. Exxon Corp. v. Governor of Maryland held that the law is consistent with the Commerce Clause, even on the assumption that it injures consumers and investors alike. A state with the power to forbid mergers has the power to defer them for three years. Investors can turn to firms incorporated in states committed to the dominance of market forces, or they can turn on legislators who enact unwise laws. The Constitution has room for many economic policies. "[A] law can be both economic folly and constitutional." *CTS*, 481 U.S. at 96-97 (Scalia, J., concurring). Wisconsin's law may well be folly; we are confident that it is constitutional. . . .

NOTES AND QUESTIONS

1. **Meaningful opportunity for success.** Federal district courts in Delaware, cited in the case above, upheld the constitutionality of the Delaware statute basing their supremacy clause reasoning, in part, on there being a "meaningful opportunity for success." Judge Easterbrook, in the case above, moves that reasoning to the Commerce Clause part of the case, but finds that the Commerce Clause does not demand such an opportunity. How does this "meaningful opportunity for success" compare to the space that must be left for shareholders under the *Unocal* test applied earlier in the chapter?

2. **Fiduciary duty to waive?** Under §203(a)(1), if the directors approve of the transaction, the moratorium does not apply. Do directors have a fiduciary duty to remove this barrier to shareholder voting in the way that at times there has seemed to be a duty to redeem the poison pill barrier to shareholder selling? A 1988 Chancery decision denied this "novel request" as it would "usurp the managerial powers of the Board by forcing it to approve a Nomad offer which the Board has found to be inadequate." Nomad Acquisition Corp. v. Damon Corp., 1988 WL 383667, 14 Del. J. Corp. L. 814,829. Reflecting that reasoning, a 2009 paper concludes "it would seem unusual and unprecedented for a Delaware court to rule that a board's fiduciary duty prevented it from doing something that the Delaware legislature had explicitly authorized." Subramanian, Herscovici & Barbetta, *Is Delaware Antitakeover Statute Unconstitutional? Evidence from 1988-2008*, 65 Bus. Law. 685 (2010). In contrast, the law firm that popularized the poison pill has asserted, "It is clear that a board's decision whether to not to waive Section 203 is subject to fiduciary duty. In any situation

where the fiduciary duties might compel a board to redeem a rights plan they would also likely compel a board to waive Section's 203's waiting period." Wachtell, Lipton, Rosen & Katz Memorandum to Clients, *Flawed Academic Challenge to Constitutionality of Delaware's Antitakeover Statute* (Sept. 29, 2009). Query whether the link to poison pill redemption would produce a null set given the cases set out in the following chapter.

7 POISON PILLS: A CASE STUDY OF DEFENSIVE TACTICS AND JUDICIAL REVIEW

Poison pills provide a useful illustration for the broader study of defensive tactics generally and the court's response to director action in a takeover setting. Even more, the poison pill is a fascinating study of the entrepreneurial role of lawyers responding to a core takeover challenge for target companies. The challenge was to design a response that was different from what went before but drew on precedent sufficient to insulate the innovation from the legal attacks that were sure to come. Eventually, the courts would have to decide how much freedom transaction planners would have in designing defensive tactics.

A. THE CHALLENGE FACING THE DRAFTERS OF THE POISON PILL

Before getting to the specifics of a poison pill and the judicial response, it would be helpful to start with what the lawyers were trying to accomplish. Why was there a need to do anything? Or put in more concrete terms, what was going to happen if the managers and their advisers did nothing? The answer is best framed in the overview described in the previous chapters. As the takeover market became more active in the early 1980s, all sorts of companies found themselves exposed to the possibility of a takeover. As the principal cases in the previous chapters illustrate, the managers of the target faced a mixed set of issues. To some degree there was the concern that animates the Delaware Supreme Court's presentation in *Unocal*, that the bidder or raider was seeking to take advantage of shareholders, or acting through shareholders to bust up the corporation in a way that could harm other stakeholders. In addition, there was also the possibility that the managers were responding to more selfish concerns of their own in resisting a takeover that might be good for shareholders and the entity as a whole. For either reason, the managers and their advisers wanted to defeat the hostile bid, and the lawyer's job was defined in those terms. In the face of a tender offer providing a premium of 30-40 percent over existing market prices, it was likely that shareholders (or at least 51 percent of them) would tender to the hostile bidder, and existing managers would quickly find themselves out of a job.

What did a defense need to do? This can best be seen in the context of the core legal rules of Chapter 3. Recall that Delaware's corporate law structure (and that of corporate law in the other states) starts with putting all corporate powers in the hands of directors (dubbed Rule #1 in an effort to drive home its centrality). Rule #2 was that shareholders are enabled to sometimes check director decision-making but only in the limited aspects of selling, suing, and voting. The goal of a defensive tactic, as seen very specifically in the poison pill, was to close off "selling," which was then the most threatening way that shareholders could act, and thereby return decision-making to corporate governance Rule #1, directors making the decisions. The "solution" was to dramatically increase the costs of a bidder making a tender offer so that it would no longer be profitable. The actual method by which this was accomplished is a good bit more complicated and is worth examining in more detail, but you should not lose sight of the core strategy reflected in this action.

The New York law firm of Wachtell, Lipton, Rosen and Katz, and its name partner, Martin Lipton, were most visible in the creation of the poison pill. The basic terms are set out in a memo by the firm. They prefer to call it a share purchase rights plan as opposed to a poison pill, but the colloquial name provides a better guide as to how the defensive tactic works.

Wachtell, Lipton, Rosen & Katz, The Share Purchase Rights Plan
March 1994

... Our recommended plan includes a "flip-in" feature designed to deter creeping accumulations of a company's stock. The "flip-in" feature is structured to be available from a 10% to a 20% ownership threshold. The plan also has the "flip-over" feature which provides shareholders protection against squeeze out. Appendix A contains a summary of the terms of our recommended plan. . . .

The basic objectives of the rights plan are to deter abusive takeover tactics by making them unacceptably expensive to the raider and to encourage prospective acquirors to negotiate with the board of directors of the target by making the rights issued pursuant to the plan redeemable for a nominal amount prior to a change of effective control through the acquisition of a large block of the target's shares. The plan was designed not to interfere, and has not interfered, with the day-to-day operations of the companies that have adopted it. Prior to its being activated by an acquisition of a large block of the target company's shares, it has no effect on a company's balance sheet or income statement and it is not taxable to the company or the shareholders. Companies have split their stock, issued stock dividends and combined their stock without interference from the plan. While the plan requires special care in such transactions, it has not hindered public offerings of common stock (including associated rights). . . .

The plan was first developed to deal with the then current two-tier, front-end loaded tender offer and related techniques. The "flip-over" provision of the plan stopped the two-tier, the partial and the creeping tender offers that were intended to be followed by a second-step merger. It accomplished this by giving the target's shareholders rights [upon the raider crossing the triggering threshold, typically 20%, but often as low as 10%], that would have to be assumed by a raider in a second-step merger, to buy the raider's common stock at half of its market price. The raider was faced with unacceptable dilution unless it either offered a price that was sufficient to attract the tender of substantially all of the shares and the rights, or negotiated a merger at a price acceptable to the target's board of directors so that the rights were redeemed and thereby removed as an impediment to the acquisition. . . . The effectiveness of the flip-in, unlike the flip-over, is dependent upon its discriminatory feature, without which the flip-in would not result in dilution to the raider since the raider would be able to buy additional shares on the same basis as the other shareholders. The flip-in feature provides greater protection against the takeover abuses described above. . . .

Our recommended plan combines the flip-over with a flip-in that is triggered by an acquisition at the 20% level. The flip-in at a 20% threshold will provide greater protection against current takeover abuses involving partial and creeping accumulations. The plan also allows the board of directors to lower the threshold to not less than 10% if appropriate in light of specific circumstances.

If the flip-in is triggered, each holder of rights (other than the raider, whose rights become void) will be able to exercise such rights for common stock of the target having a market value, at the time the raider crosses the 20% threshold, of twice the right's exercise price. This would result in dilution to the raider both economically and in terms of its percentage ownership of the target's shares. The exact level of the dilution would depend on the market value of the target's common stock in relation to the exercise price of the rights.

Our recommended plan also contains a feature that gives the board of directors the option, after the flip-in is triggered by an acquisition at the 20% level (or such lower threshold down to 10% as shall have been set by the board) but before there has been a 50% acquisition, to exchange one new share of common stock of the corporation for each then valid right (which would exclude rights held by the raider that have become void). This provision will have an economically dilutive effect on the acquiror, and provide a corresponding benefit to the remaining rights holders, that is comparable to the flip-in without requiring rights holders to go through the process and expense of exercising their rights. . . .

Appendix A
Terms of Flip-In Rights Plan

Issuance: One right to buy one one-hundredth of a share of a new series of preferred stock as a dividend on each outstanding share of common stock of the company. Until the rights become exercisable, all further issuances of common stock, including common stock issuable upon exercise of outstanding options, would include issuances of rights.

Term: 10 years.

Exercise Price: An amount per one one-hundredth of a share of the preferred stock which approximates the board's view of the long-term value of the company's common stock. Factors to be considered in setting the exercise price include; the company's business and prospects, its long-term plans and market conditions. For most companies that have adopted rights plans, the exercise price has been between three and five times current market price. The exercise price is subject to certain anti-dilution adjustments. For illustration only, assume an exercise price of $150 per one one-hundredth of a share.

Rights Detach and Become Exercisable: The rights are not exercisable and are not transferable apart from the company's common stock until the tenth day after such time as a person or group acquires beneficial ownership of 20% or more of the company's common stock or the tenth business day (or such later time as the board of directors may determine) after a person or group announces its intention to commence or commences a tender or exchange offer the consummation of which would result in beneficial ownership by a person or group of 20% or more of the company's common stock. As soon as practicable after the rights become exercisable, separate right certificates would be issued and the

A. The Challenge Facing the Drafters of the Poison Pill

rights would become transferable apart from the company's common stock.

Protection Against Squeeze Out: If, after the rights have been triggered, an acquiring company were to merge or otherwise combine with the company, or the company were to sell 50% or more of its assets or earning power, each right then outstanding would "flip over" and thereby would become a right to buy that number of shares of common stock of the acquiring company which at the time of such transaction would have a market value of two times the exercise price of the rights. Thus, if the acquiring company's common stock at the time of such transaction were trading at $75 per share and the exercise price of the rights at such time were $150, each right would thereafter be exercisable at $150 for four shares (*i.e.*, the number of shares that could be purchased for $300, or two times the exercise price of the rights) of the acquiring company's common stock.

Protection Against Creeping Acquisition/Open Market Purchases: In the event a person or group were to acquire a 20% or greater position in the company, each right then outstanding would "flip in" and become a right to buy that number of shares of common stock after the company which at the time of such acquisition would have a market value of two times the price of the rights. The acquiror who triggered the rights would be excluded from the "flip-in" because his rights would have become null and void upon his triggering acquisition. Thus, if the company's common stock at the time of the "flip-in" were trading at $75 per share and the exercise price of the rights at such time were $150, each right would thereafter be exercisable for $150 for four shares of the company's common stock. As described below, the amendment provision of the Rights Agreement provides that the 20% threshold can be lowered to not less than 10%. The board can utilize this provision to provide additional protection against creeping accumulations.

Exchange: At any time after the acquisition by a person or group of affiliated or associated persons of beneficial ownership of 20% or more of the outstanding common stock of the company and before the acquisition by a person or group of 50% or more of the outstanding common stock of the company, the board of directors may exchange the rights (other than rights owned by such person or group which have become void), in whole or in part, at an exchange ratio of one share of the company's common stock (or one one-hundredth of a share of junior participating preferred stock) per right, subject to adjustment.

Redemption: The rights are redeemable by the company's board of directors at a price of $.01 per right at any time prior to the acquisition by a person or group of beneficial ownership of 20% or more of the company's common stock. The redemption of the rights may be made effective at such time on such basis and with such conditions as the board of directors in its sole discretion may establish. Thus, the rights would not interfere with a negotiated merger or a white knight transaction, even after a hostile tender offer has been commenced. The rights may prevent a white knight transaction after a 20% acquisition.

Voting: The rights would not have any voting rights.

Terms of Preferred Stock: The preferred stock issuable upon exercise of the rights would be non-redeemable and rank junior to all other series of the company's preferred stock. The dividend, liquidation and voting rights, and the non-redemption feature, of the preferred stock are designed so that the value of one one-hundredth interest in a share of the new preferred stock purchasable with each right will approximate the value of one share of common stock. Each whole share of preferred stock would be entitled to receive a quarterly preferential dividend of $1 per share but would be entitled to receive, in the aggregate, a dividend of 100 times the dividend declared on the common stock. In the event of liquidation, the holders of the new preferred stock would be entitled to receive a preferential liquidation payment of $100 per share but would be entitled to receive, in the aggregate, a liquidation payment equal to 100 times the payment made per share of common stock. Each preferred stock would have 100 votes, voting together with the common stock. Finally, in the event of any merger, consolidation or other transaction in which shark of common stock are exchanged for or changed into other stock or securities, cash and/or other property, each share of preferred stock would be entitled to receive 100 times the amount received per share of common stock. The foregoing rights are protected against dilution in the event additional shares of common stock are issued. Since the "out of the money" rights would not be exercisable immediately, registration of the preferred issuable upon exercise of the rights with the Securities and Exchange Commission need not be effective until the rights become exercisable and are "in the money" or are so close to being "in the money" so as to make exercise economically possible.

Federal Income Tax Consequences: The Internal Revenue Service has published a revenue ruling holding that the adoption of a rights plan is not a taxable event for the company or its shareholders under the federal income tax laws. The physical distribution of rights certificates upon the rights becoming exercisable should not result in any tax. After such physical distribution, the rights would be treated for tax purposes as capital assets in the hands of most shareholders, the tax basis of each

A. The Challenge Facing the Drafters of the Poison Pill

right would be zero in most cases (or, in certain cases, an allocable part of the tax basis of the stock with respect to which the right was issued) and the holding period of each right would include the holding period of the stock with respect to which such right was issued. Upon the rights becoming rights to purchase an acquiror's common stock, holders of rights probably would be taxed even if the rights were not exercised. Upon the rights becoming rights to purchase additional common stock of the company, holders of rights probably would not have a taxable event. The redemption of the rights for cash and, most likely, the acquisition of the rights by the company for its stock would each be taxable events. The use of company stock (with the rights attached) will not interfere with the company's ability to engage in tax-free acquisitions nor will it affect any net operating losses of the company.

Accounting Consequences: The initial issuance of the rights has no accounting or financial reporting impact. Since the rights would be "out of the money" when issued, they would not dilute earnings per share. Because the redemption date of the rights is neither fixed nor determinable, the accounting guidelines do not require the redemption amount to be accounted for as a long-term obligation of the company....

Miscellaneous: The Rights Agreement provides that the company may not enter into any transaction of the sort which would give rise to the "flip-over" right if in connection therewith there are outstanding securities or there are agreements or arrangements intended to counteract the protective provisions of the rights. The Rights Agreement may be amended from time to time in any manner prior to the acquisition of a 20% position.

Comparison of Rights Plans

	"Flip-Over" Rights Plan	*"Flip-In" Rights Plan*
Prior to 20% Acquisition or Tender Offer	Rights "trade with" common	Rights "trade with" common
"Flip-Over"	On merger or sale of assets	On merger or sale of assets
"Flip-In"	In some plans, in the event of self-dealing transactions by a 20% holder — no status flip-in	Status flip-in if 20% acquired (threshold can be reduced to 10% by amendment)
Redeemable	By the Board prior to 20% acquisition	By the Board prior to 20% acquisition

Comparison of Rights Plans

	"Flip-Over" Rights Plan	"Flip-In" Rights Plan
Exchange	None	After 20% acquisition (but before 50% acquisition), the Board may exchange each Right (other than Rights held by the 20% acquiror) for one newly issued common share of the Company or 1/100 of a share or junior participating preferred

NOTES AND QUESTIONS

1. **Unpacking the plan.** The Appendix provides a useful summary of the issues covered in the poison pill, but even such a summary remains dense and off-putting on first reading. Just taking the headings of the paragraphs in the Appendix, it is possible to group the details into a small number of core issues:

   a. **The feint.** Several of the key terms relate to the shareholders' right to purchase preferred shares. See, for example:
   - *Issuance.* A dividend declared for each share of common stock to allow the owner the right to purchase 1/100 of a new share of preferred stock;
   - *Exercise price.* The price (to acquire a 1/100 preferred share) is specified and it seems large, tied to the board's opinion of the long-term value of a share of common stock, often three to five times current value; and
   - *Terms of preferred stock.* What would a shareholder get for such a price? A series of rights designed to make the value of the 1/100 share approximately equal to one share of common stock in terms of liquidation and voting rights.

   How attractive are such rights to purchase preferred shares? On the surface, it doesn't appear to be particularly attractive, but the reality is that the flip-in/flip-over rights discussed below do the heavy lifting in terms of providing the defense, and these preferred rights are never exercised. Why then are they there at all? This reflects the fact that the poison pill was a new defense, for which a judicial challenge would be a certainty, and the planners were likely looking for ways to defend the board's authority to take the

A. The Challenge Facing the Drafters of the Poison Pill

defensive actions. Consider this part in light of the *Moran* case discussed below.

b. The poison. A second set of terms from the Appendix describes the poison:

- *Rights detach.* Upon the occurrence of a triggering event, (defined as a bidder acquiring 20 percent of the target's stock in this memo but often 15 percent in the time since) or the bidder making a tender offer, the right to purchase preferred stock detaches from the common and morphs into a new rights, either "flip-in" rights or "flip-over" rights.
- *Protection against creeping acquisition (flip-in) and protection against squeeze out (flip-over).* The two provisions essentially permit the shareholders of the target company to purchase shares at half price of either the company into which the target will merge (the flip-over) or the target company itself (the flip-in). The mechanics are a good bit more complicated. For example, in part of the plan described in the excerpt, each right holder can buy the number of shares of common stock which at the time of the acquisition would have a market value of 2 times the exercise price of the rights (described in "a" above). Thus, if a company's common stock were trading at $75 per share and the exercise rights as specified above were $150/share, each right would be exercisable for $150 and would flip in to a right to purchase four shares of the company's common stock. The flip-over does something similar, but now the right is for target shareholders to purchase shares in the acquiring company directly.
- *The poison.* At this point, we have to depart from the heading provided in the memo and dig a bit deeper to find the actual poison. For simplicity's sake, let's take the "flip-in" example. What advantage would a shareholder gain in this 2-for-1 sale having put out $150? It turns out nothing, *if* every other shareholder did the same thing. The result would be only to subdivide the existing claims to the corporation's assets into smaller pieces, having added a bit of transactions cost for this change. Can every shareholder do this? As it turns out, no. The key language is the second sentence in the flip-in paragraph specifying that the acquiring company is denied the right to exercise the flip-in rights. A similar result occurs in the flip-over because only the target company shareholders (other than the bidder) are able to partake in the 2-for-1 purchase as to the acquiring company shares, not the preexisting shareholders of that company. The discriminatory provision would be challenged in court. See *Moran v. Household Int'l, Inc.*, below, on this issue.

c. **Redemption.** Of the remaining provisions, redemption ends up being a crucial characteristic, although it may not have seemed so at the time of initial drafting. Look how this is treated in the opinions that follow and how redemption would change the strategy and incentives of the bidder.

2. How much of a deterrent? The poison pill has been an effective deterrent in that only two have been triggered, one that occurred very early on when the form had not yet matured and the second in 2008 in an unusual context discussed below. It turns out that the poison pill dilutes both the cash flow rights and the voting rights of a bidder who has acquired a toehold position. As an exercise, compute the amount of dilution in the following hypothetical:

- a poison pill in a target with 1 million shares outstanding;
- a bidder who acquires up to 15 percent of those shares, as the point at which the flip-in is triggered;
- a pre-bid target share price of $10/share;
- and a flip-in price of the preferred of $40 with a 2-for-1 flip-in right as to being able to purchase new common stock.

Compute how much the share value of the target's toehold will be reduced once the flip-in has been triggered and how much the vote will be reduced. This will require you to do a little bit of math to compute how many shares each target shareholder, other than the bidder, will be able to purchase and how much that will dilute the bidder's investment. This will tell you how much of a financial hit a bidder would take in proceeding with a takeover that would trigger a poison pill.

B. JUDICIAL REVIEW OF DIRECTOR ACTION TO IMPLEMENT OR CONTINUE A POISON PILL

Moran v. Household International, Inc.
500 A.2d 1346 (Del. Sup. Ct. 1985)

McNeilly, Justice:

This case presents to this Court for review the most recent defensive mechanism in the arsenal of corporate takeover weaponry—the Preferred Share Purchase Rights Plan ("Rights Plan" or "Plan"). The validity of this mechanism has attracted national attention. *Amici curiae* briefs have been filed in support of appellants by the Securit[ies] and Exchange Commission ("SEC") and the Investment Company Institute. An *amicus curiae* brief has been filed in support of appellees ("Household") by the United Food and Commercial Workers International Union.

B. Judicial Review of Director Action

In a detailed opinion, the Court of Chancery upheld the Rights Plan as a legitimate exercise of business judgment by Household. *Moran v. Household International, Inc.*, Del. Ch., 490 A.2d 1059 (1985). We agree, and therefore, affirm the judgment below.

I...

On August 14, 1984, the Board of Directors of Household International, Inc. adopted the Rights Plan by a fourteen to two vote. The intricacies of the Rights Plan are contained in a 48-page document entitled "Rights Agreement." Basically, the Plan provides that Household common stockholders are entitled to the issuance of one Right per common share under certain triggering conditions. There are two triggering events that can activate the Rights. The first is the announcement of a tender offer for 30 percent of Household's shares ("30% trigger") and the second is the acquisition of 20 percent of Household's shares by any single entity or group ("20% trigger").

If an announcement of a tender offer for 30 percent of Household's shares is made, the Rights are issued and are immediately exercisable to purchase 1/100 share of new preferred stock for $100 and are redeemable by the Board for $.50 per Right. If 20 percent of Household's shares are acquired by anyone, the Rights are issued and become non-redeemable and are exercisable to purchase 1/100 of a share of preferred. If a Right is not exercised for preferred, and thereafter, a merger or consolidation occurs, the Rights holder can exercise each Right to purchase $200 of the common stock of the tender offeror for $100. This "flip-over" provision of the Rights Plan is at the heart of this controversy.

Household is a diversified holding company with its principal subsidiaries engaged in financial services, transportation and merchandising. HFC, National Car Rental and Vons Grocery are three of its wholly-owned entities.

Household did not adopt its Rights Plan during a battle with a corporate raider, but as a preventive mechanism to ward off future advances. The Vice-Chancellor found that as early as February 1984, Household's management became concerned about the company's vulnerability as a takeover target and began considering amending its charter to render a takeover more difficult. After considering the matter, Household decided not to pursue a fair price amendment.

In the meantime, appellant Moran, one of Household's own Directors and also Chairman of the Dyson-Kissner-Moran Corporation ("D-K-M"), which is the largest single stockholder of Household, began discussions concerning a possible leveraged buy-out of Household by D-K-M. D-K-M's financial studies showed that Household's stock was significantly undervalued in relation to the company's break-up value. It is uncontradicted that Moran's suggestion of a leveraged buy-out never progressed beyond the discussion stage.

Concerned about Household's vulnerability to a raider in light of the current takeover climate, Household secured the services of Wachtell, Lipton, Rosen and Katz ("Wachtell, Lipton") and Goldman, Sachs & Co. ("Goldman, Sachs") to formulate a takeover policy for recommendation to the Household Board at its August 14 meeting. After a July 31 meeting with a Household Board member and a pre-meeting distribution of material on the potential takeover problem and the proposed Rights Plan, the Board met on August 14, 1984.

Representatives of Wachtell, Lipton and Goldman, Sachs attended the August 14 meeting. The minutes reflect that Mr. Lipton explained to the Board that his recommendation of the Plan was based on his understanding that the Board was concerned about the increasing frequency of "bust-up"[4] takeovers, the increasing takeover activity in the financial service industry, such as Leucadia's attempt to take over Arco, and the possible adverse effect this type of activity could have on employees and others concerned with and vital to the continuing successful operation of Household even in the absence of any actual bust-up takeover attempt. Against this factual background, the Plan was approved.

Thereafter, Moran and the company of which he is Chairman, D-K-M, filed this suit. On the eve of trial, Gretl Golter, the holder of 500 shares of Household, was permitted to intervene as an additional plaintiff. The trial was held, and the Court of Chancery ruled in favor of Household.

II

The primary issue here is the applicability of the business judgment rule as the standard by which the adoption of the Rights Plan should be reviewed. Much of this issue has been decided by our recent decision in *Unocal Corp. v. Mesa Petroleum Co.*, Del. Supr., 493 A.2d 946 (1985)....

This case is distinguishable from the ones cited, since here we have a defensive mechanism adopted to ward off possible future advances and not a mechanism adopted in reaction to a specific threat. This distinguishing factor does not result in the Directors losing the protection of the business judgment rule. To the contrary, pre-planning for the contingency of a hostile takeover might reduce the risk that, under the pressure of a takeover bid, management will fail to exercise reasonable judgment. Therefore, in reviewing a pre-planned defensive mechanism it seems even more appropriate to apply the business judgment rule. *See Warner Communications v. Murdoch*, D. Del., 581 F. Supp. 1482, 1491 (1984).

Of course, the business judgment rule can only sustain corporate decision making or transactions that are within the power or authority of the Board. Therefore, before the business judgment rule can be applied

---

4. "Bust-up" takeover generally refers to a situation in which one seeks to finance an acquisition by selling off pieces of the acquired company.

it must be determined whether the Directors were authorized to adopt the Rights Plan.

III.

Appellants vehemently contend that the Board of Directors was unauthorized to adopt the Rights Plan. First, appellants contend that no provision of the Delaware General Corporation Law authorizes the issuance of such Rights. Secondly, appellants, along with the SEC, contend that the Board is unauthorized to usurp stockholders' rights to receive hostile tender offers. Third, appellants and the SEC also contend that the Board is unauthorized to fundamentally restrict stockholders' rights to conduct a proxy contest. We address each of these contentions in turn.

A.

While appellants contend that no provision of the Delaware General Corporation Law authorizes the Rights Plan, Household contends that the Rights Plan was issued pursuant to 8 Del. C. §§151(g) and 157. It explains that the Rights are authorized by §157 and the issue of preferred stock underlying the Rights is authorized by §151. Appellants respond by making several attacks upon the authority to issue the Rights pursuant to §157.

Appellants begin by contending that §157 cannot authorize the Rights Plan since §157 has never served the purpose of authorizing a takeover defense. Appellants contend that §157 is a corporate financing statute, and that nothing in its legislative history suggests a purpose that has anything to do with corporate control or a takeover defense. Appellants are unable to demonstrate that the legislature, in its adoption of §157, meant to limit the applicability of §157 to only the issuance of Rights for the purposes of corporate financing. Without such affirmative evidence, we decline to impose such a limitation upon the section that the legislature has not. *Compare Providence & Worcester Co. v. Baker*, Del. Supr., 378 A.2d 121, 124 (1977) (refusal to read a bar to protective voting provisions into 8 Del. C. §212(a)).

As we noted in *Unocal*:

> [O]ur corporate law is not static. It must grow and develop in response to, indeed in anticipation of, evolving concepts and needs. Merely because the General Corporation Law is silent as to a specific matter does not mean that it is prohibited.

493 A.2d at 957. *See also Cheff v. Mathes*, Del. Supr., 199 A.2d 548 (1964).

Secondly, appellants contend that §157 does not authorize the issuance of sham rights such as the Rights Plan. They contend that the Rights were designed never to be exercised, and that the Plan has no economic value. In addition, they contend the preferred stock made subject to the Rights is also illusory, citing *Telvest, Inc. v. Olson*, Del. Ch., C.A. No. 5798, Brown, V.C. (March 8, 1979).

Appellants' sham contention fails in both regards. As to the Rights, they can and will be exercised upon the happening of a triggering mechanism, as we have observed during the current struggle of Sir James Goldsmith to take control of Crown Zellerbach. *See* WALL STREET JOURNAL, July 26, 1985, at 3, 12. As to the preferred shares, we agree with the Court of Chancery that they are distinguishable from sham securities invalidated in *Telvest, supra*. The Household preferred, issuable upon the happening of a triggering event, have superior dividend and liquidation rights.

Third, appellants contend that §157 authorizes the issuance of Rights "entitling holders thereof to purchase from the corporation any shares of *its* capital stock of any class . . ." (emphasis added). Therefore, their contention continues, the plain language of the statute does not authorize Household to issue rights to purchase another's capital stock upon a merger or consolidation.

Household contends, *inter alia*, that the Rights Plan is analogous to "anti-destruction" or "anti-dilution" provisions which are customary features of a wide variety of corporate securities. While appellants seem to concede that "anti-destruction" provisions are valid under Delaware corporate law, they seek to distinguish the Rights Plan as not being incidental, as are most "anti-destruction" provisions, to a corporation's statutory power to finance itself. We find no merit to such a distinction. We have already rejected appellants' similar contention that §157 could only be used for financing purposes. We also reject that distinction here.

"Anti-destruction" clauses generally ensure holders of certain securities of the protection of their right of conversion in the event of a merger by giving them the right to convert their securities into whatever securities are to replace the stock of their company. *See Broad v. Rockwell International Corp.*, 5th Cir., 642 F.2d 929, 946, *cert. denied*, 454 U.S. 965, 102 S. Ct. 506, 70 L. Ed. 2d 380 (1981); *Wood v. Coastal States Gas Corp.*, Del. Supr., 401 A.2d 932, 937-39 (1979); *B.S.F. Co. v. Philadelphia National Bank*, Del. Supr., 204 A.2d 746, 750-51 (1964). The fact that the rights here have as their purpose the prevention of coercive two-tier tender offers does not invalidate them. . . .

B.

Appellants contend that the Board is unauthorized to usurp stockholders' rights to receive tender offers by changing Household's fundamental structure. We conclude that the Rights Plan does not prevent stockholders from receiving tender offers, and that the change of Household's structure was less than that which results from the implementation of other defensive mechanisms upheld by various courts.

Appellants' contention that stockholders will lose their right to receive and accept tender offers seems to be premised upon an understanding of the Rights Plan which is illustrated by the SEC *amicus* brief which states: "The Chancery Court's decision seriously understates the impact of this plan. In fact, as we discuss below, the Rights Plan will deter not only two-tier offers, but virtually all hostile tender offers."

The fallacy of that contention is apparent when we look at the recent takeover of Crown Zellerbach, which has a similar Rights Plan, by Sir James Goldsmith. WALL STREET JOURNAL, July 26, 1985, at 3, 12. The evidence at trial also evidenced many methods around the Plan ranging from tendering with a condition that the Board redeem the Rights, tendering with a high minimum condition of shares and Rights, tendering and soliciting consents to remove the Board and redeem the Rights, to acquiring 50% of the shares and causing Household to self-tender for the Rights. One could also form a group of up to 19.9% and solicit proxies for consents to remove the Board and redeem the Rights. These are but a few of the methods by which Household can still be acquired by a hostile tender offer.

In addition, the Rights Plan is not absolute. When the Household Board of Directors is faced with a tender offer and a request to redeem the Rights, they will not be able to arbitrarily reject the offer. They will be held to the same fiduciary standards any other board of directors would be held to in deciding to adopt a defensive mechanism, the same standard as they were held to in originally approving the Rights Plan. *See Unocal*, 493 A.2d at 954-55, 958.

In addition, appellants contend that the deterrence of tender offers will be accomplished by what they label "a fundamental transfer of power from the stockholders to the directors." They contend that this transfer of power, in itself, is unauthorized.

The Rights Plan will result in no more of a structural change than any other defensive mechanism adopted by a board of directors. The Rights Plan does not destroy the assets of the corporation. The implementation of the Plan neither results in any outflow of money from the corporation nor impairs its financial flexibility. It does not dilute earnings per share and does not have any adverse tax consequences for the corporation or its stockholders. The Plan has not adversely affected the market price of Household's stock.

Comparing the Rights Plan with other defensive mechanisms, it does less harm to the value structure of the corporation than do the other mechanisms. Other mechanisms result in increased debt of the corporation. *See Whittaker Corp. v. Edgar, supra* (sale of "prize asset"), *Cheff v. Mathes, supra* (paying greenmail to eliminate a threat), *Unocal Corp. v. Mesa Petroleum Co., supra* (discriminatory self-tender).

There is little change in the governance structure as a result of the adoption of the Rights Plan. The Board does not now have unfettered discretion in refusing to redeem the Rights. The Board has no more discretion in refusing to redeem the Rights than it does in enacting any defensive mechanism.

The contention that the Rights Plan alters the structure more than do other defensive mechanisms because it is so effective as to make the corporation completely safe from hostile tender offers is likewise without merit. As explained above, there are numerous methods to successfully launch a hostile tender offer.

C.

Appellants' third contention is that the Board was unauthorized to fundamentally restrict stockholders' rights to conduct a proxy contest. Appellants contend that the "20% trigger" effectively prevents any stockholder from first acquiring 20% or more shares before conducting a proxy contest and further, it prevents stockholders from banding together into a group to solicit proxies if, collectively, they own 20% or more of the stock.[12] In addition, at trial, appellants contended that read literally, the Rights Agreement triggers the Rights upon the mere acquisition of the right to vote 20% or more of the shares through a proxy solicitation, and thereby precludes any proxy contest from being waged.[13]

Appellants seem to have conceded this last contention in light of Household's response that the receipt of a proxy does not make the recipient the "beneficial owner" of the shares involved which would trigger the Rights. In essence, the Rights Agreement provides that the Rights are triggered when someone becomes the "beneficial owner" of 20% or more of Household stock. Although a literal reading of the Rights Agreement definition of "beneficial owner" would seem to include those shares which one has the right to vote, it has long been recognized that the relationship between grantor and recipient of a proxy is one of agency, and the agency is revocable by the grantor at any time. Henn, CORPORATIONS §196, at 518. Therefore, the holder of a proxy is not the "beneficial owner" of the stock. As a result, the mere acquisition of the right to vote 20% of the shares does not trigger the Rights.

The issue, then, is whether the restriction upon individuals or groups from first acquiring 20% of shares before waging a proxy contest fundamentally restricts stockholders' right to conduct a proxy contest. Regarding this issue the Court of Chancery found:

---

12. Appellants explain that the acquisition of 20% of the shares trigger the Rights, making them non-redeemable, and thereby would prevent even a future friendly offer for the ten-year life of the Rights.

13. The SEC still contends that the mere acquisition of the right to vote 20% of the shares through a proxy solicitation triggers the rights. We do not interpret the Rights Agreement in that manner.

Thus, while the Rights Plan does deter the formation of proxy efforts of a certain magnitude, it does not limit the voting power of individual shares. On the evidence presented it is highly conjectural to assume that a particular effort to assert shareholder views in the election of directors or revisions of corporate policy will be frustrated by the proxy feature of the Plan. Household's witnesses, Troubh and Higgins described recent corporate takeover battles in which insurgents holding less than 10% stock ownership were able to secure corporate control through a proxy contest or the threat of one.

Moran, 490 A.2d at 1080.

We conclude that there was sufficient evidence at trial to support the Vice-Chancellor's finding that the effect upon proxy contests will be minimal. Evidence at trial established that many proxy contests are won with an insurgent ownership of less than 20%, and that very large holdings are no guarantee of success. There was also testimony that the key variable in proxy contest success is the merit of an insurgent's issues, not the size of his holdings.

IV.

Having concluded that the adoption of the Rights Plan was within the authority of the Directors, we now look to whether the Directors have met their burden under the business judgment rule.

The business judgment rule is a "presumption that in making a business decision the directors of a corporation acted on an informed basis, in good faith and in the honest belief that the action taken was in the best interests of the company." *Aronson v. Lewis*, Del. Supr., 473 A.2d 805, 812 (1984) (citations omitted). Notwithstanding, in *Unocal* we held that when the business judgment rule applies to adoption of a defensive mechanism, the initial burden will lie with the directors. The "directors must show that they had reasonable grounds for believing that a danger to corporate policy and effectiveness existed.... [T]hey satisfy that burden 'by showing good faith and reasonable investigation....'" *Unocal*, 493 A.2d at 955 (citing *Cheff v. Mathes*, 199 A.2d at 554-55). In addition, the directors must show that the defensive mechanism was "reasonable in relation to the threat posed." *Unocal*, 493 A.2d at 955. Moreover, that proof is materially enhanced, as we noted in *Unocal*, where, as here, a majority of the board favoring the proposal consisted of outside independent directors who have acted in accordance with the foregoing standards. *Unocal*, 493 A.2d at 955; *Aronson*, 473 A.2d at 815. Then, the burden shifts back to the plaintiffs who have the ultimate burden of persuasion to show a breach of the directors' fiduciary duties. *Unocal*, 493 A.2d at 958.

There are no allegations here of any bad faith on the part of the Directors' action in the adoption of the Rights Plan. There is no allegation that the Directors' action was taken for entrenchment purposes. Household has adequately demonstrated, as explained above, that the adoption of the

Rights Plan was in reaction to what it perceived to be the threat in the market place of coercive two-tier tender offers. Appellants do contend, however, that the Board did not exercise informed business judgment in its adoption of the Plan....

To determine whether a business judgment reached by a board of directors was an informed one, we determine whether the directors were grossly negligent. *Smith v. Van Gorkom*, Del. Supr., 488 A.2d 858, 873 (1985). Upon a review of this record, we conclude the Directors were not grossly negligent. The information supplied to the Board on August 14 provided the essentials of the Plan. The Directors were given beforehand a notebook which included a three-page summary of the Plan along with articles on the current takeover environment. The extended discussion between the Board and representatives of Wachtell, Lipton and Goldman, Sachs before approval of the Plan reflected a full and candid evaluation of the Plan. Moran's expression of his views at the meeting served to place before the Board a knowledgeable critique of the Plan. The factual happenings here are clearly distinguishable from the actions of the directors of Trans Union Corporation who displayed gross negligence in approving a cash-out merger. *Id.*

In addition, to meet their burden, the Directors must show that the defensive mechanism was "reasonable in relation to the threat posed." The record reflects a concern on the part of the Directors over the increasing frequency in the financial services industry of "boot-strap" and "bust-up" takeovers. The Directors were also concerned that such takeovers may take the form of two-tier offers. In addition, on August 14, the Household Board was aware of Moran's overture on behalf of D-K-M. In sum, the Directors reasonably believed Household was vulnerable to coercive acquisition techniques and adopted a reasonable defensive mechanism to protect itself.

V ...

While we conclude for present purposes that the Household Directors are protected by the business judgment rule, that does not end the matter. The ultimate response to an actual takeover bid must be judged by the Directors' actions at that time, and nothing we say here relieves them of their basic fundamental duties to the corporation and its stockholders. *Unocal*, 493 A.2d at 954-55, 958; *Smith v. Van Gorkom*, 488 A.2d at 872-73; *Aronson*, 473 A.2d at 812-13; *Pogostin v. Rice*, Del. Supr., 480 A.2d 619, 627 (1984). Their use of the Plan will be evaluated when and if the issue arises.

AFFIRMED.

NOTES AND QUESTIONS

1. **The court's response to an innovative defense.** The opinion was handed down shortly after *Unocal* and the similarities of the court's

approach in the two cases should be apparent. What is distinctive about this case is the treatment of the board's authority before the court gets to judicial review of the board's actions under the business judgment rule and alternative doctrines. To what extent did the lawyers' creativity in drafting the plan set the stage for arguments that the court incorporated?

2. **The *Unocal* test.** When the court got to the application of the *Unocal* test, note the board action that was subjected to judicial review. Since this case, initial adoption of poison pills by a board of directors have passed judicial review with little difficulty, even if adopted on short notice in the face of receipt of a hostile offer. Instead, the last paragraph of the court's opinion shifts the focus of judicial review to a second decision, as discussed in more detail in the following case.

City Capital Associates Ltd. Partnership v. Interco Inc.
551 A.2d 787 (Del. Ch. 1988)

ALLEN, Chancellor.

This case, before the court on an application for a preliminary injunction, involves the question whether the directors of Interco Corporation are breaching their fiduciary duties to the stockholders of that company in failing to now redeem certain stock rights originally distributed as part of a defense against unsolicited attempts to take control of the company. In electing to leave Interco's "poison pill" in effect, the board of Interco seeks to defeat a tender offer for all of the shares of Interco for $74 per share cash, extended by plaintiff Cardinal Acquisition Corporation. The $74 offer is for all shares and the offeror expresses an intent to do a back-end merger at the same price promptly if its offer is accepted. Thus, plaintiffs' offer must be regarded as noncoercive.

As an alternative to the current tender offer, the board is endeavoring to implement a major restructuring of Interco that was formulated only recently. The board has grounds to conclude that the alternative restructuring transaction may have a value to shareholders of at least $76 per share. The restructuring does not involve a Company self-tender, a merger or other corporate action requiring shareholder action or approval.

It is significant that the question of the board's responsibility to redeem or not to redeem the stock rights in this instance arises at what I will call the end-stage of this takeover contest. That is, the negotiating leverage that a poison pill confers upon this company's board will, it is clear, not be further utilized by the board to increase the options available to shareholders or to improve the terms of those options. Rather, at this stage of this contest, the pill now serves the principal purpose of "protecting the restructuring" — that is, precluding the shareholders from choosing an alternative to the restructuring that the board finds less valuable to shareholders.

Accordingly, this case involves a further judicial effort to pick out the contours of a director's fiduciary duty to the corporation and its shareholders when the board has deployed the recently innovated and powerful antitakeover device of flip-in or flip-over stock rights. That inquiry is, of course, necessarily a highly particularized one.

In *Moran v. Household International, Inc.*, Del. Supr., 500 A.2d 1346 (1985), our Supreme Court acknowledged that a board of directors of a Delaware corporation has legal power to issue corporate securities that serve principally not to raise capital for the firm, but to create a powerful financial disincentive to accumulate shares of the firm's stock. Involved in that case was a board "reaction to what [it] perceived to be the threat in the market place of coercive two-tier tender offers." 500 A.2d at 1356. In upholding the board's power under Sections 157 and 141 of our corporation law to issue such securities or rights, the court, however, noted that:

> When the Household Board of Directors is faced with a tender offer and a request to redeem rights, they will not be able to arbitrarily reject the offer. They will be held to the same fiduciary standards any other board of directors would be held to in deciding to adopt a defensive mechanism, the same standard they were held to in originally approving the Rights Plan. *See Unocal*, 493 A.2d at 954-55, 958.

Moran v. Household International, Inc., Del. Supr., 500 A.2d at 1354. Thus, the Supreme Court in *Moran* has directed us specifically to its decision in *Unocal Corp. v. Mesa Petroleum Co.*, Del. Supr., 493 A.2d 946 (1985), as supplying the appropriate legal framework for evaluation of the principal question posed by this case.[1]

In addition to seeking an order requiring the Interco board to now redeem the Company's outstanding stock rights, plaintiffs seek an order restraining any steps to implement the Company's alternative restructuring transaction.

For the reasons that follow, I hold that the board's determination to leave the stock rights in effect is a defensive step that, in the circumstances of this offer and at this stage of the contest for control of Interco, cannot be justified as reasonable in relationship to a threat to the corporation or its shareholders posed by the offer; that the restructuring itself does represent a reasonable response to the perception that the offering price is "inadequate"; and that the board, in proceeding as it has done, has not breached

---

1. In saying that *Unocal* supplies the framework for decision of this aspect of the case, I reject plaintiffs' argument that the board bears a burden to demonstrate the entire fairness of its decision to keep the pill in place while its recapitalization is effectuated. *Ivanhoe Partners v. Newmont Mining Corp.*, Del. Supr., 535 A.2d 1334, 1341 (1987). While the recapitalization does represent a transaction in which the 14 person board (and most intensely, its seven inside members) has an interest — in the sense referred to in *Unocal* — it does not represent a self-dealing transaction in the sense necessary to place upon the board the heavy burden of the intrinsic fairness test. *See Weinberger v. U.O.P., Inc.*, Del. Supr., 457 A.2d 701 (1983); *Sinclair Oil Corp. v. Levien*, Del. Supr., 280 A.2d 717 (1971).

any duties derivable from the Supreme Court's opinion in *Revlon v. MacAndrews & Forbes Holdings, Inc.*, Del. Supr., 506 A.2d 173 (1986)....

I.

Interco Incorporated.

Interco is a diversified Delaware holding company that comprises 21 subsidiary corporations in four major business areas: furniture and home furnishings, footwear, apparel and general retail merchandising. Its principal offices are located in St. Louis, Missouri. The Company's nationally recognized brand names include London Fog raincoats; Ethan Allen, Lane and Broyhill furniture; Converse All Star athletic shoes and Le Tigre and Christian Dior sportswear. The Company's sales for fiscal 1988 were $3.34 billion, with earnings of $3.50 a share. It has approximately 36 million shares of common stock outstanding.

The Company's subsidiaries operate as autonomous units. Rather than seeing the subsidiaries as parts of an integrated whole, the constituent companies are viewed by Interco management as "a portfolio of assets whose investment merits have to be periodically reviewed." Owing to the lack of integration between its operating divisions, the Company is, in management's opinion, particularly vulnerable to a highly leveraged "bust-up" takeover of the kind that has become prevalent in recent years. To combat this perceived danger, the Company adopted a common stock rights plan, or poison pill, in late 1985, which included a "flip-in" provision.

The board of directors of Interco is comprised of 14 members, seven of whom are officers of the Company or its subsidiaries.

The Rales Brothers' Accumulation of Interco Stock; the Interco Board's Response.

In May, 1988, Steven and Mitchell Rales began acquiring Interco stock through CCA. The stock had been trading in the low 40's during that period. Alerted to the unusual trading activity taking place in the Company's stock, the Interco board met on July 11, 1988, to consider the implications of that news. At that meeting, the board redeemed the rights issued pursuant to the 1985 rights plan and adopted a new rights plan that contemplated both "flip-in" and "flip-over" rights.

In broad outline, the "flip-in" provision contained in the rights plan adopted on July 11 provides that, if a person reaches a threshold shareholding of 30% of Interco's outstanding common stock, rights will be exercisable entitling each holder of a right to purchase from the Company that number of shares per right as, at the triggering time, have a market value of twice the exercise price of each right. The "flip-over" feature of the rights plan provides that, in the event of a merger of the Company or the acquisition of 50% or more of the Company's assets or earning power, the rights may be exercised to acquire common stock of the acquiring company having a value of twice the exercise price of the right. The exercise price of each right is $160. The redemption price is $.01 per share.

On July 15, 1988, soon after the adoption of the new rights plan, a press release was issued announcing that the Chairman of the Company's board, Mr. Harvey Saligman, intended to recommend a major restructuring of Interco to the board at its next meeting.

On July 27, 1988, the Rales brothers filed a Schedule 13D with the Securities and Exchange Commission disclosing that, as of July 11, they owned, directly or indirectly, 3,140,300 shares, or 8.7% of Interco's common stock. On that day, CCA offered to acquire the Company by merger for a price of $64 per share in cash, conditioned upon the availability of financing. On August 8, before the Interco board had responded to this offer, CCA increased its offering price to $70 per share, still contingent upon receipt of the necessary financing.

At the Interco board's regularly scheduled meeting on August 8, Wasserstein Perella, Interco's investment banker, informed the board that, in its view, the $70 CCA offer was inadequate and not in the best interests of the Company and its shareholders. This opinion was based on a series of analyses, including discounted cash flow, comparable transaction analysis, and an analysis of premiums paid over existing stock prices for selected tender offers during early 1988. Wasserstein Perella also performed an analysis based upon selling certain Interco businesses and retaining and operating others. This analysis generated a "reference range" for the Company of $68-$80 per share. Based on all of these analyses, Wasserstein Perella concluded the offer was inadequate. The board then resolved to reject the proposal. Also at that meeting, the board voted to decrease the threshold percentage needed to trigger the flip-in provision of the rights plan from 30% to 15% and elected to explore a restructuring plan for the Company.

The Initial Tender Offer for Interco Stock.

On August 15, the Rales brothers announced a public tender offer for all of the outstanding stock of Interco at $70 cash per share. The offer was conditioned upon (1) receipt of financing, (2) the tender of sufficient shares to give the offeror a total holding of at least 75% of the Company's common stock on a fully diluted basis at the close of the offer, (3) the redemption of the rights plan, and (4) a determination as to the inapplicability of 8 Del. C. §203.

The board met to consider the tender offer at a special meeting a week later on August 22. Wasserstein Perella had engaged in further studies since the meeting two weeks earlier. It was prepared to give a further view about Interco's value. Now the studies showed a "reference range" for the whole Company of $74-$87. The so-called reference ranges do not purport to be a range of fair value; but just what they purport to be is (deliberately, one imagines) rather unclear.

In all events, after hearing the banker's opinion, the Interco board resolved to recommend against the tender offer. In rejecting the offer, the board also declined to redeem the rights plan or to render 8 Del. C. §203 inapplicable to the offer. Finally, the board refused to disclose confidential information requested by CCA in connection with its tender offer unless and until CCA indicated a willingness to enter into a confidentiality and standstill agreement with the Company.

The remainder of the meeting was devoted to an exploration of strategic alternatives to the CCA proposal. Wasserstein Perella presented the board with a detailed valuation of each operating component of the Company. The board adopted a resolution empowering management "... to explore all appropriate alternatives to the CCA offer, including, without limitation, the recapitalization, restructuring or other reorganization of the company, the sale of assets of the company in addition to the Apparel Manufacturing Group, and other extraordinary transactions, to maximize the value of the company to the stockholders. ..."

On August 23, 1988, a letter was sent to CCA informing it that Interco intended to explore alternatives to the offer and planned to make confidential information available to third parties in connection with that endeavor. Interco informed CCA that it would not disclose information to it absent compliance with a confidentiality agreement and a standstill agreement. Interco's proposal was met with an August 26, 1988 counterproposal by CCA suggesting an alternative confidentiality agreement — without standstill provisions.

Apart from the exchange of letters, there were no communications between CCA and Interco between the time the $70 offer was made on August 22 and a later, higher offer at $72 per share was made on September 10. There is some dispute as to why this occurred; one side claims that CCA did place a phone call to Mr. Saligman on September 7 that was never returned. Mr. Saligman asserts that the call was returned by him and that there was no response from CCA.

In all events, on September 10, the Rales brothers did amend their offer, increasing the price offered to $72 per share. The Interco board did not consider that offer until September 19 when its investment banker was ready to report on a proposed restructuring. At that meeting, the board rejected the $72 offer on grounds of financial inadequacy and adopted the restructuring proposal.

The Proposed Restructuring.

Under the terms of the restructuring designed by Wasserstein Perella, Interco would sell assets that generate approximately one-half of its gross sales and would borrow $2.025 billion. It would make very substantial distributions to shareholders, by means of a dividend, amounting to a stated aggregate value of $66 per share. The $66 amount would consist of (1) a $25 dividend payable November 7 to shareholders of record on October 13, consisting of $14 in cash and $11 in face amount of senior subordinated debentures, and (2) a second dividend, payable no earlier than November 29, which was declared on October 19, of (a) $24.15 in cash, (b) $6.80 principal amount of subordinated discount debentures, (c) $5.44 principal amount of junior subordinated debentures, (d) convertible preferred stock with a liquidation value of $4.76, and (e) a remaining equity interest or stub that Wasserstein Perella estimates (based on projected earnings of the then remaining businesses) will trade at a price of at least $10 per share. Thus, the total value of the restructuring to shareholders would, in the opinion of Wasserstein Perella, be at least $76 per share on a fully distributed basis.

The board had agreed to a compensation arrangement with Wasserstein Perella that gives that firm substantial contingency pay if its restructuring is successfully completed. Thus, Wasserstein Perella has a rather straightforward and conventional conflict of interest when it opines that the inherently disputable value of its restructuring is greater than the all cash alternative offered by plaintiffs. The market has not, for whatever reason, thought the prospects of the Company quite so bright. It has, in recent weeks, consistently valued Interco stock at about $70 a share. (The value at which Drexel Burnham has valued the restructuring in this litigation.) Steps have now been taken to effectuate the restructuring. On September 15, the Company announced its plans to sell the Ethan Allen furniture division, which is said by the plaintiffs to be the Company's "crown jewel." Ethan Allen, the Company maintains, has a unique marketing approach which is not conducive to integration of that business with Interco's other furniture businesses, Lane and Broyhill. Moreover, the Company says that Ethan Allen is not a suitable candidate for the cost cutting measures which must be undertaken in connection with the proposed restructuring.

Since Interco announced the terms of the restructuring on September 20, it has made two changes with respect to it. It announced on September 27 first that the dividend declared on October 13, 1988 would accrue interest at 12% per annum from that date to the payment date; and second, that the second phase dividend would similarly accrue interest (currently expected to be at a rate of 13 3/4% per annum) from the date of its declaration.

The Present CCA Offer and the Interco Board's Reaction.

In its third supplemental Offer to Purchase dated October 18, 1988, CCA raised its bid to $74. Like the preceding bid, the proposal is an all cash

B. Judicial Review of Director Action

offer for all shares with a contemplated back-end merger for the same consideration.

At its October 19, 1988 board meeting, the board rejected the $74 offer as inadequate and agreed to recommend that shareholders reject the offer. The board based its rejection both on its apparent view that the price was inadequate and on its belief that the proposed restructuring will yield shareholder value of at least $76 per share....

III.

The pending motion purports to seek a preliminary injunction. The test for the issuance of such a provisional remedy is well established. It is necessary for the applicant to demonstrate both a reasonable probability of ultimate success on the claims asserted and, most importantly, the threat of an injury that will occur before trial which is not remediable by an award of damages or the later shaping of equitable relief. Beyond that, it is essential for the court to consider the offsetting equities, if any, including the interests of the public and other innocent third parties, as well as defendants. *See generally Ivanhoe Partners v. Newmont Mining Corp.*, Del. Supr., 535 A.2d 1334 (1987).

With respect to plaintiffs' request that steps in furtherance of the restructuring transaction be enjoined *pendente lite*, the relief now sought is classically awarded on such a motion where the elements of this test are satisfied. The relief now sought with respect to the board's decision not to redeem the stock rights, however, is another matter. That relief, if awarded now, would constitute affirmative relief. *Steiner v. Simmons*, Del. Supr., 111 A.2d 574 (1955). Moreover, if it is awarded (and if a majority of shares are tendered into plaintiffs' offer thereafter), it would, in effect, constitute relief that could not later effectively be reversed following trial. It would in that event, in effect, constitute final relief. Therefore, in my opinion, that relief ought not be awarded at this time unless plaintiffs can show that it is warranted based upon facts that are not legitimately in dispute.

It is appropriate, therefore, before subjecting the board's decision not to redeem the pill to the form of analysis mandated by *Unocal*, to identify what relevant facts are not contested or contestable, and what relevant facts may appropriately be assumed against the party prevailing on this point. They are as follows:

First. The value of the Interco restructuring is inherently a debatable proposition, most importantly (but not solely) because the future value of the stub share is unknowable with reasonable certainty.

Second. The board of Interco believes in good faith that the restructuring has a value of "at least" $76 per share.

Third. The City Capital offer is for $74 per share cash.

Fourth. The board of Interco has acted prudently to inform itself of the value of the Company.

Fifth. The board believes in good faith that the City Capital offer is for a price that is "inadequate."

Sixth. City Capital cannot, as a practical matter, close its tender offer while the rights exist; to do so would be to self-inflict an enormous financial injury that no reasonable buyer would do.

Seventh. Shareholders of Interco have differing liquidity preferences and different expectations about likely future economic events.

Eighth. A reasonable shareholder could prefer the restructuring to the sale of his stock for $74 in cash now, but a reasonable shareholder could prefer the reverse.

Ninth. The City Capital tender offer is in no respect coercive. It is for all shares, not for only a portion of shares. It contemplates a prompt follow-up merger, if it succeeds, not an indefinite term as a minority shareholder. It proposes identical consideration in a follow-up merger, not securities or less money.

Tenth. While the existence of the stock rights has conferred time on the board to consider the City Capital proposals and to arrange the restructuring, the utility of those rights as a defensive technique has, given the time lines for the restructuring and the board's actions to date, now been effectively exhausted except in one respect: the effect of those rights continues to "protect the restructuring."

These facts are sufficient to address the question whether the board's action in electing to leave the defensive stock rights plan in place qualifies for the deference embodied in the business judgment rule.

IV.

I turn then to the analysis contemplated by *Unocal*, the most innovative and promising case in our recent corporation law. That case, of course, recognized that in defending against unsolicited takeovers, there is an "omnipresent specter that a board may be acting primarily in its own interest." 493 A.2d at 954. That fact distinguishes takeover defense measures from other acts of a board which, when subject to judicial review, are customarily upheld once the court finds the board acted in good faith and after an appropriate investigation. *E.g., Aronson v. Lewis*, Del. Supr., 473

A.2d 805 (1984). *Unocal* recognizes that human nature may incline *even one acting in subjective good faith* to rationalize as right that which is merely personally beneficial. Thus, it created a new intermediate form of judicial review to be employed when a transaction is neither self-dealing nor wholly disinterested. That test has been helpfully referred to as the "proportionality test."[8]

The test is easy to state. Where it is employed, it requires a threshold examination "before the protections of the business judgment rule may be conferred." 493 A.2d 954. That threshold requirement is in two parts. First, directors claiming the protections of the rule "must show that they had reasonable grounds for believing that a danger to corporate policy and effectiveness existed." The second element of the test is the element of balance. "If a defensive measure is to come within the ambit of the business judgment rule, it must be reasonable in relationship to the threat posed." 493 A.2d 955.

Delaware courts have employed the *Unocal* precedent cautiously.[9] The promise of that innovation is the promise of a more realistic, flexible and, ultimately, more responsible corporation law. See *generally*, Gilson & Kraakman, n.8, *supra*. The danger that it poses is, of course, that courts — in exercising some element of substantive judgment — will too readily seek to assert the primacy of their own view on a question upon which reasonable, completely disinterested minds might differ. Thus, inartfully applied, the *Unocal* form of analysis could permit an unraveling of the well-made fabric of the business judgment rule in this important context. Accordingly, whenever, as in this case, this court is required to apply the *Unocal* form of review it should do so cautiously, with a clear appreciation for the risks and special responsibility this approach entails.

A.

Turning to the first element of the *Unocal* form of analysis, it is appropriate to note that, in the special case of a tender offer for all shares, the threat posed, if any, is not importantly to corporate policies (as may well be the case in a stock buy-back case such as *Cheff v. Mathes*, Del. Supr., 199 A.2d 548 (1964), or a partial tender offer case such as *Unocal* itself), but rather the threat, if any, is most directly to shareholder interests. Broadly speaking,

---

8. *See* Gilson & Kraakman, *Delaware's Intermediate Standard for Defensive Tactics: Is There Substance to the Proportionality Review?*, John M. Olin Program in Law & Economics, Stanford Law School (Working Paper No. 45, August, 1988), 44 Bus. Law. [247] (forthcoming February, 1989). Professors Gilson and Kraakman offer a helpful structure for reviewing problems of this type and conclude with a perceptive observation concerning the beneficial impact upon corporate culture that the *Unocal* test might come to have.

9. Only two cases have found defensive steps disproportionate to a threat posed by a takeover attempt. *See AC Acquisitions Corp. v. Anderson, Clayton & Co.*, Del. Ch., 519 A.2d 103 (1986); *Robert M. Bass Group, Inc. v. Evans*, Del. Ch., C.A. No. 9953, Jacobs, V.C. (July 14, 1988) [1988 WL 73744].

threats to shareholders in that context may be of two types: threats to the voluntariness of the choice offered by the offer, and threats to the substantive, economic interest represented by the stockholding.

1. *Threats to voluntariness.* It is now universally acknowledged that the structure of an offer can render mandatory in substance that which is voluntary in form. The so-called "front-end" loaded partial offer—already a largely vanished breed—is the most extreme example of this phenomenon. An offer may, however, be structured to have a coercive effect on a rational shareholder in any number of different ways. Whenever a tender offer is so structured, a board may, or perhaps should, perceive a threat to a stockholder's interest in exercising choice to remain a stockholder in the firm. The threat posed by structurally coercive offers is typically amplified by an offering price that the target board responsibly concludes is substantially below a fair price.[10]

Each of the cases in which our Supreme Court has addressed a defensive corporate measure under the *Unocal* test involved the sharp and palpable threat to shareholders posed by a coercive offer. *See Unocal Corp. v. Mesa Petroleum Co.*, Del. Supr., 493 A.2d 946 (1985); *Moran v. Household International, Inc.*, Del. Supr., 500 A.2d 1346 (1985); *Ivanhoe Partners v. Newmont Mining Corp.*, Del. Supr., 535 A.2d 1334 (1987).

2. *Threats from "inadequate" but noncoercive offers.* The second broad classification of threats to shareholder interests that might be posed by a tender offer for all shares relates to the "fairness" or "adequacy" of the price.[11] It would not be surprising or unreasonable to claim that where an offer is not coercive or deceptive (and, therefore, what is in issue is essentially whether the consideration it offers is attractive or not), a board—even though it may expend corporate funds to arrange alternatives or to inform shareholders of its view of fair value—is not authorized to take preclusive action. By preclusive action I mean action that, as a practical matter, withdraws from the shareholders the option to choose between the offer and the status quo or some other board sponsored alternative.

Our law, however, has not adopted that view and experience has demonstrated the wisdom of that choice. We have held that a board is not required simply by reason of the existence of a noncoercive offer to redeem outstanding poison pill rights. *See Facet Enterprises, Inc. v. Prospect Group, Inc.*, Del. Ch., C.A. No. 9746, Jacobs, V.C. (April 15, 1988) [1988 WL 36140]; *Nomad Acquisition Corp. v. Damon Corporation*, Del. Ch., C.A. No. 10173, Hartnett, V.C. (September 16, 1988) [1988 WL 96192]; *Doskocil*

---

10. A different form of threat relating to the voluntariness of the shareholder's choice would arise in a structurally noncoercive offer that contained false or misleading material information.

11. Timing questions may be seen as simply a special case of price inadequacy. That is, the price offered is seen as inadequate because the firm's prospects will appear better later; thus, a fair price now would be higher than that offered.

B. Judicial Review of Director Action

Companies Incorporated v. Griggy, Del. Ch., C.A. No. 10095, Berger, V.C. (October 7, 1988) [1988 WL 105751]. The reason is simple. Even where an offer is noncoercive, it may represent a "threat" to shareholder interests in the special sense that an active negotiator with power, in effect, to refuse the proposal may be able to extract a higher or otherwise more valuable proposal, or may be able to arrange an alternative transaction or a modified business plan that will present a more valuable option to shareholders. *See, e.g., In re J.P. Stevens & Co., Inc. Shareholders Litigation*, Del. Ch., 542 A.2d 770 (1988) and *CFRT v. Federated Department Stores, Inc.*, 683 F. Supp. 422 (S.D.N.Y. 1988), where defensive stock rights were used precisely in this way. *See also* Gilson & Kraakman, *supra*, n.8 at pp. 26-30. Our cases, however, also indicate that in the setting of a noncoercive offer, absent unusual facts, there may come a time when a board's fiduciary duty will require it to redeem the rights and to permit the shareholders to choose. *See Doskocil Companies Incorporated v. Griggy, supra*, slip op. at 11; *Mills Acquisition Co. v. Macmillan, Inc.*, Del. Ch., C.A. No. 10168, Jacobs, V.C. (October 17, 1988), slip op. at 49-50 [1988 WL 108332].

B.

In this instance, there is no threat of shareholder coercion. The threat is to shareholders' economic interests posed by an offer the board has concluded is "inadequate." If this determination is made in good faith (as I assume it is here, *supra*), it alone will justify leaving a poison pill in place, even in the setting of a noncoercive offer, for a period while the board exercises its good faith business judgment to take such steps as it deems appropriate to protect and advance shareholder interests in light of the significant development that such an offer doubtless is. That action may entail negotiation on behalf of shareholders with the offeror, the institution of a *Revlon*-style auction for the Company, a recapitalization or restructuring designed as an alternative to the offer, or other action.[13]

Once that period has closed, and it is apparent that the board does not intend to institute a *Revlon*-style auction, or to negotiate for an increase in the unwanted offer, and that it has taken such time as it required in good faith to arrange an alternative value-maximizing transaction, then, in most instances, the legitimate role of the poison pill in the context of a noncoercive offer will have been fully satisfied. The only function then left for the pill at this end-stage is to preclude the shareholders from exercising a judgment about their own interests that differs from the judgment of the directors, who will have some interest in the question. What then is the "threat" in this instance that might justify such a result? Stating that "threat" at this

---

13. I leave aside the rare but occasionally encountered instance in which the board elects to do nothing at all with respect to an any and all tender offer.

stage of the process most specifically, it is this: *Wasserstein Perella may be correct in their respective valuations of the offer and the restructuring but a majority of the Interco shareholders may not accept that fact and may be injured as a consequence.*

C.

Perhaps there is a case in which it is appropriate for a board of directors to in effect permanently foreclose their shareholders from accepting a non-coercive offer for their stock by utilization of the recent innovation of "poison pill" rights. If such a case might exist by reason of some special circumstance, a review of the facts here show this not to be it. The "threat" here, when viewed with particularity, is far too mild to justify such a step in this instance.

Even assuming Wasserstein Perella is correct that when received (and following a period in which full distribution can occur), each of the debt securities to be issued in the restructuring will trade at par, that the preferred stock will trade at its liquidation value, and that the stub will trade initially at $10 a share, the difference in the values of these two offers is only 3%, and the lower offer is all cash and sooner. Thus, the threat, at this stage of the contest, cannot be regarded as very great even on the assumption that Wasserstein Perella is correct.

More importantly, it is incontestable that the Wasserstein Perella value is itself a highly debatable proposition. Their prediction of the likely trading range of the stub share represents one obviously educated guess. Here, the projections used in that process were especially prepared for use in the restructuring. Plaintiffs claim they are rosy to a fault, citing, for example, a $75 million cost reduction from remaining operations once the restructuring is fully implemented. This cost reduction itself is $2 per share; 20% of the predicted value of the stub. The Drexel Burnham analysis, which offers no greater claim to correctness, estimates the stub will trade at between $4.53 and $5.45. Moreover, Drexel opines that the whole package of restructure consideration has a value between $68.28 and $70.37 a share, which, for whatever reason, is quite consistent with the stock market price of a share of Interco stock during recent weeks.

The point here is not that, in exercising some restrained substantive review of the board's decision to leave the pill in place, the court finds Drexel's opinion more persuasive than Wasserstein Perella's. I make no such judgment. What is apparent — indeed inarguable — is that one could do so. More importantly, without access to Drexel Burnham's particular analysis, a shareholder could prefer a $74 cash payment now to the complex future consideration offered through the restructuring. The defendants understand this; it is evident.

The information statement sent to Interco shareholders to inform them of the terms of the restructuring accurately states and repeats the admonition:

> There can be no assurances as to actual trading values of [the stub shares].
>
> * * *
>
> It should be noted that the value of securities, including newly-issued securities and equity securities in highly leveraged companies, are subject to uncertainties and contingencies, all of which are difficult to predict and therefore any valuation [of them] may not necessarily be indicative of the price at which such securities will actually trade.

October 1, 1988 Interco Information Statement, at 3.

Yet, recognizing the relative closeness of the values and the impossibility of knowing what the stub share will trade at, the board, having arranged a value maximizing restructuring, elected to preclude shareholder choice. It did so not to buy time in order to negotiate or arrange possible alternatives, but asserting in effect a right and duty to save shareholders from the consequences of the choice they might make, if permitted to choose.

Without wishing to cast any shadow upon the subjective motivation of the individual defendants, I conclude that reasonable minds not affected by an inherent, entrenched interest in the matter, could not reasonably differ with respect to the conclusion that the CCA $74 cash offer did not represent a threat to shareholder interests sufficient in the circumstances to justify, in effect, foreclosing shareholders from electing to accept that offer.

Our corporation law exists, not as an isolated body of rules and principles, but rather in a historical setting and as a part of a larger body of law premised upon shared values. To acknowledge that directors may employ the recent innovation of "poison pills" to deprive shareholders of the ability effectively to choose to accept a noncoercive offer, after the board has had a reasonable opportunity to explore or create alternatives, or attempt to negotiate on the shareholders' behalf, would, it seems to me, be so inconsistent with widely shared notions of appropriate corporate governance as to threaten to diminish the legitimacy and authority of our corporation law.

I thus conclude that the board's decision not to redeem the rights following the amendment of the offer to $74 per share cannot be justified in the way *Unocal* requires.[17] This determination does not rest upon disputed facts and I conclude that affirmative relief is therefore permissible at this stage.

---

17. By that point, it was apparent that the board sought, by leaving the rights in place, only to "protect the restructuring"; and while not utterly clear, it by then appeared that CCA's frustrated, self-induced successive bids had come to about the top of their range.

VI.

Plaintiffs also seek an order enjoining any act in furtherance of the restructuring *pendente lite*. Specifically, they seek to stop the shopping of Ethan Allen Company (or *a fortiori* its sale) and the dividend distribution of cash and securities to be accomplished no sooner than November 7. The theory offered is essentially the same as that put forward in support of the poison pill relief: these actions are defensive; they are taken by a board that is interested (recall that half of the board members are officers of the Company, or its subsidiaries); that the board is motivated to entrench itself for selfish reasons; it cannot demonstrate the fairness of these acts and, even if it need not, they cannot be justified under *Unocal* as reasonable in relation to any threat posed by the CCA offer.

I take up the specific acts sought to be preliminarily enjoined separately. Before doing so, I refer to note 1 above. Here too, the appropriate test to determine whether these steps qualify for the deferential business judgment form of review is set forth in *Unocal*. Each of the steps quite clearly was taken defensively as part of a reaction to the Rales brothers' efforts to buy Interco, but neither is a self-dealing transaction of the classic sort.

As to the sale of Ethan Allen, I conclude that that step does appear clearly to be reasonable in relation to the threat posed by the CCA offer. Above I indicated that it was the case that one could regard either of these alternatives as the more desirable, depending upon one's liquidity preference, expectation about future events, etc. The board itself was, of course, supplied with specific expert advice that stated that the CCA offer was inadequate. I assumed that the board acted in good faith in adopting that view.

I make some additional assumptions about the effort to sell the Ethan Allen business. First, the business is being competently shopped. The record suggests that. Second, the board will not sell it for less than the best available price. Third, the board will not sell it for less than a fair price (*i.e.*, there will be no fire sale price). In the absence of indications by plaintiffs to the contrary, the board is entitled to these assumptions.

The question of reasonableness in this setting seems rather easy. Of course, a board acts reasonably in relation to an offer, albeit a noncoercive offer, it believes to be inadequate when it seeks to realize the full, market value of an important asset. Moreover, here the board puts forth sensible reasons why Ethan Allen should be sold under its new business plan. (*See supra*). Finally, as a defensive measure, the sale of Ethan Allen is not a "show stopper" insofar as this offer is concerned. This is not a "crown jewel" sale to a favored bidder; it is a public sale. On my assumption that the price will be a fair price, the corporation will come out no worse from a financial point of view. Moreover, the Rales' interests are being supplied the same information as others concerning Ethan Allen and they may bid for it. I do understand that this step complicates their life and indeed might imperil CCA's ability to complete its transaction. CCA, however, has no right to demand that its chosen target remain in status quo while its offer is formulated, gradually increased and, perhaps, accepted. I therefore conclude that the proposed sale of Ethan Allen Company is a defensive step that is reasonable in relation to the mild threat posed by this noncoercive $74 cash offer.

As to the dividend question, I will reserve judgment. It is, however, difficult for me to imagine how a pro rata distribution of cash to shareholders could itself ever constitute an unreasonable response to a bid believed to be inadequate. (Collateral agreements respecting use of such cash would raise a more litigable issue). *Cf. Ivanhoe Partners v. Newmont Mining Corp., supra*. I reserve judgment here, however, because I have not found in the record, and thus have not studied, the covenants contained in the various debt securities. They perhaps have not yet been drafted. Those covenants may contain provisions offering antitakeover protection. In the event they do, the question whether distribution of such securities was a reasonable step in reaction to the threat of an inadequate offer (of the specific proportions involved here) will be one that should be reviewed with particularity. The efficient adjudication of this case, however, warrants issuing an order on what has been decided. Should plaintiffs want a ruling on this issue, they will have to submit a written statement outlining any antitakeover effect the securities proposed to be dividended may contain.

NOTES AND QUESTIONS

1. Recalibrating the amount of judicial protection for shareholders under *Unocal*. Chancellor Allen's discussion in *Interco* adds to the development of the *Unocal* test in two important ways. First, as to threat, it broadens the menu of possible threats beyond the substantive coercion of Unocal's two-tier, front-end loaded offer to include other types of threats including shareholder ignorance of the relative value of a bidder's alternative to the incumbent's continued control. At the same time, he combines that broadening of threat with a narrowing of proportionality, suggesting there may come a time when directors' duty requires redemption of the pill. Certainly, the langue of his analysis suggests there will be real limits on the use of the poison pill.

2. The deal: What comes next. The Chancery Court restricted the board's space in one sense, by saying the time had come to remove the poison pill and let the shareholders decide, but at the same time, gave the green light to the board's other major defense of a radical restructuring of the company in a way that would make the target much less attractive to a financial bidder such as the Rales brothers. Consider how the company they would acquire would be changed. The Rales brothers' financing relied on Drexel Burnham, the investment banking firm where Michael Milken had achieved notice for his junk bond financing. During the same month, however, the Milken empire suffered a significant hit as the Department of Justice notified the firm that the firm would be indicted. Milken himself would go to jail the following year. For either reason, or both, the Rales brothers decided not to pursue their tender offer even though a large percentage of shareholders had tendered into the offer.

3. The Supreme Court's response. The Rales brothers' decision not to go forward with the deal meant that the Delaware Supreme Court never got the opportunity to review the Chancery Court's more aggressive assertion of the *Unocal* test as applied to the poison pill. In the *Time-Warner* decision, considered in more detail in Chapter 6, the Supreme Court suggested how it might have come down had the appeal gone forward:

> The Court of Chancery has suggested that an all-cash, all-shares offer, falling within a range of values that a shareholder might reasonably prefer, cannot constitute a legally recognized "threat" to shareholder interests sufficient to withstand a *Unocal* analysis. *AC Acquisitions Corp. v. Anderson, Clayton & Co.*, Del. Ch., 519 A.2d 103 (1986); *see Grand Metropolitan, PLC v. Pillsbury Co.*, Del. Ch., 558 A.2d 1049 (1988); *City Capital Associates v. Interco, Inc.*, Del. Ch., 551 A.2d 787 (1988). In those cases, the Court of Chancery determined that whatever threat existed related only to the shareholders and only to price and not to the corporation.
>
> From those decisions by our Court of Chancery, Paramount and the individual plaintiffs extrapolate a rule of law that an all-cash, all-shares offer with values reasonably in the range of acceptable price cannot pose any objective threat to a corporation or its shareholders. Thus, Paramount would have us hold that only if the value of Paramount's offer were determined to be clearly inferior to the value created by management's plan to merge with Warner could the offer be viewed — objectively — as a threat.
>
> Implicit in the plaintiffs' argument is the view that a hostile tender offer can pose only two types of threats: the threat of coercion that results from a two-tier offer promising unequal treatment for nontendering shareholders; and the threat of inadequate value from an all-shares, all-cash offer at a price below what a target board in good faith deems to be the present value of its shares. *See, e.g., Interco*, 551 A.2d at 797; *see also BNS, Inc. v. Koppers*, D. Del., 683 F. Supp. 458 (1988). Since Paramount's offer was all-cash, the only conceivable "threat," plaintiffs argue, was inadequate value. We disapprove of such a narrow and rigid construction of *Unocal*, for the reasons which follow.
>
> Plaintiffs' position represents a fundamental misconception of our standard of review under *Unocal* principally because it would involve the court in substituting its judgment as to what is a "better" deal for that of a corporation's board of directors. To the extent that the Court of Chancery has recently done so in certain of its opinions, we hereby reject such approach as not in keeping with a proper *Unocal* analysis. *See, e.g., Interco*, 551 A.2d 787, and its progeny; *but see TW Services, Inc. v. SWT Acquisition Corp.*, Del. Ch., C.A. No. 1047, Allen, C. 1989 WL 20290 (March 2, 1989).

Paramount Communications, Inc. v. Time Inc., 571 A.2d 1140, 1152-53 (Del. 1989).

B. Judicial Review of Director Action

Later in the opinion, the court opined as to the role of shareholders and directors generally:

> Paramount argues that, assuming its tender offer posed a threat, Time's response was unreasonable in precluding Time's shareholders from accepting the tender offer or receiving a control premium in the immediately foreseeable future. Once again, the contention stems, we believe, from a fundamental misunderstanding of where the power of corporate governance lies. Delaware law confers the management of the corporate enterprise to the stockholders' duly elected board representatives. 8 Del. C. §141(a). The fiduciary duty to manage a corporate enterprise includes the selection of a time frame for achievement of corporate goals. That duty may not be delegated to the stockholders. *Van Gorkom*, 488 A.2d at 873. Directors are not obliged to abandon a deliberately conceived corporate plan for a short-term shareholder profit unless there is clearly no basis to sustain the corporate strategy. *See, e.g., Revlon,* 506 A.2d at 173.

Id. at 1154

Air Products and Chemicals, Inc. v. Airgas, Inc.
16 A.3d 48 (Del. Ch. 2011)

CHANDLER, Chancellor:

This case poses the following fundamental question: Can a board of directors, acting in good faith and with a reasonable factual basis for its decision, when faced with a structurally non-coercive, all-cash, fully financed tender offer directed to the stockholders of the corporation, keep a poison pill in place so as to prevent the stockholders from making their own decision about whether they want to tender their shares—even after the incumbent board has lost one election contest, a full year has gone by since the offer was first made public, and the stockholders are fully informed as to the target board's views on the inadequacy of the offer? If so, does that effectively mean that a board can "just say never" to a hostile tender offer?

The answer to the latter question is "no." A board cannot "*just* say no" to a tender offer. Under Delaware law, it must first pass through two prongs of exacting judicial scrutiny by a judge who will evaluate the actions taken by, and the motives of, the board. Only a board of directors found to be acting in good faith, after reasonable investigation and reliance on the advice of outside advisors, which articulates and convinces the Court that a hostile tender offer poses a legitimate threat to the corporate enterprise, may address that perceived threat by blocking the tender offer and forcing the bidder to elect a board majority that supports its bid.

In essence, this case brings to the fore one of the most basic questions animating all of corporate law, which relates to the allocation of power between directors and stockholders. That is, "when, if ever, will a board's duty to 'the corporation and its shareholders' require [the board] to abandon concerns for 'long term' values (and other constituencies) and enter a current share value maximizing mode?" More to the point, in the context of a hostile tender offer, who gets to decide when and if the corporation is for sale?

Since the Shareholder Rights Plan (more commonly known as the "poison pill") was first conceived and throughout the development of Delaware corporate takeover jurisprudence during the twenty-five-plus years that followed, the debate over who ultimately decides whether a tender offer is adequate and should be accepted—the shareholders of the corporation or its board of directors—has raged on. Starting with Moran v. Household International, Inc. in 1985, when the Delaware Supreme Court first upheld the adoption of the poison pill as a valid takeover defense, through the hostile takeover years of the 1980s, and in several recent decisions of the Court of Chancery and the Delaware Supreme Court, this fundamental question has engaged practitioners, academics, and members of the judiciary, but it has yet to be confronted head on.

For the reasons much more fully described in the remainder of this Opinion, I conclude that, as Delaware law currently stands, the answer must be that the power to defeat an inadequate hostile tender offer ultimately lies with the board of directors. As such, I find that the Airgas board has met its burden under Unocal to articulate a legally cognizable threat (the allegedly inadequate price of Air Products' offer, coupled with the fact that a majority of Airgas's stockholders would likely tender into that inadequate offer) and has taken defensive measures that fall within a range of reasonable responses proportionate to that threat. I thus rule in favor of defendants. Air Products' and the Shareholder Plaintiffs' requests for relief are denied, and all claims asserted against defendants are dismissed with prejudice.

This is the Court's decision after trial, extensive post-trial briefing, and a supplemental evidentiary hearing in this long-running takeover battle between Air Products & Chemicals, Inc. ("Air Products") and Airgas, Inc. ("Airgas"). The now very public saga began quietly in mid-October 2009 when John McGlade, President and CEO of Air Products, privately approached Peter McCausland, founder and CEO of Airgas, about a potential acquisition or combination. After McGlade's private advances were rebuffed, Air Products went hostile in February 2010, launching a public tender offer for all outstanding Airgas shares.

Now, over a year since Air Products first announced its all-shares, all-cash tender offer, the terms of that offer (other than price) remain essentially unchanged. After several price bumps and extensions, the offer currently stands at $70 per share and is set to expire today, February 15, 2011—Air Products' stated "best and final" offer. The Airgas board unanimously rejected that offer as being "clearly inadequate." The Airgas board has repeatedly expressed the view that Airgas is worth at least $78 per share in a sale transaction—and at any rate, far more than the $70 per share Air Products is offering.

B. Judicial Review of Director Action

So, we are at a crossroads. Air Products has made its "best and final" offer—apparently its offer to acquire Airgas has reached an end stage. Meanwhile, the Airgas board believes the offer is clearly inadequate and its value in a sale transaction is at least $78 per share. At this stage, it appears, neither side will budge. Airgas continues to maintain its defenses, blocking the bid and effectively denying shareholders the choice whether to tender their shares. Air Products and Shareholder Plaintiffs now ask this Court to order Airgas to redeem its poison pill and other defenses that are stopping Air Products from moving forward with its hostile offer, and to allow Airgas's stockholders to decide for themselves whether they want to tender into Air Products' (inadequate or not) $70 "best and final" offer.

A week-long trial in this case was held from October 4, 2010 through October 8, 2010. Hundreds of pages of post-trial memoranda were submitted by the parties. After trial, several legal, factual, and evidentiary questions remained to be answered. In ruling on certain outstanding evidentiary issues, I sent counsel a Letter Order on December 2, 2010 asking for answers to a number of questions to be addressed in supplemental post-trial briefing. On the eve of the parties' submissions to the Court in response to that Letter Order, Air Products raised its offer to the $70 "best and final" number. At that point, defendants vigorously opposed a ruling based on the October trial record, suggesting that the entire trial (indeed, the entire case) was moot because the October trial predominantly focused on the Airgas board's response to Air Products' then-$65.50 offer and the board's decision to keep its defenses in place with respect to that offer. Defendants further suggested that any ruling with respect to the $70 offer was not ripe because the board had not yet met to consider that offer.

I rejected both the mootness and ripeness arguments. As for mootness, Air Products had previously raised its bid several times throughout the litigation but the core question before me—whether Air Products' offer continues to pose a threat justifying Airgas's continued maintenance of its poison pill—remained, and remains, the same. And as for ripeness, by the time of the December 23 Letter Order the Airgas board had met and rejected Air Products' revised $70 offer. I did, however, allow the parties to take supplemental discovery relating to the $70 offer. A supplemental evidentiary hearing was held from January 25 through January 27, 2011, in order to complete the record on the $70 offer. Counsel presented closing arguments on February 8, 2011.

Now, having thoroughly read, reviewed, and reflected upon all of the evidence presented to me, and having carefully considered the arguments made by counsel, I conclude that the Airgas board, in proceeding as it has since October 2009, has not breached its fiduciary duties owed to the Airgas stockholders. I find that the board has acted in good faith and in the honest belief that the Air Products offer, at $70 per share, is inadequate.

Although I have a hard time believing that inadequate price alone (according to the target's board) in the context of a non-discriminatory, all-cash, all-shares, fully financed offer poses any "threat"—particularly given the wealth of information available to Airgas's stockholders at this point in time—under existing Delaware law, it apparently does. Inadequate price has become a form of "substantive coercion" as that concept has been developed by the Delaware Supreme Court in its takeover jurisprudence. That is, the idea that Airgas's stockholders will disbelieve the board's views on value (or in the case of merger arbitrageurs who may have short-term profit goals in mind, they may simply ignore the board's recommendations), and so they may mistakenly tender into an inadequately priced offer. Substantive coercion has been clearly recognized by our Supreme Court as a valid threat.

Trial judges are not free to ignore or rewrite appellate court decisions. Thus, for reasons explained in detail below, I am constrained by Delaware Supreme Court precedent to conclude that defendants have met their burden under Unocal to articulate a sufficient threat that justifies the continued maintenance of Airgas's poison pill. That is, assuming defendants have met their burden to articulate a legally cognizable threat (prong 1), Airgas's defenses have been recognized by Delaware law as reasonable responses to the threat posed by an inadequate offer—even an all-shares, all-cash offer (prong 2).

In my personal view, Airgas's poison pill has served its legitimate purpose. Although the "best and final" $70 offer has been on the table for just over two months (since December 9, 2010), Air Products' advances have been ongoing for over sixteen months, and Airgas's use of its poison pill—particularly in combination with its staggered board—has given the Airgas board over a full year to inform its stockholders about its view of Airgas's intrinsic value and Airgas's value in a sale transaction. It has also given the Airgas board a full year to express its views to its stockholders on the purported opportunistic timing of Air Products' repeated advances and to educate its stockholders on the inadequacy of Air Products' offer. It has given Airgas *more time than any litigated poison pill in Delaware history*—enough time to show stockholders four quarters of improving financial results,8 demonstrating that Airgas is on track to meet its projected goals. And it has helped the Airgas board push Air Products to raise its bid by $10 per share from when it was first publicly announced to what Air Products has now represented is its highest offer. The record at both the October trial and the January supplemental evidentiary hearing confirm that Airgas's stockholder base is sophisticated and well-informed, and that essentially all the information they would need to make an informed decision is available to them. In short, there seems to be no threat here—the stockholders know what they need to know (about both the offer and the Airgas board's opinion of the offer) to make an informed decision.

That being said, however, as I understand binding Delaware precedent, I may not substitute my business judgment for that of the Airgas board. The Delaware Supreme Court has recognized inadequate price as a valid threat to corporate policy and effectiveness. The Delaware Supreme Court has also made clear that the "selection of a time frame for achievement of corporate goals . . . may not be delegated to the stockholders." [citing Paramount] Furthermore, in powerful dictum, the Supreme Court has stated that "[d]irectors are not obliged to abandon a deliberately conceived corporate plan for a short-term shareholder profit unless there is clearly no basis to sustain the corporate strategy."[citing Paramount] Although I do not read that dictum as eliminating the applicability of heightened Unocal scrutiny to a board's decision to block a non-coercive bid as underpriced, I do read it, along with the actual holding in Unitrin, as indicating that a board that has a good faith, reasonable basis to believe a bid is inadequate may block that bid using a poison pill, irrespective of stockholders' desire to accept it.

Here, even using heightened scrutiny, the Airgas board has demonstrated that it has a reasonable basis for sustaining its long term corporate strategy — the Airgas board is independent, and has relied on the advice of three different outside independent financial advisors in concluding that Air Products' offer is inadequate. Air Products' *own three nominees* who were elected to the Airgas board in September 2010 have joined wholeheartedly in the Airgas board's determination, and when the Airgas board met to consider the $70 "best and final" offer in December 2010, it was one of those Air Products Nominees who said, "We have to protect the pill." Indeed, one of Air Products' *own directors* conceded at trial that the Airgas board members had acted within their fiduciary duties in their desire to "hold out for the proper price," and that "if an offer was made for Air Products that [he] considered to be unfair to the stockholders of Air Products . . . [he would likewise] use every legal mechanism available" to hold out for the proper price as well. Under Delaware law, the Airgas directors have complied with their fiduciary duties. Thus, as noted above, and for the reasons more fully described in the remainder of this Opinion, I am constrained to deny Air Products' and the Shareholder Plaintiffs' requests for relief. . . .

NOTES AND QUESTIONS

1. The deal. Air Products, a producer of atmospheric and specialty gases and other products, and Airgas, whose core business was packaged gas, were each headquartered in eastern Pennsylania. Air Products's CEO had first approached Airgas' founder and CEO in the fall of 2009 and proposed a $60 per share all equity deal at a time the Airgas share price was in the mid $40s after recovering from a post financial crisis low of $29 in the spring of that year. After the board rejected that offer and follow-ups. Air

Products went public with a $60 tender offer in February 2010 and the following month announced a proxy contest for a slate of independent directors to fill three of the nine seats in Airgas' classified board that were up for election at the annual meeting scheduled for August. Air Products also sought approval of three bylaw proposals, including a requirement that the 2011 annual meeting occur in January. Several bumps in the offer raised the Air Products price to $65.50 by the time of the annual meeting, at which the Air Products nominees were elected and the bylaws were passed. The Delaware Supreme Court, invalidated the bylaws and impermissible cutting short of the terms of existing directors. Airgas, Inc. v. Air Products & Chemicals, Inc., 8 A.3d 1182 (De. 2010). Air Products continued its suit to have the Chancellor find the failure to redeem the poison pill as a breach of fiduciary duty.

2. **"Just Say No"**. Delaware law has long used the phrase, borrowed from former First Lady Nancy Regan's suggested approach to the war on drugs, to identify the debate as to the breadth of a board's power to use a poison pill defense. Recall Chancellor Allen's suggestion in Interco that "there may come a time" when redemption is required. What parts of Chancellor Chandler's opinion suggest the time has come in this case? What possible reasons do you see for his not requiring redemption here — the force of precedent? The position of the directors joining the board after the last annual meeting? What does the case suggest about redemption of pills going forward?

C. EVOLUTION IN THE POISON PILL AND JUDICIAL RESPONSES

The Supreme Court's decision in *Paramount* appears to give substantial room to directors in refusing to redeem a poison pill in the face of a bid that the directors believe is inadequate (a set that likely will cover almost all bids that the target board does not accept). But recall from Chapter 5 the antidote available to the poison pill. The redemption feature built in to the pill that became so important under the *Moran* analysis was a ready-made entry point if the insurgents gained control of a board by a proxy contest (discussed in more detail in Chapter 8). Planners cognizant of this vulnerability of the poison pill sought to further narrow the channel for shareholder action by modifying the plans. In turn, Delaware courts had to respond whether such board actions could be sustained as the poison pill had been. Two prime illustrations were the dead-hand pill and the slow-hand pill, which are described in the two cases excerpted below.

Carmody v. Toll Brothers, Inc.
723 A.2d 1180 (Del. Ch. 1998)

JACOBS, Vice Chancellor.

... The firm whose rights plan is being challenged is Toll Brothers (sometimes referred to as "the company"), a Pennsylvania-based Delaware corporation that designs, builds, and markets single family luxury homes in thirteen states and five regions in the United States. The company was founded in 1967 by brothers Bruce and Robert Toll, who are its Chief Executive and Chief Operating Officers, respectively, and who own approximately 37.5% of Toll Brothers' common stock. The company's board of directors has nine members, four of whom (including Bruce and Robert Toll) are senior executive officers. The remaining five members of the board are "outside" independent directors.

From its inception in 1967, Toll Brothers has performed very successfully, and "went public" in 1986. ...

The Rights Plan was adopted on June 12, 1997.... The complaint alleges that the purpose and effect of the company's Rights Plan, as with most poison pills, is to make any hostile acquisition of Toll Brothers prohibitively expensive, and thereby to deter such acquisitions unless the target company's board first approves the acquisition proposal. The target board's "leverage" derives from another critical feature found in most rights plans: the directors' power to redeem the Rights at any time before they expire, on such conditions as the directors "in their sole discretion" may establish. To this extent there is little to distinguish the company's Rights Plan from the "standard model." What is distinctive about the Rights Plan is that it authorizes only a specific, defined category of directors—the "Continuing Directors"—to redeem the Rights. The dispute over the legality of this "Continuing Director" or "dead hand" feature of the Rights Plan is what drives this lawsuit.

2. The "Dead Hand" Feature of the Rights Plan

In substance, the "dead hand" provision operates to prevent any directors of Toll Brothers, except those who were in office as of the date of the Rights Plan's adoption (June 12, 1997) or their designated successors, from redeeming the Rights until they expire on June 12, 2007....

According to the complaint, this "dead hand" provision has a twofold practical effect. First, it makes an unsolicited offer for the company more unlikely by eliminating a proxy contest as a useful way for a hostile acquiror to gain control, because even if the acquiror wins the contest, its newly-elected director representatives could not redeem the Rights. Second, the "dead hand" provision disenfranchises, in a proxy contest, all shareholders that wish the company to be managed by a board empowered to redeem the Rights, by depriving those shareholders of any practical choice except to vote for the incumbent directors. Given these effects, the plaintiff claims that the only purpose that the "dead hand" provision could serve is to discourage future acquisition activity by making any proxy contest to replace incumbent board members an exercise in futility.

II. Overview of the Problem and the Parties' Contentions

A. Overview

The critical issue on this motion is whether a "dead hand" provision in a "poison pill" rights plan is subject to legal challenge on the basis that it is invalid as *ultra vires*, or as a breach of fiduciary duty, or both. Although that issue has been the subject of scholarly comment, it has yet to be decided under Delaware law, and to date it has been addressed by only two courts applying the law of other jurisdictions.

Some history may elucidate the issue by locating its relevance within the dynamic of state corporate takeover jurisprudence. Since the 1980s, that body of law, largely judge-made, has been racing to keep abreast of the ever-evolving and novel tactical and strategic developments so characteristic of this important area of economic endeavor that is swiftly becoming a permanent part of our national (and international) economic landscape.

For our purposes, the relevant history begins in the early 1980s with the advent of the "poison pill" as an antitakeover measure. That innovation generated litigation focused upon the issue of whether any poison pill rights plan could validly be adopted under state corporation law. The seminal case, *Moran v. Household International, Inc.* answered that question in the affirmative....

It being settled that a corporate board could permissibly adopt a poison pill, the next litigated question became: under what circumstances would the directors' fiduciary duties require the board to redeem the rights in the face of a hostile takeover proposal? That issue was litigated, in Delaware and elsewhere, during the second half of the 1980s. The lesson taught by that experience was that courts were extremely reluctant to order the redemption of poison pills on fiduciary grounds. The reason was the prudent deployment of the pill proved to be largely beneficial to shareholder interests: it often resulted in a bidding contest that culminated in an acquisition on terms superior to the initial hostile offer.

Once it became clear that the prospects were unlikely for obtaining judicial relief mandating a redemption of the poison pill, a different response to the pill was needed. That response, which echoed the Supreme Court's suggestion in *Moran*, was the foreseeable next step in the evolution of takeover strategy: a tender offer coupled with a solicitation for shareholder proxies to remove and replace the incumbent board with the

C. Evolution in the Poison Pill and Judicial Responses

acquiror's nominees who, upon assuming office, would redeem the pill. Because that strategy, if unopposed, would enable hostile offerors to effect an "end run" around the poison pill, it again was predictable and only a matter of time that target company boards would develop counterstrategies. With one exception — the "dead hand" pill — these counterstrategies proved "successful" only in cases where the purpose was to delay the process to enable the board to develop alternatives to the hostile offer. The counterstrategies were largely unsuccessful, however, where the goal was to stop the proxy contest (and as a consequence, the hostile offer) altogether.

For example, in cases where the target board's response was either to (i) amend the by-laws to delay a shareholders' meeting to elect directors, or (ii) delay an annual meeting to a later date permitted under the by-laws, so that the board and management would be able to explore alternatives to the hostile offer (but not entrench themselves), those responses were upheld. On the other hand, where the target board's response to a proxy contest (coupled with a hostile offer) was (i) to move the shareholders meeting to a later date to enable the incumbent board to solicit revocations of proxies to defeat the apparently victorious dissident group, or (ii) to expand the size of the board, and then fill the newly created positions so the incumbents would retain control of the board irrespective of the outcome of the proxy contest, those responses were declared invalid.[17]

. . . This litigation experience taught that a target board, facing a proxy contest joined with a hostile tender offer, could, in good faith, employ non-preclusive defensive measures to give the board time to explore transactional alternatives. The target board could not, however, erect defenses that would either preclude a proxy contest altogether or improperly bend the rules to favor the board's continued incumbency.

In this environment, the only defensive measure that promised to be a "show stopper" (*i.e.*, had the potential to deter a proxy contest altogether) was a poison pill with a "dead hand" feature. The reason is that if only the incumbent directors or their designated successors could redeem the pill, it would make little sense for shareholders or the hostile bidder to wage a proxy contest to replace the incumbent board. Doing that would eliminate from the scene the only group of persons having the power to give the hostile bidder and target company shareholders what they desired: control

---

17. *See*, Aprahamian v. HBO & Co., Del Ch., 531 A.2d 1204 (1987) (shareholders' meeting moved to later date for the purpose of defeating the apparent victors in proxy contest. Held: invalid); Blasius Indus. v. Atlas Corp., Del. Ch., 564 A.2d 651(1988) (in response to an announced proxy contest, target board amended bylaws to create two new board positions, then filled those positions to retain board control, irrespective of outcome of proxy contest. Held: invalid).

Another statutorily permissible defensive device — the "staggered" or classified board — was useful, but still of limited effectiveness. Because only one third of a classified board would stand for election each year, a classified board would delay — but not prevent — a hostile acquiror from obtaining control of the board, since a determined acquiror could wage a proxy contest and obtain control of two thirds of the target board over a two year period, as opposed to seizing control in a single election.

of the target company (in the case of the hostile bidder) and the opportunity to obtain an attractive price for their shares (in the case of the target company stockholders). It is against that backdrop that the legal issues presented here, which concern the validity of the "dead hand" feature, attain significance. . . .

III. ANALYSIS . . .

B. The Validity of the "Dead Hand" Provision

1. The Invalidity Contentions

The plaintiff's complaint attacks the "dead hand" feature of the Toll Brothers poison pill on both statutory and fiduciary duty grounds. The statutory claim is that the "dead hand" provision unlawfully restricts the powers of future boards by creating different classes of directors—those who have the power to redeem the poison pill, and those who do not. Under 8 Del. C. §§141(a) and (d), any such restrictions and director classifications must be stated in the certificate of incorporation. The complaint alleges that because those restrictions are not stated in the Toll Brothers charter, the "dead hand" provision of the Rights Plan is ultra vires and, consequently, invalid on its face.

The complaint also alleges that even if the Rights Plan is not *ultra vires*, its approval constituted a breach of the Toll Brothers board's fiduciary duty of loyalty in several respects. It is alleged that the board violated its duty of loyalty because (a) the "dead hand" provision was enacted solely or primarily for entrenchment purposes; (b) it was also a disproportionate defensive measure, since it precludes the shareholders from receiving tender offers and engaging in a proxy contest, in contravention of the principles of *Unocal Corp. v. Mesa Petroleum Co.* (*"Unocal"*), as elucidated in *Unitrin, Inc. v. American General Corp.* (*"Unitrin"*) and (c) the "dead hand" provision purposefully interferes with the shareholder voting franchise without any compelling justification, in derogation of the principles articulated in *Blasius Indus. v. Atlas Corp.* (*"Blasius"*). . . .

2. The Statutory Invalidity Claims

. . . [T]he complaint states legally sufficient claims that the "dead hand" provision of the Toll Brothers Rights Plan violates 8 Del. C. §§141(a) and (d). There are three reasons.

First, it cannot be disputed that the Rights Plan confers the power to redeem the pill only upon some, but not all, of the directors. But under §141(d), the power to create voting power distinctions among directors exists only where there is a classified board, and where those voting

C. Evolution in the Poison Pill and Judicial Responses 269

power distinctions are expressed in the certificate of incorporation. Section 141(d) pertinently provides:

> . . . *The certificate of incorporation may confer upon holders of any class or series of stock the right to elect 1 or more directors who shall* serve for such term, *and have such voting powers as shall be stated in the certificate of incorporation.* The terms of office and voting powers of the directors elected in the manner so provided in the certificate of incorporation may be greater than or less than those of any other director or class of directors. . . . (Emphasis added.)

The plain, unambiguous meaning of the quoted language is that if one category or group of directors is given distinctive voting rights not shared by the other directors, those distinctive voting rights must be set forth in the certificate of incorporation. In the case of Toll Brothers (the complaint alleges), they are not.

Second, §141(d) mandates that the "right to elect 1 or more directors who shall . . . have such [greater] voting powers" is reserved to the stockholders, not to the directors or a subset thereof. Absent express language in the charter, nothing in Delaware law suggests that some directors of a public corporation may be created less equal than other directors, and certainly not by unilateral board action. Vesting the pill redemption power exclusively in the Continuing Directors transgresses the statutorily protected shareholder right to elect the directors who would be so empowered. For that reason, and because it is claimed that the Rights Plan's allocation of voting power to redeem the Rights is nowhere found in the Toll Brothers certificate of incorporation, the complaint states a claim that the "dead hand" feature of the Rights Plan is *ultra vires,* and hence, statutorily invalid under Delaware law.

Third, the complaint states a claim that the "dead hand" provision would impermissibly interfere with the directors' statutory power to manage the business and affairs of the corporation. That power is conferred by 8 Del. C. §141(a), which mandates:

> The business and affairs of every corporation organized under this chapter shall be managed by or under the direction of a board of directors, *except as may be otherwise provided in this chapter or in its certificate of incorporation.* . . . (Emphasis added.)

The "dead hand" poison pill is intended to thwart hostile bids by vesting shareholders with preclusive rights that cannot be redeemed except by the Continuing Directors. Thus, the one action that could make it practically possible to redeem the pill — replacing the entire board — could make that pill redemption legally impossible to achieve. The "dead hand" provision would jeopardize a newly-elected future board's ability to achieve a business combination by depriving that board of the power to redeem the pill without obtaining the consent of the "Continuing Directors," who (it may be assumed) would constitute a minority of the board. In this manner, it is claimed, the "dead hand" provision would interfere with the board's power to protect fully the corporation's (and its shareholders') interests in a transaction that is one of the most fundamental and important in the life of a business enterprise....

The defendants offer two arguments in response.... Neither contention has merit. The first is basically an argument that the Rights Plan does not violate any fiduciary duty of the board. That is unresponsive to the statutory invalidity claim. The second argument rests upon an analogy that has no basis in fact. In adopting the Rights Plan, the board did not, nor did it purport to, create a special committee having the exclusive power to redeem the pill. The analogy also ignores fundamental structural differences between the creation of a special board committee and the operation of the "dead hand" provision of the Rights Plan. The creation of a special committee would not impose long term structural power-related distinctions between different groups of directors of the same board. The board that creates a special committee may abolish it at any time, as could any successor board. On the other hand, the Toll Brothers "dead hand" provision, if legally valid, would embed structural power-related distinctions between groups of directors that no successor board could abolish until after the Rights expire in 2007.

For these reasons, the statutory invalidity claims survive the motion to dismiss.

3. The Fiduciary Duty Invalidity Claims . . .

a) The *Blasius* Fiduciary Duty Claim

[Omitted, given the developments in the *Blasius* line of cases discussed in Chapter 8.]

b) The *Unocal/Unitrin* Fiduciary Duty Claim

The final issue is whether the complaint states a legally cognizable claim that the inclusion of the "dead hand" provision in the Rights Plan was an unreasonable defensive measure within the meaning of *Unocal*. I conclude that it does.

As a procedural matter, it merits emphasis that a claim under *Unocal* requires enhanced judicial scrutiny. In that context, the board has the burden to satisfy the Court that the board (1) "had reasonable grounds for believing that a danger to corporate policy and effectiveness existed," and (2) that its "defensive response was reasonable in relation to the threat posed." Such scrutiny is, by its nature, fact-driven and requires a factual record. For that reason, as the Supreme Court recently observed, enhanced scrutiny "will usually not be satisfied by resting on a defense motion merely attacking the pleadings." Only "conclusory complaints without well-pleaded facts [may] be dismissed early under Chancery Rule 12."

The complaint at issue here is far from conclusory. Under *Unitrin*, a defensive measure is disproportionate (*i.e.*, unreasonable) if it is either coercive or preclusive. The complaint alleges that the "dead hand" provision "disenfranchises shareholders by forcing them to vote for incumbent directors or their designees if shareholders want to be represented by a board entitled to exercise its full statutory prerogatives." That is sufficient to claim that the "dead hand" provision is coercive. The complaint also alleges that that provision "makes an offer for the Company much more unlikely since it eliminates use of a proxy contest as a possible means to gain control . . . [because] . . . any directors elected in such a contest would still be unable to vote to redeem the pill"; and the provision "renders future contests for corporate control of Toll Brothers prohibitively expensive and effectively impossible." A defensive measure is preclusive if it makes a bidder's ability to wage a successful proxy contest and gain control either "mathematically impossible" or "realistically unattainable." These allegations are sufficient to state a claim that the "dead hand" provision makes a proxy contest "realistically unattainable," and therefore, disproportionate and unreasonable under *Unocal*.

IV. Conclusion

The Court concludes that for the reasons discussed above, the complaint states claims under Delaware law upon which relief can be granted. Accordingly, the defendants' motion to dismiss is denied.

Quickturn Design Systems, Inc. v. Shapiro
721 A.2d 1281 (Del. Sup. Ct. 1998)

HOLLAND, Justice.

. . . Quickturn's Delayed Redemption Provision

At the time Mentor commenced its bid, Quickturn had in place a Rights Plan that contained a so-called "dead hand" provision. That provision had a limited "continuing director" feature that became operative only if an insurgent that owned more than 15% of Quickturn's common stock successfully waged a proxy contest to replace a majority of the board. In that event, only the "continuing directors" (those directors in office at the time the poison pill was adopted) could redeem the rights.

During the same August 21, 1998 meeting at which it amended the special meeting by-law, [discussion of which is omitted here] the Quickturn board also amended the Rights Plan to eliminate its "continuing director" feature, and to substitute a "no hand" or "delayed redemption provision" into its Rights Plan. The Delayed Redemption Provision provides that, if a majority of the directors are replaced by stockholder action, the newly elected board cannot redeem the rights for six months if the purpose or effect of the redemption would be to facilitate a transaction with an "Interested Person."[21]

It is undisputed that the DRP would prevent Mentor's slate, if elected as the new board majority, from redeeming the Rights Plan for six months following their election, because a redemption would be "reasonably likely to have the purpose or effect of facilitating a Transaction" with Mentor, a party that "directly or indirectly proposed, nominated or financially supported" the election of the new board. Consequently, by adopting the DRP, the Quickturn board built into the process a six-month delay period in addition to the 90 to 100 day delay mandated by the By-Law Amendment.

Court of Chancery Invalidates Delayed Redemption Provision

When the board of a Delaware corporation takes action to resist a hostile bid for control, the board of directors' defensive actions are subjected to "enhanced" judicial scrutiny. For a target board's actions to be entitled to business judgment rule protection, the target board must first establish that it had reasonable grounds to believe that the hostile bid constituted a threat to corporate policy and effectiveness; and second, that the defensive measures adopted were "proportionate," that is, reasonable in relation to the threat that the board reasonably perceived. The Delayed Redemption Provision was reviewed by the Court of Chancery pursuant to that standard.

The Court of Chancery found: "the evidence, viewed as a whole, shows that the perceived threat that led the Quickturn board to adopt the DRP, was the concern that Quickturn shareholders might mistakenly, in ignorance of Quickturn's true value, accept Mentor's inadequate offer, and elect a new board that would prematurely sell the company before the new board could adequately inform itself of Quickturn's fair value and before the shareholders could consider other options." The Court of Chancery concluded that Mentor's combined tender offer and proxy contest amounted to substantive coercion. Having concluded that the Quickturn board reasonably perceived a cognizable threat, the Court of Chancery

---

21. The "no hand" or Delayed Redemption Provision is found in a new Section 23(b) of the Rights Plan, which states:

> (b) Notwithstanding the provisions of Section 23(a), in the event that a majority of the Board of Directors of the Company is elected by stockholder action at an annual or special meeting of stockholders, then until the 180th day following the effectiveness of such election (including any postponement or adjournment thereof), the Rights shall not be redeemed if such redemption is reasonably likely to have the purpose or effect of facilitating a Transaction with an Interested Person.

Substantially similar provisions were added to Sections 24 ("Exchange") and 27 ("Supplements and Amendments") of the Rights Plan.

C. Evolution in the Poison Pill and Judicial Responses

then examined whether the board's response—the Delayed Redemption Provision—was proportionate in relation to that threat.

In assessing a challenge to defensive measures taken by a target board in response to an attempted hostile takeover, enhanced judicial scrutiny requires an evaluation of the board's justification for each contested defensive measure and its concomitant results. The Court of Chancery found that the Quickturn board's "justification or rationale for adopting the Delayed Redemption Provision was to force *any* newly elected board to take sufficient time to become familiar with Quickturn and its value, and to provide shareholders the opportunity to consider alternatives, before selling Quickturn to *any* acquiror." The Court of Chancery concluded that the Delayed Redemption Provision could not pass the proportionality test. Therefore, the Court of Chancery held that "the DRP cannot survive scrutiny under *Unocal* and must be declared invalid."

Delayed Redemption Provision Violates Fundamental Delaware Law

In this appeal, Mentor argues that the judgment of the Court of Chancery should be affirmed because the Delayed Redemption Provision is invalid as a matter of Delaware law. According to Mentor, the Delayed Redemption Provision, like the "dead hand" feature in the Rights Plan that was held to be invalid in *Toll Brothers* will impermissibly deprive any newly elected board of both its statutory authority to manage the corporation under 8 Del. C. §141(a) and its concomitant fiduciary duty pursuant to that statutory mandate. We agree.

Our analysis of the Delayed Redemption Provision in the Quickturn Rights Plan is guided by the prior precedents of this Court with regard to a board of directors authority to adopt a Rights Plan or "poison pill." In *Moran* [*v. Household International, Inc.*, Del. Supr., 500 A.2d 1346, 1353 (1985)], this Court held that the "inherent powers of the Board conferred by 8 Del. C. §141(a) concerning the management of the corporation's 'business and affairs' provides the Board additional authority upon which to enact the Rights Plan." Consequently, this Court upheld the adoption of the Rights Plan in *Moran* as a legitimate exercise of business judgment by the board of directors. In doing so, however, this Court also held "the rights plan is not absolute."

When the Household Board of Directors is faced with a tender offer and a request to redeem the Rights [Plan], they will not be able to arbitrarily reject the offer. They will be held to the same fiduciary standards any other board of directors would be held to in deciding to adopt a defensive mechanism, the same standards as they were held to in originally approving the Rights Plan.

In *Moran*, this Court held that the "ultimate response to an actual takeover bid must be judged by the Directors' actions at the time and nothing we say relieves them of their fundamental duties to the corporation and its shareholders." Consequently, we concluded that the use of the Rights Plan would be evaluated when and if the issue arises.

One of the most basic tenets of Delaware corporate law is that the board of directors has the ultimate responsibility for managing the business and affairs of a corporation. Section 141(a) requires that any limitation on the board's authority be set out in the certificate of incorporation. The Quickturn certificate of incorporation contains no provision purporting to limit the authority of the board in any way. The Delayed Redemption Provision, however, would prevent a newly elected board of directors from *completely* discharging its fundamental management duties to the corporation and its stockholders for six months. While the Delayed Redemption Provision limits the board of directors' authority in only one respect, the suspension of the Rights Plan, it nonetheless restricts the board's power in an area of fundamental importance to the shareholders—negotiating a possible sale of the corporation. Therefore, we hold that the Delayed Redemption Provision is invalid under Section 141(a), which confers upon any newly elected board of directors *full* power to manage and direct the business and affairs of a Delaware corporation.

In discharging the statutory mandate of Section 141(a), the directors have a fiduciary duty to the corporation and its shareholders. This unremitting obligation extends equally to board conduct in a contest for corporate control. The Delayed Redemption Provision prevents a newly elected board of directors from completely discharging its fiduciary duties to protect fully the interests of Quickturn and its stockholders.

This Court has recently observed that "although the fiduciary duty of a Delaware director is unremitting, the exact course of conduct that must be charted to properly discharge that responsibility will change in the specific context of the action the director is taking with regard to either the corporation or its shareholders." This Court has held "[t]o the extent that a contract, or a provision thereof, purports to require a board to act *or not act* in such a fashion as to limit the exercise of fiduciary duties, it is invalid and unenforceable." The Delayed Redemption Provision "tends to limit in a substantial way the freedom of [newly elected] directors' decisions on matters of management policy." Therefore, "it violates the duty of each [newly elected] director to exercise his own best judgment on matters coming before the board."

In this case, the Quickturn board was confronted by a determined bidder that sought to acquire the company at a price the Quickturn board concluded was inadequate. Such situations are common in corporate takeover efforts In *Revlon* [*Inc. v. MacAndrews & Forbes Holdings, Inc.*, 506 A.2d at 185], this Court held that no defensive measure can be sustained when it represents a breach of the directors' fiduciary duty. *A fortiori*, no defensive measure can be sustained which would require a new board of directors to breach its fiduciary duty. In that regard, we note Mentor has properly acknowledged that in the event its slate of directors is elected, those newly elected directors will be required to discharge their unremitting fiduciary duty to manage the corporation for the benefit of Quickturn and its stockholders

Conclusion

The Delayed Redemption Provision would prevent a new Quickturn board of directors from managing the corporation by redeeming the Rights Plan to facilitate a transaction that would serve the stockholders' best interests, even under circumstances where the board would be required to do so because of its fiduciary duty to the Quickturn stockholders. Because the Delayed Redemption Provision impermissibly circumscribes the board's statutory power under Section 141(a) and the directors' ability to fulfill their concomitant fiduciary duties, we hold that the Delayed Redemption Provision is invalid. On that alternative basis, the judgment of the Court of Chancery is AFFIRMED.

NOTES AND QUESTIONS

1. **Challenge facing planners for the target.** Even if "just say no" was the rule as to redemption of poison pills, were targets completely protected? The context is again what was set forth in Chapter 5. The directors seek to rely on Rule #1 that leaves corporate decisions in their hands. The shareholders seek to use the levers of selling or voting to countermand the directors. "Just say no" effectively neutralizes one avenue because of the cost, but not the other. So, lawyers sought to tweak the poison pill so that shareholder voting could not be used to remove the defense.

2. **The mode of judicial review.** Note the form of judicial review of the two innovations. Vice-Chancellor Jacobs (before joining the Supreme Court) tests the dead hand against two standards, statute and common law, and finds it violative of both. Compare the two as to how they protect shareholders against managers. The menu would include shareholder self-help via the ballot box or board protection of shareholders as defined by judges in setting out fiduciary duties. The Vice-Chancellor in *Quickturn* found the slow hand a violation of *Unocal*, but the Supreme Court relied only on the statutory invalidity argument. What does this tell you about *Unocal*? What does it tell you about the Supreme Court's vision as the breadth of alternative protections for shareholders in Delaware corporate law?

3. **Triggering an NOL pill; poison pill + a classified board.** In 2010, the Delaware Supreme Court upheld a poison pill triggered by the acquirer crossing a threshold of 5 percent of the corporation's stock. *See* Versata Enterprises, Inc. v. Selectica, Inc., 5 A.3d 586 (Del. 2010) *aff'g*, 2010 WL 703062 (Del Ch. 2010). In that case, the acquirer purposely triggered

the pill. It had purchased about 7 percent of the company's stock, an investment of something over $1 million. The purchaser was a competitor owed $7.1 million by the target based on prior intellectual property litigation who sought "intentionally to impair corporate assets or else to coerce the Company into meeting certain business demands." 2010 WL. at *23. Selectica lowered the threshold for the pill from 15 percent because it feared additional purchases would trigger a change of control under tax rules that would block use of net operating losses ("NOL") that totaled $160 million for a company with a market capitalization of $23 million. The Supreme Court found that the potential loss of NOLs was a sufficient threat and that the response met the *Unocal* proportionality standard as reflected in the preclusive/coercive language of earlier cases. Even though the pill was triggered, the board in that case chose to implement the exchange portion of the pill (see the Appendix in the excerpt at the beginning of this chapter) as opposed to the more severe flip-in rights. The company then inserted a "reloaded pill" to apply to any future additional purchases and that action was also upheld. In applying *Unitrin*, the court addressed the plaintiff argument (Trilogy was the parent of Versata) that, even if a 4.99 percent shareholder could realistically win a proxy contest, "the preclusiveness question focuses on whether a challenger could realistically attain sufficient board control to remove the pill."

> Here, Trilogy contends, Selectica's charter-based classified board effectively forecloses a bid conditioned upon a redemption of the NOL Poison Pill, because it requires a proxy challenger to launch and complete two successful proxy contests in order to change control. Therefore, Trilogy argues that even if a less than 5% shareholder could win a proxy contest, Selectica's Rights Plan with a 4.99% trigger in combination with Selectica's charter-based classified board, makes a successful proxy contest for control of the board "realistically unattainable."
>
> Trilogy's preclusivity argument conflates two distinct questions: first, is a successful proxy contest realistically attainable; and second, will a successful proxy contest result in gaining control of the board at the next election? Trilogy argues that unless both questions can be answered affirmatively, a Rights Plan and a classified board, viewed collectively, are preclusive. If that preclusivity argument is correct, then it would apply whenever a corporation has both a classified board and a Rights Plan, irrespective whether the trigger is 4.99%, 20%, or anywhere in between those thresholds.
>
> Classified boards are authorized by statute and are adopted for a variety of business purposes. Any classified board also operates as an antitakeover defense by preventing an insurgent from obtaining control of the board in one election. More than a decade ago, in *Carmody*, the Court of Chancery noted "because only one-third of a classified board would stand for election each year, a classified board would delay—but not prevent—a hostile acquiror from obtaining control of the board, since a determined acquiror could wage a proxy contest and obtain control of two-thirds of the target board over a two-year period, as opposed to seizing control in a single election." The fact that a combination of defensive measures makes it more difficult for an acquirer to obtain control of a board does not make such measures realistically unattainable, i.e., preclusive.

In *Moran*, we rejected the contention "that the Rights Plan strips stockholders of their rights to receive tender offers, and that the Rights Plan fundamentally restricts proxy contests." We explained that "the Rights Plan will not have a severe impact upon proxy contests and it will not preclude all hostile acquisitions of Household." In this case, we hold that the combination of a classified board and a Rights Plan do not constitute a preclusive defense.

Range of Reasonableness
If a defensive measure is neither coercive nor preclusive, the *Unocal* proportionality test "requires the focus of enhanced judicial scrutiny to shift to 'the range of reasonableness.'" Where all of the defenses "are inextricably related, the principles of *Unocal* require that such actions be scrutinized collectively as a unitary response to the perceived threat." Trilogy asserts that the NOL Poison Pill, the Exchange, and the Reloaded NOL Poison Pill were not a reasonable collective response to the threat of the impairment of Selectica's NOLs.

The critical facts do not support that assertion. On November 20, within days of learning of the NOL Poison Pill, Trilogy sent Selectica a letter, demanding a conference to discuss an alleged breach of a patent settlement agreement between the parties. The parties met on December 17, and the following day, Trilogy resumed its purchases of Selectica stock. . . .

[Trilogy CFO Sean] Fallon described Trilogy's relationship with Selectica as a "three-legged stool," referring to Trilogy's status as a competitor, a creditor, and a stockholder of Selectica. The two companies had settled prior patent disputes in 2007 under terms that included a cross-license of intellectual property and quarterly payments from Selectica to Trilogy based on Selectica's revenues from certain products. Selectica argues that Trilogy took the unprecedented step of deliberately triggering the NOL Poison Pill — exposing its equity investment of under $2 million to dilution — primarily to extract substantially more value for the other two "legs" of the stool.

Trilogy's deliberate trigger started a ten business day clock under the terms of the NOL Poison Pill. If the Board took no action during that time, then the rights (other than those belonging to Trilogy) would "flip-in" and become exercisable for deeply discounted common stock. Alternatively, the Board had the power to exchange the rights (other than those belonging to Trilogy) for newly-issued common stock, or to grant Trilogy an exemption. Three times in the two weeks following the triggering, Selectica offered Trilogy an exemption in exchange for an agreement to stand still and to withdraw its threat to impair the value and usability of Selectica's NOLs. Three times Trilogy refused and insisted instead that Selectica repurchase its stock, terminate a license agreement with an important client, sign over intellectual property, and pay Trilogy millions of dollars. After three failed attempts to negotiate with Trilogy, it was reasonable for the Board to determine that they had no other option than to implement the NOL Poison Pill.

The Exchange employed by the Board was a more proportionate response than the "flip-in" mechanism traditionally envisioned for a Rights Plan. Because the Board opted to use the Exchange instead of the traditional "flip-in" mechanism, Trilogy experienced less dilution of its position than a Rights Plan is traditionally designed to achieve.

The implementation of the Reloaded NOL Poison Pill was also a reasonable response. The Reloaded NOL Poison Pill was considered a necessary defensive measure because, although the NOL Poison Pill and the Exchange effectively thwarted Trilogy's immediate threat to Selectica's NOLs, they did not eliminate the general threat of a Section 382 change-in-control. Following implementation of the

Exchange, Selectica still had a roughly 40% ownership change for Section 382 purposes and there was no longer a Rights Plan in place to discourage additional acquisitions by 5% holders. Selectica argues that the decision to adopt the Reloaded NOL Poison Pill was reasonable under those circumstances. We agree.

The record indicates that the Board was presented with expert advice that supported its ultimate findings that the NOLs were a corporate asset worth protecting, that the NOLs were at risk as a result of Trilogy's actions, and that the steps that the Board ultimately took were reasonable in relation to that threat. Outside experts were present and advised the Board on these matters at both the November 16 meeting at which the NOL Poison Pill was adopted and at the Board's December 29 meeting. The Committee also heard from expert advisers a third time at the January 2 meeting prior to instituting the Exchange and adopting the Reloaded NOL Poison Pill.

Under part two of the *Unocal* test, the Court of Chancery found that the combination of the NOL Poison Pill, the Exchange, and the Reloaded NOL Poison Pill was a proportionate response to the threatened loss of Selectica's NOLs. Those findings are not clearly erroneous. They are supported by the record and the result of a logical deductive reasoning process. Accordingly, we hold that the Selectica directors satisfied the second part of the *Unocal* test by showing that their defensive response was proportionate by being "reasonable in relation to the threat" identified.

Context Determines Reasonableness
Under a *Unocal* analysis, the reasonableness of a board's response is determined in relation to the "specific threat," at the time it was identified. Thus, it is the specific nature of the threat that "sets the parameters for the range of permissible defensive tactics" at any given time. The record demonstrates that a longtime competitor sought to increase the percentage of its stock ownership, not for the purpose of conducting a hostile takeover but, to intentionally impair corporate assets, or else coerce Selectica into meeting certain business demands under the threat of such impairment. Only in relation to that specific threat have the Court of Chancery and this Court considered the reasonableness of Selectica's response.

The Selectica Board carried its burden of proof under both parts of the *Unocal* test. Therefore, at this time, the Selectica Board has withstood the enhanced judicial scrutiny required by the two-part *Unocal* test. That does not, however, end the matter.

As we held in *Moran*, the adoption of a Rights Plan is not absolute. In other cases, we have upheld the adoption of Rights Plans in specific defensive circumstances while simultaneously holding that it may be inappropriate for a Rights Plan to remain in place when those specific circumstances change dramatically. The fact that the NOL Poison Pill was reasonable under the specific facts and circumstances of this case, should not be construed as generally approving the reasonableness of a 4.99% trigger in the Rights Plan of a corporation with or without NOLs.

To reiterate *Moran*, "the ultimate response to an actual takeover bid must be judged by the Directors' actions at that time." If and when the Selectica Board "is faced with a tender offer and a request to redeem the [Reloaded NOL Poison Pill], they will not be able to arbitrarily reject the offer. They will be held to the same fiduciary standards any other board of directors would be held to in deciding to adopt a defensive mechanism." The Selectica Board has no more discretion in refusing to redeem the Rights Plan "than it does in enacting any defensive mechanism."55 Therefore, the Selectica Board's future use of the Reloaded NOL Poison Pill must be evaluated if and when that issue arises.

C. Evolution in the Poison Pill and Judicial Responses 279

5 A.3d 586, 604-607(Del. 2010)

What if a poison pill had a higher trigger for institutional shareholders who take a passive stake and a lower limit for activist shareholders? *See* Steven M. Davidoff, *Netflix's Poison Pill Has a Shareholder-Friendly Flavor*, N.Y. Times DealBook (Nov. 6, 2012, 2:14 P.M.), http:// dealbook.nytimes .com/2012/11/06/netflixs-poison-pill-has-a-shareholder-friendly-flavor.

8 IS A DEFENSE AFFECTING VOTING DIFFERENT?

The roadmap set out in Chapter 3 presented the prevailing legal structure as to corporate governance in which directors get to make corporate decisions, shareholders can discipline their behavior via voting or selling their shares, and judges hold directors accountable via fiduciary duty. In the prior chapter, we focused on takeover defensive tactics by which directors and managers usually sought to prevent the use of shareholder selling to interfere with director decision-making. Now we turn our attention to the parallel avenue of shareholder voting and examine director action that seeks to constrain such shareholder action. Over the last two decades, the most effective method to constrain shareholder voting was to have a staggered board provision in the firm's articles of incorporation that subjected only one-third of the director seats to election at each annual meeting. The result was to require a bidder opposed by managers to conduct proxy fights at two annual meetings so as to get a majority of the board seats that could provide control of the corporation (absent shareholder power to call a special meeting or act by written consent which often are blocked in public corporations by planning done at the time the corporation went public). For the last two decades or so, institutional shareholders have refused to support midstream additions of staggered board provisions to the articles. Since 2005 or so, there has been effective institutional pressure to remove staggered boards so that it is no longer as prevalent as it was.

The case law concerning defensive tactics related to voting has arisen in the context of staggered boards and other election situations. It is older than *Unocal*, and it has taken some time to work out how defensive tactics as to voting relate to defensive tactics as to selling.

Schnell v. Chris-Craft Industries, Inc.
285 A.2d 437 (Del. Sup. Ct. 1971)

HERRMANN, Justice (for the majority of the Court):

This is an appeal from the denial by the Court of Chancery of the petition of dissident stockholders for injunctive relief to prevent management* from advancing the date of the annual stockholders' meeting from January 11, 1972, as set by the by-laws, to December 8, 1971.

The opinion below is reported at 285 A.2d 430. This opinion is confined to the frame of reference of the opinion below for the sake of brevity and because of the strictures of time imposed by the circumstances of the case.

[The Court of Chancery reported the facts of this case as follows:

"Plaintiffs, who are stockholders of the defendant, seek a preliminary injunction against the carrying out by such corporation of a change in the date of its annual meeting of stockholders which was ostensibly accomplished by an amendment to its by-laws adopted at a directors' meeting held on October 18, 1971. As a result of such change in by-law and the fixing of a new date by the directors, such annual meeting is now scheduled to be held on December 8, 1971, instead of on the date fixed in the by-law in question before its amendment, namely the second Tuesday in January, 1972.

"Plaintiffs and other dissident stockholders, who constitute a stockholders committee on which the plaintiff Schnell serves, are dissatisfied with defendant's recent business performance, which has been poor, plaintiffs contending that defendant has sustained losses of over $6,500,000 over the past two years. Accordingly, they have embarked on a proxy contest against present management with the purpose in mind of electing new directors and installing new management at Chris-Craft.

"The stockholders committee in question has had a formal existence since September, 1971. However, certain of its members have sought to impose their views on Chris-Craft's management since 1970, arguing that new management, achieved in one way or another, would be able to lift the defendant corporation from its slough of business losses. . . .

"Plaintiffs contend that by advancing the date of defendant's annual meeting by over a month and by the selection of an allegedly isolated town in up-state New York as the place for such meeting, defendant's board has deliberately sought to handicap the efforts of plaintiffs and other stockholders sympathetic to plaintiffs' views adequately to place their case before their fellow stockholders for decision because of the exigencies of time. Plaintiffs accordingly pray for the entry of a Preliminary injunction enjoining the convening of the annual meeting of stockholders of Chris-Craft as now scheduled for December 8, 1971, on the ground that the change in defendant's by-laws made on October 18, 1971, was improperly accomplished and constitutes a manipulation of corporate machinery

---
*We use this word as meaning "managing directors."

Chapter 8. Is a Defense Affecting Voting Different?

solely to insure that present management may be perpetuated in office to Chris-Craft's detriment. Plaintiffs further pray that the order which they seek to have entered reinstate the former annual meeting date of January 11, 1972, as provided for in the by-laws before the October 18, 1971, amendment, or that the Court fix such other date and place as the Court may deem to be fair and reasonable for such annual meeting....

"On October 18, 1971, at a meeting of seven members of defendant's board of' directors held in New York, notice of which, according to defendant's secretary, was given as required by the by-laws to every member of the board (minutes of which, however, were unjustifiably withheld from plaintiffs until the Court orally directed their production), Section 1 of Article 1 of Chris-Craft's by-laws was ended pursuant to the provisions of 8 Del. C. §211(b) allegedly to give more flexibility in fixing the date of the annual meeting and to permit the directors to set a convenient date within a specified period rather than having a fixed date set by the by-laws. Such by-law amendment reads in part as follows:

> 1. Annual Meeting. The annual meeting of stockholders of Chris-Craft Industries, Inc. (hereinafter called the "Corporation") shall be held for the election of the directors... in the two-month period commencing December 1 and ending on January 31 and at such time as shall be designated by the Board....

"At the same October 18 meeting, at which two directors, Linowes and Rochlis, were absent, the directors present fixed December 8, 1971, at 9:30 A.M. as the date and time for the annual meeting of the stockholders of Chris-Craft. Such meeting also named the Holiday Inn at Cortland, New York, where defendant operates a plant, as the place of such annual meeting of stockholders, and October 29, 1971, as the record date for stockholders eligible to vote at such meeting.

"As a result of such by-law amendment adopted pursuant to statutory authority and action taken thereunder, defendant's stockholders, to whom notice was mailed on November 8, will have received thirty days notice of the annual meeting, as now scheduled under the terms of the applicable by-law, as amended on October 18, 1971, a change accomplished more than sixty days before the date of annual meeting fixed in the pertinent by-law before its amendment, namely January 11, 1972.

"Plaintiffs contend, however, that notwithstanding defendant's compliance with the Delaware law having to do with the fixing and noticing of annual meetings, the obvious design of defendant's management has been to impede the efforts of plaintiffs and others aligned with them to solicit votes in favor of a rival slate of directors and thus constitutes a use of corporate machinery to retain present management's control and not for a purpose beneficial to the defendant and its stockholders.

"In support of such contention, plaintiffs cite Condec Corporation v. Lunkenheimer Company, 43 Del. Ch. 353, 230 A.2d 769, a case in which the plaintiffs clear majority of Lunkenheimer stock was sought to be nullified by the simple expedient of the issuance by Lunkenheimer's management of 75,000 additional shares, thereby apparently breaking Condec's majority after it had legitimately acquired control. The Court caused such improperly issued stock, authorized, as it were, at the last minute, to be cancelled. Likewise the attempted freezing out of a minority stockholder interest by a majority is actionable, Bennett v. Breuil Petroleum Corp., 34 Del. Ch. 6, 99 A.2d 236. Compare McPhail v. L.S. Starrett Co., 257 F.2d 388 (1st Cir.).

"Defendant for its part does not concede that its management has taken advantage of a change in the Delaware Corporation Law in order to blunt the attack on it of a substantial group of dissident stockholders, arguing, in addition to its contentions about weather conditions in Cortland, New York in January, as opposed to early December, that the normal delays in delivery of notices to stockholders resulting from Christmas mails supply another reason for choosing a pre-Christmas date for the annual meeting. Finally, defendant argues that as a result of its current financial records having been put in final form in connection with the settlement of a lawsuit in New York, defendant's final financial statements through August 31, 1971, are now ready for the December meeting but would be stale by mid-January."]

It will be seen that the Chancery Court considered all of the reasons stated by management as business reasons for changing the date of the meeting; but that those reasons were rejected by the Court below in making the following findings:

> I am satisfied, however, in a situation in which present management has disingenuously resisted the production of a list of its stockholders to plaintiffs or their confederates and has otherwise turned a deaf ear to plaintiffs' demands about a change in management designed to lift defendant from its present business doldrums, management has seized on a relatively new section of the Delaware Corporation Law for the purpose of cutting down on the amount of time which would otherwise have been available to plaintiffs and others for the waging of a proxy battle. Management thus enlarged the scope of its scheduled October 18 directors' meeting to include the by-law amendment in controversy after the stockholders committee had filed with the S.E.C. its intention to wage a proxy fight on October 16.
>
> Thus plaintiffs reasonably contend that because of the tactics employed by management (which involve the hiring of two established proxy solicitors as well as a refusal to produce a list of its stockholders, coupled with its use of an amendment to the Delaware Corporation Law to limit the time for contest), they are given little chance, because of the exigencies of time, including that required to clear material at the S.E.C., to wage a successful proxy fight between now and December 8. . . .

In our view, those conclusions amount to a finding that management has attempted to utilize the corporate machinery and the Delaware Law for the purpose of perpetuating itself in office; and, to that end, for the purpose of obstructing the legitimate efforts of dissident stockholders in the exercise of their rights to undertake a proxy contest against management. These are inequitable purposes, contrary to established principles of corporate democracy. The advancement by directors of the by-law date of a stockholders' meeting, for such purposes, may not be permitted to stand. Compare *Condec Corporation v. Lunkenheimer Company*, Del. Ch., 230 A.2d 769 (1967).

When the by-laws of a corporation designate the date of the annual meeting of stockholders, it is to be expected that those who intend to contest the reelection of incumbent management will gear their campaign to the by-law date. It is not to be expected that management will attempt to advance that date in order to obtain an inequitable advantage in the contest.

Management contends that it has complied strictly with the provisions of the new Delaware Corporation Law in changing the by-law date. The answer to that contention, of course, is that inequitable action does not become permissible simply because it is legally possible.

Management relies upon American Hardware Corp. v. Savage Arms Corp., 37, Del. Ch. 10, 135 A.2d 725, aff'd 37 Del. Ch. 59, 136 A.2d 690 (1957). That case is inapposite for two reasons: it involved an effort by stockholders, engaged in a proxy contest, to have the stockholders' meeting adjourned and the period for the proxy contest enlarged; and there was no finding there of inequitable action on the part of management. We agree with the rule of *American Hardware* that, in the absence of fraud or inequitable conduct, the date for a stockholders' meeting and notice thereof, duly established under the by-laws, will not be enlarged by judicial interference at the request of dissident stockholders solely because of the circumstance of a proxy contest. That, of course, is not the case before us.

We are unable to agree with the conclusion of the Chancery Court that the Stockholders' application for injunctive relief here was tardy and came too late. The stockholders learned of the action of management unofficially on Wednesday, October 27, 1971; they filed this action on Monday, November 1, 1971. Until management changed the date of the meeting, the stockholders had no need of judicial assistance in that connection. There is no indication of any prior warning of management's intent to take such action; indeed, it appears that an attempt was made by management to conceal its action as long as possible. Moreover, stockholders may not be charged with the duty of anticipating inequitable action by management, and of seeking anticipatory injunctive relief to foreclose such action simply because the new Delaware Corporation Law makes such inequitable action legally possible.

Accordingly, the judgment below must be reversed and the cause remanded, with instructions to nullify the December 8 date as a meeting date for stockholders; to reinstate January 11, 1972, as the sole date of the next annual meeting of the stockholders of the corporation; and to take such other proceedings and action as may be consistent herewith regarding the stock record closing date and any other related matters.

WOLCOTT, Chief Justice (dissenting):

I do not agree with the majority of the Court in its disposition of this appeal. The plaintiff stockholders concerned in this litigation have, for a considerable period of time, sought to obtain control of the defendant corporation. These attempts took various forms.

In view of the length of time leading up to the immediate events which caused the filing of this action, I agree with the Vice Chancellor that the application for injunctive relief came too late.

I would affirm the judgment below on the basis of the Vice Chancellor's opinion.

Blasius Industries, Inc. v. Atlas Corp.
564 A.2d 651 (Del. Ch. 1988)

ALLEN, Chancellor.

...

[This suit] challenges the validity of board action taken at a telephone meeting of December 31, 1987 that added two new members to Atlas' seven member board. That action was taken as an immediate response to the delivery to Atlas by Blasius the previous day of a form of stockholder consent that, if joined in by holders of a majority of Atlas' stock, would have increased the board of Atlas from seven to fifteen members and would have elected eight new members nominated by Blasius.

As I find the facts of this first case, they present the question whether a board acts consistently with its fiduciary duty when it acts, in good faith and with appropriate care, for the primary purpose of preventing or impeding an unaffiliated majority of shareholders from expanding the board and electing a new majority. For the reasons that follow, I conclude that, even though defendants here acted on their view of the corporation's interest and not selfishly, their December 31 action constituted an offense to the relationship between corporate directors and shareholders that has traditionally been protected in courts of equity. As a consequence, I conclude that the board action taken on December 31 was invalid and must be voided. . . .

I.

Blasius Acquires a 9% Stake in Atlas.

Blasius is a new stockholder of Atlas. It began to accumulate Atlas shares for the first time in July, 1987. On October 29, it filed a Schedule 13D with the Securities Exchange Commission disclosing that, with affiliates, it then owed 9.1% of Atlas' common stock. It stated in that filing that it intended to encourage management of Atlas to consider a restructuring of the Company or other transaction to enhance shareholder values. It also disclosed that Blasius was exploring the feasibility of obtaining control of Atlas, including instituting a tender offer or seeking "appropriate" representation on the Atlas board of directors.

Blasius has recently come under the control of two individuals, Michael Lubin and Warren Delano, who after experience in the commercial banking industry, had, for a short time, run a venture capital operation for a small investment banking firm. Now on their own, they apparently came to control Blasius with the assistance of Drexel Burnham's well noted junk bond mechanism. Since then, they have made several attempts to effect leveraged buyouts, but without success. . . .

The prospect of Messrs. Lubin and Delano involving themselves in Atlas' affairs, was not a development welcomed by Atlas' management. Atlas had a new CEO, defendant Weaver, who had, over the course of the past year or so, overseen a business restructuring of a sort. Atlas had sold three of its five divisions. It had just announced (September 1, 1987) that it would close its once important domestic uranium operation. The goal was to focus the Company on its gold mining business. By October, 1987, the structural changes to do this had been largely accomplished. Mr. Weaver was perhaps thinking that the restructuring that had occurred should be given a chance to produce benefit before another restructuring (such as Blasius had alluded to in its Schedule 13D filing) was attempted, when he wrote in his diary on October 30, 1987:

> 13D by Delano & Lubin came in today. Had long conversation w/MAH & Mark Golden [of Goldman, Sachs] on issue. All agree we must dilute these people down by the acquisition of another Co. w/stock, or merger or something else.

The Blasius Proposal of a Leverage Recapitalization or Sale.

Immediately after filing its 13D on October 29, Blasius' representatives sought a meeting with the Atlas management. Atlas dragged its feet. A meeting was arranged for December 2, 1987 following the regular meeting of the Atlas board. . . .

At that meeting, Messrs. Lubin and Delano suggested that Atlas engage in a leveraged restructuring and distribute cash to shareholders. In such a transaction, which is by this date a commonplace form of transaction, a corporation typically raises cash by sale of assets and significant borrowings and makes a large one time cash distribution to shareholders. The shareholders are typically left with cash and an equity interest in a smaller, more highly leveraged enterprise. Lubin and Delano gave the outline of a leveraged recapitalization for Atlas as they saw it.

Immediately following the meeting, the Atlas representatives expressed among themselves an initial reaction that the proposal was infeasible. On December 7, Mr. Lubin sent a letter detailing the proposal. In general, it proposed the following: (1) an initial special cash dividend to Atlas' stockholders in an aggregate amount equal to (a) $35 million, (b) the aggregate proceeds to Atlas from the exercise of option warrants and stock options, and (c) the proceeds from the sale or disposal of all of Atlas' operations that are not related to its continuing minerals operations; and (2) a special non-cash dividend to Atlas' stockholders of an aggregate $125 million principal amount of 7% Secured Subordinated Gold-Indexed Debentures. The funds necessary to pay the initial cash dividend were to principally come from (i) a "gold loan" in the amount of $35,625,000, repayable over a three to five year period and secured by 75,000 ounces of gold at a price of $475 per ounce, (ii) the proceeds from the sale of the discontinued Brockton Sole and Plastics and Ready-Mix Concrete businesses, and (iii) a then expected January, 1988 sale of uranium to the Public Service Electric & Gas Company....

The proposal met with a cool reception from management. On December 9, Mr. Weaver issued a press release expressing surprise that Blasius would suggest using debt to accomplish what he characterized as a substantial liquidation of Atlas at a time when Atlas' future prospects were promising. He noted that the Blasius proposal recommended that Atlas incur a high debt burden in order to pay a substantial one time dividend consisting of $35 million in cash and $125 million in subordinated debentures. Mr. Weaver also questioned the wisdom of incurring an enormous debt burden amidst the uncertainty in the financial markets that existed in the aftermath of the October crash.

Blasius attempted on December 14 and December 22 to arrange a further meeting with the Atlas management without success. During this period, Atlas provided Goldman Sachs with projections for the Company. Lubin was told that a further meeting would await completion of Goldman's analysis. A meeting after the first of the year was proposed.

The Delivery of Blasius' Consent Statement.

On December 30, 1987, [Atlas received the Blasius consent, which proposed to shareholders that they expand the board from 7 to 15 and add 8 new members identified in the consent. It also proposed the adoption of a precatory resolution encouraging restructuring or sale of the Company.] The reaction was immediate. Mr. Weaver conferred with Mr. Masinter, the Company's outside counsel and a director, who viewed the consent as an attempt to take control of the Company. They decided to call an emergency meeting of the board, even though a regularly scheduled meeting was to occur only one week hence, on January 6, 1988. The point of the emergency meeting was to act on their conclusion (or to seek to have the board act on their conclusion) "that we should add at least one and probably two directors to the board . . ." (Tr. 85, Vol. II). A quorum of directors, however, could not be arranged for a telephone meeting that day. A telephone meeting was held the next day. At that meeting, the board voted to amend the bylaws to increase the size of the board from seven to nine and appointed John M. Devaney and Harry J. Winters, Jr. to fill those newly created positions. Atlas' Certificate of Incorporation creates staggered terms for directors; the terms to which Messrs. Devaney and Winters were appointed would expire in 1988 and 1990, respectively.

The Motivation of the Incumbent Board in Expanding the Board and Appointing New Members.

In increasing the size of Atlas' board by two and filling the newly created positions, the members of the board realized that they were thereby precluding the holders of a majority of the Company's shares from placing a majority of new directors on the board through Blasius' consent solicitation, should they want to do so. Indeed the evidence establishes that that was the principal motivation in so acting.

The conclusion that, in creating two new board positions on December 31 and electing Messrs. Devaney and Winters to fill those positions the board was principally motivated to prevent or delay the shareholders from possibly placing a majority of new members on the board, is critical to my analysis. . . . If the board in fact was not so motivated, but rather had taken action completely independently of the consent solicitation, which merely had an incidental impact upon the possible effectuation of any action authorized by the shareholders, it is very unlikely that such action would be subject to judicial nullification. *See, e.g., Frantz Manufacturing Company v. EAC Industries*, Del. Supr., 501 A.2d 401, 407 (1985); *Moran v. Household International, Inc.*, Del. Ch., 490 A.2d 1059, 1080, *aff'd*, Del. Supr., 500 A.2d 1346 (1985). The board, as a general matter, is under no fiduciary obligation to suspend its active management of the firm while the consent solicitation process goes forward. . . .

In this setting, I conclude that, while the addition of these qualified men would, under other circumstances, be clearly appropriate as an independent step, such a step was in fact taken in order to impede or preclude a majority of the shareholders from effectively adopting the course proposed by Blasius. . . .

The January 6 Rejection of the Blasius Proposal.

On January 6, the board convened for its scheduled meeting. At that time, it heard a full report from its financial advisor concerning the feasibility of the Blasius restructuring proposal. The Goldman Sachs presentation included a summary of five year cumulative cash flows measured against a base case and the Blasius proposal, an analysis of Atlas' debt repayment capacity under the Blasius proposal, and pro forma income and cash flow statements for a base case and the Blasius proposal, assuming prices of $375, $475 and $575 per ounce of gold.

After completing that presentation, Goldman Sachs concluded with its view that if Atlas implemented the Blasius restructuring proposal (i) a severe drain on operating cash flow would result, (ii) Atlas would be unable to service its long-term debt and could end up in bankruptcy, (iii) the common stock of Atlas would have little or no value, and (iv) since Atlas would be unable to generate sufficient cash to service its debt, the debentures contemplated to be issued in the proposed restructuring could have a value of only 20% to 30% of their face amount. . . .

The board then voted to reject the Blasius proposal. . . .

II.

Plaintiff attacks the December 31 board action as a selfishly motivated effort to protect the incumbent board from a perceived threat to its control of Atlas. Their conduct is said to constitute a violation of the principle, applied in such cases as *Schnell v. Chris Craft Industries*, Del. Supr., 285 A.2d 437 (1971), that directors hold legal powers subjected to a supervening duty to exercise such powers in good faith pursuit of what they reasonably believe to be in the corporation's interest. . . .

Defendants, of course, contest every aspect of plaintiffs' claims. They claim the formidable protections of the business judgment rule. *See, e.g., Aronson v. Lewis*, Del. Supr., 473 A.2d 805 (1983); *Grobow v. Perot*, Del. Supr., 539 A.2d 180 (1988); *In re J.P. Stevens & Co., Inc. Shareholders Litigation*, Del. Ch., 542 A.2d 770 (1988).

They say that, in creating two new board positions and filling them on December 31, they acted without a conflicting interest (since the Blasius proposal did not, in any event, challenge *their* places on the board), they acted with due care (since they well knew the persons they put on the board and did not thereby preclude later consideration of the recapitalization), and they acted in good faith (since they were motivated, they say, to protect the shareholders from the threat of having an impractical, indeed a dangerous, recapitalization program foisted upon them). Accordingly, defendants assert there is no basis to conclude that their December 31 action constituted any violation of the duty of the fidelity that a director owes by reason of his office to the corporation and its shareholders.

Moreover, defendants say that their action was fair, measured and appropriate, in light of the circumstances. Therefore, even should the court conclude that some level of substantive review of it is appropriate under a legal test of fairness, or under the intermediate level of review authorized by *Unocal Corp. v. Mesa Petroleum Co.*, Del. Supr., 493 A.2d 946 (1985), defendants assert that the board's decision must be sustained as valid in both law and equity.

III.

One of the principal thrusts of plaintiffs' argument is that, in acting to appoint two additional persons of their own selection, including an officer of the Company, to the board, defendants were motivated not by any view that Atlas' interest (or those of its shareholders) required that action, but rather they were motivated improperly, by selfish concern to maintain their collective control over the Company. That is, plaintiffs say that the evidence shows there was no policy dispute or issue that really motivated this action, but that asserted policy differences were pretexts for entrenchment for selfish reasons. If this were found to be factually true, one would not need to inquire further. The action taken would constitute a breach of duty. *Schnell v. Chris Craft Industries*, Del. Supr., 285 A.2d 437 (1971); *Guiricich v. Emtrol Corp.*, Del. Supr., 449 A.2d 232 (1982). . . .

On balance, I cannot conclude that the board was acting out of a self-interested motive in any important respect on December 31. I conclude rather that the board saw the "threat" of the Blasius recapitalization proposal as posing vital policy differences between itself and Blasius. It acted, I conclude, in a good faith effort to protect its incumbency, not selfishly, but in order to thwart implementation of the recapitalization that it feared, reasonably, would cause great injury to the Company.

The real question the case presents, to my mind, is whether, in these circumstances, the board, even if it *is* acting with subjective good faith (which will typically, if not always, be a contestable or debatable judicial conclusion), may validly act for the principal purpose of preventing the shareholders from electing a majority of new directors. The question thus posed is not one of intentional wrong (or even negligence), but one of authority *as between the fiduciary and the beneficiary* (not simply legal authority, *i.e.*, as between the fiduciary and the world at large).

IV.

It is established in our law that a board may take certain steps—such as the purchase by the corporation of its own stock—that have the effect of defeating a threatened change in corporate control, when those steps are taken advisedly, in good faith pursuit of a corporate interest, and are reasonable in relation to a threat to legitimate corporate interests posed by the proposed change in control. *See Unocal Corp. v. Mesa Petroleum Co.*, Del. Supr., 493 A.2d 946 (1985); *Kors v. Carey*, Del. Ch., 158 A.2d 136 (1960); *Cheff v. Mathes*, Del. Supr., 199 A.2d 548 (1964); *Kaplan v. Goldsamt*, Del. Ch., 380 A.2d 556 (1977). Does this rule—that the reasonable exercise of good faith and due care generally validates, in equity, the exercise of legal authority even if the act has an entrenchment effect—apply to action designed for the primary purpose of interfering with the effectiveness of a stockholder vote? Our authorities, as well as sound principles, suggest that the central importance of the franchise to the scheme of corporate governance, requires that, in this setting, that rule not be applied and that closer scrutiny be accorded to such transaction.

1. Why the deferential business judgment rule does not apply to board acts taken for the primary purpose of interfering with a stockholder's vote, even if taken advisedly and in good faith.

A. The question of legitimacy.

The shareholder franchise is the ideological underpinning upon which the legitimacy of directorial power rests. Generally, shareholders have only two protections against perceived inadequate business performance. They may sell their stock (which, if done in sufficient numbers, may so affect security prices as to create an incentive for altered managerial performance), or they may vote to replace incumbent board members.

It has, for a long time, been conventional to dismiss the stockholder vote as a vestige or ritual of little practical importance.[1] It may be that we are now witnessing the emergence of new institutional voices and arrangements that will make the stockholder vote a less predictable affair than it has been. Be that as it may, however, whether the vote is seen functionally as an unimportant formalism, or as an important tool of discipline, it is clear that it is critical to the theory that legitimates the exercise of power by some (directors and officers) over vast aggregations of property that they do not own. Thus, when viewed from a broad, institutional perspective, it can be seen that matters involving the integrity of the shareholder voting process involve consideration not present in any other context in which directors exercise delegated power.

B. Questions of this type raise issues of the allocation of authority as between the board and the shareholders.

The distinctive nature of the shareholder franchise context also appears when the matter is viewed from a less generalized, doctrinal point of view. From this point of view, as well, it appears that the ordinary considerations to which the business judgment rule originally responded are simply not present in the shareholder voting context.[2] That is, a decision by the board to act for the primary purpose of preventing the effectiveness of a shareholder vote inevitably involves the question who, as between the principal and the agent, has authority with respect to a

---

1. *See, e.g.,* E. Rostow, *To Whom and For What Ends Is Corporate Management Responsible,* in THE CORPORATION IN MODERN SOCIETY (E.S. Mason ed. 1959). The late Professor A.A. Berle once dismissed the shareholders' meeting as a "kind of ancient, meaningless ritual like some of the ceremonies that go with the mace in the House of Lords." Berle, ECONOMIC POWER AND THE FREE SOCIETY (1957), *quoted in* Balotti, Finkelstein, Williams, MEETINGS OF SHAREHOLDERS (1987) at 2.

2. Delaware courts have long exercised a most sensitive and protective regard for the free and effective exercise of voting rights. This concern suffuses our law, manifesting itself in various settings. For example, the perceived importance of the franchise explains the cases that hold that a director's fiduciary duty requires disclosure to shareholders asked to authorize a transaction of all material information in the corporation's possession, even if the transaction is not a self-dealing one. *See, e.g., Smith v. Van Gorkom,* Del. Supr., 488 A.2d 858 (1985); *In re Anderson Clayton Shareholders' Litigation,* Del. Ch., 519 A.2d 669, 675 (1986).

matter of internal corporate governance. That, of course, is true in a very specific way in this case which deals with the question who should constitute the board of directors of the corporation, but it will be true in every instance in which an incumbent board seeks to thwart a shareholder majority. A board's decision to act to prevent the shareholders from creating a majority of new board positions and filling them does not involve the exercise of *the corporation's power* over its property, or with respect to *its* rights or obligations; rather, it involves allocation, between shareholders as a class and the board, of effective power with respect to governance of the corporation. This need not be the case with respect to other forms of corporate action that may have an entrenchment effect — such as the stock buybacks present in *Unocal, Cheff* or *Kors v. Carey*. Action designed principally to interfere with the effectiveness of a vote inevitably involves a conflict between the board and a shareholder majority. Judicial review of such action involves a determination of the legal and equitable obligations of an agent towards his principal. This is not, in my opinion, a question that a court may leave to the agent finally to decide so long as he does so honestly and competently; that is, it may not be left to the agent's business judgment.

2. What rule does apply: per se invalidity of corporate acts intended primarily to thwart effective exercise of the franchise or is there an intermediate standard?

Plaintiff argues for a rule of *per se* invalidity once a plaintiff has established that a board has acted for the primary purpose of thwarting the exercise of a shareholder vote. Our opinions in *Canada Southern Oils, Ltd. v. Manabi Exploration Co.*, Del. Ch., 96 A.2d 810 (1953), and *Condec Corporation v. Lunkenheimer Company*, Del. Ch., 230 A.2d 769 (1967), could be read as support for such a rule of *per se* invalidity. . . .

In my view, our inability to foresee now all of the future settings in which a board might, in good faith, paternalistically seek to thwart a shareholder vote, counsels against the adoption of a *per se* rule invalidating, in equity, every board action taken for the sole or primary purpose of thwarting a shareholder vote, even though I recognize the transcending significance of the franchise to the claims to legitimacy of our scheme of corporate governance. It may be that some set of facts would justify such extreme action.[5] This, however, is not such a case.

---

5. Imagine the facts of *Condec* changed very slightly and coming up in today's world of corporate control transactions. Assume an acquiring company buys 25% of the target's stock in a small number of privately negotiated transactions. It then commences a public tender offer for 26% of the company stock at a cash price that the board, in good faith, believes is inadequate. Moreover, the acquiring corporation announces that it may or may not do a second-step merger, but if it does one, the consideration will be junk bonds that will have a value, when issued, in the opinion of its own investment banker, of no more than the cash being offered in the tender offer. In the face of such an offer, the board may have a duty to seek to protect the company's shareholders from the coercive effects of this inadequate offer. Assume, for purposes of the hypothetical, that neither newly amended Section 203, nor any defensive device

3. *Defendants have demonstrated no sufficient justification for the action of December 31 which was intended to prevent an unaffiliated majority of shareholders from effectively exercising their right to elect eight new directors.*

The board was not faced with a coercive action taken by a powerful shareholder against the interests of a distinct shareholder constituency (such as a public minority). It was presented with a consent solicitation by a 9% shareholder. Moreover, here it had time (and understood that it had time) to inform the shareholders of its views on the merits of the proposal subject to stockholder vote. The only justification that can, in such a situation, be offered for the action taken is that the board knows better than do the shareholders what is in the corporation's best interest. While that premise is no doubt true for any number of matters, it is irrelevant (except insofar as the shareholders wish to be guided by the board's recommendation) when the question is who should comprise the board of directors. The theory of our corporation law confers power upon directors as the agents of the shareholders; it does not create Platonic masters. It may be that the Blasius restructuring proposal was or is unrealistic and would lead to injury to the corporation and its shareholders if pursued. Having heard the evidence, I am inclined to think it was not a sound proposal. The board certainly viewed it that way, and that view, held in good faith, entitled the board to take certain steps to evade the risk it perceived. It could, for example, expend corporate funds to inform shareholders and seek to bring them to a similar point of view. *See, e.g., Hall v. Trans-Lux Daylight Picture Screen Corporation*, Del. Ch., 171 A. 226, 227 (1934); *Hibbert v. Hollywood Park, Inc.*, Del. Supr., 457 A.2d 339 (1982). But there is a vast difference between expending corporate funds to inform the electorate and exercising power for the primary purpose of foreclosing effective shareholder action. A majority of the shareholders, who were not dominated in any respect, could view the matter differently than did the board. If they do, or did, they are entitled to employ the mechanisms provided by the corporation law and the Atlas certificate of incorporation to advance that view. They are also entitled, in my opinion, to restrain their agents, the board, from acting for the principal purpose of thwarting that action.

---

available to the target specifically, offers protection. Assume that the target's board turns to the market for corporate control to attempt to locate a more fairly priced alternative that would be available to all shareholders. And assume that just as the tender offer is closing, the board locates an all cash deal for all shares at a price materially higher than that offered by the acquiring corporation. Would the board of the target corporation be justified in issuing sufficient shares to the second acquiring corporation to dilute the 51% stockholder down so that it no longer had a practical veto over the merger or sale of assets that the target board had arranged for the benefit of all shares? It is not necessary to now hazard an opinion on that abstraction. The case is clearly close enough, however, despite the existence of the *Condec* precedent, to demonstrate, to my mind at least, the utility of a rule that permits, in some extreme circumstances, an incumbent board to act in good faith for the purpose of interfering with the outcome of a contemplated vote. *See also American International Rent-A-Car, Inc. v. Cross, supra,* n.3.

NOTES AND QUESTIONS

1. **The deal.** Compare the competing plans for the Atlas business. The incumbent, Mr. Weaver, had a restructuring plan that included selling divisions and growing the gold portion of the business. How does the Lubin/Delano plan differ? In examining the difference, articulate what kind of bidder is Blasius and who provides their backing (and where you have seen a deal like this before). What kind of risks will each plan require taking?

2. **The path to control.** Lubin and Delano's plan to gain control in order to implement their financial plan is a little bit unusual and likely reflects a gap in the Atlas defenses, which can be spotted by those schooled in corporate law. This requires you to know enough corporate law to know who can amend the bylaws and how both parties sought to make use of that authority here. Why did Atlas only fill two seats?

3. **The legal standard.**

    a. **Review of prior knowledge.** This case has pedagogical value because the parties' allegations show the traditional space within which judicial review operates. It requires the court to address business judgment review, entire fairness, the enhanced scrutiny of *Unocal*, and whatever might be different about voting.

    b. **Compelling justification.** Compare how the Chancellor places this case in the ambit of *Unocal* and *Revlon* of just a few years before. There is mention of threat and *Unocal*, but the Chancellor goes beyond *Unocal* because voting is involved. Indeed, his statement about the franchise as "the ideological underpinning upon which the legitimacy of director power rests" continues to be quoted in a variety of contexts. Does this test suggest a more intrusive judicial review if voting is involved?

    c. **How much of an impact?** How much of a deterrence was this defensive tactic to Lubin/Delano's quest for control? Chancellor Allen notes that the fact that the plan was "to prevent or delay the shareholders from possibly placing a majority of new members on the board, is critical to my analysis." So, another way to ask this question is how much of a delay is involved? If Lubin and Delano had not been able to use the consent procedure in January, when would have been their next opportunity to get control of Atlas?

Unitrin, Inc. v. American General Corp.
651 A.2d 1361 (Del. Sup. Ct. 1995)

Before VEASEY, C.J., HOLLAND and BERGER, JJ.

HOLLAND, Justice.

[American General, Inc., the largest provider of home service insurance proposed a friendly acquisition of Unitrin, Inc., the third largest provider of that insurance. When rebuffed, American General issued a press release announcing an all-cash tender offer for all Unitrin shares. The offering price reflected a 30 percent premium over the pre-announcement value of Unitrin shares. One day later, Unitrin's board approved a poison pill, an advance notice bylaw, and in a special meeting the following week, voted to authorize a Repurchase Program for up to 10 million shares of its outstanding stock. The Unitrin board expressed its belief that "Unitrin's stock is undervalued in the market and that the expanded program will tend to increase the value of the shares that remain outstanding." Before the Repurchase Program began, Unitrin's directors collectively held approximately 23 percent of Unitrin's outstanding shares. Unitrin's certificate of incorporation already included a "shark-repellent" provision barring any business combination with a more-than-15 percent stockholder unless approved by a majority of continuing directors or by a 75 percent stockholder vote ("Supermajority Vote"). Unitrin's shareholder directors announced publicly that they would not participate in the Repurchase Program and that this would result in a percentage increase of ownership for them, as well as for any other shareholder who did not participate.

The Court of Chancery preliminarily enjoined Unitrin from making further repurchases on the ground that the Repurchase Program was a disproportionate response to the threat posed by American General's inadequate all cash for all shares offer, under the standard in *Unocal Corp. v. Mesa Petroleum Co.*, Del. Supr., 493 A.2d 946 (1985).]

This Court has concluded that the Court of Chancery erred in applying the proportionality review *Unocal* requires by focusing upon whether the Repurchase Program was an "unnecessary" defensive response. *See Paramount Communications, Inc. v. QVC Network, Inc.*, 637 A.2d at 45-46. The Court of Chancery should have directed its enhanced scrutiny: first, upon whether the Repurchase Program the Unitrin Board implemented was draconian, by being either preclusive or coercive; and second, if it was not draconian, upon whether it was within a range of reasonable responses to the threat American General's Offer posed. Consequently, the interlocutory preliminary injunctive judgment of the Court of Chancery is reversed. . . .

[Prior to addressing the Repurchase Program, the Court included some preliminary comments about corporate voting.] This Court has been and remains assiduous in its concern about defensive actions designed to thwart the essence of corporate democracy by disenfranchising shareholders. *Paramount Communications, Inc. v. QVC Network, Inc.*, Del. Supr., 637 A.2d 34, 42 n.11 (1994). *See also Stroud v. Grace*, Del. Supr., 606 A.2d 75 (1992). . . .

More recently, this Court stated: "we accept the basic legal tenets," set forth in *Blasius Indus., Inc. v. Atlas Corp.*, Del. Ch., 564 A.2d 651 (1988), that "[w]here boards of directors deliberately employ[] . . . legal strategies either to frustrate or completely disenfranchise a shareholder vote, . . . [t]here can be no dispute that such conduct violates Delaware law." *Stroud v. Grace*, 606 A.2d at 91. In *Stroud*, we concluded, however, that a *Blasius* analysis was inappropriate. We reached that conclusion because it could not be said "that the 'primary purpose' of the board's action was to interfere with or impede exercise of the shareholder franchise," and because the shareholders had a "full and fair opportunity to vote." *Stroud v. Grace*, 606 A.2d at 92.

This Court also specifically noted that boards of directors often interfere with the exercise of shareholder voting when an acquiror *launches both a proxy fight and a tender offer. Id.* at 92 n.3. We then stated that such action "necessarily invoked both *Unocal* and *Blasius*" because "both [tests] recognize the inherent conflicts of interest that arise when shareholders are not permitted free exercise of their franchise." *Id.* Consequently, we concluded that, "[i]n certain circumstances, [the judiciary] must recognize the special import of protecting the shareholders' franchise within *Unocal*'s requirement that any defensive measure be proportionate and 'reasonable in relation to the threat posed.'" *Id.* (citation omitted).

TAKEOVER STRATEGY, TENDER OFFER/PROXY CONTEST

We begin our examination of Unitrin's Repurchase Program mindful of the special import of protecting the shareholder's franchise within *Unocal's* requirement that a defensive response be reasonable and proportionate. *Stroud v. Grace*, 606 A.2d at 92. For many years the "favored attack of a [corporate] raider was stock acquisition followed by a proxy contest." *Unocal*, 493 A.2d at 957. Some commentators have noted that the recent trend toward tender offers as the preferable alternative to proxy contests appears to be reversing because of the proliferation of sophisticated takeover defenses. Lucian A. Bebchuk & Marcel Kahan, *A Framework for Analyzing Legal Policy Towards Proxy Contests*, 78 CAL. L. REV. 1071, 1134 (1990). In fact, the same commentators have characterized a return to proxy contests as "the only alternative to hostile takeovers to gain control against the will of the incumbent directors." *Id.*

The Court of Chancery, in the case *sub judice*, was obviously cognizant that the emergence of the "poison pill" as an effective takeover device has resulted in such a remarkable transformation in the market for corporate control that hostile bidders who proceed when such defenses are in place will usually "have to couple proxy contests with tender offers." Joseph A. Grundfest, *Just Vote No: A Minimalist Strategy for Dealing with Barbarians Inside the Gates*, 45 STAN. L. REV. 857, 858 (1993). The Court of Chancery concluded that Unitrin's adoption of a poison pill was a proportionate response to the threat its Board reasonably perceived from American General's Offer. Nonetheless, the Court of Chancery enjoined the additional defense of the Repurchase Program as disproportionate and "unnecessary."

[The Supreme Court distinguished shareholder voting on a merger when the supermajority vote had been triggered and shareholder voting outside of such a context, as in a proxy fight for election of directors. Its focus was on the later election, and it was critical of the Chancery Court's initial conclusion that the repurchase program would provide the same veto in an ordinary proxy contest as it would where a supermajority was required for a merger. The Court noted that even American General acknowledged] a less than 15% stockholder bidder need not proceed with acquiring shares to the extent that it would ever implicate the Supermajority Vote provision. In fact, it would be illogical for American General or any other bidder to acquire more than 15% of Unitrin's stock because that would not only trigger the poison pill, but also the constraints of 8 Del. C. §203. If American General were to initiate a proxy contest *before* acquiring 15% of Unitrin's stock, it would need to amass only 45.1% of the votes assuming a 90% voter turnout. If it commenced a tender offer at an attractive price contemporaneously with its proxy contest, it could seek to acquire 50.1% of the outstanding voting stock.

The record reflects that institutional investors own 42% of Unitrin's shares. Twenty institutions own 33% of Unitrin's shares. It is generally accepted that proxy contests have re-emerged with renewed significance as a method of acquiring corporate control because "the growth in institutional investment has reduced the dispersion of share ownership." Lucian A. Bebchuk & Marcel Kahan, *A Framework for Analyzing Legal Policy Towards Proxy Contests*, 78 CAL. L. REV. 1071, 1134 (1990). "Institutions are more likely than other shareholders to vote at all, more likely to vote against manager proposals, and more likely to vote for proposals by other shareholders." Bernard S. Black, *The Value of Institutional Investor Monitoring: The Empirical Evidence*, 39 UCLA L. REV. 895, 925 (1992). *See also* John Pound, *Shareholder Activism and Share Values: The Causes and Consequences of Countersolicitations Against Management Antitakeover Proposals*, 32 J.L. & ECON. 357, 368 (1989).

WITH SUPERMAJORITY VOTE AFTER REPURCHASE PROGRAM PROXY CONTEST APPEARS VIABLE

The assumptions and conclusions American General sets forth in this appeal for a different purpose are particularly probative with regard to the effect of the institutional holdings in Unitrin's stock. American General's two predicate assumptions are a 90% stockholder turnout in a proxy contest and a bidder with 14.9% holdings, i.e., the maximum the bidder could own to avoid triggering the poison pill and the Supermajority Vote provision. American General also calculated the votes available to the Board or the bidder with and without the Repurchase Program:

Assuming no Repurchase [Program], the [shareholder directors] would hold 23%, the percentage collectively held by the [directors] and the bidder would be 37.9%, and the percentage of additional votes available to either side would be 52.1%.

Assuming the Repurchase [Program] is fully consummated, the [shareholder directors] would hold 28%, the percentage collectively held by the bidder and the [directors] would be 42.9%, and the percentage of additional votes available to either side would be 47.1%.

American General then applied these assumptions to reach conclusions regarding the votes needed for the 14.9% stockholder bidder to prevail: first, in an election of directors; and second, in the subsequent vote on a merger. With regard to the election of directors, American General made the following calculations:

Assume 90% stockholder turnout. To elect directors, a plurality must be obtained; assuming no abstentions and only two competing slates, one must obtain the votes of 45.1% of the shares.

The percentage of additional votes the bidder needs to win is: 45.1% − 14.9% (maximum the bidder could own and avoid the poison pill, §203 and supermajority) = 30.2%.

A merger requires approval of a majority of outstanding shares, 8 *Del. C.* §251, not just a plurality. In that regard, American General made the following calculations:

Assume 90% stockholder turnout. To approve a merger, one must obtain the favorable vote of 50.1% of the shares.

The percentage of additional votes the bidder needs to win is 50.1% − 14.9% = 35.2%.

Consequently, to prevail in a proxy contest with a 90% turnout, the percentage of additional shareholder votes a 14.9% shareholder bidder needs to prevail is 30.2% for directors and 35.2% in a subsequent merger. The record reflects that institutional investors held 42% of Unitrin's stock and 20 institutions held 33% of the stock. Thus, American General's own assumptions and calculations in the record support the Unitrin Board's argument that "it is hard to imagine a company more readily susceptible to a proxy contest concerning a pure issue of dollars."[33]

The conclusion of the Court of Chancery that the Repurchase Program would make a proxy contest for Unitrin a "theoretical" possibility that American General could not realistically pursue may be erroneous and appears to be inconsistent with its own earlier determination that the "repurchase program strengthens the position of the Board of Directors to defend against a hostile bidder, but will not deprive the public

---

33. That institutions held a high percentage of Unitrin's stock is not as significant as the fact that the relatively concentrated percentage of stockholdings would facilitate a bidder's ability to communicate the merits of its position.

stockholders of the 'power to influence corporate direction through the ballot.'" Even a complete implementation of the Repurchase Program, in combination with the pre-existing Supermajority Vote provision, would not appear to have a preclusive effect upon American General's ability successfully to marshal enough shareholder votes to win a proxy contest. *Accord Shamrock Holdings, Inc. v. Polaroid Corp.*, Del. Ch., 559 A.2d 278 (1989). A proper understanding of the record reflects that American General or any other 14.9% shareholder bidder could apparently win a proxy contest with a 90% turnout.

The key variable in a proxy contest would be the merit of American General's issues, not the size of its stockholdings. *Moran v. Household Int'l, Inc.*, Del. Supr., 500 A.2d 1346, 1355 (1985). If American General presented an attractive price as the cornerstone of a proxy contest, it could prevail, irrespective of whether the shareholder directors' absolute voting power was 23% or 28%. In that regard, the following passage from the Court of Chancery's Opinion is poignant:

> Harold Hook, the Chairman of American General, admitted in his deposition that the repurchase program is not a "show stopper" because the directors that own stock will act in their own best interest if the price is high enough. (Hook Dep. at 86-87.) Fayez Sarofim, one of the Unitrin directors that holds a substantial number of shares, testified that "everything has a price parameter."

Consequently, a proxy contest apparently remained a viable alternative for American General to pursue notwithstanding Unitrin's poison pill, Supermajority Vote provision, and a fully implemented Repurchase Program.

SUBSTANTIVE COERCION, AMERICAN GENERAL'S THREAT

This Court has recognized "the prerogative of a board of directors to resist a third party's unsolicited acquisition proposal or offer." *Paramount Communications, Inc. v. QVC Network, Inc.*, Del. Supr., 637 A.2d 34, 43 n.13 (1994). The Unitrin Board did not have unlimited discretion to defeat the threat it perceived from the American General Offer by any draconian means available. *See Unocal*, 493 A.2d at 955. Pursuant to the *Unocal* proportionality test, the nature of the threat associated with a particular hostile offer sets the parameters for the range of permissible defensive tactics. Accordingly, the purpose of enhanced judicial scrutiny is to determine whether the Board acted reasonably in "relation . . . to the threat which a particular bid allegedly poses to stockholder interests." *Mills Acquisition Co. v. Macmillan, Inc.*, Del. Supr., 559 A.2d 1261, 1288 (1989).

"The obvious requisite to determining the reasonableness of a defensive action is a clear identification of the nature of the threat." *Paramount Communications, Inc. v. Time, Inc.*, Del. Supr., 571 A.2d 1140, 1154 (1990). Courts, commentators and litigators have attempted to catalogue the threats posed by hostile tender offers. *Id.* at 1153. Commentators have categorized three types of threats:

> (i) *opportunity loss* . . . [where] a hostile offer might deprive target shareholders of the opportunity to select a superior alternative offered by target management [or, we would add, offered by another bidder]; (ii) *structural coercion*, . . . the risk that disparate treatment of non-tendering shareholders might distort shareholders' tender decisions; and (iii) *substantive coercion*, . . . the risk that shareholders will mistakenly accept an underpriced offer because they disbelieve management's representations of intrinsic value.

Id. at 1153 n.17 (quoting Ronald J. Gilson & Reinier Kraakman, Delaware's Intermediate Standard for Defensive Tactics: Is There Substance to Proportionality Review?, 44 BUS. LAW. 247, 267 (1989)).

This Court has held that the "inadequate value" of an all cash for all shares offer is a "legally cognizable threat." *Paramount Communications, Inc. v. Time, Inc.*, 571 A.2d at 1153. In addition, this Court has specifically concluded that inadequacy of value is *not* the only legally cognizable threat from "an all-shares, all-cash offer at a price below what a target board in good faith deems to be the present value of its shares." *Id.* at 1152-53. In making that determination, this Court held that the Time board of directors had reasonably determined that inadequate value was not the only threat that Paramount's all cash for all shares offer presented, but was *also* reasonably concerned that the Time stockholders might tender to Paramount in ignorance or based upon a mistaken belief, *i.e.*, yield to substantive coercion.

The record reflects that the Unitrin Board perceived the threat from American General's Offer to be a form of substantive coercion. The Board noted that Unitrin's stock price had moved up, on higher than normal trading volume, to a level slightly below the price in American General's Offer. The Board also noted that some Unitrin shareholders had publicly expressed interest in selling at or near the price in the Offer. The Board determined that Unitrin's stock was undervalued by the market at current levels and that the Board considered Unitrin's stock to be a good long-term investment. The Board also discussed the speculative and unsettled market conditions for Unitrin stock caused by American General's public disclosure. The Board concluded that a Repurchase Program would provide additional liquidity to those stockholders who wished to realize short-term gain, and would provide enhanced value to those stockholders who wished to maintain a long-term investment. Accordingly, the Board voted to authorize the Repurchase Program for up to ten million shares of its outstanding stock on the open market.

In *Unocal*, this Court noted that, pursuant to Delaware corporate law, a board of directors' duty of care required it to respond actively to protect the corporation and its shareholders from perceived harm. *Unocal*, 493 A.2d at 955. In *Unocal*, when describing the proportionality test, this Court listed several examples of concerns that boards of directors should consider in evaluating and responding to perceived threats. Unitrin's Board deemed three of the concerns exemplified in *Unocal* relevant in deciding to authorize the Repurchase Program: first, the inadequacy of the price offered; second, the nature and timing of American General's Offer; and third, the basic stockholder interests at stake, including those of short-term speculators whose actions may have fueled the coercive aspect of the Offer at the expense of the long-term investor. *Unocal,* 493 A.2d at 955-56. *Accord Ivanhoe Partners v. Newmont Mining Corp.,* Del. Supr., 535 A.2d 1334, 1341-42 (1987).

The record appears to support Unitrin's argument that the Board's justification for adopting the Repurchase Program was its reasonably perceived risk of substantive coercion, *i.e.,* that Unitrin's shareholders might accept American General's inadequate Offer because of "ignorance or mistaken belief" regarding the Board's assessment of the long-term value of Unitrin's stock. . . .

RANGE OF REASONABLENESS, PROPER PROPORTIONALITY BURDEN

. . . The Court of Chancery applied an incorrect legal standard when it ruled that the Unitrin decision to authorize the Repurchase Program was disproportionate because it was "unnecessary." The Court of Chancery stated:

> Given that the Board had already implemented the poison pill and the advance notice provision, the repurchase program was unnecessary to protect Unitrin from an inadequate bid.

In *QVC*, this Court recently elaborated upon the judicial function in applying enhanced scrutiny, citing *Unocal* as authority, albeit in the context of a sale of control and the target board's consideration of one of several reasonable alternatives. That teaching is nevertheless applicable here:

> a court applying enhanced judicial scrutiny should be deciding whether the directors made *a reasonable* decision, not *a perfect* decision. If a board selected one of several reasonable alternatives, a court should not second guess that choice even though it might have decided otherwise or subsequent events may have cast doubt on the board's determination. Thus, courts will not substitute their business judgment for that of the directors, but will determine if the directors' decision was, on balance, within a range of reasonableness. *See Unocal,* 493 A.2d at 955-56; *Macmillan,* 559 A.2d at 1288; *Nixon,* 626 A.2d at 1378.

Paramount Communications, Inc. v. QVC Network, Inc., Del. Supr., 637 A.2d 34, 45-46 (1994) (emphasis in original). The Court of Chancery did not determine whether the Unitrin Board's decision to implement the Repurchase Program fell within a "range of reasonableness."

The record reflects that the Unitrin Board's adoption of the Repurchase Program was an apparent recognition on its part that all shareholders are not alike. This Court has stated that distinctions among types of shareholders are neither inappropriate nor irrelevant for a board of directors to make, *e.g.*, distinctions between long-term shareholders and short-term profit-takers, such as arbitrageurs, and their stockholding objectives. *Id.* In *Unocal* itself, we expressly acknowledged that "a board may reasonably consider the basic stockholder interests at stake, including those of short term speculators, whose actions may have fueled the coercive aspect of the offer at the expense of the long term investor." *Unocal*, 493 A.2d at 955-56. *See also Ivanhoe Partners v. Newmont Mining Corp.*, Del. Supr., 535 A.2d 1334, 1341-42 (1987).

The Court of Chancery's determination that the Unitrin Board's adoption of the Repurchase Program was unnecessary constituted a substitution of its business judgment for that of the Board, contrary to this Court's "range of reasonableness" holding in *Paramount Communications, Inc. v. QVC Network, Inc.*, 637 A.2d at 45-46. . . .

In assessing a challenge to defensive actions by a target corporation's board of directors in a takeover context, this Court has held that the Court of Chancery should evaluate the board's overall response, including the justification for each contested defensive measure, and the results achieved thereby. Where all of the target board's defensive actions are inextricably related, the principles of *Unocal* require that such actions be scrutinized collectively as a unitary response to the perceived threat. *Gilbert v. El Paso Co.*, Del. Supr., 575 A.2d 1131, 1145 (1990). Thus, the Unitrin Board's adoption of the Repurchase Program, in addition to the poison pill, must withstand *Unocal*'s proportionality review. *Id.*

In *Unocal*, the progenitor of the proportionality test, this Court stated that the board of directors' "duty of care extends to protecting the corporation and its [stockholders] from perceived harm whether a threat originates from third parties or other shareholders." *Unocal*, 493 A.2d at 955. We then noted that "such powers are not absolute." *Id.* Specifically, this Court held that the board "does not have unbridled discretion to defeat any perceived threat by any Draconian means available." *Id.* Immediately following those observations in *Unocal*, when exemplifying the parameters of a board's authority in adopting a restrictive stock repurchase, this Court held that "the directors may not have acted *solely* or *primarily* out of a desire to perpetuate themselves in office" (preclusion of the stockholders' corporate franchise right to vote) and, further, that the stock repurchase plan must not be inequitable. *Unocal*, 493 A.2d at 955 (emphasis added).

If a defensive measure is not draconian, however, because it is not either coercive or preclusive, the *Unocal* proportionality test requires the focus of enhanced judicial scrutiny to shift to "the range of reasonableness." *Paramount Communications, Inc. v. QVC Network, Inc.*, Del. Supr., 637 A.2d 34, 45-46 (1994). Proper and proportionate defensive responses are intended and permitted to thwart perceived threats. When a corporation is not for sale, the board of directors is the defender of the metaphorical medieval corporate bastion and the protector of the corporation's shareholders. The fact that a defensive action must not be coercive or preclusive does not prevent a board from responding defensively before a bidder is at the corporate bastion's gate.[38]

The *ratio decidendi* for the "range of reasonableness" standard is a need of the board of directors for latitude in discharging its fiduciary duties to the corporation and its shareholders when defending against perceived threats. The concomitant requirement is for judicial restraint. Consequently, if the board of directors' defensive response is not draconian (preclusive or coercive) and is within a "range of reasonableness," a court must not substitute its judgment for the board's. *Paramount Communications, Inc. v. QVC Network, Inc.*, 637 A.2d at 45-46.

THIS CASE, REPURCHASE PROGRAM PROPORTIONATE WITH POISON PILL

In this case, the initial focus of enhanced judicial scrutiny for proportionality requires a determination regarding the defensive responses by the Unitrin Board to American General's offer. We begin, therefore, by ascertaining whether the Repurchase Program, as an addition to the poison pill, was draconian by being either coercive or preclusive.

A limited nondiscriminatory self-tender, like some other defensive measures, may thwart a current hostile bid, but is not inherently coercive. Moreover, it does not necessarily preclude future bids or proxy contests by stockholders who decline to participate in the repurchase. *Cf. AC Acquisitions Corp. v. Anderson, Clayton & Co.*, Del. Ch., 519 A.2d 103 (1986) (enjoining a coercive self-tender and restructuring plan). A selective repurchase of shares in a public corporation on the market, such as Unitrin's Repurchase Program, generally does not discriminate because all shareholders can voluntarily realize the same benefit by selling. See Larry E. Ribstein, *Takeover Defenses and the Corporate Contract*, 78 GEO. L.J. 71, 129-31 (1989). See also Michael Bradley & Michael Rosenzweig, *Defensive Stock Repurchases*, 99 HARV. L. REV. 1377 (1986). Here, there is no showing on this record that the Repurchase Program was coercive.

We have already determined that the record in this case appears to reflect that a proxy contest remained a viable (if more problematic) alternative for American General even if the Repurchase Program were to be completed in its entirety. Nevertheless, the Court of Chancery

---

38. This Court's choice of the term draconian in *Unocal* was a recognition that the law affords boards of directors substantial latitude in defending the perimeter of the corporate bastion against perceived threats. Thus, continuing with the medieval metaphor, if a board reasonably perceives that a threat is on the horizon, it has broad authority to respond with a panoply of individual or combined defensive precautions, e.g., staffing the barbican, raising the drawbridge, and lowering the portcullis. Stated more directly, depending upon the circumstances, the board may respond to a reasonably perceived threat by adopting individually or sometimes in combination: advance notice by-laws, supermajority voting provisions, shareholder rights plans, repurchase programs, etc.

must determine whether Unitrin's Repurchase Program would only inhibit American General's ability to wage a proxy fight and institute a merger or whether it was, in fact, preclusive[39] because American General's success would either be mathematically impossible or realistically unattainable. If the Court of Chancery concludes that the Unitrin Repurchase Program was not draconian because it was not preclusive, one question will remain to be answered in its proportionality review: whether the Repurchase Program was within a range of reasonableness?

The Court of Chancery found that the Unitrin Board reasonably believed that American General's Offer was inadequate and that the adoption of a poison pill was a proportionate defensive response. Upon remand, in applying the correct legal standard to the factual circumstances of this case, the Court of Chancery may conclude that the implementation of the limited Repurchase Program was also within a range of reasonable additional defensive responses available to the Unitrin Board. In considering whether the Repurchase Program was within a range of reasonableness the Court of Chancery should take into consideration whether: (1) it is a statutorily authorized form of business decision which a board of directors may routinely make in a non-takeover context; (2) as a defensive response to American General's Offer it was limited and corresponded in degree or magnitude to the degree or magnitude of the threat (*i.e.*, assuming the threat was relatively "mild," was the response relatively "mild?"); (3) with the Repurchase Program, the Unitrin Board properly recognized that all shareholders are not alike, and provided immediate liquidity to those shareholders who wanted it.

Conclusion

We hold that the Court of Chancery correctly determined that the *Unocal* standard of enhanced judicial scrutiny applied to the defensive actions of the Unitrin defendants in establishing the poison pill and implementing the Repurchase Program. The Court of Chancery's finding, that the Repurchase Program was a disproportionate defensive response, was based on faulty factual predicates, unsupported by the record. This error was exacerbated by its application of an erroneous legal standard of "necessity" to the Repurchase Program as a defensive response.

The interlocutory judgment of the Court of Chancery, in favor of American General, is REVERSED. This matter is REMANDED for further proceedings in accordance with this opinion.

---

39. The record in this case, when properly understood, appears to reflect that the Repurchase Program's effect on a proxy contest would not be preclusive. *Accord Moran v. Household Int'l, Inc.*, Del. Supr., 500 A.2d 1346, 1355 (1985). If the stockholders of Unitrin are "displeased with the action of their elected representatives, the powers of corporate democracy" remain available as a viable alternative to turn the Board out in a proxy contest. *Unocal*, 493 A.2d at 959.

NOTES AND QUESTIONS

1. **What's happened to *Blasius*?** The defensive tactics in this case clearly relate to shareholder voting, either in the context of voting for directors or voting on a merger that has been proposed by directors. But *Blasius* is hardly mentioned; the court says that it accepts the basic legal tenets of *Blasius*, but that the case did not apply where the primary purpose was not to interfere or impede with the shareholder vote. While the court observes that interference with shareholder voting where an acquirer launches both a proxy fight and a tender offer "necessarily involves both *Unocal* and *Blasius*," what follows is then entirely a *Unocal* analysis. Note, however, how the court's approach to the *Unocal* factors seems to shape how it decides when *Blasius* is not to apply: Because institutional investors own 42 percent of the outstanding stock, the court posits that a bidder that had already acquired a 14.9 percent toe-hold (assuming none of those shares came from institutional investors, which seems a somewhat heroic assumption), would need only attract 30.2 percent more of the shares (assuming a 90 percent turnout) to win a proxy fight to replace directors. Since shareholders retained sufficient voting power to challenge the incumbent board, which the court phrases here as lacking a "preclusive" effect in the language from the *Unocal* line of cases, the primary purpose has not been met. In a subsequent case applying *Unocal*, the court cited a footnote from *Carmody*, excerpted in Chapter 7, that distinguished defensive tactics that would "delay but not prevent" voting as opposed to stopping the proxy contest altogether. *See* Versata Enterprises, Inc. v. Selectica, Inc. 5 A.3d 586, 604 (Del. 2010), (quoting from *Carmody* n.17). Can defensive tactics against voting survive so long as some avenue for an "effective" vote remains?

2. **How many voting (or selling) avenues for shareholders must be available?** At one point in the opinion, not reproduced here, the court observes a difference among the parties as to whether it is permissible to leave potential bidders with a proxy battle as the sole avenue of acquiring an entity. The court's answer to this question seems to be yes, even if the corporation has a staggered board (not discussed in this case) that will mean the only avenue for control will be a campaign at two annual meetings. The result is that the court here was not concerned about the possible preclusion of a shareholder voting on an interested merger via the Supermajority Provision, so long as a proxy fight alternative was available. Contrast this base to *Blasius* where the defensive tactic closed off the shareholder's opportunity to vote only until the next annual meeting. The court here did not view it as dispositive that the Repurchase Program would possibly increase the burden of a potential bidder (in an election to replace directors) from having to acquire 58 percent of the nonaffiliated voters to 64 percent of the nonaffiliated voters since institutional shareholders could be expected to respond to the merits of the offer. Compare this approach to

the poison pill of the previous chapter when courts have permitted a board to not redeem the pill so long as some voting channel remains open to replace the board and enable that new board to redeem the pill, which in turn would permit the shareholders to sell their shares into a tender offer.

3. **Are the shareholders smart or dumb?** The opinion actually contains two contrasting views of shareholders that are difficult to reconcile. In the part of the opinion just discussed, the court points to a large portion of institutional shareholding (42 percent of the stock, with a group of 20 institutions owning 33 percent themselves) and affirms the conclusion, "it is hard to imagine a company more readily susceptible to a proxy contest concerning a pure issue of dollars." 651 A.2d at 1383. Yet just a few paragraphs later, it finds sufficient showing of the "threat" prong of the *Unocal* test where there is substantive coercion because of "shareholder ignorance or mistaken belief" presumably of these same shareholders. The court describes the adoption of the Repurchase Program as based on the board's apparent recognition "that all shareholders are not alike." Does that mean that directors can simultaneously rely on the dumbness of some shareholders to insert a powerful defensive tactic such as a poison pill, but defend their decision not to redeem the pill by arguing that the smart shareholders will overcome that hurdle via a proxy fight to replace the board who will then redeem the poison pill?

4. **Shareholder voting versus shareholder selling.** The *Unitrin* opinion seems to move the judicial treatment of defensive tactics into one test that absorbs both defenses to shareholder voting and to shareholder selling, but the court has not yet addressed whether the two contexts are the same. Shareholder voting is explicitly covered in the Delaware corporations code, whereas shareholder selling is left to the background rules of property law. It is possible that a future court might conclude that there is a different vulnerability when shareholders sell than when they vote and that directors have more room to invoke defensive tactics in the selling context, but that would seem to reopen the separate *Blasius* avenue that the court seems to have worked to cut off.

5. **The evolution of the *Unocal* test.** The opinion marks the further refinement of the two parts of the *Unocal* test. As to the threat, the court reaffirms the breadth of threat that will satisfy this prong. As to proportionality, the court's treatment suggests two points of evolution. First, "draconian" has taken on an increased importance as the indicator that will trigger the more intensive judicial review. In a subsequent case the court has focused on "realistically unattainable" as the standard for "preclusive" and used the "delay but not prevent" standard discussed in the previous note to define that term. *See* Versata Enterprises, Inc. v. Selectica, Inc., 5 A.3d 586 (Del. 2010). If a tactic does not come within "draconian," for which preclusive and coercive become illustrations, then judicial review under *Revlon*, the *Unitrin* court tells us, should be whether the directors' conduct was in a range of reasonableness. This phrasing of the second prong

suggests something closer to business judgment rule deference for the second prong of *Unocal* if draconian has not been met.

MM Companies, Inc. v. Liquid Audio, Inc.
813 A.2d 1118 (Del. Sup. Ct. 2003)

HOLLAND, Justice:

This is an expedited appeal from a final judgment entered by the Court of Chancery. That final judgment permitted an incumbent board of directors to adopt defense measures which changed the size and composition of the board's membership. The record reflects that those defensive actions were taken for the primary purpose of impeding the shareholders' right to vote effectively in an impending election for successor directors. We have concluded that the judgment of the Court of Chancery must be reversed. . . .

BACKGROUND FACTS

Liquid Audio is a publicly traded Delaware corporation, with its principal place of business in Redwood City, California. Liquid Audio's primary business consists of providing software and services for the digital transmission of music over the Internet. MM is a publicly traded Delaware corporation with its principal place of business in New York, New York. As of October 2002, MM was part of a group that collectively held slightly over 7% of Liquid Audio's common stock.

For more than a year, MM has sought to obtain control of Liquid Audio. On October 26, 2001, MM sent a letter to the Liquid Audio board of directors indicating its willingness to acquire the company at approximately $3 per share. Liquid Audio's board rejected MM's offer as inadequate, after an analysis of the offer and consultation with its investment banker, Broadview International LLC ("Broadview").

Liquid Audio's bylaws provide for a staggered board of directors that is divided into three classes. Only one class of directors is up for election in any given year. The effect is to prevent an insurgent from obtaining control of the company in under two years.

From November 2001 until August 2002, the Liquid Audio board of directors consisted of five members divided into three classes. Class I had two members (defendants Flynn and Imbler), whose terms expire in 2003; Class II had one member (defendant Winblad), whose term expires in 2004; and Class III had two members (defendants Kearby and Doig), whose terms expired in 2002. Defendants Flynn, Doig and Imbler were not elected to the Board by the stockholders of Liquid Audio. They were appointed to the Board by the directors of Liquid Audio to fill vacancies on the Board.

In October 2001, prior to the appointment of defendants Doig and Imbler to the Board, MM requested the Liquid Audio board to call a special meeting of the company's stockholders to consider filling the existing vacancies on the Board and to consider other proposals to be presented to the stockholders. On October 24, 2001, the Liquid Audio board issued a press release which stated that it had denied MM's request to call a special meeting because the Board believed that under the Liquid Audio bylaws stockholders are not permitted to call special meetings. Thereafter, the Board appointed defendants Doig and Imbler to the Liquid Audio board of directors.

MM's Various Actions

On November 13, 2001, MM announced its intention to nominate its own candidates for the two seats on Liquid Audio's board of directors that were up for election at the next annual meeting.

[In the ensuing months, MM took various steps to seek to take control of Liquid Audio, including filing a §220 action seeking access to a list of Liquid Audio shareholders.]

On June 10, 2002, MM filed proxy materials with the Securities and Exchange Commission ("SEC") and commenced soliciting proxies for a shareholder meeting Liquid Audio planned to have on July 1, 2002. In addition to proposing two nominees for the Board, MM's proxy statement included a takeover proposal to increase the size of the Board by an additional four directors and to fill those positions with its nominees. As outlined in its initial proxy materials, MM's takeover proposal sought to expand the Board from five members to nine. If MM's two directors were elected and its four proposed directors were also placed on the Board, MM would control a majority of the Board.

Alliance Merger

On June 13, 2002, Liquid Audio announced a stock-for-stock merger transaction with Alliance Entertainment Corp. ("Alliance"). This announcement came three days after MM mailed its proxy statement and other materials to the stockholders of Liquid Audio, and one day before the scheduled Court of Chancery hearing in connection with the Section 220 complaint. In addition to announcing the merger, the Liquid Audio board also announced that: the July 1, 2002, meeting would be postponed; a special meeting of stockholders of Liquid Audio would be held sometime in the future to vote upon the merger; and, if the merger received the requisite stockholder and regulatory approval, the merger would "close in the Fall of 2002." Based upon this announcement, the annual meeting was postponed indefinitely by the Liquid Audio board. . . .

After Liquid Audio announced that the annual meeting would be postponed indefinitely, MM filed an amended complaint, seeking an order of the Court of Chancery directing Liquid Audio to hold the annual meeting as soon as possible....

After expedited discovery, a trial was held on July 15, 2002. The Court of Chancery ordered that the annual meeting of Liquid Audio's shareholders occur on September 26, 2002. The record date for the meeting was August 12, 2002.

BOARD ADDS TWO DIRECTORS

By the middle of August 2002, it was apparent that MM's nominees, Holtzman and Mitarotonda, would be elected at the annual meeting, to serve in place of the two incumbent nominees, as members of the Liquid Audio board. On August 23, 2002, Liquid Audio announced that the Board had amended the bylaws to increase the size of the Board to seven members from five members. The Board also announced that defendants James D. Somes and Judith N. Frank had been appointed to fill the newly created directorships. Defendant Somes was appointed to serve as a Class II member of the Board and defendant Frank was appointed to serve as a Class I member of the Board. After the Board expanded from five directors to seven, MM revised its proxy statement to note that its proposal to add four directors, if successful, would have resulted in a board with eleven directors, instead of nine.

MM CHALLENGES BOARD EXPANSION

On August 26, 2002, MM filed its initial lawsuit challenging the Board's decision to add two directors. In the initial complaint, MM alleged that the Board expansion interfered with MM's ability to solicit proxies in favor of its two nominees for election to the Liquid Audio board at the annual meeting. In support of this claim, MM alleged that "some stockholders would believe that electing two members of a seven-member board, rather than two members of a five-member board, would not be worthwhile, and, thus, such stockholders simply would not vote."

At the September 26, 2002, annual meeting, the two directors proposed by MM, Holtzman and Mitarotonda, were elected to serve as directors of the Board. Liquid Audio's stockholders, however, did not approve MM's takeover proposals that would have expanded the Board and placed MM's four nominees on the Board. The stockholders' vote on both issues was consistent with the recommendation of Institutional Investor Services ("ISS"), a proxy voting advisory service, which had recommended that the stockholders vote in favor of MM's two nominees, but recommended against stockholders voting to give MM outright and immediate control of the Board.

Following the election of MM's two nominees to the Liquid Audio board of directors at the annual meeting, MM filed an amended lawsuit, challenging the Board's appointment of directors Somes and Frank. In the amended complaint, MM alleged that the expansion of the Liquid Audio board, its timing, and the Board's appointment of two new directors violated the principles of *Blasius* and *Unocal*. According to MM, that action frustrated MM's attempt to gain a "substantial presence" on the Board for at least one year and guaranteed that Liquid Audio's management will have control of, or a substantial presence on, the Board for at least two years.

BOARD'S PRIMARY PURPOSE: IMPEDE EFFECTIVE VOTE

The expedited trial was held by the Court of Chancery, as scheduled. . . .

[The testimony of each member of the Board] reflects that the Director Defendants were concerned that incumbent directors Winblad and Imbler would resign from the Liquid Audio board if MM's nominees were elected to the board at the annual meeting, which would result in MM gaining control of the Board. The record also reflects that the timing of the Director Defendants' decision to expand the Board was to accomplish its primary purpose: to minimize the impact of the election of MM's nominees to the Board. The Court of Chancery's post-trial ruling from the bench states:

> The board's concern was that given the past acrimonious relationship between MM and Liquid Audio, a relationship characterized by litigation, if MM's two nominees were elected, the possibility of continued acrimony might cause one or more of the current board members to resign. If one director resigned, that would deadlock the board two-to-two; and if two directors resigned, then MM would gain control on a two-to-one basis. Either scenario could jeopardize the pending merger, which the incumbent board favored. That was the *primary* reason (emphasis added).

After making that factual determination, the Court of Chancery recognized the effect of the Board's action in changing the size and composition of its membership immediately prior to the election of directors at the annual meeting:

> By adding two additional directors, the board foreclosed the result that it feared: The possibility of a deadlock or of MM taking control of the board. The reason is that even if MM's two nominees were elected at the 2002 annual meeting, the current directors would still constitute a majority of five. The result of the board's action was to *diminish the influence of any nominees of MM* that were elected, at least in numerical terms.

Thus, based upon the evidence presented at trial, including an assessment of the witnesses' credibility, the Court of Chancery concluded that the Director Defendants amended the bylaws to expand the Board from five to seven, appointed two additional members of the Board, and timed those actions for the *primary purpose* of diminishing the influence of MM's nominees, if they were elected at the annual meeting.

CORPORATE GOVERNANCE PRINCIPLES

The most fundamental principles of corporate governance are a function of the allocation of power within a corporation between its stockholders and its board of directors. The stockholders' power is the right to vote on specific matters, in particular, in an election of directors. The power of managing the corporate enterprise is vested in the shareholders' duly elected board representatives. Accordingly, while these "fundamental tenets of Delaware corporate law provide for a separation of control and ownership," the stockholder franchise has been characterized as the "ideological underpinning" upon which the legitimacy of the directors managerial power rests. [*Blasius* at 659.]

Maintaining a proper balance in the allocation of power between the stockholders' right to elect directors and the board of directors' right to manage the corporation is dependent upon the stockholders' unimpeded right to vote effectively in an election of directors. This Court has repeatedly stated that, if the stockholders are not satisfied with the management or actions of their elected representatives on the board of directors, the power of corporate democracy is available to the stockholders to replace the incumbent directors when they stand for re-election. Consequently, two decades ago, this Court held:

> The Courts of this State will not allow the wrongful subversion of corporate democracy by manipulation of the corporate machinery or by machinations under the cloak of Delaware law. Accordingly, careful judicial scrutiny will be given a situation in which the right to vote for the election of successor directors has been *effectively frustrated* and denied. [Giuricich v. Emtrol Corp., 449 A.2d 232, 239 (Del. 1982).]

This Court and the Court of Chancery have remained assiduous in carefully reviewing any board actions designed to interfere with or impede the effective exercise of corporate democracy by shareholders, especially in an election of directors. [*Unitrin* at 1378.]

CORPORATE GOVERNANCE REVIEW STANDARDS

The "defining tension" in corporate governance today has been characterized as "the tension between deference to directors' decisions and the scope of judicial review." The appropriate standard of judicial review is dispositive of which party has the burden of proof as any litigation proceeds from stage to stage until there is a substantive determination on the merits. Accordingly, identification of the correct analytical framework is essential to a proper judicial review of challenges to the decision-making process of a corporation's board of directors. [*Unitrin* at 1374.] . . .

Chapter 8. Is a Defense Affecting Voting Different? 313

In *Blasius*, Chancellor Allen set forth a cogent explanation of why judicial review under the deferential traditional business judgment rule standard is inappropriate when a board of directors acts for the *primary* purpose of impeding or interfering with the effectiveness of a shareholder vote, especially in the specific context presented in *Blasius* of a contested election for directors:

> [T]he ordinary considerations to which the business judgment rule originally responded are simply not present in the shareholder voting context. That is, a decision by the board to act for the primary purpose of preventing the effectiveness of a shareholder vote inevitably involves the question who, as between the principal and the agent, has authority with respect to a matter of internal corporate governance. That, of course, is true in a very specific way in this case which deals with the question who should constitute the board of directors of the corporation, but it will be true in every instance in which an incumbent board seeks to thwart a shareholder majority. A board's decision to act to prevent the shareholders from creating a majority of new board positions and filling them does not involve the exercise of the corporation's power over its property, or with respect to its rights or obligations; rather, it involves allocation, between shareholders as a class and the board, of effective power with respect to governance of the corporation. . . . Action designed principally to interfere with the effectiveness of a vote inevitably involves a conflict between the board and shareholder majority. Judicial review of such action involves a determination of the legal and equitable obligations of an agent towards his principal. This is not, in my opinion, a question that a court may leave to the agent finally to decide so long as he does so honestly and competently; that is, it may not be left to the agent's business judgment.

In *Blasius*, the Chancellor did not adopt a rule of *per se* invalidity once a plaintiff has established that a board of directors has acted for the primary purpose of interfering with or impeding the effective exercise of a shareholder vote. Instead, the Chancellor concluded that such situations required enhanced judicial scrutiny, pursuant to which the board of directors "bears the heavy burden of demonstrating a compelling justification for such action."

In *Blasius*, the Chancellor then applied that compelling justification standard of enhanced judicial review in examining a board's action to expand its size in the context of a contested election of directors, exactly what the Liquid Audio board did in this case. In *Blasius*, notwithstanding the fact that the incumbent board of directors believed in good faith that the leveraged recapitalization proposed by the plaintiff was ill-advised and less valuable than the company's business plan, Chancellor Allen explained why the incumbent board of directors' good faith beliefs were not a proper basis for interfering with the stockholder franchise in a contested election for successor directors.

> The only justification that can be offered for the action taken is that the board knows better than do the shareholders what is in the corporation's best interest. While that premise is no doubt true for any number of matters, it is irrelevant (except insofar as

the shareholders wish to be guided by the board's recommendation) when the question is who should comprise the board.... It may be that the Blasius restructuring proposal was or is unrealistic and would lead to injury to the corporation and its shareholders if pursued.... The board certainly viewed it in that way, and that view, held in good faith, entitled the board to take certain steps to evade the risk it perceived. It could, for example, expend corporate funds to inform shareholders and seek to bring them to a similar point of view. But there is a vast difference between expending corporate funds to inform the electorate and exercising power for the primary purpose of foreclosing effective shareholder action. A majority of shareholders, who were not dominated in any respect, could view the matter differently than did the board. If they do, or did, they are entitled to employ the mechanisms provided by the corporation law and the Atlas certificate of incorporation to advance that view.

In *Blasius*, the Chancellor set aside the board's action to expand the size of its membership for the primary purpose of impeding and interfering with the effectiveness of a shareholder vote in a contested election for directors. In this case, not only did the Liquid Audio board of directors take similar action in expanding the size of its membership and appointing two new directors to fill those positions, but it took that action for the same *primary* purpose.

COMPELLING JUSTIFICATION WITHIN *UNOCAL*

The *Blasius* compelling justification standard of enhanced judicial review is based upon accepted and well-established legal tenets. This Court and the Court of Chancery have recognized the substantial degree of congruence between the rationale that led to the *Blasius* "compelling justification" enhanced standard of judicial review and the logical extension of that rationale *within* the context of the *Unocal* enhanced standard of judicial review. Both standards recognize the inherent conflicts of interest that arise when a board of directors acts to prevent shareholders from effectively exercising their right to vote either contrary to the will of the incumbent board members generally or to replace the incumbent board members in a contested election.

In *Gilbert*, we held that a reviewing court must apply the *Unocal* standard of review whenever a board of directors adopts any defensive measure "in response to some threat to corporate policy and effectiveness which touches upon issues of control."[Gilbert v. El Paso Co., 575 A.2d 1131, 1144 (Del. 1990).] Later, in *Stroud*, this Court acknowledged that board action interfering with the exercise of the shareholder franchise often arises during a hostile contest for control when an acquiror launches both a proxy fight and a tender offer. [Stroud v. Grace, 606 A.2d 75, 92 n.3 Del. 1992).] Accordingly, in *Stroud*, we held that "such action necessarily invoked both *Unocal* and *Blasius*."

In *Stroud*, we emphasized, however, that the *Blasius* and *Unocal* standards of enhanced judicial review ("tests") are *not* mutually exclusive. In

Stroud, we then explained why our holding in *Gilbert* did not render *Blasius* and its progeny meaningless:

> In certain circumstances, a court must recognize the special import of protecting the shareholders' franchise within *Unocal's* requirement that any defensive measure be proportionate and "reasonable in relation to the threat posed." A board's unilateral decision to adopt a defensive measure touching "upon issues of control" that purposefully disenfranchises its shareholders is strongly suspect under *Unocal*, and cannot be sustained without a "compelling justification."

Thus, the same circumstances must be extant before the *Blasius* compelling justification enhanced standard of judicial review is required to sustain a board's action either independently, in the absence of a hostile contest for control, or within the *Unocal* standard of review when the board's action is taken as a defensive measure. The "compelling justification" standard set forth in *Blasius* is applied independently or within the *Unocal* standard only where "the primary purpose of the board's action is to interfere with or impede exercise of the shareholder franchise and the shareholders are not given a full and fair opportunity to vote" effectively. Accordingly, this Court has noted that the non-deferential *Blasius* standard of enhanced judicial review, which imposes upon a board of directors the burden of demonstrating a compelling justification for such actions, is rarely applied either independently or within the *Unocal* standard of review.

In *Unitrin*, for example, although the board's action in adopting a repurchase program was a defensive measure that implicated the shareholders' franchise and called for an application of the *Unocal* standard of review, it did not require the board to demonstrate a compelling justification for that action. In *Unitrin*, the primary purpose of the repurchase program was not to interfere with or impede the shareholders' right to vote; the shareholders' right to vote effectively remained extant; and, in particular, we noted that the shareholders retained sufficient voting power to challenge the incumbent board by electing new directors with a successful proxy contest.

In this case, however, the Court of Chancery was presented with the ultimate defensive measure touching upon an issue of control. It was a defensive action taken by an incumbent board of directors for the primary purpose of interfering with and impeding the effectiveness of the shareholder franchise in electing successor directors. Accordingly, the incumbent board of directors had the burden of demonstrating a compelling justification for that action to withstand enhanced judicial scrutiny *within* the *Unocal* standard of reasonableness and proportionality.

Unocal Required Compelling Justification

This case presents a paragon of when the compelling justification standard of *Blasius* must be applied within *Unocal*'s requirement that any defensive measure be proportionate and reasonable in relation to the threat posed. The *Unocal* standard of review applies because the Liquid Audio board's action was a "defensive measure taken in response to some threat to corporate policy and effectiveness which touches upon issues of control." The compelling justification standard of *Blasius* also had to be applied *within* an application of the *Unocal* standard to that specific defensive measure because the primary purpose of the Board's action was to interfere with or impede the effective exercise of the shareholder franchise in a contested election for directors.

The Court of Chancery properly decided to examine the Board's defensive action to expand from five to seven members and to appoint two new members in accordance with the *Unocal* standard of enhanced judicial review. Initially, the Court of Chancery concluded that defensive action was not preclusive or coercive. If a defensive measure is not draconian, because it is neither coercive nor preclusive, proportionality review under *Unocal* requires the focus of enhanced judicial scrutiny to shift to the range of reasonableness.

After the Court of Chancery determined that the Board's action was not preclusive or coercive, it properly proceeded to determine whether the Board's action was reasonable and proportionate in relation to the threat posed. Under the circumstances presented in this case, however, the Court of Chancery did not "recognize the special [importance] of protecting the shareholder's franchise within *Unocal*'s requirement that any defensive measure be proportionate and reasonable in relation to the threat posed." Since the Court of Chancery had already concluded that the *primary* purpose of the Liquid Audio board's defensive measure was to interfere with or impede an effective exercise of the shareholder's franchise in a contested election of directors, the Board had the burden of demonstrating a compelling justification for that action.

When the *primary purpose* of a board of directors' defensive measure is to interfere with or impede the effective exercise of the shareholder franchise in a contested election for directors, the board must first demonstrate a compelling justification for such action as a condition precedent to any judicial consideration of reasonableness and proportionately. As this case illustrates, such defensive actions by a board need not actually prevent the shareholders from attaining any success in seating one or more nominees in a contested election for directors and the election contest need not involve a challenge for outright control of the board of directors. To invoke the *Blasius* compelling justification standard of review *within* an application of the *Unocal* standard of review, the defensive actions of the board only need to be taken for the primary purpose of interfering with or impeding the effectiveness of the stockholder vote in a contested election for directors.

BOARD EXPANSION INVALID

The record reflects that the primary purpose of the Director Defendants' action was to interfere with and impede the effective exercise of the stockholder franchise in a contested election for directors. The Court of Chancery concluded that the Director Defendants amended the bylaws to provide for a board of seven and appointed two additional members of the Board for the primary purpose of diminishing the influence of MM's two nominees on a five-member Board by eliminating either the possibility of a deadlock on the board or of MM controlling the Board, if one or two Director Defendants resigned from the Board. That defensive action by the Director Defendants compromised the essential role of corporate democracy in maintaining the proper allocation of power between the shareholders and the Board, because that action was taken in the context of a contested election for successor directors. Since the Director Defendants did not demonstrate a compelling justification for that defensive action, the bylaw amendment that expanded the size of the Liquid Audio board, and permitted the appointment of two new members on the eve of a contested election, should have been invalidated by the Court of Chancery.

One of the most venerable precepts of Delaware's common law corporate jurisprudence is the principle that "inequitable action does not become permissible simply because it is legally possible."[*Schnell v. Chris-Craft* at 439.] At issue in this case is not the validity generally of either a bylaw that permits a board of directors to expand the size of its membership or a board's power to appoint successor members to fill board vacancies. In this case, however, the incumbent Board timed its utilization of these otherwise valid powers to expand the size and composition of the Liquid Audio board for the primary purpose of impeding and interfering with the efforts of the stockholders' power to effectively exercise their voting rights in a contested election for directors. As this Court held more than three decades ago, "these are inequitable purposes, contrary to established principles of corporate democracy... and may not be permitted to stand."[*Schnell v. Chris Craft*, 285 A.2d 437, 439 (Del. 1971)]

NOTES AND QUESTIONS

1. Whither *Blasius*? We learn from this case that the compelling justification standard of *Blasius* is to be applied *within* an application of the *Unocal* standard. The Court of Chancery had concluded in this case that defensive action was not preclusive or coercive. Under *Unitrin*, if a defensive measure is not draconian, because it is neither coercive nor preclusive, proportionality review under *Unocal* requires the focus of enhanced judicial scrutiny to shift to the range of reasonableness. In the Court's view, "to invoke the *Blasius* compelling justification standard of review *within* an application of the *Unocal* standard of review, the defensive actions of the board only need to be taken for the primary purpose of interfering with or impeding the effectiveness of the stockholder vote in a contested election for directors."

2. Determining primary purpose. The court here distinguishes *Unitrin* as not triggering *Blasius*, "In *Unitrin*, the primary purpose of the repurchase program was not to interfere with or impede the shareholders' right to vote; the shareholders' right to vote effectively remained extant; and, in particular, we noted that the shareholders retained sufficient voting power to challenge the incumbent board by electing new directors with a successful proxy contest." To what extent have we returned to *Schnell*? Do the cases since *Unocal* provide any clarity as to when the *Schnell* standard will be applied?

9 FINANCE FOUNDATION FOR VALUATION

A. INTRODUCTION

In some acquisition contexts, such as the appraisal proceeding discussed in Chapter 3, valuation is a specific prerequisite to a legal proceeding. Other times, such as in judicial review of whether directors have met their fiduciary duty under *Revlon* to obtain the highest value in a sale or in a judicial evaluation of defensive tactics or deal protection devices, valuation may be involved a bit more indirectly. But beyond these specific questions, a transactional lawyer needs to understand the basics of valuation in order to perform a strategic and advising role at a sophisticated level.

This chapter focuses on the Discounted Cash Flow (DCF) valuation method, which is drawn from finance theory. The discussion which follows is embedded in how finance theory has evolved over the last 50 years. Deal comparables and company comparables methods, as well as other valuation theories, may also appear in a financial and legal discussion.

Weinberger v. UOP, Inc., a 1983 appraisal decision by the Delaware Supreme Court, was an important fulcrum in the development of the law's approach to valuation. 457 A.2d 701. Until that time, Delaware (and many other states) followed the "Delaware block method" of valuing a company. This was a mechanistic formula that required a judge to determine separate values of the company—e.g., asset value, market value, and earnings value; to assign a percentage to each of the three methods (so their sum added up to 100 percent); and then to do a weighted average calculation to come up with the valuation number. Because this method excluded "other generally accepted techniques used in the financial community and the courts," the Supreme Court said "it is now clearly outmoded." 457 A.2d at 712. Instead, the court accepted "proof of value by any techniques or methods which are generally considered acceptable in the financial community and otherwise admissible in court and consistent with the merger statute." *Id.* at 713.

Valuation is still more of an art than a science, so your aim here should be to understand the key value drivers and likely ways that the financial process may be distorted or reflect assumptions by one of the parties that are not likely to bear close scrutiny. Keep in mind, too, that this valuation necessarily is in an acquisition context, when the deal itself is expected to produce additional value, so that it will usually be necessary to value the target (and bidder) as standalone companies and then as part of an integrated enterprise. This increased value of a target, given changes sought in the acquisition, will set the maximum price that a rational bidder could offer without destroying the wealth of its own shareholders.

B. A PRIMER ON FINANCIAL THEORY UNDERLYING THE DISCOUNTED CASH FLOW METHOD OF VALUATION

The Capital Assets Pricing Model (CAPM), first developed by financial economists in the mid-twentieth century, posits return and risk as the two key components for investors in valuing capital assets, which can also be applied to companies in an acquisition setting. Return is fairly straightforward, referring to what an investor receives in exchange for the amount put into the venture. The expectation is that rational investors will pay more for higher returns and less for lower returns in comparing various investments open to them. In an acquisition setting, as well as for other investments, what matters to the investor is the return going forward, or expected return. Past returns may be an indicator of what returns may be in the future, but in and of themselves, they are not determinative of the value of a company going forward. Of course, the future necessarily is wrapped in uncertainty, so that return in CAPM's expected return is a weighted average of the expected returns under all the possible states of the world multiplied by the expected probability for that particular state of the world. Thus, if a particular enterprise, Investment A for our discussion, expected a return of $60 in good times, $30 in medium times, and a loss of $30 in bad times, and each had a one-third chance of occurring, the expected value of that investment would be $60(.33) + $30(.33) − $30(.33), or $20 + $10 − $10, for an expected value of $20.

The meaning of risk, as used in financial theory, may not be as intuitive for you. It is used to describe the variance of the actual returns from the expected return, which, as just described, is a weighted average. Two different investments can have the same expected return but a much different variance under the different states of the world. For example,

B. A Primer on Financial Theory

consider Investment B with an expected return of $90 in good times, $30 in medium times and a loss of $60 in bad times, again with a one-third chance of each occurring. The expected return of that investment would be $90(.33) + $30(.33) − $60(.33), or $30 + $10 − $20, for an expected value of $20. This sum is the same as before in Investment A, but you should be able to see that the variance (over a range from making $90 to losing $60) is much greater. CAPM posits that, all else being equal, an investor would prefer the investment with the same return but less risk.

To these core concepts of return and risk, one additional element is the impact of diversification and portfolio theory. Risk, or variance from the expected return, can be divided into two components: systematic risk and unsystematic risk. Systematic refers to the variance in the return of the investment or company that can be attributed to systematic or market-based factors that affect all stocks, not just this particular investment. Unsystematic risk is firm-specific, the part of the variance that can be attributed to factors specific to this particular investment and not affecting investments or companies as a whole. Investors will care about variance from either source, but it turns out that they can reduce the unsystematic risk to close to zero by diversifying their portfolio, i.e., splitting it between companies that do better or worse in offsetting economic times. For example, you could take half your portfolio and put it in PeaceCo and the other half in WarCo and thereby smooth out the variance that would occur if you owned just one company over an economic cycle that included equal periods of war and peace. Similarly, a law practice focused on issuance of securities will tend to perform opposite to what one's bankruptcy practice might do in different parts of the economic cycle. A firm equally divided between the two could get the same expected return but without the variance that would occur if the practice was limited to just one specialty. Portfolio theory has shown that a relatively small number of investments (as few as 20) can reduce unsystematic risk to a very small amount. Such investments are available through a mutual fund where the costs are relatively small, a fraction of one percent of the investment. Since such diversification is easily available to remove almost all of this unsystematic risk, investors cannot expect that they will receive any kind of market premium for bearing such risk, so that the focus on valuation is on systematic risk and the return that must be offered to persuade investors to take such risk.

From this foundational assumption that these two elements, expected return and systematic risk, will determine value, economists can express (and compare) various possible portfolio investments in a graph in which return is measured on the vertical axis and risk along the horizontal axis. In Figure 9-1, Investment I has a return of 13 and a variance of 14. Any investment with *both* a higher return and a lower variance (the quadrant above and to the left of I) would definitely be preferable to I. Any investment in the quadrant below and to the right of I would be less desirable. For the other two quadrants, the division of portfolios better and worse than I would

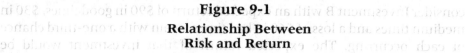

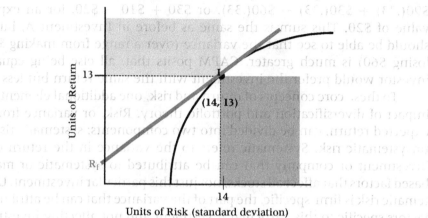

turn on the tradeoff of return for risk (how many additional units of return would be required for taking on an additional unit of risk?).

Apart from investing in various portfolios of investments available on the market, investors can put their money in a risk-free investment, usually defined as federal government obligations, which are assumed to have a certain or near-certain expectation of payment of the agreed amount without the variance that would create risk. In Figure 9-1, that point would be found on the vertical axis (since risk-free has a risk of 0) and a return significantly below that of the market portfolio (since investors expect to get a lower return for lower risk). The line between the risk-free rate and the market portfolio is called the security market line, along which all portfolio investments will have to be if they are to be competitive for investor dollars. If, for example, an investment is priced above that line, with an attractive combination of return and risk, investor demand for such a combination can be expected to push the price up and thereby reduce the return on the investment to a point along the line.

From these core principles, financial economists can model what they expect the value of an investment or portfolio or company to be, which is usually expressed as follows:

$$E(R_p) = R_f + \beta[E(R_m - R_f)]$$

$E(R_p)$ is the expected return of the portfolio or company in question, the item usually to be solved for in an acquisitions transaction.

R_f is the risk-free rate of return, usually determined by looking online for the current rate of U.S. treasury offerings.

R_m is the return of a market portfolio of stock measured historically.

$[E(R_m - R_f)]$, the bracketed computation, is referred to as the market premium, again usually measured historically. It is the difference between what a diversified stock portfolio has earned as compared to the same investment in government securities. Over time, this has been in the 6 percent range (9 percent return for stocks and 3 percent return for government bonds). Of course, these are long-term averages and are not as accurate for short-term periods of bubbles or depression or inflation in government bonds.

β is the Greek letter beta and is the part of the equation that needs the most explanations for law students without a financial background. A firm's beta is a measure of comparing how an individual firm compares to the market on the dimensions of systematic risk and return discussed above. Beta is always a relative number presented in relation to the market, where the market has a beta of 1.0. A company or investment with a variance or systematic risk that is double the market has a beta of 2.0; a company with a risk or variance that is half of the market has a beta of 0.5. Airlines are an example of an industry where companies have much higher fluctuations than the market with a resulting high beta. Utilities, with their steady income flow and not much variation, are likely to have a low beta. The expectation of financial theory is that investors are going to demand higher returns for investments that carry more risk, so that valuation of a particular company's returns must be adjusted by how much risk is being taken.

PROBLEM 9-1:

Compute the expected return for a company with a beta of 1.50 at a time when the 90-day government bond rate is 2.0 and the historical market premium for stock over government bonds is 6.0.

C. THE MECHANICS OF A DISCOUNTED CASH FLOW ANALYSIS

A discounted cash flow approach to valuation uses the two key theoretical factors for valuation just discussed—expected return and risk. On the return side, the focus is on cash flow to estimate the cash that will be generated by the business going forward if it were to be purchased. For risk, the focus is on a discount rate, to adjust for how investors would value this expected income stream given the level of risk. The particular measure used here is WACC, or Weighted Average Cost of Capital, which requires more detailed knowledge and is discussed further below. Our study of this process, which only scratches the surface of this topic, focuses on three primary points: (1) How do we forecast the free cash flow? This is a search that takes us into spreadsheets and concepts from accounting; (2) What is the appropriate discount rate for the cash flow that we estimate? This reflects the finance theory set out above; and (3) What adjustments might need to be made, for example, to take into account tax effects or specific contexts? The process is sufficiently complex and full of numbers as to cause pain for most law students, but if you focus on the key processes just described, it will improve your understanding of the deals you will be asked to evaluate. Focus on the key value drivers of the valuation and look for which factors could be manipulated in a contested acquisitions setting or judicial contest that may follow such an acquisition.

1. Forecasting Free Cash Flow

The return element of valuation is typically computed from free cash flow. Why? Because it is seen as better than the alternatives as a realistic measure of return. It is *future* cash flow, because an investor is buying future returns, not what has happened in the past. It is *free* cash flow, to describe cash the business will generate that is not already committed to particular obligations. Estimates of cash flow typically start with a historical number and are projected going forward based on certain predictions about growth. Free cash flow estimates typically are divided chronologically into an explicit forecast period, often the next five years, in which computations are made on a year-by-year basis, and then a terminal value which lumps together the expected cash flow for the remainder of the estimated investment period. Typically, this terminal value computation will have lower growth rates, based on the expectation that after the explicit forecast period, the growth will return to or near the industry average as competition erodes particular competitive advantage that may exist at the outset.

a. The Explicit Forecast Period (i.e., the First Five Years)

It should not be surprising that a spreadsheet eases working through such a process. The example which follows is best understood if you spend some time creating your own simple spreadsheet and working through the numbers line by line.

Start with current revenue or sales, which you can get from historical data, including periodic reports filed by a public company. Since you want to estimate future income, you will need to determine what you expect the growth rate to be going forward based on your best estimate of this company's prospects, the position of the industry as a whole, and the state of the economy. With these assumptions, you can fill in this row across each year of the explicit forecast period on the spreadsheet in Table 9-1.

C. The Mechanics of a Discounted Cash Flow Analysis

Table 9-1

	Year 0	Year 1	Year 2	Year 3	Year 4	Year 5
Revenue ($ thousands)	9750	10000	10500	11025	11576.3	12155.06
COGS		5400	5670	5953.5	6251.18	6563.73
Gross Profit		4600	4830	5071.5	5325.08	5591.32
SG&A		1900	1995	2094.75	2199.49	2309.46
Depreciation		1050	1050	1050	1050	1050
Operating Profit (pre-tax)		1650	1785	1926.75	2075.59	2231.86
Taxes		643.5	696.15	751.433	809.479	870.42
NOPAT		1006.5	1088.9	1175.32	1266.11	1361.43
Add: Depreciation		1050	1050	1050	1050	1050
Less: Capital Expenditure		1000	1000	1000	1000	1000
Less: Increase in NWC		55	110	116	121	127
Free Cash Flow		1001.5	1028.9	1109.32	1195.11	1284.43
Terminal Value						17361.83

Estimates for Computation

Revenue Growth Rate (per year): 0.05
Terminal Value Growth Rate (per year): 0.03
COGS (Costs of Goods Sold) (as percentage of revenue): 0.54
SG&A (Selling, General, and Administrative Expenses) (as percentage of revenue): 0.19
Taxes (as percentage of profit): 0.39
NWC (Net Working Capital): 0.22
WACC (Weighted Average Cost of Capital): 0.1062

From the top revenue line, you will need to subtract various costs, since they consume cash that will not be available to pay investors. The most obvious is COGS, or Costs of Goods Sold. This number will typically be a function of sales, so that the spreadsheet function will derive from the previous row.

Another deduction is fixed expenses, such as building and overhead, not necessarily changing in proportion to sales. This may well be inserted in the spreadsheet as a fixed number as opposed to a function of sales.

Depreciation is an accounting estimate of the wearing out of the assets used in the business and will likely be included as a function of some other number, such as size of assets.

The sum of Revenue (sales) less COGS, Fixed Expenses, and Depreciation produces Pretax Operating Profit.

Taxes, of course, will reduce the amount available for investors. They usually are a function of the income on the previous line.

The result after taxes is a net operating profit for the company.

But recall that we have chosen to measure free cash flow as the best indicator of return, so that it will be necessary to adjust the numbers just computed to take out depreciation, since it is only a paper adjustment, not an actual reduction of cash.

Similarly, capital expenses (used to produce future profits) will reduce the cash flow and will need to be removed. This number may be a fixed estimate in particular years or a function of some other number.

Similarly, if there is to be a change in the amount of working capital to be carried by the company (which can occur with a change in management), that, too, will affect cash flow and needs to be subtracted.

The result of these various calculations will be free cash flow for that year. Subsequent columns perform a similar computation for the remaining years of the explicit period, based on the assumptions about growth or change in the various factors that have been made. The bottom line of expected cash flow for each year will need to be adjusted to reflect the time value of money using an inflation rate as may be appropriate.

b. Terminal Value

The cash flow for which investors are paying will continue beyond the explicit forecast period, and these expected returns are usually collapsed into one figure. Usually, the growth rate for the various factors for use in this period will be closer to market returns. Since an investor will want to know today's value of this future income stream, it too will need to be adjusted to present dollars.

2. Picking an Appropriate Discount Rate

To determine what an investor would expect to pay for the income stream just computed, financial theory would tell us to take into account the risk or variance of this investment as compared to other possible investments using the security market line formula set out above. The method used here is WACC, or Weighted Average Cost of Capital. The weighted average part of the title refers to the fact that a company gets capital in two distinct markets, debt and equity, and that its cost of capital will be a function of its costs in each. As a result, you will want to compute its cost of debt capital (usually determined by its recent borrowing costs as a percent of the amount borrowed) and its cost of equity capital (usually determined by the security market line equitation above). The weights for the weighted average come from the debt/equity ratio of the company (or what you expect it will be after closing). The free cash flow number from the previous part is then discounted by this rate to get to free cash flow.

3. Adjustments

While the free cash flow computation and selection of the discount rate are the key variables in this computation, there may be a need still to make some adjustments. Commonly, an adjustment is made for taxes, since the government-provided deduction for taxes can multiply the benefits of the cash flow.

4. Forecasting Change in Free Cash Flow from the Merger

What we have done so far is only account for the free cash flow of an existing company with its assets in current use. As discussed in Chapter 2, an acquisition can produce value either by synergy or control benefits, so that any computation of value must also include these benefits. This would require valuing synergy benefits or control benefits and taking out costs. It is typical in a merger analysis to present scenario analysis, in which valuation is presented across a range using different discount rates, for example.

D. DEAL COMPARABLES, COMPANY COMPARABLES, AND OTHER MEASURES

Valuations may include alternative methods to a discounted cash flow-based method or may include additional computations alongside a DCF. This section focuses on Deal Comparables (looking at measures from other deals) and Company Comparables (looking at measures from other target companies), with a mention of liquidation values. Each of the first two methods assumes that our deal will have the same ratio on some key metrics as the comparable deals or companies. For each it will be important to understand how comparables are picked that will justify such an assumption and markers that would make you uncomfortable with making such an assumption.

Deal comparables or transaction multiples. Here, the value of the target or its equity is estimated from the average acquisition price or takeover premium across similar M&A deals. The first step is to compile comparable M&A deals in the target's industry or related industries. Information is available in data sets such as Thomson Reuters' Financial Merger Data set. You will want to watch for possible skewing of the data set as discussed in more detail below. Second, you want to determine a ratio of relevant measures in these comparable deals that can be used to determine the value of your target. It is common to produce an average of comparable deals to guide valuation of your target. For example, a valuation might look at purchase price/asset value (measured by book) or takeover premium/book value or takeover premium/cash flow. To take the first measure, for example, your target's purchase price will equal [the average ratio of the comparables' purchase price/the comparable company's total assets] × the target's total assets.

To insure comparability, it is common to scale the comparable deals numbers so that size variations don't skew the results using total assets or a cash flow measure for size scaling. You also want to make sure that you distinguish between whether you are estimating the value of the equity in the firm (which is often what will be purchased in a takeover transaction) or whether the entire firm is being valued (which will include debt as well as the equity).

Sometimes, the focus will be shortened even further to focus on the ratio of premiums by measuring the ratio for comparable target companies between the takeover bid and the comparable target's price before the merger announcement, such as one 30 days before the announcement.

Consider characteristics of the sample that would raise questions. Recent deals usually are more relevant, so that you avoid comparables that may have been shaped by different economic fundamentals in different time periods. If comparables were financial bidders and your deal was an offer by a strategic bidder, there may be a disconnect in terms of comparables. If your target were the smallest competitor in its area, you might question a comparable that was by far the largest company in its field. If the comparable were a merger of equals and your deal was not, or a hostile bid and your deal was not, or vice versa, you would have reason to worry about the comparables. An acquisition of a 20 percent minority stake would not be useful to guide estimates for purchase of a majority block. A private deal would not necessarily be useful for a public target or vice versa.

Beyond such obvious points of disputes, there will often be a variety of other issues such as do you use an average or the median deal. When would you want to throw out the outliers?

Company comparables/trading multiples. This method follows a similar ratio approach to deal comparables but focuses on company characteristics as opposed to deal characteristics. Just as before, your valuation expert will seek out a set of comparables, such as companies that share similar characteristics to your target. Here, the ratio will focus on accounting presentations of the company, such as the Price/Earnings (P/E) ratio or the Price to Sales ratio or the Price to Book Value ratio. As before, you will want to scale whatever measuring factor is chosen so that the different sizes of the companies does not skew the result. As before, you will want to pick comparables from the target's industry, or similar industry, and for time periods that reflect similar economic risks. If you were using a ratio of price to earnings, for example, your target's estimated stock value would equal (T's price/earnings ratio) × the comparable companies' trading multiple of (price/earnings ratio).

Parallel to the process for deal comparables, you will want to train yourself as to what factors to look for that would make you uncomfortable with using a ratio from the comparable companies to determine the value of your target. Comparables should have similar characteristics to the target in terms of risk, market share, and the growth rate of things like sales and profits.

These variables use accounting numbers so that you would want to adjust for any major accounting differences between T and the comparable companies, such as inventory policies, treatment of intangible assets, and treatment of leases (e.g., to capitalize or include in operating expenses). You would also want to adjust for off-balance-sheet items or non-recurring extraordinary items. Recent major acquisitions or divestitures by your target or the comparable companies could also skew your comparisons and should be excluded.

What differences do you see between deal comparables and company comparables? One important difference is that the company comparables do not specifically include the value of a takeover premium. A comparable deal approach will include the deal premiums in the comparison.

Other measures of valuations. If the target is to be liquidated, it may be appropriate to include a valuation that focuses on value in a winding down as opposed to a going concern basis. Assets may lose value if removed from a going concern, such that valuation may be different in such a context.

10 CASH-OUT MERGERS

A. MAJORITY POWER, MINORITY RIGHTS TO EXIT VIA APPRAISAL OR GAIN JUDICIAL REVIEW FOR BREACH OF FIDUCIARY DUTY

Weinberger v. UOP, Inc.
457 A.2d 701 (Del. Sup. Ct. en banc 1983)

MOORE, Justice:

This post-trial appeal was reheard en banc from a decision of the Court of Chancery. It was brought by the class action plaintiff below, a former shareholder of UOP, Inc., who challenged the elimination of UOP's minority shareholders by a cash-out merger between UOP and its majority owner, The Signal Companies, Inc.

In ruling for the defendants, the Chancellor re-stated his earlier conclusion that the plaintiff in a suit challenging a cash-out merger must allege specific acts of fraud, misrepresentation, or other items of misconduct to demonstrate the unfairness of the merger terms to the minority. We approve this rule and affirm it.

The Chancellor also held that even though the ultimate burden of proof is on the majority shareholder to show by a preponderance of the evidence that the transaction is fair, it is first the burden of the plaintiff attacking the merger to demonstrate some basis for invoking the fairness obligation. We agree with that principle. However, where corporate action has been approved by an informed vote of a majority of the minority shareholders, we conclude that the burden entirely shifts to the plaintiff to show that the transaction was unfair to the minority. *See, e.g., Michelson v. Duncan,* Del. Supr., 407 A.2d 211, 224 (1979). But in all this, the burden clearly remains on those relying on the vote to show that they completely disclosed all material facts relevant to the transaction.

Here, the record does not support a conclusion that the minority stockholder vote was an informed one. Material information, necessary to acquaint those shareholders with the bargaining positions of Signal and UOP, was withheld under circumstances amounting to a breach of fiduciary duty. We therefore conclude that this merger does not meet the test of fairness, at least as we address that concept, and no burden thus shifted to the plaintiff by reason of the minority shareholder vote. Accordingly, we reverse and remand for further proceedings consistent herewith.

In considering the nature of the remedy available under our law to minority shareholders in a cash-out merger, we believe that it is, and hereafter should be, an appraisal under 8 Del. C. §262 as hereinafter construed. We therefore overrule *Lynch v. Vickers Energy Corp.*, Del. Supr., 429 A.2d 497 (1981) (*Lynch II*) to the extent that it purports to limit a stockholder's monetary relief to a specific damage formula. *See Lynch II*, 429 A.2d at 507-08 (McNeilly & Quillen, JJ., dissenting). But to give full effect to section 262 within the framework of the General Corporation Law we adopt a more liberal, less rigid and stylized, approach to the valuation process than has heretofore been permitted by our courts. While the present state of these proceedings does not admit the plaintiff to the appraisal remedy per se, the practical effect of the remedy we do grant him will be co-extensive with the liberalized valuation and appraisal methods we herein approve for cases coming after this decision.

Our treatment of these matters has necessarily led us to a reconsideration of the business purpose rule announced in the trilogy of *Singer v. Magnavox Co., supra; Tanzer v. International General Industries, Inc.*, Del. Supr., 379 A.2d 1121 (1977); and *Roland International Corp. v. Najjar*, Del. Supr., 407 A.2d 1032 (1979). For the reasons hereafter set forth we consider that the business purpose requirement of these cases is no longer the law of Delaware.

I.

Signal is a diversified, technically based company operating through various subsidiaries. Its stock is publicly traded on the New York, Philadelphia and Pacific Stock Exchanges. UOP, formerly known as Universal Oil Products Company, was a diversified industrial company engaged in various lines of business, including petroleum and petro-chemical services and related products, construction, fabricated metal products, transportation equipment products, chemicals and plastics, and other products and services including land development, lumber products and waste disposal. Its stock was publicly held and listed on the New York Stock Exchange.

In 1974 Signal sold one of its wholly-owned subsidiaries for $420,000,000 in cash. *See Gimbel v. Signal Companies, Inc.*, Del. Ch., 316

A.2d 599, *aff'd*, Del. Supr., 316 A.2d 619 (1974). While looking to invest this cash surplus, Signal became interested in UOP as a possible acquisition. Friendly negotiations ensued, and Signal proposed to acquire a controlling interest in UOP at a price of $19 per share. UOP's representatives sought $25 per share. In the arm's length bargaining that followed, an understanding was reached whereby Signal agreed to purchase from UOP 1,500,000 shares of UOP's authorized but unissued stock at $21 per share.

This purchase was contingent upon Signal making a successful cash tender offer for 4,300,000 publicly held shares of UOP, also at a price of $21 per share. This combined method of acquisition permitted Signal to acquire 5,800,000 shares of stock, representing 50.5% of UOP's outstanding shares. The UOP board of directors advised the company's shareholders that it had no objection to Signal's tender offer at that price. Immediately before the announcement of the tender offer, UOP's common stock had been trading on the New York Stock Exchange at a fraction under $14 per share.

The negotiations between Signal and UOP occurred during April 1975, and the resulting tender offer was greatly oversubscribed. However, Signal limited its total purchase of the tendered shares so that, when coupled with the stock bought from UOP, it had achieved its goal of becoming a 50.5% shareholder of UOP.

Although UOP's board consisted of thirteen directors, Signal nominated and elected only six. Of these, five were either directors or employees of Signal. The sixth, a partner in the banking firm of Lazard Freres & Co., had been one of Signal's representatives in the negotiations and bargaining with UOP concerning the tender offer and purchase price of the UOP shares.

However, the president and chief executive officer of UOP retired during 1975, and Signal caused him to be replaced by James V. Crawford, a long-time employee and senior executive vice president of one of Signal's wholly-owned subsidiaries. Crawford succeeded his predecessor on UOP's board of directors and also was made a director of Signal.

By the end of 1977 Signal basically was unsuccessful in finding other suitable investment candidates for its excess cash, and by February 1978 considered that it had no other realistic acquisitions available to it on a friendly basis. Once again its attention turned to UOP.

The trial court found that at the instigation of certain Signal management personnel, including William W. Walkup, its board chairman, and Forrest N. Shumway, its president, a feasibility study was made concerning the possible acquisition of the balance of UOP's outstanding shares. This study was performed by two Signal officers, Charles S. Arledge, vice president (director of planning), and Andrew J. Chitiea, senior vice president (chief financial officer). Messrs. Walkup, Shumway, Arledge and Chitiea were all directors of UOP in addition to their membership on the Signal board.

Arledge and Chitiea concluded that it would be a good investment for Signal to acquire the remaining 49.5% of UOP shares at any price up to

$24 each. Their report was discussed between Walkup and Shumway who, along with Arledge, Chitiea and Brewster L. Arms, internal counsel for Signal, constituted Signal's senior management. In particular, they talked about the proper price to be paid if the acquisition was pursued, purportedly keeping in mind that as UOP's majority shareholder, Signal owed a fiduciary responsibility to both its own stockholders as well as to UOP's minority. It was ultimately agreed that a meeting of Signal's executive committee would be called to propose that Signal acquire the remaining outstanding stock of UOP through a cash-out merger in the range of $20 to $21 per share.

The executive committee meeting was set for February 28, 1978. As a courtesy, UOP's president, Crawford, was invited to attend, although he was not a member of Signal's executive committee. On his arrival, and prior to the meeting, Crawford was asked to meet privately with Walkup and Shumway. He was then told of Signal's plan to acquire full ownership of UOP and was asked for his reaction to the proposed price range of $20 to $21 per share. Crawford said he thought such a price would be "generous," and that it was certainly one which should be submitted to UOP's minority shareholders for their ultimate consideration. He stated, however, that Signal's 100% ownership could cause internal problems at UOP. He believed that employees would have to be given some assurance of their future place in a fully-owned Signal subsidiary. Otherwise, he feared the departure of essential personnel. Also, many of UOP's key employees had stock option incentive programs which would be wiped out by a merger. Crawford therefore urged that some adjustment would have to be made, such as providing a comparable incentive in Signal's shares, if after the merger he was to maintain his quality of personnel and efficiency at UOP.

Thus, Crawford voiced no objection to the $20 to $21 price range, nor did he suggest that Signal should consider paying more than $21 per share for the minority interests. Later, at the executive committee meeting the same factors were discussed, with Crawford repeating the position he earlier took with Walkup and Shumway. Also considered was the 1975 tender offer and the fact that it had been greatly oversubscribed at $21 per share. For many reasons, Signal's management concluded that the acquisition of UOP's minority shares provided the solution to a number of its business problems.

Thus, it was the consensus that a price of $20 to $21 per share would be fair to both Signal and the minority shareholders of UOP. Signal's executive committee authorize its management "to negotiate" with UOP "for a cash acquisition of the minority ownership in UOP, Inc., with the intention of presenting a proposal to [Signal's] board of directors . . . on March 6, 1978." . . .

Between Tuesday, February 28, 1978 and Monday, March 6, 1978, a total of four business days, Crawford spoke by telephone with all of UOP's non-Signal, i.e., outside, directors. Also during that period, Crawford retained Lehman Brothers to render a fairness opinion as to the price offered the minority for its stock. He gave two reasons for this choice. First, the time schedule between the announcement and the board meetings was short (by then only three business days) and since Lehman Brothers had been acting as UOP's investment banker for many years, Crawford felt that it would be in the best position to respond on such brief notice. Second, James W. Glanville, a long-time director of UOP and a partner in Lehman Brothers, had acted as a financial advisor to UOP for many years. Crawford believed that Glanville's familiarity with UOP, as a member of its board, would also be of assistance in enabling Lehman Brothers to render a fairness opinion within the existing time constraints.

Crawford telephoned Glanville, who gave his assurance that Lehman Brothers had no conflicts that would prevent it from accepting the task. Glanville's immediate personal reaction was that a price of $20 to $21 would certainly be fair, since it represented almost a 50% premium over UOP's market price. Glanville sought a $250,000 fee for Lehman Brothers' services, but Crawford thought this too much. After further discussions Glanville finally agreed that Lehman Brothers would render its fairness opinion for $150,000.

During this period Crawford also had several telephone contacts with Signal officials. In only one of them, however, was the price of the shares discussed. In a conversation with Walkup, Crawford advised that as a result of his communications with UOP's non-Signal directors, it was his feeling that the price would have to be the top of the proposed range, or $21 per share, if the approval of UOP's outside directors was to be obtained. But again, he did not seek any price higher than $21.

Glanville assembled a three-man Lehman Brothers team to do the work on the fairness opinion. These persons examined relevant documents and information concerning UOP, including its annual reports and its Securities and Exchange Commission filings from 1973 through 1976, as well as its audited financial statements for 1977, its interim reports to shareholders, and its recent and historical market prices and trading volumes. In addition, on Friday, March 3, 1978, two members of the Lehman Brothers team flew to UOP's headquarters in Des Plaines, Illinois, to perform a "due diligence" visit, during the course of which they interviewed Crawford as well as UOP's general counsel, its chief financial officer, and other key executives and personnel.

As a result, the Lehman Brothers team concluded that "the price of either $20 or $21 would be a fair price for the remaining shares of UOP." They telephoned this impression to Glanville, who was spending the weekend in Vermont.

On Monday morning, March 6, 1978, Glanville and the senior member of the Lehman Brothers team flew to Des Plaines to attend the scheduled UOP directors meeting. Glanville looked over the assembled information during the flight. The two had with them the draft of a "fairness opinion letter" in which the price had been left blank. Either during or immediately prior to the directors' meeting, the two-page "fairness opinion letter" was typed in final form and the price of $21 per share was inserted.

On March 6, 1978, both the Signal and UOP boards were convened to consider the proposed merger. Telephone communications were maintained between the two meetings. Walkup, Signal's board chairman, and also a UOP director, attended UOP's meeting with Crawford in order to present Signal's position and answer any questions that UOP's non-Signal directors might have. Arledge and Chitiea, along with Signal's other designees on UOP's board, participated by conference telephone. All of UOP's outside directors attended the meeting either in person or by conference telephone.

First, Signal's board unanimously adopted a resolution authorizing Signal to propose to UOP a cash merger of $21 per share as outlined in a certain merger agreement and other supporting documents. This proposal required that the merger be approved by a majority of UOP's outstanding minority shares voting at the stockholders meeting at which the merger would be considered, and that the minority shares voting in favor of the merger, when coupled with Signal's 50.5% interest would have to comprise at least two-thirds of all UOP shares. Otherwise the proposed merger would be deemed disapproved.

UOP's board then considered the proposal. Copies of the agreement were delivered to the directors in attendance, and other copies had been forwarded earlier to the directors participating by telephone. They also had before them UOP financial data for 1974-1977, UOP's most recent financial statements, market price information, and budget projections for 1978. In addition they had Lehman Brothers' hurriedly prepared fairness opinion letter finding the price of $21 to be fair. Glanville, the Lehman Brothers partner, and UOP director, commented on the information that had gone into preparation of the letter.

Signal also suggests that the Arledge-Chitiea feasibility study, indicating that a price of up to $24 per share would be a "good investment" for Signal, was discussed at the UOP directors' meeting. The Chancellor made no such finding, and our independent review of the record, detailed *infra*, satisfies us by a preponderance of the evidence that there was no discussion of this document at UOP's board meeting. Furthermore, it is clear beyond peradventure that nothing in that report was ever disclosed to UOP's minority shareholders prior to their approval of the merger.

After consideration of Signal's proposal, Walkup and Crawford left the meeting to permit a free and uninhibited exchange between UOP's non-Signal directors. Upon their return a resolution to accept Signal's offer was then proposed and adopted. While Signal's men on UOP's board participated in various aspects of the meeting, they abstained from voting. However, the minutes show that each of them "if voting would have voted yes."

Despite the swift board action of the two companies, the merger was not submitted to UOP's shareholders until their annual meeting on May 26, 1978. In the notice of that meeting and proxy statement sent to shareholders in May, UOP's management and board urged that the merger be approved. The proxy statement ... also advised the shareholders that Lehman Brothers had given its opinion that the merger price of $21 per share was fair to UOP's minority. However, it did not disclose the hurried method by which this conclusion was reached.

As of the record date of UOP's annual meeting, there were 11,488,302 shares of UOP common stock outstanding, 5,688,302 of which were owned by the minority. At the meeting only 56%, or 3,208,652, of the minority shares were voted. Of these, 2,953,812, or 51.9% of the total minority, voted for the merger, and 254,840 voted against it. When Signal's stock was added to the minority shares voting in favor, a total of 76.2% of UOP's outstanding shares approved the merger while only 2.2% opposed it.

By its terms the merger became effective on May 26, 1978, and each share of UOP's stock held by the minority was automatically converted into a right to receive $21 cash.

II.

A.

A primary issue mandating reversal is the preparation by two UOP directors, Arledge and Chitiea, of their feasibility study for the exclusive use and benefit of Signal. This document was of obvious significance to both Signal and UOP. Using UOP data, it described the advantages to Signal of ousting the minority at a price range of $21-$24 per share. Mr. Arledge, one of the authors, outlined the benefits to Signal:[6]

Purpose of the Merger

1) Provides an outstanding investment opportunity for Signal — (Better than any recent acquisition we have seen.)
2) Increases Signal's earnings.
3) Facilitates the flow of resources between Signal and its subsidiaries — (Big factor — works both ways.)
4) Provides cost savings potential for Signal and UOP.
5) Improves the percentage of Signal's "operating earnings" as opposed to "holding company earnings."
6) Simplifies the understanding of Signal.
7) Facilitates technological exchange among Signal's subsidiaries.
8) Eliminates potential conflicts of interest.

---

6. The parentheses indicate certain handwritten comments of Mr. Arledge.

Having written those words, solely for the use of Signal, it is clear from the record that neither Arledge nor Chitiea shared this report with their fellow directors of UOP. We are satisfied that no one else did either. This conduct hardly meets the fiduciary standards applicable to such a transaction....

The Arledge-Chitiea report speaks for itself in supporting the Chancellor's finding that a price of up to $24 was a "good investment" for Signal. It shows that a return on the investment at $21 would be 15.7% versus 15.5% at $24 per share. This was a difference of only two-tenths of one percent, while it meant over $17,000,000 to the minority. Under such circumstances, paying UOP's minority shareholders $24 would have had relatively little long-term effect on Signal, and the Chancellor's findings concerning the benefit to Signal, even at a price of $24, were obviously correct. *Levitt v. Bouvier*, Del. Supr., 287 A.2d 671, 673 (1972).

Certainly, this was a matter of material significance to UOP and its shareholders. Since the study was prepared by two UOP directors, using UOP information for the exclusive benefit of Signal, and nothing whatever was done to disclose it to the outside UOP directors or the minority shareholders, a question of breach of fiduciary duty arises. This problem occurs because there were common Signal-UOP directors participating, at least to some extent, in the UOP board's decision-making processes without full disclosure of the conflicts they faced.[7]

B.

In assessing this situation, the Court of Chancery was required to:

> examine what information defendants had and to measure it against what they gave to the minority stockholders, in a context in which "complete candor" is required. In other words, the limited function of the Court was to determine whether defendants had disclosed all information in their possession germane to the transaction in issue. And by "germane" we mean, for present purposes, information such as a reasonable shareholder would consider important in deciding whether to sell or retain stock.
>
> ... Completeness, not adequacy, is both the norm and the mandate under present circumstances.

---

7. Although perfection is not possible, or expected, the result here could have been entirely different if UOP had appointed an independent negotiating committee of its outside directors to deal with Signal at arm's length. *See, e.g., Harriman v. E.I. duPont de Nemours & Co.*, 411 F. Supp. 133 (D. Del. 1975). Since fairness in this context can be equated to conduct by a theoretical, wholly independent, board of directors acting upon the matter before them, it is unfortunate that this course apparently was neither considered nor pursued. *Johnston v. Greene*, Del. Supr., 121 A.2d 919, 925 (1956). Particularly in a parent-subsidiary context, a showing that the action taken was as though each of the contending parties had in fact exerted its bargaining power against the other at arm's length is strong evidence that the transaction meets the test of fairness. *Getty Oil Co. v. Skelly Oil Co.*, Del. Supr., 267 A.2d 883, 886 (1970); *Puma v. Marriott*, Del. Ch., 283 A.2d 693, 696 (1971).

Lynch v. Vickers Energy Corp., Del. Supr., 383 A.2d 278, 281 (1977) (*Lynch I*). This is merely stating in another way the long-existing principle of Delaware law that these Signal designated directors on UOP's board still owed UOP and its shareholders an uncompromising duty of loyalty. The classic language of *Guth v. Loft, Inc.*, Del. Supr., 5 A.2d 503, 510 (1939), requires no embellishment:

> A public policy, existing through the years, and derived from a profound knowledge of human characteristics and motives, has established a rule that demands of a corporate officer or director, peremptorily and inexorably, the most scrupulous observance of his duty, not only affirmatively to protect the interests of the corporation committed to his charge, but also to refrain from doing anything that would work injury to the corporation, or to deprive it of profit or advantage which his skill and ability might properly bring to it, or to enable it to make in the reasonable and lawful exercise of its powers. The rule that requires an undivided and unselfish loyalty to the corporation demands that there shall be no conflict between duty and self-interest.

Given the absence of any attempt to structure this transaction on an arm's length basis, Signal cannot escape the effects of the conflicts it faced, particularly when its designees on UOP's board did not totally abstain from participation in the matter. There is no "safe harbor" for such divided loyalties in Delaware. When directors of a Delaware corporation are on both sides of a transaction, they are required to demonstrate their utmost good faith and the most scrupulous inherent fairness of the bargain. *Gottlieb v. Heyden Chemical Corp.*, Del. Supr., 91 A.2d 57, 57-58 (1952). The requirement of fairness is unflinching in its demand that where one stands on both sides of a transaction, he has the burden of establishing its entire fairness, sufficient to pass the test of careful scrutiny by the courts. *Sterling v. Mayflower Hotel Corp.*, Del. Supr., 93 A.2d 107, 110 (1952); *Bastian v. Bourns, Inc.*, Del. Ch., 256 A.2d 680, 681 (1969), *aff'd*, Del. Supr., 278 A.2d 467 (1970); *David J. Greene & Co. v. Dunhill International Inc.*, Del. Ch., 249 A.2d 427, 431 (1968).

There is no dilution of this obligation where one holds dual or multiple directorships, as in a parent-subsidiary context. *Levien v. Sinclair Oil Corp.*, Del. Ch., 261 A.2d 911, 915 (1969). Thus, individuals who act in a dual capacity as directors of two corporations, one of whom is parent and the other subsidiary, owe the same duty of good management to both corporations, and in the absence of an independent negotiating structure (see note 7, *supra*), or the directors' total abstention from any participation in the matter, this duty is to be exercised in light of what is best for both companies. *Warshaw v. Calhoun*, Del. Supr., 221 A.2d 487, 492 (1966). The record demonstrates that Signal has not met this obligation.

C.

The concept of fairness has two basic aspects: fair dealing and fair price. The former embraces questions of when the transaction was timed, how it was initiated, structured, negotiated, disclosed to the directors, and how the approvals of the directors and the stockholders were obtained. The latter aspect of fairness relates to the economic and financial considerations of the proposed merger, including all relevant factors: assets, market value, earnings, future prospects, and any other elements that affect the intrinsic or inherent value of a company's stock. Moore, *The "Interested" Director or Officer Transaction*, 4 DEL. J. CORP. L. 674, 676 (1979); Nathan & Shapiro, *Legal Standard of Fairness of Merger Terms Under Delaware Law*, 2 DEL. J. CORP. L. 44, 46-47 (1977). *See Tri-Continental Corp. v. Battye*, Del. Supr., 74 A.2d 71, 72 (1950); 8 Del. C. §262(h). However, the test for fairness is not a bifurcated one as between fair dealing and price. All aspects of the issue must be examined as a whole since the question is one of entire fairness. However, in a non-fraudulent transaction we recognize that price may be the preponderant consideration outweighing other features of the merger. Here, we address the two basic aspects of fairness separately because we find reversible error as to both.

D.

Part of fair dealing is the obvious duty of candor required by *Lynch I, supra*. Moreover, one possessing superior knowledge may not mislead any stockholder by use of corporate information to which the latter is not privy. *Lank v. Steiner*, Del. Supr., 224 A.2d 242, 244 (1966). Delaware has long imposed this duty even upon persons who are not corporate officers or directors, but who nonetheless are privy to matters of interest or significance to their company. *Brophy v. Cities Service Co.*, Del. Ch., 70 A.2d 5, 7 (1949). With the well-established Delaware law on the subject, and the Court of Chancery's findings of fact here, it is inevitable that the obvious conflicts posed by Arledge and Chitiea's preparation of their "feasibility study," derived from UOP information, for the sole use and benefit of Signal, cannot pass muster.

The Arledge-Chitiea report is but one aspect of the element of fair dealing. How did this merger evolve? It is clear that it was entirely initiated by Signal. The serious time constraints under which the principals acted were all set by Signal. It had not found a suitable outlet for its excess cash and considered UOP a desirable investment, particularly since it was now in a position to acquire the whole company for itself. For whatever reasons, and they were only Signal's, the entire transaction was presented to and approved by UOP's board within four business days. Standing alone, this is not necessarily indicative of any lack of fairness by a majority shareholder. It was what occurred, or more properly, what did not occur, during this brief period that makes the time constraints imposed by Signal relevant to the issue of fairness.

The structure of the transaction, again, was Signal's doing. So far as negotiations were concerned, it is clear that they were modest at best. Crawford, Signal's man at UOP, never really talked price with Signal, except to accede to its management's statements on the subject, and to convey to Signal the UOP outside directors' view that as between the $20-$21 range under consideration, it would have to be $21. The latter is not a surprising outcome, but hardly arm's length negotiations. Only the protection of benefits for UOP's key employees and the issue of Lehman Brothers' fee approached any concept of bargaining.

As we have noted, the matter of disclosure to the UOP directors was wholly flawed by the conflicts of interest raised by the Arledge-Chitiea report. All of those conflicts were resolved by Signal in its own favor without divulging any aspect of them to UOP.

This cannot but undermine a conclusion that this merger meets any reasonable test of fairness. The outside UOP directors lacked one material piece of information generated by two of their colleagues, but shared only with Signal. True, the UOP board had the Lehman Brothers' fairness opinion, but that firm has been blamed by the plaintiff for the hurried task it performed, when more properly the responsibility for this lies with Signal. There was no disclosure of the circumstances surrounding the rather cursory preparation of the Lehman Brothers' fairness opinion. Instead, the impression was given UOP's minority that a careful study had been made, when in fact speed was the hallmark, and Mr. Glanville, Lehman's partner in charge of the matter, and also a UOP director, having spent the weekend in Vermont, brought a draft of the "fairness opinion letter" to the UOP directors' meeting on March 6, 1978 with the price left blank. We can only conclude from the record that the rush imposed on Lehman Brothers by Signal's timetable contributed to the difficulties under which this investment banking firm attempted to perform its responsibilities. Yet, none of this was disclosed to UOP's minority.

Finally, the minority stockholders were denied the critical information that Signal considered a price of $24 to be a good investment. Since this would have meant over $17,000,000 more to the minority, we cannot conclude that the shareholder vote was an informed one. Under the circumstances, an approval by a majority of the minority was meaningless. *Lynch I*, 383 A.2d at 279, 281; *Cahall v. Lofland*, Del. Ch., 114 A. 224 (1921).

Given these particulars and the Delaware law on the subject, the record does not establish that this transaction satisfies any reasonable concept of fair dealing, and the Chancellor's findings in that regard must be reversed.

E.

Turning to the matter of price, plaintiff also challenges its fairness. His evidence was that on the date the merger was approved the stock was worth at least $26 per share. In support, he offered the testimony of a chartered investment analyst who used two basic approaches to valuation:

a comparative analysis of the premium paid over market in ten other tender offer-merger combinations, and a discounted cash flow analysis.

In this breach of fiduciary duty case, the Chancellor perceived that the approach to valuation was the same as that in an appraisal proceeding. Consistent with precedent, he rejected plaintiff's method of proof and accepted defendants' evidence of value as being in accord with practice under prior case law. This means that the so-called "Delaware block" or weighted average method was employed wherein the elements of value, i.e., assets, market price, earnings, etc., were assigned a particular weight and the resulting amounts added to determine the value per share. This procedure has been in use for decades. *See In re General Realty & Utilities Corp.*, Del. Ch., 52 A.2d 6, 14-15 (1947). However, to the extent it excludes other generally accepted techniques used in the financial community and the courts, it is now clearly outmoded. It is time we recognize this in appraisal and other stock valuation proceedings and bring our law current on the subject.

While the Chancellor rejected plaintiff's discounted cash flow method of valuing UOP's stock, as not corresponding with "either logic or the existing law" (426 A.2d at 1360), it is significant that this was essentially the focus, i.e., earnings potential of UOP, of Messrs. Arledge and Chitiea in their evaluation of the merger. Accordingly, the standard "Delaware block" or weighted average method of valuation, formerly employed in appraisal and other stock valuation cases, shall no longer exclusively control such proceedings. We believe that a more liberal approach must include proof of value by any techniques or methods which are generally considered acceptable in the financial community and otherwise admissible in court, subject only to our interpretation of 8 Del. C. §262(h), *infra*. *See also* D.R.E. 702-05. This will obviate the very structured and mechanistic procedure that has heretofore governed such matters. *See Jacques Coe & Co. v. Minneapolis-Moline Co.*, Del. Ch., 75 A.2d 244, 247 (1950); *Tri-Continental Corp. v. Battye*, Del. Ch., 66 A.2d 910, 917-18 (1949); *In re General Realty and Utilities Corp., supra*.

Fair price obviously requires consideration of all relevant factors involving the value of a company. This has long been the law of Delaware as stated in *Tri-Continental Corp.*, 74 A.2d at 72:

> The basic concept of value under the appraisal statute is that the stockholder is entitled to be paid for that which has been taken from him, viz., his proportionate interest in a going concern. By value of the stockholder's proportionate interest in the corporate enterprise is meant the true or intrinsic value of his stock which has been taken by the merger. In determining what figure represents this true or intrinsic value, the appraiser and the courts must take into consideration all factors and elements which reasonably might enter into the fixing of value. Thus, market value, asset value, dividends, earning prospects, the nature of the enterprise and any other facts which were known or which could be ascertained as of the date of merger and which throw any light on *future prospects* of the merged corporation are not

A. Majority Power, Minority Rights to Exit Via Appraisal

only pertinent to an inquiry as to the value of the dissenting stockholders' interest, but *must be considered* by the agency fixing the value. (Emphasis added.)

This is not only in accord with the realities of present day affairs, but it is thoroughly consonant with the purpose and intent of our statutory law. Under 8 Del. C. §262(h), the Court of Chancery:

shall appraise the shares, determining their *fair* value exclusive of any element of value arising from the accomplishment or expectation of the merger, together with a fair rate of interest, if any, to be paid upon the amount determined to be the *fair* value. In determining such *fair* value, the Court shall take into account *all relevant factors*. . . . (Emphasis added.)

See also Bell v. Kirby Lumber Corp., Del. Supr., 413 A.2d 137, 150-51 (1980) (Quillen, J., concurring).

It is significant that section 262 now mandates the determination of "fair" value based upon "all relevant factors." Only the speculative elements of value that may arise from the "accomplishment or expectation" of the merger are excluded. We take this to be a very narrow exception to the appraisal process, designed to eliminate use of *pro forma* data and projections of a speculative variety relating to the completion of a merger. But elements of future value, including the nature of the enterprise, which are known or susceptible of proof as of the date of the merger and not the product of speculation, may be considered. When the trial court deems it appropriate, fair value also includes any damages, resulting from the taking, which the stockholders sustain as a class. If that was not the case, then the obligation to consider "all relevant factors" in the valuation process would be eroded. We are supported in this view not only by *Tri-Continental Corp.*, 74 A.2d at 72, but also by the evolutionary amendments to section 262. . . .

It was not until the 1981 amendment to section 262 that the reference to "fair value" was repeatedly emphasized and the statutory mandate that the Court "take into account all relevant factors" appeared [section 262(h)]. Clearly, there is a legislative intent to fully compensate shareholders for whatever their loss may be, subject only to the narrow limitation that one can not take speculative effects of the merger into account.

Although the Chancellor received the plaintiff's evidence, his opinion indicates that the use of it was precluded because of past Delaware practice. While we do not suggest a monetary result one way or the other, we do think the plaintiff's evidence should be part of the factual mix and weighed as such. Until the $21 price is measured on remand by the valuation standards mandated by Delaware law, there can be no finding at the present stage of these proceedings that the price is fair. Given the lack of any candid disclosure of the material facts surrounding establishment of the $21 price, the majority of the minority vote, approving the merger, is meaningless.

The plaintiff has not sought an appraisal, but rescissory damages of the type contemplated by *Lynch v. Vickers Energy Corp.*, Del. Supr., 429 A.2d 497, 505-06 (1981) (*Lynch II*). In view of the approach to valuation that we announce today, we see no basis in our law for *Lynch II*'s exclusive monetary formula for relief. On remand the plaintiff will be permitted to test the fairness of the $21 price by the standards we herein establish, in conformity with the principle applicable to an appraisal—that fair value be determined by taking "into account all relevant factors" [see 8 Del. C. §262(h), supra]. In our view this includes the elements of rescissory damages if the Chancellor considers them susceptible of proof and a remedy appropriate to all the issues of fairness before him. To the extent that *Lynch II*, 429 A.2d at 505-06, purports to limit the Chancellor's discretion to a single remedial formula for monetary damages in a cash-out merger, it is overruled.

While a plaintiff's monetary remedy ordinarily should be confined to the more liberalized appraisal proceeding herein established, we do not intend any limitation on the historic powers of the Chancellor to grant such other relief as the facts of a particular case may dictate. The appraisal remedy we approve may not be adequate in certain cases, particularly where fraud, misrepresentation, self-dealing, deliberate waste of corporate assets, or gross and palpable overreaching are involved. *Cole v. National Cash Credit Association*, Del. Ch., 156 A. 183, 187 (1931). Under such circumstances, the Chancellor's powers are complete to fashion any form of equitable and monetary relief as may be appropriate, including rescissory damages. Since it is apparent that this long completed transaction is too involved to undo, and in view of the Chancellor's discretion, the award, if any, should be in the form of monetary damages based upon entire fairness standards, i.e., fair dealing and fair price.

Obviously, there are other litigants, like the plaintiff, who abjured an appraisal and whose rights to challenge the element of fair value must be preserved. Accordingly, the quasi-appraisal remedy we grant the plaintiff here will apply only to: (1) this case; (2) any case now pending on appeal to this Court; (3) any case now pending in the Court of Chancery which has not yet been appealed but which may be eligible for direct appeal to this Court; (4) any case challenging a cash-out merger, the effective date of which is on or before February 1, 1983; and (5) any proposed merger to be presented at a shareholders' meeting, the notification of which is mailed to the stockholders on or before February 23, 1983. Thereafter, the provisions of 8 Del. C. §262, as herein construed, respecting the scope of an appraisal and the means for perfecting the same, shall govern the financial remedy available to minority shareholders in a cash-out merger. Thus, we return to the well established principles of *Stauffer v. Standard Brands, Inc.*, Del. Supr., 187 A.2d 78 (1962) and *David J. Greene & Co. v. Schenley Industries, Inc.*, Del. Ch., 281 A.2d 30 (1971), mandating a stockholder's recourse to the basic remedy of an appraisal.

III.

Finally, we address the matter of business purpose. The defendants contend that the purpose of this merger was not a proper subject of inquiry by the trial court. The plaintiff says that no valid purpose existed—the entire transaction was a mere subterfuge designed to eliminate the minority. The Chancellor ruled otherwise, but in so doing he clearly circumscribed the thrust and effect of *Singer*. *Weinberger v. UOP*, 426 A.2d at 1342-43, 1348-50. This has led to the thoroughly sound observation that the business purpose test "may be . . . virtually interpreted out of existence, as it was in *Weinberger*."

The requirement of a business purpose is new to our law of mergers and was a departure from prior case law. See *Stauffer v. Standard Brands, Inc.*, supra; *David J. Greene & Co. v. Schenley Industries, Inc.*, supra.

In view of the fairness test which has long been applicable to parent-subsidiary mergers, *Sterling v. Mayflower Hotel Corp.*, Del. Supr., 93 A.2d 107, 109-10 (1952), the expanded appraisal remedy now available to shareholders, and the broad discretion of the Chancellor to fashion such relief as the facts of a given case may dictate, we do not believe that any additional meaningful protection is afforded minority shareholders by the business purpose requirement of the trilogy of *Singer, Tanzer, Najjar,* and their progeny. Accordingly, such requirement shall no longer be of any force or effect.

NOTES AND QUESTIONS

1. **The deal as a §251 merger.** This transaction fits within the merger template presented in Chapter 3, but it is different in at least one important way. First, think about the deal in light of the statutory requirements set out in §251: What can you tell about the plan of merger that is required by §251(a)? Focus particularly on who the parties were, which entity was to survive, and the type of consideration to be used. Second, how did the deal satisfy the requirements of director approval specified in §251(b)? Focus here on how the deal was negotiated. Third, how did the deal satisfy the shareholder approval requirements of §251(c)? Focus here on the additional requirement at this level beyond the statutory minimum inserted in the plan of merger. Fourth, did this transaction come within the appraisal statute? That question is discussed in more detail below.

Putting yourself in the role of the planner of this merger, how big a risk did either of these approval requirements pose on the facts of this case?

Putting yourself in the role of the plaintiff minority shareholders, what risk do you see given the economic reality of this transaction?

2. **"Bringing our law current" on valuation.** *Weinberger* is an important fulcrum in corporate law's approach to valuation in an acquisition. As discussed in Part II.E of the case, prior Delaware law (and that of many other states) had used a mechanistic approach. The "Delaware block" method required a trial judge, in effect, to solve for a valuation number using three different components: assets, market value, and earnings.

Having done that, the judge was to assign a weight to each (33 percent for each or 50/40/10, etc.) and then compute a weighted average of the three. This differs substantially from what we used in Chapter 9. In the Chancery Court trial in the *Weinberger* case, the plaintiff's offer of a discounted cash flow valuation was rejected as outside of Delaware law. The Supreme Court here describes the traditional Delaware block as "completely outmoded" and said it was "time to bring our law current" using methods accepted in the financial community. Thereafter, for example, in the *Interco* case discussed in Chapter 7, the Delaware court accepted discounted cash flow as the preferred method of valuation, and it has become a baseline for valuation cases.

3. The §262 exclusion. *Weinberger's* liberalized approach to valuation and its reference to methods developed in financial markets is subject, of course, to the limits of statute. The merger statute in §262(h) specifies that valuation is not to include "any element of value arising from the accomplishment or expectation of the merger." What would be included in such a term? Consider the elements raised in Chapter 2 as to where value comes from in a typical merger. Where would the value come from in this merger? The Arledge-Chitiea report in Part II.A of the opinion is helpful here. Should those elements be excluded?

4. Narrowing the exclusion. The court discusses this exclusion at the end of Part II.E of its opinion, first describing the exclusion as capturing "only the speculative elements of value" and providing the following guidance: "We take this to be a very narrow exception to the appraisal process, designed to eliminate the use of pro forma data and projections of a speculative variety relating to the completion of the merger. But elements of future value, including the nature of the enterprise, which are known or susceptible to proof as of the date of the merger, and not the product of speculation, may be considered." Does that language include matters such as those in the Arledge-Chitiea report?

5. The changing role of appraisal. The seemingly strange fit of the court's phrasing of this exclusion with the words of the statute can be better understood with a bit of history, which falls in three periods.

Period I—Pre-1890: Unanimity as a Merger Requirement. At common law, unanimous shareholder consent was a prerequisite to fundamental changes in a corporation; courts viewed each individual shareholder as having a contract with the corporation creating vested rights that could not be changed without the shareholder's consent.

Period II—The Move Away from Unanimity to Facilitate the Growth of American Business (and Use of Appraisal to Provide Exit for Shareholders Who Wanted Out). The unanimity rule empowered arbitrary or unscrupulous shareholders, often a small minority, to establish a high "nuisance" value for their shares and exact unfair concessions from the majority by blocking or threatening to block desirable corporate change. In response, most states

A. Majority Power, Minority Rights to Exit Via Appraisal

enacted statutes authorizing non-unanimous approval of charter amendments, mergers, consolidations, sale of substantially all corporate assets, and certain other fundamental corporate action. Initially, these statutes required a supermajority shareholder approval for such action, i.e., an affirmative vote of holders of a high percentage (usually three-fourths or two-thirds) of the corporation's shares. In addition, the required vote was often measured as a percentage of all outstanding shares, including shares designated as nonvoting in the corporation's charter. Now, many corporations' statutes, including that of Delaware and the Model Business Corporation Act, permit fundamental corporate action upon the approval of a bare majority of shares given voting rights by the corporate charter.

The early statutes authorizing merger and consolidation contemplated that shareholders of the constituent companies in the transaction would continue as shareholders in the surviving corporation. Dissenting shareholders who did not want to remain in the modified enterprise had the option to have their shares appraised and purchased by the corporation, but corporate directors and controlling shareholders could not directly eliminate the minority shareholders against their will.

Appraisal thus served to provide minority shareholders liquidity as a protection if the majority sought to force them into a new enterprise against their will. The focus was on the minority's right to exit to avoid a fundamental change in the business, but not the majority's power to force the minority out of the business. Yet, as a vehicle to provide minority shareholder liquidity, it also had adverse effects on the corporate treasury, which led to tight procedural limits on the use of this right. The procedural provisions of appraisal, still visible today, reflect this context in which exit rights are provided to the minority, but that exit is conditioned so as to make it not too easy and thereby harm the corporation:

- Appraisal value was to be determined as of the date of merger, exclusive of any value attributed to the merger; the basic concept was that the shareholder was entitled to that which had been taken from the shareholder and thereby to avoid any change from the corporate transaction that was to occur.
- Any shareholder seeking appraisal had to follow an exacting set of procedures to perfect appraisal (e.g., delivering written demand before the vote, not voting in favor, making a separate demand after the vote, filing a lawsuit, and submitting the stock certificate). Failure to satisfy any of these would destroy the appraisal rights and relegate the shareholder to the amount specified in the plan of merger.
- Payment was made at the end of the litigation and interest was often not provided.
- Class action status was not available.

Period III — The Expansion of Majority Power to Include Expulsion of Minority Shareholders. During the 1960s, important commercial jurisdictions in the United States authorized cash as consideration in their regular (long-form) merger statutes. Thereafter, courts permitted mergers between a parent corporation and a wholly owned subsidiary pursuant to a plan of merger that provided shares to the majority shareholder and cash to the minority. As a result, formerly popular forms of squeeze-outs, such as dissolution, sale of assets, or use of debt or redeemable stock in mergers, which excluded the minority in an indirect or circuitous fashion, gave way to more direct squeeze-outs such as cash-out mergers. Courts that earlier had been hostile to the use of majority power to eliminate minority shareholders from an enterprise interpreted these legislative changes as authorizing the majority to eliminate minority shareholders from a corporation as long as the minority was given "fair value" for their shares. Thus appraisal became focused on an entirely different context, one now in which the minority no longer was choosing to exit, but rather was being expelled on terms and at a time chosen by the majority. The definition of value and the various procedural limitations did not necessarily change as this context did, leading courts to decades of trying to sort out what should be the terms of appraisal and whether it should be exclusive or whether minority shareholders should also be able to pursue a remedy for breach of fiduciary duty. Judicial willingness to permit an alternative remedy has been influenced in part by whether fair value in appraisal can be manipulated to the advantage of the majority The "business purpose" requirement of *Singer v. Magnavox Co.* (removed in *Weinberger*) reflects this concern, as did federal cases finding director action to be a breach of Rule 10b-5, which the U.S. Supreme Court ended based on federalism grounds in Santa Fe Indus., Inc. v. Green., 430 U.S. 462 (1977).

6. Fiduciary duty as alternatives to appraisal. Once you struggle through the meaning of valuation in appraisal, you have not exhausted the law you need to get from *Weinberger*. In fact, much of the court's opinion deals with the fiduciary duty obligations of a controlling shareholder on both sides of a transaction to show entire fairness and the fair dealing and fair price prongs of that obligation. How does the court suggest this duty could have been met in the facts of this case? Does the parent have to offer its best price? Should it have to disclose the internal report which it used to determine value?

7. Remedy and the possible exclusivity of appraisal. The remedy portion of the opinion can create confusion. The last portion of Part II suggests that a plaintiff's monetary remedy "ordinarily" should be confined to appraisal followed by a sentence noting appraisal may not be adequate in certain cases, in which case the trial court can fashion any form of equitable or monetary relief "as may be appropriate." Shortly after *Weinberger*, the Delaware Supreme Court reversed a Chancery Court opinion that had limited plaintiffs to appraisal as their exclusive remedy in a cash-out merger. Rabkin v. Philip A. Hunt Chemical Corp., 498 A.2d 1099 (Del. 1985). Since then, fiduciary duty claims have regularly been available for minority transactions shareholders when controlling shareholders have cashed them out in a merger under Section 251.

Outside of Delaware the results are mixed. Under the current Model Business Corporation Act (MBCA) and in states such as California, the statute specifically excludes controlling shareholder transactions from a statutory provision that makes appraisal exclusive. In other states, including those that use earlier versions of the MBCA where statutory language provides for exclusivity except for unlawful or fraudulent conduct, many courts have ruled like Delaware that appraisal is not exclusive, but a few are to the contrary. In states that have not updated their appraisal statutes this can create a risk that a controlling shareholder can use the cash-out form and the appraisal process to obtain shares at a low-ball price.

Cede & Co. v. Technicolor, Inc.
684 A.2d 289 (Del. Sup. Ct. 1996)

Before WALSH and HOLLAND, JJ., and HORSEY, Justice, Retired.

HOLLAND, Justice:

This appeal is from a final judgment of the Court of Chancery in an appraisal action. The proceeding arises from a cash-out merger of the minority shareholders of Technicolor Incorporated ("Technicolor"), a Delaware corporation. With the approval from a majority of Technicolor's shareholders, MacAndrews & Forbes Group Incorporated ("MAF") merged its wholly-owned subsidiary, Macanfor Corporation ("Macanfor"), into Technicolor. The only defendant-appellee in this appraisal action is Technicolor, the surviving corporation of the merger. The plaintiffs-appellants are Cinerama, Incorporated, the beneficial owner of 201,200 shares of Technicolor common stock, and Cede & Company, the record owner of those shares (collectively "Cinerama.")

Cinerama contends, *inter alia*, that the Court of Chancery erred, as a matter of law, in appraising the fair value of its Technicolor shares. According to Cinerama, that legal error was a refusal to include in the valuation calculus "MAF's new business plans and strategies for Technicolor, which the [C]ourt [of Chancery] *found* were not speculative but had been developed, adopted and implemented" between the date of the merger agreement and the date of the merger. That contention is correct and dispositive of this appeal. *Weinberger v. UOP, Inc.*, Del. Supr., 457 A.2d 701 (1983). Accordingly, the appraisal action will be remanded for further proceedings in accordance with this opinion. Cinerama's other contentions are addressed only to the extent they are relevant to the remand.

FACTS

... Technicolor was a corporation with a long and prominent history in the film/audio-visual industries. By the early eighties, Technicolor's increase in market share had leveled off. The company's core business earnings had stagnated.

Technicolor engaged in a number of distinct businesses through separate operating units. Technicolor's Professional Services Group was its main source of revenue and profit. The Videocassette Duplicating Division operated one of the largest duplicating facilities in the world. The Consumer Services Group operated film processing laboratories ("Consumer Photo Processing Division" or "CPPD"), which provided film processing services to other photofinishers. CPPD also operated the Standard Manufacturing Company ("Standard"), which manufactured film splicers and associated equipment. The Government Services Group ("Government Services") provided photographic and non-photographic support and management services under contract to governmental agencies. Technicolor's Gold Key Entertainment Division ("Gold Key"), licensed motion pictures and other programs for television exhibition. The Audio Visual Division ("Audio Visual") distributed film and video equipment.

Morton Kamerman ("Kamerman"), Technicolor's Chief Executive Officer and Board Chairman, concluded that Technicolor's principal business, theatrical film processing, did not offer sufficient long-term growth for Technicolor. Kamerman proposed that Technicolor enter the field of rapid processing of consumer film by establishing a network of stores across the country offering one-hour development of film. The business, named One Hour Photo ("OHP"), would require Technicolor to open approximately 1,000 stores over five years and to invest about $150 million.

In May 1981, Technicolor's Board of Directors approved Kamerman's plan. The following month, Technicolor announced its ambitious venture with considerable fanfare. On the date of its OHP announcement, Technicolor's stock had risen to a high of $22.13.

In the months that followed, Technicolor fell behind on its schedule for OHP store openings. The few stores that did open reported operating losses. At the same time, Technicolor's other major divisions were experiencing mixed, if not disappointing, results.

As of August 1982, Technicolor had opened only twenty-one of a planned fifty OHP retail stores. Its Board was anticipating a $5.2 million operating loss for OHP in fiscal 1983. On August 25, 1982, the Technicolor Board "authorized the company's officers to seek a buyer for Gold Key." During 1982, Technicolor also decided to terminate the Audio Visual Division. Nevertheless, Kamerman remained committed to OHP. In Technicolor's Annual Report, issued September 7, 1982, Kamerman stated, "We remain optimistic that the One Hour Photo business represents a significant growth opportunity for the Company."

Technicolor's September 1982 financial statements, for the fiscal year ending June 1982, reported an eighty percent decline of consolidated net income — from $17.073 million in fiscal 1981 to $3.445 million in 1982. Profits had declined in Technicolor's core business, film processing. Technicolor's management also attributed the decline in profits to write-offs for losses in its Gold Key and Audio Visual divisions, which had already been targeted for sale. By September 1982, Technicolor's stock had reached a new low of $8.37 after falling by the end of June to $10.37 a share.

In the late summer of 1982, Ronald O. Perelman ("Perelman"), MAF's controlling stockholder, concluded that Technicolor would be an attractive candidate for a takeover or acquisition by MAF. Kamerman and Perelman met for the first time on October 4, 1982 at Technicolor's offices in Los Angeles. Perelman informed Kamerman that MAF would be willing to pay $20 per share to acquire Technicolor. Kamerman replied that he would not consider submitting the matter to Technicolor's Board at a price below $25 a share.

Perelman met with Kamerman in Los Angeles for a second time on October 12, 1982. MAF's Chief Financial Officer also attended the meeting. The meeting's principal purposes were: (1) to allow MAF's Chief Financial Officer to review Technicolor financial data; and (2) to give Perelman a tour of Technicolor's Los Angeles facilities.

On October 27, Kamerman and Perelman reached an agreement by telephone. Perelman initially offered $22.50 per share for Technicolor's stock. Kamerman countered with a figure of $23 per share. He also stated that he would recommend its acceptance to the Technicolor Board. Perelman agreed to the $23 per share price.

The Technicolor Board convened on October 29, 1982 to consider MAF's proposal. All nine directors of Technicolor attended the meeting. Kamerman outlined the history of his negotiations with Perelman. Kamerman explained the basic structure of the transaction: a tender offer by MAF at $23 per share for all the outstanding shares of common stock of Technicolor; and a second-step merger with the remaining outstanding shares converted into $23 per share, with Technicolor becoming a wholly owned subsidiary of MAF. Kamerman recommended that MAF's $23 per share offer be accepted in view of the present market value of Technicolor's shares. Kamerman stated that accepting $23 a share was "advisable rather than shooting dice" on the prospects of Technicolor's OHP venture.

On October 29, 1982, the Technicolor Board agreed to the acquisition proposal by MAF. The Technicolor Board: approved the Agreement and Plan of Merger with MAF; recommended to the stockholders of Technicolor the acceptance of the offer of $23 per share; and recommended the repeal of the supermajority provision in Technicolor's Certificate of Incorporation. Technicolor filed forms 14D-9 and 13D with the Securities and Exchange Commission which reflected those Board actions and recommendations.

In November 1982, MAF commenced an all-cash tender offer of $23 per share to the shareholders of Technicolor. When the tender offer closed on November 30, 1982, MAF had gained control of Technicolor. By December 3, 1982, MAF had acquired 3,754,181 shares, or 82.19%, of Technicolor's shares. Thereafter, MAF and Technicolor were consolidated for tax and financial reporting purposes.

The Court of Chancery made a factual finding that, "upon acquiring control" of Technicolor, Perelman and his associates "began to dismember what they saw as a badly conceived mélange of businesses." Perelman testified: "Presumably we made the evaluation of the business of Technicolor before we made the purchase, not after." That evaluation assumed the retention of the Professional and Government Services Groups and the disposition of OHP, CPPD, Gold Key and Audio Visual.

Consequently, immediately after becoming Technicolor's controlling shareholder, MAF "started looking for buyers for several of the [Technicolor] divisions." Bear Stearns & Co. was also retained by MAF in December 1982 to assist it in disposing of Technicolor assets. A target date of June 30, 1983 was set for liquidating all of Technicolor's excess assets. As of December 31, 1982, MAF was projecting that $54 million would be realized from asset sales.

In December 1982, the Board of Technicolor notified its stockholders of a special shareholders meeting on January 24, 1983. At the meeting, the Technicolor shareholders voted to repeal the supermajority amendment and in favor of the proposed merger. MAF and Technicolor completed the merger.

VALUATION OF TECHNICOLOR

Perelman Plan or Kamerman Plan

The merger was accomplished on January 24, 1983. The parties agree that the appraised value of Technicolor must be fixed as of that date. *See Alabama By-Products Corp. v. Neal*, Del. Supr., 588 A.2d 255, 256-57 (1991). There is a fundamental disagreement between the litigants, however, concerning the nature of the enterprise to be appraised.

Cinerama argues that the Court of Chancery should have valued Technicolor as it existed on the date of the merger and, in particular, with due regard for the strategies that had been conceived and implemented following the merger agreement by MAF's controlling shareholder, Ronald O. Perelman ("Perelman Plan"). Technicolor argues that the Court of Chancery properly considered Technicolor without regard to the Perelman Plan and only as it existed on or before October 29, 1982, with the then extant strategies that had been conceived and implemented by Technicolor's Chairman, Morton Kamerman ("Kamerman Plan"). According to Cinerama:

> Reduced to its simplest form, the dispute was whether the trial court should value Perelman's Technicolor—a company whose business plans and strategies focused on the processing and duplication of film and videotape and the provision of services to

the United States Government and which planned and expected to generate $50 million in cash during 1983 from the sale of unwanted and/or unsuccessful businesses, namely, OHP, CPPD, Gold Key and Audio Visual; or Kamerman's Technicolor—a company whose business plans and strategies assumed diversification away from a concentration on film processing and videotape duplication for the professional market toward consumer oriented businesses, especially OHP.

The economic experts for both parties used a form of discounted cash flow methodology to value Technicolor. Cinerama's expert was John Torkelsen ("Torkelsen"), a financial analyst with Princeton Venture Research, Inc. Technicolor's primary expert witness was Alfred Rappaport ("Rappaport"), a professor at Northwestern University Graduate Business School and a consultant with The Alcar Group ("Alcar"). The fundamental nature of the disagreement between the parties about the Perelman Plan and the Kamerman Plan, however, resulted in different factual assumptions by their respective experts.

QUESTION OF LAW

Perelman Plan or Kamerman Plan

The Court of Chancery recognized that the parties' disagreement about valuing Technicolor based upon either the Perelman Plan or the Kamerman Plan presented a question of law with regard to the proper interpretation of the appraisal statute. *See* 8 Del. C. §262(h). According to the Court of Chancery, that legal issue is whether in valuing Technicolor as of January 24, 1983, the court should assume the business plan for Technicolor that MAF is said by [Cinerama] to have had in place at that time [Perelman Plan], or whether a proper valuation is premised upon ignoring such changes as Mr. Perelman had in mind because to the extent they create value they are "elements of value arising from the accomplishment or expectation of the merger." 8 Del. C. §262(h).

The Court of Chancery also recognized that legal issue was "particularly pertinent when considering One Hour Photo, Standard Manufacturing and [the Consumer Photo Processing Division]." Torkelsen's valuation assumed each of those businesses would be sold by MAF. Rappaport assumed that, but for the MAF acquisition, those businesses would have continued operating. Therefore, the Rappaport valuations included those businesses as going concerns. Predictably, the different assumptions factored into each expert's discounted cash flow model yielded disparate valuation results.[3]

---

3. Cinerama's expert opined that the statutory appraisal fair value of Technicolor on a per share basis as of January 24, 1983, was $62.75. Technicolor's expert opined that the statutory appraisal fair value of Technicolor at the time of the merger was $13.14 per share.

THE PARTIES' CONTENTIONS
Perelman Plan or Kamerman Plan

In the Court of Chancery, Cinerama argued that the Perelman Plan — which contemplated the sale of several businesses, focusing the company on film processing, and the new videocassette duplication business — was governing the operation of Technicolor on January 24, 1983. Consequently, Cinerama argued Perelman's Plan had to govern any expert's projection of net cash flow. For example, according to Cinerama, Technicolor's previous projections of negative cash flow from OHP's operation would be irrelevant in the appraisal valuation. In support of its position, Cinerama presented evidence that, prior to the merger date, Perelman had not only formulated, but had also implemented, a plan for how OHP and certain other Technicolor assets would be sold.

Technicolor argued to the Court of Chancery that the Perelman Plan, which it admitted called for the liquidation of OHP and a number of its other businesses, was not sufficiently defined on the date of the merger to form the factual premise for the Cinerama expert's cash flow projections from asset sales. The Court of Chancery unequivocally rejected that assertion by Technicolor. The Court of Chancery made a specific factual finding that "the record supports the conclusion that MAF intended from the outset to realize by one technique or another the capital value of One Hour Photo and to terminate that division's drain on the company's cash flow. Insofar as sale of that enterprise is involved, the 'Perelman Plan' was fixed by the merger date."

In view of that adverse factual determination, Technicolor's alternative contention was a legal argument. According to Technicolor, any value attributable to the Perelman Plan as of the merger date had to be excluded as arising from the expectation of the merger. *See* 8 Del. C. §262(h). Thus, Technicolor argued that the net cash flows which followed from the Perelman Plan should be excluded from the statutory appraisal valuation, as a matter of law.

In response, Cinerama argued to the Court of Chancery that this Court had construed the statutory phrase "exclusive of any element of value arising from the accomplishment or expectation of the merger" to exclude "[o]nly the speculative elements of value that may arise from the 'accomplishment or expectation' of the merger.... But elements of future value ... which are known or susceptible of proof as of the date of the merger and not the product of speculation, may be considered." *Weinberger v. UOP, Inc.*, Del. Supr., 457 A.2d 701, 713 (1983). Thus, Cinerama argued any nonspeculative element of future value that could be proven may be considered in a statutory appraisal proceeding, even if it is an "element of value arising from the accomplishment or expectation of the merger." *See* 8 Del. C. §262(h).

Court of Chancery's Holding

Majority Acquiror Principle/Proximate Cause Exception

The Court of Chancery acknowledged that, based upon the quoted language from *Weinberger*, Cinerama's legal argument appeared to be persuasive. The Court of Chancery concluded, however, "that reading [of *Weinberger*] is too difficult to square with the plain words of the statute to permit the conclusion that that is what was intended." The Court of Chancery then stated "in order to understand the quoted passage [from *Weinberger*] when read together with the statutory language, I assume an unexpressed phrase to the effect 'unless, but for the merger, such elements of future value would not exist.'" According to the Court of Chancery, the language in *Weinberger* would read: "But elements of future value, including the nature of the enterprise, which are known or susceptible of proof as of the date of the merger and not the product of speculation, may be considered [unless, but for the merger, such elements of future value would not exist]." *Weinberger v. UOP, Inc.*, Del. Supr., 457 A.2d 701, 713 (1983).

In explaining the "but for" caveat that it had superimposed upon this Court's holding in *Weinberger*, the Court of Chancery reasoned that, as a matter of policy, the valuation process in a statutory appraisal proceeding should be the same irrespective of whether a merger is accomplished in one or two steps:

> Delaware law traditionally and today accords to a dissenting shareholder "his proportionate interest in a going concern" and that going concern is the corporation in question, with its asset deployment, business plan and management unaffected by the plans or strategies of the acquiror. When value is created by substituting new management or by redeploying assets "in connection with the accomplishment or expectation" of a merger, that value is not, in my opinion, a part of the "going concern" in which a dissenting shareholder has a legal (or equitable) right to participate.
>
> If one accepts this principle, the question arises how is it to be applied in a two-step arm's-length acquisition transaction. In such a transaction there will be a period following close [to] the first-step tender offer in which the [majority] acquiror may, as a practical matter, be in a position to influence or change the nature of the corporate business, or to freeze controversial programs until they are reviewed following the second-step merger.

Accordingly, the Court of Chancery concluded that "[f]uture value that would not exist *but for* the merger . . . even if it is capable of being proven on the date of the merger," is irrelevant in a Delaware statutory appraisal proceeding. (Emphasis added.) Consequently, the Court of Chancery held "that value added to [Technicolor] by the implementation or the expectation of the implementation of Mr. Perelman's new business plan for [Technicolor] is not value to which, in an appraisal action, [Cinerama] is entitled to a *pro rata* share, but is value that is excluded from consideration by the statutory exclusion for value arising from the merger or its expectation."

Legal scholars have written extensively with regard to the economic desirability of including or excluding certain valuation elements in an appraisal proceeding, especially with regard to cash-out two-step mergers. The Court of Chancery's construction of "fair value" followed logically from its concept of what was economically desirable and efficient. However, the majority acquiror principle and correlative proximate cause exception for two-step mergers, upon which the Court of Chancery premised its holding, are inconsistent with this Court's interpretation of the appraisal statute in *Weinberger*. . . .

PERELMAN PLAN
Susceptible of Proof/Non-Speculative

The underlying assumption in an appraisal valuation is that the dissenting shareholders would be willing to maintain their investment position had the merger not occurred. *Cavalier Oil Corp. v. Harnett*, Del. Supr., 564 A.2d 1137, 1145 (1989). Accordingly, the Court of Chancery's task in an appraisal proceeding is to value what has been taken from the shareholder, *i.e.*, the proportionate interest in the going concern. *Id.* at 1144 (citing *Tri-Continental Corp. v. Battye*, Del. Supr., 74 A.2d 71, 72 (1950)). To that end, this Court has held that the corporation must be valued as an operating entity. *Id.* We conclude that the Court of Chancery did not adhere to this principle.

The Court of Chancery determined that Perelman "had a fixed view of how [Technicolor's] assets would be sold before the merger and had begun to implement it" prior to January 24, 1983. Consequently, the Court of Chancery found that the Perelman Plan for Technicolor was the operative reality on the date of the merger. Nevertheless, the Court of Chancery held that Cinerama was not entitled to an appraisal of Technicolor as it was actually functioning on the date of the merger pursuant to the Perelman Plan.

The Court of Chancery reached that holding by applying its majority acquiror principle and correlative proximate cause exception. The Court of Chancery excluded any value that was admittedly part of Technicolor as a going concern on the date of the merger, if that value was created by substituting new management or redeploying assets during the transient period between the first and second steps of this two-step merger, *i.e.*, Perelman's Plan. The Court of Chancery reasoned that valuing Technicolor as a going concern, under the Perelman Plan, on the date of the merger, would be tantamount to awarding Cinerama a proportionate share of a control premium, which the Court of Chancery deemed to be both economically undesirable and contrary to this Court's holding in *Bell v.*

Kirby Lumber Corp., Del. Supr., 413 A.2d 137, 140-42 (1980). *See also Rapid-American Corp. v. Harris*, Del. Supr., 603 A.2d 796, 805-07 (1992). Thus, the Court of Chancery concluded "that value [added by a majority acquiror] is not . . . a part of the 'going concern' in which a dissenting shareholder has a legal (or equitable) right to participate."

In *Kirby* and its progeny, including *Technicolor I*, this Court has explained that the dissenter in an appraisal action is entitled to receive a proportionate share of fair value in the *going concern* on the date of the merger, rather than value that is determined on a liquidated basis. *Bell v. Kirby Lumber Corp.*, 413 A.2d at 142; *see also In re Shell Oil Co.*, Del. Supr., 607 A.2d 1213, 1219 (1992); *Technicolor I*, 542 A.2d at 1186; *Rosenblatt v. Getty Oil Co.*, Del. Supr., 493 A.2d 929, 942 (1985); *Rothschild Int'l Corp. v. Liggett Group Inc.*, Del. Supr., 474 A.2d 133, 137 (1984); *accord Rapid-American Corp. v. Harris*, 603 A.2d at 802-03 Thus, the company must first be valued as an operating entity. *Cavalier Oil Corp. v. Harnett*, 564 A.2d at 1144. In that regard, one of the most important factors to consider is the "nature of the enterprise" that is the subject of the appraisal proceeding. *Rapid-American Corp. v. Harris*, 603 A.2d at 805; *see Weinberger v. UOP, Inc.*, 457 A.2d 701, 713 (1983).

In a two-step merger, to the extent that value has been added following a change in majority control before cash-out, it is still value attributable to the going concern, *i.e.*, the extant "nature of the enterprise," on the date of the merger. *See Rapid-American Corp. v. Harris*, 603 A.2d at 805. The dissenting shareholder's proportionate interest is determined only after the company has been valued as an operating entity on the date of the merger. *Cavalier Oil Corp. v. Harnett*, 564 A.2d at 1144; *cf. Walter W.B. v. Elizabeth P.B.*, Del. Supr., 462 A.2d 414, 415 (1983). Consequently, value added to the going concern by the "majority acquiror," during the transient period of a two-step merger, accrues to the benefit of all shareholders and must be included in the appraisal process on the date of the merger. *See Rapid-American Corp. v. Harris*, 603 A.2d 796; *Cavalier Oil Corp. v. Harnett*, 564 A.2d 1137; *cf. Walter W.B. v. Elizabeth P.B.*, 462 A.2d at 415.

In this case, the question in the appraisal action was the fair value of Technicolor stock on the date of the merger, January 24, 1983, as Technicolor was operating pursuant to the Perelman Plan. The Court of Chancery erred, as a matter of law, by determining the fair value of Technicolor on the date of the merger "but for" the Perelman Plan; or, in other words, by valuing Technicolor as it was operating on October 29, 1982, pursuant to the Kamerman Plan. By failing to accord Cinerama the *full proportionate value of its shares in the going concern on the date of the merger*, the Court of Chancery imposed a penalty upon Cinerama for lack of control. *Cavalier Oil Corp. v. Harnett*, 564 A.2d at 1145; *accord Rapid-American Corp. v. Harris*, 603 A.2d at 805-07; *Bell v. Kirby Lumber Corp.*, 413 A.2d at 140-42.

The "accomplishment or expectation" of the merger exception in Section 262 is very narrow, "designed to eliminate use of *pro forma* data and projections of a speculative variety relating to the completion of a merger." *Weinberger v. UOP, Inc.*, 457 A.2d at 713. That narrow exclusion does not encompass known elements of value, including those which exist on the date of the merger because of a majority acquiror's interim action in a two-step cash-out transaction. *Cf. In re Shell Oil Co.*, 607 A.2d at 1218-19. "[O]nly the *speculative* elements of value that may arise from the 'accomplishment or expectation' of the merger" should have been excluded from the Court of Chancery's calculation of fair value on the date of the merger. *Weinberger v. UOP, Inc.*, 457 A.2d at 713 (emphasis added); *cf. In re Shell Oil Co.*, 607 A.2d at 1219.

The Court of Chancery's determination not to value Technicolor as a going concern on the date of the merger under the Perelman Plan, resulted in an understatement of Technicolor's fair value in the appraisal action. That result was inevitable when the Court of Chancery valued Technicolor pursuant to a discounted cash flow model with the negative factual input and assumptions from the Kamerman Plan rather than the Perelman Plan. Consequently, the Court of Chancery permitted MAF to "reap a windfall from the appraisal process by cashing out a dissenting shareholder [Cinerama]," for less than the fair value of its interest in Technicolor as a going concern on the date of the merger. *Cavalier Oil Corp. v. Harnett*, 564 A.2d at 1145.

Cinerama has asked this Court to make an appraisal of the fair value of its Technicolor shares on the date of the merger, rather than remand this protracted litigation to the Court of Chancery. This Court will not make an independent determination of value on appeal. *Rapid-American Corp. v. Harris*, 603 A.2d at 799. This appraisal action will be remanded to the Court of Chancery for a recalculation of Technicolor's fair value on the date of the merger. *See id.*

Upon remand, it is within the Court of Chancery's discretion to select one of the parties' valuation models as its general framework, or fashion its own, to determine fair value in the appraisal proceeding. *See Rapid-American Corp. v. Harris*, 603 A.2d at 804. The Court of Chancery has properly recognized that its choice of a framework does not require it to adopt any one expert's model, methodology, or mathematical calculations *in toto*. *See id.* The undervaluation in this appraisal proceeding resulted from negative factual assumptions that originated from an erroneous legal theory, not from either the valuation framework selected or adaptions to it by the Court of Chancery. In that regard, however, we have concluded that the Court of Chancery's erroneous majority acquiror principle and proximate cause exception permeated its factual assumptions so pervasively, that the Court of Chancery's attribution of only a $4.43 per share value difference between the Perelman Plan and the Kamerman Plan should not be considered the law of this case upon remand.

LAW OF CASE

Perelman Plan Is Valuation Element

The Court of Chancery's majority acquiror principle and proximate cause exception for two-step mergers are also contrary to the law of this case, as set forth in *Technicolor I*. *See Technicolor I*, 542 A.2d at 1186-87 & n.7. In *Technicolor I*, this Court provided specific guidance regarding the application of *Weinberger*'s holdings to the trial of Cinerama's consolidated appraisal and personal liability actions. *Id.* at 1186-88. We began by emphasizing that upon remand, the *Weinberger* "'liberalized approach' to appraisal shall be used to determine the value of a cashed-out minority's [Cinerama's] share interest *on the day of the merger, reflecting all relevant information regarding the company* [Technicolor] *and its shares.*" *Id.* at 1187 (emphasis added).

In an effort to convey this Court's comprehensive interpretation of the statutory "all relevant information," we recognized in *Technicolor I* "that the majority [MAF] may have insight into their company's [Technicolor's] future based primarily on bits and pieces of *nonmaterial* information that have value as a totality." *Id.* at 1187 n.8. Consequently, in *Technicolor I*, we said "[i]t is this information that, if available in a *statutory appraisal proceeding*, the Court of Chancery *must* evaluate to determine if future earnings will affect the fair value of shares on the day of the merger." *Id.* (emphasis added) (citing 8 Del. C. §262(h)). This Court reinforced the relevance of such information to the appraisal action, independent of the personal liability action, stating "[t]he issue we are addressing is not the manipulation of the transaction, nor the suppression or misstatement of *material* information by insiders defrauding the market." *Id.* (citations omitted). Thus, the law of this case required the Court of Chancery to consider nonspeculative information about the Perelman Plan.

The record is replete with information about Technicolor's future that was known on the date of the merger. *Cf. Rosenblatt v. Getty Oil Co.*, Del. Supr., 493 A.2d 929, 941-42 (1985). MAF's October 18, 1982 financing package presented to the lending banks, Chase Manhattan Bank and Bank of America, contemplated that MAF would realize $50 million in net proceeds from the sale of assets by the end of 1983. Moreover, the loan agreement between MAF and the banks specifically identified OHP, CPPD, Gold Key and Audio Visual as assets which could be sold by MAF on behalf of Technicolor.

The Court of Chancery found that as of the date of the merger one "would not have projected" that Technicolor would retain OHP and the other businesses (CPPD, Gold Key and Audio Visual) that Perelman had designated for elimination. Following this remand, Technicolor must be viewed and valued "as an on-going enterprise, occupying a particular market position in the light of future prospects." *In re Shell Oil Co.*, Del. Supr., 607 A.2d 1213, 1218 (1992). All "elements of future value, including the nature of the enterprise, which are known or susceptible of proof as of the date of the merger and not the product of speculation, may [and should] be considered." *Weinberger v. UOP, Inc.*, Del. Supr., 457 A.2d 701, 713 (1983); *accord Rosenblatt v. Getty Oil Co.*, 493 A.2d at 940; *cf. In re Shell Oil Co.*, 607 A.2d at 1219.

EVIDENTIARY ISSUES

Cinerama has raised several evidentiary contentions which we will address briefly because this matter will be remanded for further proceedings. Cinerama argues that the Court of Chancery's reliance upon the stock market price of Technicolor's shares in September 1982 was improper for two reasons: first, that price reflected the market's negative opinion of the Kamerman Plan; and, second, the market never had an opportunity to price Technicolor stock in the context of the Perelman Plan. This Court has recognized that the "market price of shares may not be representative of true value." *Paramount Communications, Inc. v. Time Inc.*, Del. Supr., 571 A.2d 1140, 1150 n.12 (1989). Moreover, in this case, we noted that "[i]nformation and insight not communicated to the market may not be reflected in stock prices." *Technicolor I*, 542 A.2d at 1187 n.8. Nevertheless, Cinerama's objection goes to the weight, if any, to be given to the stock market price for Technicolor stock in September 1982, rather than its admissability. *See In re Delaware Racing Ass'n*, Del. Supr., 213 A.2d 203, 211 (1965); *cf. Rapid-American Corp. v. Harris*, Del. Supr., 603 A.2d 796, 806 (1992) (rejecting "*exclusive* reliance upon market value in an appraisal action"). Upon remand, Cinerama can renew its argument that the September 1982 stock market price was of little significance to the issue of fair value on the date of the merger in January 1983.

NOTES AND QUESTIONS

1. The deal. Where is the value coming from in this deal? The bidder is Ronald Perelman, who you should remember from the *Revlon* case. He sees a company gone astray and the opportunity for making money that comes from that situation. Technicolor once had a dominant position in putting color in the movies; its logo was often the last thing you saw at the movie theater at the end of the credits. But, as the court notes, its business had stagnated, and the CEO's bright idea to fill in the gap, a string of one-hour photo retail locations, had driven the stock down from $22.13 to $8.37 over 16 months. Perelman's plan is as simple as the doctor's advice to a patient seeking relief from pain — stop doing what is causing your pain. And more so than most human patients, it is possible to do exactly that, and Perelman can offer almost three times the market price.

A. Majority Power, Minority Rights to Exit Via Appraisal

2. The plaintiff. The opinions in this litigation do not tell us very much about the plaintiff, other than that it owned about 200,000 shares (4 percent or so) that it had begun acquiring in June 1982 (when the price was $10.37, heading to $8.37 in September) and that it felt that the deal price was too low. Does the $23 price reflect the entire amount that can be squeezed out of the company by the purchaser? Although, as discussed in Chapter 2, targets usually get most of the premium in a takeover, Perelman undoubtedly expected a profit. In one of the early opinions in the case, Chancellor Allen observed "In the annals of effective use of leverage the account of MAF's original minimal cash contribution to the acquisition of Technicolor certainly deserves a place." 1990 WL 161084 (Del. Ch. Oct. 19, 1990).

How is the plaintiff here different from the plaintiffs in *Weinberger* in terms of vulnerability to possible abuse? Does the market check via shareholders deciding whether to tender give them sufficient protection? Should minority shareholders who disagree with this market process have the opportunity to contest valuation in court? Are they free-riding on Perelman's efforts?

3. The structure of the deal and its impact on control and valuation. Perelman's pursuit of Technicolor illustrates the two-step tender offer/cash-out merger. After Perelman decided Technicolor was a good candidate for a takeover, he and the target's CEO began negotiations and within the month of October settled on an all-cash price of $23 per share. But this deal was structured in two parts, first as a tender offer for at least a majority of shares and then a cash-out merger in which the remaining shareholdings would receive the same $23 cash consideration. Why split up the formalities? The tender offer began in early November and closed by the end of the month with the bidder having acquired control. In fact, its shareholders reached 82 percent by December 3. Technicolor's board fairly quickly called a special shareholders meeting to vote on the merger that took place on January 24, leaving time for solicitation of proxies and other formalities. In the mean time, MAF began implementing the steps to create value including disposing of unwanted assets. Do you see how the two steps of the transaction affected the date on which valuation would occur and why the plaintiff in this case might prefer the later date? With the 2013 addition of §251(h) to the Delaware statute, an acquiring shareholder like Perelman with no prior connection to a publicly held target corporation, who makes a tender offer open to any and all shareholders and thereby acquires at least the majority of shares necessary to approve a merger, can skip the shareholder vote normally required in a merger if an immediate second-step merger provides the same consideration as the tender offer. Such a provision would permit Perelman to close such a potential time gap as to the valuation date, but doesn't resolve elements of future value known of susceptible to proof as of the day of the merger.

4. Minority shareholder remedies. Plaintiffs in this case brought both an appraisal action and a separate action for the directors' breach of fiduciary duty, illustrating the alternative remedies that Delaware law permits for mergers occurring under §251. As noted in the notes after the previous cases, courts in some other states have held that appraisal is the exclusive remedy for minority shareholders in a merger situation. The policy question is whether appraisal, a statutory remedy that traditionally used a narrow definition of value and included numerous procedural limitations, can provide sufficient protection to minority shareholders, particularly in a self-dealing situation.

5. **Return on litigation?** The litigation in this case went on for more than 20 years. After initial skirmishes, Chancellor Allen held a 47-day trial on both the appraisal and fiduciary duty claims and found that fair value was $21.60 (in contrast to the $23 offered in the deal) and that there was no violation of fiduciary duty. On appeal, the Delaware Supreme Court held that the fiduciary duty claim should have been determined first. On remand and after the parties resubmitted the case to the Chancellor with no additional evidence, the Chancellor found again that there had been no breach of fiduciary duty and was affirmed by the Delaware Supreme Court, thus ending that part of the case. The Chancellor's now-separate appraisal opinion is the one reversed by the Delaware Supreme Court in the principal case above. Thereafter, Chancellor Chandler took over the case for the second appraisal trial and in 2003 found fair value to be $21.98. In 2005, the Delaware Supreme Court reversed this opinion finding that the WACC (Weighted Average Cost of Capital) from the 1990 appraisal was the law of the case (as opposed to a different WACC Chancellor Chandler had found) and with the result that per share value was modified to $28.41. So plaintiff, after 20 years, finally achieved some positive value for the case of about $5.6 million. The court also ruled that pre-judgment interest (at a rate of 10.32 percent compound interest as determined in 1990) would accrue through the final judgment after remand in 2005 that provided an additional $46 million. *See* Cede & Co. v. Technicolor, Inc., 884 A.2d 26 (Del. 2005).

B. VALUATION TECHNIQUES

In re Emerging Communications, Inc. Shareholders Litigation
2004 WL 1305745 (Del. Ch. 2004)

JACOBS, J. Sitting by designation as Vice Chancellor under Del. Const., art. IV, §13(2).

These actions [a consolidated statutory appraisal and class actions for breach of fiduciary duty] all arise out of the two-step "going private" acquisition of the publicly owned shares of Emerging Communications, Inc. ("ECM"), by Innovative Communications Corporation, L.L.C. ("Innovative"),

B. Valuation Techniques

ECM's majority stockholder. The first step tender offer was commenced on August 18, 1998 by Innovative for 29% of ECM's outstanding shares at a price of $10.25 per share. The balance of ECM's publicly held shares were acquired in a second-step cash-out merger of ECM into an Innovative subsidiary, at the same price, on October 19, 1998.

At the time of this two-step transaction (the "Privatization"), 52% of the outstanding shares of ECM, and 100% of the outstanding shares of Innovative, were owned by Innovative Communication Company, LLC ("ICC"). ICC, in turn, was wholly owned by ECM's Chairman and Chief Executive Officer, Jeffrey J. Prosser ("Prosser"). Thus, Prosser had voting control of both of the parties to the Privatization transaction.

In June 1998, shortly after the Privatization proposal was announced, a fiduciary duty class action was brought on behalf of the former public shareholders of ECM by Brickell Partners, an ECM shareholder. On February 10, 1999, four months after the Privatization was consummated, an appraisal action was filed by Greenlight Capital, L.P. and certain of its affiliates (collectively, "Greenlight"). . . .

There are two groups of defendants: (1) the "ECM defendants," which consist of ECM, ICC, and Innovative; and (2) the "Board defendants," who were ECM's directors at the time of the Privatization. In addition to Jeffrey Prosser, who was also ECM's Chairman and Chief Executive Officer, ECM's directors were Richard Goodwin; John Raynor; Sir Shridath Ramphal; Salvatore Muoio; John Vondras; and Terrence Todman. Each of the board defendants served as an ECM director at Prosser's request.

B. Background Leading to the Formation of ECM

ECM's corporate predecessor, Atlantic TeleNetwork, Inc. ("ATN"), was a company that Prosser and a partner, Cornelius Prior, formed in 1987 to acquire the Virgin Islands Telephone Corporation ("Vitelco").

Vitelco, which was ATN's (and later ECM's) principal subsidiary, was (and still is) the exclusive provider of local wired telephone service in the USVI [United States Virgin Islands], where Vitelco operates a modern, fully digital telecommunications network. Vitelco was an extremely valuable asset. . . .

By 1993, Prosser and Prior had a falling out. That led to a management deadlock, which effectively precluded Prosser from pursuing his acquisition strategy. With the co-CEOs at loggerheads and the ATN board deadlocked. . . . Prosser and Prior decided to split ATN into two new companies (the "Split Off"). One of those companies, to be controlled by Prosser, would consist of ATN's Virgin Islands Group. That company was ECM. . . . Although ATN had no controlling stockholder before the Split Off (Prosser and Prior owned a large but not majority position), as a result of the Split Off Prosser ended up owning 52% of ECM's 10,959,131 shares, and ECM's public shareholders were relegated to the position of minority stockholders.

On December 31, 1997, ECM began trading as a public company on the American Stock Exchange. Shortly after Prosser obtained control of ECM, he appointed his long-time ATN directors, Raynor and Ramphal, to the ECM board. Prosser also appointed Messrs. Goodwin, Muoio and Vondras to the ECM board.

C. The Proposed, but Later Aborted, Merger of Innovative into ECM

ECM's life as a public company was short—only ten and one-half months. That was not accidental: before the Split Off had been completed, Prosser indicated that he intended to merge Innovative into ECM, and he began exploring a combination of the two companies in January 1998. On January 20, 1998, ECM hired Prudential to advise it on the fairness of a potential merger of Innovative into ECM's subsidiary ATNCo (the "Proposed Merger"). During the next month, Prosser formulated the terms of the Proposed Merger, assisted by Prudential, the law firm of Cahill, Gordon and Reindel, ECM's legal advisors ("Cahill Gordon"), and director John Raynor.

. . . the ECM board also constituted a special committee, consisting of Messrs. Goodwin, Raynor, and Ramphal (the "First Special Committee"), to consider Prosser's Proposed Merger. Those persons were appointed at the suggestion of Prosser. At that time, Raynor, who was an ECM director and a Prosser business associate, was on retainer as ECM's attorney and had helped Prosser formulate the terms of the Proposed Merger.

D. Prosser Abandons the Merger in Favor of the Privatization

During the third week of May 1998, Prosser began having significant reservations about the Proposed Merger, because the low market interest in ECM's common stock had caused that stock to be undervalued.[11] On May 21, 1998, Prosser, together with Raynor, met with representatives of Prudential and Cahill Gordon to discuss the feasibility of Innovative acquiring all of the outstanding stock of ECM. By that point, Prosser had decided (in Raynor's words) to "flip the transaction." Having concluded that the market was not recognizing ECM's intrinsic value, Prosser switched from being a seller of ECM stock to becoming a buyer of that stock. Although Prosser had placed a value of $13.25 per share on ECM for purposes of the Split Off that had occurred only 5 months before, as a buyer of that same stock he was now proposing to pay only $9.125 per share.

---

11. At that time (May 1998), Prosser knew that ECM's stock price was artificially depressed, because the market was not viewing ECM as a U.S. telephone company, but, rather, as a developing nation/third world phone company. That perception, Prosser knew, was unfair, because ECM had all the characteristics of a U.S. telephone company—a stable government, dollar economy, English language, American courts and legal system—and none of the characteristics of a third-world company. Trial Tr., Vol. 10 (Prosser) at 1728-29, 1801-02, 1807. Rather than educate the market or afford it time to understand ECM's true characteristics, Prosser exploited the market unfairness by proposing the Privatization at a price that reflected a "premium" over ECM's then-current depressed market price level.

B. Valuation Techniques

Between May 22 and May 28, Prosser, Prudential and Cahill formulated the terms of a Privatization proposal to be presented to ECM's board. On May 28, Raynor, Prosser and Thomas Minnich, ECM's Chief Operating Officer, informed the RTFC [the Rural Telephone Finance Cooperative, a entity that eventually would provide financing at below-market interest rates] that they had decided to abandon the Proposed Merger and to take ECM private. The next day, Prosser delivered to the ECM board a letter withdrawing the Proposed Merger and proposing instead that Innovative acquire all the ECM shares it did not already own. The proposed Privatization was structured as a first-step cash tender offer for ECM's publicly traded shares at $9.125 per share, to be followed by a second-step cash-out merger at the same price. . . .

On the same day that Prosser proposed the Privatization, he told ECM's board that he (Prosser) had retained ECM's former advisors, Prudential and Cahill Gordon, to represent Innovative as the buyer in that transaction. Prudential was an especially valuable advisor to ECM, because it understood ECM's business and properties and had been ECM's only advisor during its brief life as a stand-alone company. Thus, the advisors that initially were retained to work *for* the interests of ECM and its minority stockholders would now be working to serve the interests of Innovative, the party now bargaining *against* ECM. There is no evidence that the ECM board objected either to Prosser's co-opting these valuable advisors, or to the timing of the proposed Privatization.

E. The Formation of the Second Special Committee and the Negotiation of the Transaction Terms

At the May 29 ECM directors' meeting, the board formed another special committee (the "Second Special Committee") to review the fairness of the proposed Privatization. The directors selected to serve as members of this Second Special Committee were Messrs. Richard Goodwin, John Vondras, and Shridath Ramphal.

There were several obstacles to the ability of these three directors to operate as a fully functioning Special Committee. Located on different continents and separated by a time difference of 14 hours, the three Committee members were never able to meet in person. Instead, they had to conduct their business by telephone and fax. Even teleconferences were difficult to arrange and as a result, the Second Special Committee never met collectively — even by telephone — to consider the $10.25 final negotiated offer whose approval it ultimately recommended.

Because one of the Second Special Committee members lived in Indonesia and the other lived in England, practicality dictated that Goodwin would be the Committee chair. In that capacity, Goodwin was designated to — and did — take the lead role in negotiating with Prosser and in selecting the Committee's legal and financial advisors. Mr. Goodwin interviewed William Schwitter of Paul, Hastings, Janofsky & Walker LLP ("Paul Hastings"), as a potential legal advisor to the Second Special Committee, and on June 5, 1998, the Committee retained the Paul Hastings firm as its legal counsel. Later, after meeting with representatives of J.P. Morgan and Houlihan Lokey Howard & Zukin ("Houlihan") at his home in Massachusetts, Goodwin recommended that the Committee retain Houlihan as its financial advisor, and in mid-July, 1998, the Second Special Committee retained Houlihan in that capacity.

As part of its pre-financial analysis investigation of ECM, Houlihan conducted (among other things) a review of ECM's financial information. That information included financial projections for ECM, dated March 25, 1998 (the "March projections"), that had been prepared by James Heying, ECM's then—Chief Financial Officer and Executive Vice President of Acquisitions. What Houlihan was *not* provided, however, were financial projections dated June 22, 1998 (the "June projections") that Prosser had caused Heying to prepare as part of Prosser's and ICC's application to the RTFC to finance the acquisition of ECM's minority shares.

The June projections forecasted substantially higher growth than did the March projections. Based on the June projections, as modified by the RFTC, the RFTC concluded in July 1998 that ECM was worth (for loan approval purposes) approximately $28 per share. Recognizing that the Privatization gave Prosser "the opportunity to retain control at a price below the true market value of the company, the RTFC approved financing that would enable Prosser to offer up to $11.40 per share. That suggests, and Prosser later confirmed, that he always planned (and gave himself sufficient elbow room) to increase his initial offer by some amount. Moreover, the $60 million RTFC loan represented the amount Prosser had asked for, not the limit of what the RTFC would have allowed him to borrow.

Although Prosser made the June projections available to his legal advisor (Cahill), his financial advisor (Prudential), and his lender (the RTFC), the June projections were never provided to the Second Special Committee, Houlihan, or the ECM board. Instead, Prosser directed Heying to send Houlihan the March projections, even though the June projections were available by that point. As a result, the Committee and its advisors believed—mistakenly—that the March projections were the most recent projections available.

On August 4, 1998, the Committee met with Houlihan to discuss Houlihan's preliminary analysis, which had been furnished to the Committee members in the form of a draft presentation booklet. After explaining in detail his firm's assumptions and methodologies, Houlihan's representative informed the Committee that it was not prepared to opine that $9.125 was a price that was fair to the minority stockholders. After further discussion, the Second Special Committee agreed that $9.125 would not provide adequate compensation to the ECM minority.

Before beginning its negotiations with Prosser, the Committee members discussed different strategies for obtaining the highest possible price for the minority shareholders. The Committee was not ready to reject Prosser's

B. Valuation Techniques

offer outright without at least attempting first to negotiate a higher price. One strategy the Committee discussed was to present Prosser with a "final price" they believed was fair and acceptable. They concluded, however, that the approach best calculated to achieve the highest price was not to demand a specific price from Prosser, but, rather, to negotiate with Prosser for the highest price he would pay for the shares and then determine whether that price represented fair value for the minority stockholders.

Between August 5 and August 10, 1998, in a series of telephone conversations, Messrs. Goodwin and Prosser negotiated the buyout price for ECM's publicly held shares. During the first conversation, which took place on August 7, Goodwin told Prosser that his initial offer of $9.125 was inadequate. According to an entry that Goodwin made in his "diary":

> After much back and forth [Prosser] said that he could go up another point (which was price Houlihan had told me privately would be acceptable). If this failed [Prosser] was considering making a private tender which he calculated would give him around 90% of all the stock. If he could not get it at what he considered a fair price [he] might withdraw his offer and let the stock go to market level.

Eventually, Prosser told Goodwin that he would consider the matter and call Goodwin back. Shortly thereafter, Prosser raised his offer by one-eighth of a point, to $9.25 per share. Goodwin reported that offer to the Second Special Committee, which rejected it as inadequate. Goodwin then called Prosser and told Prosser that he would have to improve his offer. In a later negotiation, Prosser raised his offer to $10 per share. Again, Goodwin reported that offer to his fellow Committee members and to Houlihan. The Committee rejected that revised offer, and thereafter, Prosser raised his offer to $10.125 per share. The Second Special Committee rejected that offer as well.

In response, Prosser raised his offer to $10.25 per share, but told Goodwin that $10.25 was his final offer. Because the price had been going up in roughly quarter-point increments, Goodwin countered by asking for $10.50 per share. Prosser rejected that request, pointing out that $10.25 was already "straining the limits of [his] financing" for the transaction. At that point, Goodwin made a judgment that the Committee "had reached the limits of how far we could push . . . ," and informed the other Committee members—Ramphal and Vondras—of his conclusion. Ramphal and Vondras agreed to stop the negotiations at that point.[27]

---

27. . . . Goodwin's regular practice was to send faxes to Special Committee members (or their counsel) through Prosser's secretary, Eling Joseph, and ask her to fax it to the others. Although Goodwin told Ms. Joseph that the Committee materials were confidential, this practice did create the potential of giving Prosser access to almost every document that circulated among the Special Committee, including Houlihan's financial analysis. . . . It is manifest that Goodwin's decision to route those materials through the secretary who shared the same office as Prosser—Goodwin's bargaining adversary—rather than route them through the office of the Committee's counsel, Mr. Schwitter, created a serious risk of compromising the Committee's process and its effectiveness in negotiating the highest available value.

Thereafter, Goodwin asked Houlihan if it could furnish a fairness opinion at $10.25 per share. Houlihan responded that it could, because that price was within the valuation ranges resulting from its market multiple analysis and its discounted cash flow (DCF) analysis.

The Committee having obtained what they believed was the highest available price, the question then became whether that price was fair. On August 12, 1998, Goodwin and Vondras had a telephonic meeting with Houlihan and Paul Hastings to review Prosser's $10.25 offer. Having updated its financial analysis, Houlihan concluded that the revised offer price of $10.25 was fair to ECM's public shareholders from a financial point of view. Goodwin and Vondras thereafter voted to recommend that the full ECM board approve the Privatization.

F. ECM's Directors and Shareholders Approve the Proposed Privatization

A telephonic meeting of the ECM board to consider Prosser's revised offer to buy all of ECM's publicly held stock for $10.25 per share, was held on August 13, 1998, the following day. Present at that meeting were Mr. Schwitter and Houlihan representatives. Not attending were Messrs. Prosser (at the request of the Board) and Todman (due to a scheduling conflict). The Board members who had not served on the Special Committee had received copies of Houlihan's fairness analysis before the meeting.

At the meeting, the Special Committee members described the process they had employed. Houlihan then explained its financial analysis and confirmed that in its opinion, the $10.25 per share price was fair to the minority stockholders from a financial point of view. After discussion, the board determined to approve the Privatization, but only if a majority of the shares held by the minority stockholders were tendered in the first-step tender offer.... The Tender Offer commenced on August 24, 1998. At the time of the Tender Offer, there were 10,959,131 outstanding ECM shares, of which 5,606,873 shares were owned by Prosser through ICC, and the remaining 5,352,258 were held by the public. As of September 25, 1998, 3,206,844 of those shares (*i.e.*, a majority of the minority shares) had been tendered. On October 19, 1998, a special meeting of ECM shareholders took place, at which the Merger was approved by a vote of 5,760,660 FOR, and 4,466 AGAINST, out of 10,959,131 shares entitled to vote. The Merger was consummated that same day.

These appraisal and fiduciary duty class actions followed. . . .

The parties' briefs are largely devoted to the "fair price" and appraisal issues, which in this case (as noted), are one and the same. Typical in litigation of this kind, the overriding question—what ECM was intrinsically worth on the merger date—involves a proverbial "battle of the experts." In this case, the valuation experts were University of Chicago Business School Professor Mark Zmijewski, the plaintiffs' expert who valued ECM at over $41 per share; and Daniel Bayston, a consultant at Duff

B. Valuation Techniques

and Phelps and the defendants' primary valuation expert, who valued ECM at $10.38 per share.

These widely differing valuations of the same company result from quite different financial assumptions that each sponsoring side exhorts this Court to accept. To evaluate the parties' competing approaches requires the Court to resolve a multitude of DCF-related valuation issues, some of which are factual and others of which are conceptual.

The first set of issues involve which set of management projections is appropriate to use in a discounted cash flow (DCF) valuation of ECM — the March projections that were furnished to the Special Committee, or the June projections that were created closer in time to the merger date but were furnished only to Prosser, his advisors, and the RTFC, and not the Special Committee or its advisors. Professor Zmijewski used the June projections without modification. Mr. Bayston, on the other hand, used the March projections and modified them in ways that the plaintiffs hotly dispute.

A second set of issues concerns the appropriate discount rate. In this regard, both Prof. Zmijewski and Mr. Bayston determined a discount rate using standard weighted average cost of capital ("WACC") and Capital Asset Pricing Model ("CAPM") formulas.

... [T]he Court concludes that (1) the $10.25 merger price was not fair, and (2) ECM's fair value (and fair price) on the date of the merger was $38.05 per share. ...

III. THE FAIR PRICE AND FAIR VALUE OF ECM

Although each side's experts valued ECM using both the comparable company and DCF approaches, in their briefs the parties focus almost exclusively upon DCF valuation issues. ...[36]

Both sides agree, and our case law recognizes, that a DCF valuation is based upon three inputs: (a) the projections of free cash flow for a specified number of years, (b) the estimated terminal value of the firm at the end of the "projection period," and (c) the discount rate. Although the parties raise a plethora of DCF-related issues, those disputes center around four pivotal questions: (1) which projections (March or June) provide the more appropriate free cash flow input to the DCF model; (2) what is the appropriate discount rate for ECM; (3) how much weight (if any) should the market value of ECM's stock be given in the valuation; and (4) should the value resulting from the DCF method be increased by the value of the businesses that are claimed to be corporate opportunities of ECM?

---

36. The basic flaw in the comparable company approach is that ECM had no true comparables, as Mr. Bayston conceded. The DCF methodology, on the other hand, is more appropriate because ECM had available contemporaneous management forecasts, predictable earnings and cash flow.

The issues that fall within these four groupings are addressed in this Part of the Opinion.

A. Which Set of ECM's Projections — March or June — Is More Reliable for Purposes of a DCF Valuation on the Merger Date?

Critical to any DCF valuation are the projected revenues, expenses, reserves, and other charges of the firm being valued . . . the Court determines that the unmodified June projections are the more appropriate and reliable source of inputs for a DCF valuation of ECM.

First, as a general proposition (with which defendants' expert, Gilbert Matthews, agreed), "an appraiser should rely on a company's most recent contemporaneous management forecasts unless there are compelling reasons to the contrary." Here, the facts compellingly point to reliance on the June projections, which, unlike the March projections, incorporated ECM's first quarter of actual results as a stand-alone company. . . . Also telling is that the June projections were provided to Prosser's legal and financial advisors in the Privatization (Cahill and Prudential) — but not to the Second Special Committee or its advisors.

Second, . . . Defendants argue that the June projections are inappropriate for use in an appraisal because they incorporated . . . projected annual cost savings that (defendants say) are synergistic, *i.e.*, merger-related: $2.5 million in savings from the consolidation of ECM and ICC's operations, . . . the value achieved by Prosser's existing pre-merger ability to effect those cost savings was an asset of ECM at the time of the Privatization merger. It therefore was a benefit in which all ECM stockholders, not just Prosser, were entitled to share. That entitlement cannot be defeated by Prosser's unilateral decision not to achieve those savings except as part of a going private merger that would leave him as the sole owner of the enterprise.

Third, the March projections are inappropriate for the additional reason that the defendants' expert, Mr. Bayston, initially relied on those projections, but then modified them by making large adjustments to critical inputs. The effect of those inputs was to depress the cash flows that management had contemporaneously projected. . . .

The primary modification that Bayston made to the March (and, by inference, the June) projections was to increase projected capital expenditures (CapEx). Both the March and the June projections forecasted CapEx of approximately $9 million annually throughout the projection period. Prosser explained that these forecasted capital expenditures were lower than historical levels and were reasonable over the short term, because Vitelco had recently replaced and rebuilt its equipment, thereby reducing the need for short term capital expenditures. . . . [I]n his cash flow projection Bayston unilaterally increased forecasted CapEx by $3.7 million to $5.7 million per year, because (he claimed) managements "typically" underestimate capital expenditures. Bayston could not cite any scholarly research confirming that view. Nor could he quantify the average amount of any such underestimations, and he never performed an analysis of whether ECM's management had regularly underestimated CapEx. Bayston's CapEx adjustment decreased free cash flow for each of the forecast years by the amount of the adjusted increase, and for the terminal year decreased cash flow by almost 20 percent. The result was a *negative growth* in free cash flow for years 2005 to 2007, resulting in a consequential decrease in Bayston's overall valuation.

That adjustment amounts essentially to Bayston substituting his personal judgment of what CapEx should be for the non-litigation business judgment of ECM's management. Bayston's judgment rests solely upon his opinion that "managements" in general underestimate CapEx. The defendants have nowhere demonstrated that that view is generally accepted within the financial valuation community or that *this* management habitually underestimated CapEx for ECM. Bayston's valuation approach evokes a reaction akin to that expressed by the Chancellor in *Cinerama*. There, the petitioner's expert had rejected a management forecast on unsubstantiated grounds, and the Court observed: "[The expert's] attempts to arrive at more 'realistic' results with a hindsight valuation that ... completely ignores the closest insiders' projections, and results in a strikingly [low] number. This is simply inexcusable."

B. What Is the Appropriate Discount Rate?

The second major group of issues concerns the appropriate rate for discounting the projected free cash flows. Both Prof. Zmijewski and Mr. Bayston determined their discount rate(s) using the Weighted Average Cost of Capital ("WACC") and the Capital Asset Pricing Model ("CAPM") formulas. Professor Zmijewski used the WACC formula, without adjustment, to calculate a discount rate of 8.8% during the 1998-2002 period when ECM's tax abatement would be in effect, and 8.5% thereafter, assuming that ECM's tax abatement would not be renewed. Mr. Bayston also used the WACC model, but modified the formula and the inputs to that formula by adding various premiums, substituting new debt costs, and using a different debt-to-equity weighting, to arrive at a discount rate of 11.5%.

To understand the significance of the disputes that arise under this heading, it is useful to explain how the discount rate is determined under the WACC model. Under WACC, the discount rate is calculated based upon the subject company's cost of capital. WACC is the sum of: (1) the percentage of the company's capital structure that is financed with equity, multiplied by the company's cost of equity capital, *plus* (2) the percentage of the company's capital structure that is financed with debt, multiplied by its after-tax cost of debt.[57]

One element of the WACC formula—the "cost of equity capital"—is determined by the CAPM model. Under CAPM, the cost of equity capital is the risk-free rate of return plus the subject company's risk. The subject company's risk is determined by multiplying the equity risk premium for the market by the company's beta. "Beta" is the measure of a given company's nondiversifiable risk relative to the market, specifically, the tendency of the returns on a company's security to correlate with swings in the broad market. A beta of 1, for example, means that the security's price will rise and fall with the market; a beta greater than 1 signifies that the security's price will be more volatile than the market; and a beta less than 1 indicates that it will be less volatile than the market.

The approximately 3% discrepancy between the two experts' discount rates (8.8%/ 8.5% for Zmijewski vs. 11.5% for Bayston) is attributable primarily to their different determinations of the (1) cost of debt, (2) capital structure, and (3) cost of equity. . . .

1. Cost of Debt

Professor Zmijewski calculated the weighted average cost of long term debt for ECM at 6.3%, which was ECM's actual observed cost of debt. He used that figure because of ECM's historical ability to borrow from the RTFC at below-market rates. Mr. Bayston, on the other hand, determined that ECM's weighted average cost of debt on the merger date was 6.59%, but he assigned ECM a cost of long term debt of 8%. Bayston's judgment was that ECM would not be able to borrow indefinitely from the RTFC at below-market rates and, therefore, ECM would have to borrow from another lender at rates closer to 8%. . . .

The defendants admit that there is nothing of record which shows that on the merger date, ECM would not have been able to borrow from the RTFC at the weighted average cost of its existing debt. As of the merger date, ECM had never borrowed at a rate even as high as 8%. Lending at below-market rates was the RTFC's mission, and as of the merger date management expected it could continue to borrow from the RTFC at favorable interest rates . . . that supports Bayston's contrary assumption.

For these reasons, the Court accepts Prof. Zmijewski's 6.3% cost of debt input, and rejects Mr. Bayston's 8% cost-of-debt assumption, the effect of which was to increase Bayston's calculated WACC from 10.9% to 11.16%.

2. ECM's Debt/Equity Capital Structure

Another important element of the WACC formula is the percentage of the capital structure represented by equity and by long term

---

57. In formulaic terms, WACC has been expressed as WACC = (Leveraged Cost of Equity × Equity % of Capital) + (Cost of Long Term Debt × (1 − tax rate) × Debt % of Capital).

B. Valuation Techniques

debt.... [Although] Bayston calculated ECM's actual debt-to-value ratio at approximately 63%, in his judgment ECM could not viably sustain such a highly-leveraged capital structure over the long term. Accordingly, Bayston used a 30% "target" figure, which assumed that management would reduce the debt level from 63% to 30%.

Professor Zmijewski, unlike Mr. Bayston, based his 28.2% debt-to-value capital structure upon ECM's actual debt level, as opposed to a "target" debt level. But, to arrive at his 28.2% figure, Prof. Zmijewski assumed an enterprise value of $41.16 per share, which also was the ultimate fair value that he had determined for ECM.

The finance literature supports elements, but not the entirety, of each side's approach. [The court here discusses the circularity of using figures based on the valuation of the company's debt as determined in the valuation process.]

Because the purpose of this calculation is to determine WACC based upon a reliable "value of the equity," the only sensible way (in the Court's view) to avoid the circularity in this case is to use an enterprise valuation of ECM that is not litigation-driven. On this record, the only such valuation is the $27.84 per share value, based on a 12% discount rate, that the RTFC determined and actually used for purposes of financing the Privatization. Having no better or more reliable information, the Court adopts that value for purposes of determining the percentage of ECM's capital structure represented by long term debt and by equity on the merger date.

As for the percentage represented by long term debt, the only data credibly anchored to the record is the RTFC determination of ECM (ATN)'s net-debt-to-value ratio at 38.8%. Because that ratio was conservatively determined and was calculated as of July 29, 1998, three months before the merger, the actual debt-to-value percentage as of the merger date is unknown and can only be estimated. The Court concludes that a debt-to-value ratio of 38% would have been a reasonable estimate and input for purposes of determining a discount rate as of the merger date. From that conclusion it also follows that the percentage of ECM's capital structure represented by equity would have been 62% (*i.e.*, 100% − 38%).

3. Cost of Equity

Both Prof. Zmijewski and Mr. Bayston used the CAPM formula to calculate ECM's cost of equity. Using that standard approach, Zmijewski derived a cost of equity of 10.4% (for the years when the tax abatement would be in effect), and 10.3% (when the current tax abatement expires). Bayston's initial cost of equity was somewhat lower — 9.9% — but Bayston then increased it to 14% by adding "premiums" totaling 4.1%. More specifically, Bayston added a "small stock premium" of 1.7% and a "company-specific premium" of 2.4%, the latter consisting of a 1 to 1.5% "super-small stock premium" and a .9 to 1.4% "hurricane risk premium." Those "premiums" account for most of the difference between these two experts' cost of equity inputs. Accordingly, the issue becomes whether either of these premiums is appropriate in these circumstances. The party seeking to add the premium (here, the defendants) has the burden to establish that they are appropriate.

(a) The 1.7% "Small Firm/Small Stock" Premium

Although plaintiffs contend that there is no basis in the finance literature or theory for adding a "small firm/small stock" premium to the cost of equity, that is not entirely accurate. There is finance literature supporting the position that stocks of smaller companies are riskier than securities of large ones and, therefore, command a higher expected rate of return in the market. Our case law also recognizes the propriety of a small firm/small stock premium in appropriate circumstances. The issue, therefore, is not whether a small firm/small stock premium is permissible theoretically, but whether the defendants have shown that a premium of 1.7% is appropriate in this particular case. The Court concludes that the defendants have made that showing.

Mr. Bayston computed a 1.7% small stock premium by a two-step process. First, he determined qualitatively that such a premium was warranted by the size and business of ECM. Second, after reviewing data from the Ibbotson Associates publication, *Stocks, Bonds, Bills and Inflation 1998 Yearbook* ("Ibbotson"), Bayston quantified that premium by subtracting the 11% geometric mean return for large company stocks from the 12.7% mean return for small company stocks.

Plaintiffs do not attack the amount of the premium. Rather, they argue that no small stock/small company premium should have been added at all. They contend that Bayston mechanically and non-qualitatively applied a premium solely because of ECM's size, even though ECM did not fit the typical profile of a "small company." Moreover, plaintiffs argue, recent research data show that contrary to the empirical assumption that implicitly underlies the small stock/small firm premium, small firms have in fact under performed large firms.

The answer to the plaintiffs' second argument is that although large-cap companies may have outperformed small-cap companies for discrete, short periods of time, over the last 10 (indeed, the last 75) years, the mean returns for small companies have exceeded the returns for large-cap companies. The short answer to the plaintiffs' first argument is that although the favorable characteristics of ECM are reasons not to apply the second ("supersmall firm") premium that Bayston layered atop the 1.7% small stock/small company premium, those characteristics do not justify ignoring the incremental risk, not fully captured by beta, that typically accompanies a small sized firm.

Accordingly, the Court accepts the 1.7% small stock/small firm premium that Mr. Bayston added to his 9.9% cost of equity, and arrives at a total cost of equity for ECM of 11.6%.

B. Valuation Techniques 375

(b) The 2.4% "Supersmall Firm" and "Hurricane Risk" Premium

Far more controversial, and less grounded in finance theory and legal precedent, is the additional 2.4% premium added by Bayston to account for what he determined was the incremental risk of ECM being both a "supersmall" firm and also subject to unusually hazardous weather risk, specifically, hurricanes.

Defendants' support for an incremental premium that if accepted would further increase ECM's cost of capital, falls woefully short of the showing that is required. The defendants offer nothing to persuade the Court that ECM's risk profile fits what they contend is the "reality" of investment returns for micro-cap companies. ECM may be small, but it is also a utility that was unusually protected from the hazards of the marketplace. ECM was well established, it had no competition, it was able to borrow at below-market rates, and it was cushioned by regulators from extraordinary hazards (for example, by tax abatements). Implicit in the defendants' position, but nowhere straightforwardly argued, is the assumption that these advantages, however extraordinary, were not enough to offset the added risk created by ECM's "supersmall" size. It is the defendant's burden to support that assumption, and they have not done that. . . .

Apart from the "supersmall firm" premium, Bayston also added a company-specific incremental premium for hurricane risk. The effect was to increase the cost of equity by 1-1.5%, to increase the discount rate by a range of .7% to 1.05%, and to decrease enterprise value by $18 to $24 million (*i.e.*, by $1.64 to $2.19 per share). Bayston's justification for this incremental premium was that (1) as a result of Hurricane Hugo in 1989 and Hurricane Marilyn in 1995, Vitelco (ATN) suffered losses, not reimbursed by insurance or Universal Service Fund revenues, of approximately $80 million; and (2) ECM's management believed that hurricanes would pose a significant risk to ECM's business in the future, in that future storm losses would not be reimbursable by insurance because (management was informed) coverage would no longer be available.

This analysis is faulty on factual and conceptual grounds. First, it overstates the amount of unreimbursed hurricane damage. That amount, Mr. Heying testified, totaled about $55 million for the entire 70 years preceding the merger. Second, defendants' claim that management knew as of the merger date that its hurricane insurance would not continue, relies entirely on Prosser's trial testimony, which is not corroborated by any contemporaneous document and is inconsistent with ECM's SEC filings and RTFC loan documents, none of which indicate any impending loss of hurricane loss coverage. Third, assuming that the risk of future storm losses should be accounted for in some way, the defendants have not supported their argument that the appropriate way to do that is by increasing the cost of equity. Defendants cite no finance literature supporting that approach, nor have they supported their argument empirically, such as (for example) by comparing ECM's company-specific weather-related risk (net of mitigation factors) to the "average" or "mean" weather-related risk for all companies, or even for all "small" companies.

The absence of theoretical and evidentiary support leaves this Court unpersuaded that the risk of unrecoverable hurricane damage loss is so embedded in ECM's business as to require a structural increase in ECM's cost of equity. Absent theoretical and empirical guidance, a more rational approach would be to factor that risk into ECM's cash flow projections such as (for example) by dividing the net hurricane-related loss by a statistically representative number of years to arrive at a loss deduction from projected cash flow for each forecast year. Unfortunately, neither side performed such a calculation.

To summarize, the Court determines that the correct cost of equity for ECM at the merger date was 11.6% (Bayston's initial 9.9% plus a 1.7% small firm/small stock premium). That cost of equity figure does not include a premium for hurricane damage risk. That risk shall be accounted for by deducting $18 million ($1.64 per share) from the enterprise value calculated (independent of that risk) with the DCF inputs as determined in this Opinion. The result will be to reduce the enterprise value by that $18 million ($1.64 per share) amount.

C. What Weight Should Be Accorded to ECM's Market Price as Evidence of Fair Value?

To support their claim that the fair value of ECM on the merger date was no more than $10.38 per share, the defendants urge that "where, as here, the market for a publicly traded security is an active and efficient one, the market price [of ECM's common stock] is, at the least, important corroborative evidence of value. . . ." For that argument, the defendants rely upon the expert testimony of Professor Burton Malkiel of Princeton University. Professor Malkiel opined that ECM's stock "was trade[d] in an efficient market with enough volume and a low enough bid-asked spread, and that it reflected news without delay; and these . . . indicators led [Prof. Malkiel] to conclude that ECM was traded in an efficient market and that the [$7.00 per share] market price of ECM common stock prior to the buyout . . . was a reasonable reflection of its value." Intending no disrespect to Professor Malkiel, the Court is unable to accept his conclusion in this specific case. However sound Professor Malkiel's market price-based theory may be in other circumstances, that theory is inapplicable to these facts because its premise is not supported by either the trial record or Delaware law.

Delaware law recognizes that, although market price should be considered in an appraisal, the market price of shares is not always indicative of fair value. Our appraisal cases so confirm.

Moreover, the record undermines any assertion that ECM's common stock was traded in an efficient market. Indeed, it was precisely because

B. Valuation Techniques

ECM's stock market price did not reflect ECM's underlying values that Prosser decided to abandon the proposed merger and instead acquire the ECM minority interest in the Privatization. Prosser himself told his fellow ECM directors that the ECM stock price had failed to reach the desired appreciation as a result of the small public float and the fact that the stock was not being followed by Wall Street analysts. Moreover, because Prosser always owned the majority interest, the market price of ECM stock always reflected a minority discount.

Professor Malkiel admitted that markets occasionally make errors, that the market could have been wrong about ECM, and that it is possible for a stock that trades even in an efficient market to be mispriced, especially in the short run. Professor Malkiel also conceded that the market may be inefficient if material information is withheld from it. In the case of ECM, while the stock was trading freely (*i.e.*, before Prosser announced the Privatization), the market never had the benefit of any disclosed earnings or projections of future results, including the June Projections.

For these reasons, the Court rejects the defendants' argument that the market price of ECM stock corroborates the $10.25 price as the fair or intrinsic value of ECM on the date of the merger. In this case, ECM's unaffected stock market price merits little or no weight....

E. The Fair Value of ECM and the Unfairness of the Merger Price

As a consequence of the foregoing determinations, the fair value of ECM on the merger date is found to be $416,996,000, or $38.05 per share. Under 8 Del. C. §262, Greenlight, as the single appraisal claimant, is entitled to recover that per share amount, multiplied by the 750,300 shares for which it seeks appraisal, plus interest....

From that fair value finding it further follows that the $10.25 per share merger price was not a "fair price" within the meaning of the Delaware fiduciary duty case law beginning with *Weinberger v. UOP, Inc.*

IV. WAS THE TRANSACTION THE PRODUCT OF FAIR DEALING?

B. Fair Dealing Analyzed

A fair dealing analysis requires the Court to address "issues of when the transaction was timed, how it was initiated, structured, negotiated, and disclosed to the board, and how director and shareholder approval was obtained.

1. Timing, Initiation and Structure

Our courts have recognized that a freeze-out merger of the minority proposed by the majority stockholder is inherently coercive. Where, as here, the freeze-out merger is initiated by the majority stockholder, that fact, even though not dispositive, is evidence of unfair dealing.

Another circumstance that evidences the absence of fair dealing is where the transaction is timed in a manner that is financially disadvantageous to the stockholders and that enables the majority stockholder to gain correspondingly. This case is the diametric opposite of *Jedwab v. MGM Grand Hotels, Inc.,* where this Court found that the timing of a merger was not unfair because there was no "persuasive indication . . . that from the minority's point of view this [was] a particularly poor time to liquidate their investment." Here, the evidence of unfair timing could not be more persuasive. Prosser's initial proposal was to merge Innovative into a wholly owned subsidiary of ECM. That would have benefited ECM stockholders and enabled them to remain as investors in a larger merged company. Because ECM's stock price was depressed, Prosser abandoned that proposal at the eleventh hour and "flipped" the deal for his sole personal benefit to take advantage of the temporarily and artificially depressed stock price. That stock price then became the "floor" for the equally depressed and unfair Privatization price, and benefited Prosser to the same extent that it disadvantaged the minority stockholders who were now being squeezed out of the enterprise.

In addition to, and apart, from the unfairness of its initiation and timing, the transaction was also unfairly structured, in that Prudential and Cahill, the firms that had been retained as advisors to ECM in the initially Proposed (but later abandoned) Merger, were co-opted by Prosser to serve as his advisors. That switch was unfair to ECM, because during ECM's entire existence, Prudential and Cahill had been its advisers and they possessed material nonpublic information about ECM's values, business and prospects. As such, Prudential and Cahill were in the best position to represent the interests of the ECM minority. Those same advisers were now switching sides to represent interests that were adverse to that same minority.

At a minimum, ECM's board (including Prosser) or the Special Committee should have insisted that Prudential and Cahill remain as advisors to ECM, and that Prosser retain other financial and legal advisors. Failing that, the board—or at the very least the Special Committee—should have insisted that Prudential and Cahill recuse themselves from the negotiations. By doing neither, ECM was deprived of the advantage of knowledgeable advisors. That advantage was conferred upon ECM's controlling stockholder and to-be-adversary in the transaction—Prosser. There is no evidence that either the full board or the Special Committee ever considered that issue.

2. The Adequacy of the Minority Shareholders' Representation

(a) The Independence of the Board and of the Special Committee

A critical aspect of any fair dealing analysis is the adequacy of the representation of the minority stockholders' interests. In this case, that

B. Valuation Techniques

issue is particularly critical, because a majority of the ECM board members were not independent of Prosser, making it necessary to appoint a Special Committee to negotiate on the minority stockholders' behalf. Unfortunately, a majority of the Special Committee members also lacked independence, and the one Committee member who arguably was independent did not function effectively as a champion of the minority's interests.

Besides Prosser, the ECM board had six members, all of whom Prosser had directly appointed: Raynor, Ramphal, Muoio, Goodwin, Vondras, and Todman. It is undisputed that Prosser, whose wholly-owned entity was the acquirer of ECM's minority interest, was conflicted. But, most of the remaining directors also had disabling conflicts because they were economically beholden to Prosser. Directors who "through personal or other relationships are beholden to the controlling person[]" lack independence from that person.

Raynor, who was Prosser's long time lawyer, was clearly conflicted. In 1996, 1997, and 1998, virtually one hundred percent of the legal fees that Raynor generated for his law firm were attributable to work he performed for Prosser and Prosser-owned entities. Before 1996, the percentage of total fees represented by work Raynor performed for Prosser was always greater than fifty percent. From 1987 through 1998, ATNI and its affiliates, and thereafter ECM and its affiliates, were the largest single client of Raynor's firm. In 1998, the year of the Privatization, Raynor became "of counsel" at his firm and was put on a retainer arrangement wherein ATNCo paid compensation of $25,000 per month to Raynor, and $5,000 per month to his firm, to cover Raynor's office rental cost. That amount represented all of Raynor's compensation for 1998. Raynor also served as a Prosser nominee to the ATNI board, and as a director of Innovative, ECM, ATNCo and Vitelco. As a highly paid consultant to, and later full-time employee of, Prosser and his companies, Raynor was clearly beholden to Prosser and, thus, not independent.

If further evidence of non-independence were needed, in July 1998 — during ECM's consideration of the Privatization proposal — Prosser agreed to pay Raynor $2.4 million over a five year period as compensation for his past services. There was no negotiation over that fee — Raynor requested $2.4 million and Prosser agreed to it. Nor was the $2.4 million compensation arrangement ever disclosed to the ECM board, Compensation Committee or the Special Committee, yet Raynor voted as an ECM director to approve the Privatization.

Ramphal was similarly beholden to Prosser. Ramphal was originally introduced to Prosser by his son-in-law, Sir Ronald Sanders, who had a consulting arrangement with Prosser at that time. Like Sanders, Ramphal also fell into a lucrative consultancy with Prosser. In 1993 and 1994, Ramphal was paid consulting fees of $140,000 in both years, and in 1995 he was paid $120,000. On average, those amounts represented 22.5% of Ramphal's total income for that period. Those amounts were in addition to the $30,000 directors' fee that Ramphal received annually. Moreover, in 1998, Ramphal received $115,000 for his service on the ECM Board and special committees.

Given these undisputed facts, the defendants have not shown that Ramphal was independent of, *i.e.*, not beholden to, Prosser, and the Court affirmatively finds that he was not. That finding is strengthened by the fact that the consulting arrangement of Ramphal's son-in-law, Sanders, with Prosser would be put at risk if Ramphal, as a Special Committee member, took a position overly adversarial to Prosser. Finally, both Sanders and Ramphal were appointed as directors of Innovative after the Privatization had been completed.

Muoio was also a consultant to a Prosser entity and beholden to Prosser. As of mid-1997, Muoio was on an annual $200,000 retainer for providing banking/financial advisory services and he viewed Prosser as a source of additional future lucrative consulting fees. In March 1998, Muoio sought up to an additional $2 million for serving as financial adviser on a potential acquisition by ECM of CoreComm Inc. That effort was unsuccessful only because the acquisition ultimately never took place.

Lastly, Goodwin, Vondras and Todman received annual directors' fees of $100,000, a generous amount given that ECM's board met only three or four times in 1998. Goodwin and Vondras each also received $50,000 and $15,000 for their service on the Special Committee. The $115,000 Vondras received in 1998 for serving on ECM's board and Special Committee represented approximately 10% of his income for that year.

Although the directors' fees received by Goodwin, Vondras and Todman would not, without more, necessarily constitute a disabling financial interest, the record shows that all three of these directors — indeed, all the board defendants — expected to continue as directors of Prosser entities and benefit from the substantial compensation which accompanied that status. In fact, all of ECM's directors except Muoio were appointed to the Innovative board after the Privatization. That expectation, coupled with the fact that his director and committee fees represented a sizeable portion of his income, was sufficient to vitiate Vondras' independence for purposes of considering objectively whether the Privatization was fair to the minority stockholders.

The director defendants claim that they did not know they would be invited to join the Innovative board after the Privatization closed in October 1998. The evidence shows otherwise. During the negotiations over the Privatization, the ECM directors were told that they would continue on with the company "in its new incarnation." The Merger Agreement generated by the board's counsel in connection with the Privatization disclosed that the board defendants would remain directors of the surviving corporation. The Special Committee, through its counsel, received drafts of that Merger Agreement as early as July 17, 1998, before they voted to approve the transaction.

B. Valuation Techniques

In summary, the Court finds that a majority of the full board of ECM (Prosser, Raynor, Ramphal, Vondras, and Muoio) were beholden to Prosser and, thus, were not independent of him. The Court further finds that a majority of the Special Committee (Ramphal and Vondras) were beholden to, and therefore not independent of, Prosser, leaving Goodwin as the only arguably independent Committee member and Todman as the only arguably independent non-Committee director. As previously found, Goodwin, as Committee chair, did almost all of the Committee's work himself. Unfortunately, the work that Goodwin performed in that role, including his negotiations with Prosser, were fatally compromised and, consequently, inadequate to represent the interests of ECM's minority shareholders effectively.

(b) The Committee's Ineffectiveness as the Minority's Representative

There are several reasons why Mr. Goodwin's efforts as the Special Committee's chairman, and as its sole functioning member, were doomed to failure.

The first is that Prosser withheld the June projections, and knowledge of their existence, from the Committee and its advisors, Houlihan and Paul Hastings. As a consequence, Goodwin and Houlihan were deprived of information that was essential to an informed assessment of the fair value of ECM and of the gross inadequacy of merger price Prosser was offering. Thus disabled, Goodwin was not in a position to negotiate vigorously for a substantial increase in Prosser's opening offer ($9.125 per share) or, alternatively, to make a considered judgment to shut down the negotiations, thereby preventing the Privatization from going forward at all. That nondisclosure, without more, was enough to render the Special Committee ineffective as a bargaining agent for the minority stockholders.

Second, Prosser misled Goodwin by falsely representing that $10.25 per share was already straining the limits of the financing available to him. In fact, Prosser's financing would have enabled him to increase his offer to $11.40 per share, and the record evidence indicates that the RTFC was willing to lend him more, based on its implied valuation of ECM as conservatively worth about $28 per share. There is no evidence that Goodwin knew of Prosser's financing arrangements or the RTFC's valuation (for merger financing purposes) of ECM.

Third, and finally, Goodwin was careless, if not reckless, by routing all of his communications with the other Special Committee members through Eling Joseph, Prosser's secretary. The result was to give Prosser access to the Committee's confidential deliberations and strategy. That inexplicable method of channeling communications to Goodwin's fellow Committee members further confirms the severe information imbalance that existed between the two "bargaining" sides. In fact, there was no effective bargaining, because Prosser held all the cards and misled Goodwin into believing that he (Goodwin) and the Committee's financial advisor

(Houlihan), possessed all the information that was material to negotiating a fair price. Nothing could have been further from the truth.

3. The Adequacy of the Board and Shareholder Approvals

The fourth and final aspect of fair dealing concerns the adequacy of the board and shareholder approvals of the challenged transaction. In this case, those approvals were uninformed and, accordingly, of no legal consequence.

It is undisputed that the Privatization was approved by a unanimous vote of all ECM directors, with Prosser abstaining, at a board of directors' meeting held on August 17, 1998. The board's approval was not informed, however, because the voting board members were ignorant of the existence of the June Projections and of the inadequacy of the Houlihan valuation that was based upon the March projections.

Moreover, Raynor, who was conflicted, voted in favor of the Privatization but did not disclose to the other voting board members, the $2.4 million compensation payout arrangement that he had recently negotiated with Prosser. As previously found, that nondisclosure was material.

By not disclosing these facts, Prosser and Raynor violated the fiduciary duty of disclosure they owed to their fellow directors of ECM.

The approval of the transaction by a majority of the minority shareholders was also legally ineffective, because the misdisclosures and omissions in the disclosure documents sent to shareholders in connection with the Privatization rendered that vote uninformed. Those misdisclosures and omissions also violated the fiduciary duty of disclosure owed by ECM's majority stockholder and by the ECM directors who were responsible for the accuracy of those documents. The plaintiffs claim several disclosure violations, but the Court need address only three of them.

First, the Proxy Statement omitted to disclose to the minority shareholders the existence of the June projections and the fact that those projections had been furnished to Prudential and the RTFC, but were withheld from the Special Committee and its advisors. That omission was materially misleading, not only in its own right but also because the proxy statement contained affirmative representations that the public was being provided with the same projections to which Prosser was privy. The section of the proxy statement containing the March projections (identified there only as "Company projections") disclosed that "[a]lthough the company does not as a matter of course publicly disclose projections as to future revenues or earnings, because they were received by Mr. Prosser and the parent [ICC, LLC], the purchaser [ICC] is making these projections available to all stockholders." Those misdisclosures were highly material because knowledge of the June projections would have enabled the shareholders to understand ECM's intrinsic worth and the extent of the market's undervaluation of their company.

B. Valuation Techniques

Second, the disclosure documents misled minority stockholders about the Special Committee's and the board's independence from Prosser. The Schedule 14D-9, which was disseminated in connection with the first-step tender offer, disclosed the members of the Special Committee and their compensation, but not their consulting relationships or retainer agreements with other Prosser entities. Specifically, there was no disclosure of Raynor's or Ramphal's long-standing financial relationships with Prosser, including Raynor's $2.4 million payout arrangement for past services and Ramphal's significant consulting arrangements or his conflict concerning the economic and career prospects of his son-in-law. Nor was there disclosure of Muoio's consulting fee arrangement that had resulted in payments to him of hundreds of thousands of dollars. Also, because of their role as negotiators on behalf of the minority stockholders, the prior consulting relationships of Ramphal should have been disclosed. The disclosure documents misleadingly suggested that the Special Committee, and perhaps a majority of the entire board, were independent. In fact, that was not true.

Third, that disclosure violation was compounded by the false disclosure that a majority of the board that approved the Privatization were members of the Special Committee. In fact, only six of the board's seven members voted to approve the transaction, and only three of those six were members of the Special Committee. Three is not a majority of seven. Also not disclosed was the related fact that ECM's and the Committee's original advisors who had been retained to represent the interests of all shareholders in the initially Proposed (but later abandoned) Merger, had been co-opted by Prosser and were now working against the minority stockholders whose interests that they were originally hired to further.

In short, the disclosure documents were crafted to reassure the minority stockholders that their interests had been effectively represented by a Special Committee of directors who were independent of Prosser and his entities on the other side of the transaction. That impression was materially false and misleading and was sufficient, without more, to render the approving vote of the stockholders uninformed.

For all these reasons, the Court finds that the Privatization transaction, and the $10.25 per share merger price that has been adjudicated as unfair, were the product of unfair dealing. Accordingly, the Court concludes that the Privatization was not entirely fair to the minority stockholders of ECM. Having so found, the Court must now assess the liability consequences of that determination.

V. THE DEFENDANTS' FIDUCIARY DUTY BREACHES AND LIABILITY THEREFOR

Under *Emerald Partners v. Berlin* [the Court must] adjudicate which (if any) of the director defendants is liable for money damages, because ECM's §102(b)(7) charter provision exculpates those directors found to have violated *solely* their duty of care from liability for money damages. . . . The liability of the directors must be determined on an individual basis because the nature of their breach of duty (if any), and whether they are exculpated from liability for that breach, can vary for each director.

Prosser is liable in his capacity as a director for breach of his duty of loyalty, conduct that is not exculpated under Article Seventh. Prosser is also liable on the basis that he "derived an improper personal benefit" from the Privatization transaction—which is another exception to the exculpatory coverage of Article Seventh.

Raynor also is liable for breaching his fiduciary duty of loyalty—conduct that is excluded from the exculpatory shield of Article Seventh. Raynor did not personally and directly benefit from the unfair transaction (as did Prosser), but Raynor actively assisted Prosser in carrying out the Privatization, and he acted to further Prosser's interests in that transaction, which were antithetical to the interests of ECM's minority stockholders. . . .

The Court also concludes, albeit with reluctance, that Muoio is similarly liable, even though Muoio's conduct was less egregious than that of Prosser and Raynor. Unlike Raynor, Muoio did nothing affirmatively to assist Prosser in breaching his fiduciary duties of loyalty and good faith. Like his fellow directors, Muoio was also not independent of Prosser.

Muoio is culpable because he voted to approve the transaction even though he knew, or at the very least had strong reasons to believe, that the $10.25 per share merger price was unfair. Muoio was in a unique position to know that. He was a principal and general partner of an investment advising firm, with significant experience in finance and the telecommunications sector. From 1995 to 1996, Muoio had been a securities analyst for, and a vice president of, Lazard Freres & Co. in the telecommunications and media sector. From 1985 to 1995, he was a securities analyst for Gabelli & Co., Inc., in the communications sector, and from 1993 to 1995, he was a portfolio manager for Gabelli Global Communications Fund, Inc.

Hence, Muoio possessed a specialized financial expertise, and an ability to understand ECM's intrinsic value, that was unique to the ECM board members (other than, perhaps, Prosser). Informed by his specialized expertise and knowledge, Muoio conceded that the $10.25 price was "at the low end of any kind of fair value you would put," and expressed to Goodwin his view that the Special Committee might be able to get up to $20 per share from Prosser. In these circumstances, it was incumbent upon Muoio, as a fiduciary, to advocate that the board reject the $10.25 price that the Special Committee was recommending. As a fiduciary knowledgeable of ECM's intrinsic value, Muoio should also have gone on record as voting against the proposed transaction at the $10.25 per share merger price. Muoio did neither. Instead he joined the other directors in voting, without objection, to approve the transaction.

B. Valuation Techniques

That leaves the four remaining directors — Goodwin, Ramphal, Todman, and Vondras — whose conduct, while also highly troublesome, is far more problematic from a liability standpoint than that of Prosser, Raynor, and Muoio. Like Raynor and Muoio, those directors (except possibly Goodwin) were not independent of Prosser, they all voted for the Privatization, and none had a personal conflicting financial interest in, or derived a personal benefit from, that transaction to the exclusion of the minority stockholders.

The conduct of these four directors differs from that of Raynor and Muoio, in that there is no evidence that any of those four affirmatively colluded with Prosser to effectuate the Privatization, or that they otherwise deliberately engaged in conduct disloyal to the minority stockholders' interests. Nor have the plaintiffs shown that any of those directors knew or had reason to believe, that the merger price was unfair.

This is not intended to suggest that these directors covered themselves in glory, or merit commendation, for the manner in which they discharged their responsibility as fiduciaries. But it is to say, and this Court after considerable reflection finds, that there is no persuasive evidence that the fiduciary violations of the ECM directors other than Prosser, Raynor, and Muoio implicated conduct more egregious than breaches of their duty of care....

VI. CONCLUSION

For the reasons set forth above:

1. In the appraisal action, Innovative, as the surviving corporation, is liable to Greenlight in the amount of $38.05 per share for each of the 750,300 shares that are subject to the appraisal, plus interest at the rate of 6.27%, compounded monthly, from the date of the merger to the date of the judgment.
2. In the fiduciary duty action, defendants Innovative, ICC, Prosser, Raynor and Muoio are jointly and severally liable to the plaintiff class and to Greenlight (in its capacity as holder of litigation rights assigned by former ECM shareholders) in an amount equal to $27.80 per share.[193]

NOTES AND QUESTIONS

1. The deal. This tale of international finance began with two partners who had a falling out leading to a split-up of their company by which

---

193. $27.80 per share is equal to the difference between the fair value of ECM on the merger date ($38.05 per share) and the merger price paid to the ECM minority shareholders ($10.25 per share).

ECM was left with one of the partners, Prosser, owning 52 percent and public shareholders holding a minority position. After first proposing that ECM acquire another company Prosser owned, he flipped the transaction and sought to buy out the public minority stake in ECM. Can you see why this was attractive? The form was a cash-out merger that we have already discussed and it led to two plaintiffs bringing appraisal and fiduciary duty claims. What did the investors have before? What will they have afterwards? Why might this be worrisome? Who sets the terms? How close to arm's length? How useful is the market?

2. **Valuation.** What are the key DCF drivers for experts in the case? On the equity side, what attracts your attention about CapEx? How valid are additional premiums?

On the debt side, why not the RTFC rate? Can you see where the circularity is the debt/equity ratio? How does the overall result look to you?

3. **Comparing appraisal and entire fairness.** This was a consolidated action joining a statutory claim for appraisal and a common law claim brought as a class action for breach of fiduciary duty. Compare the results under each part of the litigation. What differences can you articulate as to when the plaintiffs or the defendant would prefer one over the other (even if not in this case)?

4. **The plaintiffs.** The appraisal and fiduciary duty suits were brought by separate plaintiffs. Greenlight Capital, L.P. is a hedge fund associated with an investor who later achieved greater prominence in a successful strategy to go short as the financial crisis unfolded. Brickell Partners was at the time one of the most common repeat players among class action plaintiffs regularly associated with one of the plaintiff's firms bringing class actions in fiduciary duty cases. How do you think the different characteristics of plaintiffs would affect how they prosecute the cases?

C. SHORT-FORM MERGERS

Glassman v. Unocal Exploration Corp.
777 A.2d 242 (Del. Sup. Ct. 2001)

BERGER, Justice.

In this appeal, we consider the fiduciary duties owed by a parent corporation to the subsidiary's minority stockholders in the context of a "short-form" merger. Specifically, we take this opportunity to reconcile a fiduciary's seemingly absolute duty to establish the entire fairness of any self-dealing transaction with the less demanding requirements of the short-form merger statute. The statute authorizes the elimination of minority stockholders by a summary process that does not involve the "fair dealing" component of entire fairness. Indeed, the statute does not contemplate any "dealing" at all. Thus, a parent corporation cannot satisfy the entire fairness standard if it follows the terms of the short-form merger statute without more.

Unocal Corporation addressed this dilemma by establishing a special negotiating committee and engaging in a process that it believed would pass muster under traditional entire fairness review. We find that such steps were unnecessary. By enacting a statute that authorizes the elimination of the minority without notice, vote, or other traditional indicia of procedural fairness, the General Assembly effectively circumscribed the parent corporation's obligations to the minority in a short-form merger. The parent corporation does not have to establish entire fairness, and, absent fraud or illegality, the only recourse for a minority stockholder who is dissatisfied with the merger consideration is appraisal.

I. Factual and Procedural Background

Unocal Corporation is an earth resources company primarily engaged in the exploration for and production of crude oil and natural gas. At the time of the merger at issue, Unocal owned approximately 96% of the stock of Unocal Exploration Corporation ("UXC"), an oil and gas company operating in and around the Gulf of Mexico. In 1991, low natural gas prices caused a drop in both companies' revenues and earnings. Unocal investigated areas of possible cost savings and decided that, by eliminating the UXC minority, it would reduce taxes and overhead expenses.

In December 1991 the boards of Unocal and UXC appointed special committees to consider a possible merger. The UXC committee consisted of three directors who, although also directors of Unocal, were not officers or employees of the parent company. The UXC committee retained financial and legal advisors and met four times before agreeing to a merger exchange ratio of .54 shares of Unocal stock for each share of UXC. Unocal and UXC announced the merger on February 24, 1992, and it was effected, pursuant to 8 Del. C. §253, on May 2, 1992. The Notice of Merger and Prospectus stated the terms of the merger and advised the former UXC stockholders of their appraisal rights.

Plaintiffs filed this class action, on behalf of UXC's minority stockholders, on the day the merger was announced. They asserted, among other claims, that Unocal and its directors breached their fiduciary duties of entire fairness and full disclosure. The Court of Chancery conducted a two day trial and held that: (i) the Prospectus did not contain any material misstatements or omissions; (ii) the entire fairness standard does not control in a short-form merger; and (iii) plaintiffs' exclusive remedy in this case was appraisal. The decision of the Court of Chancery is affirmed.

II. Discussion

The short-form merger statute, as enacted in 1937, authorized a parent corporation to merge with its wholly-owned subsidiary by filing and recording a certificate evidencing the parent's ownership and its merger resolution. In 1957, the statute was expanded to include parent/subsidiary mergers where the parent company owns at least 90% of the stock of the subsidiary. The 1957 amendment also made it possible, for the first time and only in a short-form merger, to pay the minority cash for their shares, thereby eliminating their ownership interest in the company....

This Court first reviewed §253 in *Coyne v. Park & Tilford Distillers Corporation*.[1] There, minority stockholders of the merged-out subsidiary argued that the statute could not mean what it says because Delaware law "never has permitted, and does not now permit, the payment of cash for whole shares surrendered in a merger and the consequent expulsion of a stockholder from the enterprise in which he has invested." The *Coyne* court held that §253 plainly does permit such a result and that the statute is constitutional.

The next question presented to this Court was whether any equitable relief is available to minority stockholders who object to a short-form merger. In *Stauffer v. Standard Brands Incorporated*,[3] minority stockholders sued to set aside the contested merger or, in the alternative, for damages. They alleged that the merger consideration was so grossly inadequate as to constitute constructive fraud and that Standard Brands breached its fiduciary duty to the minority by failing to set a fair price for their stock. The Court of Chancery held that appraisal was the stockholders' exclusive remedy, and dismissed the complaint. This Court affirmed, but explained that appraisal would not be the exclusive remedy in a short-form merger tainted by fraud or illegality:

> [T]he exception [to appraisal's exclusivity] ... refers generally to all mergers, and is nothing but a reaffirmation of the ever-present power of equity to deal with illegality or fraud. But it has no bearing here. No illegality or overreaching is shown. The dispute reduces to nothing but a difference of opinion as to value. Indeed it is difficult to imagine a case under the short merger statute in which there could be such actual fraud as would entitle a minority to set aside the merger. This is so because the very purpose of the statute is to provide the parent corporation with a means of eliminating the minority shareholder's interest in the enterprise. Thereafter the former stockholder has only a monetary claim.

The *Stauffer* doctrine's viability rose and fell over the next four decades. Its holding on the exclusivity of appraisal took on added significance in 1967, when the long-form merger statute—§251—was amended to allow cash-out mergers. In *David J. Greene & Co. v. Schenley*

---

1. Del. Supr., 154 A.2d 893 (1959).
3. Del. Supr., 187 A.2d 78 (1962).

C. Short-Form Mergers

Industries, Inc.,[5] the Court of Chancery applied *Stauffer* to a long-form cash-out merger. *Schenley* recognized that the corporate fiduciaries had to establish entire fairness, but concluded that fair value was the plaintiff's only real concern and that appraisal was an adequate remedy....

In 1977, this Court started retreating from *Stauffer* (and *Schenley*). *Singer v. Magnavox Co.* held that a controlling stockholder breaches its fiduciary duty if it effects a cash-out merger under §251 for the sole purpose of eliminating the minority stockholders....

Singer's business purpose test was extended to short-form mergers two years later in *Roland International Corporation v. Najjar*.[9] The *Roland* majority wrote:

> The short form permitted by §253 does simplify the steps necessary to effect a merger, and does give a parent corporation some certainty as to result and control as to timing. But we find nothing magic about a 90% ownership of outstanding shares which would eliminate the fiduciary duty owed by the majority to the minority....

After *Roland*, there was not much of *Stauffer* that safely could be considered good law. But that changed in 1983, in *Weinberger v. UOP, Inc.*, when the Court dropped the business purpose test, made appraisal a more adequate remedy, and said that it was "return[ing] to the well established principles of *Stauffer* ... and *Schenley* ... mandating a stockholder's recourse to the basic remedy of an appraisal." *Weinberger* focused on two subjects-the "unflinching" duty of entire fairness owed by self-dealing fiduciaries, and the "more liberalized appraisal" it established.

By referencing both *Stauffer* and *Schenley*, one might have thought that the *Weinberger* court intended appraisal to be the exclusive remedy "ordinarily" in non-fraudulent mergers where "price ... [is] the preponderant consideration outweighing other features of the merger." In *Rabkin v. Philip A. Hunt Chemical Corp.*,[18] however, the Court dispelled that view. The *Rabkin* plaintiffs claimed that the majority stockholder breached its fiduciary duty of fair dealing by waiting until a one year commitment to pay $25 per share had expired before effecting a cash-out merger at $20 per share. The Court of Chancery dismissed the complaint, reasoning that, under *Weinberger*, plaintiffs could obtain full relief for the alleged unfair dealing in an appraisal proceeding. This Court reversed, holding that the trial court read *Weinberger* too narrowly and that appraisal is the exclusive remedy only if stockholders' complaints are limited to "judgmental factors of valuation."

Rabkin, through its interpretation of *Weinberger*, effectively eliminated appraisal as the exclusive remedy for any claim alleging breach of the duty of entire fairness. But *Rabkin* involved a long-form merger, and the Court did not discuss, in that case or any others, how its refinement of *Weinberger*

---

5. Del. Ch., 281 A.2d 30 (1971)
9. Del. Supr., 407 A.2d 1032 (1979).
18. Del. Supr., 498 A.2d 1099 (1985).

impacted short-form mergers. Two of this Court's more recent decisions that arguably touch on the subject are *Bershad v. Curtiss-Wright Corp.*,[20] and *Kahn v. Lynch Communication Systems, Inc.*,[21] both long-form merger cases. In *Bershad*, the Court included §253 when it identified statutory merger provisions from which fairness issues flow:

> In parent-subsidiary merger transactions the issues are those of fairness-fair price and fair dealing. These flow from the statutory provisions permitting mergers, 8 Del. C. §§251-253 (1983), and those designed to ensure fair value by an appraisal, 8 Del. C. §262 (1983) . . . "; and in *Lynch*, the Court described entire fairness as the "exclusive" standard of review in a cash-out, parent/subsidiary merger.

Mindful of this history, we must decide whether a minority stockholder may challenge a short-form merger by seeking equitable relief through an entire fairness claim. Under settled principles, a parent corporation and its directors undertaking a short-form merger are self-dealing fiduciaries who should be required to establish entire fairness, including fair dealing and fair price. The problem is that §253 authorizes a summary procedure that is inconsistent with any reasonable notion of fair dealing. In a short-form merger, there is no agreement of merger negotiated by two companies; there is only a unilateral act—a decision by the parent company that its 90% owned subsidiary shall no longer exist as a separate entity. The minority stockholders receive no advance notice of the merger; their directors do not consider or approve it; and there is no vote. Those who object are given the right to obtain fair value for their shares through appraisal.

The equitable claim plainly conflicts with the statute. If a corporate fiduciary follows the truncated process authorized by §253, it will not be able to establish the fair dealing prong of entire fairness. If, instead, the corporate fiduciary sets up negotiating committees, hires independent financial and legal experts, etc., then it will have lost the very benefit provided by the statute—a simple, fast and inexpensive process for accomplishing a merger. We resolve this conflict by giving effect the intent of the General Assembly. In order to serve its purpose, §253 must be construed to obviate the requirement to establish entire fairness.

Thus, we again return to *Stauffer*, and hold that, absent fraud or illegality, appraisal is the exclusive remedy available to a minority stockholder who objects to a short-form merger. In doing so, we also reaffirm *Weinberger's* statements about the scope of appraisal. The determination of fair value must be based on *all* relevant factors, including damages and elements of future value, where appropriate. So, for example, if the merger was timed to take advantage of a depressed market, or a low point in the company's cyclical earnings, or to precede an anticipated positive

---

20. Del. Supr., 535 A.2d 840 (1987).
21. Del. Supr., 638 A.2d 1110 (1994).

development, the appraised value may be adjusted to account for those factors. We recognize that these are the types of issues frequently raised in entire fairness claims, and we have held that claims for unfair dealing cannot be litigated in an appraisal.[26] But our prior holdings simply explained that equitable claims may not be engrafted onto a statutory appraisal proceeding; stockholders may not receive rescissionary relief in an appraisal. Those decisions should not be read to restrict the elements of value that properly may be considered in an appraisal.

Although fiduciaries are not required to establish entire fairness in a short-form merger, the duty of full disclosure remains, in the context of this request for stockholder action. Where the only choice for the minority stockholders is whether to accept the merger consideration or seek appraisal, they must be given all the factual information that is material to that decision. The Court of Chancery carefully considered plaintiffs' disclosure claims and applied settled law in rejecting them. We affirm this aspect of the appeal on the basis of the trial court's decision.

III. Conclusion

Based on the foregoing, we affirm the Court of Chancery and hold that plaintiffs' only remedy in connection with the short-form merger of UXC into Unocal was appraisal.

NOTES AND QUESTIONS

1. **The deal.** This is a merger between a parent and subsidiary pursuant to a short-form merger procedure that has been part of the Delaware statute since the early twentieth century. The parent here owns 96 percent of the subsidiary and says it seeks to reduce taxes and overhead expenses at a time of low industry earnings. What protection might there be against possible overreaching by the majority shareholders? The vote of the subsidiary's board as required by §251(b)? The vote of the subsidiary's shareholders as required by §251(c)? Judicial enforcement of fiduciary duty of the directors and majority shareholders? Fair value under section §262? Given the wording of the statute, the court rules only the last is available, but no fiduciary duty. Are there any worrisome facts that strike you in the context?

2. **Changing metrics for appraisal.** Notice how the court modifies the appraisal right. It says explicitly that appraisal value may be adjusted to take into account whether the transaction was timed to take advantage of a depressed market and other items that would appear to come under the fair dealing aspect of *Weinberger*. Later, it suggests a duty of full disclosure that

---

26. *Alabama By-Products Corporation v. Neal*, Del. Supr., 588 A.2d 255, 257 (1991).

could be the basis for relief in appropriate cases. Consider the remedial options that might be available as discussed in the case that follows.

Berger v. Pubco Corp.
976 A.2d 132 (Del. Sup. Ct. 2009) (en banc)

JACOBS, Justice.

The issue on this appeal is what remedy is appropriate in a "short form" merger under 8 *Del. C.* §253, where the corporation's minority stockholders are involuntarily cashed out without being furnished the factual information material to an informed shareholder decision whether or not to seek appraisal. The Court of Chancery held that because the notice of merger did not disclose those material facts, the minority shareholders were entitled to a "quasi-appraisal" remedy, wherein those shareholders who elect appraisal must "opt in" to the proceeding and escrow a portion of the merger proceeds they received. We conclude that although the Court of Chancery correctly found that the majority stockholder had violated its disclosure duty, the court erred as a matter of law in prescribing this specific form of remedy.

Under *Glassman v. Unocal Exploration Corporation*, [777 A.2d 242 (Del. 2001),] the exclusive remedy for minority shareholders who challenge a short form merger is a statutory appraisal, provided that there is no fraud or illegality, and that all facts are disclosed that would enable the shareholders to decide whether to accept the merger price or seek appraisal. But where, as here, the material facts are not disclosed, the controlling stockholder forfeits the benefit of that limited review and exclusive remedy, and the minority shareholders become entitled to participate in a "quasi-appraisal" class action to recover the difference between "fair value" and the merger price without having to "opt in" to that proceeding or to escrow any merger proceeds that they received. Because the trial court declined to order that remedy, we must reverse.

FACTUAL AND PROCEDURAL BACKGROUND

The facts pivotal to this appeal, all drawn from the Court of Chancery's Opinion deciding cross motions for summary judgment, are undisputed. Pubco Corporation ("Pubco" or "the company") is a Delaware corporation whose common shares were not publicly traded. Over 90 percent of Pubco's shares were owned by defendant Robert H. Kanner, who was Pubco's president and sole director. The plaintiff, Barbara Berger, was a Pubco minority shareholder.

Sometime before October 12, 2007, Kanner decided that Pubco should "go private." As the owner of over 90% of Pubco's outstanding shares, Kanner was legally entitled to effect a "short form" merger under 8 Del. C. §253. Because that short form procedure is available only to corporate

C. Short-Form Mergers

controlling shareholders, Kanner formed a wholly-owned shell subsidiary, Pubco Acquisition, Inc., and transferred his Pubco shares to that entity to effect the merger. In that merger, which took place on October 12, 2007, Pubco's minority stockholders received $20 cash per share.

Under the short form merger statute (8 Del. C. §253), the only relevant corporate action required to effect a short term merger is for the board of directors of the parent corporation to adopt a resolution approving a certificate of merger, and to furnish the minority shareholders a notice advising that the merger has occurred and that they are entitled to seek an appraisal under 8 Del. C. §262. Section 253 requires that the notice include a copy of the appraisal statute, and Delaware case law requires the parent company to disclose in the notice of merger all information material to shareholders deciding whether or not to seek appraisal.

In November 2007, the plaintiff received a written notice (the "Notice") from Pubco, advising that Pubco's controlling shareholder had effected a short form merger and that the plaintiff and the other minority stockholders were being cashed out for $20 per share. The Notice explained that shareholder approval was not required for the merger to become effective, and that the minority stockholders had the right to seek an appraisal. The Notice also disclosed some information about the nature of Pubco's business, the names of its officers and directors, the number of its shares and classes of stock, a description of related business transactions, and copies of Pubco's most recent interim and annual unaudited financial statements. The Notice also disclosed that Pubco's stock, although not publicly traded, was sporadically traded over-the-counter, and that in the twenty-two months preceding the merger there were thirty open market trades that ranged in price from $12.55 to $16.00 per share, at an average price of $13.32. Finally, the Notice provided telephone, fax and e-mail contact information where shareholders could request and obtain additional information.

In its summary judgment opinion, the Court of Chancery found that except for the financial statements, the disclosures in the Notice provided no significant detail. For example, the description of the Company comprised only five sentences, one of which vaguely stated that "[t]he Company owns other income producing assets." No disclosures relating to the company's plans or prospects were made, nor was there any meaningful discussion of Pubco's actual operations or disclosure of its finances by division or line of business. Rather, the unaudited financial statements lumped all of the company's operations together. The financial statements did indicate that Pubco held a sizeable amount of cash and securities, but did not explain how those assets were, or would be, utilized. Finally, the Notice contained no disclosure of how Kanner had determined the $20 per share merger price that he unilaterally had set.

As our law required, the company attached to the Notice a copy of the appraisal statute, but the copy attached was outdated and, therefore, incorrect. The appraisal statute had been updated by changes that became effective in August 2007—two months before the Notice was sent to shareholders—but the version attached to the Notice did not reflect those changes. Pubco never sent a corrected copy of the updated appraisal statute to its former minority stockholders.

On December 14, 2007, the plaintiff initiated this lawsuit as a class action on behalf of all Pubco minority stockholders, claiming that the class is entitled to receive the difference between the $20 per share paid to each class member and the fair value of his or her shares, irrespective of whether any class member demanded appraisal. Pubco and Kanner . . . filed a cross-motion for summary judgment.

ANALYSIS
A. The Claims, Issues, and Standard of Review

Because the plaintiff challenges a short form cash-out merger under Section 253, the starting point for analysis is *Glassman*, which holds that in a short-form merger there is no "entire fairness" review and that the exclusive remedy is a statutory appraisal. *Glassman* cautions, however, that those limited review and exclusive remedy protections are not absolute or unqualified. They are available only "absent fraud or illegality." Moreover, "[a]lthough fiduciaries are not required to establish entire fairness in a short-form merger, the duty of full disclosure remains. . . . Where the only choice for the minority stockholders is whether to accept the merger consideration or seek appraisal, they must be given all the factual information that is material to that decision."

The question not reached, and therefore not addressed, by *Glassman* is: what consequence should flow where the fiduciary fails to observe its "duty of full disclosure"? That is the only issue before us and it is one of first impression.

The Court of Chancery held that where minority shareholders who are cashed out in a short form merger are deprived of information material to deciding whether or not to seek appraisal, they are entitled to a "quasi-appraisal" remedy with the following features. First, the shareholders must be furnished the material information of which they were deprived. Second, the shareholders must then be afforded an opportunity to choose whether or not to participate in an action to determine the "fair value" of their shares. Third, shareholders who choose to participate must formally "opt in" to the proceeding and place into escrow a prescribed portion of the merger consideration that they received. Paraphrasing *Gilliland* [v. *Motorola, Inc.*, 873 A.2d 305 (Del. Ch. 2005)], the Court of Chancery identified the purpose of the escrow requirement as to "replicate a modicum of the risk that would inhere" if the proceeding were an actual appraisal.[17]

On appeal, the plaintiff-appellant does not contest the supplemental disclosure requirement of the order awarding the quasi-appraisal remedy, only its opt in and escrow features. The appellant claims that as a matter of law, all minority shareholders should have been treated as members of a class entitled to seek the quasi-appraisal recovery, without being burdened by any precondition or requirement that they opt in or escrow any portion of the merger proceeds paid to them. That, the plaintiff contends, is the only proper application of both *Glassman* and the short form merger statute, 8 Del. C. §253.

The defendants-appellees, not surprisingly, take the opposite position. They contend that the adjudicated remedy, modeled after the Court of Chancery's earlier *Gilliland*, is the only outcome that properly implements the policies which underlie the Delaware appraisal statute and animate the rulings in *Glassman*. . . .

B. Discussion

(1) The Remedial Alternatives

. . . In the abstract, four possible alternatives present themselves, of which only two are advocated by either side. The remaining two alternatives are advocated by no party. We nonetheless identify and consider them, because to do otherwise would render our analysis truncated and incomplete.

The alternatives advocated by each side, respectively, are the two forms of "quasi-appraisal" remedy earlier described. . . .

Of the remaining two remedial alternatives (those advocated by neither side), the first would be a "replicated appraisal" proceeding that would duplicate the precise sequence of events and requirements of the appraisal statute. Under the "replicated appraisal" approach, the minority shareholders would receive (in a supplemental disclosure) all information material to making an informed decision whether to elect appraisal. Shareholders who elect appraisal would then make a formal demand for appraisal and remit to the corporation their stock certificates and the entire merger consideration that they received. Thereafter, the corporation would have the opportunity, as contemplated by the appraisal statute, to attempt to reach a settlement with the appraisal claimants. Where no settlement is

---

17. Chancery Opinion, at *5. The risk being referred to is that "'a stockholder who seeks appraisal must forego all of the transactional consideration and essentially place his investment in limbo until the appraisal action is resolved.' As part of this risk, a minority stockholder faces the prospect of receiving less than the merger price in the appraisal action." *Gilliland*, 873 A.2d at 312 (quoting *Turner v. Bernstein*, 776 A.2d 530, 547-48 (Del. Ch. 2000)).

reached, a formal appraisal action could then be commenced by the dissenting shareholders or by the corporation.

Under the fourth alternative (also not advocated by either side), there would be no remedial appraisal proceeding at all. Rather, the consequence of the fiduciary's adjudicated failure to disclose material facts would be to render *Glassman* inapplicable. As a result, the remedy would be the same as in a "long form" cash out merger under 8 Del. C. §251 — a shareholder class action for breach of fiduciary duty, where the legality of the merger (and the liability of the controlling stockholder fiduciaries) are determined under the traditional "entire fairness" review standard.

(2) Selecting the Most Appropriate Alternative

The four alternative possibilities having been identified, the question then becomes: which remedy is the most appropriate — the one ordered by the Court of Chancery or one of the three alternative forms? To decide that issue, we must first answer a predicate question: by what analytical standard do we determine which remedial alternative is optimal? We conclude that the optimal alternative would be the remedy that best effectuates the policies underlying the short form merger statute (Section 253), the appraisal statute (Section 262) and the *Glassman* decision, taking into account considerations of practicality of implementation and fairness to the litigants. A reasoned application of that standard permits the remedial alternatives to be ranked in an objective and transparent way.

Applying that standard leads us to conclude that the fourth alternative would merit the lowest priority. Under that alternative, a violation of the disclosure requirement would render *Glassman* inapplicable and deprive the majority stockholder fiduciary of the benefit of *Glassman*'s limited review and exclusive remedy. In that setting (to reiterate), the minority shareholders would be entitled to the same remedies as are available in a fiduciary duty class action challenging a long form merger.

The strongest argument favoring this approach would run as follows: under *Glassman*, full disclosure of all material facts is a necessary condition for the fiduciary to enjoy *Glassman*'s limited review and exclusive appraisal remedy. Therefore, a violation of that disclosure condition should deprive the fiduciary of those benefits. That argument, although unassailable in terms of logic and equity, is flawed in one highly important respect. To accept it would disregard the intent of the General Assembly, as described in *Glassman* and *Stauffer v. Standard Brands, Incorporated*, that in a legally valid, non-fraudulent, short form merger the minority shareholders' remedy should be limited to an appraisal. Moreover, validating such an approach would disserve the purpose of *Glassman*'s disclosure requirement, which is to enable the minority stockholders to make an informed decision whether or not to seek an appraisal. A remedy that sidesteps appraisal altogether would frustrate that purpose.

C. Short-Form Mergers

Unlike this approach, the remaining three alternative remedies would give effect (albeit in varying degrees) to that legislative intent. Therefore, in the hierarchy those alternative remedies should rank above the one that abjures appraisal.

That observation brings into focus a second alternative-the "replicated appraisal" remedy that would duplicate precisely the sequence of events and requirements of the appraisal statute. Under that approach, the minority shareholders would receive a supplemental disclosure, to enable them to make an informed decision whether or not to elect an appraisal. Shareholders who elect that remedy must then make a formal demand for an appraisal, and then remit to the corporation their stock certificates and all the merger consideration they received.

This approach would place the minority shareholders in the situation they would find themselves had they received proper disclosure to begin with. The strongest argument favoring this alternative is that it would give maximum effect to the legislative intent recognized in *Glassman*. The flaw of this approach, however, is that it would effectuate that legislative intent at an unacceptable cost measured in terms of practicality of application and fairness to the minority. In *Gilliland*, the Court of Chancery so recognized, implicitly acknowledging the impracticality of such an approach by refusing to order a "replicated appraisal" remedy:

> The opt-in procedures to be followed, however, will not be as stringent as those under the statute. For example, the court will not require beneficial or "street name" owners to "demand" quasi-appraisal through their record holder. The court is concerned that, given the substantial passage of time since the merger, it would be difficult for stockholders to secure the cooperation of the former record holders or nominees needed to perfect demand in accordance with the statute. Instead, stockholders seeking to opt-in will need to provide only proof of beneficial ownership of [their] shares on the merger date.

The *Gilliland* court also recognized (again, implicitly) that it would be unfair to require shareholders who desire an appraisal to remit the entire merger consideration they received *to the corporation*, as would occur in a replicated appraisal. Instead, the court required only that "those stockholders who choose to participate in the action to pay *into escrow a portion* of the merger consideration they have already received." The *Gilliland* court thereby acknowledged the unfairness of requiring the minority stockholders to bear the risk of the corporation's creditworthiness, which would result from their having to pay back a portion of the merger proceeds to the company. Instead, the court ordered that the proceeds be placed into an escrow account, with the escrowed funds representing only a portion of the merger consideration the minority actually received.

Implicit in the *Gilliland* remedy is the recognition that it is unfair to the minority shareholders, on whose behalf significant litigation expense and effort were successfully devoted, to limit their relief to requiring the fiduciary merely to fulfill the disclosure obligation it had all along. A remedy limited to awarding a second statutory appraisal would deny the minority any credit for that expense and effort, after having been forced to prosecute that litigation solely because the controlling shareholder had violated its fiduciary duty. A replicated appraisal remedy would also give controlling shareholders little incentive to observe their disclosure duty in future cases, since the cost of the remedy to the controllers would be negligible. Both in *Gilliland* and in this case the Court of Chancery eschewed that approach, concluding instead that the appropriate remedy should be a "quasi appraisal." Both parties agree with that conclusion, and so do we.

That requires us to choose between the two dueling forms of quasi-appraisal advocated by the parties on this appeal. Both forms would entitle the minority stockholders to supplemental disclosure enabling them to make an informed decision whether to participate in the lawsuit or to retain the merger proceeds. Both forms would entitle those who elect to participate to seek a recovery of the difference between the fair value of their shares and the merger consideration they received, without having to establish the controlling shareholders' personal liability for breach of fiduciary duty. The difference between the two quasi-appraisal approaches is that under the defendants' approach (which the Court of Chancery approved), the minority shareholders who elect to participate would be required to "opt in" and to escrow a prescribed portion of the merger proceeds they received. Under the plaintiff's approach, all minority stockholders would automatically become members of the class without being required to "opt in" or to escrow any portion of the merger proceeds.

As thus narrowed, the final issue may be stated as follows: under the standard we have applied, which remedy is the more appropriate—the one that imposes the opt in and partial escrow requirements or the one that does not? Considerations of utility and fairness impel us to conclude that the latter is the more appropriate remedy for the disclosure violation that occurred here. Because neither the opt-in nor the escrow requirement is mandated as a matter of law and because those requirements involve different equities, we analyze each requirement separately.

We start with the "opt in" issue. The approach adopted by the Court of Chancery requires the minority shareholders to opt in to become members of the plaintiff class. The other choice would treat those shareholders automatically as members of the class—that is, as having already opted in. Those shareholders would continue as members of the class, unless and until individual members opt out after receiving the remedial supplemental disclosure and the Rule 23 notice of class action informing them of their opt out right. From the minority's standpoint, the first alternative is potentially more burdensome than the second, because shareholders that fail either to opt in or to opt in within a prescribed time, forfeit the opportunity to seek an appraisal recovery. On the other hand, structuring the remedy as an "opt out" class action avoids that risk of forfeiture, and thus benefits the minority shareholders. To the corporation, however, neither alternative is more burdensome than the other. Under either alternative the company will know at a relatively early stage which shareholders are (and are not) members of the class.

Given these choices, it is self evident which alternative is optimal. As between an opt in requirement that would potentially burden shareholders desiring to seek an appraisal recovery but would impose no burden on the corporation, and an opt out requirement that would impose a lesser burden on the shareholders but again no burden on the corporation, the latter alternative is superior and is the remedy that the trial court should have ordered.

That leaves the requirement that the minority shareholders electing to participate in the quasi-appraisal must escrow a portion of the merger proceeds that they received. The rationale for this requirement, as stated in *Gilliland*, is "to mimic, at least in small part, the risks of a statutory appraisal . . . to promote well-reasoned judgments by potential class members and to avoid awarding a 'windfall' to those shareholders who made an informed decision [after receiving the original notice of merger] to take the cash rather than pursue their statutory appraisal remedy."

The defendants-appellees argue that it is fair and equitable to require the minority shareholders to escrow some portion of the merger proceeds. Otherwise (defendants say), the shareholders would have it both ways: they could retain the merger proceeds they received and at the same time litigate to recover a higher amount — a dual benefit they would not have in an actual appraisal. It is true that the minority shareholders would enjoy that "dual benefit." But, does that make it inequitable from the fiduciary's standpoint? We think not. No positive rule of law cited to us requires replicating the burdens imposed in an actual statutory appraisal. Indeed, our law allows the minority to enjoy that dual benefit in the related setting of a class action challenging a long form merger on fiduciary duty grounds. In that setting the shareholder class members may retain the merger proceeds and simultaneously pursue the class action remedy. The defendants cite no case authority, nor are we aware of any, holding that that in the long form merger context that benefit is inequitable to the majority shareholder accused of breaching its fiduciary duty.

Lastly, fairness requires that the corporation be held to the same strict standard of compliance with the appraisal statute as the minority shareholders. Our case law is replete with examples where dissenting minority shareholders that failed to comply strictly with certain technical requirements of the appraisal statute, were held to have lost their entitlement to an appraisal, and, consequently, lost the opportunity to recover the difference between the fair value of their shares and the merger price. These technical statutory violations were not curable, so that irrespective of the equities the unsuccessful appraisal claimant could not proceed anew. That result effectively allowed the corporation to retain the entire difference between fair value and the merger price attributable to the shares for which appraisal rights were lost. The appraisal statute should be construed even-handedly, not as a one-way street. Minority shareholders who fail to observe the appraisal statute's technical requirements risk forfeiting their statutory entitlement to recover the fair value of their shares. In fairness, majority stockholders that deprive their minority shareholders of material information should forfeit their statutory right to retain the merger proceeds payable to shareholders who, if fully informed, would have elected appraisal.

In cases where the corporation does not comply with the disclosure requirement mandated by *Glassman*, the quasi-appraisal remedy that operates in the fairest and most balanced way and that best effectuates the legislative intent underlying Section 253, is the one that does not require the minority shareholders seeking a recovery of fair value to escrow a portion of the merger proceeds they received. We hold, for these reasons, that the quasi-appraisal remedy ordered by the Court of Chancery was legally erroneous in the circumstances presented here.

To summarize: where there is a breach of the duty of disclosure in a short form merger, the *Gilliland* approach does not appropriately balance the equities. If only a technical and non-prejudicial violation of 8 Del. C. §253 had occurred, the result might be different. In some circumstances, for example, where stockholders receive an incomplete copy of the appraisal statute with their notice of merger, the *Gilliland* remedy might arguably be supportable. But the majority stockholder's duty of disclosure provides important protection for minority stockholders being cashed out in a short form merger. This protection — the quasi-appraisal remedy for a violation of that fiduciary disclosure obligation — should not be restricted by opt-in or escrow requirements.

D. PLANNING TO MINIMIZE JUDICIAL REVIEW

In re Cox Communications, Inc. Shareholders Litigation
879 A.2d 604 (Del. Ch. 2005)

STRINE, Vice Chancellor.

II. FACTUAL BACKGROUND

Cox is one of the nation's largest broadband communications companies, with a particularly strong cable television franchise. Throughout its history, the eponymous Cox has been controlled by its founding family, the Coxes. At various times, the Family has found it convenient to take Cox public, in order to raise money from the public capital markets. At other times, the Family has found it preferable to run Cox as a private company.

As of the summer of 2004, Cox was a public company, whose shares were listed on the New York Stock Exchange. The Cox Family controlled 74% of Cox's voting power. By summer 2004, the Family decided that it would be in its best interest to acquire the remaining shares of Cox that it did not own — some 245.5 million shares — and to take Cox private again. This idea was broached with top management of Cox by Family representatives on the Cox board, including the Chairman James C. Kennedy. On August 1, 2004, a Cox board meeting was held at which the Family previewed its intention to offer to pay $32 per share as an initial bid in a merger transaction whereby the Family would acquire all of the public shares of Cox (the "Proposal"). In a letter that followed the meeting, the Family made clear that it expected that Cox would form a special committee of independent Cox directors (the "Special Committee") to respond to and negotiate its Proposal. Indeed, the Proposal specifically required approval by the Special Committee. The Family did not threaten to change the board in order to pursue a merger if the Special Committee did not find favor with its Proposal. But the Family did state that it would not sell its Cox shares or support a sale of Cox to a third party.

At 4:06 a.m. on the next morning, August 2, the Proposal was announced publicly before the markets opened. The Proposal set in course two separate strands of activity. One involved the formation and start of work by the Special Committee. The other involved a race to the courthouse by various plaintiffs. I describe the latter activity first because it took place largely without any consideration of what the Special Committee was planning to do. After describing the initial jockeying among the plaintiffs, I will return to discuss the key events that led to an actual transaction between the Family and Cox, and the settlement of this litigation.

A. The Plaintiffs Rush to Court to Challenge the Negotiable Proposal

Beginning at 8:36 a.m. on August 2, and continuing throughout the day, a flurry of hastily drafted complaints were filed with this court. The first of the complaints consisted of paragraphs cobbled together from public documents, and rested on the core premises that Cox was poised for growth, that the Family's Proposal undervalued the company, that the offer was timed to allow the Family to reap for itself Cox's expected profits from heavy capital investments made in recent years, and that the directors of Cox were acquiescing to the Family's wishes. At 9:28 a.m., the Abbey Gardy firm, which is lead counsel in this action, filed its initial complaint, the second complaint filed that morning. That complaint was even less meaty than the first filed complaint. It is exemplary of hastily-filed, first-day complaints that serve no purpose other than for a particular law firm and its client to get into the medal round of the filing speed (also formerly known as the lead counsel selection) Olympics. The complaint's allegations were entirely boilerplate, with no particular relevance to the situation facing Cox. Most notably, the complaint's strained accusations of wrongdoing reflected, but did not maturely and thoughtfully confront, the reality that the Family's Proposal was just that, a proposal, subject to the expected evaluation of a Special Committee of independent directors, which would soon be formed and have the chance to hire advisors.

By the end of the day, six complaints of this ilk were filed in this court. . . .

A food fight then ensued among the plaintiffs' firms for lead counsel status. The Prickett Jones firm filed motions to expedite and to consolidate the cases under a committee structure it would lead. The rest of the filing plaintiffs lined up behind Abbey Gardy. The fight was resolved at a hearing on August 24, and confirmed in an order dated August 30, in which the court determined that Abbey Gardy would be lead counsel. . . .

The court largely denied the motion to expedite, for the obvious reason that there was as yet no transaction to enjoin. The only thing on the table was a Proposal by the Family that was subject to ongoing examination and negotiation by the Cox board through its Special Committee. . . .

As it turns out, the denial of the motion to expedite was the last substantial activity that would occur in the litigation challenging the Proposal until the consideration of the settlement itself. All the important events were transpiring on the business front, even those that involved the plaintiffs themselves. I therefore describe the course of those events next.

B. Getting to a Deal and Settlement: A Tale of Two Negotiation Paths Leading to the Same Place at the Same Time

After the public announcement of the Proposal, the Cox board formed the Special Committee as anticipated in the Family's Proposal. It was comprised of three Cox directors who were not employees or officers of Cox, or otherwise affiliates of the Family, including Janet M. Clarke who was the Chairwoman. The board resolution creating the Special Committee specifically stated that the Cox board would not authorize or recommend any transaction with the Family unless the transaction was recommended to the full board by the Special Committee.

On August 5, 2004, the Special Committee selected Fried, Frank, Harris, Shriver & Jacobson LLP as its legal counsel. On August 16, the Special Committee retained Goldman, Sachs & Co. as its financial advisor. After that, the Special Committee, with the aid of its advisors, gathered public and non-public financial information about Cox and its prospects, including non-public projections of the company's future performance. The Special Committee did so for the evident purposes of considering the

D. Planning to Minimize Judicial Review

attractiveness of Cox's opening bid and determining how to respond to that bid. During this stage, the Special Committee communicated with representatives of the Family to understand the basis for the Proposal and to hear their views about value. Goldman Sachs used this input and other information to develop valuation information to help its clients develop a bargaining position.

By late September, the Special Committee had worked with Goldman Sachs to develop a presentation to the Family's financial advisors. That presentation was designed to impress upon the Family the Special Committee's view that Cox had a bright future and should be valued much higher than the Proposal's $32 per share price. In other words, the presentation was a negotiation document designed to help the Special Committee convince the Family of the sincerity of its view that it should substantially increase its initial bid. After the meeting with the financial advisors, Fried Frank met with the Family's legal advisors and expressed the Special Committee's desire that any merger or tender offer transaction be subject to a non-waivable majority of minority approval condition or "Minority Approval Condition."

On October 4, 2004, the Special Committee initiated the beginning of real negotiations by sending a letter to the Family unanimously rejecting the $32 price as unacceptable. Various rounds of discussions were had, at which the Family's and the Special Committee's financial advisors jousted over value. On October 11, the Family raised its bid to $33.50 per share and hinted that this might be its final bid. The next day, the Special Committee communicated to the Family that if the $33.50 bid was the Family's final bid, it would be rejected, and if that bid was intended to lead to a deal at $35.00, then the Family should know that the Special Committee would reject that price as well.

By this time, the plaintiffs in this case, through their lead counsel, Arthur N. Abbey of Abbey Gardy, had been invited into the negotiation dance by the Family's litigation counsel, Kevin G. Abrams of Richards Layton & Finger, but on a separate track from the Special Committee. On October 12, the plaintiffs' counsel and their financial advisor, Richard L. Smithline, met with the financial and legal advisors for the Family. Smithline presented valuation materials designed to support the plaintiffs' position that the Family should raise its bid to at least $38 per share. The plaintiffs were not informed, apparently, that the Family had already told the Special Committee that it was prepared to raise its bid to $33.50.

This established a pattern. The Special Committee dealt with the Family in a direct manner: Clarke had direct contact with the Family's key representative, Kennedy as well as through communications between the Special Committee's advisors and the Family's advisors. By contrast, the plaintiffs, as might be expected, dealt exclusively with litigation counsel for the Family, aside from the one meeting at which the plaintiffs' financial advisors were given the opportunity to make a presentation to the Family's financial advisors. Litigation counsel for the Family decided what, if any, information the plaintiffs would be told about the bargaining dynamic between the Special Committee and the Family.

Consistent with this pattern, on October 12, Kennedy called Clarke and told her that the Family would withdraw its $33.50 offer unless an in-person meeting between principals for the Family and the Special Committee members themselves resulted in an agreement. It was eventually agreed that this meeting would occur on October 15.

Meanwhile, on October 13, Abrams told Abbey that the Family might raise its offer to $33.50 and might agree to a majority of the minority condition. Later that day, Abbey told Abrams that the plaintiffs would accept a settlement at $37 per share with a Minority Approval Condition.

On October 15, Kennedy and one of his top subordinates for the Family's Holding Company met with the Special Committee. No advisors were present. After some discussion, Kennedy indicated that the Family might raise its offer to $34 per share. After even more talk, Kennedy signaled a willingness to offer $34.50 with the proviso that if the Special Committee did not accept that price, the Family would cease consideration of taking Cox private.

The Special Committee adjourned to caucus with their advisors. Upon their return, Clarke told Kennedy that the Special Committee would not recommend a price lower than $35.25 per share. Kennedy responded that if that was the Special Committee's position, the Family would withdraw its Proposal.

The Special Committee then caucused again with its advisors. Clarke was empowered to negotiate the best obtainable price, subject to a confirming opinion as to financial fairness by Goldman Sachs, agreement to a Minority Approval Condition, settlement of this litigation, and negotiation of a merger agreement.

Clarke met with Kennedy later that day. She said the Special Committee would accept a deal at $35 per share. Naturally, having framed the bidding this way, Clarke opened the door to Kennedy offering to split the difference between his previous $34.50 overture and her $35 price. Kennedy did so and Clarke agreed that the Special Committee would recommend that $34.75 per share price, subject to the conditions described.

After that occurred, Abrams was informed of the state of play. He called Abbey and told him that the Family's "best and final offer" was $34.75 per share and that the Family would not settle this case at any higher price. Abbey remembers being told that this was the Family's "best and absolutely final offer." I have little doubt that, without being explicitly told so, Abbey knew that this meant that the Family had likely reached the end of its bargaining process with the Special Committee. As Abrams stated in court, he told Abbey that the Family was "prepared to proceed with this transaction without you." As Abrams also noted, "[Mr. Abbey] knows that when I say best and final, that's it, and he was

D. *Planning to Minimize Judicial Review*

not going to get an additional penny from me." In other words, Abbey was told that the proverbial "train was leaving the station."

Abbey told Abrams that he would consider the offer in consultation with the plaintiffs' financial advisor but that the deal would also have to include a Minority Approval Condition. The next morning Abbey orally agreed to these terms. Abrams promptly informed the Special Committee's lawyers and the transactional counsel for the Family that the litigation was settled in principle and that a formal Memorandum of Understanding would be prepared.

As of that time, the Special Committee's financial advisors were finalizing their analysis in advance of determining whether they could deliver a fairness opinion. The Special Committee and the Family were also negotiating the terms of the actual merger agreement.

By October 18, the Special Committee and the Family reached accord on a final merger contract. The Special Committee met and received a favorable fairness presentation from Goldman Sachs. After receiving that, the Special Committee unanimously recommended the merger to the full board. At a later meeting, the full Cox board also voted to approve the deal based upon the recommendation of the Special Committee.

That same day, Abrams and Abbey reached agreement on an MOU stating that the Family acknowledged that the desirability of settling this action and the efforts of the plaintiffs' counsel in this action were causal factors that led to the Family increasing its bid to $34.75, and agreeing to the Minority Approval Condition. A similar MOU was also executed with a group of plaintiffs who had filed similar actions in Georgia. The negotiations involving those plaintiffs are not described in the record before me in any detail.

The next day, October 19, Cox and the Family signed the merger agreement.

C. *The Settlement Is Presented to the Court for Approval and the Merger Closes*

The parties moved promptly to complete confirmatory discovery and negotiate a final stipulation of settlement. Only after that was done, they swear, was there any discussion of the amount of attorneys fees the plaintiffs' counsel would seek.

In the attorneys' fee negotiations, the Family eventually agreed not to oppose a fee request of up to $4.95 million. Separately, the Family forged a deal by which it agreed not to oppose a fee request from the Georgia plaintiffs of more than $1.25 million. In both cases, the Family agreed to pay whatever fee was awarded rather than to require that any fee award be withheld from the merger consideration to be paid to the public stockholders of Cox. According to the plaintiffs' counsel Arthur Abbey, he would have sought a fee much larger than $4.95 million had the defendants refused to agree not to oppose a fee request up to that amount.

The Stipulation of Settlement was presented to the court on November 10, 2004. Notice was promptly issued to the public stockholders on November 24, 2004. By that time, the Family had already commenced their tender offer at $34.75 per share.

On December 2, 2004, the tender offer expired. Approximately 189.7 million of Cox's 245.5 million public shares were tendered, satisfying the Minority Approval Condition and giving the Family over 90% of the Cox shares. On December 8, 2004, a back end, short-form merger was executed taking Cox private.

III. OBJECTORS TO THE PLAINTIFFS' FEE EMERGE

When the deadline to object to the proposed settlement expired, no objections to the settlement itself had been filed. But an objection was made to the plaintiffs' counsel request for an award of attorneys' fees....

The points that the objectors make, in other words, have less to do with this case in particular, and more to do with concerns about how the common law rules that Delaware uses to govern mergers with controlling stockholders create inefficient incentives for plaintiffs' lawyers and corporate defense counsel, leading to lawsuits that exist, in [the objector's] view, almost entirely as a vehicle for the payment of attorneys' fees and the entry of a judgment of the court providing the defendants with a broad release from any future lawsuits relating to the underlying transactions.

IV. LEGAL ANALYSIS

A. The Delaware Law of Mergers with Controlling Stockholders...

In the important case of *Kahn v. Lynch Communication, Inc.*, the Court held that regardless of the procedural protections employed, a merger with a controlling stockholder would always be subject to the entire fairness standard. Even if the transaction was 1) negotiated and approved by a special committee of independent directors; and 2) subject to approval by a majority of the disinterested shares (i.e., those shares not held by the controller or its affiliates), the best that could be achieved was a shift of the burden of persuasion on the issue of fairness from the defendants to the plaintiffs. In reaching this decision, the Supreme Court expressly relied on *Citron's* reasoning about the implicit coercion thought to be felt by minority stockholders in this transactional context. Less clear is why the Supreme Court refused to give weight to independent director approval, given that *Aronson v. Lewis* had held that independent directors were presumed to be capable of exercising a disinterested business judgment in deciding whether to cause the company to sue a controlling stockholder. In part, *Lynch*'s decision on this score seemed to turn on a vestigial concept

D. Planning to Minimize Judicial Review

from a discarded body of case law; namely, that because there no longer needed to be a "business purpose" for a merger with a controlling stockholder, it was somehow not a "business judgment" for independent directors to conclude that a merger was in the best interests of the minority stockholders.

That is an odd and unsatisfying rationale, which, if taken seriously, would have implications for all decisions by directors who agree to cash mergers. All in all, it is perhaps fairest and more sensible to read *Lynch* as being premised on a sincere concern that mergers with controlling stockholders involve an extraordinary potential for the exploitation by powerful insiders of their informational advantages and their voting clout. Facing the proverbial 800 pound gorilla who wants the rest of the bananas all for himself, chimpanzees like independent directors and disinterested stockholders could not be expected to make sure that the gorilla paid a fair price.

Therefore, the residual protection of an unavoidable review of the financial fairness whenever plaintiffs could raise a genuine dispute of fact about that issue was thought to be a necessary final protection. But, in order to encourage the use of procedural devices such as special committees and Minority Approval Conditions that tended to encourage fair pricing, the Court did give transactional proponents a modest procedural benefit — the shifting of the burden of persuasion on the ultimate issue of fairness to the plaintiffs — if the transaction proponents proved, in a factually intensive way, that the procedural devices had, in fact, operated with integrity. In the case of a special committee, later case law held that the defendants would only be relieved of the burden of proving fairness if it first proved that "the committee function[ed] in a manner which indicates that the controlling shareholder did not dictate the terms of the transaction and that the committee exercised real bargaining power." In the case of a Minority Approval Condition, the defendants had the usual ratification burden — to show that all material facts had been disclosed and the absence of coercive threats. But in either event, or in the exceedingly rare case in which both protections were employed in advance of, and not as part of a negotiated settlement, the most the defendants could get was a burden shift.

Although it is an undeniable reality that *Lynch* stated that any merger with a controlling stockholder, however structured, was subject to a fairness review, it would be unfair not to make explicit another reality. No defendant in *Lynch*, and no defendant since, has argued that the use of an independent special committee *and* a Minority Approval Condition sufficiently alleviates any implicit coercion as to justify invocation of the business judgment rule. For this reason, it is important not to assume that the Supreme Court has already rejected this more precisely focused contention.

B. A Tempered Description of the Objectors' Criticism of the Incentive Effects Created by Lynch

The incentive system that *Lynch* created for plaintiffs' lawyers is its most problematic feature, however, and the consequence that motivates the objectors' contentions here. After *Lynch*, there arose a pattern of which this case is simply one of the latest examples.

As the objectors point out and this court has often noted in settlement hearings regarding these kind of cases in the past, the ritualistic nature of a process almost invariably resulting in the simultaneous bliss of three parties—the plaintiffs' lawyers, the special committee, and the controlling stockholders—is a jurisprudential triumph of an odd form of tantra. I say invariably because the record contains a shocking omission—the inability of the plaintiffs, despite their production of expert affidavits, to point to one instance in the precise context of a case of this kind (i.e., cases started by attacks on negotiable going-private proposals) of the plaintiffs' lawyers refusing to settle once a special committee has agreed on price with a controller.

That bears repeating. In no instance has there been a situation when the controller's lawyer told the plaintiffs' lawyer this is my best and final offer and received the answer, "sign up your deal with the special committee, and we'll meet you in the Chancellor's office for the scheduling conference on our motion to expedite." Rather, in every instance, the plaintiffs' lawyers have concluded that the price obtained by the special committee was sufficiently attractive, that the acceptance of a settlement at that price was warranted.[39]

The objectors use this admittedly material fact to buttress another argument they make about *Lynch*. That argument, which is again something members of this court have grasped for some time, rests in the ease for the plaintiffs' lawyers of achieving "success" in this ritual. When a controlling stockholder announces a "proposal" to negotiate a going private merger, the controller is, like any bidder, very unlikely to present his full reserve price as its opening bid. Moreover, given the nature of *Lynch* and its progeny, and their emphasis on the effectiveness of the special committee as a bargaining agent, the controller knows, and special committee members will demand, that real price negotiations proceed after the opening bid, and that those negotiations will almost certainly result in any consummated deal occurring at a higher price.

For plaintiffs' lawyers, the incentives are obvious.[40] By suing on the proposal, the plaintiffs' lawyers can claim that they are responsible, in part,

---

39. *See* Elliott J. Weiss & Lawrence J. White, *File Early, Then Free Ride: How Delaware Law (Mis)-Shapes Shareholder Class Actions*, 57 VAND. L. REV. 1797, 1820 & n.84, 1833-34 (2004); Weiss Aff. ¶15.

40. *Cf.* Weiss & White, 57 VAND. L. REV. at 1857 n.183 (stating that the rule of *Lynch* "appears to have had the effect of encouraging plaintiffs' attorneys to settle cases challenging squeeze outs, largely without regard to whether the merger terms agreed to by an SNC [special negotiating committee] are entirely fair").

D. Planning to Minimize Judicial Review

for price increases in a deal context in which price increases are overwhelmingly likely to occur. Added to this incentive is the fact that the plaintiffs' lawyers know that the *Lynch* standard gives them the ability, on bare satisfaction of notice pleading standards and Rule 11, to defeat a motion to dismiss addressed to any complaint challenging an actual merger agreement with a special committee, even one conditioned on Minority Approval. Because of this ability, the plaintiffs' claims always have settlement value because of the costs of discovery and time to the defendants. Add to this another important ingredient, which is that once a special committee has negotiated a material price increase with the aid of well-regarded financial and legal advisors, the plaintiffs' lawyers can contend with a straight face that it was better to help get the price up to where it ended than to risk that the controller would abandon the deal. Abandonment of the deal, the plaintiffs' lawyers will say with accuracy, will result in the company's stock price falling back to its pre-proposal level, which is always materially lower as it does not reflect the anticipation of a premium-generating going private transaction. Having vigorously aided the special committee to get into the range of fairness and having no reason to suspect that the special committee was disloyal to its mission, the plaintiffs' lawyers can say, in plausible good faith, that it was better for the class to take this improved bid, which is now well within the range of fairness, rather than to risk abandonment of the transaction. Moreover, for those stockholders who wish to challenge the price, appraisal still remains an option.

C. Siliconix: Another Road to Going Private Is Paved

Of course, things cannot be quite that simple. And they are not. To describe why, I must add more jurisprudential context and then bring in the arguments raised by the plaintiffs' experts.

Under Delaware law, the doctrine of independent legal significance exists. That doctrine permits corporations to take, if the DGCL permits it, a variety of transactional routes to the same destination. For years, there had existed a strand of Delaware law that stated that a controlling stockholder who made a tender offer—as opposed to a merger proposal—to acquire the rest of the controlled company's shares had no duty to offer a fair price. So long as the controller did not actually coerce the minority stockholders or commit a disclosure violation, its tender offer was immune from equitable intervention for breach of fiduciary duty. *Lynch v. Vickers Energy Corp.* stands for this basic proposition, which was reaffirmed in *Solomon v. Pathe Communications Corp.*,[45] less than two years after *Lynch* was decided. In the tender offer context, the doctrine of implicit coercion that *Lynch* is premised upon was unrecognized, but the form of the transaction, rather than any

---

45. 672 A.2d 35, 39 (Del. 1996).

reasoned analysis, apparently formed the implicit justification for the discrepancy.

The opportunity that the tender offer line of cases presented for transactional planners interested in deal certainty was tempered, however, by the unsettled nature of a related question. . . . whether the short-form merger would be subject to the *Lynch* standard. In *In re Unocal Exploration Corp. Shareholders Litigation*,[46] that uncertainty was resolved. . . . In that transactional context, stockholders who believed that the price was unfair had an exclusive remedy: appraisal.

After *Unocal Exploration* was decided by this court, transactional lawyers put together the *Solomon* strand of authority with that new certainty and generated a new, and less negotiation- and litigation-intensive route to going private: a front tender offer designed to get the controller 90% of the shares, coupled with a back-end short form merger. In subsequent cases in this Court, it was held that this method of transaction — which came to be known by the first written decision addressing it — *In re Siliconix Inc. Shareholders Litigation*[47] — did not trigger entire fairness review so long as the offer was not actually coercive and there was full disclosure. In the later case of *Pure Resources*,[48] this Court held that the mere fact that the controller had taken the *Siliconix* route did not relieve it of fiduciary duties.[49] Although those duties did not include a duty to pay a fair price, the court held that a *Siliconix* transaction could be subject to fairness review to protect the minority unless:

(i) the offer is subject to a nonwaivable majority of the minority tender condition,
(ii) the controlling shareholder commits to consummate a short-form merger promptly after increasing its holdings above ninety percent,
(iii) the controlling shareholder "has made no retributive threats," and
(iv) the independent directors are given complete discretion and sufficient time "to react to the tender offer, by (at the very least) hiring their own advisors," providing a recommendation to the non-controlling shareholders, and disclosing adequate information to allow the non-controlling shareholders an opportunity for informed decision making.[50]

Since *Siliconix* was decided, controllers have therefore had two different transactional methods to choose between in attempting to go

---

46. 793 A.2d 329 (Del. Ch. 2000), *aff'd*, [*sub nom.* Glassman v. Unocal Exploration, Corp.,] 777 A.2d 242 (Del. 2001).
47. 2001 WL 716787 (Del. Ch. June 19, 2001).
48. 808 A.2d 421 (Del. Ch. 2002).
49. 808 A.2d at 444-46.
50. Ronald J. Gilson & Jeffrey N. Gordon, *Controlling Controlling Stockholders*, 152 U. Pa. L. Rev. 785, 827-28 (2003) (paraphrasing and distilling the holdings of *Pure Resources*, 808 A.2d at 445).

private. One can imagine various reasons why a controller might prefer one route or the other, depending on variables like the controller's ownership stake, the extent of the public float, the presence of big holders, the desire for certainty and closure, and which route might yield the best price for it. For example, the further a controller was from 90% to begin with, the more attractive the merger route might be, and vice versa, simply for efficiency reasons in both cases.

D. The Plaintiffs' Expert Counter Attack

For present purposes, however, what is relevant is the empirical evidence that the plaintiffs have submitted to counter the objectors' position. To confront the scholarly work of Weiss and White, who are of the view that litigation of this kind is of no material benefit to minority stockholders, the plaintiffs have submitted an affidavit from Professor Guhan Subramanian of the Harvard Law School.

Subramanian makes two major arguments. First, Subramanian cites to his own recent scholarly studies to support his view that the *Lynch* form of transaction results, on average, in going private transactions that pay the minority a higher premium in comparison to the pre-announcement market price than do *Siliconix* deals. Second, Subramanian attempts to show that the filing of lawsuits under *Lynch* challenging going private merger proposals by controlling stockholders are a material factor in producing these more favorable results. . . .

In recent work, Professor Subramanian studied the prices at which going-private transactions occurred since *Siliconix*, breaking them down between merger, or *Lynch*, transactions and tender offer, or *Siliconix*, transactions. Subramanian finds that the final premium paid over the pre-announcement market price was on average higher in *Lynch* deals than *Siliconix* deals, and that the difference was statistically significant.[52] Likewise, he finds that controllers, on average, increase their opening bids more when pursuing a *Lynch* merger than a *Siliconix* tender offer and that the difference is statistically significant. Subramanian, after controlling for other possible factors, concludes that these outcomes differ primarily because of the stronger bargaining hand given to the special committee in the *Lynch* context versus the *Siliconix* context. Because the *Lynch* transaction can only proceed with the special committee's approval unless the controller wants to take on the affirmative burden to prove fairness and because a merger transaction presupposes a negotiated price and a tender offer does not, Subramanian believes that minority stockholders do better in *Lynch* deals.

---

52. Subramanian, *Post-Siliconix Freeze-Outs: Theory & Evidence*, at Table 1 (Working Draft, Jan. 2005).

The active bargaining agency of the special committee is, Subramanian concludes, the critically absent feature in *Siliconix* deals. . . .

Subramanian infers that the controller can pay a lower price in the *Siliconix* context because the weaker hand of the special committee and plaintiffs, *combined*, will enable controllers to keep more nickels in their pockets and still close deals. For that reason, Subramanian thinks *Lynch*, and the role that it provides to plaintiffs as a watchdog, "polices the worst control shareholder deals, and benefits target company shareholders. . . ."[54]

E. The Court's Distillation of the Expert Input

Where does this leave us? By this point, the reader has probably accurately sensed that I have been dragged into an academic debate of considerable complexity. The lawyers did not ask for an opportunity for the experts to testify and the experts' dueling over minutia in affidavits has been less than clear and helpful. That is not to say that the input they have provided is without decisional utility. It has value if used with appropriate caution. And from it I make the following observations.

First, the record supports the proposition that *Lynch* deals tend to generate higher final premiums than *Siliconix* deals. One would suspect that this would be so for several reasons, including: 1) the greater leverage that the form of transaction gives to special committees; 2) the fact that the governing standard of review always gives the plaintiffs settlement value; 3) the reality that signing up a merger when the votes are locked up results in the greatest certainty for a controller; and 4) signing up a merger with a special committee and a settlement with plaintiffs' lawyer provides not only deal certainty, but a broad release and the most effective discouragement of appraisal claims. One cannot tell, of course, how important each of them is as a factor, but one awkward fact strongly suggests that the threat of bare knuckles litigation over fairness is not as important as the special committee's role as an negotiating force.

That awkward fact is the absence of evidence that "traditional" plaintiffs' lawyers, who attacked going private proposals by controllers, have ever refused to settle once they have received the signal that the defendants have put on the table their best and final offer — i.e., an offer that is acceptable to the special committee. There are examples of when the plaintiffs have settled at a lower price than the special committee demanded, but no examples of when the iron fist of the plaintiffs' bar demanded more than

---

54. Subramanian Aff. ¶ 31 (quoting Robert B. Thompson & Randall S. Thomas, *The New Look Of Shareholder Litigation: Acquisition Oriented Class Actions*, 57 VAND. L. REV. 133, 202 (2004)).

D. Planning to Minimize Judicial Review

the velvet glove of the special committee. The plaintiffs' bar would say, of course, this is because they did such a good job in each case that the price concessions they helped the special committee extract was of such inarguable fairness that it would been silly to fight on.

Perhaps what can be most charitably said is that the pendency of litigation and the theoretical threat that the plaintiffs will press on provides special committee members with additional clout that they wield to get good results, and that gives lawyers for controllers leverage to get their clients to pay a higher price to ensure deal closure and the utmost reduction of litigation risk.

Second, there is much that remains to be explored about the actual price differences between *Lynch* and *Siliconix* deals. Many *Siliconix* deals are quite small and involve very troubled companies. . . .

Third, litigation under *Lynch* never seems to involve actual litigation conflict if the lawsuit begins with a suit attacking a negotiable proposal. These cases almost invariably settle or are dismissed voluntarily by the plaintiffs. In those instances when there is actual litigation conflict in an "attack" on a going private transaction that has occurred because the complaint actually sought to stop a real transaction—an agreed-upon merger or a tender offer that was actively been pressed. In those situations, it is also much more likely that a plaintiff with a large stake who has hired a non-traditional law firm will mount a challenge. The *Pure Resources* and *Emerging Communications* transactions are good examples of these realities. Indeed, in *Emerging Communications*, the original plaintiffs pressed forward with a settlement after confirmatory discovery that would have resulted in a final price of $10.25 binding those stockholders who did not seek appraisal to the same price negotiated by the special committee. Only after objection by a large holder represented by a very large firm that more usually represents corporate defendants than stockholders was the settlement abandoned. The ultimate result was an award of damages based on a $38.05 per share value, in a detailed opinion by Vice Chancellor (Justice) Jacobs that found glaringly obvious procedural and substantive problems with the special committee process.

Fourth, minority stockholders seem to be doing more than tolerably well under both the *Lynch* and *Siliconix* regimes. Even if premiums to market are lower in *Siliconix* transactions, the premiums paid are large in comparison to the routine, day-to-day trading prices, in which minority and liquidity discounts will be suffered. For that reason, at every settlement, the plaintiffs' lawyers say that they could not risk pushing farther, lest the controller decide not to press on and offer a deal, and the stockholders suffer the fate of continuing as owners of minority shares in a going concern. After all, events that generate liquidity for all minority stockholders at substantial premiums are usually welcomed by stockholders.

V. Are the Plaintiffs Entitled to an Award of Attorneys' Fees and In What Amount?

[The Court awarded attorneys' fees and expenses, substantially less than requested, on the grounds that the attorneys played at least a small role in achieving the price increase negotiated by the Special Committee.]

VI. A Coda on the Jurisprudential Elephant in the Corner

Before concluding, I feel obliged to add a coda. The present case illustrates, in my view, the need to adjust our common law of corporations to take appropriate account of the positive and negative consequences flowing from the standard of review governing going private mergers. . . .

In this corner of our law, a relatively modest alteration of *Lynch* would do much to ensure this type of integrity, while continuing to provide important, and I would argue, *enhanced*, protections for minority stockholders. That alteration would permit the invocation of the business judgment rule for a going private merger that involved procedural protections that mirrored what is contemplated in an arms-length merger under independent, disinterested director *and* stockholder approval. Put simply, if a controller proposed a merger, subject from inception to negotiation and approval of the merger by an independent special committee *and* a Minority Approval Condition, the business judgment rule should presumptively apply. In that situation, the controller and the directors of the affected company should be able to obtain dismissal of a complaint unless: 1) the plaintiffs plead particularized facts that the special committee was not independent or was not effective because of its own breach of fiduciary duty or wrongdoing by the controller (e.g., fraud on the committee); or 2) the approval of the minority stockholders was tainted by misdisclosure, or actual or structural coercion.

This alteration would promote the universal use of a transactional structure that is very favorable to minority stockholders—one that deploys an active, disinterested negotiating agent to bargain for the minority coupled with an opportunity for the minority to freely decide whether to accept or reject their agent's work product. Indeed, the plaintiffs' own expert, Professor Subramanian, supports reform of precisely this kind. And *Lynch* in its current form could be retained to govern any merger in which the controller refuses to use both of these techniques from the inception of the process, allowing for the controller to proceed, get appropriate burden-shifting credit for use of special committee or a Minority Approval Condition, but remain subject to the entire fairness standard.

Importantly, this revised standard would not diminish the integrity-enforcing potential of litigation in any material way, in my view. Plaintiffs who believed that a special committee breached its fiduciary duties in agreeing to a merger would continue to have the practical ability to press a claim. . . .

This standard would also encourage the filing of claims only by plaintiffs and plaintiffs' lawyers who genuinely believed that a wrong had been committed. The chance to free ride on the expected increase in the controller's original proposal would be eliminated and therefore litigation would only be filed by those who believed that they possessed legal claims with value.

Importantly, a revision along these lines would leave in place another remedial option that is viable for stockholders who believe that the ultimate price paid in a negotiated merger is unfair appraisal. . . .

Of course, a revision in *Lynch* alone is arguably not complete. The plaintiffs have presented a cogent argument that the negotiating leverage wielded by special committees in mergers with controlling stockholders results in better outcomes for stockholders than does the ability of stockholders to reject a structurally non-coercive tender offer made by a controlling stockholder. The jarring doctrinal inconsistency between the equitable principles of fiduciary duty that apply to *Lynch* and *Siliconix* deals has been noted by this court before in *Pure Resources* and *Cysive*. It was thought preferable in *Pure Resources* to keep the strands separate until there is an alteration in *Lynch*, lest the less than confidence inspiring pattern of "*Lynch* litigation" replicate itself across-the-board in all going private transactions, thereby deterring the procession of offers that provide valuable liquidity to minority stockholders and efficiency for the economy in general.

A principled reconciliation of the two lines of authority could center on much the same solution articulated above, as Professors Gilson and Gordon have suggested in an important scholarly article.[92] In the case of a tender offer by a controlling stockholder, the controlling stockholder could be relieved of the burden of proving entire fairness if: 1) the tender offer was recommended by an independent special committee; 2) the tender offer was structurally non-coercive in the manner articulated by *Pure Resources*; and 3) there was a disclosure of all material facts. In that case, the transaction should be immune from challenge in a breach of fiduciary duty action unless the plaintiffs pled particularized facts from which it could be inferred that the special committee's recommendation was tainted by a breach of fiduciary duty or that there was a failure in disclosure. That is, an alteration on the *Lynch* line could be accompanied by a strengthening of equitable review in the *Siliconix* line. But in both cases, there would remain a strong incentive for controllers to afford stockholders the procedural protection *of both* a special committee with real clout and of non-coerced, fully informed approval by the minority stockholders.

---

92. Ronald J. Gilson & Jeffrey N. Gordon, *Controlling Controlling Stockholders*, 152 U. PA. L. REV. 785, 827-28 (2003).

As important, this incentive would enable transactional planners to know that they can structure transactions in a way that affords them the opportunity to obtain a dismissal on the complaint. In this way, the alteration brings this area of our law into harmony with the rest of Delaware corporate law that gives substantial deference to decisions made by disinterested, independent directors and approved by disinterested, non-coerced stockholders. . . .

NOTES AND QUESTIONS

1. The deal. The family owning 74 percent of the shares proposes a going-private transaction for reasons similar to those we have already studied. A special committee is appointed with financial and legal advisers and vigorous negotiations ensue. In addition, representatives of plaintiffs who filed lawsuits when the possibility of the deal was announced seek a seat at the table. A deal results. It is implemented first by a tender offer and then a short-form merger. Why? Chancellor Strine describes a familiar pattern of enterprising lawyers reacting to a judicial opinion, here the *Glassman* short-form merger opinion set out earlier in this chapter, that creates new strategic opportunities, here the then newly-declared absence of fiduciary duties in a short form merger. The planners combine that transaction with a tender offer for which traditionally there had not been the same fiduciary duty as in a merger. Unlike a cash-out merger in which there is a corporate-action in which the controlling shareholder is on both sides and all shareholders are involuntarily bound by the merger terms once the specified majority vote has been obtained, a tender offer is just a series of contracts between two shareholders (the controlling shareholder and the various minority shareholder), which each shareholder is free to accept or reject. The *Cox* opinion also describes the judicial response that follows in this interactive dance between lawyer and judge. Judges on the Chancery Court, in *Siliconix* and *Pure Resources*, described in the opinion, and later in other cases, fill in gaps by subjecting such a two-step transaction to a fairness review that is similar, but not the same as what you have already seen. One focus, but not the only one, in the Coda, is the "jarring inconsistency" between the fiduciary duty principles applicable in this two-step form and in the more traditional cash-out merger illustrated by *Kahn v. Lynch Communications*, a structure the Delaware Supreme Court has not yet resolved.

2. Do minority shareholders require different protections in a tender offer than a merger? The larger question is whether shareholders need a different kind of protection in one form versus the other (recall the discussion of *Unitrin* in Chapter 8). The issue was also addressed in the *Emerging Communications* case:

D. Planning to Minimize Judicial Review

The defendants argue that the burden must shift, nonetheless, because the minimum tender condition, *i.e.*, the condition that a majority of the minority shareholders tender into the offer, was the functional equivalent of a shareholder ratification of the transaction. But no Delaware case has held that burden-shifting can be accomplished by a tender of shares rather than by an actual vote. Nor should a tender be treated as the equivalent of an informed vote. Shareholders cannot be deemed to have ratified board action unless they are afforded the opportunity to express their approval of the precise conduct being challenged. [*In re Santa Fe Pac. S'holders Litig.*, 669 A.2d 59, 69 (Del. 1995); *see also In re Cencom Cable Income Partners, L.P.*, No. 14634, 2000 WL 640676, at *5 (Del. C. May 5, 2000) ("Ratification can effectively occur only where the specific transaction is clearly delineated to the investor whose approval is sought and that approval has been put to a vote.").] Stockholders have materially different interests at stake when tendering, as opposed to voting their shares. In considering whether to tender, stockholders must evaluate the risk of being left worse off, *i.e.*, left vulnerable to being frozen out at an even lower price, if the other stockholders were to tender into an inadequate offer. As Vice Chancellor Strine incisively observed in *In re Pure Resources S'holders Litig.*

> Indeed, many commentators would argue that the tender offer form is more coercive than a merger vote. In a merger vote, stockholders can vote no and still receive the transactional consideration if the merger prevails. In a tender offer, however, a nontendering shareholder faces an uncertain fate. That stockholder could be one of the few who holds out, leaving herself in an even more thinly traded stock with little hope of liquidity and subject to a §253 merger at a lower price or at the same price or . . . at a later (and, given the time value of money, a less valuable) time. [808 A.2d 421, 442-43 (Del. Ch. 2002), *appeal refused*, 812 A.2d 224 (Del. 2002) (footnotes omitted).]

Accordingly, the burden of proving fair dealing remains with the defendants.

2004 WL at *31-32.

3. Changing the standard of review in cash-out mergers with cleansing protections. The first part of the Coda suggests an even more dramatic change in the law of cash-out mergers—shifting the judicial standard of review from entire fairness to the business judgment rule for a going private merger with procedural protections that mirrored an arm's length merger, particularly, action by an independent committee of the board and a majority of the minority shareholder approval condition for the merger. In In re MFW Shareholders Litigation, 67 A.3d 496 (Del. Ch. 2013), Chancellor (now Chief Justice) Strine got such a case, which differed from prior cash-out cases discussed in this chapter in which the planners were found to have used one of the two cleansing devices, but not to have successfully implemented both. In *MFW*, the Chancellor in part based his argument, as he had in the Coda, on providing incentives for deal structures from the controlling shareholder that could provide enhanced protections for minority shareholders.

> By giving controlling stockholders the opportunity to have a going private transaction reviewed under the business judgment rule, a strong incentive is created to give minority stockholders much broader access to the transactional structure that is most likely to effectively protect their interests. In fact, this incentive may make

this structure the common one, which would be highly beneficial to minority stockholders. That structure, it is important to note, is critically different than a structure that uses only *one* of the procedural protections. The "or" structure does not replicate the protections of a third-party merger under the DGCL approval process, because it only requires that one, and not both, of the statutory requirements of director and stockholder approval be accomplished by impartial decision makers. . . .

When these two protections are established up-front, a potent tool to extract good value for the minority is established. From inception, the controlling stockholder knows that it cannot bypass the special committee's ability to say no. And, the controlling stockholder knows it cannot dangle a majority-of-the-minority vote before the special committee late in the process as a deal-closer rather than having to make a price move. From inception, the controller has had to accept that any deal agreed to by the special committee will also have to be supported by a majority of the minority stockholders. That understanding also affects the incentives of the special committee in an important way. The special committee will understand that those for whom it is bargaining will get a chance to express whether they think the special committee did a good or poor job. . . . [M]ost directors will want to procure a deal that their minority stockholders think is a favorable one, and virtually all will not want to suffer the reputational embarrassment of repudiation at the ballot box. That is especially so in a market where many independent directors serve on several boards, and where institutional investors and their voting advisors, such as ISS and Glass Lewis, have computer-aided memory banks available to remind them of the past record of directors when considering whether to vote for them or withhold votes at annual meetings of companies on whose boards they serve.

. . . [E]mpirical evidence indicates that special committees have played a valuable role in generating outcomes for minority investors in going private transactions that compare favorably with the premiums received in third-party merger transactions.

If . . . the special committee approves a transaction that the minority investors do not like, the minority investors get to vote it down, on a full information base and without coercion. In the *Unitrin* case nearly a generation ago, our Supreme Court noted the prevalence of institutional investors in the target company's stockholder base in concluding that a proxy contest centering on the price of a takeover offer was viable, despite insiders having increased their stock ownership to 28%, stating that "[i]nstitutions are more likely than other shareholders to vote at all [and] more likely to vote against manager proposals." Market developments in the score of years since have made it far easier, not harder, for stockholders to protect themselves. With the development of the internet, there is more public information than ever about various commentators', analysts', institutional investors', journalists' and others' views about the wisdom of transactions. Likewise, the internet facilitates campaigns to defeat management recommendations. Not only that, institutional investor holdings have only grown since 1994, making it easier for a blocking position of minority investors to be assembled.[164] Perhaps most important, it is difficult to look at the past generation of experience and conclude that stockholders are reluctant to express positions contrary to those espoused by company management. Stockholders have been effective in using their voting rights to adopt precatory proposals that have resulted in a sharp increase in so-called majority voting policies and a sharp decrease in structural takeover defenses. Stockholders have mounted more proxy fights, and, as important, wielded the threat of a proxy fight or a "withhold vote" campaign to secure changes

---

164. See . . . Matteo Tonello & Stephan Rabimov, *The 2010 Institutional Investment Report: Trends In Asset Allocation and Portfolio Composition*, Conference Bd. (2009), at 26 (showing that institutional ownership of equities in the 1,000 largest U.S. companies increased from 57% in 1994 to 69% in 2008).

in both corporate policies and the composition of corporate boards. Stockholders have voted against mergers they did not find favorable, or forced increases in price. Nor has timidity characterized stockholder behavior in companies with large blockholders or even majority stockholders; such companies still face stockholder activism in various forms, and are frequently the subject of lawsuits if stockholders suspect wrongdoing. . . .

In re MFW Shareholders Litigation, 67 A.3d 496, 528-531 (Del. Ch. 2013).

4. The approach of the Delaware Supreme Court. Prior to hearing the appeal of MFW, the Delaware Supreme Court had provided less of a carrot to controlling shareholders in a cash-out merger, flipping the burden of persuasion as to the fairness of the transaction from the defendant to the plaintiff, if, as set forth at the beginning of the *Weinberger* case, the corporate action had been approved by an informed vote of the majority of the minority shareholders or in *Kahn v. Lynch Communication Systems, Inc.*, 638 A.2d 1110 (Del. 1994), if approved by a well-functioning committee of independent directors. In 2012, the Delaware Supreme Court had reaffirmed the use of entire fairness:

Delaware has long adhered to the principle that the controlling shareholders have the burden of proving an interested transaction was entirely fair. However, in order to encourage the use of procedural devices that foster fair pricing, such as special committees and minority stockholder approval conditions, this Court has provided transactional proponents with what has been described as a "*modest procedural benefit*—the shifting of the burden of persuasion on the ultimate issue of entire fairness to the plaintiffs—if the transaction proponents proved, in a factually intensive way, that the procedural devices had, in fact, operated with integrity." We emphasize that in *Cox*, the procedural benefit of burden shifting was characterized as "modest."

. . . [W]e recognize that the purpose of providing defendants with the opportunity to seek a burden shift is not only to encourage the use of special committees, but also to provide a reliable pretrial guide for the parties regarding who has the burden of persuasion. Therefore, which party bears the burden of proof must be determined, if possible, before the trial begins. The Court of Chancery has noted that, in the interest of having certainty, "it is unsurprising that few defendants have sought a pretrial hearing to determine who bears the burden of persuasion on fairness" given "the factually intense nature of the burden-shifting inquiry" and the "modest benefit" gained from the shift.

The failure to shift the burden is not outcome determinative under the entire fairness standard of review. We have concluded that, because the only "modest" effect of the burden shift is to make the plaintiff prove unfairness under a preponderance of the evidence standard, the benefits of clarity in terms of trial presentation outweigh the costs of continuing to decide either during or after trial whether the burden has shifted. Accordingly, we hold prospectively that, if the record does not permit a pretrial determination that the defendants are entitled to a burden shift, the burden of persuasion will remain with the defendants throughout the trial to demonstrate the entire fairness of the interested transaction.

The Defendants argue that if the Court of Chancery rarely determines the issue of burden shifting on the basis of a pretrial record, corporations will be dissuaded from forming special committees of independent directors and from seeking approval of an interested transaction by an informed vote of a majority of the minority shareholders.

That argument underestimates the importance of either or both actions to the process component—fair dealing—of the entire fairness standard. This Court has repeatedly held that any board process is materially enhanced when the decision is attributable to independent directors. Accordingly, judicial review for entire fairness of how the transaction was structured, negotiated, disclosed to the directors, and approved by the directors will be significantly influenced by the work product of a properly functioning special committee of independent directors. Similarly, the issue of how stockholder approval was obtained will be significantly influenced by the affirmative vote of a majority of the minority stockholders.

A fair process usually results in a fair price. Therefore, the proponents of an interested transaction will continue to be incentivized to put a fair dealing process in place that promotes judicial confidence in the entire fairness of the transaction price. Accordingly, we have no doubt that the effective use of a properly functioning special committee of independent directors and the informed conditional approval of a majority of minority stockholders will continue to be integral parts of the best practices that are used to establish a fair dealing process.

Americas Mining Corp. v. Theriault. 51.A. 3d 1213, 1239-1244 (Del. 2012).

5. Shareholder litigation. The *Cox* opinion expresses some concern about lawyer incentives in litigation of the kind illustrated in this case. This is what might be called litigation agency costs, which occur in representative litigation when one shareholder sues on behalf of the entire class of shareholders harmed in the transaction, and the lawyers who represent the lead plaintiff have the greatest amount riding on the suit and the largest impact on its prosecution. Similar worries have been expressed about derivative suits and federal securities fraud class actions. A study of two years of cases filed in the Delaware Chancery Court showed that 85 percent of public company litigation in Delaware were class actions (as opposed to derivative or direct suits) and 94 percent of class actions arose in an acquisitions setting. Thompson & Thomas, *The New Look of Shareholder Litigation: Acquisition-Oriented Class Actions*, 57 VAND. L. REV. 133 (2004). More recent empirical work shows that almost all merger activity generates shareholder lawsuits. See e.g., Matthew D. Cain & Steven M. Davidoff, *A Great Game: The Dynamics of State Competition and Litigation* (Apr. 1, 2012) (unpublished manuscript) (available at http:// ssrn.com/ abstract=1984758).

The litigation pattern shows several indicia that might reinforce the worry about lawyer incentives:

- Suits are filed very quickly. Two-thirds of suits are filed the first day after a deal announcement or within the first three days (in contrast to only 12 percent of derivative suits filed that close to the challenged conduct).
- There are multiple suits filed for most deals. On average, a deal will generate four class action suits, but it is not unusual for that number to exceed five or more (even up to 41 suits); the larger

number of suits is correlated with the size of the company and with the presence of another bidder having filed suit.
- The same law firms bring most of these cases, with 16 firms filing three-quarters of the complaints; there are also some repeat players among the plaintiffs bringing the cases. The general pattern is that plaintiffs are dispersed with institutional shareholders not showing up in these cases as often as they do in federal securities class actions.

The pattern of settlements shows that affirmative relief is not spread evenly across all kinds of deals nor spread evenly over the suits brought in different contexts. Control shareholder acquisitions are statistically significantly more likely to result in additional monetary consideration being paid than settlements in other types of suits or in suits that are dismissed with no relief. Control shareholder deals and MBOs (management buyouts), where there would be reasons to worry about conflict of interest, make up 80 percent of the cases in which affirmative money relief is given even though they make up 50 percent of the deals in which litigation is brought.

Type of Deal	Total Deals w/Litigation	Total Deals w/Relief	$ Added to Deal	Relief other than $ to Deal
Controlling SH	65	25	20	5
MBO	41	10	5	5
Third Party	72	20	6	14
2d Bidder/ Hostile	34	5	0	5
Total	212	60	31	29

Source: Thompson & Thomas, 57 VAND. L. REV. 133, 199 Table. (2004).

Data from the period before and after the financial crisis shows a drop in the number of cases providing recovery to shareholders and more in which the remedy is only additional disclosure and fees for attorneys. Matthew D. Cain & Steven M. Davidoff, *A Great Game: The Dynamics of State Competition and Litigation* (Apr. 1, 2012) (unpublished manuscript), available at http:// ssrn.com/abstract=1984758).

The remaining question, posed by the principal case, is the source of this additional money. Did the bidder hold back some amount anticipating litigation? Did the special committee do the heavy lifting with the class free-riding on the committee's work? Does the litigation spur the special committee to do something that they would otherwise not do? To what extent do Coda and the results in the MFW litigation seek to modify the prior litigation pattern?

6. Bylaws providing an exclusive forum for shareholder litigation. A significant part of the increase in shareholder litigation described in Note 5 has occurred in forums outside of Delaware, even though the affected corporation often is incorporated in Delaware and the substantive law to be applied in the forum state will be the law of Delaware under the internal affairs doctrine. What would be gained from such filings? Often it is a way for a different set of law firms to get a seat at the table and to participate in settlement. In response, the boards of directors of some Delaware corporations added provisions to their bylaws specifying Delaware courts as the forum for suits raising fiduciary duty claims. In Boilermakers, Local 154 v. Chevron Corp., 73A.3d 934 (Del. Ch, 2013) the Delaware Chancery Court upheld such a bylaw. Would you predict a decline in the number of mergers that attract litigation?

11 SALE OF CONTROL FOR A PREMIUM

If value is created in an acquisition by any of the reasons specified in Chapter 2, how should that increase be shared? Our focus here is not between the shareholders of the buying company and the shareholders of the selling company as discussed earlier, but rather among the shareholders of the seller, particularly between a controlling shareholder, when there is one, and the remaining (or minority) shareholders.

A shareholder who owns a controlling interest in a company faces a substantially different (lower) risk than owners of minority shares, so that it would not be surprising if that lower risk was reflected in a higher per share price for the shares in such a position. A controlling shareholder can control the board and through it the economic strategy of the business. Such a shareholder is in a position to execute a change in strategy that will produce value (for example, the implementation of the Perelman plan in the *Technicolor* case) without the uncertainty that ordinarily would accompany any investor's expectations about the policy a board will follow. Similarly, the controlling shareholder's position permits it to better monitor managers and thereby reduce the uncertainty that would accompany the degrees of possible losses from agency costs.

Thus, it would not be surprising if those buying control would pay more (on a per share basis) than in buying minority shares in the same company. Similarly, those selling such a position would seek such a higher price. Empirical evidence reflects such premiums:

- Premiums are paid for controlling blocks of shares.
- If there is not a controlling block and a contest for control emerges, the price for shares tends to rise.
- When there is a contest for corporate control, the price per share falls on the day after the shares begin to trade without voting rights (a point that corresponds to the record date).

As an example, consider a corporation with 1 million shares with a control value estimated to be $5 million. How much would you expect the value of each share to increase if the control value were realized? $10 per share? $5 per share? $0 per share? Would your answer change if one shareholder were to own 50.1 percent of the shares? What is the value of each of her shares that can be attributed to the control value? What is the control portion value of each minority share in that context?

Until now the discussion has focused on finance. To this structure we need to add any legal constraints that may limit actions relating to distribution of acquisition gains. First, fiduciary duty principles limit officers and directors in their control of other people's money in the corporation. Insider transactions with the corporation are intensely scrutinized by an entire fairness test if the transaction has not been cleansed through statutory or judicially approved procedures. Similarly, fiduciaries cannot take for themselves an opportunity that belongs to the corporation.

Shareholders traditionally were not subjected to the same fiduciary rules. Actions which they take as owners of shares relate to their personal property, not collective assets belonging to the group. However, courts have extended the fiduciary duties of directors and officers to controlling shareholders when they, because of their controlling position, cause the corporation to take action that would otherwise be a violation of the traditional fiduciary duties of directors and officers.

A second set of legal rules that you should keep in mind are those relating to distribution of assets in a merger. In a typical merger setting, the merger plan will usually specify that shares are to receive a stated amount of consideration (or sometimes a choice between considerations such as cash or stock). In a cash-out, where the terms of the merger typically specify that the minority shareholders will receive a specified amount of cash for their shares, the dissenting shareholders are entitled to contest the amount in court via an appraisal action or a fiduciary duty action where the controlling shareholder will typically have to prove the entire fairness. *See Weinberger v. UOP, Inc.*, in Chapter 10. Case law has made clear that under either measure the dissenting shareholders are entitled to receive a proportionate share of a going concern without any discount for a minority interest. As you read the cases below, consider how the transactions proposed by the planners differ from the traditional merger setting and if that affects what non-controlling shareholders are to receive.

Perlman v. Feldmann
219 F.2d 173 (2d Cir. 1955)

CLARK, Chief Judge.

This is a derivative action brought by minority stockholders of Newport Steel Corporation to compel accounting for, and restitution of,

Chapter 11. Sale of Control for a Premium 425

allegedly illegal gains which accrued to defendants as a result of the sale in August, 1950, of their controlling interest in the corporation. The principal defendant, C. Russell Feldmann, who represented and acted for the others, members of his family,[1] was at that time not only the dominant stockholder, but also the chairman of the board of directors and the president of the corporation. Newport, an Indiana corporation, operated mills for the production of steel sheets for sale to manufacturers of steel products, first at Newport, Kentucky, and later also at other places in Kentucky and Ohio. The buyers, a syndicate organized as Wilport Company, a Delaware corporation, consisted of end-users of steel who were interested in securing a source of supply in a market becoming ever tighter in the Korean War. Plaintiffs contend that the consideration paid for the stock included compensation for the sale of a corporate asset, a power held in trust for the corporation by Feldmann as its fiduciary. This power was the ability to control the allocation of the corporate product in a time of short supply, through control of the board of directors; and it was effectively transferred in this sale by having Feldmann procure the resignation of his own board and the election of Wilport's nominees immediately upon consummation of the sale.

. . . Jurisdiction below was based upon the diverse citizenship of the parties. Plaintiffs argue here, as they did in the court below, that in the situation here disclosed the vendors must account to the non-participating minority stockholders for that share of their profit which is attributable to the sale of the corporate power. Judge Hincks denied the validity of the premise, holding that the rights involved in the sale were only those normally incident to the possession of a controlling block of shares, with which a dominant stockholder, in the absence of fraud or foreseeable looting, was entitled to deal according to his own best interests. Furthermore, he held that plaintiffs had failed to satisfy their burden of proving that the sales price was not a fair price for the stock per se. Plaintiffs appeal from these rulings of law which resulted in the dismissal of their complaint.

The essential facts found by the trial judge are not in dispute. Newport was a relative newcomer in the steel industry with predominantly old installations which were in the process of being supplemented by more modern facilities. Except in times of extreme shortage Newport was not in a position to compete profitably with other steel mills for customers not in its immediate geographical area. Wilport, the purchasing syndicate, consisted of geographically remote end-users of steel who were interested in buying more steel from Newport than they had been able to obtain during recent periods of tight supply. The price of $20 per share was found by

---

1. The stock was not held personally by Feldmann in his own name, but was held by the members of his family and by personal corporations. The aggregate of stock thus had amounted to 33% of the outstanding Newport stock and gave working control to the holder. The actual sale included 55,552 additional shares held by friends and associates of Feldmann, so that a total of 37% of the Newport stock was transferred.

Judge Hincks to be a fair one for a control block of stock, although the over-the-counter market price had not exceeded $12 and the book value per share was $17.03. But this finding was limited by Judge Hincks' statement that "what value the block would have had if shorn of its appurtenant power to control distribution of the corporate product, the evidence does not show." It was also conditioned by his earlier ruling that the burden was on plaintiffs to prove a lesser value for the stock.

Both as director and as dominant stockholder, Feldmann stood in a fiduciary relationship to the corporation and to the minority stockholders as beneficiaries thereof. *Pepper v. Litton*, 308 U.S. 295, 60 S. Ct. 238, 84 L. Ed. 281; *Southern Pac. Co. v. Bogert*, 250 U.S. 483, 39 S. Ct. 533, 63 L. Ed. 1099. His fiduciary obligation must in the first instance be measured by the law of Indiana, the state of incorporation of Newport. *Rogers v. Guaranty Trust Co. of New York*, 288 U.S. 123, 136, 53 S. Ct. 295, 77 L. Ed. 652; *Mayflower Hotel Stockholders Protective Committee v. Mayflower Hotel Corp.*, 89 U.S. App. D.C. 171, 193 F.2d 666, 668. Although there is no Indiana case directly in point, the most closely analogous one emphasizes the close scrutiny to which Indiana subjects the conduct of fiduciaries when personal benefit may stand in the way of fulfillment of trust obligations. In *Schemmel v. Hill*, 91 Ind. App. 373, 169 N.E. 678, 682, 683, McMahan, J., said: 'Directors of a business corporation act in a strictly fiduciary capacity. Their office is a trust. *Stratis v. Andreson*, 1926, 254 Mass. 536, 150 N.E. 832, 44 A.L.R. 567; *Hill v. Nisbet*, 1885, 100 Ind. 341, 353. When a director deals with his corporation, his acts will be closely scrutinized. *Bossert v. Geis*, 1914, 57 Ind. App. 384, 107 N.E. 95. Directors of a corporation are its agents, and they are governed by the rules of law applicable to other agents, and, as between themselves and their principal, the rules relating to honesty and fair dealing in the management of the affairs of their principal are applicable. They must not, in any degree, allow their official conduct to be swayed by their private interest, which must yield to official duty. *Leader Publishing Co. v. Grant Trust Co.*, 1915, 182 Ind. 651, 108 N.E. 121. "In a transaction between a director and his corporation, where he acts for himself and his principal at the same time in a matter connected with the relation between them, it is presumed, where he is thus potentially on both sides of the contract, that self-interest will overcome his fidelity to his principal, to his own benefit and to his principal's hurt." And the judge added: "Absolute and most scrupulous good faith is the very essence of a director's obligation to his corporation. The first principal duty arising from his official relation is to act in all things of trust wholly for the benefit of his corporation."

In Indiana, then, as elsewhere, the responsibility of the fiduciary is not limited to a proper regard for the tangible balance sheet assets of the corporation, but includes the dedication of his uncorrupted business judgment for the sole benefit of the corporation, in any dealings which may adversely affect it. *Young v. Higbee Co.*, 324 U.S. 204, 65 S. Ct. 594, 89 L. Ed. 890; *Irving Trust Co. v. Deutsch*, 2 Cir., 73 F.2d 121, certiorari denied 294 U.S. 708, 55 S.

Ct. 405, 79 L. Ed. 1243; *Seagrave Corp. v. Mount,* 6 Cir., 212 F.2d 389; *Meinhard v. Salmon,* 249 N.Y. 458, 164 N.E. 545, 62 A.L.R. 1; *Commonwealth Title Ins. & Trust Co. v. Seltzer,* 227 Pa. 410, 76 A. 77. Although the Indiana case is particularly relevant to Feldmann as a director, the same rule should apply to his fiduciary duties as majority stockholder, for in that capacity he chooses and controls the directors, and thus is held to have assumed their liability. *Pepper v. Litton,* supra, 308 U.S. 295, 60 S. Ct. 238. This, therefore, is the standard to which Feldmann was by law required to conform in his activities here under scrutiny.

It is true, as defendants have been at pains to point out, that this is not the ordinary case of breach of fiduciary duty. We have here no fraud, no misuse of confidential information, no outright looting of a helpless corporation. But on the other hand, we do not find compliance with that high standard which we have just stated and which we and other courts have come to expect and demand of corporate fiduciaries. In the often-quoted words of Judge Cardozo: "Many forms of conduct permissible in a workaday world for those acting at arm's length, are forbidden to those bound by fiduciary ties. A trustee is held to something stricter than the morals of the market place. Not honesty alone, but the punctilio of an honor the most sensitive, is then the standard of behavior. As to this there has developed a tradition that is unbending and inveterate. Uncompromising rigidity has been the attitude of courts of equity when petitioned to undermine the rule of undivided loyalty by the 'disintegrating erosion' of particular exceptions." *Meinhard v. Salmon,* supra, 249 N.Y. 458, 464, 164 N.E. 545, 546, 62 A.L.R. 1. The actions of defendants in siphoning off for personal gain corporate advantages to be derived from a favorable market situation do not betoken the necessary undivided loyalty owed by the fiduciary to his principal.

The corporate opportunities of whose misappropriation the minority stockholders complain need not have been an absolute certainty in order to support this action against Feldmann. . . .

This rationale is equally appropriate to a consideration of the benefits which Newport might have derived from the steel shortage. In the past Newport had used and profited by its market leverage by operation of what the industry had come to call the "Feldmann Plan." This consisted of securing interest-free advances from prospective purchasers of steel in return for firm commitments to them from future production. The funds thus acquired were used to finance improvements in existing plants and to acquire new installations. In the summer of 1950 Newport had been negotiating for cold-rolling facilities which it needed for a more fully integrated operation and a more marketable product, and Feldmann plan funds might well have been used toward this end.

Further, as plaintiffs alternatively suggest, Newport might have used the period of short supply to build up patronage in the geographical area in which it could compete profitably even when steel was more abundant.

Either of these opportunities was Newport's, to be used to its advantage only. Only if defendants had been able to negate completely any possibility of gain by Newport could they have prevailed. It is true that a trial court finding states: "Whether or not, in August, 1950, Newport's position was such that it could have entered into 'Feldmann Plan' type transactions to procure funds and financing for the further expansion and integration of its steel facilities and whether such expansion would have been desirable for Newport, the evidence does not show." This, however, cannot avail the defendants, who — contrary to the ruling below — had the burden of proof on this issue, since fiduciaries always have the burden of proof in establishing the fairness of their dealings with trust property. *Pepper v. Litton*, supra, 308 U.S. 295, 60 S. Ct. 238; *Geddes v. Anaconda Copper Mining Co.*, 254 U.S. 590, 41 S. Ct. 209, 65 L. Ed. 425; *Mayflower Hotel Stockholders Protective Committee v. Mayflower Hotel Corp.*, 84 U.S. App. D.C. 275, 173 F.2d 416.

Defendants seek to categorize the corporate opportunities which might have accrued to Newport as too unethical to warrant further consideration. It is true that reputable steel producers were not participating in the gray market brought about by the Korean War and were refraining from advancing their prices, although to do so would not have been illegal. But Feldmann plan transactions were not considered within this self-imposed interdiction; the trial court found that around the time of the Feldmann sale Jones & Laughlin Steel Corporation, Republic Steel Company, and Pittsburgh Steel Corporation were all participating in such arrangements. In any event, it ill becomes the defendants to disparage as unethical the market advantages from which they themselves reaped rich benefits.

We do not mean to suggest that a majority stockholder cannot dispose of his controlling block of stock to outsiders without having to account to his corporation for profits or even never do this with impunity when the buyer is an interested customer, actual or potential, for the corporation's product. But when the sale necessarily results in a sacrifice of this element of corporate good will and consequent unusual profit to the fiduciary who has caused the sacrifice, he should account for his gains. So in a time of market shortage, where a call on a corporation's product commands an unusually large premium, in one form or another, we think it sound law that a fiduciary may not appropriate to himself the value of this premium. Such personal gain at the expense of his coventurers seems particularly reprehensible when made by the trusted president and director of his company. In this case the violation of duty seems to be all the clearer because of this triple role in which Feldmann appears, though we are unwilling to say, and are not to be understood as saying, that we should accept a lesser obligation for any one of his roles alone.

Hence to the extent that the price received by Feldmann and his codefendants included such a bonus, he is accountable to the minority stockholders who sue here. Restatement, Restitution §§190, 197 (1937);

Seagrave Corp. v. Mount, supra, 6 Cir., 212 F.2d 389. And plaintiffs, as they contend, are entitled to a recovery in their own right, instead of in right of the corporation (as in the usual derivative actions), since neither Wilport nor their successors in interest should share in any judgment which may be rendered. See *Southern Pacific Co. v. Bogert,* 250 U.S. 483, 39 S. Ct. 533, 63 L. Ed. 1099. Defendants cannot well object to this form of recovery, since the only alternative, recovery for the corporation as a whole, would subject them to a greater total liability.

The case will therefore be remanded to the district court for a determination of the question expressly left open below, namely, the value of defendants' stock without the appurtenant control over the corporation's output of steel. We reiterate that on this issue, as on all others relating to a breach of fiduciary duty, the burden of proof must rest on the defendants. *Bigelow v. RKO Radio Pictures,* 327 U.S. 251, 265-266, 66 S. Ct. 574, 90 L. Ed. 652; *Package Closure Corp. v. Sealright Co.,* 2 Cir., 141 F.2d 972, 979. Judgment should go to these plaintiffs and those whom they represent for any premium value so shown to the extent of their respective stock interests.

The judgment is therefore reversed and the action remanded for further proceedings pursuant to this opinion.

NOTES AND QUESTIONS

1. Source of the gain in the transaction. What was the source of gain in the Wilport/Newport transaction? What gains such as synergies identified earlier in your mergers study can you see in this acquisition? This transaction also contains a second set of value creation drivers related to "soft" price controls. During the Korean War, when military demand for steel increased, the government pushed steel suppliers not to raise prices, and the case tells us that "reputable" steel producers were complying. Plotted on a classic supply and demand curve graph, this was to cap prices at a point where demand exceeded supply and at a point P bar where end users would be willing to pay considerably more.

2. The Feldmann plan. Those who had steel to sell had an incentive to look for ways to capture some or all of that difference. The "Feldmann plan" was such a technique. Interest-free cash payments from potential buyers effectively increased the cash the sellers would receive and captured some or all of the difference between P bar and P^D. Newport has used such a technique in the past, and the opinion reports that the reputable steel producers were participating in such arrangements at the time of the transaction. The method chosen by the planners of this transaction is an alternative method of securing the amount attributable to control that was effectively blocked by the soft cap from price controls. Wilport may not be able to buy the steel itself at the higher market price, but it could buy the shares of the company which would produce the same result of control of

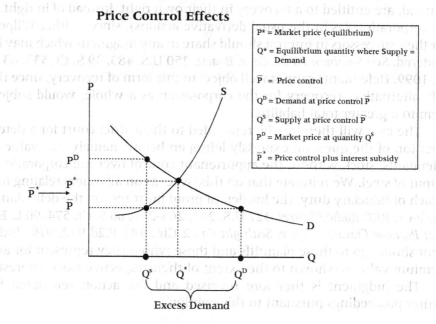

Figure 11-1

Price Control Effects

P^* = Market price (equilibrium)
Q^* = Equilibrium quantity where Supply = Demand
$\bar{P}$ = Price control
Q^D = Demand at price control $\bar{P}$
Q^S = Supply at price control $\bar{P}$
P^D = Market price at quantity Q^S
$\bar{P}^*$ = Price control plus interest subsidy

the supply of steel. How much would Wilport pay to achieve such a control of the supply of steel by acquiring control of the Newport Corporation? Up to the amount P^D.

3. The form of the transaction. Once you have in mind how much an acquirer such as Wilport would pay to acquire Newport, would such an acquirer care about the form the transaction took? Or asked another way, would the total purchase price be different if the form of the acquisition was not a sale of shares, but rather a merger, as we have previously studied. It is likely that Wilport would have offered the same control premium, reflecting what the steel was worth to it, but now spread over the entire outstanding shares as opposed to just the 37 percent. In fact, there was just such an alternative transaction for Newport itself at the time. A contemporary federal case, Birnbaum v. Newport Steel Corp., 193 F.2d 461, 462 (2d Cir. 1952), one of the most important early Rule 10b-5 cases, reported that during this same period, Newport was negotiating with another company, Follansbee Steel Corporation, over a merger "which would have been highly profitable to all the stockholders of Newport." The Second Circuit reports that "in August 1950, Feldmann, acting in his official capacity as president of Newport, rejected the Follansbee offer, and on August 31, 1950, sold his stock to the defendant Wilport Company at a price of $22 per share which was twice the then market value of the stock." So what is it about this transaction that leads to the Second Circuit striking it down on corporate law principles in Perlman? Does it forbid controlling shareholders to sell for a control premium? No, the opinion is explicit about that four paragraphs from the end. Is it the source of the control premium such that gains from synergy would by retained but not gains from avoiding soft price controls? Does it matter that the control premium holder had less than 50 percent?

4. What about the non-controlling shareholders? Consider the position of the non-controlling or minority shareholders. What would you expect happened to their share value after this transaction and should that matter? Easterbrook and Fischel assert that the going price of Newport shares (prior to the Wilport transaction) would have reflected "the full value of Newport, including the value of the advances under the Feldmann plan." Easterbrook & Fischel, *Corporate Control Transactions*, 91 YALE L.J. 698, 717-18 (1982). Easterbrook and Fischel conclude that the price of Newport shares in fact rose substantially after the Wilport transaction and point to an unpublished paper by Charles Cope that reports an increase in price for the remainder of 1950, a gain that remained after accounting for the rising fortunes of the steel industry at the time. Should controlling shareholders be able to receive a premium if the other shareholders are no worse off, or must there be equal sharing? Consider a later opinion below from the Delaware chancellor.

Mendel v. Carroll
651 A.2d 297 (Del. Ch. 1994)

ALLEN, Chancellor.

... [T]stockholder plaintiffs in these consolidated actions seek an unprecedented remedy: an order requiring the board of directors of a Delaware corporation to grant an option to buy 20% of its stock to a third party for the primary purpose of diluting the voting power of an existing control block of stock. The order sought would direct the Board of Directors of Katy Industries, Inc. ("Katy") to grant to an affiliate of Pensler Capital Corporation (together with Pensler Capital Partners L.L.P., referred to here as "Pensler") an option to purchase up to 20% of Katy's outstanding common stock at $27.80 per share. The granting of such an option is a condition of an offer for a $27.80 per share cash merger extended by Pensler to Katy. The proposed merger is said by plaintiffs to be without other material conditions.

Katy's board of directors has declined to grant the option sought. The board took this position in the face of a claim by a group of related shareholders (the Carroll Family) that granting such an option would deprive them of their legitimate and dominant voice in corporate affairs, and would in the circumstances constitute a breach of fiduciary duty.

Plaintiffs' theory, stated most summarily, is that when the Katy board had earlier resolved to accept the terms of a $25.75 cash-out merger proposed by the Carroll Family, the company was put up "for sale," and that as a result the board now has a single duty: to exercise its active and informed judgment in a good faith effort to get the best available value for the stockholders. Plaintiffs contend that rejection of Pensler's $27.80 merger proposal is not consistent with that goal. They posit that granting the option sought is a necessary step for the board to satisfy its special duty (which plaintiffs call a "*Revlon* duty"), and thus it is obligated in these circumstances to do so.

The notable fact in this case is that at all relevant times a small group of Carroll Family members has controlled between 48% and 52% of Katy's voting stock. In fact, this group has coordinated its activities informally and through legal agreements. With a single exception, accounting for about 5% of the stock, this group has steadily taken the position that it would buy, but it would not voluntarily sell Katy stock. Thus, members of the Carroll Family early and continually announced active resistance to Pensler's proposal.

Following Pensler's September 1993 initial proposal, the Special Committee of the Katy Board withdrew its recommendation of the Carroll Merger. In December 1993 the Carroll Family withdrew its offer. To evidence its *bona fides* in withdrawing the offer, the Carroll Family further offered to execute a standstill agreement stating that it would not acquire additional Katy shares beyond some open market purchases certain family members had made in December.

The dilutive option sought by Pensler as a condition of its $27.80 offer is, of course, a means of overcoming the resistance of the Carroll shareholders. Exercise of the option sought would reduce the voting power of the Carrolls from their current level of 50.6% to approximately 40% and thus make feasible stockholder approval of the Pensler transaction. A Special Committee of the Katy board of directors, delegated to deal first with the Carroll Family proposal and then with Pensler, after obtaining advice from legal counsel, declined to recommend to the full board the granting of the dilutive option.

Plaintiffs filed this suit in February 1994, after the full board announced its intention to declare an extraordinary $14.00 per share dividend. In addition to the mandatory granting of a stock option, plaintiffs also seek an order: requiring the defendants to negotiate fairly with Pensler; prohibiting the voting of certain shares recently acquired on the market by certain members of the Carroll Family; prohibiting Katy from making certain payments; and prohibiting Katy from distributing the $14.00 special dividend authorized in March 1994 by the board of directors. On the last point, it is plaintiffs' contention that the special dividend is in fact an alternative to Pensler's value-maximizing proposal, and for that reason constitutes a violation of what they take to be the on-going special duties arising from the board's decision to approve the now withdrawn Carroll Family proposal.

For the reasons that follow, I conclude that the board of Katy Industries is not under any special duty at this time to maximize the current value of the public shares or of the company's stock as a whole. Thus, I reject the premise of the principal theory offered by plaintiffs to justify the strong relief they seek. More broadly, assuming that the radical step of granting stock for the primary purpose of affecting the outcome of a shareholder vote or tender could be justified under some set of circumstances, I can see here no overreaching or palpable breach of fiduciary duty by a controlling shareholder that might justify such a protective reaction....

I.

Katy is a New York Stock Exchange listed firm, founded in 1968 by Wallace E. Carroll, Sr. As a practical matter, control of Katy has always rested in the hands of Mr. Carroll, Sr. or his children. During periods relevant to this suit, the Carroll Family (defined here as Mr. Carroll, his three sons, his daughter Lelia Carroll Johnson and her former husband Philip, and affiliated trusts or other interests) has owned between 48% and 52% of Katy's outstanding common stock. Traditionally these interests were held in a coordinated way. In 1983, all of the Carroll Family Members entered into a Stock Purchase Agreement. That agreement granted a right of first refusal to other signatories with respect to all Katy stock owned, but contained no restrictions on the exercise of voting rights.

In August 1988, the Carroll Family's holdings of Katy stood at approximately 48%. At that time, the board of directors authorized the Company to repurchase up to 500,000 of the nine million shares outstanding. No shares, however, were acquired under that authority at that time.

Wallace Carroll, Sr. died in September 1990. In March 1991 Katy retained Dillon, Read & Co., Inc. to conduct a financial review of the company, and "to advise the board on a variety of financial alternatives available to [Katy]." Kurowski Aff. Ex. A. Among the Dillon, Read personnel assigned to that project was Mr. Sanford Pensler, now a principal in Pensler Capital Corp. In its August 1991 report Dillon, Read noted that "Katy appears to be awash in capital" and that "[i]t is unlikely the public markets will give full value to this collection of assets in its present configuration." Kahn Aff. Ex. B at 307. Several strategic options were presented, including a "split off" of operating subsidiaries and the repurchase of "substantial amounts of equity." *Id.* at 321-22. Dillon, Read noted that "investment in Katy's own shares appears to be very attractive." *Id.* at 323.

In fact, Katy had already privately repurchased a substantial block of common stock in June 1991. It made another negotiated purchase in September, after receiving the investment bank's analyses. The June repurchase brought the Carroll Family's aggregate common stock ownership to over 50%; the September repurchase increased that aggregate interest to over 52%. Katy later repurchased another 5,800 shares in the market in April 1992.

A. The Family Buyout Proposal

Members of the Carroll Family retained Morgan Stanley & Co. to advise them with respect to their holdings in Katy. In June 1992 the Carroll Family publicly announced that it was reviewing its options concerning Katy. At that time Katy stock had been trading at about $16.00 per share. On September 1, 1992, the Carroll Family executed a Participation Agreement in which they agreed to act in concert in the acquisition of the publicly held shares of Katy.[5] On that same day, the Carroll Family offered to acquire all non-Carroll shares of Katy common stock at $22.00 per share.[6] In the intervening months the stock had risen to trade on the day prior to the announcement at $24.00 per share.

In presenting its proposal, the Carroll Family advised the board that it had no interest in selling any of its approximately 52.6% of Katy's common stock. In response to the offer, the board appointed a Special Committee comprised of directors who were apparently disinterested in the proposal. They retained the investment bank Goldman Sachs & Co., as well as the Dallas law firm Jenkens & Gilchrist, P.C., as counsel. After consideration, the Special Committee rejected the $22.00 offer as inadequate and attempted to negotiate a higher price with the Carroll Family. The Carroll Family offered $24.00 per share, but the Special Committee insisted on $26.00 per share. No agreement was reached and the Carroll Family withdrew its offer. The Special Committee was disbanded in December 1992.

On March 11, 1993, the Carroll Family made a new offer to purchase all outstanding non-Carroll Katy shares at $25.75 per share. In conjunction with the new offer, the Carroll Family amended the Participation Agreement to enable Barry Carroll and his affiliates to sell their 4.6% holding in Katy stock (hereinafter, "Barry Carroll's shares").[8] The Special Committee was reinstituted and advised of the treatment of Barry Carroll's shares.

---

5. The Participation Agreement generally provides that Carroll Family members: (i) will transfer shares only to a newly formed acquisition entity or to other family members; (ii) will vote in favor of a Carroll Merger and other measures to facilitate it; and (iii) will not solicit or vote in favor of any third party proposal. Kahn Aff. Ex. A at 57.

6. On September 2, 1992, six class action complaints were filed in this court, alleging that the $22.00 per share offer was grossly inadequate. . . .

8. This fact is important to plaintiffs because they wish to establish that at this or some later point the "non-selling" members of the Carroll Family held less than 50% of Katy's voting stock. From this premise they then try to build an argument that "control" was at such time in the public shares and thus at the time of the March 15 acceptance by the board of the Family's $25.75 proposal, the transaction represented a change in corporate control as contemplated by *Paramount Communications Inc. v. QVC Network Inc.*, Del. Supr., 637 A.2d 34 (1993), thus, in their theory triggering "*Revlon* duties." It is their view of the impact here of "*Revlon* duties" that leads to relief they seek.

After Goldman Sachs indicated that it would render an opinion that $25.75 represented a price within a range of fair prices for the public stock, the Special Committee concluded that the new offer was in the best interests of Katy's shareholders, and recommended the offer to the full board. The board approved that offer on March 15, 1993, and authorized the officers of Katy to enter into a merger agreement with a Carroll Family-controlled entity on March 23. A proxy statement was mailed to shareholders on August 23, 1993.

B. A Rosecliff Pensler Proposal Emerges

In a September 1, 1993 letter to Mr. Jacob Saliba, Katy's Chairman, a venture called Rosecliff Pensler Partners L.P. ("Rosecliff Pensler")[9] proposed to purchase, on a friendly basis only, all of Katy's outstanding shares for at least $29.00 per share, subject to completing due diligence, obtaining financing, and receiving necessary government approvals. On September 2, Barry Carroll wrote to Mr. Saliba that he thought the Rosecliff Pensler offer was attractive and should be pursued.

At a special meeting of the board of directors of September 17, 1993, representatives of the Special Committee advised the Board that Goldman Sachs had stated, in effect, that until the Rosecliff Pensler proposal could be more clearly defined and evaluated, the Special Committee could not rely upon Goldman's August 23, 1993 opinion concerning the fairness of the Carroll Family Merger. As a result, the Special Committee advised the full board that it was not then in a position to continue its endorsement of the Carroll Family Merger. At that meeting Philip Johnson reiterated that as shareholders the members of the Carroll Family were not interested in selling their shares; there was therefore no way in which a Rosecliff Pensler merger proposal could be effectuated; and thus no reason for Katy to permit Rosecliff Pensler to conduct a due diligence investigation.

Notwithstanding Mr. Johnson's position, the Katy board resolved at a further September 23, 1993 meeting to permit Rosecliff Pensler access to Company information on the same basis as it had been made available to the Carroll Family's advisors.

C. Steinhardt Pensler Proposal

By mid-November 1993, Rosecliff Inc. appears to have lost interest in a Katy transaction, but Pensler found a new joint venturer in Steinhardt Enterprise Inc. On November 29, 1993, a new partnership of Pensler Capital Corporation and Steinhardt Enterprise Inc. ("Steinhardt Pensler")

---

9. Rosecliff Pensler was a partnership of Rosecliff, Inc. and Pensler Capital Corporation.

proposed to purchase all of Katy's outstanding shares at $28.00 per share, purportedly without financing or due diligence conditions. The offer was scheduled to expire on December 6, 1993.

Also on November 29, Barry Carroll advised Mr. Saliba and the board of directors that he would not sign another extension of the Participation Agreement, scheduled to terminate on November 30, 1993, and that he intended to sell his shares pursuant to the 1983 Stock Purchase Agreement. The withdrawal of Barry Carroll's shares from the Participation Agreement left the Carroll Family, excluding Barry Carroll (hereinafter, the "Carroll Group"), with ownership of approximately 47.9% of Katy's outstanding common stock.

D. Carroll Family Market Purchases

On December 1, 1993, Philip Johnson wrote to Mr. Saliba that the Carroll Family was exercising its right to terminate the merger agreement.

Also on December 1, the Carroll Group (i.e., the family minus Barry Carroll and affiliates) filed a Schedule 13D amendment with the Securities and Exchange Commission disclosing that it intended to acquire additional shares of common stock "to establish the position of the [Carroll Group] as the holders, in the aggregate, of a majority of the outstanding Shares and thereby to assure the control of the Company by the members of the Carroll Family regardless of the level of Share holdings of Mr. Barry Carroll. . . ." Kahn Aff. Ex. F at 38. The Carroll Group further stated that it had no present intention of engaging in any transaction to take Katy private. On December 2 and 3, 1993, Wallace Carroll, Jr. and Lelia Carroll Johnson purchased shares in the market with the result that the Carroll Group's ownership rose again to 50.6% of the outstanding common stock of Katy.

E. Further Negotiations with Steinhardt Pensler and the Requested Dilution of Carroll Group Control

On December 3, 1993, the Special Committee requested authority from the board to meet and negotiate with Steinhardt Pensler. After a spirited discussion during which Mr. Johnson reiterated that the Carroll Group was in no event interested in selling its Katy stock, and over the objection of certain directors, the board granted the permission requested.

On December 5, 1993, Steinhardt Pensler presented the Special Committee with a proposed Merger Agreement that contemplated a $28.00 per share cash merger and a proposed Stock Option Agreement. The Stock Option Agreement would grant Steinhardt Pensler an irrevocable option to purchase up to 1.8 million shares of authorized but unissued shares of

Katy at a price equal to the merger consideration; it would also grant Steinhardt Pensler the right to put the shares to Katy if the shareholders subsequently failed to approve the merger. Both agreements would require Katy to indemnify Steinhardt Pensler and pay damages if the option was found to be improper.

On December 11, while the Special Committee and its legal and financial advisors were evaluating the offer, Steinhardt Pensler made another offer at a reduced price of $27.80, claiming that it had just learned that Goldman Sachs' fee arrangement with Katy was tied to the merger price.

Steinhardt Pensler offered to increase the bid to $28.00 per share if Goldman Sachs agreed to cap its fee at $1 million, and stated that the new offer would expire on December 15, 1993. Odoner Aff. ¶ 4.

On December 13, the Special Committee met with Steinhardt Pensler and its advisors. Later that same day, the Special Committee reported to the full board. The board then authorized the Special Committee to continue to meet and negotiate concerning the proposed Merger and Stock Option Agreements with Steinhardt Pensler. Mr. Johnson voiced the Carroll Group's objection to the dilutive option in strong terms, claiming it would constitute a breach of fiduciary duty to the Carrolls by diluting their controlling position just to favor others.

The Special Committee sent a revised draft of the proposed agreements to Steinhardt Pensler on December 14. The proposed changes included provisions: insuring that Steinhardt Pensler had the financial commitments necessary to close the deal; prohibiting Steinhardt Pensler from further altering or withdrawing from the transaction based on due diligence; and imposing further conditions on the receipt of termination and breakup fees. There was no timely response and, by its terms, the $27.80 Steinhardt Pensler offer expired on December 15, 1993.

Nevertheless, the two sides' representatives remained in contact regarding Steinhardt Pensler's financing and other matters through December 1993 and early January 1994. On January 18, 1994, the Special Committee reported to the full board that a "log jam" in negotiations with Steinhardt Pensler over the bidders' financing had broken when the Special Committee received letters, and Goldman Sachs confirmed, that the partners had access to capital sufficient for the commitment. Minor points arising from due diligence required further negotiation. The purchase price remained $27.80, but would rise to $28.00 if Goldman Sachs would cap its fee at $1 million. The legality of the grant of the dilutive option continued to be a crucial issue to the Special Committee. At the January 18 meeting, the board unanimously agreed, though it did not formally resolve that, without an opinion from the Special Committee's Delaware counsel, to the effect that the option would be valid and would not constitute a breach of duty, the Committee could not negotiate a merger agreement including such an option with Steinhardt Pensler.

F. Legal Opinions on the Dilutive Option

... The Special Committee now turned to that counsel for advice on the question whether granting an option of the type sought would, in the circumstances, constitute a violation of the board's fiduciary duty to the Carroll Group as shareholders. The Special Committee's Delaware attorneys produced a thirty-two-page opinion analyzing the relevant facts and law, and essentially concluded that it was unclear whether granting the option would be legal.

Following the receipt of the inconclusive opinion of its counsel, the Special Committee made two recommendations at a January 28, 1994 special meeting of the full board. Given the uncertain validity of the option, the Special Committee first recommended that it was no longer in the best interests of Katy and its shareholders to pursue negotiations with Steinhardt Pensler. Second, the Special Committee recommended that the board appoint another committee to explore other methods to maximize shareholder value, including: (i) a self-tender by Katy; (ii) a Dutch auction of Katy shares; and/or (iii) a dividend in excess of $10.00 per share on Katy's common stock. In accordance with these recommendations, the board directed the Special Committee's counsel to notify Steinhardt Pensler that Katy would no longer discuss a merger with a dilutive option. The board further established a new committee to consider strategies to enhance shareholder value.

On March 8, 1994, the new committee recommended that the board approve a special cash dividend of $14.00 per share of Katy common stock. The board has endorsed that recommendation but has not yet declared such a dividend, pending outcome of this motion. This suit had been filed on February 18, 1994 and on March 17, 1994 the court heard plaintiffs' motion for preliminary injunction....

IV.

I turn then to the core issue: whether Katy's board of directors has or had a legal or equitable obligation to facilitate a closing of Pensler's $27.80 cash merger proposal by granting the option that Pensler seeks. To provide an answer to such a question, particularly in the setting of a preliminary injunction application, does not require one to formulate an answer to the abstract question whether a board of directors could ever, consistent with its fiduciary obligations, grant an option to buy stock for the principal purpose of affecting the outcome of an expected shareholder action, such as an election, a consent solicitation, or a tender offer. Surely if the principal motivation for such dilution is simply to maintain corporate control ("entrenchment") it would violate the norm of loyalty. *See Condec Corp. v. Lunkenheimer Co.,* Del. Ch., 230 A.2d 769 (1967); *Canada Southern Oils, Ltd. v. Manabi Exploration Co.,* Del. Ch., 96 A.2d 810 (1953). Where, however, a board of directors acts in good faith and on the reasonable belief that a controlling shareholder is abusing its power and is exploiting or threatening to exploit the vulnerability of minority shareholders, I suppose, for reasons touched upon in the cases cited in the margin, that the board might permissibly take such an action. *See Unocal Corp. v. Mesa Petroleum Co.*, Del. Supr., 493 A.2d 946 (1985).

Here, of course, plaintiffs' core argument can be understood to be that the controlling shareholders *are* exploiting the vulnerability of the minority shares in a very particular way. The gist of plaintiffs' complaint is that the minority shareholders could get more cash for their stock in a Pensler cash deal than they would have gotten in the proposed $25.75 Carroll Group deal. Thus, plaintiffs would contend that the foregoing protective principle grounded in fiduciary obligation would apply to this situation, and that the board is, as a result, under a current obligation to take the radical step of intentionally diluting the control of the controlling block of stock.

In my opinion, this view is mistaken. I apprehend in the facts recited above no threat of exploitation or even unfairness towards a vulnerable minority that might arguably justify discrimination against a controlling block of stock. Plaintiffs see in the Carroll Group's unwillingness to sell at $27.80 or to buy at that price, a denial of plaintiffs' ability to realize such a price, and see this as exploitation or breach of duty. This view implicitly regards the $27.80 per share price and the Carroll Family Merger price of $25.75 as comparable sorts of things. But they are legally and financially quite different. *It is, for example, quite possible that the Carroll $25.75 price may have been fair, even generous, while the $27.80 Pensler price may be inadequate.* If one understands why this is so, one will understand one reason why the injunction now sought cannot be granted.

The fundamental difference between these two possible transactions arises from the fact that the Carroll Family already in fact had a committed block of controlling stock. Financial markets in widely traded corporate stock accord a premium to a block of stock that can assure corporate control. Analysts differ as to the source of any such premium but not on its existence. Optimists see the control premium as a reflection of the efficiency enhancing changes that the buyer of control is planning on making to the organization.[15] Others tend to see it, at least sometimes, as the price that a prospective wrongdoer is willing to pay in order to put himself in the position to exploit vulnerable others,[16] or simply as a function of a downward sloping demand curve demonstrating investors' heterogeneous

---

15. Frank H. Easterbrook and Daniel R. Fischel, THE ECONOMIC STRUCTURE OF CORPORATE LAW 126-44 (1991); Frank H. Easterbrook and Daniel R. Fischel, *Corporate Control Transactions*, 91 YALE L.J. 698 (1982).

16. *See* Robert W. Hamilton, *Private Sale of Control Transactions: Where We Stand Today*, 36 CASE W. RES. L. REV. 248 (1985); *see, e.g., Gerdes v. Reynolds*, 28 N.Y.S.2d 622, 650-52 (N.Y. App. Div. 1941).

beliefs about the subject stock's value.[17] In all events, it is widely understood that buyers of corporate control will be required to pay a premium above the market price for the company's traded securities.

The law has acknowledged, albeit in a guarded and complex way, the legitimacy of the acceptance by controlling shareholders of a control premium. See *Cheff v. Mathes*, Del. Supr., 199 A.2d 548, 555 (1964); *Hecco Ventures v. Sea-Land Corp.*, Del. Ch., C.A. No. 8486, 1986 WL 5840, Jacobs, V.C. (May 19, 1986); *Zetlin v. Hanson Holdings, Inc.*, 48 N.Y.2d 684, 421 N.Y.S.2d 877, 878, 397 N.E.2d 387, 388-89 (1979).[18]

The significant fact is that in the Carroll Family Merger, the buyers were not buying corporate control. With either 48% or 52% of the outstanding stock they already had it. Therefore, in evaluating the fairness of the Carroll proposal, the Special Committee and its financial advisors were in a distinctly different position than would be a seller in a transaction in which corporate control was to pass.

The Pensler offer, of course, was fundamentally different. It was an offer, in effect, to the controlling shareholder to purchase corporate control, and to all public shareholders, to purchase the remaining part of the company's shares, all at a single price. It distributed the control premium evenly over all shares. Because the Pensler proposed $27.80 price was a price that contemplated not simply the purchase of non-controlling stock, as did the Carroll Family Merger, but complete control over the corporation, it was not fairly comparable to the per-share price proposed by the Carroll Group. . . .

To note that these proposals are fundamentally different does not, of course, mean that the board owes fiduciary duties in one instance but not in the other. That is not the case. But to describe the duty that corporate directors bear in any particular situation one must first consider the circumstances that give rise to the occasion for judgment. When the Katy board or its Special Committee evaluated the Carroll Family Merger, it was obligated to take note of the circumstance that the proposal was being advanced by a group of shareholders that constituted approximately 50% of all share ownership, and who arguably had the power to elect the board. In this circumstance, in my opinion, the board's duty was to respect

---

17. See Lynn A. Stout, *Are Takeover Premiums Really Premiums? Market Price, Fair Value, and Corporate Law*, 99 Yale L.J. 1235, 1244-52 (1990).

18. The doctrine applicable to a sale of corporate control at a premium is far more complex than it may at first appear. Indeed one might conclude that courts afford it somewhat grudging recognition. A number of liability creating doctrines have been applied which have the effect of creating risks to the controlling shareholder who attempts to realize a control premium. These doctrines include negligence, see *Harris v. Carter*, Del. Ch., 582 A.2d 222, 232-36 (1990); *Insuranshares Corp. v. Northern Fiscal Corp.*, 35 F. Supp. 22, 25-27 (E.D. Pa. 1940); sale of corporate office, see *Essex Universal Corp. v. Yates*, 305 F.2d 572, 581-82 (2d Cir. 1962) (Friendly, J., concurring); and sale of corporate opportunity, see *Brown v. Halbert*, 271 Cal. App. 2d 252, 76 Cal. Rptr. 781, 791-94 (1969); *Jones v. H.F. Ahmanson & Co.*, 1 Cal. 3d 93, 81 Cal. Rptr. 592, 604, 460 P.2d 464, 476 (1969). See generally E. Elhauge, *The Triggering Function of Sale of Control Doctrine*, 59 U. Chi. L. Rev. 1465 (1992).

the rights of the Carroll Family, while assuring that if any transaction of the type proposed was to be accomplished, it would be accomplished only on terms that were fair to the public shareholders and represented the best available terms from their point of view. *See, e.g., Kahn v. Lynch Communication Sys., Inc.*, Del. Supr., 638 A.2d 1110, 1119 (1994); *In re First Boston, Inc. Shareholders Litig.*, Del. Ch., C.A. No. 10338 (Cons.), 1990 WL 78836, Allen, C. (June 7, 1990).

This obligation the board faces is rather similar to the obligation that the board assumes when it bears what have been called "*Revlon* duties," but the obligations are not identical. When presented with the controlling stockholders' proposal, the obligation of the Katy board was in some respects similar to that faced by a board when it elects to sell the corporation, because *if* the board were to approve a proposed cash-out merger, it would have to bear in mind that the transaction is a final-stage transaction for the public shareholders. Thus, the time frame for analysis, insofar as those shareholders are concerned, is immediate value maximization. The directors are obliged in such a situation to try, within their fiduciary obligation, to maximize the current value of the minority shares. In this respect the obligation is analogous to the board's duty when it is engaged in a process of "selling" the corporation, as for example in the recent *Paramount Communications Inc. v. QVC Network Inc.*, Del. Supr., 637 A.2d 34 (1994). But the duty is somewhat different because of the existence of the controlling Carroll Family block.

The Carroll Family made it clear throughout these events that, for the most part, its members were completely uninterested in being sellers in any transaction.[19] No part of their fiduciary duty as controlling shareholders requires them to sell their interest. *See Bershad v. Curtiss-Wright Corp.*, Del. Supr., 535 A.2d 840 (1987); *Jedwab v. MGM Grand Hotels, Inc.*, Del. Ch., 509 A.2d 584 (1986) (self sacrifice not required). The board's fiduciary obligation to the corporation and its shareholders, in this setting, requires it to be a protective guardian of the rightful interest of the public shareholders. But while that obligation may authorize the board to take extraordinary steps to protect the minority from plain overreaching, it does not authorize the board to deploy corporate power *against* the majority stockholders, in the absence of a threatened serious breach of fiduciary duty by the controlling stock.

To acknowledge that the Carroll Family has no obligation to support a transaction in which they would in effect sell their stock is not, of course, to suggest that they can use their control over the corporation to effectuate a self-interested merger at an unfair price. *See Weinberger v. U.O.P., Inc.*, Del. Supr., 457 A.2d 701 (1983). There is nothing in the present record,

---

19. The fact that Mr. Barry Carroll parted company with his family does not appear to have affected the practical fact of control — which of course is the predicate fact for the existence of a control premium.

however, that suggests to me that the $25.75 price the Carroll Group proposed to pay for the public shares was an inadequate or unfair price for the non-controlling stock. For the reasons stated above, the fact that Pensler was willing to pay more for all of the shares does not, logically, support an inference that the Carroll proposal for the non-controlling public shares was not fair.

Thus, while I continue to hold open the possibility that a situation might arise in which a board could, consistently with its fiduciary duties, issue a dilutive option in order to protect the corporation or its minority shareholders from exploitation by a controlling shareholder who was in the process or threatening to violate his fiduciary duties to the corporation,[20] such a situation does not at all appear to have been faced by the Katy board of directors.

In my opinion, far from "*Revlon* duties" requiring such action, the Katy board could not, consistent with its fiduciary obligations to all of the stockholders of Katy Industries, have issued the dilutive option for the purpose sought in this instance. Therefore, that the board considered the matter and declined to do so could in no event be considered to constitute a breach of duty to the minority shareholders.

V.

The Carroll Group withdrew its proposed merger on December 1, 1993. Thereafter, on March 8, 1994, the board authorized the payment of an extraordinary $14.00 per share cash dividend. Plaintiffs seek to enjoin the payment of this dividend.

It is elementary that the declaration of dividends out of available corporate funds is a matter left to the discretion of the board of directors and that the declaration or payment of a dividend will be reviewed by a court only on the basis of fraud or gross abuse of discretion. *See Gabelli & Co. v. Liggett Group, Inc.*, Del. Supr., 479 A.2d 276, 280 (1984) (quoting *Eshleman v. Keenan*, Del. Ch., 194 A. 40, 43 (1937) (Wolcott, C.)).

The only argument plaintiffs can advance in support of the position that the declaration and payment of the special dividend is "a gross abuse," is again predicated upon the assertion that "*Revlon* duties" require the board now to maximize the current value of the stock. The proposed dividend, they say, is inconsistent with a transaction with Pensler, and thus does not satisfy this *Revlon* duty. Concluding as I do above, it follows that plaintiffs have shown no gross abuse in the declaration of the special dividend, nor have plaintiffs shown any other ground for the grant of preliminary injunction at this time. Therefore the application will be denied.

---

20. In such an instance the board would bear a heavy burden to establish the justification for any steps purposely taken to affect the outcome of shareholder action. *See Blasius Indus., Inc. v. Atlas Corp.*, Del. Ch., 564 A.2d 651 (1988).

NOTES AND QUESTIONS

1. **The two transactions.** Compare the two transactions embedded in the case. First in time was a cash-out merger. From the prior chapter, what will be the legal standard by which such a transaction will be reviewed and to whom and to what transaction does it apply? Why does the deal not go through? Second was an outsider transaction (from a financial adviser initially retained to advise the company who then decided to make a bid for the company). What is the legal standard asserted to apply? What was keeping this deal from going through?

2. **Control premiums.** What does this opinion say about control premiums? Beyond the Chancellor's summary statement of the law, what does his analysis of the two transactions and the laws relation to them tell you about the acceptability of control premiums? Does it tell you how *Perlman* might be decided in Delaware?

In re Synthes, Inc. Shareholder Litigation
50 A.3d 1022 (Del. Ch. 2012)

STRINE, Chancellor.

I. INTRODUCTION

On this motion to dismiss, plaintiff stockholders argue that they have stated a claim for breach of fiduciary duty because a controlling stockholder refused to consider an acquisition offer that would have cashed out all the minority stockholders of the defendant Synthes, Inc., but required the controlling stockholder to remain as an investor in Synthes. Instead, the controlling stockholder worked with the other directors of Synthes and, after affording a consortium of private equity buyers a chance to make an all-cash, all-shares offer, ultimately accepted a bid made by Johnson & Johnson for 65% stock and 35% cash, and consummated a merger on those terms (the "Merger"). The controlling stockholder received the same treatment in the Merger as the other stockholders. In other words, although the controller was allowed by our law to seek a premium for his own controlling position, he did not and instead allowed the minority to share ratably in the control premium paid by J & J. The Synthes board of directors did not accept J & J's initial bid, but instead engaged in extended negotiations that resulted in J & J raising its bid substantially. The private equity group's bid for only a part of the company's equity never reached a price level as high as J & J's bid and the private equity group never made an offer to buy all of Synthes' equity.

In this decision, I dismiss the complaint. Contrary to the plaintiffs, I see no basis to conclude that the controlling stockholder had any conflict with the minority that justifies the imposition of the entire fairness standard. The controlling stockholder had more incentive than anyone to maximize the sale price of the company, and Delaware does not require a controlling stockholder to penalize itself and accept less than the minority, in order to afford the minority better terms. Rather, pro rata treatment remains a form of safe harbor under our law.

Furthermore, this case is not governed by Revlon, under the settled authority of our Supreme Court in In re Santa Fe Pacific Corp. Shareholder Litigation.[1] And even if it were, the complaint fails to plead facts supporting an inference that Synthes' board failed to take reasonable steps to maximize the sale price of the company. The complaint in fact illustrates that the board actively solicited logical strategic and private equity buyers over an unhurried time period, and afforded these parties access to due diligence to formulate offers, cites no discrimination among interested buyers, and reveals that the board did not accept J & J's offer even after it seemed clear no other bidder would top that offer, but instead bargained for more....

II. FACTUAL BACKGROUND

A. Synthes, Its Board, and Its Controlling Stockholder

Before the Merger, Synthes was a global medical device company incorporated in Delaware with its headquarters in Switzerland, and whose common stock traded on the SIX Swiss Exchange....

Synthes' board (the "Board") was composed of ten directors, each of whom is a defendant in this action. The most notable of the directors for purposes of this motion is Swiss billionaire Hansjoerg Wyss, the 76-year-old Chairman of the Board and Synthes' alleged controlling stockholder. Mr. Wyss founded Synthes in the 1970s and served as its CEO for thirty years until his retirement in 2007. The plaintiffs allege that Wyss controlled a majority of the board by dominating five other members through a mix of alleged close familial and business ties.[5] The plaintiffs effectively concede the independence of the remaining four directors. In terms of voting control, Wyss owned 38.5% of the company's stock, making him the company's largest stockholder. The plaintiffs further allege, however, that Wyss

---

1. 669 A.2d 59 (Del.1995).
5. These directors include: (i) Mr. Wyss' daughter, Amy Wyss; (ii) Robert Bland, trustee for certain Wyss family trusts; (iii) Charles Hedgepeth, who supposedly "owes lucrative and prestigious positions to [Wyss], who presided as Synthes CEO during the time frame that Hedgepeth held his executive positions with the [c]ompany," Compl. ¶ 100; (iv) David Helfet, trustee for a non-profit foundation which allegedly has a close connection with Wyss; (v) and Amin Khoury, who is said to have been Wyss' "right-hand-man" throughout the Merger process, id. ¶ 98. No fact allegations are directed towards the remaining four directors aside from those listing their title: Daniel Eicher, Andre Mueller, Felix Pardo, and Jobst Wagner.

controlled approximately 52% of Synthes' shares through his control of 13.25% of the company's shares owned by family members and trusts.

According to the plaintiffs, Wyss was well past retirement age and getting ready at some point to step down as Chairman of the Board from the company he spent many years of his life building. As part of that plan, he wanted to divest his stockholdings in Synthes and free up that wealth in order to achieve certain estate planning and tax goals. Doing so piecemeal would be problematic, however, because unloading that much stock on the public market in blocs would cause the share price to drop, thus reducing his sale profits. So, the plaintiffs contend, in order to achieve his liquidity goals in view of Synthes' allegedly thin public float, Wyss needed to sell his personal holdings to a single buyer. Wyss was by far the largest stockholder of Synthes (with the next largest non-affiliated stockholder holding only a 6% stake), and thus was the only stockholder who could not liquidate his entire Synthes stake on the public markets without affecting the share price. The plaintiffs contend that this "unique" liquidity dilemma infected the entire sale process ultimately consummated by the Merger.

B. The Board Embarks on the Merger Process

The idea to find a potential buyer for Synthes arose in April 2010 as part of the Board's ongoing review of the company's strategic initiatives. . . .

Following Wyss' approval of the Board's desire to explore strategic alternatives, the Board appointed independent director Amin Khoury as lead director, and it hired Credit Suisse Securities (USA) LLC as its financial advisor.

Belying any crisis need to sell, the complaint indicates that the Board and its financial advisor were deliberate in the marketing of the company. [The Board contacted nine logical strategic buyers with the financial capacity to acquire a company of Synthes' large size, which at the time exceeded $15 billion and entered into confidentiality agreements with the three strategics who expressed continuing interest (one of which was J & J) and shared financial due diligence information with them.]

J & J is a global manufacturer of healthcare products and provider of related services, and is one of the last few remaining AAA-rated companies in the U.S. With a market capitalization exceeding $167 billion, its common stock is widely held and traded on the NYSE. . . . J & J would be the only strategic buyer to emerge as a bidder.

Although it was engaged in talks with J & J, the Board was also open to pursuing a deal with a financial buyer. . . . [Credit Suisse opened a second negotiating front by reaching out to six private equity firms that were considered to have the resources necessary to buy Synthes and three submitted separate non-binding proposals to acquire the company at ranges of up to CHF (Swiss Franc) 150 per share in cash. But, the firms indicated that they could not finance an acquisition of Synthes independently and would need to form a consortium in order to proceed with a transaction. After an additional round of meetings in January 2011 at which Wyss was present, Synthes authorized the three firms to club for bidding purposes.]

In the meantime, on December 23, 2010, J & J submitted its first non-binding offer to acquire Synthes at an indicative price range of CHF 145-150 per share, with more than 60% of the consideration to be paid in the form of J & J stock. . . .

Negotiations also moved forward with the private equity buyers. On February 9, 2011, the newly formed consortium (the "PE Club") submitted a revised bid, reflecting an increased all-cash purchase price of CHF 151 per share (the "Partial Company Bid"). Even as a consortium, however, the PE Club did not have deep enough pockets to make a bid for the whole company. Rather, the proposal "required" Wyss to "convert a *substantial* portion of his equity investment in Synthes into an equity investment in the post-merger company." In other words, the Partial Company Bid was contingent on Wyss' financing part of the transaction with his own equity stake in order to lower the acquisition cost of an already expensive purchase, and Wyss remaining as a major investor in Synthes. . . .

Following the receipt of these bids, the Board met with its advisors on February 10 and 11, 2011 to compare the competing proposals in view of its strategic alternatives, such as foregoing a transaction in favor of growing by acquisition, or maintaining the status quo. The Board recognized that the Partial Company Bid represented greater value certainty because it was all cash. . . . The Board also recognized that the Partial Company Bid was riskier because the ability of the PE Club to close the deal would depend on the health of the financing markets. At that meeting, the Board also discussed the Partial Company Bid's requirement that Wyss roll a "substantial portion of his equity" in order to finance a cash buy-out of Synthes. The plaintiffs allege that Wyss was opposed to this aspect of the deal because he wanted to cash out alongside the rest of Synthes' shareholders rather than trade one illiquid bloc of stock (his Synthes shares) for another (shares in the private post-merger entity) [and] caused the Board to cease consideration of the Partial Company Bid at that time. The Board then authorized Khoury, as the lead director, to continue discussions with J & J exclusively. On February 14, 2011, Khoury spoke with J & J regarding its proposal of CHF 145-150 per share, and proceeded to bid it up. Specifically, Khoury used the Partial Company Bid as leverage to get J & J to sweeten its bid. He informed J & J that Synthes had received all-cash proposals in amounts higher than CHF 150 per share, and so J & J's offer was unacceptable, and that it would only accept a proposal at CHF 160 per share.

[J & J eventually] agreed to increase its offer to CHF 159 per share, with a consideration mix of 65% stock (subject to a collar) and 35% cash. All stockholders, including Wyss, would receive the same per share Merger consideration. J & J required certain deal protections as part of the Merger. First, J & J required that Wyss, along with his daughter (who was also a director) and two Wyss family trusts, enter into a voting agreement binding them to collectively vote approximately 37% of Synthes' outstanding stock in favor of the Merger (the "Voting Agreement"), which was less than the 48.83% that they held collectively. Second, the Board agreed to a no-solicitation provision but retained a fiduciary out to consider a superior proposal. Third, the Board agreed to hold a stockholder vote on the Merger regardless of whether the Board exercised its fiduciary out and changed its recommendation in favor of a superior proposal. In that event, however, the percentage of shares subject to the Voting Agreement would be reduced from approximately 37% to 33%. Fourth, the Board agreed to certain matching rights, allowing J & J five business days to match a superior proposal and two days to match an amendment to a superior proposal. Fifth, the Board agreed to a termination fee of $650 million, which represented approximately 3.05% of the equity value of the Merger at the time of signing, and an even lower percentage of enterprise value (approximately 2.9%), which is typically the more relevant measure for assessing the preclusive effect of a termination fee on a materially better topping bid.

[In April 2011, the boards of both companies separately met and approved the Merger Agreement which implied an equity value of $21.3 billion, representing a 26% premium to Synthes' average trading price during the month preceding the announcement. After shareholder approval and regulatory review, the Merger closed in June 2012, more than one year after the Merger Agreement was signed, and more than two years after the Board first began exploring a potential sale transaction. The PE Club provided no higher expression of interest during the months of negotiation or during the months leading up to shareholder approval.] . . .

IV. LEGAL ANALYSIS . . .

B. The Business Judgment Rule Applies to a Merger Resulting from an Open and Deliberative Sale Process When a Controlling Stockholder Shares the Control Premium Ratably with the Minority

A core tenet of Delaware corporate law is that the directors of a corporation are presumed to have acted "independently, with due care, in good faith and in the honest belief that [their] actions were in the stockholders' best interests." The burden is on the plaintiff challenging the corporate decision to allege facts that rebut the presumption that a board's decision is entitled to the protection of the business judgment rule. One traditional way of doing so, of course, is for a plaintiff to allege that the merger transaction she challenges was an interested one in which the corporation was on the other side from its majority stockholder. When a merger transaction is with a third party, however, plaintiffs have sought to invoke the entire fairness standard by arguing that the controlling stockholder received materially different terms from the third party in the merger than the minority stockholders and that the third-party merger should therefore be subject to fairness review irrespective of the fact that the controlling stockholder was not on both sides of the table. The argument in that context is that the controller used its power over the company to cause the company to enter into a transaction that was not equal to all the stockholders, and unfair to the minority because the controller unfairly diverted proceeds that should have been shared ratably with all stockholders to itself.

In this case, a chutzpah version of that theory is advanced. That theory involves the notion that if a controlling stockholder like Wyss has a liquidity issue not shared by small stockholders and does not wish to continue to be a stockholder in the selling corporation, and expresses its desire for a transaction that affords it the same liquidity and ability to sell out as all the other stockholders get, the controlling stockholder nonetheless has a disabling conflict if it refuses to assent to an alternative proposal on terms that afford all of these benefits to the minority, but not to itself, even if the ultimate transaction that is agreed to shares the control premium ratably between the controller and the other stockholders. By the same theory, the independent directors who assented to the transaction that treated all stockholders equally and that gave the minority its full pro rata share of the control premium have supposedly violated the duty of loyalty by subordinating the best interests of the minority to the outrageous demand of the controller for equal treatment. Their support of the pro rata Merger supposedly evidenced their "domination and control" by the controller. . . .

Under venerable and sound authority, the plaintiffs must plead that Wyss had a conflicting interest in the Merger in the sense that he derived a personal financial benefit "to the exclusion of, and detriment to, the minority stockholders." The plaintiffs unconvincingly try to gin up a conflict of interest by asserting that Wyss received liquidity benefits that were not shared equally with the rest of the stockholders and colored his decision to support the Merger and to supposedly improperly reject further consideration of the Partial Company Bid.

C. Does a Controller's Desire for the Same Liquidity as Other Stockholders Amount to a Conflicting Interest?

The major argument that the plaintiffs make is that Wyss was a really rich dude who wanted to turn the substantial wealth he had tied up in Synthes into liquid form—and fast. . . . If ever there be a case to indulge the unusual and counterintuitive notion that a controlling stockholder has a conflict because the controller supported a board's desire to consider strategic options and its ultimate negotiation of a merger that provides equal consideration to all stockholders, this is not that case. Generally speaking, a fiduciary's financial interest in a transaction as a stockholder (such as receiving liquidity value for her shares) does not establish a disabling conflict of interest when the transaction treats all stockholders equally, as does the Merger. This notion stems from the basic understanding that when a stockholder who is also a fiduciary receives the same consideration for her shares as the rest of the shareholders, their interests are aligned. It also stems from the desire of the common law of corporations to make common sense. Controlling stockholders typically are well-suited to help the board extract a good deal on behalf of the other stockholders because they usually have the largest financial stake in the transaction and thus have a natural incentive to obtain the best price for their shares. As a general matter, therefore, if one wishes to protect minority stockholders, there is a good deal of utility to making sure that when controlling stockholders afford the minority pro rata treatment, they know that they have docked within the safe harbor created by the business judgment rule. If, however, controlling stockholders are subject to entire fairness review when they share the premium ratably with everyone else, they might as well seek to obtain a differential premium for themselves or just to sell their control bloc, and leave the minority stuck-in. How this incentive scheme would benefit minority stockholders more than a system creating an incentive for pro rata treatment is something the plaintiffs have not explained, and my limited mind cannot conjure why it would.

It may be that there are very narrow circumstances in which a controlling stockholder's immediate need for liquidity could constitute a disabling conflict of interest irrespective of pro rata treatment. Those circumstances would have to involve a crisis, fire sale where the controller, in order to satisfy an exigent need (such as a margin call or default in a larger investment) agreed to a sale of the corporation without any effort to make logical buyers aware of the chance to sell, give them a chance to do due diligence, and to raise the financing necessary to make a bid that would reflect the genuine fair market value of the corporation. . . . That sort of uncommon scenario, however, has no application here. Specifically, there are no well-pled facts to suggest that Wyss forced a crisis sale of Synthes to J & J in order to satisfy some urgent need for cash. By the plaintiffs' own admission, Wyss was loaded. . . . The plaintiffs' argument about Wyss' interests also runs into the pled facts about the strategic process in which Synthes engaged. Not only was that process one suggested by the Board and not Wyss, the pled facts indicate that it was a patient process reasonably calculated to generate the highest value the market would pay for Synthes. Contrary to Synthes rushing into the arms of any particular buyer fast, Synthes took its time, gave bidders access to non-public information, and the chance to consider the risks of making a bid and to raise financing for a bid.

That sale effort also did not discriminate against any class of buyers. Logical strategic buyers with wallets large enough to plausibly purchase Synthes were approached. So were the private equity buyers in that category....

[At oral argument plaintiffs argued conflict in different terms: The plaintiffs say that they were unfairly deprived of the chance to sell all of their Synthes shares for cash because Wyss refused to support a deal where he did not get to sell all his shares, but had to remain a substantial investor in Synthes. But this] supposed liquidity conflict was not really a conflict at all because he and the minority stockholders wanted the same thing: liquid currency and, all things being equal, at the highest dollar value amount of that currency. If there is anything even more liquid than J & J stock, it's cash. Thus, *on the plaintiffs' own theory*, Wyss had little reason not to prefer an all-cash deal if the PE Club was willing to out-bid J & J on terms equally available to all shareholders.

... [W]hat is revealed is that the plaintiffs' main gripe is that Wyss refused to consider an all-cash offer that might have delivered a better deal for the minority shareholders *at Wyss' expense.* In other words, they complain that Wyss refused to facilitate a potentially better deal for the minority because he was not willing to roll a "substantial" part of his equity stake into the post-merger entity and thereby accept a different, less liquid, and less value-certain form of consideration than that offered to the minority stockholders. That is an astonishing argument that reflects a misguided view of the duties of a controlling stockholder under Delaware law.

A primary focus of our corporate jurisprudence has been ensuring that controlling stockholders do not use the corporate machinery to unfairly advantage themselves at the expense of the minority. It is, of course, true that controlling stockholders are putatively free under our law to sell their own bloc for a premium or even to take a different premium in a merger. As a practical matter, however, that right is limited in other ways that tend to promote equal treatment, for example, by the appraisal remedy that requires pro rata treatment of minority stockholders without regard to minority discounts, by certain substantive and procedural doctrines,[84] and, in a good illustration of the law of unintended consequences, §203 of the DGCL. These realities not only make it riskier for a controller to seek a premium but limit buyers' willingness to pay one. Particularly in the context of third-party transactions, the effect of these factors is to encourage majority stockholders to use their negotiating power in a way that gives the minority stockholders the opportunity to share in the benefits the majority stockholder obtains for itself. Thus, when a controlling stockholder acts in

---

[84]. *See* Mendel, 651 A.2d at 305 (citing doctrines of negligence, sale of corporate office, and sale of corporate opportunity); *see also* In re John Q. Hammons Hotels Inc. S'holder Litig., 2009 WL 3165613, at *12 (Del.Ch. Oct. 2, 2009) (concluding that the plaintiffs invoked entire fairness review when the evidence suggested that the controlling stockholder was effectively "competing" with the minority for portions of the consideration that the acquiror was willing to pay).

accordance with those incentives and shares its control premium evenly with the minority stockholders, courts typically view that as a "powerfu[l]" indication "that the price received was fair."

Delaware law does not, however, go further than that and impose on controlling stockholders a duty to engage in self-sacrifice for the benefit of minority shareholders. That is, the duty to put the "best interest of the corporation and its shareholders" above "any interest . . . not shared by the stockholders generally" does not mean that the controller has to subrogate his own interests so that the minority stockholders can get the deal that they want. As Chancellor Allen aptly wrote in *Thorpe v. CERBCO, Inc.*, "[c]ontrolling shareholders, while not allowed to use their control over corporate property or processes to exploit the minority, are not required to act altruistically towards them." Wyss was thus entitled to oppose a deal that required him to subsidize a better deal for the minority stockholders by subjecting him to a different and worse form of consideration. To hold otherwise would turn on its head the basic tenet that controllers have a right to vote their shares in their own interest. Put simply, minority stockholders are not entitled to get a deal on better terms that what is being offered to the controller, and the fact that the controller would not accede to that deal does not create a disabling conflict of interest. . . .

[The Court also rejected another theory plaintiff raised of Wyss' supposed failure to suggest that the Board continue negotiating with the PE Club noting:] Private equity buyers are not middle schoolers nervous about asking a date to a dance. And the private equity buyers here were not uninvited, on the pled facts. They were invited by Synthes and Wyss to make a bid. Not only that, they were allowed to club together to make a better bid because in isolation they didn't have the wallet to make a favorable bid for a company as large as Synthes. The PE Club then put in a bid that involved it paying approximately $14.7 billion for control of Synthes, which it stated was the best it could do. That bid was not for all of Synthes, but required Wyss to remain a substantial investor. . . . Silence is a form of negotiation. Synthes had been actively engaging with the individual private equity firms for months and allowed them to club. If Synthes felt the Partial Company Bid was not good, the PE Club would know that it needed to do better. If the PE Club decided not to do so, there is no rational basis on the pled facts to conceive that was because it was too shy to make a new bid, rather than that the PE Club was adhering to its prior statement that it could not raise its price and needed Wyss to roll a substantial part of his equity. . . .

D. The Plaintiffs' Revlon and Unocal Arguments Fail as Well

The plaintiffs contend that the business judgment rule does not apply on the separate ground that the Merger implicates enhanced scrutiny under Revlon, because it is an "end stage" transaction in which Synthes' shareholders will only own 7% of the surviving entity. According to them, this is the last chance for the Synthes minority stockholders to receive a premium for their Synthes shares and thus on the basis of transcript dictum cited by the plaintiffs in their brief, the Merger invokes the Revlon standard of review.

As an initial matter, I note that even if Revlon applied, for the reasons discussed at length above, there are no pled facts from which I could infer that Wyss and the Board did not choose a reasonable course of action to ensure that Synthes stockholders received the highest value reasonably attainable. Thus, even if Revlon applied, the complaint fails to state a viable claim.

But, the plaintiffs are also wrong on the merits of their argument that Revlon applies. Their sole basis for claiming that Revlon applies is that the Synthes stockholders are receiving mixed consideration of 65% J & J stock and 35% cash for their Synthes stock, and that this blended consideration represents the last chance they have to get a premium for their Synthes shares. But under binding authority of our Supreme Court as set forth in QVC and its progeny, Revlon duties only apply when a corporation undertakes a transaction that results in the sale or change of control. Putting aside the reality that the plaintiffs (under their own theory) were moving from a company under the control of Wyss to receiving stock in company that had no controlling stockholder, and thus is already an odd case to apply Revlon,[114] the mixed consideration Merger does not qualify as a change of control under our Supreme Court's precedent. A change of control "does not occur for purposes of Revlon where control of the corporation remains, post-merger, in a large, fluid market."[115] Here, the Merger consideration consists of a mix of 65% stock and 35% cash, with the stock portion being stock in a company whose shares are held in large, fluid market. In the case of In re Santa Fe Pacific Corp. Shareholder Litigation, the Supreme Court held that a merger transaction involving nearly equivalent consideration of 33% cash and 67% stock did not trigger Revlon review when there was no basis to infer that the stock portion of that consideration was stock in a controlled company.[116]

Similarly, the plaintiffs' half-hearted challenge to the Merger Agreement's deal protections fails too. They have made no attempt to show how the deal protections would have unreasonably precluded the emergence of a genuine topping bidder willing to make a materially higher bid, and thus

---

114. In this regard, the court's comments in In re NCS Healthcare, Inc., Shareholders Litigation ("Omnicare"), are particularly appropriate. In that case, the court noted that:

> The situation presented on this motion does not involve a change of control. On the contrary, this case can be seen as the obverse of a typical *Revlon* case. Before the transaction . . . is completed, [the target company] remains controlled by the [controlling stockholder]. The record shows that, as a result of the proposed . . . merger, [the target's] stockholders will become stockholders in a company that has no controlling stockholder or group. Instead, they will be stockholders in a company subject to an open and fluid market for control.

825 A.2d 240, 254-55 (Del.Ch.2002), *rev'd on other grounds, Omni Care, Inc. v. NCS Healthcare, Inc.*, 822 A.2d 397 (Del. 2002).

115. *In re NYMEX S'holder Litig.*, 2009 WL 3206051, at *5 (Del. Ch. Sept. 30, 2009).
116. 669 A.2d 59, 71 (Del.1995).

fail to state a claim. Although J & J had locked up a large number of Wyss' shares in favor of the Merger, that level was far less than a majority, and even less in a force-the-vote context. If a better topping bid was available, Synthes' stockholders could have voted down the Merger and opened the door to that better bid. Likewise, the plaintiffs acknowledge that the deal protections that J & J granted came at the end of an open process whereby logical buyers were invited to obtain due diligence on Synthes and to make bids free from the inhibiting effect of any deal with an initial bidder. Thus, because the Board had deliberately searched the market and was seeking to close a favorable deal with the last remaining bidder, it had a firm market basis to make the decision about how likely a later emerging bid was and to judge what concessions in terms of deal protections were necessary in order to land the one huge fish it actually had on the hook. This court should be particularly reluctant to deem unreasonable a board's decision to use deal protections as part of the negotiating strategy to pull the best bid from the final bidder or bidders who emerge from an open process on the theory that some party that has already had a chance to make a real bid without having to hurdle any deal protection barrier at all will somehow come to a different realization of the company's value, or that some unexpected bidder will emerge from an unexplored and overlooked dusty corner of our well-scoured capital markets. That sort of tactical judgment is freighted with none of the concerns about disloyalty that animate *Unocal* and *Revlon*, and is one that courts are ill-equipped to second guess as unreasonable. For that reason, this court has made clear that when there has been a "good faith negotiation process in which the target board has reasonably granted [deal] protections in order to obtain a good result for the stockholders, there [are] no grounds for judicial intrusion." I adhere to that principle here.

NOTES AND QUESTIONS

1. **The deal.** How did the economic motivations of the two sets of bidders differ?

2. ***Revlon* revisited.** What are the director actions being challenged and what standard of review does the court use? What does the court's refusal to apply *Revlon* tell you about the various justifications for *Revlon* discussed in the cases in chapter 6? Separately, consider the court's alternative holding of what it takes to satisfy the *Revlon* standard if the court finds it is applicable.

3. **Standard of Review.** This is another example, like *MFW* discussed at the end of the last chapter in which "cleansing" leads to the more deferential judicial review under the business judgment rule. Are these facts ore or less worrisome in terms of risks to minority shareholders? Or put another way are the two cases equally compelling to you in terms of business judgment review?

12 DISCLOSURE AND LIMITS ON THE USE OF INFORMATION

A. RISK ARBITRAGE, MANDATORY DISCLOSURE, AND THE SEARCH FOR INFORMATION

The possibility of an acquisition changes the expected value of a business as the market reacts to the anticipated changes from the possible combination. Recall from Chapter 2 that takeover targets typically receive a premium of 30 percent or more as compared to their pre-announcement price. Certainly, it would be extremely valuable to know when a takeover deal would occur. Even for acquirer stock, where event studies show break even or a slight decline in return, knowledge about a takeover can be relevant to an investor's decisions. This chapter looks at the value of information in a takeover setting, examining first how arbitrage illustrates the value of information and then how law shapes this information market, first with a positive stimulus by requiring disclosure of information and second via a negative stimulus through insider trading prohibitions.

Once an acquisition is announced (or even before if the information leaks into the marketplace), there is an immediate upward pressure on the target's stock price. Risk arbitrageurs immediately buy shares of the target pushing its price up toward the bidder's offer price. Yet the target's price rise stops short of the bidder's offer. Why? Because there is some uncertainty in the acquisition, the deal-break risk, such that if the deal does not happen, the higher value will not be realized and the stock could return to its pre-announcement level. Many target shareholders are willing to sell their shares at less than the offer price because they don't want to take the deal-break risk and potentially lose the entire takeover premium. Arbitrageurs thus are supplying deal-break insurance. Their motivation is the short-term profits that could be achieved by buying a target's stock at a price below the bidder's offer price (the deal spread) and then selling at the offer price at the deal's conclusion.

The deal spread can widen and narrow in the post-announcement period as new events occur that make the completion of the deal more or less likely. Chart 12-1 shows the deal spread on Compaq stock, the target in a well-known acquisition by Hewlett-Packard. The spread was fairly low immediately after the deal's announcement but quadrupled two months later when the son of one of the HP founders announced his opposition to the merger. The spread then bounced around until the merger vote, reflecting the ebbs and flows of a very hotly contested race on the HP side of the voting. HP management eventually prevailed in a contest that led to litigation over vote-buying. See Hewlett v. Hewlett-Packard Co., 2002 WL 818091 (Del. Ch. 2002).

For risk arbitrage to be profitable, the arbitrageur wants there to be a positive deal spread and for the deal to be completed. An arbitrageur's expected return from this activity will be the weighted average of two figures, first, the expected purchase price if the deal closes multiplied by the probability of the deal's success and second, the target's expected price if the deal were to break multiplied by that probability of a deal break. That means the key economic variables for the arbitrageur's decisions are: (1) the probabilities of a deal break or conversely, a deal completion; (2) the expected target purchase price on deal completion; and (3) the expected target share price upon a deal break. If a second bidder enters the picture, the arbitrageur's decision-tree analysis has to expand to include the probabilities of either the second bidder winning or the initial bidder

Chart 12-1

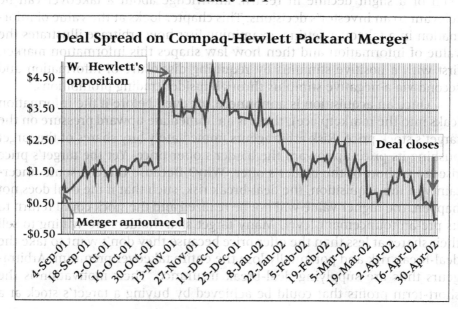

winning at a higher price, in addition to the original two outcomes of deal success or deal failure.

Depending upon when the arbitrageur bought into the stock, the downside loss could be much larger than the upside gain. Losses during the time after announcement can occur not just because of problems between the two companies but also because of market risks or industry risks. This position can affect the dynamic of a takeover contest, as arbitrageurs are often the primary buyer of target stock after an announcement and often acquire a substantial share of the pool of target stock. The high cost of capital of the arbitrageurs and their desire to liquidate their position quickly to make their business plan successful inclines them to not to want to hold stock for a long period. This itself can increase the chances of a bid's success.

If the consideration is stock of the acquirer as opposed to cash and there is a fixed exchange rate, the arbitrageur's approach varies somewhat. Consider the stock market reaction to stock prices after two large, New York-based banks, Chase Manhattan and J.P. Morgan, announced a combination.

The deal was announced on September 13, and there was a spike in J.P. Morgan's price and a drop in Chase's, as typically occurs after a takeover. What do you make of the post-announcement changes in the stock of the two companies? Was it a market downturn? A decline in the industry? The market's negative assessment of the deal? Arbitrageurs care about a

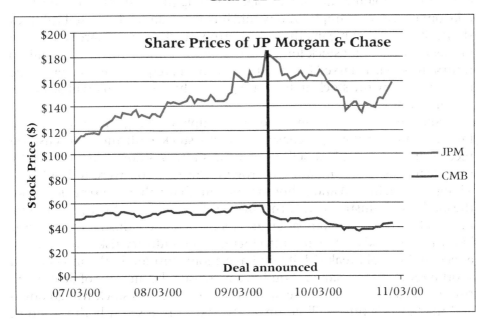

Chart 12-2

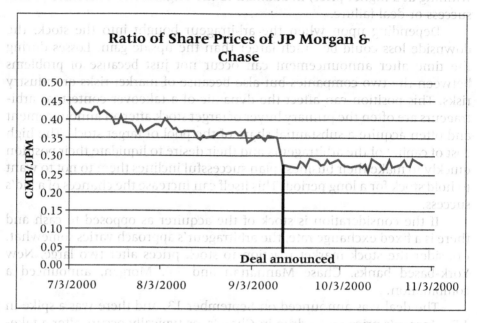

Chart 12-3
Ratio of Share Prices of JP Morgan & Chase

decline for any of those reasons. Had they only owned J.P. Morgan stock during this period they would have taken a loss.

Consider the ratio of the two companies' shares and the impact on an arbitrageur's risk. In such a setting, an arbitrageur would not only buy the target after the announcement of the takeover but would also hedge some of the risk of holding the target stock by selling the bidder's stock short. To take our previous example, you would buy Compaq stock and sell HP stock short. Short-selling means that you borrow stock from a shareholder and immediately sell that stock for its current market price. You also commit to return the stock at a fixed future date, which will require you to reenter the market and buy the stock at its future price, which you think will be below its current price.

Shorting in such a context does a couple of things. First, it lets you finance much of your purchase of target's stock with the proceeds you receive from your initial selling of your short position. This lowers the immediate cost by eliminating borrowing costs. If you were to hold both a long position in JPM and a short position in Chase, there is no net loss from the market or industry downturn. The rise in one will be offset by the decline in the other. If the two companies are not in the same industry, this hedge is likely not as good as you are introducing more industry risk. But note the effect on the deal break risk if you have a long position in the target and a short position in the bidder. You have increased the amount of deal-break risk that you are taking. If the deal craters, the target's stock will go down and the bidder's price will go up so that you can lose on both positions.

B. LAW'S EFFECT ON INFORMATION

1. Mandatory Disclosure from Federal Law

Disclosure is the core approach found in the federal securities laws. The Supreme Court has repeatedly described the "fundamental purpose" of Congress in enacting the Securities Exchange Act of 1934 Act as "to substitute a philosophy of full discourse for the philosophy of caveat emptor and thus to achieve a high standard of business ethics in the securities industry." SEC v. Capital Gains Research Bureau, Inc., 375 U.S. 180, 186 (1963). In rejecting an argument that information about a merger was not material until an agreement-in-principle as to price and structure had occurred, the Court said, "Disclosure and not paternalistic withholding of accurate information, is the policy chosen and expressed by Congress." Basic, Inc. v. Levinson, 485 U.S. 224 (1988). The disclosure required by the Securities Acts requires issuers to put information into the public domain for all to use, on the premise that the costs will create greater benefits to companies, investors, and society in terms of more capital directed toward business.

Having absorbed such broad statements of purpose, you should also recall the learning from Chapter 4 that our mandatory disclosure is episodic, not continuous, and that disclosure obligations are triggered in a specific set of contexts:

- *Issuance of securities.* The Securities Act of 1933, the first of the federal securities laws, focused on providing investors with full disclosure before they could be asked to purchase securities in a new issuance of securities, traditionally through a prospectus that would be put in the hands of an investor before the investment decision was made.
- *Solicitation of proxies.* The Securities Exchange Act of 1934, §14(a), extended disclosure to the setting in which shareholders of public companies were asked for their proxies in connection with matters to be voted on by shareholders, matters traditionally determined by state law.
- *Tender offers.* Tender offers grew up as alternatives to the forms of acquisition where state corporations law required a vote of the shareholders, at least of the target company. The New Deal securities laws imposed disclosure requirements when proxies were

solicited, such as in connection with a state-required vote of shareholders. But until 1968, no similar requirement was required when the form of the transaction was a tender offer, and the form of the shareholder participation was by voting with their feet by selling in response to a tender offer. A House committee explained the need for the new legislation this way:

> When one company seeks control of another by means of a stock-for-stock exchange, the offer must be registered under the Securities Act of 1933. The shareholder gets a prospectus setting forth all material facts about the offer. He know who the purchaser is, and what plans have been made for the company, He is thus placed in a position to make an informed decision whether to hold his stock or to exchange it for the stock of the other company. . . .
>
> In contrast when a cash tender offer is made, no information need be filed or disclosed to shareholders. Such an offer can be made on the most minimal disclosure, yet the investment decision — whether to retain the security or to sell it — is in substance little difference from the decision made on the original purchase of a security, or on an offer to exchange once security for another. . . .
>
> The persons seeking control . . . have information about themselves and about their plans which if known to the investors, might substantially change the assumptions on which the market price is based, This bill is designed to make the relevant facts known so that the shareholders have a fair opportunity to make their decision.

H. Rep. No. 1711, 90th Cong., 2d Sess., reprinted in 2 U.S. CODE CONG. & AD. NEWS 2811, 2812-13 (1968).

The Williams Act imposed disclosure requirements in connection with a tender offer (§14(d) of the Securities Exchange Act of 1934) or if a person/potential bidder crossed the 5 percent threshold of ownership in a publicly traded company, something of an early warning tripwire that a company was in play (§13(d)). An additional provision (§14(e)) prohibits any fraudulent, deceptive, or manipulative acts or practices in connection with a tender offer. Such disclosure addresses the plans of a potential takeover and gives target defenders an additional point of possible litigation in an effort to protect the company.

The regulation of tender offers under the Williams Act amendments to the Securities Exchange Act of 1934 shares the disclosure approach that is the core of the 1934 Act, but these more recent provisions go beyond the pure disclosure realm to provide some substantive regulation of tender offers that respond to some potentially coercive contexts that were seen to arise in tender offers. For example, prior to the Williams Act it was common for tender offers to occur via a "Saturday night special," a bid announced after the markets closed on Friday and intended to entice a majority of

B. Law's Effect on Information

shares to tender before the markets opened again on Monday. Such offers would seek to pressure a shareholder decision by offering a premium over current market price to a minority of the target company's shares on a first-come, first-served basis. §14(d)(6) requires that purchases be prorated from all those who tendered during the offering period, and Rule 14e-1 specifies that an offer must stay open for 20 business days. Section 14(d)(5), as supplemented by Rule 14(d)(7), permits a shareholder to withdraw tendered securities during the offer period, thus freeing a shareholder of one peril of an immediate decision.

- *Going private transactions.* A particular subset of deals, discussed in more detail in the next chapter, relates to a change of control in which a publicly held entity is bought out by a private entity, often with the participation of the incumbent management. The particular risks to investors in that type of transaction were seen as justifying particular disclosure and other regulation as discussed in more detail in the next chapter.
- *Periodic disclosure on 10-K (annual reports), 10-Q (quarterly reports), and 8-K (current reports).* The most comprehensive disclosure required by the federal securities laws is not triggered by a particular transaction but by the calendar. Publicly traded companies are required to provide their shareholders with annual reports and quarterly reports with extensive information about the company's business, property, its management, including their compensation, and conflicts of interest. See, particularly, Regulation S-K and the various items covered in that disclosure that provide the basis of 10-K and 10-Q reports. In addition to these periodic reports, public companies must also make current reports on Form 8-K within days after a series of specific events. The size of this list grew considerably after the Enron scandals and the Sarbanes-Oxley reforms that followed.

2. Mandatory Disclosure's Impact on Information About Merger Transactions and the Additional Effect of Antifraud Prohibitions

a. When Will Merger Information Have to Be Disclosed?

Consider how the various iterations of mandatory disclosure described in the prior section will require disclosure of merger negotiations. Planners typically want to keep negotiations quiet until there has been agreement between the two sets of managers and their two boards of directors. Substantial disclosure is required when an acquiring firm issues securities (as would occur in a stock-for-stock deal, for example) or because of a proxy solicitation (when the deal is to occur by a vote of the target shareholders on a merger, for example), but the timing of that disclosure will be well after there has been an agreement among the principles. The same is true for disclosure required by going-private regulations. The disclosure required by a tender offer will be required when a bidder goes public, but the timing of that is within the control of the bidder. So, from our initial list, that leaves the periodic reports that are triggered by the calendar as raising possible disclosure obligations prior to the directors agreeing on a deal. What if your negotiations straddle one of those reporting dates? Even here, the SEC has provided guidance suggesting that companies could withhold merger discussions from their periodic reports if it would adversely impact the negotiations. See SEC Release 33-6835 (May 18, 1989) ("known trends" in Item 303 of Regulation S-K, the MD&A or Management's Discussion and Analysis section, does not require disclosure of pending merger talks if not otherwise required to be disclosed).

So why not simply withhold discussion until the deal is approved by the boards. The dilemma for deal planners is revealed by *Basic, Inc. v. Levinson* arising out of a two-year-long discussion between two firms making refractory equipment. Over a 13-month period, the target company issued three statements denying that it was engaged in merger negotiations:

> On October 21, 1977, after heavy trading and a new high in Basic stock, the following news item appeared in the Cleveland Plain Dealer: "[Basic] President Max Muller said the company knew no reason for the stock's activity and that no negotiations were under way with any company for a merger. He said Flintkote recently denied Wall Street rumors that it would make a tender offer of $25 a share for control of the Cleveland-based maker of refractories for the steel industry."
>
> On September 25, 1978, in reply to an inquiry from the New York Stock Exchange, Basic issued a release concerning increased activity in its stock and stated that
>
>> "management is unaware of any present or pending company development that would result in the abnormally heavy trading activity and price fluctuation in company shares that have been experienced in the past few days."
>
> On November 6, 1978, Basic issued to its shareholders a "Nine Months Report 1978." This Report stated:
>
>> "With regard to the stock market activity in the Company's shares we remain unaware of any present or pending developments which would account for the high volume of trading and price fluctuations in recent months."

Basic Inc. v. Levinson, 485 U.S. 224, 228, note 4 (1988).

When a deal was announced at a nice premium for Basic shareholders, a class action was brought on behalf of all Basic shareholders who had sold their shares after the first statement in what was said to be an artificially depressed market. Had the truth been told, the argument would be that all those sellers would have received the $46 contained in the eventual

B. Law's Effect on Information

agreement, as opposed to the much smaller amount they sold for at the earlier time.

The Supreme Court was clear in how the company could have avoided Rule 10b-5 liability: "Silence, absent a duty to disclose, is not misleading under Rule 10b-5." Why, then, did not the company just remain silent? Look back again at the three examples and what triggered them. The first was in response to a newspaper inquiry, the second in response to the stock exchange inquiry, and the third in a nine-month report. If you were the lawyer for the company, how would you have presented the options to the company executives in response to those calls from the newspaper and the stock exchange? Option #1 would be to tell the truth about the negotiations. What could be wrong with that? Given what you have already seen about how target company prices respond to a takeover announcement, it is likely that the price of Basic would have risen to the point that planners may have feared that it would endanger the ability of the bidder to pay a premium that would entice target shareholders to vote or tender. Planners may have felt they were risking the loss of what may be a good deal for all shareholders. Or the stock exchange might have suspended trading, as it often does until a pending takeover announcement can be made. Option #2 would be to do what the company did here, to say it is unaware of any company developments that would explain the abnormal trading activity and price fluctuation in the company's shares. This choice, the Court says, is foreclosed by the Congressional choice for truth. Option #3 would be a "no comment" in response to the inquiries. As the court recognized in Basic, "No comment statements are generally the functional equivalent of silence" in the eyes of the law so as to not trigger liability. But the court also recognized the dilemma that would follow.

> To be actionable, of course, a statement must also be misleading. Silence, absent a duty to disclose, is not misleading under Rule 10b-5. "No comment" statements are generally the functional equivalent of silence. See *In re Carnation Co.*, Exchange Act Release No. 22214, 33 S.E.C. Docket 1025 (1985). See also NEW YORK STOCK EXCHANGE LISTED COMPANY MANUAL §202.01, reprinted in 3 CCH FED. SEC. L. REP. ¶23,515 (1987) (premature public announcement may properly be delayed for valid business purpose and where adequate security can be maintained); AMERICAN STOCK EXCHANGE COMPANY GUIDE §§401-405, reprinted in 3 CCH FED. SEC. L. REP. ¶¶23,124A-23,124E (1985) (similar provisions). It has been suggested that given current market practices, a "no comment" statement is tantamount to an admission that merger discussions are underway. See *Flamm v. Eberstadt*, 814 F.2d, at 1178. That may well hold true to the extent that issuers adopt a policy of truthfully denying merger rumors when no discussions are underway, and of issuing "no comment" statements when they are in the midst of negotiations. There are, of course, other statement policies firms could adopt; we need not now advise issuers as to what kind of practice to follow, within the range permitted by law. Perhaps more importantly, we think that creating an exception to a regulatory scheme founded on a pro-disclosure legislative philosophy, because complying with the regulation might be "bad for business," is a role for Congress, not this Court.

Basic Inc. v. Levinson, 485 U.S. 224, 230, note 17 (1988).

So where does that leave you? Most planners try to avoid being put in this dilemma by preventing the phone call from occurring. Not by refusing to answer the phone (or now electronic inquiries), but by clamping a lid on discussion and, when a deal gets close, to arrange a timetable to force key agreements to be done over a weekend while markets are not open, so that announcements can be made before the opening of the market. The result can be long weekends for merger advisers, but fewer dilemmas as occurred in *Basic*.

b. Remedies for Failure to Comply with Mandatory Disclosure or Antifraud Provisions Relating to Mergers

The federal securities statutes include express and severe private remedies for violations of the 1933 Act (*see* Sections 11 and 12 of that Act). The parallel express remedial portions of the 1934 Act are much less encompassing and have given way to implied private rights of action. The Supreme Court's 1964 decision in *J.I. Case v. Borak Co.* provided an implied private right of action for violation of the proxy provisions. By the time cases enforcing the Williams Act got to the Supreme Court, the tide had turned as to judicial willingness to accept implied private actions that had not been expressed by Congress, and the Supreme Court declined to provide implied rights of action. Lower federal courts have permitted equitable actions such as injunctions. See, for example, the discussion in the *CSX* case in Chapter 14.

Class actions under Rule 10b-5 have been the most prevalent vehicle for enforcing disclosure obligations of the federal securities laws both for the mandatory disclosure provisions discussed above and for misrepresentations or omissions in voluntary disclosures such as those discussed in *Basic*.

3. Disclosure Duties Arising from State Law Fiduciary Duty

State statutes typically provide very little specific disclosure that must be made in a merger. Such legislation is limited to things like notice. But common law has filled in much of the gap, as discussed in this excerpt from the *Topps* case included in the next chapter:

> When directors of a Delaware corporation seek approval for a merger, they have a duty to provide the stockholders with the material facts relevant to making an

B. Law's Effect on Information

informed decision.[3] In that connection, the directors must also avoid making materially misleading disclosures, which tell a distorted rendition of events or obscure material facts.[4] In determining whether the directors have complied with their disclosure obligations, the court applies well-settled standards of materiality, familiar to practitioners of our law and federal securities law.[5]

Note particularly how Delaware common law of fiduciary duty of disclosure piggy backs on the federal disclosure obligations. The *Topps* case illustrates how Delaware uses that federal disclosure to develop a unique state law approach to takeovers.

Delaware law also provides a cause of action for insider trading discussed in Section C below. But the claim is a derivative claim based on breach of fiduciary duty and the unjust enrichment of the trader. See the classic case of Brophy v. Cities Service Co., 70 A.2d 5 (Del Ch. 1949). A 2010 Chancery Court decision cast doubt on *Brophy* as a "misguided vehicle for recovering the same trading losses that are addressed by federal securities law." Pfeiffer v. Toll, 987 A.2d 683 (Del Ch. 2010). The Delaware Supreme Court in Kahn v. Kohlberg Kravis Roberts & Co. L.P., 23 A. 3d 831 (Del. 2011) rejected the Chancery Court's view of *Brophy* and permitted the traditional claim to continue even if no actual harm to the corporation and irrespective of arguably parallel federal remedies:

> We decline to adopt *Pfeiffer*'s thoughtful, but unduly narrow, interpretation of *Brophy* and its progeny. We also disagree with the *Pfeiffer* court's conclusion that the purpose of *Brophy* is to "remedy harm to the corporation." In fact, *Brophy* explicitly held that the corporation did not need to suffer an actual loss for there to be a viable claim. Importantly, *Brophy* focused on preventing a fiduciary wrongdoer from being unjustly enriched. Moreover, we have found no cases requiring that the corporation suffer actual harm for a plaintiff to bring a *Brophy* claim. To read *Brophy* as applying only where the corporation has suffered actual harm improperly limits its holding.
>
> We decline to adopt *Pfeiffer*'s interpretation that would limit the disgorgement remedy to a usurpation of corporate opportunity or cases where the insider used confidential corporate information to compete directly with the corporation. *Brophy* was not premised on either of those rationales. Rather, *Brophy* focused on the public policy of preventing unjust enrichment based on the misuse of confidential corporate information. Just as the *Brophy* court relied on the seminal decision in *Guth v. Loft*, we also rely on the *Guth* court's rationale in this case, and refuse to restrict disgorgement in *Brophy* cases as *Pfeiffer* suggests.
>
> The rule, inveterate and uncompromising in its rigidity, does not rest upon the narrow ground of injury or damage to the corporation resulting from a betrayal of

---

3. *E.g.*, Arnold v. Society for Savings Bancorp., Inc., 650 A.2d 1270, 1277 (Del. 1994).

4. *E.g.*, Emerald Partners v. Berlin, 726 A.2d 1215, 1223 (Del. Supr. 1999) ("When stockholder action is requested, directors are required to provide shareholders with all information that is material to the action being requested and to provide a balanced truthful account of all matters disclosed in the communication with shareholders.") (quotation omitted).

5. *See, e.g.*, Rosenblatt v. Getty Oil Co., 493 A.2d 929, 944 (Del. 1985) (explaining that information is material if "there is a substantial likelihood that a reasonable investor would consider it important in deciding how to vote") (citing *TSC Industries, Inc. v. Northway, Inc.*, 426 U.S. 438, 449, 96 S. Ct. 2126, 48 L. Ed. 2d 757 (1976)).

confidence, but upon a broader foundation of a wise public policy that, for the purpose of removing all temptation, extinguishes all possibility of profit flowing from a breach of the confidence imposed by the fiduciary relation.

Given *Guth*'s eloquent articulation of Delaware's public policy and the fact that "Delaware law dictates that the scope of recovery for a breach of the duty of loyalty is not to be determined narrowly," we find no reasonable public policy ground to restrict the scope of disgorgement remedy in *Brophy* cases—irrespective of arguably parallel remedies grounded in federal securities law.

C. LAW'S LIMITS ON THE USE OF INSIDE INFORMATION

1. Classic Insiders

Chiarella v. United States
445 U.S. 222 (1980)

Mr. Justice POWELL delivered the opinion of the Court.

The question in this case is whether a person who learns from the confidential documents of one corporation that it is planning an attempt to secure control of a second corporation violates §10(b) of the Securities Exchange Act of 1934 if he fails to disclose the impending takeover before trading in the target company's securities.

I

Petitioner is a printer by trade. In 1975 and 1976, he worked as a "markup man" in the New York composing room of Pandick Press, a financial printer. Among documents that petitioner handled were five announcements of corporate takeover bids. When these documents were delivered to the printer, the identities of the acquiring and target corporations were concealed by blank spaces or false names. The true names were sent to the printer on the night of the final printing.

The petitioner, however, was able to deduce the names of the target companies before the final printing from other information contained in the documents. Without disclosing his knowledge, petitioner purchased stock in the target companies and sold the shares immediately after the takeover attempts were made public. By this method, petitioner realized a gain of slightly more than $30,000 in the course of 14 months. Subsequently, the Securities and Exchange Commission (Commission or SEC) began an investigation of his trading activities. In May 1977, petitioner entered into a consent decree with the Commission in which he agreed to return his profits to the sellers of the shares. On the same day, he was discharged by Pandick Press [and later convicted of criminal violation of §10(b) receiving a sentence of one year, suspended except for one month, and five years probation, the first criminal conviction for insider trading under the section].

II

... This case concerns the legal effect of the petitioner's silence. The District Court's charge permitted the jury to convict the petitioner if it found that he willfully failed to inform sellers of target company securities that he knew of a forthcoming takeover bid that would make their shares more valuable....

Thus, administrative and judicial interpretations have established that silence in connection with the purchase or sale of securities may operate as a fraud actionable under §10(b) despite the absence of statutory language or legislative history specifically addressing the legality of nondisclosure. But such liability is premised upon a duty to disclose arising from a relationship of trust and confidence between parties to a transaction. Application of a duty to disclose prior to trading guarantees that corporate insiders, who have an obligation to place the shareholder's welfare before their own, will not benefit personally through fraudulent use of material, nonpublic information.[12]

III

In this case, the petitioner was convicted of violating §10(b) although he was not a corporate insider and he received no confidential information from the target company. Moreover, the "market information" upon which he relied did not concern the earning power or operations of the target company, but only the plans of the acquiring company. Petitioner's use of that information was not a fraud under §10(b) unless he was subject to an affirmative duty to disclose it before trading. In this case, the jury instructions failed to specify any such duty. In effect, the trial court instructed the jury that petitioner owed a duty to everyone; to all sellers, indeed, to the market as a whole. The jury simply was told to decide whether petitioner used material, nonpublic information at a time when "he knew other people trading in the securities market did not have access to the same information."

The Court of Appeals affirmed the conviction by holding that "[a]nyone— corporate insider or not—who regularly receives material

---

12. "Tippees" of corporate insiders have been held liable under §10(b) because they have a duty not to profit from the use of inside information that they know is confidential and know or should know came from a corporate insider, Shapiro v. Merrill Lynch, Pierce, Fenner & Smith, Inc., 495 F.2d 228, 237-238 (C.A.2 1974). The tippee's obligation has been viewed as arising from his role as a participant after the fact in the insider's breach of a fiduciary duty. ...

nonpublic information may not use that information to trade in securities without incurring an affirmative duty to disclose." 588 F.2d, at 1365 (emphasis in original). Although the court said that its test would include only persons who regularly receive material, nonpublic information, its rationale for that limitation is unrelated to the existence of a duty to disclose. The Court of Appeals, like the trial court, failed to identify a relationship between petitioner and the sellers that could give rise to a duty. Its decision thus rested solely upon its belief that the federal securities laws have "created a system providing equal access to information necessary for reasoned and intelligent investment decisions." The use by anyone of material information not generally available is fraudulent, this theory suggests, because such information gives certain buyers or sellers an unfair advantage over less informed buyers and sellers.

This reasoning suffers from two defects. First, not every instance of financial unfairness constitutes fraudulent activity under §10(b). See Santa Fe Industries, Inc. v. Green, 430 U.S. 462, 474-477 (1977). Second, the element required to make silence fraudulent—a duty to disclose—is absent in this case. No duty could arise from petitioner's relationship with the sellers of the target company's securities, for petitioner had no prior dealings with them. He was not their agent, he was not a fiduciary, he was not a person in whom the sellers had placed their trust and confidence. He was, in fact, a complete stranger who dealt with the sellers only through impersonal market transactions.

We cannot affirm petitioner's conviction without recognizing a general duty between all participants in market transactions to forgo actions based on material, nonpublic information. Formulation of such a broad duty, which departs radically from the established doctrine that duty arises from a specific relationship between two parties, should not be undertaken absent some explicit evidence of congressional intent.

As we have seen, no such evidence emerges from the language or legislative history of §10(b). Moreover, neither the Congress nor the Commission ever has adopted a parity-of-information rule. Instead the problems caused by misuse of market information have been addressed by detailed and sophisticated regulation that recognizes when use of market information may not harm operation of the securities markets. For example, the Williams Act[15] limits but does not completely prohibit a tender offeror's purchases of target corporation stock before public announcement of the offer. Congress' careful action in this and other areas contrasts, and is in some tension, with the broad rule of liability we are asked to adopt in this case.

Indeed, the theory upon which the petitioner was convicted is at odds with the Commission's view of §10(b) as applied to activity that has the

---

15. Title 15 U.S.C. §78m(d)(1) (1976 ed., Supp. 11) permits a tender offeror to purchase 5% of the target company's stock prior to disclosure of its plan for acquisition.

C. Law's Limits on the Use of Inside Information   **469**

same effect on sellers as the petitioner's purchases. "Warehousing" takes place when a corporation gives advance notice of its intention to launch a tender offer to institutional investors who then are able to purchase stock in the target company before the tender offer is made public and the price of shares rises. In this case, as in warehousing, a buyer of securities purchases stock in a target corporation on the basis of market information which is unknown to the seller. In both of these situations, the seller's behavior presumably would be altered if he had the nonpublic information. Significantly, however, the Commission has acted to bar warehousing under its authority to regulate tender offers after recognizing that action under §10(b) would rest on a "somewhat different theory" than that previously used to regulate insider trading as fraudulent activity.

We see no basis for applying such a new and different theory of liability in this case. As we have emphasized before, the 1934 Act cannot be read "'more broadly than its language and the statutory scheme reasonably permit.'" Touche Ross & Co. v. Redington, 442 U.S. 560, 578 (1979), quoting SEC v. Sloan, 436 U.S. 103, 116 (1978). Section 10(b) is aptly described as a catchall provision, but what it catches must be fraud. When an allegation of fraud is based upon nondisclosure, there can be no fraud absent a duty to speak. We hold that a duty to disclose under §10(b) does not arise from the mere possession of nonpublic market information. The contrary result is without support in the legislative history of §10(b) and would be inconsistent with the careful plan that Congress has enacted for regulation of the securities markets. Cf. Santa Fe Industries, Inc. v. Green, 430 U.S., at 479.[20]

[The concurring opinions of Justices Brennan and Stevens and the dissenting opinion of Chief Justice Burger are omitted.]

Mr. Justice BLACKMUN with whom Mr. Justice MARSHALL joins, dissenting:

... [T]he Court's approach unduly minimizes the importance of petitioners *access* to confidential information that the honest investor, no matter how diligently he tried, could not legally obtain.... Even at common law, ... there has been a trend away from strict adherence to the harsh maxim caveat emptor and toward a more flexible, less formalistic understanding of the duty to disclose.... By its narrow construction of §10(b) and Rule 10b-5, the Court places the federal securities laws in the

---

20. Mr. Justice Blackmun's dissent would establish the following standard for imposing criminal and civil liability under §10(b) and Rule 10b-5: "[P]ersons having access to confidential material information that is not legally available to others generally are prohibited . . . from engaging in schemes to exploit their structural informational advantage through trading in affected securities." This view is not substantially different from the Court of Appeals' theory that anyone "who regularly receives material nonpublic information may not use that information to trade in securities without incurring an affirmative duty to disclose," and must be rejected for the reasons stated in Part III. Additionally, a judicial holding that certain undefined activities "generally are prohibited" by §10(b) would raise questions whether either criminal or civil defendants would be given fair notice that they have engaged in illegal activity.

rearguard of this movement, a position opposite to the expectations of Congress at the time the securities laws were enacted.

2. Tippee Liability and Constructive Insiders

Dirks v. Securities and Exchange Commission
463 U.S. 646 (1983)

Justice POWELL delivered the opinion of the Court

Petitioner Raymond Dirks received material nonpublic information from "insiders" of a corporation with which he had no connection. He disclosed this information to investors who relied on it in trading in the shares of the corporation. The question is whether Dirks violated the antifraud provisions of the federal securities laws by this disclosure.

I

In 1973, Dirks was an officer of a New York broker-dealer firm who specialized in providing investment analysis of insurance company securities to institutional investors. On March 6, Dirks received information from Ronald Secrist, a former officer of Equity Funding of America. Secrist alleged that the assets of Equity Funding, a diversified corporation primarily engaged in selling life insurance and mutual funds, were vastly overstated as the result of fraudulent corporate practices. Secrist also stated that various regulatory agencies had failed to act on similar charges made by Equity Funding employees. He urged Dirks to verify the fraud and disclose it publicly.

Dirks decided to investigate the allegations. He visited Equity Funding's headquarters in Los Angeles and interviewed several officers and employees of the corporation. The senior management denied any wrongdoing, but certain corporation employees corroborated the charges of fraud. Neither Dirks nor his firm owned or traded any Equity Funding stock, but throughout his investigation he openly discussed the information he had obtained with a number of clients and investors. Some of these persons sold their holdings of Equity Funding securities, including five investment advisers who liquidated holdings of more than $16 million.[2]

While Dirks was in Los Angeles, he was in touch regularly with William Blundell, the Wall Street Journal's Los Angeles bureau chief. Dirks

---

2. Dirks received from his firm a salary plus a commission for securities transactions above a certain amount that his clients directed through his firm. But "[i]t is not clear how many of those with whom Dirks spoke promised to direct some brokerage business through [Dirks' firm] to compensate Dirks, or how many actually did so." 681 F.2d, at 831: The Boston Company Institutional Investors, Inc., promised Dirks about $25,000 in commissions, but it is unclear whether Boston actually generated any brokerage business for his firm.

urged Blundell to write a story on the fraud allegations. Blundell did not believe, however, that such a massive fraud could go undetected and declined to write the story. He feared that publishing such damaging hearsay might be libelous.

During the 2-week period in which Dirks pursued his investigation and spread word of Secrist's charges, the price of Equity Funding stock fell from $26 per share to less than $15 per share. This led the New York Stock Exchange to halt trading on March 27. Shortly thereafter California insurance authorities impounded Equity Funding's records and uncovered evidence of the fraud. Only then did the Securities and Exchange Commission (SEC) file a complaint against Equity Funding and only then, on April 2, did the Wall Street Journal publish a front-page story based largely on information assembled by Dirks. Equity Funding immediately went into receivership.[4]

The SEC began an investigation into Dirks' role in the exposure of the fraud. After a hearing by an Administrative Law Judge, the SEC found that Dirks had aided and abetted violations of §17(a) of the Securities Act of 1933, 48 Stat. 84, as amended, 15 U.S.C. §77q(a), §10(b) of the Securities Exchange Act of 1934, 48 Stat. 891, 15 U.S.C. §78j(b), and SEC Rule 10b-5, 17 C.F.R. §240.10b-5 (1983), by repeating the allegations of fraud to members of the investment community who later sold their Equity Funding stock. The SEC concluded: "Where 'tippees'—regardless of their motivation or occupation—come into possession of material 'corporate information that they know is confidential and know or should know came from a corporate insider,' they must either publicly disclose that information or refrain from trading." 21 S.E.C. Docket 1401, 1407 (1981) (footnote omitted) (quoting Chiarella v. United States, 445 U.S. 222, 230, n.12 (1980)). Recognizing, however, that Dirks "played an important role in bringing [Equity Funding's] massive fraud to light," 21 S.E.C. Docket, at 1412, the SEC only censured him.

Dirks sought review in the Court of Appeals for the District of Columbia Circuit. The court entered judgment against Dirks. . . .

III

We were explicit in *Chiarella* in saying that there can be no duty to disclose where the person who has traded on inside information "was not [the corporation's] agent, was not a fiduciary, [or] was not a person in whom the sellers [of the securities] had placed their trust and confidence." Not to require such a fiduciary relationship, we recognized, would "depar[t] radically from the established doctrine that duty arises from a

---

4. A federal grand jury in Los Angeles subsequently returned a 105-count indictment against 22 persons, including many of Equity Funding's officers and directors. All defendants were found guilty of one or more counts, either by a plea of guilty or a conviction after trial.

specific relationship between two parties" and would amount to "recognizing a general duty between all participants in market transactions to forgo actions based on material, nonpublic information." This requirement of a specific relationship between the shareholders and the individual trading on inside information has created analytical difficulties for the SEC and courts in policing tippees who trade on inside information. Unlike insiders who have independent fiduciary duties to both the corporation and its shareholders, the typical tippee has no such relationships.[14] In view of this absence, it has been unclear how a tippee acquires the *Cady, Roberts* duty to refrain from trading on inside information.

A.

The SEC's position, as stated in its opinion in this case, is that a tippee "inherits" the *Cady, Roberts* obligation to shareholders whenever he receives inside information from an insider:

> In tipping potential traders, Dirks breached a duty which he had assumed as a result of knowingly receiving confidential information from [Equity Funding] insiders. Tippees such as Dirks who receive non-public, material information from insiders become "subject to the same duty as [the] insiders." Shapiro v. Merrill Lynch, Pierce, Fenner & Smith, Inc.[, 495 F.2d 228, 237 (C.A.2 1974) (quoting Ross v. Licht, 263 F. Supp. 395, 410 (S.D.N.Y. 1967))]. Such a tippee breaches the fiduciary duty which he assumes from the insider when the tippee knowingly transmits the information to someone who will probably trade on the basis thereof. . . . Presumably, Dirks' informants were entitled to disclose the [Equity Funding] fraud in order to bring it to light and its perpetrators to justice. However, Dirks—standing in their shoes—committed a breach of the fiduciary duty which he had assumed in dealing with them, when he passed the information on to traders. (21 S.E.C. Docket, at 1410, n.42.)

This view differs little from the view that we rejected as inconsistent with congressional intent in *Chiarella*. In that case, the Court of Appeals agreed with the SEC and affirmed Chiarella's conviction, holding that "[a]nyone—corporate insider or not—who regularly receives material nonpublic information may not use that information to trade in securities

---

14. Under certain circumstances, such as where corporate information is revealed legitimately to an underwriter, accountant, lawyer, or consultant working for the corporation, these outsiders may become fiduciaries of the shareholders. The basis for recognizing this fiduciary duty is not simply that such persons acquired nonpublic corporate information, but rather that they have entered into a special confidential relationship in the conduct of the business of the enterprise and are given access to information solely for corporate purposes. When such a person breaches his fiduciary relationship, he may be treated more properly as a tipper than a tippee. See Shapiro v. Merrill Lynch, Pierce, Fenner & Smith, Inc., 495 F.2d 228, 237 (C.A.2 1974) (investment banker had access to material information when working on a proposed public offering for the corporation). For such a duty to be imposed, however, the corporation must expect the outsider to keep the disclosed nonpublic information confidential, and the relationship at least must imply such a duty.

C. Law's Limits on the Use of Inside Information

without incurring an affirmative duty to disclose." United States v. Chiarella, 588 F.2d 1358, 1365 (C.A.2 1978) (emphasis in original). Here, the SEC maintains that anyone who knowingly receives nonpublic material information from an insider has a fiduciary duty to disclose before trading.[15]

In effect, the SEC's theory of tippee liability in both cases appears rooted in the idea that the antifraud provisions require equal information among all traders. This conflicts with the principle set forth in *Chiarella* that only some persons, under some circumstances, will be barred from trading while in possession of material nonpublic information. Judge Wright correctly read our opinion in *Chiarella* as repudiating any notion that all traders must enjoy equal information before trading: "[T]he 'information' theory is rejected. Because the disclose-or-refrain duty is extraordinary, it attaches only when a party has legal obligations other than a mere duty to comply with the general antifraud proscriptions in the federal securities laws." 681 F.2d, at 837. See *Chiarella*, 445 U.S., at 235, n.20. We reaffirm today that "[a] duty [to disclose] arises from the relationship between parties . . . and not merely from one's ability to acquire information because of his position in the market." Id., at 231-232, n.14. Imposing a duty to disclosure or abstain solely because a person knowingly receives material nonpublic information from an insider and trades on it could have an inhibiting influence on the role of market analysts, which the SEC itself recognizes is necessary to the preservation of a healthy market.[17] It is common-place for analysts to "ferret out and analyze information," 21 S.E.C. Docket, at

---

15. Apparently, the SEC believes this case differs from *Chiarella* in that Dirks' receipt of inside information from Secrist, an insider, carried Secrist's duties with it, while Chiarella received the information without the direct involvement of an Insider and thus inherited no duty to disclose or abstain. The SEC fails to explain, however, why the receipt of nonpublic information from an insider automatically carries with it the fiduciary duty of the insider. As we emphasized in *Chiarella*, mere possession of nonpublic information does not give rise to a duty to disclose or abstain; only a specific relationship does that. And we do not believe that the mere receipt of information from an insider creates such a special relationship between the tippee and the corporation's shareholders.

Apparently recognizing the weakness of its argument in light of *Chiarella*, the SEC attempts to distinguish that case factually as involving not "inside" information, but rather "market" information, i.e., "information originating outside the company and usually about the supply and demand for the company's securities." This Court drew no such distinction in *Chiarella* and, as The Chief Justice noted, "[i]t is clear that §10(b) and Rule 10b-5 by their terms and by their history make no such distinction." 445 U.S., at 241, n.1 (dissenting opinion). See ALI, Federal Securities Code §1603, Comment (2)(j) (Prop. Off. Draft 1978).

17. The SEC expressly recognized that "[t]he value to the entire market of [analysts'] efforts cannot be gainsaid; market efficiency in pricing is significantly enhanced by [their] initiatives to ferret out and analyze information, and thus the analyst's work redounds to the benefit of all investors." 21 S.E.C. Docket, at 1406. The SEC asserts that analysts remain free to obtain from management corporate information for purposes of "filling in the 'interstices in analysis.' . . ." Brief for Respondent 42 (quoting Investors Management Co., 44 S.E.C., at 646). But this rule is inherently imprecise, and imprecision prevents parties from ordering their actions in accord with legal requirements. Unless the parties have some guidance as to where the line is between permissible and impermissible disclosures and uses, neither corporate insiders nor analysts can be sure when the line is crossed.

1406,[18] and this often is done by meeting with and questioning corporate officers and others who are insiders. And information that the analysts obtain normally may be the basis for judgments as to the market worth of a corporation's securities. The analyst's judgment in this respect is made available in market letters or otherwise to clients of the firm. It is the nature of this type of information, and indeed of the markets themselves, that such information cannot be made simultaneously available to all of the corporation's stockholders or the public generally.

B.

The conclusion that recipients of inside information do not invariably acquire a duty to disclose or abstain does not mean that such tippees always are free to trade on the information. The need for a ban on some tippee trading is clear. Not only are insiders forbidden by their fiduciary relationship from personally using undisclosed corporate information to their advantage, but they also may not give such information to an outsider for the same improper purpose of exploiting the information for their personal gain. See 15 U.S.C. §78t(b) (making it unlawful to do indirectly "by means of any other person" any act made unlawful by the federal securities laws). Similarly, the transactions of those who knowingly participate with the fiduciary in such a breach are "as forbidden" as transactions "on behalf of the trustee himself." Mosser v. Darrow, 341 U.S. 267, 272 (1951). See Jackson v. Smith, 254 U.S. 586, 589 (1921); Jackson v. Ludeling, 21 Wall. 616, 631-632 (1874). As the Court explained in *Mosser*, a contrary rule "would open up opportunities for devious dealings in the name of others that the trustee could not conduct in his own." 341 U.S., at 271. See SEC v. Texas Gulf Sulphur Co., 446 F.2d 1301, 1308 (C.A.2), cert. denied, 404 U.S. 1005 (1971). Thus, the tippee's duty to disclose or abstain is derivative from that of the insider's duty. Cf. *Chiarella*, 445 U.S., at 246, n.1 (Blackmun, J., dissenting). As we noted in *Chiarella*, "[t]he tippee's obligation has been viewed as arising from his role as a participant after the fact in the insider's breach of a fiduciary duty." Id., at 230, n.12.

---

18. On its facts, this case is the unusual one. Dirks is an analyst in a broker-dealer firm, and he did interview management in the course of his investigation. He uncovered, however, startling information that required no analysis or exercise of judgment as to its market relevance. Nonetheless, the principle at issue here extends beyond these facts. The SEC's rule—applicable without regard to any breach by an insider—could have serious ramifications on reporting by analysts of investment views.

Despite the unusualness of Dirks' "find," the central role that he played in uncovering the fraud at Equity Funding, and that analysts in general can play in revealing information; that corporations may have reason to withhold from the public, is an important one. Dirks careful investigation brought to light a massive fraud at the corporation. And until the Equity Funding fraud was exposed, the information in the trading market was grossly inaccurate. But for Dirks' efforts, the fraud might well have gone undetected longer.

Thus, some tippees must assume an insider's duty to the shareholders not because they receive inside information, but rather because it has been made available to them *improperly*. And for Rule 10b-5 purposes, the insider's disclosure is improper only where it would violate his *Cady, Roberts* duty. Thus, a tippee assumes a fiduciary duty to the shareholders of a corporation not to trade on material nonpublic information only when the insider has breached his fiduciary duty to the shareholders by disclosing the information to the tippee and the tippee knows or should know that there has been a breach. As Commissioner Smith perceptively observed in *In re Investors Management Co.*, 44 S.E.C. 633 (1971): "[T]ippee responsibility must be related back to insider responsibility by a necessary finding that the tippee knew the information was given to him in breach of a duty by a person having a special relationship to the issuer not to disclose the information. . . ." Id., at 651 (concurring in result). Tipping thus properly is viewed only as a means of indirectly violating the *Cady, Roberts* disclose-or-abstain rule.[21]

C.

In determining whether a tippee is under an obligation to disclose or abstain, it thus is necessary to determine whether the insider's "tip" constituted a breach of the insider's fiduciary duty. All disclosures of confidential corporate information are not inconsistent with the duty insiders owe to shareholders. In contrast to the extraordinary facts of this case, the more typical situation in which there will be a question whether disclosure violates the insider's *Cady, Roberts* duty is when insiders disclose information to analysts. In some situations, the insider will act consistently with his fiduciary duty to shareholders, and yet release of the information may affect the market. For example, it may not be clear — either to the corporate insider or to the recipient analyst — whether the information will be viewed as material nonpublic information. Corporate officials may mistakenly think the information already has been disclosed or that it is not material enough to affect the market. Whether disclosure is a breach of duty therefore depends in large part on the purpose of the disclosure. This standard was identified by the SEC itself in *Cady, Roberts*: a purpose of the securities laws was to eliminate "use of inside information for personal advantage." 40 S.E.C., at 912, n.15. Thus, the test is whether the insider

---

21. We do not suggest that knowingly trading on inside information is ever "socially desirable or even that it is devoid of moral considerations." Dooley, *Enforcement of Insider Trading Restrictions*, 66 VA. L. REV. 1, 55 (1980). Nor do we imply an absence of responsibility to disclose promptly indications of illegal actions by a corporation to the proper authorities — typically the SEC and exchange authorities in cases involving securities. Depending on the circumstances, and even where permitted by law, one's trading on material nonpublic information is behavior that may fall below ethical standards of conduct. But in a statutory area of the law such as securities regulation, where legal principles of general application must be applied, there may be "significant distinctions between actual legal obligations and ethical ideals."

personally will benefit, directly or indirectly, from his disclosure. Absent some personal gain, there has been no breach of duty to stockholders. And absent a breach by the insider, there is no derivative breach.[22] As Commissioner Smith stated in *Investors Management Co.*: "It is important in this type of case to focus on policing insiders and what they do . . . rather than on policing information per se and its possession. . . ." 44 S.E.C., at 648 (concurring in result).

The SEC argues that, if inside-trading liability does not exist when the information is transmitted for a proper purpose but is used for trading, it would be a rare situation when the parties could not fabricate some ostensibly legitimate business justification for transmitting the information. We think the SEC is unduly concerned. In determining whether the insider's purpose in making a particular disclosure is fraudulent, the SEC and the courts are not required to read the parties' minds. Scienter in some cases is relevant in determining whether the tipper has violated his *Cady, Roberts* duty. But to determine whether the disclosure itself "deceive[s], manipulate[s], or defraud[s]" shareholders, Aaron v. SEC, 446 U.S. 680, 686 (1980), the initial inquiry is whether there has been a breach of duty by the insider. This requires courts to focus on objective criteria, i.e., whether the insider receives a direct or indirect personal benefit from the disclosure, such as a pecuniary gain or are reputational benefit that will translate into future earnings. Cf. 40 S.E.C., at 912, n.15; Brudney, *Insiders, Outsiders, and Informational Advantages Under the Federal Securities Laws*, 93 HARV. L. REV. 332, 348 (1979) ("The theory . . . is that the insider, by giving the information out selectively, is in effect selling the information to its recipient for cash, reciprocal information, or other things of value for himself. . . ."). There are objective facts and circumstances that often justify such an inference. For example, there may be a relationship the insider and the particular recipient. The elements of fiduciary duty and exploitation of nonpublic information also exist when an insider makes a gift of confidential information to a trading relative or friend. The tip and trade resemble trading by the insider himself followed by a gift of the profits to the recipient.

Determining whether an insider personally benefits from a particular disclosure, a question of fact, will not always be easy for courts. But it is essential, we think, to have a guiding principle for those whose daily

---

22. An example of a case turning on the court's determination that the disclosure did not impose any fiduciary duties on the recipient of the inside information is *Walton v. Morgan Stanley & Co.*, 623 F.2d 796 (C.A.2 1980). There, the defendant investment banking firm, representing one of its own corporate clients, investigated another corporation that was a possible target of a takeover bid by its client. In the course of negotiations the investment banking firm was given, on a confidential basis, unpublished material information. Subsequently, after the proposed takeover was abandoned, the firm was charged with relying on the information when it traded in the target corporation's stock. For purposes of the decision, it was assumed that the firm knew the information was confidential, but that it had been received in arm's-length negotiations. In the absence of any fiduciary relationship, the Court of Appeals found no basis for imposing tippee liability on the investment firm.

activities must be limited and instructed by the SEC's inside-trading rules, and we believe that there must be a breach of the insider's fiduciary duty before the tippee inherits the duty to disclose or abstain. In contrast, the rule adopted by the SEC in this case would have no limiting principle.

IV

Under the inside-trading and tipping rules set forth above, we find that there was no actionable violation by Dirks. It is undisputed that Dirks himself was a stranger to Equity Funding, with no pre-existing fiduciary duty to its shareholders. He took no action, directly or indirectly, that induced the shareholders or officers of Equity Funding to repose trust or confidence in him. There was no expectation by Dirks' sources that he would keep their information in confidence. Nor did Dirks misappropriate or illegally obtain the information about Equity Funding. Unless the insiders breached their *Cady, Roberts* duty to shareholders in disclosing the nonpublic information to Dirks, he breached no duty when he passed it on to investors as well as to the Wall Street Journal.

It is clear that neither Secrist nor the other Equity Funding employees violated their *Cady, Roberts* duty to the corporation's shareholders by providing information to Dirks. The tippers received no monetary or personal benefit for revealing Equity Funding's secrets, nor was their purpose to make a gift of valuable information to Dirks. As the facts of this case clearly indicate, the tippers were motivated by a desire to expose the fraud. In the absence of a breach of duty to shareholders by the insiders, there was no derivative breach by Dirks. Dirks therefore could not have been "a participant after the fact in [an] insider's breach of a fiduciary duty." *Chiarella*, 445 U.S., at 230, n.12. . . .

Justice BLACKMUN, with whom Justice BRENNAN and Justice MARSHALL join dissenting

. . . The fact that the insider himself does not benefit from the breach does not eradicate the shareholder's injury. Cf. Restatement (Second) of Trusts §205, Comments c and d (1959) (trustee liable for acts causing diminution of value of trust); 3 A. Scott, Law of Trusts §205, p. 1665 (3d ed. 1967) (trustee liable for any losses to trust caused by his breach). It makes no difference to the shareholder whether the corporate insider gained or intended to gain personally from the transaction; the shareholder still has lost because of the insider's misuse of non-public information. The duty is addressed not to the insider's motives, but to his actions and their consequences on the shareholder. Personal gain is not an element of the breach of this duty. . . .

The improper-purpose requirement not only has no basis in law, but it also rests implicitly on a policy that I cannot accept. The Court justifies Secrist's and Dirks' action because the general benefit derived from the violation of Secrist's duty to shareholders outweighed the harm caused to those shareholders, see Heller, Chiarella, *SEC Rule 14e-3 and* Dirk: *"Fairness" versus Economic Theory,* 37 Bus. LAWYER 517, 550 (1982); Easterbrook, *Insider Trading, Secret Agents, Evidentiary Privileges, and the Production of Information,* 1981 S. CT. REV. 309, 338—in other words, because the end justified the means. Under this view, the benefit conferred on society by Secrist's and Dirks' activities may be paid for with the losses caused by shareholders trading with Dirks' clients.

Although Secrist's general motive to expose the Equity Funding fraud was laudable, the means he chose were not. Moreover, even assuming that Dirks played a substantial role in exposing the fraud, he and his clients should not profit from the information they obtained from Secrist. Misprision of a felony long has been against public policy. Branzburg v. Hayes, 408 U.S. 665, 696-697 (1972); see 18 U.S.C. §4. A person cannot condition his transmission of information of a crime on a financial award. As a citizen, Dirks had at least an ethical obligation to report the information to the proper authorities. The Court's holding is deficient in policy terms not because it fails to create a legal norm out of that ethical norm, but because it actually rewards Dirks for his aiding and abetting. . . .

In my view, Secrist violated his duty to Equity Funding shareholders by transmitting material nonpublic information to Dirks with the intention that Dirks would cause his clients to trade on that information. Dirks, therefore, was under a duty to make the information publicly available or to refrain from actions that he knew would lead to trading. Because Dirks caused his clients to trade, he violated §10(b) and Rule 10b-5. Any other result is a disservice to this country's attempt to provide fair and efficient capital markets. I dissent.

NOTE

As suggested in Part B of this chapter, mandatory disclosure provides something of a public good to arbs and other traders active in securities markets. Law prohibiting insider trading discussed in this part likewise is an information-forcing legal rule. The protection received by Dirks retains the incentive for market professionals and Dirks to pursue information. *See* David Haddock & Jonathan Macey, *Regulation on Demand: A Private Interest Model with an Application to Insider Trading Regulation,* 30 J.L. & ECON. 311 (1986) (the fiduciary duty restrictions on insiders remove the market professionals' chief competition for information). SEC rule-making in Regulation FD, 17 CFR §§243-100 to 103, limits some of the traditional space in which traders such as Dirks operated by banning selective disclosure by an issuer or persons acting on its behalf of material non-public information.

3. Misappropriation and Rule 14e-3 Liability

Justice Powell's majority opinion in *Chiarella* declined to address an argument made in that case that Chiarella could be liable on the basis of his having misappropriated the information because that theory was not presented to the jury that convicted Chiarella. In separate opinions, two Justices suggested there could be such liability. Chief Justice Burger's broad misappropriation theory would reach informational advantage obtained by an *unlawful* means. The focus was on the stealing and not the fiduciary relationship to the person whose shares are traded. Justice Stevens defined misappropriation more narrowly, suggesting that actions, as in *Chiarella*, could constitute a fraud or deceit of the acquiring companies that had entrusted confidential information to Chiarella's employer. He noted, however, that the fraud on the source, who was neither a purchaser nor seller of securities, might negate a Rule 10b-5 claim because of Blue Chip Stamps v. Manor Drug Stores, 421 U.S. 723 (1975), a classic securities case that limited the reach of Rule 10b-5 to cases brought by actual purchasers and sellers of securities.

Several appellate courts later upheld misappropriation liability. *See e.g.*, U.S. v. Chestman, 947 F.2d 551 (2d Cir. 1991) (en banc); S.E.C. v. Cherif, 933 F.2d 403 (7th Cir. 1991). Prior to *O'Hagan* set out below, two circuit courts used *Blue Chip Stamps* and Santa Fe Industries, Inc. v. Green, 430 U.S. 462 (1977), to assert that §10(b) is concerned with the deception of purchasers and sellers of securities and to extend it to breach of duty outside of that context would render meaningless the statutory requirement that the fraud be in connection with the purchase and sale of a security. *See, e.g.*, United States v. Bryan, 58 F.3d 933 (4th Cir. 1995) (overturning the conviction of the former director of the West Virginia lottery for securities fraud arising from his trading on inside information as to companies that would receive state lottery contracts); United States v. O'Hagan, 92 F.3d 612 (8th Cir. 1996).

In the case that follows, the Supreme Court addressed that split and also liability based on SEC Rule 14e-3, which had been promulgated in the months after *Chiarella*. It derives its statutory authority not from §10(b), but §14(e), an antifraud provision regulating tender offers in which an acquiring company purchases shares directly from the shareholders of a target in contrast to a merger when the acquisition occurs by a vote of the directors and shareholders.

United States v. O'Hagan
521 U.S. 642 (1997)

Justice GINSBURG delivered the opinion of the Court.

This case concerns the interpretation and enforcement of §10(b) and §14(e) of the Securities Exchange Act of 1934, and rules made by the

Securities and Exchange Commission pursuant to these provisions, Rule 10b-5 and Rule 14e-3(a). Two prime questions are presented.... (1) Is a person who trades in securities for personal profit, using confidential information misappropriated in breach of a fiduciary duty to the source of the information, guilty of violating §10(b) and Rule 10b-5? (2) Did the Commission exceed its rulemaking authority by adopting Rule 14e-3(a), which proscribes trading on undisclosed information in the tender offer setting, even in the absence of a duty to disclose? Our answer to the first question is yes, and to the second question, viewed in the context of this case, no.

I

Respondent James Herman O'Hagan was a partner in the law firm of Dorsey & Whitney in Minneapolis, Minnesota. In July 1988, Grand Metropolitan PLC (Grand Met), a company based in London, England, retained Dorsey & Whitney as local counsel to represent Grand Met regarding a potential tender offer for the common stock of the Pillsbury Company, headquartered in Minneapolis. Both Grand Met and Dorsey & Whitney took precautions to protect the confidentiality of Grand Met's tender offer plans. O'Hagan did no work on the Grand Met representation.... By the end of September, [O'Hagan had purchased] 2,500 unexpired Pillsbury options, apparently more than any other individual investor. O'Hagan also purchased, in September 1988, some 5,000 shares of Pillsbury common stock, at a price just under $39 per share. When Grand Met announced its tender offer in October, the price of Pillsbury stock rose to nearly $60 per share. O'Hagan then sold his Pillsbury call options and common stock, making a profit of more than $4.3 million.

The Securities and Exchange Commission (SEC or Commission) initiated an investigation into O'Hagan's transactions, culminating in a 57-count indictment [for mail fraud, 10b-5 securities fraud, violating Rule 14e-3, and money laundering statutes]. The indictment alleged that O'Hagan defrauded his law firm and its client, Grand Met, by using for his own trading purposes material, nonpublic information regarding Grand Met's planned tender offer. According to the indictment, O'Hagan used the profits he gained through this trading to conceal his previous embezzlement and conversion of unrelated client trust funds.[1] ... A jury convicted O'Hagan on all 57 counts, and he was sentenced to a 41-month term of imprisonment....

---

1. O'Hagan was convicted of theft in state court, sentenced to 30 months imprisonment, and fined. See State v. O'Hagan, 474 N.W.2d 613, 615, 623 (Minn. App. 1991). The Supreme Court of Minnesota disbarred O'Hagan from the practice of law. See In re O'Hagan, 450 N.W.2d 571 (Minn. 1990).

C. Law's Limits on the Use of Inside Information

II

We address first the Court of Appeals' reversal of O'Hagan's convictions under §10(b) and Rule 10b-5....

A.

[Section 10(b)] proscribes (1) using any deceptive device (2) in connection with the purchase or sale of securities, in contravention of rules prescribed by the Commission. The provision, as written, does not confine its coverage to deception of a purchaser or seller of securities, see United States v. Newman, 664 F.2d 12, 17 (C.A.2 1981); rather, the statute reaches any deceptive device used "in connection with the purchase or sale of any security."...

Under the "traditional" or "classical theory" of insider trading liability, §10(b) and Rule 10b-5 are violated when a corporate insider trades in the securities of his corporation on the basis of material, nonpublic information. Trading on such information qualifies as a "deceptive device" under §10(b), we have affirmed, because "a relationship of trust and confidence [exists] between the shareholders of a corporation and those insiders who have obtained confidential information by reason of their position with that corporation." Chiarella v. United States, 445 U.S. 222, 228 (1980). That relationship, we recognized, "gives rise to a duty to disclose [or to abstain from trading] because of the 'necessity of preventing a corporate insider from ... tak[ing] unfair advantage of ... uninformed ... stockholders.'" (citation omitted). The classical theory applies not only to officers, directors, and other permanent insiders of a corporation, but also to attorneys, accountants, consultants, and others who temporarily become fiduciaries of a corporation. See Dirks v. SEC, 463 U.S. 646, 655, n.14 (1983).

The "misappropriation theory" holds that a person commits fraud "in connection with" a securities transaction, and thereby violates §10(b) and Rule 10b-5, when he misappropriates confidential information for securities trading purposes, in breach of a duty owed to the source of the information. See Brief for United States 14. Under this theory, a fiduciary's undisclosed, self-serving use of a principal's information to purchase or sell securities, in breach of a duty of loyalty and confidentiality, defrauds the principal of the exclusive use of that information. In lieu of premising liability on a fiduciary relationship between company insider and purchaser or seller of the company's stock, the misappropriation theory premises liability on a fiduciary-turned-trader's deception of those who entrusted him with access to confidential information.

The two theories are complementary, each addressing efforts to capitalize on nonpublic information through the purchase or sale of securities. The classical theory targets a corporate insider's breach of duty to shareholders with whom the insider transacts; the misappropriation theory outlaws trading on the basis of nonpublic information by a corporate "outsider" in breach of a duty owed not to a trading party, but to the source of the information. The misappropriation theory is thus designed to "protec[t] the integrity of the securities markets against abuses by 'outsiders' to a corporation who have access to confidential information that will affect th[e] corporation's security price when revealed, but who owe no fiduciary or other duty to that corporation's shareholders." Ibid.

In this case, the indictment alleged that O'Hagan, in breach of a duty of trust and confidence he owed to his law firm, Dorsey & Whitney, and to its client, Grand Met, traded on the basis of nonpublic information regarding Grand Met's planned tender offer for Pillsbury common stock. This conduct, the Government charged, constituted a fraudulent device in connection with the purchase and sale of securities.[5]

B.

We agree with the Government that misappropriation, as just defined, satisfies §10(b)'s requirement that chargeable conduct involve a "deceptive device or contrivance" used "in connection with" the purchase or sale of securities. We observe, first, that misappropriators, as the Government describes them, deal in deception. A fiduciary who "[pretends] loyalty to the principal while secretly converting the principal's information for personal gain," Brief for United States 17, "dupes" or defrauds the principal. See Aldave, *Misappropriation: A General Theory of Liability for Trading on Nonpublic Information*, 13 HOFSTRA L. REV. 101, 119 (1984).

We addressed fraud of the same species in Carpenter v. United States, 484 U.S. 19 (1987), which involved the mail fraud statute's proscription of "any scheme or artifice to defraud," 18 U.S.C. §1341. Affirming convictions under that statute, we said in *Carpenter* that an employee's undertaking not to reveal his employer's confidential information "became a sham" when the employee provided the information to his co-conspirators in a scheme to obtain trading profits. A company's confidential information, we recognized in *Carpenter*, qualifies as property to which the company has a right of exclusive use. The undisclosed misappropriation of such information, in violation of a fiduciary duty, the Court said in *Carpenter*, constitutes fraud akin to embezzlement — "the fraudulent appropriation to one's own use of

---

5. The Government could not have prosecuted O'Hagan under the classical theory, for O'Hagan was not an "insider" of Pillsbury, the corporation in whose stock he traded. Although an "outsider" with respect to Pillsbury, O'Hagan had an intimate association with, and was found to have traded on confidential information from, Dorsey & Whitney, counsel to tender offeror Grand Met. Under the misappropriation theory, O'Hagan's securities trading does not escape Exchange Act sanction, as it would under the dissent's reasoning, simply because he was associated with, and gained nonpublic information from, the bidder, rather than the target.

the money or goods entrusted to one's care by another." (quoting Grin v. Shine, 187 U.S. 181, 189 (1902)); see Aldave, 13 HOFSTRA L. REV., at 119. Carpenter's discussion of the fraudulent misuse of confidential information, the Government notes, "is a particularly apt source of guidance here, because [the mail fraud statute] (like Section 10(b)) has long been held to require deception, not merely the breach of a fiduciary duty."

Deception through nondisclosure is central to the theory of liability for which the Government seeks recognition. As counsel for the Government stated in explanation of the theory at oral argument: "To satisfy the common law rule that a trustee may not use the property that [has] been entrusted [to] him, there would have to be consent. To satisfy the requirement of the Securities Act that there be no deception, there would only have to be disclosure." See generally Restatement (Second) of Agency §§390, 395 (1958) (agent's disclosure obligation regarding use of confidential information).....[6]

Similarly, full disclosure forecloses liability under the misappropriation theory: because the deception essential to the misappropriation theory involves feigning fidelity to the source of information, if the fiduciary discloses to the source that he plans to trade on the nonpublic information, there is no "deceptive device" and thus no §10(b) violation, although the fiduciary-turned-trader may remain liable under state law for breach of a duty of loyalty.

We turn next to the §10(b) requirement that the misappropriator's deceptive use of information be "in connection with the purchase or sale of [a] security." This element is satisfied because the fiduciary's fraud is consummated, not when the fiduciary gains the confidential information, but when, without disclosure to his principal, he uses the information to purchase or sell securities. The securities transaction and the breach of duty thus coincide. This is so even though the person or entity defrauded is not the other party to the trade, but is, instead, the source of the nonpublic information. See Aldave, 13 HOFSTRA L. REV., at 120 ("a fraud or deceit can be practiced on one person, with resultant harm to another person or group of persons"). A misappropriator who trades on the basis of material, nonpublic information, in short, gains his advantageous market position through deception; he deceives the source of the information and simultaneously harms members of the investing public.

The misappropriation theory targets information of a sort that misappropriators ordinarily capitalize upon to gain no-risk profits through the

---

6. Under the misappropriation theory urged in this case, the disclosure obligation runs to the source of the information, here, Dorsey & Whitney and Grand Met. Chief Justice Burger, dissenting in *Chiarella*, advanced a broader reading of §10(b) and Rule 10b-5; the disclosure obligation, as he envisioned it, ran to those with whom the misappropriator trades. 445 U.S., at 240 ("a person who has misappropriated nonpublic information has an absolute duty to disclose that information or to refrain from trading"). The Government does not propose that we adopt a misappropriation theory of that breadth.

purchase or sale of securities. Should a misappropriator put such information to other use, the statute's prohibition would not be implicated. The theory does not catch all conceivable forms of fraud involving confidential information; rather, it catches fraudulent means of capitalizing on such information through securities transactions. . . .

The misappropriation theory comports with §10(b)'s language, which requires deception "in connection with the purchase or sale of any security," not deception of an identifiable purchaser or seller. The theory is also well-tuned to an animating purpose of the Exchange Act: to insure honest securities markets and thereby promote investor confidence. See 45 Fed. Reg. 60412 (1980) (trading on misappropriated information "undermines the integrity of, and investor confidence in, the securities markets"). Although informational disparity is inevitable in the securities markets, investors likely would hesitate to venture their capital in a market where trading based on misappropriated nonpublic information is unchecked by law. An investor's informational disadvantage vis-à-vis a misappropriator with material, nonpublic information stems from contrivance, not luck; it is a disadvantage that cannot be overcome with research or skill. See Brudney, *Insiders, Outsiders, and Informational Advantages Under the Federal Securities Laws*, 93 HARV. L. REV. 322, 356 (1979) ("If the market is thought to be systematically populated with . . . transactors [trading on the basis of misappropriated information] some investors will refrain from dealing altogether, and others will incur costs to avoid dealing with such transactors or corruptly to overcome their unerodable informational advantages.").

In sum, considering the inhibiting impact on market participation of trading on misappropriated information, and the congressional purposes underlying §10(b), it makes scant sense to hold a lawyer like O'Hagan a §10(b) violator if he works for a law firm representing the target of a tender offer, but not if he works for a law firm representing the bidder. The text of the statute requires no such result.[9] . . .

III

. . . Did the Commission, as the Court of Appeals held, exceed its rulemaking authority under §14(e) when it adopted Rule 14e-3(a) without

---

9. As noted earlier, however, the textual requirement of deception precludes §10(b) liability when a person trading on the basis of nonpublic information has disclosed his trading plans to, or obtained authorization from, the principal, even though such conduct may affect the securities markets in the same manner as the conduct reached by the misappropriation theory. Contrary to the dissent's suggestion, the fact that §10(b) is only a partial antidote to the problems it was designed to alleviate does not call into question its prohibition of conduct that falls within its textual proscription. Moreover, once a disloyal agent discloses his imminent breach of duty, his principal may seek appropriate equitable relief under state law. Furthermore, in the context of a tender offer, the principal who authorizes an agent's trading on confidential information may, in the Commission's view, incur liability for an Exchange Act violation under Rule 14e-3(a).

C. Law's Limits on the Use of Inside Information

requiring a showing that the trading at issue entailed a breach of fiduciary duty? We hold that the Commission, in this regard and to the extent relevant to this case, did not exceed its authority. . . .

Section 14(e)'s first sentence prohibits fraudulent acts in connection with a tender offer. This self-operating proscription was one of several provisions added to the Exchange Act in 1968 by the Williams Act. The section's second sentence delegates definitional and prophylactic rulemaking authority to the Commission. Congress added this rulemaking delegation to §14(e) in 1970 amendments to the Williams Act.

Through §14(e) and other provisions on disclosure in the Williams Act, Congress sought to ensure that shareholders "confronted by a cash tender offer for their stock [would] not be required to respond without adequate information." Rondeau v. Mosinee Paper Corp., 422 U.S. 49, 58 (1975) [see Lewis v. McGraw, 619 F.2d 192, 195 (C.A.2 1980) (per curiam) ("very purpose" of Williams Act was "informed decisionmaking by shareholders")]. As we recognized in Schreiber v. Burlington Northern, Inc., 472 U.S. 1 (1985), Congress designed the Williams Act to make "disclosure, rather than court-imposed principles of 'fairness' or 'artificiality,' . . . the preferred method of market regulation." Section 14(e), we explained, "supplements the more precise disclosure provisions found elsewhere in the Williams Act, while requiring disclosure more explicitly addressed to the tender offer context than that required by §10(b)." . . .

As characterized by the Commission, Rule 14e-3(a) is a "disclose or abstain from trading" requirement.[15] The Second Circuit concisely described the rule's thrust:

> One violates Rule 14e-3(a) if he trades on the basis of material nonpublic information concerning a pending tender offer that he knows or has reason to know has been acquired "directly or indirectly" from an insider of the offeror or issuer, or someone working on their behalf. Rule 14e-3(a) is a disclosure provision. It creates a duty in those traders who fall within its ambit to abstain or disclose, *without regard to whether trader owes a pre-existing fiduciary duty* to respect the confidentiality of the information.

United States v. Chestman, 947 F.2d 551, 557 (1991) (en banc) (emphasis added), cert. denied, 503 U.S. 1004 (1992).

In the Eighth Circuit's view, because Rule 14e-3(a) applies whether or not the trading in question breaches a fiduciary duty, the regulation exceeds the SEC's §14(e) rulemaking authority. . . . [T]he SEC may "identify and regulate," in the tender offer context, "acts and practices" the law already defines as "fraudulent"; but, the Eighth Circuit maintained, the SEC may not "create its own definition of fraud." . . . Section 10(b) interpretations guide construction of §14(e), the Eighth Circuit added, citing this Court's acknowledgment in Schreiber that §14(e)'s "'broad antifraud

---

15. The rule thus adopts for the tender offer context a requirement resembling the one Chief Justice Burger would have adopted in *Chiarella* for misappropriators under §10(b). See supra, n.6.

prohibition' . . . [is] modeled on the antifraud provisions of §10(b) . . . and Rule 10b-5."

For the meaning of "fraudulent" under §10(b), the Eighth Circuit looked to *Chiarella*. In that case, the Eighth Circuit recounted, this Court held that a failure to disclose information could be "fraudulent" under §10(b) only when there was a duty to speak arising out of "'a fiduciary or other similar relationship of trust and confidence.'" *Chiarella*, 445 U.S., at 228 (quoting Restatement (Second) of Torts §551(2)(a) (1976)). Just as §10(b) demands a showing of a breach of fiduciary duty, so such a breach is necessary to make out a §14(e) violation, the Eighth Circuit concluded. . . .

We need not resolve in this case whether the Commission's authority under §14(e) to "define . . . such acts and practices as are fraudulent" is broader than the Commission's fraud-defining authority under §10(b), for we agree with the United States that Rule 14e-3(a), as applied to cases of this genre, qualifies under §14(e) as a "means reasonably designed to prevent" fraudulent trading on material, nonpublic information in the tender offer context.[17] A prophylactic measure, because its mission is to prevent, typically encompasses more than the core activity prohibited. . . . We hold, accordingly, that under §14(e), the Commission may prohibit acts, not themselves fraudulent under the common law or §10(b), if the prohibition is "reasonably designed to prevent . . . acts and practices [that] are fraudulent."[18]

The United States emphasizes that Rule 14e-3(a) reaches trading in which "a breach of duty is likely but difficult to prove." "Particularly in the context of a tender offer," as the Tenth Circuit recognized, "there is a fairly wide circle of people with confidential information," *Peters*, 978 F.2d, at 1167, notably, the attorneys, investment bankers, and accountants involved in structuring the transaction. The availability of that information may lead to abuse, for "even a hint of [a] tender offer may send the price of the target company's stock soaring." *SEC v. Materia*, 745 F.2d 197, 199 (C.A.2 1984). Individuals entrusted with nonpublic information, particularly if they have no long-term loyalty to the issuer, may find the temptation to trade on that information hard to resist in view of "the very large short-term profits potentially available [to them]." *Peters*, 978 F.2d, at 1167.

---

17. We leave for another day, when the issue requires decision, the legitimacy of Rule 14e-3(a) as applied to "warehousing," which the Government describes as "the practice by which bidders leak advance information of a tender offer to allies and encourage them to purchase the target company's stock before the bid is announced." As we observed in *Chiarella*, one of the Commission's purposes in proposing Rule 14e-3(a) was "to bar warehousing under its authority to regulate tender offers." 445 U.S., at 234. The Government acknowledges that trading authorized by a principal breaches no fiduciary duty. The instant case, however, does not involve trading authorized by a principal; therefore, we need not here decide whether the Commission's proscription of warehousing falls within its §14(e) authority to define or prevent fraud.

18. The Commission's power under §10(b) is more limited. See supra (Rule 10b-5 may proscribe only conduct that §10(b) prohibits).

C. Law's Limits on the Use of Inside Information 487

"[I]t may be possible to prove circumstantially that a person [traded on the basis of material, nonpublic information], but almost impossible to prove that the trader obtained such information in breach of a fiduciary duty owed either by the trader or by the ultimate insider source of the information." Ibid. The example of a "tippee" who trades on information received from an insider illustrates the problem. Under Rule 10b-5, "a tippee assumes a fiduciary duty to the shareholders of a corporation not to trade on material nonpublic information only when the insider has breached his fiduciary duty to the shareholders by disclosing the information to the tippee and the tippee knows or should know that there has been a breach." *Dirks*, 463 U.S., at 660. To show that a tippee who traded on nonpublic information about a tender offer had breached a fiduciary duty would require proof not only that the insider source breached a fiduciary duty, but that the tippee knew or should have known of that breach. "Yet, in most cases, the only parties to the [information transfer] will be the insider and the alleged tippee." *Peters*, 978 F.2d, at 1167.

In sum, it is a fair assumption that trading on the basis of material, nonpublic information will often involve a breach of a duty of confidentiality to the bidder or target company or their representatives. The SEC, cognizant of the proof problem that could enable sophisticated traders to escape responsibility, placed in Rule 14e-3(a) a "disclose or abstain from trading" command that does not require specific proof of a breach of fiduciary duty. That prescription, we are satisfied, applied to this case, is a "means reasonably designed to prevent" fraudulent trading on material, nonpublic information in the tender offer context. See *Chestman*, 947 F.2d, at 560 ("While dispensing with the subtle problems of proof associated with demonstrating fiduciary breach in the problematic area of tender offer insider trading, [Rule 14e-3(a)] retains a close nexus between the prohibited conduct and the statutory aims."); [accord, *Maio*, 51 F.3d, at 635, and n.14; *Peters*, 978 F.2d, at 1167]. Therefore, insofar as it serves to prevent the type of misappropriation charged against O'Hagan, Rule 14e-3(a) is a proper exercise of the Commission's prophylactic power under §14(e)....

[The opinions of Justice Scalia, concurring in part and dissenting in part, and of Justice Thomas, with whom The Chief Justice joins, concurring in the judgment in part and dissenting in part are omitted.]

NOTES AND QUESTIONS

1. The Court stated that the misappropriation theory applies to a person who "misappropriates confidential information for securities trading purposes, in breach of a duty owed to the source of the information." Does the misappropriation theory have the breadth of the information

theory rejected in *Chiarella* or does agency law act as a recognizable limit that prevents misappropriation from becoming a parity of information rule? Consider whether the following relationships would satisfy that duty (this list is drawn from appellate cases prior to *O'Hagan*):

- Between an employer and employee or former employee, *see* United States v. Newman, 664 F.2d 12 (2d Cir. 1981); S.E.C. v. Cherif, 933 F.2d 403 (7th Cir. 1991).
- Between a newspaper and its reporter, *see* United States v. Carpenter, 791 F.2d 1024 (2d Cir. 1986), *aff'd* (as to 10b-5 claims) by an equally divided court, 484 U.S. 19 (1987).
- Between a psychiatrist and patient, *see* United States v. Willis, 737 F. Supp. 269 (S.D.N.Y. 1990).
- Between a government official and his constituency, *see* United States v. Bryan, 58 F.3d 933 (4th Cir. 1995).
- Between a father and son, *see* United States v. Reed, 601 F. Supp. 685 (S.D.N.Y.), rev'd on other grounds, 773 F.2d 477 (2d Cir. 1985).
- Between a husband and wife, *see* United States v. Chestman, 947 F.2d 551 (2d Cir. 1991) (en banc).

Rule 10b5-2, a post-*O'Hagan* rule, provides a non-exclusive definition of circumstances in which a person has a duty of trust or confidence for purposes of the "misappropriation" theory of insider trading. Three groups are included: (1) a person who agrees to maintain information in confidence; (2) where there is a history, pattern or practice of sharing confidences such that the recipient knows or reasonably should know of the expectation of confidentiality; or (3) a spousal, parent/child or sibling relationship. This last category contains language narrowing this group where the recipient negates the recipient's knowledge of the communicator's expectation of confidentiality by showing an absence of either of the first two factual patterns, an agreement to maintain confidentiality, or a pattern or practice of sharing and maintaining confidences.

4. Assembling the Bases for Insider Trading Liability

From the reading above you should have identified multiple bases of liability for insider trading that you should be able to apply to an acquisition merger setting:

Which theory is likely to attach to insiders of the target?

Which theories are likely to attach to insiders of the acquirer?

C. Law's Limits on the Use of Inside Information

Can you distinguish information conveyed by an insider to another in breach of duty versus the information conveyed for a legitimate corporate purpose?

Are you more susceptible to insider trading liability in a tender offer or a merger?

After all the theories are in play, describe the space in which you could have and trade on inside information and not face liability?

FINANCIAL REORGANIZATIONS: HIGHLY LEVERAGED TRANSACTIONS, GOING PRIVATE, ASSET RESTRUCTURING

The focus in this chapter is on deals where financial motives drive the gain rather than synergistic or other gains that could be produced by combining the assets of the target with others in the same business. In simplest terms, these transactions start with the same assets and the same management as before but seek to create additional value through various financial-based changes. Going-private transactions via a leveraged buyout (LBO) are the most visible of such transactions. Such a deal involving RJR Nabisco at the end of the 1980s takeovers boom provided the setting for *Barbarians at the Gate* that has become a classic read for those studying the history of deals and thinking about pursuing this line of work.

This chapter begins with a look at the financial factors that are needed for such transactions and how they create value. Subsequent sections address how valuation is different in such a setting and the law that shapes these deals. A case study from one of the largest such deals of the new century provides an accessible vehicle to understand the finance and the law. The last section explores variations of financial restructuring that focus more on rearranging the assets of the company as opposed to its money.

A. LEVERAGED BUYOUTS, GOING PRIVATE, AND OTHER TRANSACTIONS MAKING USE OF LEVERAGE

During the late 1980s and thereafter, private equity firms such as KKR (Kohlberg, Kravis & Roberts) and Forstmann Little regularly sought to take over companies (e.g., RJR) in financial transactions characterized by (1) borrowing large amounts of money (often using high-yield loans and junk bonds) and (2) using the new funds to buy back most of the stock and/or to fund a large cash dividend. In the twenty-first century, a growing group of funds, such as Thomas H. Lee, the Blackstone Group, and Apollo Advisers, found this to be a very profitable venue, at least until the credit crisis in 2007-2008.

Consider an example from the earlier period involving Congoleum, Inc., a conglomerate that had interests in flooring, shipbuilding, and auto parts. At the time of the transaction, the company had an equity value of $150 million and outstanding debt of $125 million. The planners offered shareholders a buyout of their equity worth $460 million, financed with $380 million in debt and $95 million in excess cash of the company. The firm's CEO and CFO invested their existing stock options to purchase shares in the LBO. Future earnings from the company's business enabled it to pay off the debt. At that time, the company did a second LBO and again borrowed money, which was used to return cash to shareholders. The two top executives reinvested their profits to own half of the equity. Two years later, the firm liquidated and equity holders received $850 million. For the two top executives, what had been an investment of $100,000 or so procured gains of hundreds of millions.

1. Economic Factors Used to Create Wealth in LBOs

How can a leveraged buyout create such value, given that no additional assets or synergies are being added to the enterprise and the management often is the same as before? There are several economic rationales that can produce value:

- *Improving the bottom line because of the tax shield and saving the costs of public ownership.* The change in the firm's capital structure, with debt replacing equity, can increase the firm's return on equity to the extent that interest paid on debt reduces the firm's taxable income and the amount due in taxes. Less noticeable can be the savings by avoiding the costs of public registration and the distractions of having to manage the firm to meet analysts' quarterly expectations.
  - *Improving management incentives.* This can happen in several ways. First, management often acquires a greater ownership position because of the LBO in contrast to the minuscule percentage of equity that managers frequently own in a publicly held company. This added ownership percentage gives the executives a greater incentive to produce returns on their shares and manage in a way that improves the bottom line and accrues value to all of

A. Leveraged Buyouts, Going Private, and Other Transactions

the equity investors as the residual claimants. This incentive is multiplied because the leverage makes the stock price (and the managers' stock) highly sensitive to any change in the firm's value. Since equity provides only a minority of the firm's capital, but receives the entire gain after the fixed debt claimants are paid, earnings improvements produce a large return on the equity invested. Assume, to take a simple example, a firm with $100 in revenue that owes $75 on its debt obligations for that reporting period leaving $25 for the shareholders. If the $100 increases by 10 percent to $110, the amount available to equity increases by 40 percent from $25 to $35. Since the firm's debt is a fixed claim that will not increase with the additional cash, the 10 percent return can increase the equity's return by 40 percent, thus multiplying the equity owners' incentive to wrench more profits out of the business.

- *Improving monitoring of managers.* Even with incentives, the interests of managers are not perfectly aligned with owners such that additional monitoring can improve performance. An LBO does this in several ways. First, the large increase in interest payments regularly due on the debt severely limits management's freedom and subjects them to the discipline of the credit markets. They simply do not have the free cash flow available to spend on projects that don't produce a sufficient return. This, itself, reduces managers' ability to engage in empire building that may appeal to the manager's individual interest but not produce an increase in shareholder value. The lack of free cash flow means that managers have to subject their plans to the discipline of the market in persuading lenders to provide funds for new projects. Second, there is potential for more effective monitoring by shareholders or directors than existed before. The LBO results in concentrated ownership by private equity investors and others whose business plan means that to prosper they have to ensure the company can meet its large debt payments. With such incentives, shareholders are likely to be more demanding than those in a typical publicly held corporation with dispersed share ownership. This more intense monitoring will also show up at the board of directors' level where, unlike the typical public corporation with independent but, perhaps, uninvolved directors, the directors now are the owners or are directly accountable to the owners. Concentrated owners who are repeat players in the going-private business can hire more specialized board members. *See* Masulis & Thomas, *Does Private Equity Create Wealth? The Effects of Private Equity and Derivatives on Corporate Governance*, 76 U. Chi. L. Rev. 219 (2009).

- *Increasing share value at the expense of other stakeholders.* To the extent that increased equity value comes from another stakeholder, as already illustrated by the possible decline in the government's receipt of corporate income taxes paid by the firm, LBOs raise additional concerns, which has most focused on existing bondholders and employees. Existing debt holders of the company received a rate of return commensurate with the anticipated risk and return at the time of the borrowing. What does the leveraged transaction do? It usually substantially raises the risk of bankruptcy in a way that is likely to drive down the value of existing debt. Debt holders could negotiate for contractual protection against such a change, if they are willing to incur the costs and their lawyers can draft provisions sufficiently complete to fill the gaps. Whether or not additional legal protection is available through corporate law principles is discussed below. Employees may feel like they are paying for the added value if jobs or wages are adversely affected. Separating such losses that occur from change in the industry and other causes from that due to change in the firm's financial structure can be difficult. Other stakeholders, think suppliers and car dealerships of Chrysler in 2009, for example, suffered in the context of that company's bankruptcy after going private, but similar travails fell on the suppliers, dealers, and employees of General Motors, which had not gone through a leveraged transaction.

2. It's Not for Everyone: The Ideal Candidate for an LBO; Empirical Evidence on Post-Transaction Performance

The increased leverage of the firms that have undergone a financial transaction increases the bankruptcy risk of these companies because they have less of the cushion that equity provides in a typical publicly held company. If a downturn were to occur in the economy and sales were to drop 25 percent, or if a firm were to have a major reversal in its product line or lose a major customer, a firm capitalized with more equity than debt would see the value of its equity drop but would still be able to meet the payments to the debt holders as they came due. In contrast, a highly leveraged firm has in effect pledged a much greater percentage of its expected cash flow to support fixed payments to lenders. Any appreciable loss in that cash flow could permit the lenders to take over the business.

What kind of business would be an ideal LBO target? A company with a large and stable cash flow (both from its own sources of revenue and its costs of capital expenses and research & development) would be preferred as opposed to a firm who saw its income swing wildly as the economy fluctuates and would be vulnerable to the first hiccup in the economy after the LBO. Capable management is often a characteristic of these transactions (hence the name Management Buyouts or MBOs for a large segment of them) as opposed to firms that are underperforming, because management does not understand the business. Given the discussion of management incentives above, a capable management with low equity holdings and a poor compensation plan offers greater potential arising from the introduction of LBO efficiencies. A firm already making high tax payments and with low leverage/unused debt capacity would more likely be a candidate for a LBO.

A core concern of the planner of a LBO is to control distress costs, which typically requires an immediate effort to reduce risk of bankruptcy. One way is to rapidly reduce expenses and expand revenues so the business has a greater cushion separating its revenue from its fixed payment obligations. A LBO firm would be more inclined to sell assets that have a greater value to other investors. For that reason, firms with a larger percentage of tangible assets or even unrelated divisions provide opportunities in a LBO context. A privately held firm may also make use of private debt, involving a smaller number of unsophisticated lenders that makes it easier to explain the business to lenders and to renegotiate as the business evolves.

Empirical evidence suggests LBO firms are able to realize some of the efficiencies from the economic factors described above. LBO firms appear to become more profitable while privately held as compared to industry competitors. As measured by what happens when they go public again (see below), LBO firms outperformed competitors in operating income and stock returns for the years after the transactions. LBO firms show improved focus in terms of shedding excess assets and using less working capital (but not reducing research & development and maintenance). Not surprisingly given the discussion above, tax payments are reduced substantially. While management is usually retained, board composition substantially changes in the direction of more specialization, and its size is reduced.

3. Exit

Although there have been some suggestions that the privately held firm could replace the public corporation in large parts of our economy, exit remains a key part of the business plan for most firms implementing highly leveraged transactions. Once the efficiency gains have been realized and in a time period of under a decade, the LBO firm is likely to be sold off in one of several ways. The private firm may go public again, so that the LBO is an interlude between two publicly held phases of the company. Alternatively, once the debt has been paid down, the sponsors and managers may engage in a second LBO that returns the leverage and the discipline to the prior position. The firm may get sold to a strategic buyer in the industry or even to another private equity firm. Finally, piecemeal divestiture and liquidation is possible, including the variations discussed in section C of this chapter.

4. Law Shaping the LBO Deal

Law has less of a footprint for LBO deals than for other types of transactions that we have studied. As for acquisitions generally, there are multiple forms to use in accomplishing the LBO, but the impact is much less than we saw in Chapter 3. Possible conflicts of interest in the transaction are a major concern, visible in both disclosure obligations and the possibility of fiduciary duty, but overall, we do not see the same level of legal involvement as for acquisitions generally.

Going private, as in a leveraged buyout, can be accomplished by a merger, a sale of assets, an issuer tender offer, or a reverse stock split. In each of the settings, the economic exchange is similar: existing shareholders receive cash or other consideration for their ownership interest. In each, the shareholders of the target must provide their assent — in the merger by the vote of shareholders that is required by state corporations statutes like Delaware §251; in a sale of assets by a similar requirement in statutes such as Delaware §271. There, the consideration is actually paid to the corporate treasury, but the shareholders have usually voted to dissolve, so that amount in the treasury will be distributed to the shareholders pro rata. A reverse stock split is actually an amendment to the firm's articles or certificate of incorporation, which says something like every 1 share of the corporation's stock becomes 1/100 or 1/1000 or a smaller fraction of a new share and all shareholders who end up with less than a whole share will be cashed out at a set price. Amendments to the certificate require approval by a vote of the majority of shareholders under state corporations law. If the tender offer is chosen, the new investors offer cash to the public shareholders, usually conditioning the offer on acceptance by at least a majority and then employing a cash-out merger if there are any hold-out shareholders.

The requirement for majority approval by the shareholders, either by vote or tender, is the first line of defense against a LBO on terms that aren't beneficial to the equity holders. But in many highly leveraged transactions, the key managers, to whom shareholders would ordinarily look for advice, are on the other side of the transaction, as buyers of what the shareholders are selling. What protections would you expect against such possible conflict of interest? Corporate law principles say that the insiders who are buyers cannot speak or act for the entity in any corporate actions that may be required. Fiduciary duty under state corporate law requires directors to disclose before the shareholders vote, as described by the Delaware Supreme Court in Gantler v. Stephens, 965 A.2d 695 (Del. 2009).

> It is well-settled law that "directors of Delaware corporations [have] a fiduciary duty to disclose fully and fairly all material information within the board's control when it seeks shareholder action." That duty "attaches to proxy statements and any other disclosures in contemplation of stockholder action." The essential inquiry here is

A. Leveraged Buyouts, Going Private, and Other Transactions

whether the alleged omission or misrepresentation is material. The burden of establishing materiality rests with the plaintiff, who must demonstrate "a substantial likelihood that the disclosure of the omitted fact would have been viewed by the reasonable investor as having significantly altered the 'total mix' of information made available."

We have defined "materiality" as follows:

> An omitted fact is material if there is a substantial likelihood that a reasonable shareholder would consider it important in deciding how to vote.... It does not require proof of a substantial likelihood that disclosure of the omitted fact would have caused a reasonable investor to change his vote. What the standard does contemplate is a showing of a substantial likelihood that, under all the circumstances, the omitted fact would have assumed actual significance in the deliberations of the reasonable shareholder. Put another way, there must be a substantial likelihood that the disclosure of the omitted fact would have been viewed by the reasonable investor as having significantly altered the "total mix" of information made available.

Arnold, 650 A.2d at 1277 (citations and emphasis omitted).

... In the Reclassification Proxy, the Board disclosed that "[a]fter careful deliberations, the board determined in its business judgment that the [First Place merger] proposal was not in the best interest of the Company or our shareholders and rejected the [merger] proposal." Although boards are "not required to disclose all available information[,] ..." "once [they] travel[] down the road of partial disclosure of ... [prior bids] us[ing] ... vague language ... , they ha[ve] an obligation to provide the stockholders with an accurate, full, and fair characterization of those historic events."

By stating that they "careful[ly] deliberat[ed]," the Board was representing to the shareholders that it had considered the Sales Process on its objective merits and had determined that the Reclassification would better serve the Company than a merger. The Court of Chancery found, however, that the Board's Reclassification Proxy disclosure of "careful deliberations" about terminating the Sales Process was immaterial, because it would not alter the total mix of information to "omit[] that phrase in its entirety." We disagree and conclude that that disclosure was materially misleading.

The Reclassification Proxy specifically represented that the First Niles officers and directors "ha[d] a conflict of interest with respect to the [Reclassification] because he or she is in a position to structure it in a way that benefits his or her interests differently from the interests of unaffiliated shareholders." Given the defendant fiduciaries' admitted conflict of interest, a reasonable shareholder would likely find significant—indeed, reassuring—a representation by a conflicted Board that the Reclassification was superior to a potential merger which, after "careful deliberations," the Board had "carefully considered" and rejected. In such circumstances, it cannot be concluded as a matter of law, that disclosing that there was little or no deliberation would not alter the total mix of information provided to the shareholders.

The Vice Chancellor's finding that the challenged phrase could have been omitted in its entirety has the same infirmity. Had the "careful deliberations" representation never been made, the shareholders might well have evaluated the Reclassification more skeptically, and perhaps even less favorably on its merits, for two reasons. First, the shareholders would have had no information about the Reclassification's desirability vis-à-vis other alternatives. Second, they were told that the Board and Management had a conflict of interest in the one transaction that their fiduciaries had determined to endorse.

We are mindful of the case law holding that a corporate board is not obligated to disclose in a proxy statement the details of merger negotiations that have "gone south," since such information "would be [n]either viably practical [n]or material to shareholders in the meaningful way intended by . . . case law." Even so, a board cannot properly claim in a proxy statement that it had carefully deliberated and decided that its preferred transaction better served the corporation than the alternative, if in fact the Board rejected the alternative transaction without serious consideration. The complaint's allegation that at its March 9, 2005, meeting the Board voted to reject a merger with First Place without any discussion, supports a reasonable inference that the Board did not "carefully deliberate" on the merits of that transaction.

965 A.2d at 710-11.

Federal securities law has added specific disclosure obligations for going-private transactions to the state law requirements just discussed because of the perceived additional vulnerability of shareholders in making such a decision, Rule 13e-3 is triggered by many of the forms of transactions identified above (for example, merger, sale of assets, reorganization, etc.) that will result in a deregistration of the equity securities from the public disclosure obligations of the Securities Exchange Act of 1934 or other events such as a material change in dividends, indebtedness, or capitalization. In such a transaction, the rule requires disclosure as to the source of funds to be used in the transaction, managers' equity participation and employment arrangements going forward, potential conflicts of interest, offers by unaffiliated parties over the past 18 months, alternatives to an MBO/LBO considered, and the positions of outside directors. Those disclosures are not unlike disclosure required in transactions generally, but Rule 13(e) does include a requirement beyond that which is found elsewhere: The directors in a going-private transaction must disclose their view about the fairness of the transaction, a departure from the usual SEC approach that does not get to the substance of a deal, but lets shareholders decide once they have received full disclosure.

In addition to these fiduciary duties focused on the conflict of interest, what about the intermediate judicial review discussed in Chapter 6, particularly the directors duties under *Revlon*? Should a LBO trigger a *Revlon* duty? In this regard, the *Topps* and *Netsmart* cases discussed below look at the intersection of disclosure and *Revlon*.

Highly leveraged transactions raise an additional legal element not seen before in terms of the ability of other constituents to raise legal claims. The *RJR* case itself provoked litigation by Metropolitan Life Insurance Company.

Metropolitan Life Insurance Co. v. RJR Nabisco, Inc.
716 F. Supp. 1504 (S.D.N.Y. 1989)

WALKER, District Judge:

The corporate parties to this action are among the country's most sophisticated financial institutions, as familiar with the Wall Street

A. Leveraged Buyouts, Going Private, and Other Transactions

investment community and the securities market as American consumers are with the Oreo cookies and Winston cigarettes made by defendant RJR Nabisco, Inc. (sometimes "the company" or "RJR Nabisco"). The present action traces its origins to October 20, 1988, when F. Ross Johnson, then the Chief Executive Officer of RJR Nabisco, proposed a $17 billion leveraged buy-out ("LBO") of the company's shareholders, at $75 per share. Within a few days, a bidding war developed among the investment group led by Johnson and the investment firm of Kohlberg Kravis Roberts & Co. ("KKR"), and others. On December 1, 1988, a special committee of RJR Nabisco directors, established by the company specifically to consider the competing proposals, recommended that the company accept the KKR proposal, a $24 billion LBO that called for the purchase of the company's outstanding stock at roughly $109 per share. . . .

Plaintiffs now allege, in short, that RJR Nabisco's actions have drastically impaired the value of bonds previously issued to plaintiffs by, in effect, misappropriating the value of those bonds to help finance the LBO and to distribute an enormous windfall to the company's shareholders. As a result, plaintiffs argue, they have unfairly suffered a multimillion dollar loss in the value of their bonds. . . .

Although the numbers involved in this case are large, and the financing necessary to complete the LBO unprecedented, the legal principles nonetheless remain discrete and familiar. Yet while the instant motions thus primarily require the Court to evaluate and apply traditional rules of equity and contract interpretation, plaintiffs do raise issues of first impression in the context of an LBO. At the heart of the present motions lies plaintiffs' claim that RJR Nabisco violated a restrictive covenant — not an explicit covenant found within the four corners of the relevant bond indentures, but rather an *implied* covenant of good faith and fair dealing — not to incur the debt necessary to facilitate the LBO and thereby betray what plaintiffs claim was the fundamental basis of their bargain with the company. The company, plaintiffs assert, consistently reassured its bondholders that it had a "mandate" from its Board of Directors to maintain RJR Nabisco's preferred credit rating. Plaintiffs ask this Court first to imply a covenant of good faith and fair dealing that would prevent the recent transaction, then to hold that this covenant has been breached, and finally to require RJR Nabisco to redeem their bonds.

RJR Nabisco defends the LBO by pointing to express provisions in the bond indentures that, *inter alia*, permit mergers and the assumption of additional debt. These provisions, as well as others that could have been included but were not, were known to the market and to plaintiffs, sophisticated investors who freely bought the bonds and were equally free to sell them at any time. Any attempt by this Court to create contractual terms *post hoc*, defendants contend, not only finds no basis in the controlling law and undisputed facts of this case, but also would constitute an impermissible invasion into the free and open operation of the marketplace.

For the reasons set forth below, this Court agrees with defendants. There being no express covenant between the parties that would restrict the incurrence of new debt, and no perceived direction to that end from covenants that are express, this Court will not imply a covenant to prevent the recent LBO and thereby create an indenture term that, while bargained for in other contexts, was not bargained for here and was not even within the mutual contemplation of the parties.

B. The Indentures

The bonds implicated by this suit are governed by long, detailed indentures, which in turn are governed by New York contract law. No one disputes that the holders of public bond issues, like plaintiffs here, often enter the market after the indentures have been negotiated and memorialized. Thus, those indentures are often not the product of face-to-face negotiations between the ultimate holders and the issuing company. What remains equally true, however, is that underwriters ordinarily negotiate the terms of the indentures with the issuers. Since the underwriters must then sell or place the bonds, they necessarily negotiate in part with the interests of the buyers in mind. Moreover, these indentures were not secret agreements foisted upon unwitting participants in the bond market. No successive holder is required to accept or to continue to hold the bonds, governed by their accompanying indentures; indeed, plaintiffs readily admit that they could have sold their bonds right up until the announcement of the LBO. Instead, sophisticated investors like plaintiffs are well aware of the indenture terms and, presumably, review them carefully before lending hundreds of millions of dollars to any company.

Indeed, the prospectuses for the indentures contain a statement relevant to this action:

> The Indenture contains no restrictions on the creation of unsecured short-term debt by [RJR Nabisco] or its subsidiaries, no restriction on the creation of unsecured Funded Debt by [RJR Nabisco] or its subsidiaries which are not Restricted Subsidiaries, and no restriction on the payment of dividends by [RJR Nabisco].

Further, as plaintiffs themselves note, the contracts at issue "[do] not impose debt limits, since debt is assumed to be used for productive purposes."...

2. The Elimination of Restrictive Covenants

In its Amended Complaint, MetLife lists the six debt issues on which it bases its claims. Indentures for two of those issues — the 10.25 percent Notes due in 1990, of which MetLife continues to hold $10 million, and the 8.9 percent Debentures due in 1996, of which MetLife continues to hold $50 million — once contained express covenants that, among other things, restricted the company's ability to incur precisely the sort of debt involved in the recent LBO. In order to eliminate those restrictions, the parties to this action renegotiated the terms of those indentures, first in 1983 and then again in 1985.

MetLife acquired $50 million principal amount of 10.25 percent Notes from Del Monte in July of 1975. [The loan] agreement restricted Del Monte's ability, among other things, to incur the sort of indebtedness involved in the RJR Nabisco LBO. In 1979, R.J. Reynolds—the corporate predecessor to RJR Nabisco—purchased Del Monte and assumed its indebtedness. Then, in December of 1983, R.J. Reynolds requested MetLife to agree to deletions of those restrictive covenants in exchange for various guarantees from R.J. Reynolds. A few months later, MetLife and R.J. Reynolds entered into a guarantee and amendment agreement reflecting those terms. Pursuant to that agreement, and in the words of Robert E. Chappell, Jr., MetLife's Executive Vice President, MetLife thus "gave up the restrictive covenants applicable to the Del Monte debt...in return for [the parent company's] guarantee and public covenants."

MetLife acquired the 8.9 percent Debentures from R.J. Reynolds in October of 1976 in a private placement. A promissory note evidenced MetLife's $100 million loan. That note, like the Del Monte agreement, contained covenants that restricted R.J. Reynolds' ability to incur new debt. In June of 1985, R.J. Reynolds announced its plans to acquire Nabisco Brands in a $3.6 billion transaction that involved the incurrence of a significant amount of new debt. R.J. Reynolds requested MetLife to waive compliance with these restrictive covenants in light of the Nabisco acquisition.

In exchange for certain benefits, MetLife agreed to exchange its 8.9 percent debentures-which *did* contain explicit debt limitations—for debentures issued under a public indenture—which contain no explicit limits on new debt. An internal MetLife memorandum explained the parties' understanding:

> [MetLife's $100 million financing of the Nabisco Brands purchase] had its origins in discussions with RJR regarding potential covenant violations in the 8.90% Notes. More specifically, *in its acquisition of Nabisco Brands, RJR was slated to incur significant new long-term debt, which would have caused a violation in the funded indebtedness incurrence tests in the 8.90% Notes.* In the discussions regarding [MetLife's] willingness to consent to the additional indebtedness, *it was determined that a mutually beneficial approach to the problem* was to 1) agree on a new financing having a rate and a maturity desirable for [MetLife] and 2) modify the 8.90% Notes. The former was accomplished with agreement on the proposed financing, while the latter was accomplished by [MetLife] agreeing to substitute RJR's public indenture covenants for the covenants in the 8.90% Notes. In addition to the covenant substitution, RJR has agreed to "debenturize" the 8.90% Notes upon [MetLife's] request. This will permit [MetLife] to sell the 8.90% Notes to the public.

3. The Recognition and Effect of the LBO Trend

Other internal MetLife documents help frame the background to this action, for they accurately describe the changing securities markets and the responses those changes engendered from sophisticated market participants, such as MetLife and Jefferson-Pilot. At least as early as 1982, MetLife recognized an LBO's effect on bond values. In the spring of that year, MetLife participated in the financing of an LBO of a company called Reeves Brothers ("Reeves"). At the time of that LBO, MetLife also held bonds in that company. Subsequent to the LBO, as a MetLife memorandum explained, the "Debentures of Reeves were downgraded by Standard & Poor's from BBB to B and by Moody's from Baa1 to Ba3, thereby lowering the value of the Notes and Debentures held by MetLife. . . .

MetLife further recognized its "inability to force any type of payout of the [Reeves'] Notes or the Debentures as a result of the buy-out [which] was somewhat disturbing at the time we considered a participation in the new financing. However," the memorandum continued,

> our concern was tempered since, as a stockholder in [the holding company used to facilitate the transaction], we would benefit from the increased net income attributable to the continued presence of the low coupon indebtedness. The recent downgrading of the Reeves Debentures and the consequent "loss" in value has again raised questions regarding our ability to have forced a payout. *Questions have also been raised about our ability to force payouts in similar future situations, particularly when we would not be participating in the buy-out financing.*

Id. (emphasis added). In the memorandum, MetLife sought to answer those very "questions" about how it might force payouts in "similar future situations."

> *A method of closing this apparent "loophole," thereby forcing a payout of [MetLife's] holdings, would be through a covenant dealing with a change in ownership.* Such a covenant is fairly standard in financings with privately-held companies. . . . It provides the lender with an option to end a particular borrowing relationship via some type of special redemption. . . .

Id., at 2 (emphasis added).

A more comprehensive memorandum, prepared in late 1985, evaluated and explained several aspects of the corporate world's increasing use of mergers, takeovers and other debt-financed transactions. That memorandum first reviewed the available protection for lenders such as MetLife:

> Covenants are incorporated into loan documents to ensure that after a lender makes a loan, the creditworthiness of the borrower and the lender's ability to reach the borrower's assets do not deteriorate substantially. *Restrictions on the incurrence of debt,* sale of assets, mergers, dividends, restricted payments and loans and advances to affiliates *are some of the traditional negative covenants that can help protect lenders in the event their obligors become involved in undesirable merger/takeover situations.*

A. Leveraged Buyouts, Going Private, and Other Transactions   503

MetLife Northeastern Office Memorandum, dated November 27, 1985, attached as Bradley Aff. Exh. U, at 1-2 (emphasis added). The memorandum then surveyed market realities:

> Because almost any industrial company is apt to engineer a takeover or be taken over itself, *Business Week* says that investors are beginning to view debt securities of high grade industrial corporations as Wall Street's riskiest investments. In addition, *because public bondholders do not enjoy the protection of any restrictive covenants*, owners of high grade corporates face substantial losses from takeover situations, if not immediately, then when the bond market finally adjusts. . . . [T]here have been 10-15 merger/takeover/LBO situations where, *due to the lack of covenant protection, [MetLife] has had no choice but to remain a lender to a less creditworthy obligor.* . . . The fact that the quality of our investment portfolio is greater than the other large insurance companies . . . may indicate that we have negotiated better covenant protection than other institutions, thus generally being able to require prepayment when situations become too risky. . . . [However,] a problem exists. And *because the current merger craze is not likely to decelerate* and because there exist vehicles to circumvent traditional covenants, the problem will probably continue. Therefore, *perhaps it is time to institute appropriate language designed to protect Metropolitan from the negative implications of mergers and takeovers.*

Id. at 2-4 (emphasis added).

Indeed, MetLife does not dispute that, as a member of a bondholders' association, it received and discussed a proposed model indenture, which included a "comprehensive covenant" entitled "Limitations on Shareholders' Payments." . . .

Apparently, that provision — or provisions with similar intentions — never went beyond the discussion stage at MetLife. That fact is easily understood; indeed, MetLife's own documents articulate several reasonable, undisputed explanations:

> While it would be possible to broaden the change in ownership covenant to cover any acquisition-oriented transaction, *we might well encounter significant resistance in implementation with larger public companies.* . . . With respect to implementation, we would be faced with the task of imposing a non-standard limitation on potential borrowers, *which could be a difficult task in today's highly competitive marketplace. Competitive pressures notwithstanding, it would seem that management of larger public companies would be particularly opposed to such a covenant since its effect would be to increase the cost of an acquisition* (due to an assumed debt repayment), a factor that could well lower the price of any tender offer (thereby impacting shareholders).

Bradley Reply Aff. Exh. D, at 3 (emphasis added). The November 1985 memorandum explained that

> [o]bviously, our ability to implement methods of takeover protection will vary between the public and private market. In that public securities do not contain any meaningful covenants, it would be very difficult for [MetLife] to demand takeover protection in public bonds. Such a requirement would effectively take us out of the public industrial market. A recent *Business Week* article does suggest, however, that

there is increasing talk among lending institutions about requiring blue chip companies to compensate them for the growing risk of downgradings. *This talk, regarding such protection as restrictions on future debt financings, is met with skepticism by the investment banking community which feels that CFO's are not about to give up the option of adding debt and do not really care if their companies' credit ratings drop a notch or two.*

Bradley Resp. Aff. Exh. A, at 8 (emphasis added).

The Court quotes these documents at such length not because they represent an "admission" or "waiver" from MetLife, or an "assumption of risk" in any tort sense, or its "consent" to any particular course of conduct—all terms discussed at even greater length in the parties' submissions. Rather, the documents set forth the background to the present action, and highlight the risks inherent in the market itself, for any investor. Investors as sophisticated as MetLife and Jefferson-Pilot would be hard-pressed to plead ignorance of these market risks. Indeed, MetLife has not disputed the facts asserted in its own internal documents. Nor has Jefferson-Pilot—presumably an institution no less sophisticated than MetLife—offered any reason to believe that its understanding of the securities market differed in any material respect from the description and analysis set forth in the MetLife documents. Those documents, after all, were not born in a vacuum. They are descriptions of, and responses to, the market in which investors like MetLife and Jefferson-Pilot knowingly participated.

These documents must be read in conjunction with plaintiffs' Amended Complaint. That document asserts that the LBO "undermines the foundation of the investment grade debt market..."; that, although "the indentures do not purport to limit dividends or debt ... [s]uch covenants were believed unnecessary with blue chip companies..."; that "the transaction contradicts the premise of the investment grade market...", and, finally, that "[t]his buy-out was not contemplated at the time the debt was issued, contradicts the premise of the investment grade ratings that RJR Nabisco actively solicited and received, and is inconsistent with the understandings of the market ... which [p]laintiffs relied upon."

III. Discussion

A. Plaintiffs' Case Against the RJR Nabisco LBO

1. Count One: The Implied Covenant

In their first count, plaintiffs assert that

[d]efendant RJR Nabisco owes a continuing duty of good faith and fair dealing in connection with the contract [i.e., the indentures] through which it borrowed money from MetLife, Jefferson-Pilot and other holders of its debt, including a duty not to frustrate the purpose of the contracts to the debtholders or to deprive the debtholders of the intended object of the contracts—purchase of investment-grade securities.

... [T]he question of whether or not an *implied* covenant has been violated ... surfaces where, while the express terms may not have been technically breached, one party has nonetheless effectively deprived the other of those express, explicitly bargained-for benefits. In such a case, a court will read an implied covenant of good faith and fair dealing into a contract to ensure that neither party deprives the other of "the fruits of the agreement." *See, e.g., Greenwich Village Assoc. v. Salle*, 110 A.D.2d 111, 115, 493 N.Y.S.2d 461, 464 (1st Dep't 1985). *See also Van Gemert v. Boeing Co.*, 553 F.2d 812, 815 ("*Van Gemert II*") (2d Cir. 1977). Such a covenant is implied only where the implied term "is consistent with other mutually agreed upon terms in the contract." *Sabetay v. Sterling Drug, Inc.*, 69 N.Y.2d 329, 335, 514 N.Y.S.2d 209, 212, 506 N.E.2d 919, 922 (1987). In other words, the implied covenant will only aid and further the explicit terms of the agreement and will never impose an obligation "'which would be inconsistent with other terms of the contractual relationship.'" *Id.* (citation omitted). Viewed another way, the implied covenant of good faith is breached only when one party seeks to prevent the contract's performance or to withhold its benefits. *See Collard v. Incorporated Village of Flower Hill*, 75 A.D.2d 631, 632, 427 N.Y.S.2d 301, 302 (2d Dep't 1980). As a result, it thus ensures that parties to a contract perform the substantive, bargained-for terms of their agreement. *See, e.g., Wakefield v. Northern Telecom, Inc.*, 769 F.2d 109, 112 (2d Cir. 1985) (Winter, J.).

In contracts like bond indentures, "an implied covenant ... derives its substance directly from the language of the Indenture, and 'cannot give the holders of Debentures any rights inconsistent with those set out in the Indenture.' [Where] *plaintiffs' contractual rights [have not been] violated, there can have been no breach of an implied covenant.* "*Gardner & Florence Call Cowles Foundation v. Empire Inc.*, 589 F. Supp. 669, 673 (S.D.N.Y. 1984), *vacated on procedural grounds*, 754 F.2d 478 (2d Cir. 1985) (quoting *Broad v. Rockwell*, 642 F.2d 929, 957 (5th Cir.) (*en banc*), *cert. denied*, 454 U.S. 965, 102 S. Ct. 506, 70 L. Ed. 2d 380 (1981)) (emphasis added).

Thus, in cases like *Van Gemert v. Boeing Co.*, 520 F.2d 1373 (2d Cir.), *cert. denied*, 423 U.S. 947, 96 S. Ct. 364, 46 L. Ed. 2d 282 (1975) ("*Van Gemert I*"), and *Pittsburgh Terminal Corp. v. Baltimore & Ohio Ry. Co.*, 680 F.2d 933 (3d Cir.), *cert. denied*, 459 U.S. 1056, 103 S. Ct. 475, 74 L. Ed. 2d 621 (1982) — both relied upon by plaintiffs — the courts used the implied covenant of good faith and fair dealing to ensure that the bondholders received the benefit of their bargain as determined from the face of the contracts at issue. In *Van Gemert I*, the plaintiff bondholders alleged inadequate notice to them of defendant's intention to redeem the debentures in question and hence an inability to exercise their conversion rights before the applicable deadline. The contract itself provided that notice would be given in the first place. *See, e.g., id.* at 1375 ("A number of provisions in the debenture, the Indenture Agreement, the prospectus, the registration statement ... and the Listing Agreement ... dealt with the possible redemption of the debentures ... and the notice debenture-holders were to receive. ..."). Faced with those provisions, defendants in that case unsurprisingly admitted that the indentures specifically required the company to provide the bondholders with notice. *See id.* at 1379. While defendant there issued a press release that mentioned the possible redemption of outstanding convertible debentures, that limited release did not "mention even the tentative dates for redemption and expiration of the conversion rights of debenture holders." *Id.* at 1375. Moreover, defendant did not issue any general publicity or news release. Through an implied covenant, then, the court fleshed out the full extent of the more skeletal right that appeared in the contract itself, and thus protected plaintiff's bargained-for right of conversion. As the court observed,

> What one buys when purchasing a convertible debenture in addition to the debt obligation of the company ... is principally the expectation that the stock will increase sufficiently in value that the conversion right will make the debenture worth more than the debt. ... *Any loss* occurring to him from failure to convert, as here, *is not from a risk inherent in his investment but rather from unsatisfactory notification procedures.*

Id. at 1385 (emphasis added, citations omitted). I also note, in passing, that *Van Gemert I* presented the Second Circuit with "less sophisticated investors." *Id.* at 1383. Similarly, the court in *Pittsburgh Terminal* applied an implied covenant to the indentures at issue because defendants there "took steps to prevent the Bondholders from receiving information which they needed *in order to receive the fruits of their conversion option should they choose to exercise it.*" *Pittsburgh Terminal*, 680 F.2d at 941 (emphasis added).

The appropriate analysis, then, is first to examine the indentures to determine "the fruits of the agreement" between the parties, and then to decide whether those "fruits" have been spoiled — which is to say, whether plaintiffs' contractual rights have been violated by defendants.

The American Bar Foundation's *Commentaries on Indentures* ("the Commentaries"), relied upon and respected by both plaintiffs and defendants, describes the rights and risks generally found in bond indentures like those at issue:

> The most obvious and important characteristic of long-term debt financing is that the holder ordinarily has not bargained for and does not expect any substantial gain in the value of the security to compensate for the risk of loss. ... [T]he significant fact, *which accounts in part for the detailed protective provisions of the typical long-term debt financing instrument*, is that *the lender (the purchaser of the debt security) can expect only interest at the prescribed rate plus the eventual return of the principal.* Except for possible increases in the market value of the debt security because of changes in interest rates, the debt security will seldom be worth more than the lender paid for it. ... It may, of course, become worth much less. Accordingly, the typical investor in a long-term debt security is primarily interested in every reasonable assurance that the principal and interest

A. Leveraged Buyouts, Going Private, and Other Transactions

will be paid when due. . . . Short of bankruptcy, *the debt security holder can do nothing to protect himself against actions of the borrower which jeopardize its ability to pay the debt unless he . . . establishes his rights through contractual provisions set forth in the debt agreement or indenture.*

Id. at 1-2 (1971) (emphasis added).

A review of the parties' submissions and the indentures themselves satisfies the Court that the substantive "fruits" guaranteed by those contracts and relevant to the present motions include the periodic and regular payment of interest and the eventual repayment of principal. *See, e.g.,* Bradley Aff. Exh. L, §3.1 ("The Issuer covenants . . . that it will duly and punctually pay . . . the principal of, and interest on, each of the Securities . . . at the respective times and in the manner provided in such Securities. . . ."). According to a typical indenture, a default shall occur if the company either (1) fails to pay principal when due; (2) fails to make a timely sinking fund payment; (3) fails to pay within 30 days of the due date thereof any interest on the date; or (4) fails duly to observe or perform any of the express covenants or agreements set forth in the agreement. *See, e.g.,* Brad. Aff. Exh. L, §5.1. Plaintiffs' Amended Complaint nowhere alleges that RJR Nabisco has breached these contractual obligations; interest payments continue and there is no reason to believe that the principal will not be paid when due.

It is not necessary to decide that indentures like those at issue could never support a finding of additional benefits, under different circumstances with different parties. Rather, for present purposes, it is sufficient to conclude what obligation is *not* covered, either explicitly or implicitly, by these contracts held by these plaintiffs. Accordingly, this Court holds that the "fruits" of these indentures do not include an implied restrictive covenant that would prevent the incurrence of new debt to facilitate the recent LBO. To hold otherwise would permit these plaintiffs to straightjacket the company in order to guarantee their investment. These plaintiffs do not invoke an implied covenant of good faith to protect a legitimate, mutually contemplated benefit of the indentures; rather, they seek to have this Court create an additional benefit for which they did not bargain.

. . . While the Court stands ready to employ an implied covenant of good faith to ensure that such bargained-for rights are performed and upheld, it will not, however, permit an implied covenant to shoehorn into an indenture additional terms plaintiffs now wish had been included. *See also Broad v. Rockwell International Corp.*, 642 F.2d 929 (5th Cir.) (*en banc*) (applying New York law), *cert. denied*, 454 U.S. 965, 102 S. Ct. 506, 70 L. Ed. 2d 380 (1981) (finding no liability pursuant to an implied covenant where the terms of the indenture, as bargained for, were enforced).

Plaintiffs argue in the most general terms that the fundamental basis of all these indentures was that an LBO along the lines of the recent RJR Nabisco transaction would never be undertaken, that indeed *no* action would be taken, intentionally or not, that would significantly deplete the company's assets. Accepting plaintiffs' theory, their fundamental bargain with defendants dictated that nothing would be done to jeopardize the extremely high probability that the company would remain able to make interest payments and repay principal over the 20 to 30 year indenture term — and perhaps by logical extension even included the right to ask a court "to make sure that plaintiffs had made a good investment." *Gardner*, 589 F. Supp. at 674. But as Judge Knapp aptly concluded in *Gardner* "Defendants . . . were under a duty to carry out the terms of the contract, but not to make sure that plaintiffs had made a good investment. The former they have done; the latter we have no jurisdiction over." *Id*. Plaintiffs' submissions and MetLife's previous undisputed internal memoranda remind the Court that a "fundamental basis" or a "fruit of an agreement" is often in the eye of the beholder, whose vision may well change along with the market, and who may, with hindsight, imagine a different bargain than the one he actually and initially accepted with open eyes.

The sort of unbounded and one-sided elasticity urged by plaintiffs would interfere with and destabilize the market. And this Court, like the parties to these contracts, cannot ignore or disavow the marketplace in which the contract is performed. Nor can it ignore the expectations of that market — expectations, for instance, that the terms of an indenture will be upheld, and that a court will not, *sua sponte*, add new substantive terms to that indenture as it sees fit.[26] The Court has no reason to believe that the market, in evaluating bonds such as those at issue here, did not discount for the possibility that any company, even one the size of RJR Nabisco, might engage in an LBO heavily financed by debt. That the bonds did not lose any of their value until the October 20, 1988, announcement of a possible RJR Nabisco LBO only suggests that the market had theretofore evaluated the risks of such a transaction as slight.

The Court recognizes that the market is not a static entity, but instead involves what plaintiffs call "evolving understanding[s]." P. Opp. at 21. Just as the growing prevalence of LBO's has helped change certain ground rules and expectations in the field of mergers and acquisitions, so too it has obviously affected the bond market, a fact no one disputes. *See, e.g.*, Chappell Dep. at 136 ("I think we would have been extremely naive not to understand what was happening in the marketplace."). To support their

---

26. *Cf. Broad v. Rockwell*, 642 F.2d at 943 ("Not least among the parties 'who must comply with or refer to the indenture' are the members of the investing public and their investment advisors. A large degree of uniformity in the language of debenture indentures is essential to the effective functioning of the financial markets: uniformity of the indentures that govern competing debenture issues is what makes it possible meaningfully to compare one debenture issue with another, focusing only on the business provisions of the issue. . . .") (citation omitted); *Sharon Steel Corporation v. Chase Manhattan Bank, N.A.*, 691 F.2d 1039, 1048 (2d Cir. 1982) (Winter, J.) ("[U]niformity in interpretation is important to the efficiency of capital markets. . . . . [T]he creation of enduring uncertainties as to the meaning of boilerplate provisions would decrease the value of all debenture issues and greatly impair the efficient working of capital markets.").

argument that defendants have violated an implied covenant, plaintiffs contend that, since the October 20, 1988, announcement, the bond market has "stopped functioning." They argue that if they had "sold and abandoned the market [before October 20, 1988], the market, if everyone had the same attitude, would have disappeared." What plaintiffs term "stopped functioning" or "disappeared," however, are properly seen as natural responses and adjustments to market realities. Plaintiffs of course do not contend that no new issues are being sold, or that existing issues are no longer being traded or have become worthless.

To respond to changed market forces, new indenture provisions can be negotiated, such as provisions that were in fact once included in the 8.9 percent and 10.25 percent debentures implicated by this action. New provisions could include special debt restrictions or change-of-control covenants. There is no guarantee, of course, that companies like RJR Nabisco would accept such new covenants; parties retain the freedom to enter into contracts as they choose. But presumably, multi-billion dollar investors like plaintiffs have some say in the terms of the investments they make and continue to hold. And, presumably, companies like RJR Nabisco need the infusions of capital such investors are capable of providing.

Whatever else may be true about this case, it certainly does not present an example of the classic sort of form contract or contract of adhesion often frowned upon by courts. In those cases, what motivates a court is the strikingly inequitable nature of the parties' respective bargaining positions. *See generally*, Rakoff, *Contracts of Adhesion: An Essay in Reconstruction*, 96 HARV. L. REV. 1173 (1982). Plaintiffs here entered this "liquid trading market," with their eyes open and were free to leave at any time. Instead they remained there notwithstanding its well understood risks.

Ultimately, plaintiffs cannot escape the inherent illogic of their argument. On the one hand, it is undisputed that investors like plaintiffs recognized that companies like RJR Nabisco strenuously opposed additional restrictive covenants that might limit the incurrence of new debt or the company's ability to engage in a merger. Furthermore, plaintiffs argue that they had no choice other than to accept the indentures as written, without additional restrictive covenants, or to "abandon" the market. Tr. at 14-15.

Yet on the other hand, plaintiffs ask this Court to imply a covenant that would have just that restrictive effect because, they contend, it reflects precisely the fundamental assumption of the market and the fundamental basis of their bargain with defendants. If that truly were the case here, it is difficult to imagine why an insistence on that term would have forced the plaintiffs to abandon the market. The Second Circuit has offered a better explanation: "[a] promise by the defendant should be implied only if the court may rightfully assume that the parties would have included it in their written agreement had their attention been called to it.... *Any such assumption in this case would be completely unwarranted.* "Neuman v. Pike, 591 F.2d 191, 195 (2d Cir. 1979) (emphasis added, citations omitted).

In the final analysis, plaintiffs offer no objective or reasonable standard for a court to use in its effort to define the sort of actions their "implied covenant" would permit a corporation to take, and those it would not.[28] Plaintiffs say only that investors like themselves rely upon the "skill" and "good faith" of a company's board and management, see, e.g., P. Mem. at 35, and that their covenant would prevent the company from "destroy [ing] . . . the legitimate expectations of its long-term bondholders." Id. at 54. As is clear from the preceding discussion, however, plaintiffs have failed to convince the Court that by upholding the explicit, bargained-for terms of the indenture, RJR Nabisco has either exhibited bad faith or destroyed plaintiffs' *legitimate,* protected expectations.

. . . It is also not to say that defendants were free willfully or knowingly to misrepresent or omit material facts to sell their bonds. Relief on claims based on such allegations would of course be available to plaintiffs, if appropriate — but those claims properly sound in fraud, and come with requisite elements. Plaintiffs also remain free to assert their claims based on the fraudulent conveyance laws, which similarly require specific proof. Those burdens cannot be avoided by resorting to an overbroad, superficially appealing, but legally insufficient, implied covenant of good faith and fair dealing.

. . . [P]laintiffs advance a claim that remains based, their assertions to the contrary notwithstanding, on an alleged breach of a fiduciary duty. Defendants go to great lengths to prove that the law of Delaware, and not New York, governs this question. Defendants' attempt to rely on Delaware law is readily explained by even a cursory reading of *Simons v. Cogan,* 549 A.2d 300, 303 (Del. 1988), the recent Delaware Supreme Court ruling which held, *inter alia,* that a corporate bond "represents a contractual entitlement to the repayment of a debt and does not represent an equitable interest in the issuing corporation necessary for the imposition of a trust relationship with concomitant fiduciary duties." Before such a fiduciary duty arises, "an existing property right or equitable interest supporting such a duty must exist." *Id.* at 304. A bondholder, that court concluded, "acquires no equitable interest, and remains a creditor of the corporation whose interests are protected by the contractual terms of the indenture." *Id.* . . .

Regardless, this Court finds *Simons* persuasive, and believes that a New York court would agree with that conclusion. In the venerable case of *Meinhard v. Salmon,* 249 N.Y. 458, 164 N.E. 545 (1928), then Chief Judge Cardozo explained the obligations imposed on a fiduciary, and why those obligations are so special and rare:

---

28. Under plaintiffs' theory, bondholders might ask a court to prohibit a company like RJR Nabisco not only from engaging in an LBO, but also from entering a new line of business — with the attendant costs of building new physical plants and hiring new workers — or from acquiring new businesses such as RJR Nabisco did when it acquired Del Monte.

> Many forms of conduct permissible in a workaday world for those acting at arm's length, are forbidden to those bound by fiduciary ties. A trustee is held to something stricter than the morals of the market place. Not honesty alone, but the punctilio of an honor the most sensitive, is then the standard of behavior. As to this there has developed a tradition that is unbending and inveterate. Uncompromising rigidity has been the attitude of courts of equity when petitioned to undermine the rule of undivided loyalty. . . . Only thus has the level of conduct for fiduciaries been kept at a level higher than that trodden by the crowd.

Id. at 464 (citation omitted). Before a court recognizes the duty of a "punctilio of an honor the most sensitive," it must be certain that the complainant is entitled to more than the "morals of the market place," and the protections offered by actions based on fraud, state statutes or the panoply of available federal securities laws. This Court has concluded that the plaintiffs presently before it — sophisticated investors who are unsecured creditors — are not entitled to such additional protections.

Equally important, plaintiffs' position on this issue — that "A Company May Not Deliberately Deplete its Assets to the Injury of its Debtholders," — provides no reasonable or workable limits, and is thus reminiscent of their implied covenant of good faith. Indeed, many indisputably legitimate corporate transactions would not survive plaintiffs' theory. With no workable limits, plaintiffs' envisioned duty would extend equally to trade creditors, employees, and every other person to whom the defendants are liable in any way. Of all such parties, these informed plaintiffs least require a Court's equitable protection; not only are they willing participants in a largely impersonal market, but they also possess the financial sophistication and size to secure their own protection.

5. HCA's LBO as a Case Study

In 2006, HCA, Inc. went private in a $33 billion transaction eclipsing RJR Nabisco as the largest LBO until that time. Alluding to that earlier deal, the *Wall Street Journal* headlined its story "Barbarians at the Bedside: How Wall Street Securities Firms Plan to Profit in HCA Hospitals; Juggling Many Roles in Buyout."

The company. Founded in 1968 by two Nashville doctors — Drs. Thomas Frist Sr. & Jr. — and former Kentucky Fried Chicken Company developer, Jack Massey, Hospital Corporation of America brought a new business model to hospitals. In 1969, the company went public with 11 hospitals and developed a national chain of for-profit hospitals. Along the way, the company had gone private once before and then returned to public ownership again with a public offering. At the time of the deal, it was among the largest healthcare service providers in the United States with revenues of almost $25 billion. It operated almost

180 hospitals and more than 100 free-standing surgery centers in 21 states, England, and Switzerland.

The financial context. Why would a deal be discussed? In the period leading up to the transaction, company management and their advisors had devoted substantial attention to strategies to increase market value and to utilize the cash flow being generated by operations. The company had made capital investments of $8 billion over the previous five years. It had announced 10 divestitures of non-core assets in the previous calendar year. The management had focused on improving operations, particularly patient safety and quality. Specifically, the company had addressed patient migration to outpatient servers over hospital stays with a $260 million investment over two years. In terms of using the cash flow, the company had increased its dividend an average of 17 percent over the prior two years, and the company had itself repurchased more than $8 billion in shares over the previous five years, including a Dutch auction completed the previous November.

The market's reaction to the firm's strategy. Investment bankers advising the company noted that the prior efforts "didn't move the needle" in terms of market response to the company's value-increasing efforts. More generally, analysts following the hospital sector were negative on its then current prospects. One analyst, for example, observed, "hospital trends are still weak and we are certainly not willing to call a rebound." The bottom line was that public markets seemed to not be rewarding HCA for its strategy and cash flow.

Strategic alternatives. The company and its advisers had several financial options. One would be acquisition, of another public hospital company or various not-for-profits that had historically dominated the hospital market, or international growth or ancillary businesses. There were only a few other public hospital companies, limiting the options and increasing possible antitrust concerns. The industry had gone through a long period of not-for-profits consolidating with some traditional providers getting out of the business, such that the number of possible targets was less than in earlier periods. The company had already moved into the ancillary business of free-standing surgery centers and had some international operations, but growth prospects did not appear relatively strong. If, instead, the management were to make cash generation their focus, they could consider divesting non-core hospitals, a spinoff of outpatient centers, or even spinning off the hospital company itself.

The LBO alternative. In evaluating the LBO, the company assessed how critical was the public market to HCA. Over the prior few years, the company had been a net buyer not a seller in the public markets. If not publicly traded, a company loses the opportunity to use its stock as an acquisition currency, but as discussed above, that seemed to be a limited opportunity for HCA at the time. More generally, there seemed to be limits on the amount of leverage the company could take in a public market. Going private would permit management to be unleashed from a quarterly focus on financial results from analysts and others. Communication was likely to be easier with a small group of sophisticated lenders than a public market that includes activist shareholders. More generally, it was a favorable borrowing climate to add leverage with rates at historical lows and a likely supply of bankers willing to lend. The growth of mega funds in private equity provided more firms able to do big deals.

How big would the price be in an LBO? The firm's investment bankers were thinking of a post-deal capital structure something like the following:

Source of Capital	Amount (in millions)	
Term Debt	$11,600	
Euro Loan	1,250	
ABL Facility	1,750	
High Yield Notes	5,700	
Existing Debt	7,700	
Total Debt	$28,000	(85%)
Sponsor Equity	4,200	
Management & Family	800	
Total Equity	$ 5,000	(15%)

Where would the value come from in such a transaction? In effect, such a deal would replace $41 billion in public equity with $5 billion in private equity and a lot of new debt. The company's ratio of debt to earnings, using the EBITDA measure, would rise from 2.8 to 6.5. It would be important to pay down debt, both from the company's cash flow and from selected divestitures and other monetization strategies. In addition, the sponsors would likely want a dividend and would likely anticipate a future public offering of the stock.

The players. The company's investment banker was Merrill Lynch. The "sponsors" who would provide the private equity, determined after a small team of management and the IB talked with potential investors, included two well-known private equity firms, KKR and Bain Investments, and a unit of Merrill Lynch. The banks that provided the bank financing included Bank of America, Citigroup, and a subsidiary of Merrill Lynch. The equity investors eventually included top management of the company, including CEO and chair Jack Bovender and board member

Dr. Thomas Frist, Jr. from the founding family. Other than Bovender, the company's board was made up of independent directors with broad business, financial, and public policy experience. The company's counsel was James Cheek, a well-regarded corporate practitioner. The board's special committee that was eventually appointed was represented by Credit Suisse First Boston and Morgan Stanley on the financial side and Shearman & Sterling on the legal side.

The time line.

- *April 5:* Senior management and Merrill Lynch meet.
- *April 11:* Management/IB team meets with a small group of private equity firms.
- *May 3:* Sponsors report to management that LBO is doable and request permission to do due diligence.
- *May 24-25:* Board of directors meets and approves such an exploration.
- *June 30:* Sponsors signal definitive offer is forthcoming and board of directors forms a special committee.
- *July 11:* The sponsors and the board's special committee meet and discuss valuation.
- *July 14-18:* Sponsors and the special committee negotiate.
  - *7/14 Sponsors at $48.75* (compared to market in the high $30s)
  - *7/17 Committee: "pencils down"* until significantly higher offer
  - *7/17 Sponsors at $50.50*
  - *7/18 Committee: would consider a proposal of $52*
  - *7/18 (evening) Sponsors: $50.75 as best and final offer*
  - *7/18 (evening) Committee: $51—Take it or Leave it*
  - *7/18 (midnight) Sponsors: Deal*
- *July 19-21:* Lawyers draft a merger agreement.
- *July 23-24:* Special committee approves, and the following day the full board approves.
- *July-mid Sept:* "Go Shop" period.

Legal Issues and how to address them. What legal issues are likely to come up and how would you address them?

Given what you have already studied about LBOs, wouldn't it be likely that sponsors would want to involve managers in the new venture? In light of the financial context described above and management's previous efforts to increase value, how would you deal with some of management's potential conflict of interest at a point in time when the question is whether a LBO is a feasible or likely to be the best alternative?

A. *Leveraged Buyouts, Going Private, and Other Transactions* **515**

Who should be on the special committee of the board, and when should such a group be appointed? Should the committee hear the views of Dr. Frist, who is to be part of the equity group but is also an iconic figure in the history of the company?

Are there *Revlon* duties for the board? How long a go shop period, if any, would you think would be appropriate? What about termination fees and other potential lock-ups?

What do you make of Merrill Lynch's multiple roles? Should the company have had another investment banker or one less sponsor or lender?

Antitrust allegations. The HCA generated an antitrust claim directed to the behavior of private equity firms. In 2013 a federal district court denied summary judgment claims against eight private equity firms and let claims go forward alleging an agreement to refrain from jumping each other's proprietary deals. Dahl v. Bain Capital Partners LLC, 2013 WL 3802433 (July 18, 2003) and 937 F. Supp. 2d 119 (D. Mass. March 13, 2013):

> As a general overview, the Freescale and HCA transactions involved two consortiums: Consortium #1, which included Blackstone, Carlyle, and TPG; and Consortium #2, which included KKR and Bain. In late July of 2006, Consortium #2 was negotiating a proprietary deal for HCA. The evidence, in the light most favorable to the Plaintiffs, showed that KKR had "asked the industry to step down on HCA" and, despite strong interest in the company, Goldman Sachs, Blackstone, Carlyle, and TPG promptly "stood down" after the deal was signed.
>
> The evidence further showed that in September of 2006, Consortium #1 was close to securing a deal to purchase Freescale when Consortium #2's KKR and Bain, along with Silver Lake, sent an indication of interest to the Freescale Board, disrupting Consortium #1's deal. The Consortium #1 Defendants, shocked by Bain, KKR, and Silver Lake's action, began considering mounting, as retaliation, a competing bid for HCA. Due to the threat of the competing bids, the consortiums communicated with each other and abruptly "stood down" from each other's deals.
>
> As to Count Two. . . . [the court concluded the] evidence establishes that [Goldman Sachs, Carlyle, TPG, and Blackstone] showed interest in the HCA transaction, but promptly "stepped down" from making a topping bid within 48 hours of the commencement of the fifty-day "go-shop" period. The evidence further shows that [Goldman Sachs, Carlyle, TPG, and Blackstone] communicated their decision to "step down" on HCA to [KKR and Bain] within ninety-six hours of the commencement of the "go shop" period and subsequently lamented having forgone a potentially lucrative deal. Dahl, 2013 WL 950992 at *16.The Court also found that two statements suggested that Goldman Sachs, Carlyle, TPG, and Blackstone were acting pursuant to a prior agreement to refrain from "jumping" HCA.. The first statement was made during an intra-office email exchange between executives of Carlyle after they had learned that Consortium #2 had decided to compete for Freescale. The statement reads, "[a]nd just think, KKR asked the industry to step down on HCA." The Court held that this statement was significant because, in light of the fact that each Defendant promptly "stepped down" after the deal was signed and announced, it indicated that there was a prior agreement to refrain from "jumping" HCA. *Id.* The Court further noted that "the shock conveyed in the statement by the Carlyle

executive at KKR's decision to pursue Freescale indicates that KKR's decision was a breach of its agreement not to pursue Freescale."

The second statement was made by a Blackstone executive after Consortium #2 decided to pass on Freescale.. It reads, "Henry Kravis [of KKR] just called to say congratulations and that they were standing down because he had told me before they would not jump a signed deal of ours." The Court held that this statement suggested that there was a previous agreement not to "jump" Freescale and that KKR had ultimately decided to adhere to that agreement. *Id.* The Court also held that, in combination with the rest of the evidence, the statement provided an inference that the decision by Consortium #1 to "step down" on HCA was in exchange for KKR "stepping down" on Freescale..

As to Count One, the Court found that the evidence established a "larger picture" of an overarching conspiracy on the part of the Defendants to refrain from "jumping" each other's announced proprietary deals.. The Court singled out three fundamental pieces of evidence that connected the circumstances of the Freescale and HCA transactions to the overarching conspiracy . . . [that] indicated a continuous agreement across the proprietary deals. . . .

1. An email by a TPG executive regarding the Freescale transaction, stating that "KKR has agreed not to jump our deal since no one in private equity ever jumps an announced deal."
2. The fact that no Defendant ever "jumped" an announced proprietary deal during the "go-shop" period.
3. A Goldman Sachs executive's observation, upon learning that KKR had decided to withdraw from the Freescale transaction, that "club etiquette prevails."

The Court determined that the first two pieces of evidence indicated a uniformity of conduct within the industry to refrain from "jumping" each other's announced proprietary deals. The Court further held that the third piece of evidence indicated that such uniformity may not be the result of independent action because "the term 'club etiquette' denotes an accepted code of conduct between the Defendants."

2013 WL 3802433 at 3-4 (July 18, 2013) (on reconsideration in part August 29, 2013 dismissing two of the defendant firms).

The Subsequent IPO. In 2011, HCA did an IPO, although we probably need a new term to describe a firm doing an initial public offering for the third time. In March, the offering raised about $3.8 billion, about 30 percent for shares of the selling shareholders and the remainder for shares from the corporation. The shares sold at $30/share, at the high end of the anticipated $27-30 range for the offering; it was said to be the largest private equity based IPO in history. Several months before the IPO, the company had borrowed to pay owners a dividend of $2 billion, bringing the company's debt when it went public to about $28 billion. The amount sold by the selling shareholders was 18 percent of their holdings, which meant as of the time of the offering, they retained value of the new public company in the range of what they had invested in the going-private deal. They had received $4 billion in dividends in the year leading up to the public offering before the $2 billion dividend described above. *See generally,* Christine Alesi & Pat Wechsler, HCA Said to Seek as Much as $30/share, BLOOMBERG, February 8, 2011. Additional special dividends followed in 2012 for all shareholders including a majority still owned by the private equity funds and the family. *See* Anna Wilde Mathews, HCA Plans $1 Billion Payout to Holders, WALL STREET JOURNAL, October 17, 2012 at B8 c.6.

6. Topps *as a Case Study of the Overlap of Federal Disclosure and State Intermediate Scrutiny*

In re The Topps Co. Shareholders Litigation
926 A.2d 58 (Del. Ch. 2007)

STRINE, Vice Chancellor.

I. INTRODUCTION

The Topps Company, Inc. is familiar to all sports-loving Americans. Topps makes baseball and other cards (think Pokemon), this is Topps's so-called "Entertainment Business." It also distributes Bazooka bubble gum and other old-style confections, this is Topps's "Confectionary Business." Arthur Shorin, the son of Joseph Shorin, one of the founders of Topps and the inspiration for "Bazooka Joe," is Topps's current Chairman and Chief Executive Officer. Shorin has served in those positions since 1980 and has worked for Topps for more than half a century, though he owns only about 7% of Topps's equity. Shorin's son-in-law, Scott Silverstein, is his second-in-command, serving as Topps's President and Chief Operating Officer.

Despite its household name, Topps is not a large public company. Its market capitalization is less than a half billion dollars and its financial performance has, as a general matter, flagged over the past five years.

In 2005, Topps was threatened with a proxy contest. It settled that dispute by a promise to explore strategic options, including a sale of its Confectionary Business. Topps tried to auction off its Confectionary Business, but a serious buyer never came forward. Insurgents reemerged the next year, in a year when Shorin was among the three directors up for re-election to Topps's classified board. With the ballots about to be counted, and defeat a near certainty for the management nominees, Shorin cut a face-saving deal, which expanded the board to ten and involved his re-election along with the election of all of the insurgent nominees.

Before that happened, former Disney CEO and current private equity investor Michael Eisner had called Shorin and offered to be "helpful." Shorin understood Eisner to be proposing a going private transaction.

Once the insurgents were seated, an "Ad Hoc Committee" was formed of two insurgent directors and two "Incumbent Directors" to evaluate Topps's strategic direction. Almost immediately, the insurgent directors and the incumbent directors began to split on substantive and, it is fair to say, stylistic grounds. The insurgents then became "Dissident Directors."

In particular, the Ad Hoc Committee divided on the issue of whether and how Topps should be sold. The Dissident Directors waxed and waned on the advisability of a sale, but insisted that if a sale was to occur, it should involve a public auction process. The Incumbent Directors were also ambivalent about a sale, but were resistant to the idea that Topps should again begin an auction process, having already failed once in trying to auction its Confectionary Business.

From the time the insurgents were seated, Eisner was on the scene, expressing an interest in making a bid. Two other financial buyers also made a pass. But Topps's public message was that it was not for sale.

Eventually, the other bidders dropped out after making disappointingly low value expressions of interest. Eisner was told by a key Incumbent Director that the Incumbent Directors might embrace a bid of $10 per share. Eisner later bid $9.24 in a proposal that envisioned his retention of existing management, including Shorin's son-in-law. Eisner was willing to tolerate a post-signing Go Shop process, but not a pre-signing auction.

The Ad Hoc Committee split 2-2 over whether to negotiate with Eisner. Although offered the opportunity to participate in the negotiation process, the apparent leader of the Dissidents refused, favoring a public auction. One of the Incumbent Directors who was an independent director took up the negotiating oar, and reached agreement with Eisner on a merger at $9.75 per share. The "Merger Agreement" gave Topps the chance to shop the bid for 40 days after signing, and the right to accept a "Superior Proposal" after that, subject only to Eisner's receipt of a termination fee and his match right.

The Topps board approved the Merger Agreement in a divided vote, with the Incumbent Directors all favoring the Merger, and the Dissidents all dissenting. Because of the dysfunctional relations on the Ad Hoc Committee, that Committee was displaced from dealing with the Go Shop process by an Executive Committee comprised entirely of Incumbent Directors.

Shortly before the Merger Agreement was approved, Topps's chief competitor in the sports cards business, plaintiff The Upper Deck Company, expressed a willingness to make a bid. That likely came as no surprise to Topps since Upper Deck had indicated its interest in Topps nearly a year and half earlier. In fact, Upper Deck had expressed an unrequited ardor for a friendly deal with Topps since 1999, and Shorin knew that. But Topps signed the Merger Agreement with Eisner without responding to Upper Deck's overture. Shortly after the Merger was approved, Topps's investment banker began the Go Shop process, contacting more than 100 potential strategic and financial bidders, including Upper Deck, who was the only serious bidder to emerge.

A. Leveraged Buyouts, Going Private, and Other Transactions   519

Suffice it to say that Upper Deck did not move with the clarity and assiduousness one would ideally expect from a competitive rival seeking to make a topping bid. Suffice it also to say that Topps's own reaction to Upper Deck's interest was less than welcoming. Instead of an aggressive bidder and a hungry seller tangling in a diligent, expedited way over key due diligence and deal term issues, the story that emerges from the record is of a slow-moving bidder unwilling to acknowledge Topps's legitimate proprietary concerns about turning over sensitive information to its main competitor and a seller happy to have a bid from an industry rival go away, even if that bid promised the Topps's stockholders better value.

By the end of the Go Shop period, Upper Deck had expressed a willingness to pay $10.75 per share in a friendly merger, subject to its receipt of additional due diligence and other conditions. Although having the option freely to continue negotiations to induce an even more favorable topping bid by finding that Upper Deck's interest was likely to result in a Superior Proposal, the Topps board, with one Dissident Director dissenting, one abstaining, and one absent, voted not to make such a finding.

After the end of the Go Shop period, Upper Deck made another unsolicited overture, expressing a willingness to buy Topps for $10.75 without a financing contingency and with a strong come hell or high water promise to deal with manageable (indeed, mostly cosmetic) antitrust issues. The bid, however, limited Topps to a remedy for failing to close limited to a reverse break-up fee in the same amount ($12 million) Eisner secured as the only recourse against him. Without ever seriously articulating why Upper Deck's proposal for addressing the antitrust issue was inadequate and without proposing a specific higher reverse break-up fee, the Topps Incumbent Directors have thus far refused to treat Upper Deck as having presented a Superior Proposal, a prerequisite to putting the onus on Eisner to match that price or step aside.

In fact, Topps went public with a disclosure about Upper Deck's bid, but in a form that did not accurately represent that expression of interest and disparaged Upper Deck's seriousness. Topps did that knowing that it had required Upper Deck to agree to a contractual standstill (the "Standstill Agreement") prohibiting Upper Deck from making public any information about its discussions with Topps or proceeding with a tender offer for Topps shares without permission from the Topps board.

The Topps board has refused Upper Deck's request for relief from the Standstill Agreement in order to allow Upper Deck to make a tender offer and to tell its side of events. A vote on the Eisner Merger is scheduled to occur within a couple of weeks.

A group of "Stockholder Plaintiffs" and Upper Deck (collectively, the "moving parties") have moved for a preliminary injunction. They contend that the upcoming Merger vote will be tainted by Topps's failure to disclose material facts about the process that led to the Merger Agreement and about Topps's subsequent dealings with Upper Deck. Even more, they argue that Topps is denying its stockholders the chance to decide for themselves whether to forsake the lower-priced Eisner Merger in favor of the chance to accept a tender offer from Upper Deck at a higher price. Regardless of whether the Topps board prefers the Eisner Merger as lower risk, the moving parties contend that the principles animating *Revlon, Inc. v. MacAndrews & Forbes Holdings, Inc.* prevent the board from denying the stockholders the chance to make a mature, uncoerced decision for themselves.

In this decision, I conclude that a preliminary injunction against the procession of the Eisner Merger vote should issue until such time as: (1) the Topps board discloses several material facts not contained in the corporation's "Proxy Statement," including facts regarding Eisner's assurances that he would retain existing management after the Merger; and (2) Upper Deck is released from the standstill for purposes of: (a) publicly commenting on its negotiations with Topps; and (b) making a non-coercive tender offer on conditions as favorable or more favorable than those it has offered to the Topps board....

V. Resolution of the *Revlon* Claim and Decision on the Scope of the Injunction

... Most important, I do not believe that the substantive terms of the Merger Agreement suggest an unreasonable approach to value maximization. The Topps board did not accept Eisner's $9.24 bid. They got him up to $9.75 per share—not their desired goal but a respectable price, especially given Topps's actual earnings history and the precarious nature of its business.

Critical, of course, to my determination is that the Topps board recognized that they had not done a pre-signing market check. Therefore, they secured a 40-day Go Shop Period and the right to continue discussions with any bidder arising during that time who was deemed by the board likely to make a Superior Proposal. Furthermore, the advantage given to Eisner over later arriving bidders is difficult to see as unreasonable. He was given a match right, a useful deal protection for him, but one that has frequently been overcome in other real-world situations. Likewise, the termination fee and expense reimbursement he was to receive if Topps terminated and accepted another deal—an eventuality more likely to occur after the Go Shop Period expired than during it—was around 4.3% of the total deal value. Although this is a bit high in percentage terms, it includes Eisner's expenses, and therefore can be explained by the relatively small size of the deal. At 42 cents a share, the termination fee (including expenses) is not of the magnitude that I believe was likely to have deterred a bidder with an interest in materially outbidding Eisner. In fact, Upper Deck's expression of interest seems to prove that point—the termination fee is not even one of the factors it stresses.

Although a target might desire a longer Go Shop Period or a lower break fee, the deal protections the Topps board agreed to in the Merger Agreement seem to have left reasonable room for an effective post-signing market check. For 40 days, the Topps board could shop like Paris Hilton. Even after the Go Shop Period expired, the Topps board could entertain an unsolicited bid, and, subject to Eisner's match right, accept a Superior Proposal. The 40-day Go Shop Period and this later right work together, as they allowed interested bidders to talk to Topps and obtain information during the Go Shop Period with the knowledge that if they needed more time to decide whether to make a bid, they could lob in an unsolicited Superior Proposal after the Period expired and resume the process.

In finding that this approach to value maximization was likely a reasonable one, I also take into account the potential utility of having the proverbial bird in hand. Although it is true that having signed up with Eisner at $9.75 likely prevented Topps from securing another deal at $10, the $9.75 bird in hand might be thought useful in creating circumstances where other bidders would feel more comfortable paying something like Upper Deck now says it is willing to bid. Because a credible buying group—comprised not only of Eisner, an experienced buyer of businesses for Disney, but also the experienced private equity firm, Madison Dearborn—had promised to pay $9.75, other bidders could take some confidence in that and have some form of "sucker's insurance" for considering a bid higher than that. Human beings, for better or worse, like cover. We tend to feel better about being wrong, if we can say others made the same mistake. Stated more positively, recognizing our own limitations, we often, quite rationally, take comfort when someone whose acumen and judgment we respect validates our inclinations. A credible, committed first buyer serves that role.

In this regard, Topps's decision to enter into the Merger Agreement with Eisner despite its having received an unsolicited indication of interest from Upper Deck a few days before the signing was also likely not an unreasonable one. This is perhaps a closer call, but the suggestion of Dissident Director Brog to respond to Upper Deck only after inking the Eisner deal bolsters this conclusion. Although the facts on this point are less than clear, as discussed, Topps appears to have had rational reason to be suspicious of Upper Deck's sincerity. Upper Deck had made proposals before, but had often appeared flaky. Moreover, Upper Deck was only expressing an interest in the Entertainment Business, not the whole company at that point. A sale of the Entertainment Business would have left Topps with a floundering Confectionary Business that it had already tried to sell once, without success. Signing up a sure thing with Eisner forced Upper Deck to get serious about the whole company, and set a price floor that Upper Deck knew it had to beat by a material amount.

For all these reasons, I cannot buttress the issuance of an injunction on the alleged unreasonableness of the Topps's board decision to sign up the

Merger Agreement. I now turn to the more troubling claims raised, which are about the board's conduct after the Merger Agreement was consummated . . . [and after Upper Deck made] a formal bid for Topps at $10.75 per share two days before the close of the Go Shop. The Topps board had a fiduciary obligation to consider that bid in good faith and to determine whether it was a Superior Proposal or reasonably likely to lead to one. That is especially the case because the Topps board was duty bound to pursue the highest price reasonably attainable, given that they were recommending that the stockholders sell their shares to Eisner for cash.[26]

Because of the final-hour nature of the bid, the Topps board had to determine whether to treat Upper Deck as an Excluded Party under the Merger Agreement so that it could continue negotiations with it after the close of the Go Shop Period. The Topps board's decision not to do so strikes me as highly questionable. In reaching that conclusion, I recognize that Topps had legitimate concerns about Upper Deck's bid. Although there was no financing contingency in the proposal, Topps had reason for concern because Upper Deck has proposed to limit its liability under its proposed deal to $12 million in the event it was not able to close the transaction. Underlying Topps's skepticism of the seriousness of Upper Deck's proposal was perhaps the suspicion that Upper Deck was willing to pay $12 million simply to blow up Topps's deal with Eisner. Topps had to consider the possibility that Upper Deck was afraid that Eisner, by leveraging his reputation in the entertainment community, might be able to turn Topps into a stronger competitor than it had previously been.

Moreover, Upper Deck's initial proposal arguably did not address Topps's concerns that Upper Deck's proposal raised antitrust concerns. In its initial unsolicited overture to Topps before the Eisner deal was signed, Upper Deck acknowledged that there might be some antitrust issues associated with a merger of the two firms. Yet, in its initial bid, Upper Deck proposed placing virtually all of the antitrust risk on Topps. True, Topps had been down this road itself before, and won, but the lack of any more substantial antitrust assurance in Upper Deck's initial bid arguably gave Upper Deck too easy an out in the event that regulators raised even a minor objection because of the optics of the transaction.

That said, Upper Deck was offering a substantially higher price, and rather than responding to Upper Deck's proposal by raising these legitimate concerns, the Topps board chose to tie its hands by failing to declare Upper Deck an Excluded Party in a situation where it would have cost Topps nothing to do so. Eisner would have had no contractual basis to complain about a Topps board decision to treat Upper Deck as an Excluded Party in light of Upper Deck's 10% higher bid price.

Upper Deck's first bid may not have been a Superior Proposal. But Topps had no reason to believe that the terms of Upper Deck's bid were

---

26. *Revlon*, 506 A.2d at 184 n.16; *QVC*, 637 A.2d at 34.

A. Leveraged Buyouts, Going Private, and Other Transactions   523

non-negotiable, and it would have been reasonable for the Topps directors to have believed that their financing and antitrust concerns were manageable ones that could and, indeed, should have been capable of reasonable resolution in subsequent negotiating rounds. Topps could have gone back to Upper Deck with a proposal to increase the reverse termination fee and could have proposed a reasonable provision to deal with the antitrust concerns. By declaring Upper Deck an Excluded Party, the Topps board would have preserved maximum flexibility to negotiate freely with Upper Deck. The downside of such a declaration is hard to perceive.

The only advantage I can perceive from the decision not to continue talking with Upper Deck was if that decision was intended to signal Topps's insistence on a better bid that satisfied its concerns. But the behavior of the Topps's Incumbent Directors and their advisors, as revealed in this record, does not suggest such a motivation. The decision of Brog to abstain from the vote on that issue is an oddment, I admit, which lends support to the decision, but is consistent with the Dissident Directors' enigmatic behavior and possibly a refusal by Brog to vote on the issue, given his exclusion from the sale process. The reason I remain troubled by the decision is that the behavior of the Topps Incumbent Directors after this point inspires no confidence that their prior actions were motivated by a desire to advance the interests of Topps stockholders.

Upper Deck came back a month later with an improved unsolicited bid. That bid again offered a price materially higher than Eisner's: $10.75 per share. That bid also was, again, not any more financially contingent than Eisner's bid; there was no financial contingency, but Topps's remedy was limited to a $12 million reverse break-up fee. This time, to address Topps's antitrust concerns, Upper Deck offered a strong "come hell or high water" provision offering to divest key licenses if required by antitrust regulators, as well as an opinion by a respected antitrust expert addressing Topps's still unspecified antitrust concerns.

Although the Topps Incumbent Directors did obtain a waiver from Eisner to enter discussions with Upper Deck about this bid, they did not pursue the potential for higher value with the diligence and genuineness expected of directors seeking to get the best value for stockholders. Topps made no reasonable counter-offer on the antitrust issue and failed to identify why the transaction proposed a genuine antitrust concern. Instead, Topps insisted that Upper Deck agree to accept any condition, however extreme, proposed by antitrust regulators, and Topps never acknowledged its own past antitrust victories. Although Topps felt free to negotiate price with Eisner when he was promising to pay a materially lower price, cap his liability at $12 million, and condition his deal on approval by Topps licensors (which Upper Deck did not), it never made reasonable suggestions to Upper Deck about a higher reverse break-up fee, antitrust issues, or price. Furthermore, although it did a deal with Eisner with only very limited remedial recourse if he breached, largely one senses, because of the reputational damage Eisner would suffer if he failed to close, the Topps board never seems to have taken into account the reputational damage Upper Deck would suffer if it did the same, despite its knowledge that Upper Deck has acquired other businesses in the past (remember Fleer?) and may therefore wish to continue to do so.

This behavior is consistent with a record that indicates that Shorin was never enthusiastic about the idea of having his family company end up in the hands of an upstart rival. That possible motivation is one that I do not approach in the same reductivist manner as the moving parties. Quite frankly, neither of the moving parties has made the case that Shorin and Silverstein are not skilled, competent, hard-working executives. More important, it is often the case that founders (and sons of founders) believe that their businesses stand for something more than their stock price. Founders therefore often care how their family legacy—in the form of a corporate culture that treats workers and consumers well, or a commitment to product quality—will fare if the corporation is placed under new stewardship.

The record before me clearly evidences Shorin's diffidence toward Upper Deck and his comparatively much greater enthusiasm for doing a deal with Eisner. Eisner's deal is premised on continuity of management and involvement of the Shorin family in the firm's business going forward. Upper Deck is in the same business line and does not need Shorin or his top managers.

Although Shorin and the other defendants claim that they truly desire to get the highest value and want nothing more than to get a topping bid from Upper Deck that they can accept, their behavior belies those protestations. In reaching that conclusion, I rely not only on the defendants' apparent failure to undertake diligent good faith efforts at bargaining with Upper Deck, I also rely on the misrepresentations of fact about Upper Deck's offer that are contained in Topps's public statements.

This raises the related issue of how the defendants have used the Standstill. Standstills serve legitimate purposes. When a corporation is running a sale process, it is responsible, if not mandated, for the board to ensure that confidential information is not misused by bidders and advisors whose interests are not aligned with the corporation, to establish rules of the game that promote an orderly auction, and to give the corporation leverage to extract concessions from the parties who seek to make a bid.[28]

But standstills are also subject to abuse. Parties like Eisner often, as was done here, insist on a standstill as a deal protection. Furthermore, a standstill can be used by a target improperly to favor one bidder over another, not

---

28. Contemplate, for example, a final round auction involving three credible, but now tired bidders, who emerged from a broad market canvass. One can easily imagine how a board striving in good faith to extract the last dollar they could for their stockholders might promise the three remaining bidders that the top bidder at 8:00 P.M. on the next Friday will get very strong deal protections including a promise from the target not to waive the Standstill as to the losers.

for reasons consistent with stockholder interest, but because managers prefer one bidder for their own motives.

In this case, the Topps board reserved the right to waive the Standstill if its fiduciary duties required. That was an important thing to do, given that there was no shopping process before signing with Eisner.

The fiduciary out here also highlights a reality. Although the Standstill is a contract, the Topps board is bound to use its contractual power under that contract only for proper purposes. On this record, I am convinced that Upper Deck has shown a reasonable probability of success on its claim that the Topps board is misusing the Standstill. As I have indicated, I cannot read the record as indicating that the Topps board is using the Standstill to extract reasonable concessions from Upper Deck in order to unlock higher value. The Topps board's negotiating posture and factual misrepresentations are more redolent of pretext, than of a sincere desire to comply with their *Revlon* duties.

Frustrated with its attempt to negotiate with Topps, Upper Deck asked for a release from the Standstill to make a tender offer on the terms it offered to Topps and to communicate with Topps's stockholders. The Topps board refused. That refusal not only keeps the stockholders from having the chance to accept a potentially more attractive higher priced deal, it keeps them in the dark about Upper Deck's version of important events, and it keeps Upper Deck from obtaining antitrust clearance, because it cannot begin the process without either a signed merger agreement or a formal tender offer.

Because the Topps board is recommending that the stockholders cash out, its decision to foreclose its stockholders from receiving an offer from Upper Deck seems likely, after trial, to be found a breach of fiduciary duty. If Upper Deck makes a tender at $10.75 per share on the conditions it has outlined, the Topps stockholders will still be free to reject that offer if the Topps board convinces them it is too conditional. Indeed, Upper Deck is not even asking for some sort of prior restraint preventing the Topps board from implementing a rights plan in the event of a tender offer (although Upper Deck has indicated that will begin round two of this litigation if Topps does). What Upper Deck is asking for is release from the prior restraint on it, a prior restraint that prevents Topps's stockholders from choosing another higher-priced deal. Given that the Topps board has decided to sell the company, and is not using the Standstill Agreement for any apparent legitimate purpose, its refusal to release Upper Deck justifies an injunction. Otherwise, the Topps stockholders may be foreclosed from ever considering Upper Deck's offer, a result that, under our precedent, threatens irreparable injury.

Similarly, Topps went public with statements disparaging Upper Deck's bid and its seriousness but continues to use the Standstill to prevent Upper Deck from telling its own side of the story. The Topps board seeks to have the Topps stockholders accept Eisner's bid without hearing the full story. That is not a proper use of a standstill by a fiduciary given the circumstances presented here. Rather, it threatens the Topps stockholders with making an important decision on an uninformed basis, a threat that justifies injunctive relief.

As this reasoning recognizes, one danger of an injunction based on the Topps board's refusal to waive the Standstill is that it will reduce the board's leverage to bargain with Upper Deck. Because this record suggests no genuine desire by the board to use the Standstill for that purpose, that danger is minimal. To address it, however, the injunction I will issue will not allow Upper Deck to go backwards as it were. The Merger vote will be enjoined until after Topps has granted Upper Deck a waiver of the Standstill to: (1) make an all shares, non-coercive tender offer of $10.75 cash or more per share, on conditions as to financing and antitrust no less favorable to Topps than contained in Upper Deck's most recent offer; and (2) communicate with Topps stockholders about its version of relevant events.

The other danger of an injunction of this kind is premised on a fear that stockholders will make an erroneous decision. In this regard, it is notable that nothing in this decision purports to compel the Topps board to enter a merger agreement with Upper Deck that it believes to be unduly conditional. What this decision does conclude is that, on this record, there is no reasonable basis for permitting the Topps board to deny its stockholders the chance to consider for themselves whether to prefer Upper Deck's higher-priced deal, taking into account its unique risks, over Eisner's lower-priced deal, which has its own risks.[31] If the Topps board sees the Upper Deck tender offer and believes it should not be accepted, it can tell the stockholders why. It can even consider the use of a rights plan to prevent the tender offer's procession, if it can square use of such a plan with its obligations under *Revlon* and *Unocal*. But it cannot at this point avoid an injunction on the unsubstantiated premise that the Topps stockholders will be unable, after the provision of full information, rationally to decide for themselves between two competing, non-coercive offers.

NOTES AND QUESTIONS

1. Voting, selling, or appraisal to cure breaches of fiduciary duty. Vice Chancellor Strine found it sufficiently likely, for purposes of meeting the preliminary injunction standard, that the board's decision to foreclose its stockholders from receiving an offer from Upper Deck would be

---

31. *See, e.g., Revlon,* 506 A.2d at 184 ("[W]hen bidders make relatively similar offers, or dissolution of the company becomes inevitable, the directors cannot fulfill their enhanced *Unocal* duties by playing favorites with the contending factions. Market forces must be allowed to operate freely to bring the target's shareholders the best price available for their equity."); *see also Robert M. Bass Group, Inc. v. Evans,* 552 A.2d 1227, 1242 (Del. Ch. 1988).

A. Leveraged Buyouts, Going Private, and Other Transactions

a breach of fiduciary duty under *Revlon*. What then should be the remedy? Money damages? For the board to accept the Upper Deck deal? The court's focus here was on letting shareholders decide for themselves, which would mean voting down the Eisner offer if they wished, and tendering into Upper Deck's higher offer. Why wouldn't a poison pill prevent such shareholder action? At the subsequent shareholders' meeting, the Eisner transaction (providing $9.75) received the approval of 65 percent of shares represented at the meeting, making up 53 percent of the outstanding shares.

The ability of shareholder voting to cure possible *Revlon* deficiencies was more starkly presented in a case that same year, In re Netsmart, Inc. Securities Litigation, 924 A. 2d 171, 175 (Del. Ch. 2007). There, Vice Chancellor Strine found that management's discussion with four possible private equity bidders, but no possible strategic bidders, was likely a *Revlon* violation. But the court was unwilling to require a search for a strategic bidder where the delay would pose a risk that the existing financial bidder would walk away or materially lower its bid. Voting, rather than judicially imposed director conduct, was preferred, "If [the shareholders] are confident that the company's prospects are sound and that a search for a strategic buyer or higher-paying financial buyer will bear fruit, they can vote no and take the risk of being wrong."

In litigation involving the *Caremark/CVS/Express Scripts* acquisition battle, Chancellor Chandler similarly emphasized ensuring a fully informed shareholder vote, La. Municipal Police Employees' Retirement Sys. v. Crawford, 918 A. 2d 1172 (Del Ch. 2007). In that case, the management of Caremark, a leading pharmacy benefits manager, entered into a merger of equals with CVS, American's largest retail pharmacy, choosing that deal over an alternative proposed by Express Scripts, another large pharmacy benefits manager. Why might Caremark managers prefer the CVS deal? The vertical combination had the obvious advantage to the Caremark managers in that the two management teams had agreed that each would continue to run their own businesses in the combined entity. How should such a possibility be checked? The focus of the court was insuring the shareholder's fully informed vote, emphasizing the value of "permitting informed shareholders to speak directly to their fiduciaries without further intervention by this Court." *Id*. at 1192. At the same time, the court placed great faith in appraisal to cure any remaining problems with the process, at least at the preliminary injunction stage. The court found that the $6 special dividend which CVS authorized Caremark to pay before the transaction in order to compete with the higher Express Scripts offer destroyed the exclusion from appraisal rights that the initial transaction had possessed as a pure stock-for-stock merger such that the vote had to be enjoined for failure to give the shareholders the statutorily required notice of their appraisal rights. Appraisal and the ability of the shareholders to vote in a fully informed fashion, in the court's view, permitted shareholder self-help and tempered the need for judicial intervention. *But see Netsmart* (suggesting appraisal more important in a micro-cap company without a full market check as opposed to a full market check in a larger company where market price would be deemed more reliable in an appraisal proceeding).

2. Disclosure in state law fiduciary duty contexts. In the *Netsmart* opinion discussed in the previous note, Vice Chancellor Strine stated his willingness to "throw the injunction flag" where there has not been complete disclosure, such that "the stockholders are about to make a decision on materially misleading or incomplete information . . . [so that] the stockholders' chance to engage in self-help on the front end would have been vitiated and lost forever." 924 A.2d at 208. The vice chancellor preferred voting over appraisal action, preferring injunction where the disabling of the vote maximized shareholders having to resort to appraisal, "the crudest of judicial tools." *Id.* at 208.

While the remedy for inadequate disclosure at state law is nuanced, the obligation is more straightforward as set out by Vice Chancellor Strine in a portion of the *Topps* case not included in the excerpt above:

> When directors of a Delaware corporation seek approval for a merger, they have a duty to provide the stockholders with the material facts relevant to making an informed decision.[3] In that connection, the directors must also avoid making materially misleading disclosures, which tell a distorted rendition of events or obscure material facts.[4] In determining whether the directors have complied with their disclosure obligations, the court applies well-settled standards of materiality, familiar to practitioners of our law and federal securities law.[5]

Note the willingness of state courts to rely on federal standards of disclosure. But consider the examples in this setting as to how state courts make greater use of *Revlon* and *Unocal*.

B. LEVERAGED RECAPITALIZATIONS

It is possible to pursue a highly leveraged status without the company leaving publicly held status. Such transactions are termed leveraged recaps or

---

3. *E.g., Arnold v. Society for Savings Bancorp., Inc.*, 650 A.2d 1270, 1277 (Del. 1994).

4. *E.g., Emerald Partners v. Berlin*, 726 A.2d 1215, 1223 (Del. Supr. 1999) ("When stockholder action is requested, directors are required to provide shareholders with all information that is material to the action being requested and to provide a balanced truthful account of all matters disclosed in the communication with shareholders.") (quotation omitted).

5. *See, e.g., Rosenblatt v. Getty Oil Co.*, 493 A.2d 929, 944 (Del. 1985) (explaining that information is material if "there is a substantial likelihood that a reasonable investor would consider it important in deciding how to vote") (citing *TSC Industries, Inc. v. Northway, Inc.*, 426 U.S. 438, 449, 96 S. Ct. 2126, 48 L. Ed. 2d 757 (1976)).

B. Leveraged Recapitalizations

leveraged recapitalizations, such as the Interco deal discussed in Chapter 7 that was important in the development of the law's response to the poison pill.

In a leveraged recap, the company takes on a large debt via new borrowing and uses the cash to pay a large dividend to the equity holders. Recall that in *Interco* the company paid a cash dividend of $38.15 plus more than $23 (face value) in senior and junior subordinated debentures, preferred stock carrying a face value of $4.76 along with the remaining common stock (termed the "stub" since most of its value had disappeared as all the obligations just described were inserted with priority to the corporation's assets in front of the stock). Alternatively, the company could distribute senior securities to stockholders, which would provide them a cash flow, but with a different anticipated payout period. Having taken on such a debt, it is likely that the company will seek to monetize existing assets, as occurred in *Interco*, with the company agreeing to sell two of its four divisions, including the furniture chain that was the "crown jewel." Even before assets are sold, the effect of the recapitalization is to substantially reduce the company's free cash flow and constrain the possible empire building of management. It is also possible to issue managers additional shares to align their interests more like what would occur in a LBO.

As the Interco deal illustrates, a leveraged recapitalization can be an effective defensive tactic, although one that can have a "scorched earth" type of impact. The company remains a public company but likely has become much less attractive because it has consumed all of its cash and likely has used up all of the firm's debt capacity. In addition, the company now carries a much larger bankruptcy risk that would change the financial calculus of any bidders. In some circumstances, an Employee Stock Ownership Plan (ESOP) can be the entity that borrows or provides the cash for the recapitalization. Such an investor is often viewed as friendly to management and thus this is a potentially effective defensive tactic.

How will the courts respond to such actions? If you recall the structure introduced in Chapter 5, a court, when faced with a challenge to director action as a breach of fiduciary duty, will start with the deference of the business judgment rule unless self-dealing can be shown or a defensive tactic or sale of business that triggers the enhanced scrutiny under the *Unocal* or *Revlon* tests. Set out below is Chancellor Allen's analysis in the *Interco* case:

> ... [T]he appropriate test to determine whether these steps qualify for the deferential business judgment form of review is set forth in *Unocal*. Each of the steps quite clearly was taken defensively as part of a reaction to the Rales brothers' efforts to buy Interco, but neither is a self-dealing transaction of the classic sort.
>
> As to the sale of Ethan Allen, I conclude that that step does appear clearly to be reasonable in relation to the threat posed by the CCA offer. Above I indicated that it was the case that one could regard either of these alternatives as the more desirable, depending upon one's liquidity preference, expectation about future events, etc. The

board itself was, of course, supplied with specific expert advice that stated that the CCA offer was inadequate. I assumed that the board acted in good faith in adopting that view.

I make some additional assumptions about the effort to sell the Ethan Allen business. First, the business is being competently shopped. The record suggests that. Second, the board will not sell it for less than the best available price. Third, the board will not sell it for less than a fair price (i.e. there will be no fire sale price). In the absence of indications by plaintiffs to the contrary, the board is entitled to these assumptions.

The question of reasonableness in this setting seems rather easy. Of course, a board acts reasonably in relation to an offer, albeit a noncoercive offer, it believes to be inadequate when it seeks to realize the full, market value of an important asset. Moreover, here the board puts forth sensible reasons why Ethan Allen should be sold under its new business plan. . . . Finally, as a defensive measure, the sale of Ethan Allen is not a "show stopper" insofar as this offer is concerned. This is not a "crown jewel" sale to a favored bidder; it is a public sale. On my assumption that the price will be a fair price, the corporation will come out no worse from a financial point of view. Moreover, the Rales' interests are being supplied the same information as others concerning Ethan Allen and they may bid for it. I do understand that this step complicates their life and indeed might imperil CCA's ability to complete its transaction. CCA, however, has no right to demand that its chosen target remain in status quo while its offer is formulated, gradually increased and, perhaps, accepted. I therefore conclude that the proposed sale of Ethan Allen Company is a defensive step that is reasonable in relation to the mild threat posed by this noncoercive $74 cash offer.

As to the dividend question, I will reserve judgment. It is, however, difficult for me to imagine how a pro rata distribution of cash to shareholders could itself ever constitute an unreasonable response to a bid believed to be inadequate. (Collateral agreements respecting use of such cash would raise a more litigable issue). Cf. Ivanhoe Partners v. Newmont Mining Corp., supra. I reserve judgment here, however, because I have not found in the record, and thus have not studied, the covenants contained in the various debt securities. They perhaps have not yet been drafted. Those covenants may contain provisions offering antitakeover protection. In the event they do, the question whether distribution of such securities was a reasonable step in reaction to the threat of an inadequate offer (of the specific proportions involved here) will be one that should be reviewed with particularity. The efficient adjudication of this case, however, warrants issuing an order on what has been decided. Should plaintiffs want a ruling on this issue, they will have to submit a written statement outlining any antitakeover effect the securities proposed to be dividended may contain.

City Capital Assocs. Ltd. Partnership v. Interco, Inc., 551 A.2d 787, 800-801 (Del. Ch. 1988).

That part of the opinion follows the material set forth in Chapter 7, where Chancellor Allen had ruled that there comes a time when a board has to be willing to redeem a poison pill and let the shareholders decide. Subsequent opinions of the Delaware Supreme Court blunted the impact of the Chancellor's poison pill holding and moved the law on that question more in the direction of letting directors "just say no." But the focus here is on the recapitalization as compared to the poison pill. Are the directors less interested in refusing to redeem the poison pill than in approving the recapitalization? Should the legal standard be different?

C. ASSET RESTRUCTURING

The prior parts of this chapter focus on creating value and cash flow by the company borrowing funds. Cash flow can also be created, sometimes equally well, by selling assets, which is the specific focus on the last part of this chapter. Here, we look at three prime examples: (1) Divestitures, in which the assets typically are sold to a third party, such as another company in the industry; (2) Carve-outs, in which the assets are moved to a separate subsidiary in which the seller maintains a dominant controlling position (often 80 percent) but a minority of the stock in the subsidiary if sold to the public; and (3) a Spinoff, in which the assets are moved into a separate company and the shares of that company are distributed as a dividend to the shareholders of the selling company. The result is that the assets remain as part of a publicly held company with initially the same set of shareholders, but it will now be managed separately from the seller. For each method, you should focus on what are the key economic drivers of such a change, who gets to decide, and what judicial review seems likely.

1. Divestitures

The most obvious economic advantage of a divestiture is usually liquidity. The selling company may dispose of a subsidiary, a division, or assets to a third party, usually for cash. Such sales can provide the cash to pay down borrowing necessary to make an acquisition in the first place, so it is not uncommon for divestitures to follow a successful acquisition, particularly LBOs. Over time, the number of divestitures rises and falls with the number of acquisition deals, with divestitures typically accounting for 40 percent of all deals. Sometimes, such sales are necessary to satisfy antitrust concerns raised by governments. (For example, when two large oil companies, Exxon and Mobil, merged, the combined company had to divest $4 billion of assets.) As discussed in the last section, it can also be part of a defensive strategy, where incumbent management feels the need to provide cash to its shareholders.

A second economic gain can come from divestitures improving management's focus. A long-standing complaint of conglomerates is that they make it easy to hide poor managerial performance, particularly if there are unrelated industries or geographically separate operations within the corporation. A divestiture can also remove negative synergies, as, for example, when a company was vertically integrated to include soft drink production and restaurants that used soft drinks, but other restaurants were less willing to use the company's soft drink brand because it was from a competitor. The restaurant portion of the business was losing business for the firm.

Third, assets restructuring often leads to better monitoring by boards, shareholders, and the markets generally. Divestitures move the company toward what analysts sometimes describe as a "pure play," an investment that provides a single kind of risk. Analysts and other investors who follow specific industries may be more willing to invest in and follow a company after a simplifying asset divestiture. Such an investment can be more easily compared to benchmark investment, and such transparency removes complexity that can make it difficult to value conglomerates.

Empirical evidence regarding divestitures shows that seller's operations generally do become more focused with a decrease in the reported lines of businesses and with most divestitures relating to unrelated lines of businesses. Seller's remaining assets become more profitable. Announcement returns to the seller's stock are positive (about two percent)—and double that when the firm used the proceeds to pay down debt versus zero if the firm is expected to retain the proceeds. Stock price reactions are larger for firms in financial distress and increases as the fraction of the firm's assets sold increases. If the buyer is known to have a comparative advantage in managing divested assets, the seller benefits in terms of an announcement return.

2. Carve-Outs

In a carve-out, the divested assets are placed in a separate subsidiary of the selling corporation, and shares of that company are offered to the public as an initial public offering. Typically, the amount sold to the public will be 20 percent, permitting tax benefits discussed below. Like a divestiture, a carve-out is a liquidity event, raising money for the seller, but in a much smaller amount. It can be a way of testing the water regarding interest in the subsidiary assets, particularly where efforts to complete a divestiture have not produced the results the seller's management might like. A carve-out offers the opportunity to provide the subsidiary's management with higher powered incentives tailored to the specific performance of their unit. The new subsidiary will provide its own public disclosure with the monitoring that can flow from that, and its directors will have their own fiduciary duties.

If the carve-out leaves 80 percent or more of the stock in the parent's hands, the two corporations can continue to file a consolidated tax return. The parent would recognize gain or loss on the amount raised in the carve-out, unless the money remains with the subsidiary. The subsidiary can borrow cash and pay it to the parent as a dividend and not disturb the tax-free status of the transactions if IRS rules are met.

Most carve-outs are followed by a second event, often associated with a positive return for the stock of the parent and the subsidiary. These could include:

C. Asset Restructuring

- Subsequent public offering of the parent's remaining stock.
- A tax-free spinoff of the parent's remaining stock.
- Sale by the parent of its remaining shares to another firm or to management of the subsidiary.
- The parent's reacquisition of the shares initially spun off.

3. Spinoff

Unlike the prior options, a spinoff is not a liquidity event for the seller. But like the carve-out, it separates the assets into a separate company with its own reporting obligations and the ability to more easily provide management incentives tailored to the performance of this entity. Even more than the carve-out, it is possible to grant complete operational control to the new corporation's management team since they will no longer have a parent corporation controlling 80 percent, but rather shares held by a dispersed set of shareholders who initially will mirror the corporation doing the spin-off. The spin-off can sometimes free the parent from regulation arising from the business of the subsidiary and free one party from national regulations in a particular country.

One attraction of a spinoff is the ability to make this operational change without incurring immediate tax recognition. Under §335 of the IRC, to get tax-free treatment the seller must be motivated by a valid business purposes, both the parent and the subsidiary must have actively conducted business for five years before the spinoff, the parent must have owned at least 80 percent of the subsidiary, and the parent, after distribution, must retain no practical control. Planners must beware the anti-Morris Trust provisions of §355(e) that can make a spinoff by a target within two years of a merger taxable to the target firm.

A prominent example of a spinoff was the 2013 announcement that Time, Inc. would be spun off from Time Warner Inc,, undoing part of the acquisition in one of the key cases described in Chapter 6. *See* Keach Hagey & Martin Peers, *New Plan: Spin Off Time Inc.*, Wall Street Journal, March 7, 2013 at B1, c1. Recall the focus in the earlier context on preserving the Time culture and observe one of the business justifications given for the spinoff: to increase revenue by building a closer partnership between business and the newsroom and for the first time having magazine editors report directly to the company's business side. *See* Leslie Kaufman, *Reshuffling at Time Inc. to Set Table for Spinoff*, New York Times, November 1, 2013 at M1, c6.

14 ACTIVIST SHAREHOLDERS

A. WHO ARE ACTIVIST SHAREHOLDERS?

Activist shareholders impact many types of deals and represent one of the notable changes in the census of shareholders over the last few decades. At the time of Berle and Means, one-third of the way through the twentieth century, shareholders were seen as a geographically dispersed group in which individual "Mom and Pop" investors were the representative members. By the late twentieth century, institutional shareholders such as public and private pension funds and mutual funds had replaced individuals as the largest group on the shareholder roster. *See* Kahan & Rock, *Embattled CEOs*, 88 Tex. L. Rev. 987 (2010) (tracing growth of institutional shareholders from 8 percent in 1950 to 60 percent in 2006). Yet even as the percentage ownership of these institutions rose, their passive approach to involvement in corporate governance, including takeovers, did not fundamentally change. *Id.* at 995 (hopes of commentators in the early 1990s as the dawn of a new era of shareholder power unfilled — at least until recently). Only with the ascension of a new subset of investors such as hedge funds, whose business plan has been to make money by actively influencing takeovers, has the change in census produced a change in terms of shaping deals.

The reasons for this new trend reflect both economics and law. Technological advances and computing power make it possible to absorb and analyze more information than in a paper-based system. Telecommunications make it possible to communicate both more quickly and more broadly than before in a way that reduces the costs of one contemplating involvement in a takeover. Financial innovation in the structure of the investment industry has permitted hedge funds to employ highly incentivized managers charged with deploying large and less regulated pools of capital. Activist investors reflect a subset of such financial firms whose business strategy has been to focus on making money by investing in target companies and influencing takeover or related transactions. Changes in law have also contributed to lowering the costs. For example, it is now easier (and cheaper) to do a solicitation electronically than in the earlier paper-based system and with the greater concentration of activist investors, it likely is easier to achieve some impact while staying within the exemption from proxy solicitation (which occurs via SEC Rule 14a-2) if the number of persons solicited does not exceed ten.

B. PATTERNS OF ENGAGEMENT

Shareholder activism is visible in at least three contexts, two of which show up in the material covered so far in this book. One context is when managers have put forward a takeover for shareholder approval and activist shareholders weigh in to oppose it either on the acquirer side, the target side, or both sides. A second is when there is no management-proposed deal on the table, but the activists seek to engage with management including obtaining seats on (but not control of) the board of directors. The goal, discussed below, is often to encourage a value increasing transaction, particularly a cash-generating transaction for shareholders, as illustrated by those transactions discussed in Chapter 13. A third context can be seen in generic governance changes, unrelated to a specific transaction.

Activism to directly influence a corporate decision on a pending deal. The legal requirements regarding corporate decision-making for mergers and similar transactions, discussed in Chapter 3, spread the responsibility for approval between the board of directors of the participating corporations and their shareholders. We have also seen in deals presented in earlier chapters how director incentives may differ from those of shareholders. For example, on the acquirer side, given the break-even or loss impact that takeovers usually produce for acquiring shareholders as discussed in Chapter 1, there may be worry that management paid too much. The Kraft/Cadbury deal discussed in Chapter 15 included legendary investor Warren Buffet warning Kraft, the acquiring company in which he owned a large block, not to overpay. On the target side, shareholders may worry that a target board is selling for too little, particularly if the deal is a management buyout or other deal where there is a potential conflict of interest by the management.

Data on activist deals suggests that this context accounts for a minority of activist engagements, less than 20 percent in one study. *See* Bratton,

B. Patterns of Engagement

Hedge Funds and Governance Targets, 95 Geo. L.J. 1375 (2007) (in a sample of firms targeted by activist shareholders between 2002 and 2006, 25 of 114 were triggered by a control transactions, with more on the sell side than the buy side). Law dramatically effects which deals provide an opportunity for such a strategy. The existence of voting rights is a crucial requirement and, as you may remember from Chapter 3, voting rights are not universal requirements, as least on the acquiring side, where the overpayment concern is likely to be greatest for investors. If there are no voting rights, such as those situations in which planners have been able to structure the transaction to avoid voting rights required by state law or stock exchange listing standards, there will be much less opportunity for activist shareholders to become involved. Similarly, on the target side, in a cash-out setting where there is already a shareholder with majority votes, there will be less incentive for an activist shareholder to become involved. Even here, however, some activist shareholders are repeat players in pursuing appraisal rights or litigation rights where they believe the deal treats the minority investors unfairly.

In some contexts, the role and incentives of investors can be less direct than in the examples just presented. Many of the institutional investors are diversified, which means that they well may hold shares in both the acquiring and target companies in a takeover. How should they vote their shares? If, as is often the case, the deal produces an immediate positive price bump for the target, but not for the acquirer, should they vote their target shares for the merger and their acquiring shares against the merger or should they vote both sets of shares depending their net position in the two companies given the impact of the takeover on each? From a macroeconomics perspective, the latter choice is more often likely to move assets to their highest and best use, but corporate law has chosen to make voting on a company-by-company basis, which suggests a different motivation. For an argument that voting in this context is not designed to aggregate social preferences but as an error-correcting device, see Thompson & Edelman, *Corporate Voting*, 62 Vand. L. Rev. 129 (2009).

What if investors who have a potential gain from the transaction on one side (e.g., the target corporation) desire to influence the vote on the other side? Developments in financial markets with derivatives and swaps have made it easier to decouple voting rights and financial interests. Thus, in a well-known takeover, Mylan Labs sought to acquire King Pharmaceuticals at a merger price that was 60 percent more than King's prior market price. Hedge fund investor Richard Perry, with an interest in King, sought to increase the chances of the merger's accomplishment by buying a 10 percent stake in Mylan. By combining that purchase with a short sale of Mylan stock, Perry ended up with votes in Mylan but no financial interest. Such possible "empty voting" creates the potential for investors to game the system. *See* Black & Hu, *The New Vote Buying: Empty Voting and Hidden (Morphable) Ownership*, 79 S. Cal. L. Rev. 811 (2006). Possible responses have included disclosure of such positions, as now occurs in the United Kingdom, or regulatory limits of nonvoting interest.

Engagement to push (perhaps reluctant) management toward a value-increasing transaction. In certain contexts, activist investors have also been highly visible before there are any announced deals. The goal here is usually to influence existing management, but not actually replace them. Thus, the activist will push for one or several seats on the board of directors, but not a majority of positions. This focus on persuasion shapes the kinds of transactions in which this activism shows up. More often, activists are advocating a cash-generation strategy, as illustrated in the previous chapter where the preferred changes in corporate practices would be selling assets or borrowing and then paying dividends or otherwise distributing additional cash.

Who would be the target of such a strategy? Likely you would expect a cash-rich company or one with assets that could be easily converted to cash without harming the operations of the company (e.g., a conglomerate or another company with distinct operating units or a company with little borrowing relative to its risk). Would you expect such a company to be underperforming relative to its peers? During the 1980s, underperforming companies were more often the target of cash-generating transactions, but in this century the targets of activist investors have been companies with relatively good management and operating performance. *See* Brav, Jiang, Thomas & Partnoy, *Hedge Fund Activism, Corporate Governance and Fund Performance*, 63 J. Fin. 1729 (2008) (large empirical study of activist investors show such investors are value investors as opposed to targeting poorly performing companies; target firms do not seem to suffer from serious operational difficulties).

Who would be the bidder in such a context? Going back to our discussion in Chapter 2, activist shareholders are more often described as financial buyers as opposed to strategic buyers. They are less likely to have any relative advantage on cost-cutting and other gains that require synergy. Such efforts are more likely to be concentrated in particular industries where economic factors have made cash-generating activities more likely to produce results. Sometimes such activist's strategies produce "wolf packs" where multiple activist investors buy shares in the same company and seek the same result.

The different goals in this context often mean that shareholder engagement looks different than the takeovers that occupy much of this book.

B. Patterns of Engagement

Activist investors often will only pursue a partial or short slate of directors to have a say at the board discussions. Many want to stay under a 10 percent ownership position to avoid triggering the short swing profit disgorgement under §16(a) of the Securities Exchange Act of 1934. Empirical data suggests that activist investors following such a strategy achieve some success. Bratton's analysis shows most who pursue board seats achieve one or more.

The fear that such investors are short-term quick buck artists does not appear to be borne out by the data. Bratton's data set shows a two-year duration for investment, longer than the average holding period for institutional investors as a whole. Bratton at 1410. The BJTP study showed that markets react favorably to an activist investment in a target, consistent with the view that it creates value. *See* Brav, Jiang, Thomas & Partnoy, supra. The authors also find that total payout and book value leverage increases in target firms.

Non-transactional efforts to change corporate governance. Institutional shareholders have, since the turn of the century, had a greater influence of bringing about changes in corporate governance. These efforts are distinguished from the earlier discussed two contexts in that the investments here typically are not oriented toward a particular transactional change, such as voting down a current merger or persuading management to purse a specific cash-generating strategy, but rather are aimed at process and changing the governance of the corporation. This difference in approach is also reflected in the subset of institutional investors who take the lead in such efforts. Public pension funds and union-related pension funds have been particularly active in the area and have been able to persuade mutual funds and other institutional investors to support some recommended changes.

This combination of investor influence has been particularly effective since 2003 in gaining the removal from corporate charters of provisions requiring staggered term elections for board members; they have also been effective in getting corporations to install provisions for majority voting for directors instead of plurality voting. *See* Kahan & Rock, *supra*, at Table 2 (showing the incidence of staggered boards among S&P 100 firms dropped from 44 percent in 2003 to 16 percent in 2008 and describing rise of majority voting provisions as "meteoric"). The persuasive efforts of these activist shareholders often have been effective after the shareholders have proven their voting clout in terms of getting precatory shareholder proposals approved or procuring no votes against directors who have opposed changes sought by the shareholders. By removing some of the most effective takeover defenses, these efforts also influence the direction of future takeovers.

CSX Corp. v. Children's Inv. Fund Management (UK) LLP
654 F. 3d 276 (2d Cir. 2011)

Before: NEWMAN, WINTER, and CALABRESI, Circuit Judges.

[Background Notes:]

1. The trial judge's description of the case and total default swaps:

See 562 F. Supp. 2d 511, 516-17, 519-523 (Lewis A. Kaplan, District Judge) (S.D. N.Y. 2008):

The defendants—two hedge funds that seek extraordinary gain, sometimes through "shareholder activism"—amassed a large economic position in CSX Corporation ("CSX"), one of the nation's largest railroads. They did so for the purpose of causing CSX to behave in a manner that they hoped would lead to a rise in the value of their holdings. And there is nothing wrong with that. But they did so in close coordination with each other and without making the public disclosure required of 5 percent shareholders and groups by the Williams Act, a statute that was enacted to ensure that other shareholders are informed of such accumulations and arrangements. They now have launched a proxy fight that, if successful, would result in their having substantial influence and perhaps practical working control of CSX.

Defendants seek to defend their secret accumulation of interests in CSX by invoking what they assert is the letter of the law. Much of their position in CSX was in the form of total return equity swaps ("TRSs"), a type of derivative that gave defendants substantially all of the indicia of stock ownership save the formal legal right to vote the shares. In consequence, they argue, they did not beneficially own the shares referenced by the swaps and thus were not obliged to disclose sooner or more fully than they did. In a like vein, they contend that they did not reach a formal agreement to act together, and therefore did not become a "group" required to disclose its collaborative activities, until December 2007 despite the fact that they began acting in concert with respect to CSX far earlier. . . .

The term "derivative," as the term is used in today's financial world, refers to a financial instrument that derives its value from the price of an underlying instrument or index. Among the different types of derivatives are swaps, instruments whereby two counterparties agree to "exchange cash flows on two financial instruments over a specific period of time." These are (1) a "reference obligation," or "underlying asset" such as a security, a bank loan, or an index, and (2) a benchmark loan, generally with an interest rate set relative to a commonly used reference rate (the "reference rate") such as the London Inter-Bank Offered Rate ("LIBOR"). A TRS is a particular form of swap.

The typical—or "plain vanilla"—TRS is represented by Figure 1.

B. Patterns of Engagement

Counterparty A—the "short" party—agrees to pay Counterparty B—the "long" party—cash flows based on the performance of a defined underlying asset in exchange for payments by the long party based on the interest that accrues at a negotiated rate on an agreed principal amount (the "notional amount"). More specifically, Counterparty B, which may be referred to as the "total return receiver" or "guarantor," is entitled to receive from Counterparty A the sum of (1) any cash distributions, such as interest or dividends, that it would have received had it held the referenced asset, and (2) either (i) an amount equal to the market appreciation in the value of the referenced asset over the term of the swap (if the TRS is cash-settled) or, what is economically the same thing, (ii) the referenced asset in exchange for its value on the last refixing date prior to the winding up of the transaction (if the TRS is settled in kind). Counterparty A, referred to as the "total return payer" or "beneficiary," is entitled to receive from Counterparty B(1) an amount equal to the interest at the negotiated rate that would have been payable had it actually loaned Counterparty A the notional amount, and (2) any decrease in the market value of the referenced asset.[14]

Figure 1

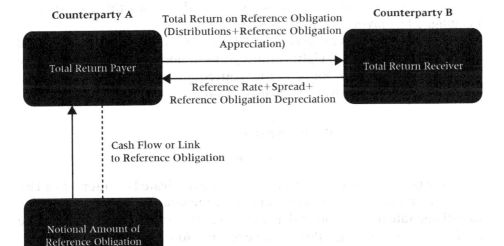

For example, in a cash-settled TRS with reference to 100,000 shares of the stock of General Motors, the short party agrees to pay to the long party an amount equal to the sum of (1) any dividends and cash flow, and (2) any increase in the market value that the long party would have realized had it

---

14. The payments occur on "refixing dates" that recur throughout the duration of the TRS as specified by the contract.

owned 100,000 shares of General Motors. The long party in turn agrees to pay to the short party the sum of (1) the amount equal to interest that would have been payable had it borrowed the notional amount from the short party, and (2) any depreciation in the market value that it would have suffered had it owned 100,000 shares of General Motors.

In practical economic terms, a TRS referenced to stock places the long party in substantially the same economic position that it would occupy if it owned the referenced stock or security. There are two notable exceptions. First, since it does not have record ownership of the referenced shares, it does not have the right to vote them. Second, the long party looks to the short party, rather than to the issuer of the referenced security for distributions and the marketplace for any appreciation in value.

The short party of course is in a different situation. It is entitled to have the long party place it in the same economic position it would have occupied had it advanced the long party an amount equal to the market value of the referenced security. But there are at least two salient distinctions, from the short party's perspective, between a TRS and a loan. First, the short party does not actually advance the notional amount to the long party. Second, it is subject to the risk that the referenced asset will appreciate during the term of the TRS. As will appear, the institutions that make a business of serving as short parties in TRSs deal with this exposure by hedging, a fact pivotal to one of CSX's claims here.

The swap agreements at issue in this case are cash-settled TRSs entered into by TCI with each of eight counterparties, most significantly Deutsche Bank AG ("Deutsche Bank") and Citigroup Global Markets Limited ("Citigroup"), and by 3G with Morgan Stanley.

B. The Purposes of TRSs...

1. Short Parties

As a generic matter, a short party may be motivated to enter into a TRS simply to obtain the cash flow generated by the long party's payment of the negotiated rate on the notional amount over the term of the swap. But the *quid pro quo* for that cash flow is the exposure to the risk of market appreciation in the referenced security.

As a matter of theory and on occasion in practice, a short party may accept that exposure either because it thinks the risk of appreciation is small—in other words, it is making its own investment decision with respect to the referenced security—or because it has a more or less offsetting long exposure that it wishes to hedge. But that is not what we are dealing with in this case.

The defendants' counterparties in this case are major financial service institutions that are in the business, among others, of offering TRSs as a product or service and seeking an economic return via the pseudo-interest, if it may be so called, that they receive on the notional amount and from other incidental revenue sources. They are not, in this aspect of their endeavors, in the business of speculating on the market fluctuation of the shares referenced by the TRSs into which they enter as short parties. Accordingly, they typically hedge their short exposures by purchasing the referenced securities in amounts identical to those referenced in their swap agreements.

Institutions that hedge short TRS exposure by purchasing the referenced shares typically have no economic interest in the securities. They are, however, beneficial owners and thus have the right to vote the referenced shares.[18]

Institutional voting practices appear to vary. As noted below, some take the position that they will not vote shares held to hedge TRS risk. Some may be influenced, at least in some cases, to vote as a counterparty desires. Some say they vote as they determine in their sole discretion. Of course, one may suppose that banks seeking to attract swap business well understand that activist investors will consider them to be more attractive counterparties if they vote in favor of the positions their clients advocate. In any case, however, the accumulation of substantial hedge positions significantly alters the corporate electorate. It does so by (1) eliminating the shares constituting the hedge positions from the universe of available votes, (2) subjecting the voting of the shares to the control or influence of a long party that does not own the shares, or (3) leaving the vote to be determined by an institution that has no economic interest in the fortunes of the issuer, holds nothing more than a formal interest, but is aware that future swap business from a particular client may depend upon voting in the "right" way.

2. Long Parties

A long party to a TRS referencing equity in a public company gains economic exposure to the equity. In other words, it is exposed to essentially the same potential benefits and detriments as would be the case if it held the referenced security, and it gains that exposure without the need for the capital to fund or maintain such a purchase directly. This may permit such investors to operate with greater leverage or a lower cost than might be the case if they bought the security directly. But those are by no means the only reasons motivating long parties to engage in TRSs. There can be tax advantages. Most importantly for purposes of this case, if the long party to a cash-settled TRS is not the beneficial owner of the referenced shares—a question hotly contested here—one interested in amassing a large economic exposure to the equity of a registered company may do so without

---

18. This decoupling of the economic and voting interests is discussed, among other places, in Henry Hu & Bernard Black, *The New Vote Buying: Empty Voting and Hidden (Morphable) Ownership*, 79 S. CAL. L. REV. 811 (2006).

making the public disclosure that is required when a person or group acquires 5 percent or more of the outstanding shares.

The avoidance of public disclosure can confer significant advantages on the long party. By concealing its activities, it may avoid other investors bidding up the referenced stock in anticipation of a tender offer or other corporate control contest and thus maximize the long party's profit potential. Second, it permits a long party who is interested in persuading an issuer to alter its policies, but desirous of avoiding an all-out battle for control, to select the time of its emergence to the issuer as a powerful player to a moment of its choosing, which may be when its exposure is substantially greater than 5 percent. In other words, it permits a long party to ambush an issuer with a holding far greater than 5 percent.

One other point bears mention here. TRSs, like all or most derivatives, are privately negotiated contracts traded over the counter. Their terms may be varied during their lives as long as the counterparties agree. In consequence, a TRS that in its inception contemplates cash settlement may be settled in kind—i.e., by delivery of the referenced shares to the long party—as long as the parties consent.

This confers another potential advantage on a long party that contemplates a tender offer, proxy fight, or other corporate control contest. By entering into cash-settled TRSs, such an investor may concentrate large quantities of an issuer's stock in the hands of its short counterparties and, when it judges the time to be right, unwind those swaps by acquiring the referenced shares from those counterparties in swiftly consummated private transactions. Moreover, even if such TRSs were settled in cash, the disposition by the short counterparties of the referenced shares held to hedge their swap exposures would afford a ready supply of shares to the market at times and in circumstances effectively chosen and known principally by the long party. The long party therefore likely would have a real advantage in converting its exposure from swaps to physical shares even if it does not unwind the swaps in kind.

2. The statutes and rules:

Section 13(d) of the Exchange Act, enacted as part of the Williams Act in 1968, was passed to address the increasing frequency with which hostile takeovers were being used to influence changes in corporate control. Section 13(d) in particular was adopted "to alert the marketplace to every large, rapid aggregation or accumulation of securities, regardless of technique employed, which might represent a potential shift in corporate control." It requires one who directly or indirectly becomes the owner of more than 5 percent of a class of equity securities of a reporting company to disclose information about the identity of the beneficial ownership, the

B. Patterns of Engagement

number of shares owned and the number of shares for which there is a right to acquire, whether the purpose is to acquire control or make major changes, and other disclosure as the SEC may require. Beneficial ownership as defined by the SEC in Rule 13d-3 includes a person who "directly or indirectly, through any contract, arrangement or understanding, relationship or otherwise" has voting power or investment power as to such security. In order to prevent circumvention of Section 13(d)(1), Section 13(d)(3) further provides that "[w]hen two or more persons act as a partnership, limited partnership, syndicate, or other group for the purpose of acquiring, holding, or disposing of securities of an issuer, such syndicate or group shall be deemed a 'person' for the purposes of this subsection."

---

3. The district court decision:

The trial judge found, "[t]here are persuasive arguments for concluding, on the facts of this case, that . . . under Rule 13d-3(a) defendants beneficially owned at least some and quite possibly all of the referenced CSX shares held by their counterparties," but the court declined to base its ruling on that section, turning instead to the adjacent Rule 13d-3(b) forbidding action "as part of a plan or scheme to evade the reporting requirements" of Section 13(d).

On that point, the court found "that TCI created and used the TRSs with the purpose and effect of preventing the vesting of beneficial ownership in TCI as part of a plan or scheme to evade the reporting requirements of Section 13(d). Under the plain language of Rule 13d-3(b), it thus is deemed to be a beneficial owner of the shares held by its counterparties to hedge their short exposures created by the TRSs."

Secondly, the trial court that the two hedge funds formed a group with respect to CSX securities no later than February 13, 2007, pointing to "the existing relationship, the admitted exchanges of views and information regarding CSX, 3G's striking patterns of share purchases immediately following meetings with Hohn and Amin, and the parallel proxy fight preparation." As a remedy the trial judge permanently enjoined future disclosure violations, but declined to enjoin the voting of hedge funds shares in CSX at the CSX annual meeting, sterilization that the company had argued was necessary to prevent the hedge funds being able to retain the fruits of their violation and to deter future violations.

---

4. The Second Circuit decisions:

Upon appeal, a panel of the second circuit (made up of a former dean of Yale Law School, a former securities professor at Yale, and a three decades-long member of the court) quickly affirmed the trial court's denial of the sterilization remedy "with opinion to follow," 292 Fed Appx. 133 (2d Cir. 2008). When the opinion eventually arrived some 33 months later it noted disagreement in the panel as to "circumstances under which the long party to such swap agreements may have or be deemed to have beneficial ownership of shares purchased by the short party as a hedge." So the panel limited the question before it to the question of group formation and limited even this question to the question of a group only between the two hedge funds without considering the question of a possible group involving the counterparties. On this question as so narrowed the panel remanded for the trial court to determine if in fact a group had been formed not just measured by its group's activities but rather was the group formed for the purpose of acquiring, holding, voting or disposing of the shares owned outright by the hedge funds. Not surprisingly, the passage of time seems to have stripped the parties of their interest in pursuing a now hypothetical question for them, but the differences among the panel do tell us something of the reach of federal securities law in an activist shareholder contest.]

NEWMAN, Circuit Judge.

This case comes to us raising issues concerning a contractual arrangement known as a "cash-settled total return equity swap agreement" although our disposition at this stage of the appeal touches only tangentially on such issues....

The parties have endeavored to frame issues that would require decision as to the circumstances under which parties to cash-settled total-return equity swap agreements must comply with the disclosure provisions of section 13(d). Such issues would turn on the circumstances under which the long party to such swap agreements may have or be deemed to have beneficial ownership of shares purchased by the short party as a hedge.

Rather than resolve such issues, as to which there is disagreement within the panel, we consider at this time only issues concerning a "group" violation of section 13(d)(3) with respect to CSX shares owned outright by the Defendants (without regard to whatever beneficial ownership, if any, they might have acquired as long parties to cash-settled total-return equity swap agreements).... [T]he panel is divided on numerous issues concerning whether and under what circumstances the long party to a cash-settled total return equity swap may be deemed, for purposes of section 13(d), the beneficial owner of shares purchased by the short party as a hedge. In view of that disagreement, we conclude that it is appropriate at this time to limit our consideration to the issue of group formation, *see* 15 U.S.C. §78m (d) (3), an issue as to which we seek further findings from the District Court. All members of the panel are in agreement as to this disposition....

II. "Group" Violation

... Although the District Court found the existence of a group "with respect to CSX securities," the Court did not explicitly find a group formed for the purpose of acquiring CSX securities. Even if many of the parties' "activities" were the result of group action, two or more entities do not become a group within the meaning of section 13(d)(3) unless they "act as a ... group for the purpose of acquiring ... securities of an issuer."

Moreover, because the District Court deemed the Funds, as long parties to cash-settled total-return equity swap agreements, to have a beneficial interest in shares acquired by hedging short parties to such agreements, the Court did not distinguish in its group finding between CSX shares deemed to be beneficially owned by the Funds and those owned outright by the Funds. However, with our current consideration of a group violation confined to CSX shares owned outright by the Funds, a precise finding, adequately supported by specific evidence, of whether a group existed for purposes of acquiring CSX shares outright during the relevant period needs to be made in order to facilitate appellate review, and we will remand for that purpose. Because the combined total outright ownership of CSX shares by TCI and 3G crossed the 5 percent threshold by April 10, 2007, a TCI/3G group, if it was formed for the statutorily defined purpose, would have been required to file a section 13(d) disclosure within ten days, *i.e.*, by April 20, 2007, *see* 15 U.S.C. §78m(d); 17 C.F.R. §240.13d-1. Thus, on remand the District Court will have to make findings as to whether the Defendants formed a group for the purpose of "acquiring, holding, voting or disposing," 17 C.F.R. §240.13d-5(b)(1), of CSX shares owned outright, and, if so, a date by which at the latest such a group was formed. Only if such a group's outright ownership of CSX shares exceeded the 5 percent threshold prior to the filing of a section 13(d) disclosure can a group violation of section 13(d) be found.

III. Appropriateness of Injunctive Relief

... If a section 13(d) violation is found, limited to a group violation with respect to purchase of the shares outright (which is the only violation considered in this opinion), the threat of future violations would be less substantial than appeared to the District Court, which based its broad injunction (*i.e.*, not limited to CSX shares) on its view that the Funds were deemed to be beneficial owners of the hedged shares purchased by the short parties to the swap agreements.

Another factor that would arguably weigh against a broad injunction is the disclosure that CSX made just prior to the expiration of the ten-day period following April 10, 2007, the date when the group's total of CSX shares owned outright crossed the 5 percent threshold. On April 18, 2007, CSX filed its Form 10-Q for the period ending March 30, 2007. The Form

10-Q reported that TCI had made a filing under the Hart-Scott-Rodino Antitrust Improvements Act, Pub.L. No. 94-435, 90 Stat. 1383 (1976), of its intention to acquire more than $500 million of CSX stock and that TCI "currently holds a significant economic position through common stock ownership and derivative contracts tied to the value of CSX stock." *CSX I*, 562 F. Supp. 2d at 527 (internal quotation marks omitted). Thus, TCI's control ambitions were known to the public before it was required to file under section 13(d), at least with respect to the group's outright ownership of shares as of April 10, 2007. We recognize that a Hart-Scott-Rodino filing does not reveal all of the information required by a section 13(d) disclosure. Nevertheless, the filing has a bearing on the scope of relief warranted for the limited section 13(d) violation we have considered in this opinion.

On the other hand, if a section 13(d) violation, even a limited one, is found on the basis of a group purchase of shares outright and non-disclosure when the group's holdings crossed the 5 percent threshold, it would continue to be relevant that the District Court has found that some of the parties "testified falsely in a number of respects, notably including incredible claims of failed recollection." The District Court was within its discretion in concluding that people who have lied about securities matters can reasonably be expected to attempt securities laws violations in the future.

Under all the circumstances, we will remand to the District Court so that it may (a) determine whether the evidence permits findings as to the formation of a group, as described above, a date by which at the latest such a group was formed, and whether such a group's outright ownership of CSX shares crossed the 5 percent threshold prior to the filing of a section 13(d) disclosure, and (b) if a group violation of section 13(d) is found, reconsider the appropriateness and scope of injunctive relief based only on the group's failure to disclose outright ownership of more than 5 percent of CSX's shares.

IV. Injunctive "Sterilization" of the Disputed Shares

... In the present matter, the Funds' section 13(d) disclosures occurred in December 2007, approximately six months before the June 25, 2008, shareholders' meeting. Therefore, following *Treadway* [*Companies, Inc. v. Care Corp.*, 638 F.2d 357 (2d Cir.1980)], we conclude that injunctive share "sterilization" was not available.

CSX, however, argues that the Williams Act does not aim merely at timely dissemination of information but more broadly "seeks to provide a level playing field and to promote compliance." Appellant's Brief at 48. For this proposition, CSX relies on a passing remark, in a footnote, in which the Supreme Court expressed skepticism about "whether 'deterrence' of §14(e) violations is a meaningful goal, except possibly with respect to the most flagrant sort of violations which no reasonable person could consider lawful." *Piper v. Chris-Craft Indus., Inc.*, 430 U.S. 1, 40 n.26 (1977). Far from

B. Patterns of Engagement

supporting CSX's claim, this remark mentions none of the goals of the Williams Act, concerns section 14(e) rather than section 13(d), and actually casts doubt upon the usefulness of determining remedies with an eye toward promoting compliance.

CSX also rests its "level playing field" claim on two Supreme Court cases that include "fair corporate suffrage" as among the original goals of the Securities Exchange Act of 1934: *Virginia Bankshares, Inc. v. Sandberg*, 501 U.S. 1083, 1103 (1991), and *J.I. Case Co. v. Borak*, 377 U.S. 426, 431 (1964). However, neither case attributed that goal to the Williams Act, and there is no reason to conclude that adequate timely disclosure of the information covered by the Williams Act would be insufficient to ensure the "fairness" of a subsequent shareholder vote....

WINTER, Circuit Judge, concurring

I concur in the judgment remanding for further findings.

The district court's finding of a February 2007 group formation that required disclosure under Rule 13d-5(b)(1) cannot be upheld for various reasons discussed *infra*. Particularly, it was based in part on a flawed analysis of the economic and legal role of cash-settled total-return equity swap agreements.

The court viewed the economic role of such swaps as an underhanded means of acquiring or facilitating access to CSX stock that could be used to gain control through a proxy fight or otherwise. In my view, without an agreement between the long and short parties permitting the long party ultimately to acquire the hedge stock or to control the short party's voting of it, such swaps are not a means of indirectly facilitating a control transaction. Rather, they allow parties such as the Funds to profit from efforts to cause firms to institute new business policies increasing the value of a firm. If management changes the policies and the firm's value increases, the Funds' swap agreements will earn them a profit for their efforts. If management does not alter the policies, however, and a proxy fight or other control transaction becomes necessary, the swaps are of little value to parties such as the Funds. Absent an agreement such as that described above, such parties must then, as happened here, unwind the swaps and buy stock at the open market price, thus paying the costs of both the swaps and the stock.

The district court's legal analysis concluded that the one role of such swaps was to avoid the disclosure requirements of Section 13(d) — no doubt true — and therefore violated Rule 13d-3. The legal conclusion, however, was also flawed, leaving unmentioned, *inter alia*, explicit legislation regarding swaps and Supreme Court decisions discussing statutory triggers involving "beneficial ownership" of a firm's stock. That legislation and those decisions, as they stood at the time, foreclosed the conclusion reached by the district court. Finally, the recent Dodd-Frank bill and SEC response thereto make it clear that the district court's analysis is not consistent with present law. Dodd-Frank Wall Street Reform Protection Act, Pub.L. No. 111-203, 124 Stat. 1376 (2010); Beneficial Ownership Reporting Requirements and Security Based Swaps, S.E.C. Release No. 64,087, 17 C.F.R. Part 240, 2011 WL 933460, at *2 (June 8, 2011).

I

In my view, cash-settled total-return equity swaps do not, without more, render the long party a "beneficial owner" of such shares with a potential disclosure obligation under Section 13(d). However, an agreement or understanding between the long and short parties to such a swap regarding the short party's purchasing of such shares as a hedge, the short party's selling of those shares to the long party upon the unwinding of the swap agreements, or the voting of such shares by the short parties renders the long party a "beneficial owner" of shares purchased as a hedge by the short party.

A. The Statutory Scheme

... Some measure of certainty should be accorded to persons subject to Section 13(d)'s disclosure requirements. Investors benefit little from case by case, prolonged, expensive and repetitive litigation that weighs amorphous standards and circumstantial evidence regarding state of mind with disparate outcomes, particularly when the underlying information quickly loses its relevance because of ever-changing commercial environments. Even where a disclosure requirement seems less than fully comprehensive, knowledge of what need be disclosed and what need not at least leaves the market with some certainty as to the unknown.

In the present case, much certainty can be provided simply by following the language of Section 13(d). The language does not impose a general disclosure requirement that is triggered by an intent to obtain control or an equity position of influence within a particular company. Nor does it purport to require, as suggested by the district court, disclosure of all steps that might be part of a control transaction in the eyes of a court Rather, it specifies precise *conduct* constituting the disclosure trigger: the acquisition, alone or in coordination with others, of "beneficial ownership" of 5 percent of any "equity security" of a company. 15 U.S.C. §78m(d)(1).

The term "beneficial owner[s] ... of any equity security" was not drawn from thin air in 1968. *Id.* It was already a familiar term from its use in Section 16, which was part of the original 1934 Act. ...

The case law under Section 16 is particularly informative with regard to whether Section 13(d) is to be interpreted as giving decisive weight to a would-be acquirer's intentions toward a target, as the district court did, or whether a more mechanical, conduct-based interpretation is appropriate. Although modern financial transactions have generated some close

B. Patterns of Engagement

cases—*e.g., Kern County Land Co. v. Occidental Petroleum Co.*, 411 U.S. 582, (1973)—the application of Section 16 is largely mechanical, that is, independent of the purposes or state of mind of parties to a transaction. . . .

A large measure of certainty is provided by this test's mechanical attributes, but, as *Reliance Electric* noted with regard to Section 16, at a cost. 404 U.S. at 422, 92 S. Ct. 596. Application of the language of Section 13(d) leads to an inevitable overbreadth—requiring disclosure where no control or influence is intended by a holder of 5 percent of shares.

There is also an inevitable underbreadth, *see id.*—not requiring disclosure of conduct that constitutes significant steps in an attempt to gain control but does not fall within the pertinent language. Without triggering any disclosure requirement, a potential acquirer can, for example, amass 4.9 percent of the target company's shares. The potential acquirer may further make inquiry of some large shareholders with an eye to learning how many shares might be available for private purchases in the future and what price ranges are likely, so long as there is no implicit or explicit agreement to buy. *Pantry Pride, Inc. v. Rooney*, 598 F. Supp. 891, 900 (S.D.N.Y.1984) ("Section 13(d) allows individuals broad freedom to discuss the possibilities of future agreements without filing under securities laws."). Such inquiries may cause—and be expected to cause—these other shareholders to keep or acquire more shares than they otherwise would, in anticipation of the potential acquirer deciding to make an acquisition.

The same potential acquirer may line up financing in anticipation of a large purchase of the target company's shares in a short period of time. The potential acquirer can then form a group with other like-minded investors and coordinate future plans to buy the target company's stock, again so long as the 5 percent ownership threshold is not yet reached. The group may then cross the threshold and acquire an unlimited amount of the company's securities over a ten-day period before being required to make disclosure. So long as "the method used to 'avoid' [disclosure] is one permitted by the statute," *Reliance Elec.*, 404 U.S. at 422, 92 S. Ct. 596, it does not matter that a firm or group of firms employing that method consciously sought to avoid disclosure under Section 13(d). That result flows from the statutory language and is not for courts to alter. . . .

The district court also did not consider the fact that Congress has been well aware of legal issues involving swaps for years and has repeatedly passed legislation regarding them, all of which is specifically relevant to the issues in this case and generally relevant to the propriety of, or need for, courts' adopting legal rules that Congress and the SEC have avoided. . . . The 2000 legislation, in effect at the time of the district court's opinion and the hearing of this appeal, included a moderately lengthy and detailed amendment to the 1934 Act broadly limiting the SEC's regulatory authority over security-based swap agreements. *See* Commodity Futures Modernization Act of 2000 §§301 & 303. In particular, that amendment prohibited the SEC from "promulgating, interpreting, or enforcing rules; [ ] or issuing orders of general applicability" in a manner that "imposes or specifies reporting or recordkeeping requirements, procedures, or standards as prophylactic measures against fraud, manipulation, or insider trading with respect to any [cash-settled total-return equity swap]." 15 U.S.C. §78c-1(b)(2). This amendment contained exceptions to this prohibition with regard to the disclosure and disgorgement provisions of Section 16 that, *inter alia*, make it clear that a long party's ownership of cash-settled total-return equity swaps was not to be calculated in determining beneficial ownership of 10 percent of equity shares. *See* 15 U.S.C. §78c-1 (b)(3).

In 2010, the Dodd-Frank bill not only included security-based swaps in the definition of security but also amended the definition of beneficial owner contained in Section 13 of the SEA. . . . However, the SEC has not exercised its new authority to promulgate rules that specifically reference swaps. Rather, it has repromulgated Rule 13(d)-3 on the ground that "[a]bsent rulemaking under Section 13(*o*), [the amendment to Section 13(*o*)] may be interpreted to render the beneficial ownership determinations made under Rule 13d-3 inapplicable to a person who purchases or sells a security-based swap." Beneficial Ownership Reporting Requirements and Security Based Swaps, 2011 WL 933460, at *2. The SEC's fear appears to be that, given the prior Congressional bar to its regulating cash-settled total-return equity based swaps, Rule 13d-3 could not apply to such swaps before the amendment and needed repromulgation pursuant to that amendment if the Rule were ever to apply to such swaps.

Two matters of significance must be noted. First, if Rule 13d-3 did not apply to such swaps before the amendment, the district court was wrong in its legal analysis. Second, the repromulgated Rule makes no mention of security-based swaps and in the words of the amendment to Section 13(*o*) regulates them "only to the extent" that it applies as written.

B. Beneficial Ownership

I turn now to the issue of whether the Funds, as long parties to the cash-settled total-return equity swaps, are beneficial owners of referenced shares bought by short parties to hedge short positions in those swaps. The district court held that if a long party to such a swap would expect that the short party would hedge its position by purchasing shares, then the long party was a beneficial owner of those shares because it "had the power to influence" the purchase. The district court further found that the "only practical alternative" for the short parties to hedge was to purchase CSX shares. *Id.* . . . In the present context, there are two SEC rules that apply: Rules 13d-3(a) and 13d-3(b). . . . These Rules were in effect at the time of the district court's decision and, as discussed *supra*, were repromulgated in 2011 pursuant to the Dodd-Frank amendment to Section 13.

1. Rule 13d-3(a)

... The issue here is whether, under Rule 13d-3(a), such swaps accord the long party investment or voting power over the hedge shares when the short party purchases referenced shares as a hedge.

a. Investment Power

CSX argues that it was "inevitable" that TCI's swap counterparties would buy CSX shares to hedge their short swap positions and then would sell those shares when TCI closed out its swaps. TCI had, CSX concludes, "the economic ability to cause its short counterparties to buy and sell the CSX shares" and therefore had "investment power" over those shares.

CSX asserts that expectations based on the incentives of counterparties to buy and sell shares qualify, for the purposes of Rule 13d-3(a), as the power to "direct the disposition" of those shares. I disagree.

Both literally and in the context of the term "beneficial ownership" and Section 13(d)'s concerns over control, this argument gives too much breadth to the term "direct the disposition of." To "direct" something, or to "influence" it, even indirectly, one generally must have some measure of active control, and, in the context of Section 13(d) and swaps, that control must be exercisable in the interests of the long party....

"Influence" must also be interpreted in the context of Section 13(d)'s concern over control transactions. No one would dream that the author of a weekly column providing stock tips that reliably cause investors to buy and sell the stocks mentioned was the beneficial owner of the shares bought and sold even though the column "influence[d]," not to say caused, the purchases and sales. A relationship that leaves short parties free to act in whatever way they deem to be in their self-interest with regard to purchases and sales of referenced shares also does not fit within the concept of "beneficial ownership" in the long party. Likewise, a swap agreement that accords complete freedom to the short parties to act in their self-interest with regard to purchases and sales of referenced shares does not confer "beneficial ownership" in the long party in any sense in which those words are commonly used.

Rather, without an agreement or understanding with regard to hedging or unwinding, cash-settled total-return equity swaps leave the short counterparty free to act solely in its self-interest. Absent an agreement or informal understanding committing the banks to buy shares to hedge their CSX-referenced swaps or to sell those shares to the long party when the swaps terminated, the Funds possessed only the power to predict with some confidence the purchase of those shares as a hedge, not the power to direct such a purchase, much less to direct those shares' disposition. The long counterparties' act of entering into a swap, therefore, falls well short of "directing" the short counterparties to purchase the stock.

Long counterparties may well expect short counterparties to hedge their swap positions by buying the shares involved in an amount roughly equal to those specified in the swap. However, as noted *supra*, alternative hedging methods exist and are sometimes used. . . . Had the banks chosen, for whatever reason, not to hedge their short swap positions with a purchase of shares, not to sell all their hedge shares once the swaps had terminated, to alter their hedging methods and sell the hedge shares before the swaps were unwound, or to sell those shares to a competing would-be acquirer of CSX, the Funds would have lacked any means, legal or moral, to compel the banks to alter that choice or even to inform the Funds of their actions. *See* Hu & Black, 79 S. Cal. L. Rev. at 839. Thus, the sort of power that CSX attributes to the Funds does not fit within the language "to direct the disposition" of the CSX shares. 17 C.F.R. §240.13d-3(a)(2).

CSX recognizes the need to establish a nexus between influencing a sale of the short party's hedge shares upon unwinding and the long party's control ambitions by arguing that, in the inducing of those sales, the Funds exercised investment power by "materially facilitat[ing] [the Funds'] rapid and low-cost acquisition of a physical position upon the termination of the swaps." Whether or not the alleged "material facilitation" would run afoul of the *Reliance Electric* test, *see supra*, or would provide a sufficient nexus to the term "investment power" to constitute "beneficial ownership," 17 C.F.R. §240.13d-3(a)(2), the "material facilitation" claimed here substantially overstates the effect of acquiring long positions in cash-settled equity swaps.

Cash-settled equity swaps allow the short party to retain its hedge shares or dispose of them at the highest price available. Thus, the long party's choices for acquiring actual shares in the referenced company are either to go into the open market or to pay the short party no less than the open market price.

Buying or selling by the short party may affect the availability and price of shares, but hardly constitutes the claimed "material facilitation." If the market for the shares is liquid, as will often be the case, then rapid acquisition of those shares would be possible regardless of the sale of shares used to hedge swap positions. Thus, such a sale would have little practical effect on the long party's ability to acquire shares. If the market is highly illiquid, then potential short parties would find it very costly to acquire the shares and thus either would not acquire shares to hedge their short swap positions or, more likely, would refuse to enter into such swap agreements.

If the market's illiquidity is more moderate, then closing out swap agreements may provide a degree of confidence that a block of shares will go on the market. However, purchasing this confidence will be very expensive, because keeping individual short parties under Section 13(d)'s 5 percent threshold may require using several short counterparties, who will be competing with each other for limited available shares and will pass the resulting increased hedging costs on to the prospective long party.

B. Patterns of Engagement 555

Moreover, if the long party's purpose is to ensure the availability of shares when making its acquisition move, the ultimate effect of these swap stratagems may be only to reduce market illiquidity for a competing acquirer—perhaps an acquirer that is in league with the firm's management or even management itself—who, having avoided the costs of the swaps, will be better positioned to make its own bid.

Moreover, cash-settled total-return equity swaps will not lower a long party's costs of acquisition. The basis for CSX's claim that these swaps allow long parties to acquire shares at a low price is unclear. It may be based on the belief that unwinding the swaps will momentarily increase the market supply of shares and thus lower those shares' market price. However, if the swap unwinding is likely to lower the prices of the referenced shares, then the short party, who, as a seller, will suffer from that downward slippage in prices, will insist on passing those foreseeable extra hedging costs along to the long party in the form of higher "interest" payments, leaving long parties on the average in much the same (or worse) economic position as if they had simply bought the shares directly, without a detour through a cash-settled equity swap position. In other words, cash-settled total-return equity swaps, without more, are not a substitute for the ownership of shares by parties seeking to control a corporation. Control still requires the purchase of shares on the open market, *as happened in the instant case*, or from the short party at the open market price, thus causing the party seeking control to bear the costs of both the swaps and the shares.

In the absence of some other agreement governing the disposition of shares purchased to hedge a swap position, merely having a long position in a cash-settled total-return equity swap does not constitute having the power, directly or indirectly, to direct the disposition of shares that a counterparty purchases to hedge its swap positions, and thus does not constitute having "investment power" for purposes of Rule 13d-3(a).

b. Voting Power

The district court found no evidence of explicit agreements between TCI and the banks committing the banks to vote their shares in a specified way. *CSX Corp*. Nevertheless, CSX argues that TCI's ability to select counterparties gave it "voting power," 17 C.F.R. §240.13d-3(a)(1), over the counterparties' hedge shares.

In fact, TCI eventually consolidated its swap holdings in Citibank and Deutsche Bank. TCI "hope[d] that Deutsche Bank would vote in [TCI's] favor" because a hedge fund internal to Deutsche Bank, Austin Friars, also had investments in CSX. CSX argues further that when TCI chose its other swap counterparties, it selected banks that it knew were "sympathetic to [its] voting objectives." CSX concedes that some of these counterparties had policies that prohibited them from voting their shares but argues that the effective removal of these counterparties' shares from the voting pool left TCI in a better position than if the votes of those shares had been left to chance. I disagree on both counts.

That a short party's self-interest predisposes it to vote in favor of positions taken by a prospective long counterparty is insufficient, on its own, to show a transfer of voting power to the long counterparty for purposes of Section 13(d) and Rule 13d-3(a)(1). To hold otherwise would distort both the term "beneficial owner" and the word "power." A short party's self-interest is not an obligation to vote as the long party would desire. Nor is it a right in the long party to compel the short party to vote in a particular way. Indeed, were another putative acquirer to appear in competition with the long party, the long party might well find that the short party's self-interest was now at odds with its own. *See* Hu & Black, 79 S. Cal. L. Rev. at 839.

Purchases by a short party with a policy against voting shares held solely as a hedge will not increase the voting power of a long party's shares. Abstaining can have influence only with regard to shares that, if not purchased by a short party as a hedge, would have been voted against the wishes of the long party. Because the hypothetical voting intentions of persons from whom the abstaining short parties purchased their shares on the open market are unknown, this asserted influence over shareholder votes is entirely speculative and hardly qualifies as voting "power."

The facts that the Funds "hoped" that Deutsche Bank would vote in the desired way, or that the Funds entered into cash-settled equity swap agreements with counterparties believed to be inclined to vote as the Funds desired, do not constitute the requisite power to direct the counterparties' vote. *See* 17 C.F.R. §240.13d-3(a)(1). Indeed, the facts indicate the opposite: when TCI realized that it needed to exercise control and decided to wage a proxy battle, it started unwinding its swaps and buying shares in order to vote the shares as it pleased, indicating that the Funds' swap positions did not give the power, directly or indirectly, to "direct the voting" of the counterparties' CSX shares. *Id.*

Finally, I note that my conclusion parallels Congress's earlier decision to exclude security-based swaps in determining whether a party is a 10 percent beneficial owner, for purposes of Section 16, triggering its reporting and disgorgement provisions, while requiring 10 percent owners to report security-based swap holdings and to disgorge short-swing profits in trading them.

2. Rule 13d-3(b)

... Rule 13d-3(b) is one of a large number of historical and contemporary rules and regulations, or preliminary notes to them, that seek to prohibit "plan[s] or scheme[s] to evade" statutory provisions or SEC rules and regulations....

Evasion provisions are catch-all methods of closing unforeseen "loopholes" that seek to use form to evade substance or to comply with technicalities while violating the "spirit" or intent of regulatory provisions.

B. Patterns of Engagement

As such, there are two important points to be made about them. First, evasion provisions do not expand the permissibly regulable area. Second, they are not subject to the canon of construction that a statutory or regulatory provision must be read to have effect and is not superfluous.... Evasion provisions may be superfluous in actual practice because there are no loopholes....

The district court found "overwhelming" evidence that the Funds entered into the swap agreements "at least in major part, for the purpose of preventing the vesting of beneficial ownership of CSX shares in TCI and as part of a plan or scheme to evade the reporting requirements of Section 13(d)...." The district court rested this conclusion upon the following evidence: (i) TCI's chief financial officer once said that a reason to use swaps is that they provide "the ability to purchase without disclosure"; (ii) TCI emails had discussed the need to limit the size of swap agreements with individual counterparties in order to avoid those counterparties' having to disclose their holdings of shares purchased for hedging purposes; (iii) TCI acquired only 4.5 percent of CSX's shares—below Section 13(d)'s 5 percent reporting threshold—until TCI was ready to disclose its position; and (iv) TCI admitted that one of its motivations for avoiding disclosure by its swap counterparties was a concern that disclosure would drive up the market price of CSX shares and thus increase TCI's cost of purchasing CSX shares later.

This view of "evasion" under Rule 13d-3(b) is extraordinarily expansive. To be sure, TCI wanted to avoid disclosure and constrained its trading activities accordingly. In fact, the intent to avoid disclosure under Section 13(d) is ubiquitous. Quite apart from wanting to conceal acquisition tactics, a desire to avoid the expense of disclosure is inevitable. But "preventing" the vesting of beneficial ownership in shares must mean more than what the district court described. At a minimum, the transaction must include a component that provides a substantial equivalence of the rights of ownership relevant to control, or include steps that stop short of, or conceal, the vesting of ownership, while nevertheless ensuring that such ownership will vest at the signal of the would-be owner. Conduct lacking such a component or steps does not violate the statute even when fully intended to avoid disclosure. *Reliance Elec.*, 404 U.S. at 422, 92 S. Ct. 596 ("Liability cannot be imposed simply because the investor structured his transaction with the intent of avoiding liability under §16(b).").

The district court's rationale depended so heavily on the Funds' intent to avoid disclosure that it found it unnecessary to decide whether cash-settled total-return equity swaps constituted the equivalence of beneficial ownership of shares absent a desire not to disclose. *CSX Corp.*, 562 F. Supp. 2d at 545-48. (The district court strongly implied that it did.) It simply held that such swaps prevented the vesting of beneficial ownership—a characteristic common to all non-purchasing acts—and was intended to avoid disclosure—an everpresent state of mind. *Id.* at 551-52. The intent to avoid disclosure cannot constitute a violation of the statute when the underlying transaction does not provide the party with the substantial equivalence of the rights of ownership relevant to control. That is clearly the meaning of *Reliance Electric*.

I am aware of no SEC guidance establishing the meaning of "evade" in Rule 13-3(b), nor has our caselaw addressed the issue. In applying evasion provisions, the Commission appears to borrow doctrine from the tax evasion context, in particular, the business purpose and substance over form doctrines. *See generally Gregory v. Helvering*, 293 U.S. 465, (holding that when the form of a transaction does not comport with its substance, the substance of the transaction controls for tax liability purposes). For example, in what is perhaps its earliest interpretive guidance, the Commission suggested that a transaction would be interpreted as an attempt to evade registration requirements under the Act if it was not deemed "bona fide," even if it "might comply with the literal conditions of [the Act]." Letters of General Counsel Discussing Application of Section 3(a)(9), Securities Act Release No. 646, 1936 WL 31995, at *2 (Feb. 3, 1936) (citing *Gregory v. Helvering*, 293 U.S. 465, 55 S. Ct. 266, 79 L. Ed. 596 (1935)).

Similar analyses can also be seen in more recent Commission statements....

Evasion provisions must be read in light of the underlying statutory or regulatory provision. As explained above, there are many perfectly legal methods of intentionally avoiding disclosure under Section 13(d). Section 13(d) is designed to compel disclosure of holdings involving 5 percent beneficial ownership interests. It does not require disclosure of control ambitions absent such holdings. In that light, "evasion" suggests a transaction with the ownership characteristics and benefits intended to be regulated, or steps to create a false appearance of the transaction or the persons entering into it, to avoid compliance with the regulation's reporting requirements. *See* Letter from Brian V. Breheny, Deputy Dir., SEC Div. of Corp. Fin., as *Amicus Curiae*.

If the transaction under scrutiny does not have substantially the characteristics or expected benefits that are intended to be regulated, then an evasion provision simply does not apply. Evasion of Section 13(d), 15 U.S.C. §78m(d), is not present in cash-settled total-return equity swaps because the swaps themselves provide no means of exercising control. As explained in the discussion of Rule 13d-3(a), an owner of such swaps cannot seek to exercise control without buying the actual shares in an open competitive market. In the present case, when the Funds could not persuade CSX to change its policies, they had to make actual purchases of CSX stock, a step that would have been unnecessary if the swaps they held were the substantial equivalent of beneficial ownership.

It is also critical to note that the swaps here were not sham transactions creating a false appearance while lacking economic substance. Long counterparties to such swaps have legitimate economic purposes. As the district

B. Patterns of Engagement

court found with regard to TCI, the swaps would enable TCI to reap a leverage-amplified profit if CSX's management, faced with the Funds' potential challenge, instituted new policies that increased the value of the company. If that occurred, a successful insurgent proxy fight or other control transaction would have been precluded, but TCI would share in the increased value resulting from its efforts. Similarly, if competing bidders appeared with a higher price for the company, TCI would share in the increased share price.

Finally, my view does no substantial damage to underlying statutory policies; indeed, it effectuates them. As noted, swaps are not instruments that have escaped Congress's attention and are a poor candidate for being labeled an unforseen device used to evade congressional purpose.

To the contrary, at the time of the district court's decision, the 2000 Act not only exempted security-based swaps from the securities laws definition of a regulable "security" but also "prohibited" the SEC from regulating security-based swaps in the extraordinarily broad language quoted *supra* . . . . Congress's then perception of a lack of an equivalence between cash-settled total-return swaps and ownership of the underlying securities was further demonstrated by Section 16's exclusion of such swaps from the calculation of the 10 percent disgorgement trigger but inclusion in the calculation of profits from short-swing trades. That scheme recognizes that ownership rights do not attach to swaps and therefore such swaps cannot afford access to inside information. Given that by statute swaps could not then be counted in calculating Section 16's disgorgement trigger for the long party, it was a bold step indeed for the district court to hold that shares purchased and owned by the short party as a hedge were to be counted as owned by the long party because swaps "evade" the statutory purpose.

The situation is not much different today. While the SEC now has authority to regulate security-based swaps, it has simply repromulgated Rule 13d-3. For the reasons stated, this hardly justifies a court treating cash-settled total-return swaps as an evasion of Section 13(d).

C. "Group" Formation

. . . The district court's finding as to the formation of a group between TCI and 3G in February 2007 cannot be upheld without adopting the district court's legal conclusions regarding swaps. It was necessarily based in part on the premise that TCI's purchase of swaps rendered TCI a beneficial owner of shares bought by the short parties as a hedge. It was that premise that led the court to conclude that TCI's goal in February 2007 was at that time to seek control of CSX through the use of swaps. Indeed, on February 13, 2007, TCI and 3G did not own in the aggregate 5% of CSX's actual shares.

The district court's finding of a group also suffers from a second error. That finding was that "the parties activities from at least as early as February 13, 2007, were products of concerted action." However, Rule 13d-5(b)(1) applies only to groups formed "for the purpose of acquiring, holding, voting or disposing" of "securities" of the target firm. The Rule does not encompass all "concerted action" with an aim to change a target firm's policies even while retaining an option to wage a proxy fight or engage in some other control transaction at a later time. Indeed, the Rule does not encompass "concerted action" with a change of control aim that does not involve one or more of the specified acts.

The overwhelming evidence is that TCI, while understanding that a hostile proxy fight might ultimately be necessary, first sought to change CSX's policies without a control change and to profit through swaps. In fact, TCI was negotiating with CSX management at the end of March, and the strongest evidence relied upon by the district court in support of the TCI-3G group finding was the "parallel proxy fight preparations," which occurred in "late September-October 2007." The finding of a group formation in February 2007 is, therefore, flawed.

There are only two pieces of evidence supporting the February 2007 finding. One is the fact of the relationship between TCI and 3G—a 3G affiliate was an investor in TCI. The other is that, on two occasions, 3G purchased shares after conversations with TCI. These are the only concrete acts relied upon by the district court that might reflect a February 2007 agreement requiring aggregation of TCI/3G shareholdings.

As to the ongoing relationship between TCI and 3G, it surely demonstrates an opportunity to form a "group," but it also provides an explanation for frequent conversations that do not involve CSX. With regard to 3G's purchases of stock, there is no claim that TCI increased its shareholdings at the same time, that is, no evidence of "concerted action" in buying actual shares. In fact, there is no evidence whatsoever that 3G's and TCI's purchases of CSX stock were coordinated in February 2007. Indeed, the district court found that, at this time, TCI was informing other funds of TCI's interest in altering CSX's business plans in the hope of "steer[ing] CSX shares into the hands of like-minded associates." There is no evidence that 3G's purchases at this time were more than the result of this sharing of information, which hardly amounts to an agreement to buy CSX shares.

The finding of a "group" owning 5% of CSX shares in February 2007 is clearly erroneous, and I concur in order to seek clarification on a remand.

Conclusion

I therefore concur in the result. I add a final word, a relief to any reader who got this far. The issue here is not fact specific. Total-return cash-settled swap agreements can be expected to cause some party to purchase the referenced shares as a hedge. No one questions that any understanding between long and short parties regarding the purchase, sale, retention, or voting of shares renders them a group—including the long party—deemed to be the beneficial owner of the referenced shares purchased as a hedge and any other shares held by the group. Whether, absent any such understanding, total-return cash-settled swaps render a long party the beneficial owner of referenced shares bought as a hedge by the immediate short party or some other party down the line is a question of law not fact. At the time of the district court opinion, the SEC had no authority to regulate such "understanding"-free swaps. It has such authority now, but it has simply repromulgated the earlier regulations. These regulations, and the SEC's repromulgation of them, offer no reasons for treating such swaps as rendering long parties subject to Sections 13 and 16 based on shares purchased by another party as a hedge. Absent some reasoned direction from the SEC, there is neither need nor reason for a court to do so.

NOTES AND QUESTIONS

1. **The deal.** There is no pending management-initiated transaction here. TCI, one of the most well-known and successful hedge funds in recent years, in pursuing activist investing, thought CSX should pursue a leveraged buyout or other going private transaction. To increase its influence, it and another activist investor each sought representatives on the CSX board of directors. The legal issues go to alleged violations of the federal securities laws. The fact pattern illustrates the difference between disclosure required by a proxy solicitation under §14(a) of the 1934 Act and disclosure required by the early warning provision of §13(d) added by the Williams Act in 1968.

2. **Swaps.** How do the swaps fit in? This fact pattern illustrates the hedging part of the hedge fund label. TCI, for example, acquired at least some of its position not by directly purchasing shares in CSX, but more indirectly by acquiring a derivative or a swap, a private contractual exchange between two parties in which TCI would be the long party to the exchange by which it would receive the economic exposure of the equity (here the CSX stock) courtesy of the counterparty who would contractually agree to provide the financial equivalent of owning the stock. It is a way for an investor like TCI to obtain the financial position as a CSX shareholder but only initially put up the fee it pays to the counterparty to enter into the exchange. This form of leveraging the investment is a frequent part of investing today, particularly with hedge funds. The issue here is whether TCI should be considered as the beneficial owner of those shares, for purposes of measuring whether it had passed the threshold for disclosure under §13(d). Were the swaps a way of evading the regulation of the Williams Act? Here the court notes the additional financial layer to

the transaction. The short party, the counterparty to TCI who has received a fee from TCI to take the risk of a future increase in the value of CSX stock, can hedge that risk by actually buying an equivalent number of shares of CSX (thereby protecting itself should CSX share value rise and it had to pay TCI, but hoping to make a profit from the fee it received if there is no change in the value of CSX stock). The district court's interpretations of this exchange was as follows: TCI knows the counterparty will make this purchase, and it knows further that when the swap is unwound (or completed) that the counterparty will then want to dispose of the stock it had purchased with the result that TCI at that point can swoop in and immediately acquire that block of stock. TCI would effectively have a large position without having to disclose it, a possible evasion that seems to concern the court (and the SEC which filed an amicus brief).

3. **Remedies.** This case also illustrates remedies available for violation of the federal securities laws in a takeover context that you should compare to remedies under state law. *See, e.g.*, the *Topps* case in Chapter 13. The outcome of the vote was that each of the hedge funds was successful in getting two nominees elected to the board of CSX. The company would argue that the noncompliance with the Williams Act's provisions gave the activists a head start that distorted the vote. Look at the remedy the district court provided, particularly its response to the petition for sterilization of the shares. Is the court letting the hedge funds retain the benefits of their noncompliance? What is the court's worry about the sterilization remedy? What about alternative relief of delaying the vote and requiring resubmitting of any proxy solicitations?

15 INTERNATIONAL TRANSACTIONS

There has been a dramatic surge in the number of deals outside the United States, particularly in the twenty-first century, as shown in Chart 15-1 below.

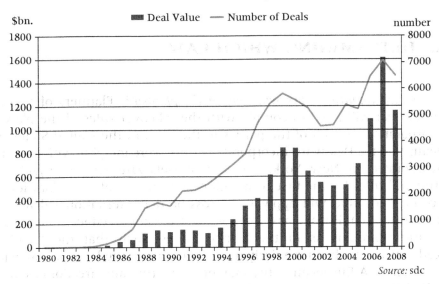

Chart 15-1

Non-US M&A activity, 1980-2008

Source: sdc

As a result, more deals are cross-border transactions in which participants in the deal come from different countries and legal systems. This chapter briefly describes several important ways in which regulation in other countries differs from what we have seen in the United States earlier in the book, but using the prior structure as a template for this cross-border discussion. Before looking at the differences in legal rules, it is important to focus on how the economic and practical incentives for deals will be different because of the different structure of share ownership across different cultures. The United States, along with the United Kingdom, Australia, and some other countries reflect a pattern of share ownership characterized by significant dispersion among individual shareholders or institutions. In many European countries, in contrast, there are large block holders that can dominate decision-making regarding takeovers. In some countries a dominant bank-centered financial system means that the takeovers market is decided among a smaller group of participants. In other countries, families or related groups provide large block holders in many public companies. As a result, takeovers in countries with widely dispersed shareholders will look different than those with substantial block holders. Yet, even within countries with shareholding patterns more oriented to takeovers through markets, there are real differences in how takeovers are regulated, including hostile takeovers. A second difference to focus on is the difference in regulation between those directed as deals put forward or involving a controlling shareholder and takeovers in the absence of a controlling shareholder. There are differences in the rules in both contexts, as compared to those discussed earlier in this book.

A. DETERMINING WHICH LAW

Which countries' laws will concern the planner? Planners of a cross-border deal will need to comply with the takeover rules of the place of incorporation of each of the parties to the deal. In the United States this means that if a Delaware-incorporated entity were merging with an entity incorporated in New York, the law of Delaware would provide the structural rules for the first corporation and the law of New York for the second. The same will apply to a cross-border international deal. One difference is that Europe has not provided the same freedom of movement for incorporations as in the United States, such that the "seat" or headquarters has been regularly used to determine the law applicable to a corporation. A European entity may not have the same freedom as in the United States to change its place of incorporation and thus pick the governance rules, although this has been relaxed after the *Centros* decisions of the European Court of Justice (Case # 212/97 decision of March 9, 1999) and the establishment of a European entity form (European company or SE). *See* Council Directive 205/56/EC on Cross Border Mergers of Limited Liability Companies, 2005 O.J. (L.310). Federal securities law in the United States has the potential to reach the transactions of entities incorporated or headquartered abroad whose business and shareholders impact the United States, even if these transactions seem to be a relatively small part of the foreign company's overall footprint. Here the deal planners look to attorneys for guidance on the possibility of coming within exemptions in the tender offer rules and related regulations under the federal securities laws. The Supreme Court has held that the antifraud provisions of the federal securities law does not have extraterritorial effect, as for a foreign plaintiff suing for a transaction on a foreign exchange. *See* Morrison v. National Australia Bank, 561 U.S. 247 (2010).

B. MORE EXPANSIVE ROLES FOR SHAREHOLDERS IN FRIENDLY DEALS

The breadth of the role for shareholders in corporate governance. Recall from Chapter 3 the American focus, as illustrated by Delaware's law, to trust directors to make most corporate decisions, including many involving takeovers. Shareholders retain rights to vote, sell, and sue but only in limited doses. Many European countries provide a greater role for shareholders generally and more particularly in relation to takeovers. This includes requirements of shareholder approval of authorization of shares or preemptive rights. Shareholders are also more able to call a shareholders' meeting without the board having a gatekeeper blocking position as usually occurs in the United States or being able to amend the bylaws more easily than has occurred in the United States. *See generally* Kraakman et al., THE ANATOMY OF CORPORATE LAW (2d ed. 2009) at 73 (the U.S. as the least shareholder centric jurisdiction among principal commercial jurisdictions presented.)

Shareholder approval of mergers. The percentage vote required for shareholder approval of fundamental corporate changes such as mergers can be higher in jurisdictions outside the United States. The European Union's Third Company Law Directive, with which member states are required to harmonize their domestic law, requires a minimum of two-thirds of the shareholder vote at a shareholder meeting or one-half of the outstanding stock. *See* European Union, Third Company Law Directive (1978). In a Delaware deal where the requirement is more than half of the outstanding shares, the European vote requirement could actually be lower if there were a large minority of shares which did not vote. Some European countries have even higher requirements, such as 75 percent in Germany or the UK. *See generally* THE ANATOMY OF CORPORATE LAW, supra, at 93.

Shareholder approval of acquiring company transactions. Recall from Chapter 3 that triangular mergers, sale of assets, and other forms of transactions permit planners to avoid the requirement for shareholder approval, at least for acquiring companies. Outside of the United States, it is more likely that the shareholder approval requirements extend to the acquiring company as well as the target.

C. ROLES FOR GROUPS OTHER THAN SHAREHOLDERS

Requirement of expert reports. The EU requires public companies to commission independent expert reports on the substantive terms of the transaction. *See* Article 10 of the Third Directive. The Tokyo Stock Exchange requires that Japanese deals include a third-party analysis to determine whether the proposed merger terms are fair. Compare this to the United States where there is no formal rule requiring such a report but "best practices" boosted by the threat of liability in Delaware Supreme Court decisions such as *Van Gorkom* have spurred dealmakers, in conflicted deals at least, to regularly include fairness opinions of investment bankers, which provide some analogous protection.

Requirement of judicial approval. The closest analogy to a United States statutory merger in the United Kingdom is called a "scheme of arrangement," which has none of the pejorative meaning that the word "scheme" carries in the United States. A UK scheme is not effective until there has been court approval, which can slow down a deal or perhaps raise additional hurdles.

Requirement of government approval. Countries worried about the loss of their local industries sometimes require government consent prior to a cross-border deal. Even the United States, which normally defers to private ordering as to structure of deals, has a statutory requirement that can block mergers where there are concerns of national security. Since 1988, the President has had the authority to block, or order the divestiture of, any acquisition of control of a U.S. business by a foreign party on a finding (non-reviewable) that the acquisition might pose a significant threat to U.S. national security. Deal review has been delegated to the Committee on Foreign Investment in the United States (CFIUS). *See* 50 U.S.C. §2170; 31 C.F.R. §§600.101 et seq. Recent years have seen deals to take over U.S. ports or oil companies undone by concern over foreign ownership. Some other countries are even more likely to intervene in such deals. In counties where state run economies have been privatized to some extent, such government controls can still be seen.

Requirements for employee participation. Germany's corporate system includes a codetermination system in which employees have half of the seats on the corporation's supervisory board, which gives them a greater formal role in approval of takeovers. The EU mandates consultation with employees. *See generally* THE ANATOMY OF CORPORATE LAW, supra, at 100.

Creditor Protection. The corporate legal system in many European countries and in Japan provides more formal protection for creditors than do the statutory laws of the United States.

D. DIFFERENT APPROACHES TO ABILITY OF MANAGEMENT TO OPPOSE DEALS FAVORED BY SHAREHOLDERS

Greater freedom for shareholders to act outside of board control. In many jurisdictions outside the United States, shareholders retain the authority to take action on their own, such as initiating an extraordinary resolution that in the U.S could be blocked by the directors' power to manage the business.

Limits on management ability to take "frustrating actions." Rule 21 of the London City Takeovers Code prohibits companies from taking frustrating actions" in a takeover setting without the approval of shareholders. Thus, British companies cannot "take any action which may result in any offer or bona fide possible offer being frustrated or its shareholders being denied the opportunity to decide on the merits." In that setting, poison pills and various other board-initiated takeover defenses would not be possible and consequently more of the takeover fight would be moved to the space provided for shareholder decision-making. This frustrating action concept is also found in some other commonwealth companies and reflects similar concerns elsewhere.

E. DIFFERENT RULES IN DEALS BY A CONTROLLING SHAREHOLDER

Fewer Appraisals. A handful of European countries use appraisal in limited circumstances, but this right to get your cash back from the company is not as common as in the United States.

Ability to follow up takeover with squeeze out. Many of the European countries do provide an express legal mechanism for bidders to follow up an acquisition offer with a compulsory transaction that squeezes out any remaining holders at the same price.

Compulsory bids once a threshold is crossed. In an effort to protect minority shareholders, it is common outside of the United States to require a bidder who acquires a block of shares that crosses a certain threshold, say 30 percent, to make an offer for all of the remaining shares.

F. DIFFERENT METHODS OF CONFLICT RESOLUTION

Takeovers code vs. courts. A major difference between the United States and the United Kingdom is the dispute resolution scheme for a takeover. The United States relies on courts for the most part, particularly the Delaware Court of Chancery, whose judges provide quick hearings on ongoing takeovers disputes under Delaware corporate law. The UK, in contrast, relies on the City Takeover Code, a non-governmental entity reflecting a degree of self-regulation by the key players in the industry. The process is designed to encourage the parties to consult with the Takeovers Panel early in the process. The Panel, in turn, works with the parties to achieve a consensual resolution. The Cadbury/Kraft deal described below illustrates the difference in approach under a takeovers panel. Australia follows a similar approach. Professors Armour and Skeel have argued that the U.K. pattern based on self-regulation led to a regime largely driven by the interests of investors while the dynamics of judicial law-making in the United States has benefited managers. *See* Armour & Skeel, *Who Writes the Rules for Hostile Takeovers and Why?* 95 GEO. L.J. 1727 (2007).

Civil law and focus on ex ante. Acquisitions in civil law countries also do not make as much use of courts as dispute resolvers in the midst of a takeover.

G. CADBURY/KRAFT AS A CASE STUDY

Differences between legal regulation of mergers and acquisitions outside of the United States can be illustrated by examining Kraft, Foods, Inc.'s bid for Cadbury in 2009/10.

G. Cadbury/Kraft as a Case Study

The Parties. Kraft Foods, Inc., a large American food company, made a surprise offer for Cadbury PLC in 2009. Kraft, maker of some of America's most well-known brands, had earlier in its life been a part of tobacco giant Phillip Morris, who merged it with Nabisco Brands. By the time of its approach to Cadbury, it was again an independent company. Legendary financier Warren Buffet owned about eight percent of Kraft at the time of the Cadbury offer.

Cadbury was begun by John Cadbury in Birmingham England in the early nineteenth century. By 1847, he and his brothers began selling its first solid chocolate, and by the 1920s, Cadbury dominated the British confectionary market. In 1969, Cadbury merged with Schweppes, a drinks maker. Cadbury and Schweppes demerged in 2008 under shareholder pressure, but Cadbury still remained a large confectionary presence in various parts of the world, including fast-growing markets such as India and Mexico. Members of the Cadbury family had led the company until the mid-1990s, but by the time of the Kraft offer did not control enough shares to determine the fate of the company.

As a British company, Cadbury was subject to the City Code on Takeovers and Mergers, which governs any firm bidding for a company that is listed on the London stock exchange and any company on the receiving end of such an approach.

The Timeline

- *August 28, 2009*—Kraft made an unsolicited offer to Cadbury's management.
- *September 9*—Kraft publicly announced its "bear hug," a "possible offer" of cash and shares to Cadbury, which it valued at 10.2 billion pounds or 745 pence a share. The possible offer includes financing and due diligence conditions that under Rule 13 of the Takeovers Code are not permitted except on limited circumstances and with prior consultation with the Takeovers Panel. As a result, at the point that the "possible" adjective were to be removed from this offer, so likely would these conditions. Cadbury says the offer "fundamentally undervalues" the company.
- *September 22*—Cadbury asks the Takeovers Panel for a "put up or shut up" deadline.
- *September 25*—UK Cabinet Secretary Peter Mandelson suggests foreign ownership of British companies could damage the economy.
- *September 30*—The Takeovers Panel gives Kraft until November 9 to make a formal bid. If Kraft does not make an offer within that deadline it cannot make another bid for six months. This illustrates the more structured time line imposed on a takeover by an outside party, as opposed to the United States where parties proceed at their

own pace and where the timing of the annual meeting will often be a crucial determinant in a bidder's strategy.

- *November 9*—Kraft makes its offer but doesn't improve the terms. Because of a decline in the stock price of Kraft since September 7, the Kraft offer is down to 9.8 billion pounds. Cadbury again rejects the bid as "derisory."
- *Mid-November*—Royal Bank of Scotland, state-owned since the 2008 financial meltdown, sustains criticism because of its role in financing Kraft.
- *Mid-November*—Hershey, Inc. and Italian confectionary company Ferrero consider an alternative bid, which would likely be as a white knight.
- *December 4*—Kraft posts its circular describing its bid. This starts the 60-day timetable under the City Code. Potential bidders who have already expressed an interest, such as Hershey and Ferrero, have until January 25 to file a bid or be barred for six months from making an offer for Cadbury.
- *December 14*—Cadbury's defense promises higher dividends and tells investors it will have higher sales and profits margins.
- *January 5, 2010*—Kraft secures more cash by selling its frozen pizza business to Nestle and increases the cash portion of its offer. Warren Buffet warns Kraft not to overpay for Cadbury and specifically warns about giving up too many Kraft shares.
- *January 7*—Cadbury holds informal talks with Hershey about a friendly deal. Because of a 2002 Pennsylvania statute, enacted after Hershey sought to merge with the William Wrigley Company, Hershey's controlling shareholder, the Hershey Trust, must obtain the approval of the Pennsylvania attorney general for any transaction that could threaten the Trust's control of Hershey. Because Hershey is considerably smaller than Kraft or Cadbury, it would likely need to use stock, which in turn could threaten the Trust's level of control.
- *January 19*—Kraft raises its offer to 850 pence. Cadbury recommends the almost 12 billion pound sale to Kraft.
- *January 25*—Deadline for the previously announced potential bidders to make their offer. By this date, the two possible alternative bidders announce they will not go forward.
- *February 2*—Deadline for Cadbury's shareholders to vote on Kraft's offer. Last day for any new bidder to launch its own offer, which if launched would have restarted the 60-day timetable. Kraft secures 71 percent of the Cadbury shares by this date and a few days later crossed the 75 percent threshold, permitting it to delist Cadbury shares from public trading.
- *February 9*—Kraft announces that it will close the Cadbury plant at Keynsham, England, that Cadbury management had earlier

announced would close, but which Kraft, during the takeover, had said it would be able to keep open. The Takeovers Panel was said to be investigating, but without the power to intervene or fine.
- *March*—Kraft CEO receives a $10.6 million performance bonus (up from $4.1 million the previous year).

The Aftermath. The Takeovers Panel did investigate Cadbury and found its conduct regarding the Keynsham plant as inconsistent with the Takeover Code. More generally, the deal helped spur changes to the Takeover Code that became effective in 2011. Cadbury's chairman had argued that existing rules favored bidders over targets and resulted in damaging periods of uncertainty. The new rules provide that the names of additional prospective bidders who have approached the target will be disclosed with a target's announcement of a bid. There is a 28-day "put up or shut up" period for bidders, more binding than in the previous rules. Break fees are prohibited. Employee representatives must have their views publicized. *See* Code Committee of the Takeover Panel, RS 2011/1 published July 21, 2011.

APPENDIX A: DELAWARE GENERAL CORPORATION LAW

Subchapter I. Formation

§109. Bylaws

Subchapter IV. Directors and Officers

§141. Board of Directors; Powers; Number, Qualifications, Terms and Quorum; Committees; Classes of Directors; Nonstock Corporations; Reliance upon Books; Action Without Meeting; Removal
§144. Interested Directors; Quorum
§146. Submission of Matters for Stockholder Vote

Subchapter VI. Stock Transfers

§203 Business Combinations with Interested Stockholders

Subchapter IX. Merger, Consolidation or Conversion

§251. Merger or Consolidation of Domestic Corporations
§252. Merger or Consolidation of Domestic and Foreign Corporations; Service of Process upon Surviving or Resulting Corporation [omitted]
§253. Merger of Parent Corporation and Subsidiary or Subsidiaries
§254. Merger or Consolidation of Domestic Corporation and Joint-Stock or Other Association [omitted]
§255. Merger or Consolidation of Domestic Nonstock Corporations [omitted]
§256. Merger or Consolidation of Domestic and Foreign Nonstock Corporations; Service of Process upon Surviving or Resulting Corporation [omitted]
§257. Merger or Consolidation of Domestic Stock and Nonstock Corporations [omitted]

§258. Merger or Consolidation of Domestic and Foreign Stock and Nonstock Corporations [omitted]
§259. Status, Rights, Liabilities, of Constituent and Surviving or Resulting Corporations Following Merger or Consolidation
§260. Powers of Corporation Surviving or Resulting from Merger or Consolidation; Issuance of Stock, Bonds or Other Indebtedness
§261. Effect of Merger upon Pending Actions
§262. Appraisal Rights
§263. Merger or Consolidation of Domestic Corporation and Limited Partnership [omitted]
§264. Merger or Consolidation of Domestic Corporation and Limited Liability Company [omitted]
§265. Conversion of Other Entities to a Domestic Corporation [omitted]
§266. Conversion of Domestic Corporation to Other Entities [omitted]

Subchapter X. Sale of Assets, Dissolution and Winding Up

§271. Sale, Lease or Exchange of Assets; Consideration; Procedure

SUBCHAPTER I. FORMATION

§109. Bylaws

(a) The original or other bylaws of a corporation may be adopted, amended or repealed by the incorporators, by the initial directors of a corporation other than a nonstock corporation or initial members of the governing body of a nonstock corporation if they were named in the certificate of incorporation, or, before a corporation other than a nonstock corporation has received any payment for any of its stock, by its board of directors. After a corporation other than a nonstock corporation has received any payment for any of its stock, the power to adopt, amend or repeal bylaws shall be in the stockholders entitled to vote. In the case of a nonstock corporation, the power to adopt, amend or repeal bylaws shall be in its members entitled to vote. Notwithstanding the foregoing, any corporation may, in its certificate of incorporation, confer the power to adopt, amend or repeal bylaws upon the directors or, in the case of a nonstock corporation, upon its governing body. The fact that such power has been so conferred upon the directors or governing body, as the case may be, shall not divest the stockholders or members of the power, nor limit their power to adopt, amend or repeal bylaws.

(b) The bylaws may contain any provision, not inconsistent with law or with the certificate of incorporation, relating to the business of the corporation, the conduct of its affairs, and its rights or powers or the rights or powers of its stockholders, directors, officers or employees.

SUBCHAPTER IV. DIRECTORS AND OFFICERS

§141. Board of Directors; Powers; Number, Qualifications, Terms and Quorum; Committees; Classes of Directors; Nonstock Corporations; Reliance upon Books; Action Without Meeting; Removal

(a) The business and affairs of every corporation organized under this chapter shall be managed by or under the direction of a board of directors, except as may be otherwise provided in this chapter or in its certificate of incorporation. If any such provision is made in the certificate of incorporation, the powers and duties conferred or imposed upon the board of directors by this chapter shall be exercised or performed to such extent and by such person or persons as shall be provided in the certificate of incorporation.

(b) The board of directors of a corporation shall consist of 1 or more members, each of whom shall be a natural person. The number of directors shall be fixed by, or in the manner provided in, the bylaws, unless the certificate of incorporation fixes the number of directors, in which case a change in the number of directors shall be made only by amendment of the certificate. Directors need not be stockholders unless so required by the certificate of incorporation or the bylaws. The certificate of incorporation or bylaws may prescribe other qualifications for directors. Each director shall hold office until such director's successor is elected and qualified or until such director's earlier resignation or removal. Any director may resign at any time upon notice given in writing or by electronic transmission to the corporation. A resignation is effective when the resignation is delivered unless the resignation specifies a later effective date or an effective date determined upon the happening of an event or events. A resignation that is conditioned upon the director failing to receive a specified vote for reelection as a director may provide that it is irrevocable. A majority of the total number of directors shall constitute a quorum for the transaction of business unless the certificate of incorporation or the bylaws require a greater number. Unless the certificate of incorporation provides otherwise, the bylaws may provide that a number less than a majority shall constitute a quorum that in no case shall be less 1/3 than of the total number of directors except that when a board of 1 director is authorized under this section, then 1 director shall constitute a quorum. The vote of the majority of the directors present at a meeting at which a quorum is present shall be the act of the board of directors unless the certificate of incorporation or the bylaws shall require a vote of a greater number.

(c) (1) All corporations incorporated prior to July 1, 1996, shall be governed by paragraph (1) of this subsection, provided that any such corporation may by a resolution adopted by a majority of the whole board elect to be governed by paragraph (2) of this subsection, in which case paragraph (1) of this subsection shall not apply to such corporation. All corporations incorporated on or after July 1, 1996, shall be governed by paragraph (2) of this subsection. The board of directors may, by resolution passed by a majority of the whole board, designate 1 or more committees, each committee to consist of 1 or more of the directors of the corporation. The board may designate 1 or more directors as alternate members of any committee, who may replace any absent or disqualified member at any meeting of the committee. The bylaws may provide that in the absence or disqualification of a member of a committee, the member or members present at any meeting and not disqualified from voting, whether or not the member or members present constitute a quorum, may unanimously appoint another member of the board of directors to act at the meeting in the place of any such absent or disqualified member. Any such committee, to the extent provided in the resolution of the board of directors, or in the bylaws of the corporation, shall have and may exercise all the powers and authority of the board of directors in the management of the business and affairs of the corporation, and may authorize the seal of the corporation to be affixed to all papers which may require it; but no such committee shall have the power or authority in reference to amending the certificate of incorporation (except that a committee may, to the extent authorized in the resolution or resolutions providing for the issuance of shares of stock adopted by the board of directors as provided in subsection (a) of §151 of this title, fix the designations and any of the preferences or rights of such shares relating to dividends, redemption, dissolution, any distribution of assets of the corporation or the conversion into, or the exchange of such shares for, shares of any other class or classes or any other series of the same or any other class or classes of stock of the corporation or fix the number of shares of any series of stock or authorize the increase or decrease of the shares of any series), adopting an agreement of merger or consolidation under §251, §252, §254, §255, §256, §257, §258, §263 or §264 of this title, recommending to the stockholders the sale, lease or exchange of all or substantially all of the corporation's property and assets, recommending to the stockholders a dissolution of the corporation or a revocation of a dissolution, or amending the bylaws of the corporation; and, unless the resolution, bylaws or certificate of incorporation expressly so provides, no such committee shall have the power or authority to declare a dividend, to authorize the issuance of stock or to adopt a certificate of ownership and merger pursuant to §253 of this title.

(2) The board of directors may designate 1 or more committees, each committee to consist of 1 or more of the directors of the corporation. The board may designate 1 or more directors as alternate members of any committee, who may replace any absent or disqualified member at any meeting of the committee. The bylaws may provide that in the absence or disqualification of a member of a committee, the member or members present at any meeting and not

disqualified from voting, whether or not such member or members constitute a quorum, may unanimously appoint another member of the board of directors to act at the meeting in the place of any such absent or disqualified member. Any such committee, to the extent provided in the resolution of the board of directors, or in the bylaws of the corporation, shall have and may exercise all the powers and authority of the board of directors in the management of the business and affairs of the corporation, and may authorize the seal of the corporation to be affixed to all papers which may require it; but no such committee shall have the power or authority in reference to the following matter: (i) approving or adopting, or recommending to the stockholders, any action or matter (other than the election or removal of directors) expressly required by this chapter to be submitted to stockholders for approval or (ii) adopting, amending or repealing any bylaw of the corporation.

(3) Unless otherwise provided in the certificate of incorporation, the bylaws, or the resolution of the board of directors designating the committee, a committee may create one or more subcommittees, each subcommittee to consist of one or more members of the committee, and delegate to a subcommittee any or all of the powers and authority of the committee.

(d) The directors of any corporation organized under this chapter may, by the certificate of incorporation or by an initial bylaw, or by a bylaw adopted by a vote of the stockholders, be divided into 1, 2, or 3 classes; the term of office of those of the first class to expire at the first annual meeting held after such classification becomes effective; of the second class 1 year thereafter; of the third class 2 years thereafter; and at each annual election held after such classification becomes effective, directors shall be chosen for a full term, as the case may be, to succeed those whose terms expire. The certificate of incorporation or bylaw provision dividing the directors into classes may authorize the board of directors to assign members of the board already in office to such classes at the time such classification becomes effective. The certificate of incorporation may confer upon holders of any class or series of stock the right to elect 1 or more directors who shall serve for such term, and have such voting powers as shall be stated in the certificate of incorporation. The terms of office and voting powers of the directors elected separately by the holders of any class or series of stock may be greater than or less than those of any other director or class of directors. In addition, the certificate of incorporation may confer upon 1 or more directors, whether or not elected separately by the holders of any class or series of stock, voting powers greater than or less than those of other directors. Any such provision conferring greater or lesser voting power shall apply to voting in any committee or subcommittee, unless otherwise provided in the certificate of incorporation or bylaws. If the certificate of incorporation provides that 1 or more directors shall have more or less than 1 vote per director on any matter, every reference in this chapter to a majority or other proportion of the directors shall refer to a majority or other proportion of the votes of the directors.

(e) A member of the board of directors, or a member of any committee designated by the board of directors, shall, in the performance of such member's duties, be fully protected in relying in good faith upon the records of the corporation and upon such information, opinions, reports or statements presented to the corporation by any of the corporation's officers or employees, or committees of the board of directors, or by any other person as to matters the member reasonably believes are within such other person's professional or expert competence and who has been selected with reasonable care by or on behalf of the corporation.

(f) Unless otherwise restricted by the certificate of incorporation or bylaws, any action required or permitted to be taken at any meeting of the board of directors or of any committee thereof may be taken without a meeting if all members of the board or committee, as the case may be, consent thereto in writing or by electronic submission, and the writing or writings or electronic transmission or transmissions are filed with the minutes of proceedings of the board, or committee.

(g) Unless otherwise restricted by the certificate of incorporation or bylaws, the board of directors of any corporation organized under this chapter may hold its meetings, and have an office or offices, outside of this State.

(h) Unless otherwise restricted by the certificate of incorporation or bylaws, the board of directors shall have the authority to fix the compensation of directors.

(i) Unless otherwise restricted by the certificate of incorporation or bylaws, members of the board of directors of any corporation, or any committee designated by the board, may participate in a meeting of such board, or committee by means of conference telephone or other communications equipment by means of which all persons participating in the meeting can hear each other, and participation in a meeting pursuant to this subsection shall constitute presence in person at the meeting.

(j) The certificate of incorporation of any nonstock corporation may provide that less than 1/3 of the members of the governing body may constitute a quorum thereof and may otherwise provide that the business and affairs of the corporation shall be managed in a manner different from that provided in this section. Except as may be otherwise provided by the certificate of incorporation, this section shall apply to such a corporation, and when so applied, all references to the board of directors, to members thereof, and to stockholders shall be deemed to refer to the governing body of the corporation, the members thereof and the members of the corporation, respectively; and all references to stock, capital stock, or shares thereof shall be deemed to refer to memberships of a non-profit nonstock corporation and to membership interests of any other nonstock corporation.

(k) Any director or the entire board of directors may be removed, with or without cause, by the holders of a majority of the shares then entitled to vote at an election of directors, except as follows:

(1) Unless the certificate of incorporation otherwise provides, in the case of a corporation whose board is classified as provided in subsection (d) of this section, stockholders may effect such removal only for cause; or

(2) In the case of a corporation having cumulative voting, if less than the entire board is to be removed, no director may be removed without cause if the votes cast against such director's removal would be sufficient to elect such director if then cumulatively voted at an election of the entire board of directors, or, if there be classes of directors, at an election of the class of directors of which such director is a part. Whenever the holders of any class or series are entitled to elect 1 or more directors by the certificate of incorporation, this subsection shall apply, in respect to the removal without cause of a director or directors so elected, to the vote of the holders of the outstanding shares of that class or series and not to the vote of the outstanding shares as a whole.

§144. Interested Directors; Quorum

(a) No contract or transaction between a corporation and 1 or more of its directors or officers, or between a corporation and any other corporation, partnership, association, or other organization in which 1 or more of its directors or officers, are directors or officers, or have a financial interest, shall be void or voidable solely for this reason, or solely because the director or officer is present at or participates in the meeting of the board or committee which authorizes the contract or transaction, or solely because any such director's or officer's votes are counted for such purpose, if:

(1) The material facts as to the director's or officer's relationship or interest and as to the contract or transaction are disclosed or are known to the board of directors or the committee, and the board or committee in good faith authorizes the contract or transaction by the affirmative votes of a majority of the disinterested directors, even though the disinterested directors be less than a quorum; or

(2) The material facts as to the director's or officer's relationship or interest and as to the contract or transaction are disclosed or are known to the stockholders entitled to vote thereon, and the contract or transaction is specifically approved in good faith by vote of the stockholders; or

(3) The contract or transaction is fair as to the corporation as of the time it is authorized, approved or ratified, by the board of directors, a committee or the stockholders.

(b) Common or interested directors may be counted in determining the presence of a quorum at a meeting of the board of directors or of a committee which authorizes the contract or transaction.

§146. Submission of Matters for Stockholder Vote

A corporation may agree to submit a matter to a vote of its stockholders whether or not the board of directors determines at any time subsequent to approving such matter that such matter is no longer advisable and recommends that the stockholders reject or vote against the matter.

SUBCHAPTER VI. STOCK TRANSFERS

§203. Business Combinations with Interested Stockholders

(a) Notwithstanding any other provisions of this chapter, a corporation shall not engage in any business combination with any interested stockholder for a period of 3 years following the time that such stockholder became an interested stockholder, unless:

(1) Prior to such time the board of directors of the corporation approved either the business combination or the transaction which resulted in the stockholder becoming an interested stockholder;

(2) Upon consummation of the transaction which resulted in the stockholder becoming an interested stockholder, the interested stockholder owned at least 85% of the voting stock of the corporation outstanding at the time the transaction commenced, excluding for purposes of determining the number of shares outstanding those shares owned (i) by persons who are directors and also officers and (ii) employee stock plans in which employee participants do not have the right to determine confidentially whether shares held subject to the plan will be tendered in a tender or exchange offer; or

(3) At or subsequent to such time the business combination is approved by the board of directors and authorized at an annual or special meeting of stockholders, and not by written consent, by the affirmative vote of at least 662/3% of the outstanding voting stock which is not owned by the interested stockholder.

(b) The restrictions contained in this section shall not apply if:

(1) The corporation's original certificate of incorporation contains a provision expressly electing not to be governed by this section;

(2) The corporation, by action of its board of directors, adopts an amendment to its bylaws within 90 days of February 2, 1988, expressly electing not to be governed by this section, which amendment shall not be further amended by the board of directors;

(3) The corporation, by action of its stockholders, adopts an amendment to its certificate of incorporation or bylaws expressly

electing not to be governed by this section; provided that, in addition to any other vote required by law, such amendment to the certificate of incorporation or bylaws must be approved by the affirmative vote of a majority of the shares entitled to vote. An amendment adopted pursuant to this paragraph shall be effective immediately in the case of a corporation that both (i) has never had a class of voting stock that falls within any of the three categories set out in subsection (b)(4) hereof, and (ii) has not elected by a provision in its original certificate of incorporation or any amendment thereto to be governed by this section. In all other cases, an amendment adopted pursuant to this paragraph shall not be effective until 12 months after the adoption of such amendment and shall not apply to any business combination between such corporation and any person who became an interested stockholder of such corporation on or prior to such adoption. A bylaw amendment adopted pursuant to this paragraph shall not be further amended by the board of directors;

(4) The corporation does not have a class of voting stock that is: (i) Listed on a national securities exchange; or (ii) held of record by more than 2,000 stockholders, unless any of the foregoing results from action taken, directly or indirectly, by an interested stockholder or from a transaction in which a person becomes an interested stockholder;

(5) A stockholder becomes an interested stockholder inadvertently and (i) as soon as practicable divests itself of ownership of sufficient shares so that the stockholder ceases to be an interested stockholder; and (ii) would not, at any time within the 3-year period immediately prior to a business combination between the corporation and such stockholder, have been an interested stockholder but for the inadvertent acquisition of ownership;

(6) The business combination is proposed prior to the consummation or abandonment of and subsequent to the earlier of the public announcement or the notice required hereunder of a proposed transaction which (i) constitutes one of the transactions described in the 2nd sentence of this paragraph; (ii) is with or by a person who either was not an interested stockholder during the previous 3 years or who became an interested stockholder with the approval of the corporation's board of directors or during the period described in paragraph (7) of this subsection (b); and (iii) is approved or not opposed by a majority of the members of the board of directors then in office (but not less than 1) who were directors prior to any person becoming an interested stockholder during the previous 3 years or were recommended for election or elected to succeed such directors by a majority of such directors. The proposed transactions referred to in the preceding sentence are limited to (x) a merger or consolidation of the corporation (except for a merger in respect of which, pursuant to §251(f)

of this title, no vote of the stockholders of the corporation is required); (y) a sale, lease, exchange, mortgage, pledge, transfer or other disposition (in 1 transaction or a series of transactions), whether as part of a dissolution or otherwise, of assets of the corporation or of any direct or indirect majority-owned subsidiary of the corporation (other than to any direct or indirect wholly-owned subsidiary or to the corporation) having an aggregate market value equal to 50% or more of either [the] aggregate market value of all of the assets of the corporation determined on a consolidated basis or the aggregate market value of all the outstanding stock of the corporation; or (z) a proposed tender or exchange offer for 50% or more of the outstanding voting stock of the corporation. The corporation shall give not less than 20 days' notice to all interested stockholders prior to the consummation of any of the transactions described in clause (x) or (y) of the 2nd sentence of this paragraph; or

(7) The business combination is with an interested stockholder who became an interested stockholder at a time when the restrictions contained in this section did not apply by reason of any of paragraphs (1) through (4) of this subsection (b), provided, however, that this paragraph (7) shall not apply if, at the time such interested stockholder became an interested stockholder, the corporation's certificate of incorporation contained a provision authorized by the last sentence of this subsection (b).

Notwithstanding paragraphs (1), (2), (3) and (4) of this subsection, a corporation may elect by a provision of its original certificate of incorporation or any amendment thereto to be governed by this section; provided that any such amendment to the certificate of incorporation shall not apply to restrict a business combination between the corporation and an interested stockholder of the corporation if the interested stockholder became such prior to the effective date of the amendment.

(c) As used in this section only, the term:

(1) "Affiliate" means a person that directly, or indirectly through 1 or more intermediaries, controls, or is controlled by, or is under common control with, another person.

(2) "Associate," when used to indicate a relationship with any person, means:

(i) Any corporation, partnership, unincorporated association or other entity of which such person is a director, officer or partner or is, directly or indirectly, the owner of 20% or more of any class of voting stock;

(ii) any trust or other estate in which such person has at least a 20% beneficial interest or as to which such person serves as trustee or in a similar fiduciary capacity; and

(iii) any relative or spouse of such person, or any relative of such spouse, who has the same residence as such person.

(3) "Business combination," when used in reference to any corporation and any interested stockholder of such corporation, means:

(i) Any merger or consolidation of the corporation or any direct or indirect majority-owned subsidiary of the corporation with (A) the interested stockholder, or (B) with any other corporation, partnership, unincorporated association or other entity if the merger or consolidation is caused by the interested stockholder and as a result of such merger or consolidation subsection (a) of this section is not applicable to the surviving entity;

(ii) Any sale, lease, exchange, mortgage, pledge, transfer or other disposition (in 1 transaction or a series of transactions), except proportionately as a stockholder of such corporation, to or with the interested stockholder, whether as part of a dissolution or otherwise, of assets of the corporation or of any direct or indirect majority-owned subsidiary of the corporation which assets have an aggregate market value equal to 10% or more of either the aggregate market value of all the assets of the corporation determined on a consolidated basis or the aggregate market value of all the outstanding stock of the corporation;

(iii) Any transaction which results in the issuance or transfer by the corporation or by any direct or indirect majority-owned subsidiary of the corporation of any stock of the corporation or of such subsidiary to the interested stockholder, except: (A) Pursuant to the exercise, exchange or conversion of securities exercisable for, exchangeable for or convertible into stock of such corporation or any such subsidiary which securities were outstanding prior to the time that the interested stockholder became such; (B) pursuant to a merger under §251(g) of this title; (C) pursuant to a dividend or distribution paid or made, or the exercise, exchange or conversion of securities exercisable for, exchangeable for or convertible into stock of such corporation or any such subsidiary which security is distributed, pro rata to all holders of a class or series of stock of such corporation subsequent to the time the interested stockholder became such; (D) pursuant to an exchange offer by the corporation to purchase stock made on the same terms to all holders of said stock; or (E) any issuance or transfer of stock by the corporation; provided however, that in no case under items (C)-(E) above shall there be an increase in the interested stockholder's proportionate share of the stock of any class or series of the corporation or of the voting stock of the corporation;

(iv) Any transaction involving the corporation or any direct or indirect majority-owned subsidiary of the corporation which has the effect, directly or indirectly, of increasing the proportionate share of the stock of any class or series, or securities convertible into the stock of any class or series, of the corporation or of any such subsidiary which is owned by the interested stockholder, except as a result of immaterial changes due to fractional share adjustments or as a result of any purchase or redemption of any shares of stock not caused, directly or indirectly, by the interested stockholder; or

(v) Any receipt by the interested stockholder of the benefit, directly or indirectly (except proportionately as a stockholder of such corporation), of any loans, advances, guarantees, pledges or other financial benefits (other than those expressly permitted in subparagraphs (i)-(iv) of this paragraph) provided by or through the corporation or any direct or indirect majority-owned subsidiary.

(4) "Control," including the terms "controlling," "controlled by" and "under common control with," means the possession, directly or indirectly, of the power to direct or cause the direction of the management and policies of a person, whether through the ownership of voting stock, by contract or otherwise. A person who is the owner of 20% or more of the outstanding voting stock of any corporation, partnership, unincorporated association or other entity shall be presumed to have control of such entity, in the absence of proof by a preponderance of the evidence to the contrary; Notwithstanding the foregoing, a presumption of control shall not apply where such person holds voting stock, in good faith and not for the purpose of circumventing this section, as an agent, bank, broker, nominee, custodian or trustee for 1 or more owners who do not individually or as a group have control of such entity.

(5) "Interested stockholder" means any person (other than the corporation and any direct or indirect majority-owned subsidiary of the corporation) that (i) is the owner of 15% or more of the outstanding voting stock of the corporation, or (ii) is an affiliate or associate of the corporation and was the owner of 15% or more of the outstanding voting stock of the corporation at any time within the 3-year period immediately prior to the date on which it is sought to be determined whether such person is an interested stockholder; and the affiliates and associates of such person; provided, however, that the term "interested stockholder" shall not include (x) any person who (A) owned shares in excess of the 15% limitation set forth herein as of, or acquired such shares pursuant to a tender offer commenced prior to, December 23, 1987, or pursuant to an exchange offer announced prior to the aforesaid date and commenced within 90 days thereafter and either (I) continued to own shares in excess of such 15% limitation or would have but for action by the corporation or (II) is an affiliate or associate of the corporation and so continued (or so would have continued but for action by the corporation) to be the

owner of 15% or more of the outstanding voting stock of the corporation at any time within the 3-year period immediately prior to the date on which it is sought to be determined whether such a person is an interested stockholder or (B) acquired said shares from a person described in item (A) of this paragraph by gift, inheritance or in a transaction in which no consideration was exchanged; or (y) any person whose ownership of shares in excess of the 15% limitation set forth herein is the result of action taken solely by the corporation; provided that such person shall be an interested stockholder if thereafter such person acquires additional shares of voting stock of the corporation, except as a result of further corporate action not caused, directly or indirectly, by such person. For the purpose of determining whether a person is an interested stockholder, the voting stock of the corporation deemed to be outstanding shall include stock deemed to be owned by the person through application of paragraph (9) of this subsection but shall not include any other unissued stock of such corporation which may be issuable pursuant to any agreement, arrangement or understanding, or upon exercise of conversion rights, warrants or options, or otherwise.

(6) "Person" means any individual, corporation, partnership, unincorporated association or other entity.

(7) "Stock" means, with respect to any corporation, capital stock and, with respect to any other entity, any equity interest.

(8) "Voting stock" means, with respect to any corporation, stock of any class or series entitled to vote generally in the election of directors and, with respect to any entity that is not a corporation, any equity interest entitled to vote generally in the election of the governing body of such entity. Every reference to a percentage of voting stock shall refer to such percentage of the votes of such voting stock.

(9) "Owner," including the terms "own" and "owned," when used with respect to any stock, means a person that individually or with or through any of its affiliates or associates:

(i) Beneficially owns such stock, directly or indirectly; or

(ii) Has (A) the right to acquire such stock (whether such right is exercisable immediately or only after the passage of time) pursuant to any agreement, arrangement or understanding, or upon the exercise of conversion rights, exchange rights, warrants or options, or otherwise; provided, however, that a person shall not be deemed the owner of stock tendered pursuant to a tender or exchange offer made by such person or any of such person's affiliates or associates until such tendered stock is accepted for purchase or exchange; or (B) the right to vote such stock pursuant to any agreement, arrangement or understanding; provided, however, that a person shall not be deemed the owner of any stock because of such person's right to vote such stock if the agreement, arrangement or understanding to vote such stock arises solely from a revocable proxy or consent given in response to a proxy or consent solicitation made to 10 or more persons; or

(iii) Has any agreement, arrangement or understanding for the purpose of acquiring, holding, voting (except voting pursuant to a revocable proxy or consent as described in item (B) of subparagraph (ii) of this paragraph), or disposing of such stock with any other person that beneficially owns, or whose affiliates or associates beneficially own, directly or indirectly, such stock.

(d) No provision of a certificate of incorporation or bylaw shall require, for any vote of stockholders required by this section, a greater vote of stockholders than that specified in this section.

(e) The Court of Chancery is hereby vested with exclusive jurisdiction to hear and determine all matters with respect to this section.

SUBCHAPTER IX. MERGER, CONSOLIDATION OR CONVERSION

§251. *Merger or Consolidation of Domestic Corporations*

(a) Any 2 or more corporations existing under the laws of this State may merge into a single corporation, which may be any 1 of the constituent corporations or may consolidate into a new corporation formed by the consolidation, pursuant to an agreement of merger or consolidation, as the case may be, complying and approved in accordance with this section.

(b) The board of directors of each corporation which desires to merge or consolidate shall adopt a resolution approving an agreement of merger or consolidation and declaring its advisability. The agreement shall state: (1) The terms and conditions of the merger or consolidation; (2) the mode of carrying the same into effect; (3) in the case of a merger, such amendments or changes in the certificate of incorporation of the surviving corporation as are desired to be effected by the merger, or, if no such amendments or changes are desired, a statement that the certificate of incorporation of the surviving corporation shall be its certificate of incorporation; (4) in the case of a consolidation, that the certificate of incorporation of the resulting corporation shall be as is set forth in an attachment to the agreement; (5) the manner, if any, of converting the shares of each of the constituent corporations into shares or other securities of the corporation surviving or resulting from the merger or consolidation, or of cancelling some or all of such shares, and, if any shares of any of the constituent corporations are not to remain outstanding, to be converted solely into shares or other securities of the surviving or resulting corporation or to be cancelled, the cash, property, rights or securities of any other corporation or entity which the holders of such shares are to receive in exchange for, or upon conversion of such shares and the surrender of any certificates evidencing them, which cash, property, rights or securities of any other corporation or entity may be in addition to or in lieu of shares or other securities of the surviving or resulting corporation; and (6) such other details or provisions as are deemed desirable, including, without limiting the generality of the foregoing, a provision for the payment of cash in lieu of the issuance or recognition of fractional shares, interest or rights, or for any other arrangement with respect thereto, consistent with §155 of this title. The agreement so adopted shall be executed and acknowledged in accordance with §103 of this title. Any of the terms of the agreement of merger or consolidation may be made dependent upon facts ascertainable outside of such agreement, provided that the manner in which such facts shall operate upon the terms of the agreement is clearly and expressly set forth in the agreement of merger or consolidation. The term "facts," as used in the preceding sentence, includes, but is not limited to, the occurrence of any event, including a determination on action by any person or body, including the corporation.

(c) The agreement required by subsection (b) of this section shall be submitted to the stockholders of each constituent corporation at an annual or special meeting for the purpose of acting on the agreement. Due notice of the time, place and purpose of the meeting shall be mailed to each holder of stock, whether voting or nonvoting, of the corporation at his address as it appears on the records of the corporation, at least 20 days prior to the date of the meeting. The notice shall contain a copy of the agreement or a brief summary thereof, as the directors shall deem advisable. At the meeting, the agreement shall be considered and a vote taken for its adoption or rejection. If a majority of the outstanding stock of the corporation entitled to vote thereon shall be voted for the adoption of the agreement, that fact shall be certified on the agreement by the secretary or assistant secretary of the corporation, provided that such certification on the agreement shall not be required if a certificate of merger or consolidation is filed in lieu of filing the agreement. If the agreement shall be so adopted and certified by each constituent corporation, it shall then be filed and shall become effective, in accordance with §103 of this title. In lieu of filing the agreement of merger or consolidation required by this section, the surviving or resulting corporation may file a certificate of merger or consolidation, executed in accordance with §103 of this title, which states:

 (1) The name and state of incorporation of each of the constituent corporations;

 (2) That an agreement of merger or consolidation has been approved, adopted, executed and acknowledged by each of the constituent corporations in accordance with this section;

 (3) The name of the surviving or resulting corporation;

 (4) In the case of a merger, such amendments or changes in the certificate of incorporation of the surviving corporation as are desired

to be effected by the merger, or, if no such amendments or changes are desired, a statement that the certificate of incorporation of the surviving corporation shall be its certificate of incorporation;

(5) In the case of a consolidation, that the certificate of incorporation of the resulting corporation shall be as set forth in an attachment to the certificate;

(6) That the executed agreement of consolidation or merger is on file at an office of the surviving corporation, stating the address thereof; and

(7) That a copy of the agreement of consolidation or merger will be furnished by the surviving corporation, on request and without cost, to any stockholder of any constituent corporation.

(d) Any agreement of merger or consolidation may contain a provision that at any time prior to the time that the agreement (or a certificate in lieu thereof) filed with the Secretary of State becomes effective in accordance with §103 of this title, the agreement may be terminated by the board of directors of any constituent corporation notwithstanding approval of the agreement by the stockholders of all or any of the constituent corporations; in the event the agreement of merger or consolidation is terminated after the filing of the agreement (or a certificate in lieu thereof) with the Secretary of State but before the agreement (or a certificate in lieu thereof) has become effective, a certificate of termination or merger or consolidation shall be filed in accordance with §103 of this title. Any agreement of merger or consolidation may contain a provision that the boards of directors of the constituent corporations may amend the agreement at any time prior to the time that the agreement (or a certificate in lieu thereof) filed with the Secretary of State becomes effective in accordance with §103 of this title, provided that an amendment made subsequent to the adoption of the agreement by the stockholders of any constituent corporation shall not (1) alter or change the amount or kind of shares, securities, cash, property and/or rights to be received in exchange for or on conversion of all or any of the shares of any class or series thereof of such constituent corporation, (2) alter or change any term of the certificate of incorporation of the surviving corporation to be effected by the merger or consolidation, or (3) alter or change any of the terms and conditions of the agreement if such alteration or change would adversely affect the holders of any class or series thereof of such constituent corporation; in the event the agreement of merger or consolidation is amended after the filing thereof with the Secretary of State but before the agreement has become effective, a certificate of amendment of merger or consolidation shall be filed in accordance with §103 of this title.

(e) In the case of a merger, the certificate of incorporation of the surviving corporation shall automatically be amended to the extent, if any, that changes in the certificate of incorporation are set forth in the agreement of merger.

(f) Notwithstanding the requirements of subsection (c) of this section, unless required by its certificate of incorporation, no vote of stockholders of a constituent corporation surviving a merger shall be necessary to authorize a merger if (1) the agreement of merger does not amend in any respect the certificate of incorporation of such constituent corporation, (2) each share of stock of such constituent corporation outstanding immediately prior to the effective date of the merger is to be an identical outstanding or treasury share of the surviving corporation after the effective date of the merger, and (3) either no shares of common stock of the surviving corporation and no shares, securities or obligations convertible into such stock are to be issued or delivered under the plan of merger, or the authorized unissued shares or the treasury shares of common stock of the surviving corporation to be issued or delivered under the plan of merger plus those initially issuable upon conversion of any other shares, securities or obligations to be issued or delivered under such plan do not exceed 20% of the shares of common stock of such constituent corporation outstanding immediately prior to the effective date of the merger. No vote of stockholders of a constituent corporation shall be necessary to authorize a merger or consolidation if no shares of the stock of such corporation shall have been issued prior to the adoption by the board of directors of the resolution approving the agreement of merger or consolidation. If an agreement of merger is adopted by the constituent corporation surviving the merger, by action of its board of directors and without any vote of its stockholders pursuant to this subsection, the secretary or assistant secretary of that corporation shall certify on the agreement that the agreement has been adopted pursuant to this subsection and, (1) if it has been adopted pursuant to the first sentence of this subsection, that the conditions specified in that sentence have been satisfied, or (2) if it has been adopted pursuant to the second sentence of this subsection, that no shares of stock of such corporation were issued prior to the adoption by the board of directors of the resolution approving the agreement of merger or consolidation, provided that such certification on the agreement shall not be required if a certificate of merger or consolidation is filed in lieu of filing the agreement. The agreement so adopted and certified shall then be filed and shall become effective, in accordance with §103 of this title. Such filing shall constitute a representation by the person who executes the agreement that the facts stated in the certificate remain true immediately prior to such filing.

(g) Notwithstanding the requirements of subsection (c) of this section, unless expressly required by its certificate of incorporation, no vote of stockholders of a constituent corporation shall be necessary to authorize a merger with or into a single director indirect wholly-owned subsidiary of such constituent corporation if: (1) such constituent corporation and the direct or indirect wholly-owned subsidiary of such constituent corporation are the only constituent entities to the merger; (2) each share or fraction of a share of the capital stock of the constituent corporation outstanding immediately prior to the effective time of the merger is converted in the merger into a share or equal fraction of share of capital stock of a holding company having the same designations, rights, powers and preferences, and the qualifications, limitations and restrictions thereof, as the share of stock of the constituent corporation being converted in the merger; (3) the holding company and the constituent corporation are corporations of this State and the direct or indirect wholly-owned subsidiary that is the other constituent entity to the merger is a corporation or limited liability company of this State; (4) the certificate of incorporation and by-laws of the holding company immediately following the effective time of the merger contain provisions identical to the certificate of incorporation and by-laws of the constituent corporation immediately prior to the effective time of the merger (other than provisions, if any, regarding the incorporator or incorporators, the corporate name, the registered office and agent, the initial board of directors and the initial subscribers for shares and such provisions contained in any amendment to the certificate of incorporation as were necessary to effect a change, exchange, reclassification, subdivision, combination or cancellation of stock, if such change, exchange, reclassification, subdivision, combination, or cancellation has become effective); (5) as a result of the merger the constituent corporation or its successor becomes or remains a direct or indirect wholly-owned subsidiary of the holding company; (6) the directors of the constituent corporation become or remain the directors of the holding company upon the effective time of the merger; (7) the organizational documents of the surviving entity immediately following the effective time of the merger contain provisions identical to the certificate of incorporation of the constituent corporation immediately prior to the effective time of the merger (other than provisions, if any, regarding the incorporator or incorporators, the corporate or entity name, the registered office and agent, the initial board of directors and the initial subscribers for shares, references to members rather than stockholders or shareholders, references to interests, units or the like rather than stock or shares, references to managers, managing members or other members of the governing body rather than directors and such provisions contained in any amendment to the certificate of incorporation as were necessary to effect a change, exchange, reclassification, subdivision, combination or cancellation of stock, if such change, exchange, reclassification, subdivision, combination or cancellation has become effective); provided, however, that (i) if the organizational documents of the surviving entity do not contain the following provisions, they shall be amended in the merger to contain provisions requiring that (A) any act or transaction by or involving the surviving entity, other than the election or removal of directors or managers, managing members or other members of the governing body of the surviving entity, that requires for its adoption under this chapter or its organizational documents the approval of the stockholders or members of the surviving entity shall, by specific reference to this subsection, require, in addition, the approval of the stockholders of the holding company (or any successor by merger), by the same vote as is required by this chapter and/or by the organizational documents of the surviving entity; provided, however, that for purposes of this clause (i)(A), any surviving entity that is not a corporation shall include in such amendment a requirement that the approval of the stockholders of the holding company be obtained for any act or transaction by or involving the surviving entity, other than the election or removal of directors or managers, managing members or other members of the governing body of the surviving entity, which would require the approval of the stockholders of the surviving entity if the surviving entity' were a corporation subject to this chapter; (B) any amendment of the organizational documents of a surviving entity that is not a corporation, which amendment would, if adopted by a corporation subject to this chapter, be required to be included in the certificate of incorporation of such corporation, shall, by specific reference to this subsection, require, in addition, the approval of the stockholders of the holding company (or any successor by merger), by the same vote as is required by this chapter and/or by the organizational documents of the surviving entity; and (C) the business and affairs of a surviving entity that is not a corporation shall be managed by or under the direction of a board of directors, board of managers or other governing body consisting of individuals who are subject to the same fiduciary duties applicable to, and who are liable for breach of such duties to the same extent as, directors of a corporation subject to this chapter; and (ii) the organizational documents of the surviving entity may be amended in the merger (A) to reduce the number of classes and shares of capital stock or other equity interests or units that the surviving entity is authorized to issue and (B) to eliminate any provision authorized by subsection (d) of §141 of this title; and (8) the stockholders of the constituent corporation do not recognize gain or loss for United States federal income tax purposes as determined by the board of directors of the constituent corporation. Neither subdivision (g)(7)(i) of this section nor any provision of a surviving entity's organizational documents required by subdivision (g)(7)(i) shall be deemed or construed to require approval of the stockholders of the holding company to elect or remove directors or managers, managing members or other members of the governing body of the surviving entity. The term "organizational documents," as used in subdivision (g)(7) and in the preceding sentence, shall, when used in reference to a corporation, mean the certificate of incorporation of such corporation, and when used in reference to a limited liability company, mean the limited liability company agreement of such limited liability company.

As used in this subsection only, the term "holding company" means a corporation which, from its incorporation until consummation of a merger governed by this subsection, was at all times a direct or indirect wholly-owned subsidiary of the constituent corporation and whose capital stock is issued in such merger. From and after the effective time of a merger adopted by a constituent corporation by action of its board of directors and without any vote of stockholders pursuant to this subsection: (i) to the extent the restrictions of §203 of this title applied to the constituent corporation and its stockholders at the effective time of the merger, such restrictions shall apply to the holding company and its stockholders immediately after the effective time of the merger as though it were the constituent corporation, and all shares of stock of the holding company acquired in the merger shall for purposes of §203 of this title be deemed to have been acquired at the time that the shares of stock of the constituent corporation converted in the merger were acquired, and provided further that any stockholder who immediately prior to the effective time of the merger was not an interested stockholder within the meaning of §203 of this title shall not solely by reason of the merger become an interested stockholder of the holding company, (ii) if the corporate name of the holding company immediately following the effective time of the merger is the same as the corporate name of the constituent corporation immediately prior to the effective time of the merger, the shares of capital stock of the holding company into which the shares of capital stock of the constituent corporation are converted in the merger shall be represented by the stock certificates that previously represented shares of capital stock of the constituent corporation capital stock of the constituent corporation and (iii) to the extent a stockholder of the constituent corporation immediately prior to the merger had standing to institute or maintain derivative litigation on behalf of the constituent corporation, nothing in this section shall be deemed to limit or extinguish such standing. If an agreement of merger is adopted by a constituent corporation by action of its board of directors and without any vote of stockholders pursuant to this subsection, the secretary or assistant secretary of the constituent corporation shall certify on the agreement that the agreement has been adopted pursuant to this subsection and that the conditions specified in the first sentence of this subsection have been satisfied, provided that such certification on the agreement shall not be required if a certificate of merger or consolidation is filed in lien of filing the agreement. The agreement so adopted and certified shall then be filed and become effective, in accordance with §103 of this title. Such filing shall constitute a representation by the person who executes the agreement that the facts stated in the certificate remain true immediately prior to such filing.

(h) Notwithstanding the requirements of subsection (c) of this section, unless expressly required by its certificate of incorporation, no vote of stockholders of a constituent corporation whose shares are listed on a national securities exchange or held of record by more than 2,000 holders immediately prior to the execution of the agreement of merger by such constituent corporation shall be necessary to authorize a merger if:

(1) The agreement of merger, which must be entered into on or after August 1, 2013, expressly provides that such merger shall be governed by this subsection and shall be effected as soon as practicable

following the consummation of the offer referred to in paragraph (h)(2) of this section;

(2) A corporation consummates a tender or exchange offer for any and all of the outstanding stock of such constituent corporation on the terms provided in such agreement of merger that, absent this subsection, would be entitled to vote on the adoption or rejection of the agreement of merger;

(3) Following the consummation of such offer, the consummating corporation owns at least such percentage of the stock, and of each class or series thereof, of such constituent corporation that, absent this subsection, would be required to adopt the agreement of merger by this chapter and by the certificate of incorporation of such constituent corporation;

(4) At the time such constituent corporation's board of directors approves the agreement of merger, no other party to such agreement is an "interested stockholder" (as defined in §203(c) of this title) of such constituent corporation;

(5) The corporation consummating the offer described in paragraph (h)(2) of this section merges with or into such constituent corporation pursuant to such agreement; and

(6) The outstanding shares of each class or series of stock of the constituent corporation not to be canceled in the merger are to be converted in such merger into, or into the right to receive, the same amount and kind of cash, property, rights or securities paid for shares of such class or series of stock of such constituent corporation upon consummation of the offer referred to in paragraph (h)(2) of this section.

If an agreement of merger is adopted without the vote of stockholders of a corporation pursuant to this subsection, the secretary or assistant secretary of the surviving corporation shall certify on the agreement that the agreement has been adopted pursuant to this subsection and that the conditions specified in this subsection (other than the condition listed in paragraph (h)(5) of this section) have been satisfied; provided that such certification on the agreement shall not be required if a certificate of merger is filed in lieu of filing the agreement. The agreement so adopted and certified shall then be filed and shall become effective, in accordance with §103 of this title. Such filing shall constitute a representation by the person who executes the agreement that the facts stated in the certificate remain true immediately prior to such filing.

§253. *Merger of Parent Corporation and Subsidiary or Subsidiaries*

(a) In any case in which at least 90% of the outstanding shares of each class of the stock of a corporation or corporations (other than a corporation which has in its certificate of incorporation the provision required by subsection (g)(7)(i) of Section 251 of this title), of which class there are outstanding shares that, absent this subsection, would be entitled to vote on such merger, is owned by another corporation and 1 of the corporations is a corporation of this State and the other or others are corporations of this State, or any other state or states, or the District of Columbia and the laws of the other state or states, or the District permit a corporation of such jurisdiction to merge with a corporation of another jurisdiction, the corporation having such stock ownership may either merge the other corporation or corporations into itself and assume all of its or their obligations, or merge itself, or itself and 1 or more of such other corporations, into 1 of the other corporations by executing, acknowledging and filing, in accordance with §103 of this title, a certificate of such ownership and merger setting forth a copy of the resolution of its board of directors to so merge and the date of the adoption; provided, however, that in case the parent corporation shall not own all the outstanding stock of all the subsidiary corporations, parties to a merger as aforesaid, the resolution of the board of directors of the parent corporation shall state the terms and conditions of the merger, including the securities, cash, property, or rights to be issued, paid, delivered or granted by the surviving corporation upon surrender of each share of the subsidiary corporation or corporations not owned by the parent corporation, or the cancellation of some or all of such shares. Any of the terms of the resolution of the board of directors to so merge may be made dependent upon facts ascertainable outside of such resolution, provided that the manner in which such facts shall operate upon the terms of the resolution is clearly and expressly set forth in the resolution. The term "facts," as used in the preceding sentence, includes, but is not limited to, the occurrence of any event, including a determination or action by any person or body, including the corporation. If the parent corporation be not the surviving corporation, the resolution shall include provision for the pro rata issuance of stock of the surviving corporation to the holders of the stock of the parent corporation on surrender of any certificates therefor, and the certificate of ownership and merger shall state that the proposed merger has been approved by a majority of the outstanding stock of the parent corporation entitled to vote thereon at a meeting duly called and held after 20 days' notice of the purpose of the meeting mailed to each such stockholder at his address as it appears on the records of the corporation if the parent corporation is a corporation of this State or state that the proposed merger has been adopted, approved, certified, executed and acknowledged by the parent corporation in accordance with the laws under which it is organized if the parent corporation is not a corporation of this State. . . .

(b) If the surviving corporation is a Delaware corporation, it may change its corporate name by the inclusion of a provision to that effect in the resolution of merger adopted by the directors of the parent corporation and set forth in the certificate of ownership and merger, and upon the effective date of the merger, the name of the corporation shall be so changed.

(c) Subsection (d) of §251 of this title shall apply to a merger under this section, and subsection (e) of §251 of this title shall apply to a merger under this section in which the surviving corporation is the subsidiary corporation and is a corporation of this State. References to "agreement of merger" in subsections (d) and (e) of §251 of this title shall mean for purposes of this subsection the resolution of merger ad opted by the board of directors of the parent corporation. Any merger which effects any changes other than those authorized by this section or made applicable by this subsection shall be accomplished under §251, 252, 257 or 258 of this tide. Section 262 of this title shall not apply to any merger effected under this section, except as provided in subsection (d) of this section.

(d) In the event all of the stock of a subsidiary Delaware corporation party to a merger effected under this section is not owned by the parent corporation immediately prior to the merger, the stockholders of the subsidiary Delaware corporation party to the merger shall have appraisal rights as set forth in §262 of this title.

(e) A merger may be effected under this section although 1 or more of the corporations parties to the merger is a corporation organized under the laws of a jurisdiction other than 1 of the United States; provided that the laws of such jurisdiction permit a corporation of such jurisdiction to merge with a corporation of another jurisdiction. . . .

§259. Status, Rights, Liabilities, of Constituent and Surviving or Resulting Corporations Following Merger or Consolidation

(a) When any merger or consolidation shall have become effective under this chapter, for all purposes of the laws of this State the separate existence of all the constituent corporations, or of all such constituent corporations except the one into which the other or others of such constituent corporations have been merged, as the case may be, shall cease and the constituent corporations shall become a new corporation, or be merged into 1 of such corporations, as the case may be, possessing all the rights, privileges, powers and franchises as well of a public as of a private nature, and being subject to all the restrictions, disabilities and duties of each of such corporations so merged or consolidated; and all and singular, the rights, privileges, powers and franchises of each of said corporations, and all property, real, personal and mixed, and all debts due to any of said constituent corporations on whatever account, as well for stock subscriptions as all other things in action or belonging to each of such corporations shall be vested in the corporation surviving or resulting from such merger or consolidation; and all property, rights, privileges, powers and franchises, and all and every other interest shall be thereafter as effectually the property of the surviving or resulting corporation as they were of the several and respective constituent corporations, and the title to any real estate vested by deed or otherwise, under the laws of this State, in any of such constituent corporations, shall not revert or be in any way impaired by reason of this chapter; but all rights of creditors and all liens upon any property of any of said constituent corporations shall be preserved unimpaired, and all debts, liabilities and duties of the respective constituent corporations shall thenceforth attach to said surviving or resulting corporation, and may be enforced against it to the same extent as if said debts, liabilities and duties had been incurred or contracted by it. . . .

§260. Powers of Corporation Surviving or Resulting from Merger or Consolidation; Issuance of Stock, Bonds or Other Indebtedness

When 2 or more corporations are merged or consolidated, the corporation surviving or resulting from the merger may issue bonds or other obligations, negotiable or otherwise, and with or without coupons or interest certificates thereto attached, to an amount sufficient with its capital stock to provide for all the payments it will be required to make, or obligations it will be required to assume, in order to effect the merger or consolidation. For the purpose of securing the payment of any such bonds and obligations, it shall be lawful for the surviving or resulting corporation to mortgage its corporate franchise, rights, privileges and property, real, personal or mixed. The surviving or resulting corporation may issue certificates of its capital stock or uncertificated stock if authorized to do so and other securities to the stockholders of the constituent corporations in exchange or payment for the original shares, in such amount as shall be necessary in accordance with the terms of the agreement of merger or consolidation in order to effect such merger or consolidation in the manner and on the terms specified in the agreement.

§261. Effect of Merger upon Pending Actions

Any action or proceeding, whether civil, criminal or administrative, pending by or against any corporation which is a party to a merger or consolidation shall be prosecuted as if such merger or consolidation had not taken place, or the corporation surviving or resulting from such merger or consolidation may be substituted in such action or proceeding.

§262. Appraisal Rights

(a) Any stockholder of a corporation of this State who holds shares of stock on the date of the making of a demand pursuant to subsection (d) of this section with respect to such shares, who continuously holds such shares through the effective date of the merger or consolidation, who has otherwise complied with subsection (d) of this section and who has neither voted in favor of the merger or consolidation nor consented thereto in writing pursuant to §228 of this title shall be entitled to an appraisal by the Court of Chancery of the fair value of his shares of stock under the circumstances described in subsections (b) and (c) of this section. As used in this section, the word "stockholder" means a holder of record of stock in a stock corporation and also a member of record of a nonstock corporation; the words "stock" and "share" mean and include what is ordinarily meant by those words and also membership or membership interest of a member of a nonstock corporation; and the words "depository receipt" means a receipt or other instrument issued by a depository representing an interest in one or more shares, or fractions thereof, solely of stock of a corporation, which stock is deposited with the depository.

(b) Appraisal rights shall be available for the shares of any class or series of stock of a constituent corporation in a merger or consolidation to be effected pursuant to §251, (other than a merger effected pursuant to §251(g) of this title and, subject to paragraph (b)(3) of this section, 251(h) of this title) its certificate of incorporation the provision required by subsection (g)(7)(i) of section 25f of this title), 252, 254, 255, 256, 257, 258, 263, or 264 of this title:

(1) Provided, however, except as provided in §363(b) of this title, that no appraisal rights under this section shall be avail able for the shares of any class or series of stock, which stock, or depository receipts in respect thereof, at the record date fixed to determine the stockholders entitled to receive notice of the meeting of stockholders to act upon the agreement of merger or consolidation, were either: (i) listed on a national securities exchange or (ii) held of record by more than 2,000 holders; and further provided that no appraisal rights shall be available for any shares of stock of the constituent corporation surviving a merger if the merger did not require for its approval the vote of the stockholders of the surviving corporation as provided in subsection (f) of §251 of this title.

(2) Notwithstanding paragraph (1) of this subsection, appraisal rights under this section shall be available for the shares of any class or series of stock of a constituent corporation if the holders thereof are required by the terms of an agreement of merger or consolidation pursuant to §251, 252, 254, 255, 256, 257, 258, 263 and 264 of this title to accept for such stock anything except:

    a. Shares of stock of the corporation surviving or resulting from such merger or consolidation, or depository receipts in respect thereof;

    b. Shares of stock of any other corporation, or depository receipts in respect thereof, which shares of stock (or depository receipts in respect there of) or depository receipts at the effective date of the merger or consolidation will be either listed on a national securities exchange or held of record by more than 2,000 holders;

c. Cash in lieu of fractional shares or fractional depository receipts described in the foregoing subparagraphs a. and b. of this paragraph; or

d. Any combination of the shares of stock, depository receipts and cash in lieu of fractional shares or fractional depository receipts described in the foregoing subparagraphs a., b. and c. of this paragraph.

(3) In the event all of the stock of a subsidiary Delaware corporation party to a merger effected under 251(h) §253 or §267 of this title is not owned by the parent corporation immediately prior to the merger, appraisal rights shall be available for the shares of the subsidiary Delaware corporation.

(4) In the event of an amendment to a corporation's certificate of incorporation contemplated by §363(a) of this title, appraisal rights shall be available as contemplated by §363(b) of this title, and the procedures of this section, including those set forth in subsections (d) and (e) of this section, shall apply as nearly as practicable, with the word "amendment" substituted for the words "merger or consolidation," and the word "corporation" substituted for the words "constituent corporation" and/or "surviving or resulting corporation."

(c) Any corporation may provide in its certificate of incorporation that appraisal rights under this section shall be available for the shares of any class or series of its stock as a result of an amendment to its certificate of incorporation, any merger or consolidation in which the corporation is a constituent corporation or the sale of all or substantially all of the assets of the corporation. If the certificate of incorporation contains such a provision, the procedures of this section, including those set forth in subsections (d) and (e) of this section, shall apply as nearly as is practicable.

(d) Appraisal rights shall be perfected as follows:

(1) If a proposed merger or consolidation for which appraisal rights are provided under this section is to be submitted for approval at a meeting of stockholders, the corporation, not less than 20 days prior to the meeting, shall notify each of its stockholders who was such on the record date for notice of such meeting . . . with respect to shares for which appraisal rights are available pursuant to subsection (b) or (c) hereof that appraisal rights are available for any or all of the shares of the constituent corporations, and shall include in such notice a copy of this section. . . . Each stockholder electing to demand the appraisal of such stockholder's shares shall deliver to the corporation, before the taking of the vote on the merger or consolidation, a written demand for appraisal of such stockholder's shares. Such demand will be sufficient if it reasonably informs the corporation of the identity of the stockholder and that the stockholder intends thereby to demand the appraisal of such stockholder's shares. A proxy or vote against the merger or consolidation shall not constitute such a demand. A

stockholder electing to take such action must do so by a separate written demand as herein provided. Within 10 days after the effective date of such merger or consolidation, the surviving or resulting corporation shall notify each stockholder of each constituent corporation who has complied with this subsection and has not voted in favor of or consented to the merger or consolidation of the date that the merger or consolidation has become effective; or

(2) If the merger or consolidation was approved pursuant to §228, §253 or §267 of this title, then either a constituent corporation before the effective date of the merger or consolidation or the surviving or resulting corporation within 10 days thereafter shall notify each of the holders of any class or series of stock of such constituent corporation who are entitled to appraisal rights of the approval of the merger or consolidation and that appraisal rights are available for any or all shares of such class or series of stock of such constituent corporation, and shall include in such notice a copy of this section. Such notice may, and, if given on or after the effective date of the merger or consolidation, shall, also notify such stockholders of the effective date of the merger or consolidation. Any stockholder entitled to appraisal rights may, within 20 days after the date of mailing of such notice, or, in the case of a merger approved pursuant to §251(h) of this title, within the later of the consummation of the tender or exchange offer contemplated by §251(h) of this title and 20 days after the date of mailing of such notice, demand in writing from the surviving or resulting corporation the appraisal of such holder's shares. Such demand will be sufficient if it reasonably informs the corporation of the identity of the stockholder and that the stockholder intends thereby to demand the appraisal of such holder's shares. If such notice did not notify stockholders of the effective date of the merger or consolidation, either (i) each such constituent corporation shall send a second notice before the effective date of the merger or consolidation notifying each of the holders of any class or series of stock of such constituent corporation that are entitled to appraisal rights of the effective date of the merger or consolidation or (ii) the surviving or resulting corporation shall send such a second notice to all such holders on or within 10 days after such effective date; provided, however, that if such second notice is sent more than 20 days following the sending of the first notice, or, in the case of a merger approved pursuant to §251(h) of this title, later than the later of the consummation of the tender or exchange offer contemplated by §251(h) of this title and 20 days following the sending of the first notice, such second notice need only be sent to each stockholder who is entitled to appraisal rights and who has demanded appraisal of such holder's shares in accordance with this subsection. An affidavit of the secretary or assistant secretary or of the transfer agent of the corporation that is required to give either notice that such

notice has been given shall, in the absence of fraud, be prima facie evidence of the facts stated therein. For purposes of determining the stockholders entitled to receive either notice, each constituent corporation may fix, in advance, a record date that shall be not more than 10 days prior to the date the notice is given; provided that, if the notice is given on or after the effective date of the merger or consolidation, the record date shall be such effective date. If no record date is fixed and the notice is given prior to the effective date, the record date shall be the close of business on the day next preceding the day on which the notice is given.

(e) Within 120 days after the effective date of the merger or consolidation, the surviving or resulting corporation or any stockholder who has complied with subsections (a) and (d) of this section hereof and who is otherwise entitled to appraisal rights, may commence an appraisal proceeding by filing a petition in the Court of Chancery demanding a determination of the value of the stock of all such stockholders. Notwithstanding the foregoing, at any time within 60 days after the effective date of the merger or consolidation, any stockholder who has not commenced an appraisal proceeding or joined that proceeding as a named party shall have the right to withdraw such stockholder's demand for appraisal and to accept the terms offered upon the merger or consolidation. Within 120 days after the effective date of the merger or consolidation, any stockholder who has complied with the requirements of subsections (a) and (d) of this section hereof, upon written request, shall be entitled to receive from the corporation surviving the merger or resulting from the consolidation a statement setting forth the aggregate number of shares not voted in favor of the merger or consolidation and with respect to which demands for appraisal have been received and the aggregate number of holders of such shares. Such written statement shall be mailed to the stockholder within 10 days after such stockholder's written request for such a statement is received by the surviving or resulting corporation or within 10 days after expiration of the period for delivery of demands for appraisal under subsection (d) of this section hereof, whichever is later. Notwithstanding subsection (a) of this section, a person who is the beneficial owner of shares of such stock held either in a voting trust or by a nominee on behalf of such person may, in such person's own name, file a petition or request from the corporation the statement described in this subsection.

(f) Upon the filing of any such petition by a stockholder, service of a copy thereof shall be made upon the sunning or resulting corporation, which shall within 20 days after such service file in the office of the Register in Chancery in which the petition was filed a duly verified list containing the names and addresses of all stockholders who have demanded payment for their shares and with whom agreements as to the value of their shares have not been reached by the surviving or resulting corporation. If the petition shall be filed by the surviving or resulting corporation, the petition shall be accompanied by such a duly verified list. The Register in Chancery, if so ordered by the Court, shall give notice of the time and place fixed for the hearing of such petition by registered or certified mail to the surviving or resulting corporation and to the stockholders shown on the list at the addresses therein stated. Such notice shall also be given by 1 or more publications at least 1 week before the day of the hearing, in a newspaper of general circulation published in the City of Wilmington, Delaware or such publication as the Court deems advisable. The forms of the notices by mail and by publication shall be approved by the Court, and the costs thereof shall be borne by the surviving or resulting corporation.

(g) At the hearing on such petition, the Court shall determine the stockholders who have complied with this section and who have become entitled to appraisal rights. The Court may require the stockholders who have demanded an appraisal for their shares and who hold stock represented by certificates to submit their certificates of stock to the Register in Chancery for notation thereon of the pendency of the appraisal proceedings; and if any stockholder fails to comply with such direction, the Court may dismiss the proceedings as to such stockholder.

(h) After the Court determines the stockholders entitled to an appraisal, the appraisal proceeding shall be conducted in accordance with the rules of the Court of Chancery, including any rules specifically governing appraisal proceedings. Through such proceeding the Court shall determine the fair value of the shares exclusive of any element of value arising from the accomplishment or expectation of the merger or consolidation, together with interest, if any, to be paid upon the amount determined to be the fair value. In determining such fair value, the Court shall take into account all relevant factors. Unless the Court in its discretion determines otherwise for good cause shown, interest from the effective date of the merger through the date of payment of the judgment shall be compounded quarterly and shall accrue at 5% over the Federal Reserve discount rate (including any surcharge) as established from time to time during the period between the effective date of the merger and the date of payment of the judgment. Upon application by the surviving or resulting corporation or by any stockholder entitled to participate in the appraisal proceeding, the Court may, in its discretion, proceed to trial upon the appraisal prior to the final determination of the stockholders entitled to an appraisal. Any stockholder whose name appears on the list filed by the surviving or resulting corporation pursuant to subsection (f) of this section and who has submitted such stockholder's certificates of stock to the Register in Chancery, if such is required, may participate fully in all proceedings until it is finally determined that such stockholder is not entitled to appraisal rights under this section.

(i) The Court shall direct the payment of the fair value of the shares, together with interest, if any, by the surviving or resulting corporation to the stockholders entitled thereto. Payment shall be so made to each such stockholder, in the case of holders of uncertificated stock forthwith, and the case of holders of shares represented by certificates upon the surrender to the corporation of the certificates representing such stock. The Court's decree may be enforced as other decrees in the Court of Chancery may be enforced, whether such surviving or resulting corporation be a corporation of this State or of any state.

(j) The costs of the proceeding may be determined by the Court and taxed upon the parties as the Court deems equitable in the circumstances. Upon application of a stockholder, the Court may order all or a portion of the expenses incurred by any stockholder in connection with the appraisal proceeding, including, without limitation, reasonable attorney's fees and the fees and expenses of experts, to be charged pro rata against the value of all the shares entitled to an appraisal.

(k) From and after the effective date of the merger or consolidation, no stockholder who has demanded appraisal rights as provided in subsection (d) of this section shall be entitled to vote such stock for any purpose or to receive payment of dividends or other distributions on the stock (except dividends or other distributions payable to stockholders of record at a date which is prior to the effective date of the merger or consolidation); provided, however, that if no petition for an appraisal shall be filed within the time provided in subsection (e) of this section, or if such stockholder shall deliver to the surviving or resulting corporation a written withdrawal of such stockholder's demand for an appraisal and an acceptance of the merger or consolidation, either within 60 days after the effective date of the merger or consolidation as provided in subsection (e) of this section or thereafter with the written approval of the corporation, then the right of such stockholder to an appraisal shall cease. Notwithstanding the foregoing, no appraisal proceeding in the Court of Chancery shall be dismissed as to any stockholder without the approval of the Court, and such approval may be conditioned upon such terms as the Court deems just; provided, however, that this provision shall not affect the right of any stockholder who has not commenced an appraisal proceeding or joined that proceeding as a named party to withdraw such stockholder's demand for appraisal and to accept the terms offered upon the merger or consolidation within 60 days after the effective date of the merger or consolidation, as set forth in subsection (e) of this section.

(1) The shares of the surviving or resulting corporation to which the shares of such objecting stockholders would have been converted had they assented to the merger or consolidation shall have the status of authorized and unissued shares of the surviving or resulting corporation.

SUBCHAPTER X. SALE OF ASSETS, DISSOLUTION AND WINDING UP

§271. Sale, Lease or Exchange of Assets; Consideration; Procedure

(a) Every corporation may at any meeting of its board of directors or governing body sell, lease or exchange all or substantially all of its property and assets, including its goodwill and its corporate franchises, upon such terms and conditions and for such consideration, which may consist in whole or in part of money or other property, including shares of stock in, and/or other securities of, any other corporation or corporations, as its board of directors or governing body deems expedient and for the best interests of the corporation, when and as authorized by a resolution adopted by the holders of a majority of the outstanding stock of the corporation entitled to vote thereon or, if the corporation is a nonstock corporation, by a majority of the members having the right to vote for the election of the members of the governing body, at a meeting duly called upon at least 20 days' notice. The notice of the meeting shall state that such a resolution will be considered.

(b) Notwithstanding authorization or consent to a proposed sale, lease or exchange of a corporation's property and assets by the stockholders or members, the board of directors or governing body may abandon such proposed sale, lease or exchange without further action by the stockholders or members, subject to the rights, if any, of third parties under any contract relating thereto.

(c) For purposes of this section only, the property and assets of the corporation include the property and assets of any subsidiary of the corporation. As used in this subsection, "subsidiary" means any entity wholly-owned and controlled, directly or indirectly, by the corporation and includes, without limitation, corporations, partnerships, limited partnerships, limited liability partnerships, limited liability companies, and/or statutory trusts. Notwithstanding subsection (a) of this section, except to the extent the certificate of incorporation otherwise provides, no resolution by stockholders or members shall be required for a sale, lease or exchange of property and assets of the corporation to a subsidiary.

APPENDIX B: FEDERAL STATUTES & REGULATIONS

Securities Exchange Act of 1934

§13(a), (d)   Periodical and Other Reports
§14(a), (d), (e)   Proxies

Rules and Regulations Under the 1934 Act

Form 10-K   Annual Report Pursuant to Section 13 or 15(d) of the Securities Exchange Act of 1934
Rule 13e-3   Going Private Transactions by Certain Issuers or Their Affiliates
Rule 13e-4   Tender Offers by Issuers
Rule 14d-10   Equal Treatment of Security Holders
Rule 14e-1   Unlawful Tender Offer Practices
Rule 14e-3   Transactions in Securities on the Basis of Material, Nonpublic Information in the Context of Tender Offers

SECURITIES EXCHANGE ACT OF 1934

§13. Periodical and Other Reports

(a) Reports by Issuer of Security; Contents

Every issuer of a security registered pursuant to section 12 of this title shall file with the Commission, in accordance with such rules and regulations as the Commission may prescribe as necessary or appropriate for the proper protection of investors and to insure fair dealing in the security—

(1) such information and documents (and such copies thereof) as the Commission shall require to keep reasonably current the information and documents required to be included in or filed with an application or registration statement filed pursuant to section 12 of this title. . . .

(2) such annual reports (and such copies thereof), certified if required by the rules and regulations of the Commission by independent public accountants, and such quarterly reports (and such copies thereof), as the Commission may prescribe.

Every issuer of a security registered on a national securities exchange shall also file a duplicate original of such information, documents, and reports with the exchange. In any registration statement, periodic report, or other reports to be filed with the Commission, an emerging growth company need not present selected financial data in accordance with section 229.301 of title 17, Code of Federal Regulations, for any period prior to the earliest audited period presented in connection with its first registration statement that became effective under this Act or the Securities Act of 1933 and, with respect to any such statement or reports, an emerging growth company may not be required to comply with any new or revised financial accounting standard until such date that a company that is not an issuer as defined under section 2(a) of the Sarbanes-Oxley Act of 2002 (15 U.S.C. 7201(a)) is required to comply with such new or revised accounting standard, if such standard applies to companies that are not issuers.

(d) Reports by Persons Acquiring More Than Five Per Centum of Certain Classes of Securities

(1) Any person who, after acquiring directly or indirectly the beneficial ownership of any equity security of a class which is registered pursuant to section 12 of this title, or any equity security of an insurance company which would have been required to be so registered except for the exemption contained in section 12(g)(2)(G) of this title, or any equity security issued by a closed-end investment company registered under the Investment Company Act of 1940 or any equity security issued by a Native Corporation pursuant to section 1629c(d)(6) of title 43 or otherwise becomes or is deemed to become a beneficial owner of any of the foregoing upon the purchase or sale of a security-based swap that the Commission may define by rule, and is directly or indirectly the beneficial owner of more than 5 per centum of such class shall, within ten days after such acquisition or within such shorter time as the Commission may establish by rule, file with the Commission, a statement containing such of the following information, and such additional information, as the Commission may by rules and regulations, prescribe as necessary or appropriate in the public interest or for the protection of investors—

(A) the background, and identity, residence, and citizenship of, and the nature of such beneficial ownership by, such person and all other persons by whom or on whose behalf the purchases have been or are to be effected;

(B) the source and amount of the funds or other consideration used or to be used in making the purchases, and if any part of the purchase price is represented or is to be represented by funds or other consideration borrowed or otherwise obtained for the purpose of acquiring, holding, or trading such security, a description of the transaction and the names of the parties thereto, except that where a source of funds is a loan made in the ordinary course of business by a bank, as defined in section 3(a)(6) of this title, if the person filing such statement so requests, the name of the bank shall not be made available to the public.

(C) if the purpose of the purchases or prospective purchases is to acquire control of the business of the issuer of the securities, any plans or proposals which such persons may have to liquidate such issuer, to sell its assets to or merge it with any other persons, or to make any other major change in its business or corporate structure;

(D) the number of shares of such security which are beneficially owned, and the number of shares concerning which there is a right to acquire, directly or indirectly, by (i) such person, and (ii) by each associate of such person, giving the background, identity, residence, and citizenship of each such associate; and

(E) information as to any contracts, arrangements, or understandings with any person with respect to any securities of the issuer, including but not limited to transfer of any of the securities, joint ventures, loan or option arrangements, puts or calls, guaranties of loans, guaranties against loss or guaranties of profits, division of losses or profits, or the giving or withholding of proxies, naming the persons with whom such contracts, arrangements, or understandings have been entered into, and giving the details thereof.

(2) If any material change occurs in the facts set forth in the statement filed with the Commission, an amendment shall be filed with the Commission, in accordance with such rules and regulations as the Commission may prescribe as necessary or appropriate in the public interest or for the protection of investors.

(3) When two or more persons act as a partnership, limited partnership, syndicate, or other group for the purpose of acquiring, holding, or disposing of securities of an issuer, such syndicate or group shall be deemed a "person" for the purposes of this subsection.

(4) In determining, for purposes of this subsection, any percentage of a class of any security, such class shall be deemed to consist of the amount of the outstanding securities of such class, exclusive of any securities of such class held by or for the account of the issuer or a subsidiary of the issuer.

(5) The Commission, by rule or regulation or by order, may permit any person to file in lieu of the statement required by paragraph (1) of this subsection or the rules and regulations thereunder, a notice stating the name of such person, the number of shares of

any equity securities subject to paragraph (1) which are owned by him, the date of their acquisition and such other information as the Commission may specify, if it appears to the Commission that such securities were acquired by such person in the ordinary course of his business and were not acquired for the purpose of and do not have the effect of changing or influencing the control of the issuer nor in connection with or as a participant in any transaction having such purpose or effect.

(6) The provisions of this subsection shall not apply to—

(A) any acquisition or offer to acquire securities made or proposed to be made by means of a registration statement under the Securities Act of 1933;

(B) any acquisition of the beneficial ownership of a security which, together with all other acquisitions by the same person of securities of the same class during the preceding twelve months, does not exceed 2 per centum of that class;

(C) any acquisition of an equity security by the issuer of such security;

(D) any acquisition or proposed acquisition of a security which the Commission, by rules or regulations or by order, shall exempt from the provisions of this subsection as not entered into for the purpose of, and not having the effect of, changing or influencing the control of the issuer or otherwise as not comprehended within the purposes of this subsection.

§14. *Proxies*

(a) Solicitation of Proxies in Violation of Rules and Regulations

(1) It shall be unlawful for any person, by the use of the mails or by any means or instrumentality of interstate commerce or of any facility of a national securities exchange or otherwise, in contravention of such rules and regulations as the Commission may prescribe as necessary or appropriate in the public interest or for the protection of investors, to solicit or to permit the use of his name to solicit any proxy or consent or authorization in respect of any security (other than an exempted security) registered pursuant to section 12 of this title.

(2) The rules and regulations prescribed by the Commission under paragraph (1) may include—

(A) a requirement that a solicitation of proxy, consent, or authorization by (or on behalf of) an issuer include a nominee submitted by a shareholder to serve on the board of directors of the issuer; and

(B) a requirement that an issuer follow a certain procedure in relation to a solicitation described in subparagraph (A).

Appendix B: Federal Statutes & Regulations **609**

(d) Tender Offer by Owner of More Than Five Per Centum of Class of Securities; Exceptions

(1) It shall be unlawful for any person, directly or indirectly, by use of the mails or by any means or instrumentality of interstate commerce or of any facility of a national securities exchange or otherwise, to make a tender offer for, or a request or invitation for tenders of, any class of any equity security which is registered pursuant to section 12 of this title, or any equity security of an insurance company which would have been required to be so registered except for the exemption contained in section 12(g)(2)(G) of this title, or any equity security issued by a closed-end investment company registered under the Investment Company Act of 1940, if, after consummation thereof, such person would, directly or indirectly, be the beneficial owner of more than 5 per centum of such class, unless at the time copies of the offer or request or invitation are first published or sent or given to security holders such person has filed with the Commission a statement containing such of the information specified in section 13(d) of this title, and such additional information as the Commission may by rules and regulations prescribe as necessary or appropriate in the public interest or for the protection of investors. All requests or invitations for tenders or advertisements making a tender offer or requesting or inviting tenders of such a security shall be filed as a part of such statement and shall contain such of the information contained in such statement as the Commission may by rules and regulations prescribe. Copies of any additional material soliciting or requesting such tender offers subsequent to the initial solicitation or request shall contain such information as the Commission may by rules and regulations prescribe as necessary or appropriate in the public interest or for the protection of investors, and shall be filed with the Commission not later than the time copies of such material are first published or sent or given to security holders. Copies of all statements, in the form in which such material is furnished to security holders and the Commission, shall be sent to the issuer not later than the date such material is first published or sent or given to any security holders.

(2) When two or more persons act as a partnership, limited partnership, syndicate, or other group for the purpose of acquiring, holding, or disposing of securities of an issuer, such syndicate or group shall be deemed a "person" for purposes of this subsection.

(3) In determining, for purposes of this subsection, any percentage of a class of any security, such class shall be deemed to consist of the amount of the outstanding securities of such class, exclusive of any securities of such class held by or for the account of the issuer or a subsidiary of the issuer.

(4) Any solicitation or recommendation to the holders of such a security to accept or reject a tender offer or request or invitation for

tenders shall be made in accordance with such rules and regulations as the Commission may prescribe as necessary or appropriate in the public interest or for the protection of investors.

(5) Securities deposited pursuant to a tender offer or request or invitation for tenders may be withdrawn by or on behalf of the depositor at any time until the expiration of seven days after the time definitive copies of the offer or request or invitation are first published or sent or given to security holders, and at any time after sixty days from the date of the original tender offer or request or invitation, except as the Commission may otherwise prescribe by rules, regulations, or order as necessary or appropriate in the public interest or for the protection of investors.

(6) Where any person makes a tender offer, or request or invitation for tenders, for less than all the outstanding equity securities of a class, and where a greater number of securities is deposited pursuant thereto within ten days after copies of the offer or request or invitation are first published or sent or given to security holders than such person is bound or willing to take up and pay for, the securities taken up shall be taken up as nearly as may be pro rata, disregarding fractions, according to the number of securities deposited by each depositor. The provisions of this subsection shall also apply to securities deposited within ten days after notice of an increase in the consideration offered to security holders, as described in paragraph (7), is first published or sent or given to security holders.

(7) Where any person varies the terms of a tender offer or request or invitation for tenders before the expiration thereof by increasing the consideration offered to holders of such securities, such person shall pay the increased consideration to each security holder whose securities are taken up and paid for pursuant to the tender offer or request or invitation for tenders whether or not such securities have been taken up by such person before the variation of the tender offer or request or invitation.

(8) The provisions of this subsection shall not apply to any offer for, or request or invitation for tenders of, any security—

(A) if the acquisition of such security, together with all other acquisitions by the same person of securities of the same class during the preceding twelve months, would not exceed 2 per centum of that class;

(B) by the issuer of such security; or

(C) which the Commission, by rules or regulations or by order, shall exempt from the provisions of this subsection as not entered into for the purpose of, and not having the effect of, changing or influencing the control of the issuer or otherwise as not comprehended within the purposes of this subsection.

(e) Untrue Statement of Material Fact or Omission of Fact with Respect to Tender Offer

It shall be unlawful for any person to make any untrue statement of a material fact or omit to state any material fact necessary in order to make the statements made, in the light of the circumstances under which they are made, not misleading, or to engage in any fraudulent, deceptive, or manipulative acts or practices, in connection with any tender offer or request or invitation for tenders, or any solicitation of security holders in opposition to or in favor of any such offer, request, or invitation. The Commission shall, for the purposes of this subsection, by rules and regulations define, and prescribe means reasonably designed to prevent, such acts and practices as are fraudulent, deceptive, or manipulative. . . .

RULES AND REGULATIONS UNDER THE 1934 ACT

Form 10-K: Annual Report Pursuant to Section 13 or 15(d) of the Securities Exchange Act of 1934

GENERAL INSTRUCTIONS

A. Rule as to Use of Form 10-K

(1) This Form shall be used for annual reports pursuant to Section 13 or 15(d) of the Securities Exchange Act of 1934 (the "Act") for which no other form is prescribed. This Form also shall be used for transition reports filed pursuant to Section 13 or 15(d) of the Act.

(2) Annual reports on this Form shall be filed within the following period:

    (a) 60 days after the end of the fiscal year covered by the report (75 days for fiscal years ending before December 15, 2006) for large accelerated filers (as defined in Rule 12b-2);

    (b) 75 days after the end of the fiscal year covered by the report for accelerated filers (as defined in Rule 12b-2); and

    (c) 90 days after the end of the fiscal year covered by the report for all other registrants.

G. Information to Be Incorporated by Reference

(1) Attention is directed to Rule 12b-23 which provides for the incorporation by reference of information contained in certain documents in answer or partial answer to any item of a report.

(2) The information called for by Parts I and II of this Form (Items 1 through 9A or any portion thereof) may, at the registrant's option, be incorporated by reference from the registrant's annual report to security holders furnished to the Commission pursuant to Rule 14a-3(b) or Rule 14c-3(a) or

from the registrant's annual report to security holders, even if not furnished to the Commission pursuant to Rule 14a-3(b) or Rule 14c-3(a), provided such annual report contains the information required by Rule 14a-3.

NOTES

1. In order to fulfill the requirements of Part I of Form 10-K, the incorporated portion of the annual report to security holders must contain the information required by Items 1-3 of Form 10-K, to the extent applicable.
2. If any information required by Part I or Part II is incorporated by reference into an electronic format document from the annual report to security holders as provided in General Instruction G, any portion of the annual report to security holders incorporated by reference shall be filed as an exhibit in electronic format, as required by Item 601(b)(13) of Regulation S-K.

(3) The information required by Part III (Items 10, 11, 12, 13 and 14) shall be incorporated by reference from the registrant's definitive proxy statement (filed or required to be filed pursuant to Regulation 14A) or definitive information statement (filed or to be filed pursuant to Regulation 14C) which involves the election of directors, if such definitive proxy statement or information statement is filed with the Commission not later than 120 days after the end of the fiscal year covered by the Form 10-K. However, if such definitive proxy or information statement is not filed with the Commission in the 120-day period or is not required to be filed with the Commission by virtue of Rule 3a12-3(b) under the Exchange Act, the Items comprising the Part III information must be filed as part of the Form 10-K, or as an amendment to the Form 10-K, not later than the end of the 120-day period. It should be noted that the information regarding executive officers required by Item 401 of Regulation S-K may be included in part I of Form 10-K under an appropriate caption. See Instruction 3 to Item 401(b) of Regulation S-K.

(4) No item numbers of captions of items need be contained in the material incorporated by reference into the report. However, the registrant's attention is directed to Rule 12b-23(e) regarding the specific disclosure required in the report concerning information incorporated by reference. When the registrant combines all of the information in Parts I and II of this Form (Items 1 through 9A) by incorporation by reference from the registrant's annual report to security holders and all of the information in Part III of this Form (Items 10 through 14) by incorporating by reference from a definitive proxy statement or information statement involving the election of directors, then, notwithstanding General Instruction C(1), this Form shall consist of the facing or cover page, those sections incorporated from the annual report to security holders, the proxy or information statement, and the information, if any, required by Part IV

of this Form, signatures, and a cross reference sheet setting forth the item numbers and captions in Parts I, II and III of this Form and the page and/or pages in the referenced materials where the corresponding information appears.

H. Integrated Reports to Security Holders

Annual reports to security holders may be combined with the required information of Form 10-K and will be suitable for filing with the Commission if the following conditions are satisfied:

(1) The combined report contains full and complete answers to all items required by Form 10-K. When responses to a certain item of required disclosure are separated within the combined report, an appropriate cross-reference should be made. If the information required by Part III of Form 10-K is omitted by virtue of General Instruction G, a definitive proxy or information statement shall be filed.

(2) The cover page and the required signatures are included. As appropriate, a cross-reference sheet should be filed indicating the location of information required by the items of the Form.

(3) If an electronic filer files any portion of an annual report to security holders in combination with the required information of Form 10-K, as provided in this instruction, only such portions filed in satisfaction of the Form 10-K requirements shall be filed in electronic format. . . .

[INFORMATION TO BE INCLUDED IN THE REPORT]
FORM 10-K . . .

Indicate by check mark whether the registrant is a large accelerated filer, an accelerated filer, a non-accelerated filer or a smaller reporting company. See definition of "accelerated filer and large accelerated filer" and "smaller reporting company" in Rule 12b-2 of the Exchange Act. (Check one):

Indicate by check mark if disclosure of delinquent filers pursuant to Item 405 of Regulation S-K is not contained herein, and will not be contained, to the best of registrant's knowledge, in definitive proxy or information statements incorporated by reference in Part III of this Form 10-K or any amendment to this Form 10-K. [ ]

Large accelerated filer _____ Accelerated filer _____ Non-accelerated filer _____ Smaller reporting company _____

Indicate by check mark if the registrant is a well-known seasoned issuer, as defined in Rule 405 of the Securities Act. Yes _____ No _____

Indicate by check mark if the registrant is not required to file reports pursuant to Section 13 or Section 15(d) of the Act. Yes _____ No _____

Note—Checking the box above will not relieve any registrant required to file reports pursuant to Section 13 or 15(d) of the Exchange Act from their obligations under those Sections.

Indicate by check mark whether the registrant has submitted electronically and posted on its corporate Web site, if any, every Interactive Data File required to be submitted and posted pursuant to Rule 405 of Regulation S-T during the preceding 12 months (or for such shorter period that the registrant was required to submit and post such files). Yes____ No____

Indicate by check mark whether the registrant (1) has filed all reports required to be filed by Section 13 or 15(d) of the Securities Exchange Act of 1934 during the preceding 12 months (or for such shorter period that the registrant was required to file such reports), and (2) has been subject to such filing requirements for the past 90 days. Yes____ No____

Indicate by check mark whether the registrant is a shell company (as defined by Rule 12b-2 of the Act). Yes____ No____

State the aggregate market value of the voting and non-voting common equity held by non-affiliates of the registrant. The aggregate market value shall be computed by reference to the price at which the common equity was sold, or the average bid and asked prices of such common equity, as of a specified date within 60 days prior to the date of filing. (See definition of affiliate in Rule 405.)

NOTE

If a determination as to whether a particular person or entity is an affiliate cannot be made without involving unreasonable effort and expense, the aggregate market value of the common stock held by non-affiliates may be calculated on the basis of assumptions reasonable under the circumstances, provided that the assumptions are set forth in this Form. ...

Documents Incorporated by Reference

List hereunder the following documents if incorporated by reference and the Part of the Form 10-K (e.g., Part I, Part II, etc.) into which the document is incorporated: (1) Any annual report to security holders; (2) Any proxy or information statement; and (3) Any prospectus filed pursuant to Rule 424(b) or (c) under the Securities Act of 1933. The listed documents should be clearly described for identification purposes (e.g., annual report to security holders for fiscal year ended December 24, 1980).

Part I [See General Instruction G(2)]

Item 1. Business

Furnish the information required by Item 101 of Regulation S-K except that the discussion of the development of the registrant's business need only include developments since the beginning of the fiscal year for which this report is filed.

Item 1A. Risk Factors

Set forth, under the caption "Risk Factors," where appropriate, the risk factors described in Item 503(c) of Regulation S-K applicable to the registrant. Provide any discussion of risk factors in plain English in accordance with Rule 421(d) of the Securities Act of 1933. Smaller reporting companies are not required to provide the information required by this Item.

Item 1B. Unresolved Staff Comments

If the registrant is an accelerated filer or a large accelerated filer, as defined in Rule 12b-2 of the Exchange Act, or is a well-known seasoned issuer as defined in Rule 405 of the Securities Act and has received written comments from the Commission staff regarding its periodic or current reports under the Act not less than 180 days before the end of its fiscal year to which the annual report relates, and such comments remain unresolved, disclose the substance of any such unresolved comments that the registrant believes are material. Such disclosure may provide other information including the position of the registrant with respect to any such comment.

Item 2. Properties

Furnish the information required by Item 102 of Regulation S-K.

Item 3. Legal Proceedings

(a) Furnish the information required by Item 103 of Regulation S-K.

(b) As to any proceeding that was terminated during the fourth quarter of the fiscal year covered by this report, furnish information similar to that required by Item 103 of Regulation S-K, including the date of termination and a description of the disposition thereof with respect to the registrant and its subsidiaries.

Item 4. Mine Safety Disclosures

If applicable, provide a statement that the information concerning mine safety violation or other regulatory matters required by Section 1503(a) of the Dodd-Frank Wall Street Reform and Consumer Protection Act and Item 104 of Regulation S-K (17 CFR 229.104) is included in exhibit 95 to the annual report.

Part II [See General Instruction G(2)]

Item 5. Market for Registrant's Common Equity and Related Stockholder Matters

(a) Furnish the information required by Item 201 of Regulation S-K and Item 701 of Regulation S-K as to all equity securities of the registrant sold by the registrant during the period covered by the report that were not registered under the Securities Act. If the Item 701 information previously has been included in a Quarterly Report on Form 10-Q or in a Current Report on Form 8-K, it need not be furnished.

(c) Furnish the information required by Item 703 of Regulation S-K for any repurchase made in a month within the fourth quarter of the fiscal year covered by the report. Provide disclosures covering repurchases made on a monthly basis. For example, if the fourth quarter began on January 16 and ended on April 15, the chart would show repurchases for the months from January 16 through February 15, February 16 through March 15, and March 16 through April 15.

Item 6. Selected Financial Data

Furnish the information required by Item 301 of Regulation S-K.

Item 7. Management's Discussion and Analysis of Financial Condition and Results of Operation

Furnish the information required by Item 303 of Regulation S-K.

Item 8. Financial Statements and Supplementary Data

(a) Furnish financial statements meeting the requirements of Regulation S-X, except §210.3-05 and Article 11 thereof, and the supplementary financial information required by Item 302 of Regulation S-K. . . .

(b) A smaller reporting company may provide the information required by Article 8 of Regulation S-X in lieu of the financial statements required by Item 8 of this Form.

Item 9. Changes in and Disagreements with Accountants on Accounting and Financial Disclosure

Furnish the information required by Item 304(b) of Regulation S-K.

Item 9A. Controls and Procedures

Furnish the information required by Items 307 and 308 of Regulation S-K.

Item 9B. Other Information

The registrant must disclose under this item any information required to be disclosed in a report on Form 8-K during the fourth quarter of the year covered by this Form 10-K, but not reported, whether or not otherwise required by this Form 10-K. If disclosure of such information is made under this item, it need not be repeated in a report on Form 8-K which would otherwise be required to be filed with respect to such information or in a subsequent report on Form 10-K.

Appendix B: Federal Statutes & Regulations **617**

Part III [See General Instruction G(3)]

Item 10. Directors, Executive Officers, and Corporate Governance

Furnish the information required by Items 401, 405, 406, and 407(c)(3), d(4), and d(5) of Regulation S-K.

Instruction. Checking the box provided on the cover page of this Form to indicate that Item 405 disclosure of delinquent Form 3, 4, or 5 filers is not contained herein is intended to facilitate Form processing and review. Failure to provide such indication will not create liability for violation of the federal securities laws. The space should be checked only if there is no disclosure in this Form of reporting person delinquencies in response to Item 405 and the registrant, at the time of filing the Form 10-K, has reviewed the information necessary to ascertain, and has determined that, Item 405 disclosure is not expected to be contained in Part III of the Form 10-K or incorporated by reference.

Item 11. Executive Compensation

Furnish the information required by Item 402 Regulation S-K and paragraphs (e)(4) and (e)(5) of Item 407 of Regulation S-K.

Item 12. Security Ownership of Certain Beneficial Owners and Management

Furnish the information required by Item 201(d) of Regulation S-K and by Item 403 of Regulation S-K.

Item 13. Certain Relationships and Related Transactions, and Director Independence

Furnish the information required by Item 404 of Regulation S-K and Item 407(a) of Regulation S-K.

Part IV

Item 14. Principal Accountant Fees and Services

Furnish the information required by Item 9(e) of Schedule 14A.

(1) Disclose, under the caption Audit Fees, the aggregate fees billed for each of the last two fiscal years for professional services rendered by the principal accountant for the audit of the registrant's annual financial statements and review of financial statements include in the registrant's Form 10-Q or services that are normally provided by the accountant in connection with statutory and regulatory fillings or engagements for those fiscal years.

(2) Disclose, under the caption Audit-Related Fees, the aggregate fees billed in each of the last two fiscal years for assurance and related services by the principal accountant that are reasonably related to the performance of the audit or review of the registrant's financial statements and are not reported under Item 9(e)(1) of Schedule 14A. Registrants shall describe the nature of the services comprising the fees disclosed under this category.

(3) Disclose, under the caption Tax Fees, the aggregate fees billed in each of the last two fiscal years for professional services rendered by the principal accountant for tax compliance, tax advice, and tax planning. Registrants shall describe the nature of the services comprising the fees disclosed under this category.

(4) Disclose, under the caption All Other Fees, the aggregate fees billed in each of the last two fiscal years for products and services provided by the principal accountant, other than the services reported in Items 9(e)(1) through 9(e)(3) of Schedule 14A. Registrants shall describe the nature of the services comprising the fees disclosed under this category.

(5) (i) Disclose the audit committee's pre-approval policies and procedures described in paragraph (c)(7)(i) of Rule 2-01 of Regulation S-X.

(ii) Disclose the percentage of services described in each of Items 9(e)(2) through 9(e)(4) of Schedule 14A that were approved by the audit committee pursuant to paragraph (c)(7)(ii)(C) of Rule 2-01 of Regulation S-X.

(6) If greater than 50 percent, disclose the percentage of hours expended on the principal accountant's engagement to audit the registrant's financial statements for the most recent fiscal year that were attributed to work performed by persons other than the principal accountant's full-time, permanent employees.

Item 15. Exhibits, Financial Statement Schedules, and Reports on Form 8-K

(a) List the following Documents filed as a part of the report:

1. All financial statements.
2. Those financial statement schedules required to be filed by Item 8 of this Form, and by paragraph (d) below.
3. Those exhibits required by Item 601 of Regulation S-K and by paragraph(c) below. Identify in the list each management contract or compensatory plan or arrangement required to be filed as an exhibit to this form pursuant to Item 14(c) of this report.

(b) Reports on Form 8-K. State whether any reports on Form 8-K have been filed during the last quarter of the period covered by this report, listing the items reported, any financial statements filed and the dates of any such reports.

(c) Registrants shall file, as exhibits to this Form, the exhibits required by Item 601 of Regulation S-K.

(d) Registrants shall file, as financial statement schedules to this Form, the financial statements required by Regulation S-X which are excluded from the annual report to shareholders by Rule 14a-3(b), including (1) separate financial statements of subsidiaries not consolidated and fifty percent or less owned persons; (2) separate financial statements of affiliates whose securities are pledged as collateral and (3) schedules.

Rule 13e-3. Going Private Transactions by Certain Issuers or Their Affiliates

(a) *Definitions.* Unless indicated otherwise or the context otherwise requires, all terms used in this section and in Schedule 13E-3 shall have the same meaning as in the Act or elsewhere in the General Rules and Regulations thereunder. In addition, the following definitions apply:

(1) An *affiliate* of an issuer is a person that directly or indirectly through one or more intermediaries controls, is controlled by, or is under common control with such issuer. For the purposes of this section only, a person who is not an affiliate of an issuer at the commencement of such person's tender offer for a class of equity securities of such issuer will not be deemed an affiliate of such issuer prior to the stated termination of such tender offer and any extensions thereof;

(2) The term *purchase* means any acquisition for value including, but not limited to, (i) any acquisition pursuant to the dissolution of an issuer subsequent to the sale or other disposition of substantially all the assets of such issuer to its affiliate, (ii) any acquisition pursuant to a merger, (iii) any acquisition of fractional interests in connection with a reverse stock split, and (iv) any acquisition subject to the control of an issuer or an affiliate of such issuer;

(3) A *Rule 13e-3* transaction is any transaction or series of transactions involving one or more of the transactions described in paragraph (a)(3)(i) of this section which has either a reasonable likelihood or a purpose of producing, either directly or indirectly, any of the effects described in paragraph (a)(3)(ii) of this section;

(i) The transactions referred to in paragraph (a)(3) of this section are:

(A) A purchase of any equity security by the issuer of such security or by an affiliate of such issuer;

(B) A tender offer for or request or invitation for tenders of any equity security made by the issuer of such class of securities or by an affiliate of such issuer; or

(C) A solicitation subject to Regulation 14A of any proxy, consent or authorization of, or a distribution subject to Regulation 14C of information statements to, any equity security holder by the issuer of the class of securities or by an affiliate of such issuer, in connection with: a merger, consolidation, reclassification, recapitalization, reorganization or similar corporate transaction of an issuer or between an issuer (or its subsidiaries) and its affiliate; a sale of substantially all the assets of an issuer to its affiliate or group of affiliates; or a reverse stock split of any class of equity securities of the issuer involving the purchase of fractional interests.

(ii) The effects referred to in paragraph (a)(3) of this section are:

(A) Causing any class of equity securities of the issuer which is subject to section 12(g) or section 15(d) of the Act to become eligible for termination of registration under Rule 12g-4 or Rule 12h-6 or causing the reporting obligations with respect to such class to become eligible for termination under Rule 12h-6; or suspension under Rule 12h-3 or section 15(d); or

(B) Causing any class of equity securities of the issuer which is either listed on a national securities exchange or authorized to be quoted in an inter-dealer quotation system of a registered national securities association to be neither listed on any national securities exchange nor authorized to be quoted on an inter-dealer quotation system of any registered national securities association.

(4) An *unaffiliated security holder* is any security holder of an equity security subject to a Rule 13e-3 transaction who is not an affiliate of the issuer of such security.

(b) *Application of section to an issuer (or an affiliate of such issuer) subject to section 12 of the Act.* (1) It shall be a fraudulent, deceptive or manipulative act or practice, in connection with a Rule 13e-3 transaction, for an issuer which has a class of equity securities registered pursuant to section 12 of the Act or which is a closed-end investment company registered under the Investment Company Act of 1940, or an affiliate of such issuer, directly or indirectly

(i) To employ any device, scheme or artifice to defraud any person;

(ii) To make any untrue statement of a material fact or to omit to state a material fact necessary in order to make the statements made, in light of the circumstances under which they were made, not misleading; or

(iii) To engage in any act, practice or course of business which operates or would operate as a fraud or deceit upon any person.

(2) As a means reasonably designed to prevent fraudulent, deceptive or manipulative acts or practices in connection with any Rule 13e-3 transaction, it shall be unlawful for an issuer which has a class of equity securities registered pursuant to section 12 of the Act, or an affiliate of such issuer, to engage, directly or indirectly, in a Rule 13e-3 transaction unless:

(i) Such issuer or affiliate complies with the requirements of paragraphs (d), (e) and (f) of this section; and

(ii) The Rule 13e-3 transaction is not in violation of paragraph (b)(1) of this section.

(c) *Application of section to an issuer (or an affiliate of such issuer) subject to section 15(d) of the Act.* (1) It shall be unlawful as a fraudulent, deceptive or manipulative act or practice for an issuer which is required to file periodic reports pursuant to Section 15(d) of the Act, or an affiliate of such issuer, to engage, directly or indirectly, in a Rule 13e-3 transaction unless such issuer or affiliate complies with the requirements of paragraphs (d), (e) and (f) of this section.

(2) An issuer or affiliate which is subject to paragraph (c)(1) of this section and which is soliciting proxies or distributing information statements in connection with a transaction described in paragraph (a)(3)(i)(A) of this section may elect to use the timing procedures for conducting a solicitation subject to Regulation 14A or a distribution subject to Regulation 14C in complying with paragraphs (d), (e) and (f) of this section, provided that if an election is made, such solicitation or distribution is conducted in accordance with the requirements of the respective regulations, including the filing of preliminary copies of soliciting materials or an information statement at the time specified in Regulation 14A or 14C, respectively.

(d) *Material required to be filed.* The issuer or affiliate engaging in a Rule 13e-3 transaction must file with the Commission:

(1) A Schedule 13E-3 including all exhibits;

(2) An amendment to Schedule 13E-3 reporting promptly any material changes in the information set forth in the schedule previously filed; and

(3) A final amendment to Schedule 13E-3 reporting promptly the results of the Rule 13e-3 transaction.

(e) *Disclosure of information to security holders.*

(1) In addition to disclosing the information required by any other applicable rule or regulation under the federal securities laws, the issuer or affiliate engaging in a Rule 13e-3 transaction must disclose to security holders of the class that is the subject of the transaction, as specified in paragraph (f) of this section, the following:

(i) The information required by Item 1 of Schedule 13E-3 (Summary Term Sheet);

(ii) The information required by Items 7, 8 and 9 of Schedule 13E-3, which must be prominently disclosed in a "Special Factors" section in the front of the disclosure document;

(iii) A prominent legend on the outside front cover page that indicates that neither the Securities and Exchange Commission nor any state securities commission has: approved or disapproved of the transaction; passed upon the merits or fairness of the transaction; or passed upon the adequacy or accuracy of the disclosure in the document. The legend also must make it clear that any representation to the contrary is a criminal offense;

(iv) The information concerning appraisal rights required by Item 1016(f) of [Regulation M-A]; and

(v) The information required by the remaining items of Schedule 13E-3, except for (exhibits), or a fair and adequate summary of the information. . . .

Rule 13e-4. Tender Offers by Issuers

(a) *Definitions.* Unless the context otherwise requires, all terms used in this section and in Schedule TO shall have the same meaning as in the Act or elsewhere in the General Rules and Regulations thereunder. In addition, the following definitions shall apply:

(1) The term *issuer* means any issuer which has a class of equity security registered pursuant to section 12 of the Act, or which is required to file periodic reports pursuant to section 15(d) of the Act, or which is a closed-end investment company registered under the Investment Company Act of 1940.

(2) The term *issuer tender offer* refers to a tender offer for, or a request or invitation for tenders of, any class of equity security, made by the issuer of such class of equity security or by an affiliate of such issuer. . . .

(b) As soon as practicable on the date of commencement of the issuer tender offer, the issuer or affiliate making the issuer tender offer must comply with:

(1) The filing requirements of paragraph (c)(2) of this section;

(2) The disclosure requirements of paragraph (d)(1) of this section; and

(3) The dissemination requirements of paragraph (e) of this section.

(c) *Material required to be filed.* The issuer or affiliate making the issuer tender offer must file with the Commission:

(1) All written communications made by the issuer or affiliate relating to the issuer tender offer, from and including the first public announcement, as soon as practicable on the date of the communication;

(2) A Schedule TO including all exhibits;

(3) An amendment to Schedule TO reporting promptly any material changes in the information set forth in the schedule previously filed; and

(4) A final amendment to Schedule TO reporting promptly the results of the issuer tender offer.

(d) *Disclosure of tender offer information to security holders.*

(1) The issuer or affiliate making the issuer tender offer must disclose, in a manner prescribed by paragraph (e)(1) of this section, the following:

(i) The information required by Item 1 of Schedule TO (summary term sheet); and

(ii) The information required by the remaining items of Schedule TO for issuer tender offers, except for Item 12 (exhibits), or a fair and adequate summary of the information.

(2) If there are any material changes in the information previously disclosed to security holders, the issuer or affiliate must disclose the changes promptly to security holders in a manner specified in paragraph (e)(3) of this section.

(3) If the issuer or affiliate disseminates the issuer tender offer by means of summary publication as described in paragraph (e)(1)(iii) of this section, the summary advertisement must not include a transmittal letter that would permit security holders to tender securities sought in the offer and must disclose at least the following information:

(i) The identity of the issuer or affiliate making the issuer tender offer;

(ii) The information required by Regulation M-A, Items 1004(a)(1) and 1006(a) of this chapter;

(iii) Instructions on how security holders can obtain promptly a copy of the statement required by paragraph (d)(1) of this section, at the issuer or affiliate's expense; and

(iv) A statement that the information contained in the statement required by paragraph (d)(1) of this section is incorporated by reference.

(e) *Dissemination of tender offers to security holders.* An issuer tender offer will be deemed to be published, sent or given to security holders if the issuer or affiliate making the issuer tender offer complies fully with one or more of the methods described in this section.

(1) For issuer tender offers in which the consideration offered consists solely of cash and/or securities exempt from registration under Section 3 of the Securities Act of 1933:

(i) Dissemination of cash issuer tender offers by long-form publication: By making adequate publication of the information required by paragraph (d)(1) of this section in a newspaper or newspapers, on the date of commencement of the issuer tender offer.

(ii) Dissemination of any issuer tender offer by use of stockholder and other lists:

(A) By mailing or otherwise furnishing promptly a statement containing the information required by paragraph (d)(1) of this section to each security holder whose name appears on the most recent stockholder list of the issuer;

(B) By contacting each participant on the most recent security position listing of any clearing agency within the possession or access of the issuer or affiliate making the issuer tender offer, and making inquiry of each participant as to the approximate number of beneficial owners of the securities sought in the offer that are held by the participant;

(C) By furnishing to each participant a sufficient number of copies of the statement required by paragraph (d)(1) of this section for transmittal to the beneficial owners; and

(D) By agreeing to reimburse each participant promptly for its reasonable expenses incurred in forwarding the statement to beneficial owners.

(iii) Dissemination of certain cash issuer tender offers by summary publication:

(A) If the issuer tender offer is not subject to Rule 13e-3, by making adequate publication of a summary advertisement containing the information required by paragraph (d)(3) of this section in a newspaper or newspapers, on the date of commencement of the issuer tender offer; and

(B) By mailing or otherwise furnishing promptly the statement required by paragraph (d)(1) of this section and a transmittal letter to any security holder who requests a copy of the statement or transmittal letter.

(2) For tender offers in which the consideration consists solely or partially of securities registered under the Securities Act of 1933, a registration statement containing all of the required information, including pricing information, has been filed and a preliminary prospectus or a prospectus that meets the requirements of Section 10(a) of the Securities Act, including a letter of transmittal, is delivered to security holders. However, for going-private transactions (as defined by Rule 13e-3) and roll-up transactions (as described by Item 901 of Regulation S-K), a registration statement registering the securities to be offered must have become effective and only a prospectus that meets the requirements of Section 10(a) of the Securities Act may be delivered to security holders on the date of commencement.

(3) If a material change occurs in the information published, sent or given to security holders, the issuer or affiliate must disseminate promptly disclosure of the change in a manner reasonably calculated to inform security holders of the change. In a registered securities offer where the issuer or affiliate disseminates the preliminary prospectus as permitted by paragraph (e)(2) of this section, the offer must remain open from the date that material changes to the tender offer materials are disseminated to security holders, as follows:

(i) Five business days for a prospectus supplement containing a material change other than price or share levels;

(ii) Ten business days for a prospectus supplement containing a change in price, the amount of securities sought, the dealer's soliciting fee, or other similarly significant change;

(iii) Ten business days for a prospectus supplement included as part of a post-effective amendment; and

(iv) Twenty business days for a revised prospectus when the initial prospectus was materially deficient.

(f) *Manner of making tender offer.* (1) The issuer tender offer, unless withdrawn, shall remain open until the expiration of:

(i) At least twenty business days from its commencement; and

(ii) At least ten business days from the date that notice of an increase or decrease in the percentage of the class of securities being sought or the consideration offered or the dealer's soliciting fee to be given is first published, sent or given to security holders. Provided, however, That, for purposes of this paragraph, the acceptance for payment by the issuer or affiliate of an additional amount of securities not to exceed two percent of the class of securities that is the subject of the tender offer shall not be deemed to be an increase. For purposes of this paragraph, the percentage of a class of securities shall be calculated in accordance with section 14(d)(3) of the Act.

(2) The issuer or affiliate making the issuer tender offer shall permit securities tendered pursuant to the issuer tender offer to be withdrawn:

(i) At any time during the period such issuer tender offer remains open; and

(ii) If not yet accepted for payment, after the expiration of forty business days from the commencement of the issuer tender offer.

(3) If the issuer or affiliate makes a tender offer for less than all of the outstanding equity securities of a class, and if a greater number of securities is tendered pursuant thereto than the issuer or affiliate is bound or willing to take up and pay for, the securities taken up and paid for shall be taken up and paid for as nearly as may be pro rata, disregarding fractions, according to the number of securities tendered by each security holder during the period such offer remains open; *Provided, however,* That this provision shall not prohibit the issuer or affiliate making the issuer tender offer from:

(i) Accepting all securities tendered by persons who own, beneficially or of record, an aggregate of not more than a specified number which is less than one hundred shares of such security and who tender all their securities, before prorating securities tendered by others; or

(ii) Accepting by lot securities tendered by security holders who tender all securities held by them and who, when tendering their securities, elect to have either all or none of at least a minimum amount or none accepted, if the issuer or affiliate first accepts all securities tendered by security holders who do not so elect;

(4) In the event the issuer or affiliate making the issuer tender increases the consideration offered after the issuer tender offer has commenced, such issuer or affiliate shall pay such increased consideration to all security holders whose tendered securities are accepted for payment by such issuer or affiliate.

(5) The issuer or affiliate making the tender offer shall either pay the consideration offered, or return the tendered securities, promptly after the termination or withdrawal of the tender offer.

(6) Until the expiration of at least ten business days after the date of termination of the issuer tender offer, neither the issuer nor any affiliate shall make any purchases, otherwise than pursuant to the tender offer, of:

(i) Any security which is the subject of the issuer tender offer, or any security of the same class and series, or any right to purchase any such securities; and

(ii) In the case of an issuer tender offer which is an exchange offer, any security being offered pursuant to such exchange offer, or any security of the same class and series, or any right to purchase any such security.

(7) The time periods for the minimum offering periods pursuant to this section shall be computed on a concurrent as opposed to a consecutive basis.

(8) No issuer or affiliate shall make a tender offer unless:

(i) The tender offer is open to all security holders of the class of securities subject to the tender offer; and

(ii) The consideration paid to any security holder for securities tendered in the tender offer is the highest consideration paid to any other security holder for securities tendered in the tender offer.

(9) Paragraph (f)(8)(i) of this section shall not:

(i) Affect dissemination under paragraph (e) of this section; or

(ii) Prohibit an issuer or affiliate from making a tender offer excluding all security holders in a state where the issuer or affiliate is prohibited from making the tender offer by administrative or judicial action pursuant to a state statute after a good faith effort by the issuer or affiliate to comply with such statute.

(10) Paragraph (f)(8)(ii) of this section shall not prohibit the offer of more than one type of consideration in a tender offer, provided that:

(i) Security holders are afforded equal right to elect among each of the types of consideration offered; and

(ii) The highest consideration of each type paid to any security holder is paid to any other security holder receiving that type of consideration.

(11) If the offer and sale of securities constituting consideration offered in an issuer tender offer is prohibited by the appropriate authority of a state after a good faith effort by the issuer or affiliate to register or qualify the offer and sale of such securities in such state:

(i) The issuer or affiliate may offer security holders in such state an alternative form of consideration; and

(ii) Paragraph (f)(10) of this section shall not operate to require the issuer or affiliate to offer or pay the alternative form of consideration to security holders in any other state.

(12) (i) Paragraph (f)(8)(ii) of this section shall not prohibit the negotiation, execution or amendment of an employment compensation, severance or other employee benefit arrangement, or payments made or to be made or benefits granted or to be granted according to such an arrangement, with respect to any security holder of the issuer, where the amount payable under the arrangement:

(A) Is being paid or granted as compensation for past services performed, future services to be performed, or future services to be refrained from performing, by the security holder (and matters incidental thereto); and

(B) Is not calculated based on the number of securities tendered or to be tendered in the tender offer by the security holder.

(ii) The provisions of paragraph (f)(12)(i) of this section shall be satisfied and, therefore, pursuant to this non-exclusive safe harbor, the negotiation, execution or amendment of an arrangement and any payments made or to be made or benefits granted or to be granted according to that arrangement shall not be prohibited by paragraph (f)(8)(ii) of this section, if the arrangement is approved as an employment compensation, severance or other employee benefit arrangement solely by independent directors as follows:

(A) The compensation committee of the board of directors that performs functions similar to a compensation committee of the issuer approves the arrangement, regardless of whether the issuer is a party to the arrangement, or, if an affiliate is a party to the arrangement, the compensation committee or a committee of the board of directors that performs functions similar to a compensation committee of the affiliate approves the arrangement; or

(B) If the issuer's or affiliate's board of directors, as applicable, does not have a compensation committee or a committee of the board of directors that performs functions similar to a compensation committee or if none of the members of the issuer's or affiliate's compensation committee or committee that performs functions similar to a compensation committee is independent, a special committee of the board of directors formed to consider and approve the arrangement approves the arrangement; or

(C) If the issuer or affiliate, as applicable, is a foreign private issuer, any or all members of the board of directors or any committee of the board of directors authorized to approve employment compensation, severance or other employee benefit arrangements under the laws or regulations of the home country approves the arrangement.

Rule 14d-10. Equal Treatment of Security Holders

(a) No bidder shall make a tender offer unless:

(1) The tender offer is open to all security holders of the class of securities subject to the tender offer; and

(2) The consideration paid to any security holder for securities tendered in the tender offer is the highest consideration paid to any other security holder for securities tendered during such tender offer....

(d)(1) Paragraph (a)(2) of this section shall not prohibit the negotiation, execution or amendment of an employment compensation, severance or other employee benefit arrangement, or payment made or to be made or benefits granted or to be granted according to such an arrangement, with respect to any security holder of the subject company, where the amount payable under the arrangement:

(i) Is being paid or granted as compensation for past services performed, future services to be performed, or future services to be refrained from performing, by the security holder (and matters incidental thereto); and

(ii) Is not calculated based on the number of securities tendered or to be tendered in the tender offer by the security holder.

(2) The provisions of paragraph (d)(1) of this section shall be satisfied and, therefore, pursuant to this non-exclusive safe harbor, the negotiation, execution or amendment of an arrangement and any payments made or to be made or benefits granted or to be granted according to that arrangement shall not be prohibited by paragraph (a)(2) of this section, if the arrangement is approved as

an employment compensation, severance or other employee benefit arrangement solely by independent directors as follows:

(i) The compensation committee or a committee of the board of directors that performs functions similar to a compensation committee of the subject company approves the arrangement, regardless of whether the subject company is a party to the arrangement, or, if the bidder is a party to the arrangement, the compensation committee or a committee of the board of directors that performs functions similar to a compensation committee of the bidder approves the arrangement; or

(ii) If the subject company's or bidder's board of directors, as applicable, does not have a compensation committee or a committee of the board of the directors that performs functions similar to a compensation committee or if none of the members of the subject company's or bidder's compensation committee or committee or committee that performs functions similar to a compensation committee is independent, a special committee of the board of directors formed to consider and approve the arrangement approves the arrangement; or

(iii) If the subject company or bidder, as applicable, is a foreign private issuer, any or all members of the board of directors or any committee of the board of directors authorized to approve employment compensation, severance or other employee benefit arrangements under the laws or regulations of the home country approves the arrangement.

REGULATION 14E

Rule 14e-1. Unlawful Tender Offer Practices

As a means reasonably designed to prevent fraudulent, deceptive or manipulative acts or practices within the meaning of section 14(e) of the Act, no person who makes a tender offer shall:

(a) Hold such tender offer open for less than twenty business days from the date such tender offer is first published or sent or given to security holders; provided, however, that if the tender offer involves a roll-up transaction as defined in Item 901(c) of Regulation S-K and the securities being offered are registered (or authorized to be registered) on Form S-4 or Form F-4, the offer shall not be open for less than sixty calendar days from the date the tender offer is first published or sent to security holders:

(b) Increase or decrease the percentage of the class of securities being sought or the consideration offered or the dealer's soliciting fee to be given in a tender offer unless such tender offer remains open for at least ten business days from the date that notice of such increase or decrease is first published or sent or given to security holders.

Provided, however, That, for purposes of this paragraph, the acceptance for payment of an additional amount of securities not to exceed two percent of the class of securities that is the subject of the tender offer shall not be deemed to be an increase. For purposes of this paragraph, the percentage of a class of securities shall be calculated in accordance with section 14(d)(3) of the Act.

(c) Fail to pay the consideration offered or return the securities deposited by or on behalf of security holders promptly after the termination or withdrawal of a tender offer. This paragraph does not prohibit a bidder electing to offer a subsequent offering period under Rule 14d-11 from paying for securities during the subsequent offering period in accordance with that section.

(d) Extend the length of a tender offer without issuing a notice of such extension by press release or other public announcement, which notice shall include disclosure of the approximate number of securities deposited to date and shall be issued no later than the earlier of: (i) 9:00 a.m. Eastern time, on the next business day after the scheduled expiration date of the offer or (ii), if the class of securities which is the subject of the tender offer is registered on one or more national securities exchanges, the first opening of any one of such exchanges on the next business day after the scheduled expiration date of the offer.

(e) The periods of time required by paragraphs (a) and (b) of this section shall be tolled for any period during which the bidder has failed to file in electronic format, absent a hardship exemption, the Schedule TO Tender Offer Statement, any tender offer material required to be filed by Item 12 of that Schedule pursuant to paragraph (a) of Item 1016 of Regulation M-A, and any amendments thereto. If such documents were filed in paper pursuant to a hardship exemption, the minimum offering periods shall be tolled for any period during which a required confirming electronic copy of such Schedule and tender offer material is delinquent.

Rule 14e-3. *Transactions in Securities on the Basis of Material, Nonpublic Information in the Context of Tender Offers*

(a) If any person has taken a substantial step or steps to commence, or has commenced, a tender offer (the "offering person"), it shall constitute a fraudulent, deceptive or manipulative act or practice within the meaning of section 14(e) of the Act for any other person who is in possession of material information relating to such tender offer which information he knows or has reason to know is non-public and which he knows or has reason to know has been acquired directly or indirectly from:

 (1) The offering person,

 (2) The issuer of the securities sought or to be sought by such tender offer, or

 (3) Any officer, director, partner or employee or any other person acting on behalf of the offering person or such issuer, to purchase or

sell or cause to be purchased or sold any of such securities or any securities convertible into or exchangeable for any such securities or any option or right to obtain or to dispose of any of the foregoing securities, unless within a reasonable time prior to any purchase or sale such information and its source are publicly disclosed by press release or otherwise.

(b) A person other than a natural person shall not violate paragraph (a) of this section if such person shows that:

(1) The individual(s) making the investment decision on behalf of such person to purchase or sell any security described in paragraph (a) of this section or to cause any such security to be purchased or sold by or on behalf of others did not know the material, nonpublic information; and

(2) Such person had implemented one or a combination of policies and procedures, reasonable under the circumstances, taking into consideration the nature of the person's business, to ensure that individual(s) making investment decision(s) would not violate paragraph (a) of this section, which policies and procedures may include, but are not limited to, (i) those which restrict any purchase, sale and causing any purchase and sale of any such security or (ii) those which prevent such individual(s) from knowing such information.

(c) Notwithstanding anything in paragraph (a) of this section to contrary, the following transactions shall not be violations of paragraph (a) of this section:

(1) Purchase(s) of any security described in paragraph (a) of this section by a broker or by another agent on behalf of an offering person; or

(2) Sale(s) by any person of any security described in paragraph (a) of this section to the offering person.

(d)(1) As a means reasonably designed to prevent fraudulent, deceptive or manipulative acts or practices within the meaning of section 14(e) of the Act, it shall be unlawful for any person described in paragraph (d)(2) of this section to communicate material, nonpublic information relating to a tender offer to any other person under circumstances in which it is reasonably foreseeable that such communication is likely to result in a violation of this section except that this paragraph shall not apply to a communication made in good faith,

(i) To the officers, directors, partners or employees of the offering person, to its advisors or to other persons, involved in the planning, financing, preparation or execution of such tender offer;

(ii) To the issuer whose securities are sought or to be sought by such tender offer, to its officers, directors, partners, employees or advisors or to other persons, involved in the planning, financing, preparation or execution of the activities of the issuer with respect to such tender offer; or

(iii) To any person pursuant to a requirement of any statute or rule or regulation promulgated thereunder.

(2) The persons referred to in paragraph (d)(1) of this section are:

(i) The offering person or its officers, directors, partners, employees or advisors;

(ii) The issuer of the securities sought or to be sought by such tender offer or its officers, directors, partners, employees or advisors;

(iii) Anyone acting on behalf of the persons in paragraph (d)(2)(i) of this section or the issuer or persons in paragraph (d)(2)(ii) of this section; and

(iv) Any person in possession of material information relating to a tender offer which information he knows or has reason to know is nonpublic and which he knows or has reason to know has been acquired directly or indirectly from any of the above.

TABLE OF CASES

Principal cases are italicized.

Airgas, Inc. v. Air Products & Chemicals, Inc., 264
Air Products & Chemicals, Inc. v. Airgas, Inc., 259
Amanda Acquisition Corp. v. Universal Foods Corp., 213
Americas Mining Corp. v. Theriault, 420
Aronson v. Lewis, 118

Basic, Inc. v. Levinson, 462, 463
Berger v. Pubco Corp., 392
Birnbaum v. Newport Steel Corp., 430
Blasius Indus., Inc. v. Atlas Corp., 286, 306, 317
Blue Chip Stamps v. Manor Drug Stores, 479
Boilermakers Local 154 v. Chevron Corp., 422
Brehm v. Eisner, 140
Brophy v. Cities Service Co., 465

Caremark International, Inc. Derivative Litigation, In re, 140
Carmody v. Toll Brothers, Inc., 265
Carpenter v. United States, 488
Cede & Co. v. Technicolor, Inc. (Chancery 1990), 361
Cede & Co. v. Technicolor, Inc. (Supreme Court 1996), 349
Cede & Co. v. Technicolor, Inc. (Supreme Court 2005), 362
Cheff v. Mathes, 141

Chiarella v. United States, 466
City Capital Assoc. Ltd. Partnership v. Interco, Inc. (3d Cir.), 581
City Capital Assoc. Ltd. Partnership v. Interco, Inc. (Delaware), 151, 242, 264, 346, 529
Cox Communications, Inc. Shareholders Litigation, In re, 400
CSX Corp. v. Children's Investment Fund Management (UK) LLP, 540
CTS Corp. v. Dynamics Corp. of America, 190

Dahl v. Bain Capital Partners LLC, 515
Dirks v. SEC, 470
Del Monte Foods Co. Shareholders Litigation, In re, 130

Edgar v. MITE Corp., 211
Emerging Communications, Inc. Shareholders Litigation, In re, 362, 417

Farris v. Glen Alden Corp., 36, 47-49
Florida Commercial Banks v. Culverhouse, 59

GAF Corp. v. Milstein, 59
Gantler v. Stephens, 119, 128, 130, 496
Glassman v. Unocal Exploration Corp., 386, 416
Good v. Lackawanna Leather Co., 50

633

Hanson Trust PLC v. SCM Corp., 61
Hariton v. Arco Electronics, Inc., 34, 48, 49
Hexion Specialty Chemicals, Inc. v. Huntsman, 139
Hewlett v. Hewlett-Packard Co., 456

IBP, Inc. Shareholder Litigation, In re, 70

J.I. Case Co. v. Borak, 464
Jewell v. Payless Drug Stores Northwest Inc., 209
Johnson v. Trueblood, 141, 142

Kahn v. Lynch Communication Systems, Inc., 419
Kahn v. Kohlberg, Kravis, Roberts & Co. LP, 465

Louisiana Municipal Police Employees' Retirement System v. Crawford, 189, 527
Lyondell Chemical Company v. Ryan, 131

MAI Basic Four Inc. v. Prime Computer, Inc., 58
Martin Marietta Materials, Inc. v. Vulcan Materials Inc., 80, 92
Mendel v. Carroll 209, 431
Metropolitan Life Ins. Co. v. RJR Nabisco, Inc., 8, 498
MM Companies, Inc. v. Liquid Audio, Inc., 308
Monty v. Leis, 209
Moran v. Household International, Inc., 234

NACCO Industries. Inc. v. Applica, Inc., 94
Netsmart Technologies, Inc. Shareholders Litigation, In re, 527
New Jersey Carpenters Pension Fund v. Infogroup, Inc., 130
Nomad Acquisition Corp. v. Damon Corp., 222

Omnicare, Inc. v. NCS Healthcare, Inc., 98, 191

Panter v. Marshall Field & Co., 142
Paramount Communications, Inc. v. QVC Network, Inc., 172
Paramount Communications, Inc. v. Time, Inc., 50, 140, 160, 258, 259
Perlman v. Feldmann, 424
Pfeiffer v. Toll, 465
Piper v. Chris-Craft Industries, Inc., 59
Plaine v. McCabe, 59
Pratt v. Ballwan-Cummings Furniture Co., 50
Prudent Real Estate Trust v. Johncamp Realty, Inc., 54, 58

Quickturn Design Systems, Inc. v. Shapiro, 271

Rabkin v. Phillip A. Hunt Chemical Corp, 349
Revlon, Inc. v. MacAndrews & Forbes Holdings, Inc., 152, 453, 498
Rondeau v. Mosinee Paper Corp., 53

Santa Fe Industries, Inc. v. Green, 348, 479
Schnell v. Chris-Craft Industries, Inc., 282, 318
SEC v. Capital Gains Research Bureau, Inc., 459
SEC v. Carter Hawley Hale Stores, Inc., 61
SEC v. Cherif, 479
Selectic, Inc. v. Versata Enterprises, Inc., 248
Singer v. Magnavox, Co., 348
Smith v. Van Gorkom, 98, 128, 130
Stone v. Ritter, 131, 140
Synthes Inc. Shareholders Litigation, In re, 130

Terry v. Penn Central Corp. (3d Cir.), 42, 48
Terry v. Penn Central Corp. (Dist. Ct.), 49
Topps Company Shareholders Litigation, In re, 464, 498, 517, 528, 562
Toys 'R' Us Shareholders Litigation, In re, 209

United States v. Bryan, 479, 488
United States v. Carpenter, 488
United States v. Chestman, 479, 488
United States v. Newman, 488
United States v. O'Hagan (8th Cir.), 479
United States v. O'Hagan (Supreme Court), 479, 488
United States v. Reed, 488
United States v. Willis, 488
Unitrin, Inc. v. American General Corp., 295, 317, 416
Unocal Corp. v. Mesa Petroleum Co., 143, 242, 257, 306

Ventas, Inc. v. HCP Inc., 93

Versata Enterprises, Inc. v. Selectica, Inc., 275, 306, 307

Walt Disney Company Derivative Litigation, In re (Chancery 2005), 140
Walt Disney Company Derivative Litigation, In re (Supreme Court 2006), 140
Wayport Inc. Litigation, In re, 130
Weinberger v. UOP, Inc., 98, 118, 319, *331,* 345, 424
Wellman v. Dickinson, 59, 61
Wheelabrator Technologies, Inc. Shareholder Litig., In re, 129

INDEX

Acquisition
   controlling shareholder, 423
   merger, 29
   sale of assets, 31
   sale of control sharers, 423
   tender offers. *See* Tender offers
   two step, 361, 416
Activist shareholders, 535
Antitakeover statutes, 211
   control share acquisition, 211
   disgorgement, 212
   moratorium/business combination, 211
   other constituencies, 212
   severance compensation, 213
   supermajority, 212
Antitrust, 2, 24, 62, 481
Appraisal rights
   antitakeover statute, 212
   costs, 48
   defined, 27, 30, 331
   exclusions, 346, 348
   procedural requirements, 347
   valuation, 345, 362, 391
Arbitrage, 455
Asset restructuring, 531
   carve-outs, 532
   divestiture, 531
   spinoffs, 533

Bankruptcy, 6, 18, 20, 494
Bear hug, 66
Blasius test, 306, 317

Board of directors. *See also* Business judgment rule; Defensive tactics; Directors; Fiduciary duty; Section 102(b)(7)
   approval of mergers, 27
   staggered elections, 97, 281, 539
Business judgment rule, 25, 118, 141, 295, 417, 453, 529
Bylaw amendments, 295
   exclusive forum, 422

Cadbury/Kraft, 536
   as a case study, 568
Cash out
   appraisal as exclusive remedy, 348
   fiduciary duty claim, 417
   historical origins, 348
Capital Assets Pricing Model (CAPM), 320
Casual pass, 66
CFIUS, 63, 566
Clayton Act, 62
Cleansing, 453
Control premiums, 423, 443
Control, sale of, 423
Corporate laws
   Delaware statute, 25
   Model Business Corporation Act, 25
Crown jewel, 96
Currency used as consideration, 17, 55

De facto. *See* Mergers
Deal break, 456
Deal dance, 65

Defensive tactics, 54, 76
  deal protection devices, 190
  financial defense, 96
  frustrating action, 568
  legal defense, 96
Directors
  Role in corporation, 25
  Exculpation, 130
Discounted Cash Flow (DCF), 323
Dissolution, 31
Due diligence, 68

Earn out, 67
Empty voting, 538
Enhanced (Intermediate) Scrutiny, 171, 295
Enron, 70
Entire fairness, 98, 118, 295, 386, 417

Fair dealing. *See* Fiduciary duty
Fair price. *See* Fiduciary duty
Fair value. *See* Appraisal rights
Fiduciary duty
  alternative to appraisal, 348
  carve-outs, 532
  disclosure, 464
  exculpation, 130
  good faith, 131, 139
  loyalty, 78
  ratification, 109
Fiduciary out, 208
Financial bidders, 14, 538
Financing decisions
  capital structure, 18
  cost of capital, 18
  currency choices, 17
  ownership structure, 18
  risk bearing, 19
  tax liability, 19
Force the vote provision, 207

Globalization, 5, 170, 563
Going private, 53, 128, 496
  federal law, 498
  Rule 13e-3, 128, 496
  state law disclosures, 498

Golden parachute, 98
Good faith. *See* Fiduciary duty

Hart-Scott-Rodino Act, 63
HCA, Inc.
  as a case study, 511
Hedge funds, 536

Incentives for mergers
  change of control, 12
  financial, 13, 491
  synergies, 11
  vertical integration, 11
Initial Public Offering, 516
Insider trading
  classic, 466
  constructive (or temporary), 470
  misappropriation, 479
  short swing profits, 488
  tender offer, 479
  tippee, 470

Junk bonds, 131
Just say no, 264, 275, 530

Leverage, 13, 20, 492, 493
Leveraged buyout (LBO), 117, 492, 494
  HCA as case study, 511
Leveraged recapitalization, 528
  ESOP, 529
Liabilities
  in merger, 26
  in sale of assets, 31
  in tender offer, 33
  in triangular merger, 32
Listing standards, 49
Litigation
  appraisal, 362
  class action, 386, 422
  representative, 386, 420
London city code, 566

Management buyout (MBO), 117, 494
Managers. *See also* Management buyout (MBO)
  empire building, 493
  monitoring of, 493

Merger agreement
  confidentiality agreement, 93
  gap filling, 80
  material adverse change (MAC)
    clause, 68, 70
  no shop, 94, 208
  representations and warranties, 69
  standstill, 93
Merger of equals, 67, 170
Mergers
  alternatives to, 28-30
  board approval, 27
  cash out, 27, 349, 386, 416
  costs, 15
  cross-border activity, 563
  de facto, 34, 51
  definitive agreement, 67
  Delaware vs. other states, 32, 48
  due diligence, 68
  economic factors, 4
  employee participation, 567
  gains from, 5
  government approval, 566
  long form, 348
  plan of merger, 29
  reverse triangular, 28, 33
  shareholder approval, 27. *See also* Shareholder voting
  short form, 386
  social issues, 67
  stakeholders, 8
  statutory, 28, 49
  statutory requirements, 26
  triangular, 28, 32, 49
  U.S. activity, 2
  upside down, 30
  voting. *See* Shareholder voting
  waves, 1

National security, 63
No shop, no talk, 94, 208

Poison pill, 97, 224, 307
  dead hand, 265
  NOL pill, 275
  redemption, 243
  reloaded, 275
  slow hand, 271
Prisoner's dilemma, 151
Proxy fight, 54
Proxy solicitation, 52, 459, 536, 562

Recapitalization, 128
Regulation FD, 478
Reverse stock split, 128, 496
Reverse triangular mergers. *See* Mergers
Revlon duties, 160, 171, 208, 453, 498, 527
Revlonland, 159, 172, 189
Rule 10b-5, 464

Sale of assets, 28, 31
Saturday night special, 460
Scorched earth, 529
Section 102(b)(7), 118, 130, 131, 140
Securities and Exchange Commission (SEC), 51, 68, 92
Securities laws
  issuance of securities, 52, 459
  mandatory disclosure, 24, 51, 459
  proxy solicitation, 3, 52, 536
  Sarbanes-Oxley Act, 3, 128, 461
  Securities Act of 1933, 3, 51, 459, 464
  Securities Exchange Act of 1934, 3, 51, 128
  Williams Act, 3, 52
Share repurchase, 67, 96
Shareholder ratification, 128
Shareholder voting, 25, 49, 69
  acquiring companies, 207
  creating uncertainty, 206
  defensive tactic, 275
  empty voting, 538
  enhanced review of defensive tactics, 348
  in mergers, 30
  in other countries, 565
  market out exception, 30
  purpose of, 537
  removing poison pill, 295
  reverse stock split, 496
  state law, 49

stock exchange listing requirements, 30
stock for stock, 67
supermajority, 496
Sherman Act, 62
Short form merger, 386
  appraisal as exclusive remedy, 391
  disclosure, 391
Short selling, 458
Staggered board, 97, 213, 539
Stalking horse, 207
Standstill agreement, 92
Strategic bidders, 14
Swaps, 561

Takeovers panel, 568, 571
Tax shield, 9, 18, 64, 492
Taxes, 15, 61
  carve-outs, 482
  spinoffs, 483
Tender offers, 3, 29, 33, 49, 52, 54, 459
  two-tier, 152, 416
Termination fee, 70, 207
Triangular mergers. *See* Mergers

Unocal test, 150, 160, 171, 189, 201, 208, 222, 281, 295, 306

proportionality, 307
threat, 307

Valuation, 150, 362. *See also* Appraisal rights
  comparable companies, 327
  comparable transactions, 327
  Delaware block, 319
  discounted cash flow (DCF), 320, 386
  diversification, 321
  fiduciary duty claim, 361
  return and risk, 321
Voting. *See* Shareholder voting

WACC (Weighted Average Cost of Capital), 323, 327
White knight, 60, 96
White squire, 96
Williams Act, 3, 52, 460, 561
  best price rule, 60, 461
  disclosures, 58, 60
  groups, 59
  remedy, 59, 562
  Rule 13d, 460, 561
Wolf packs, 538